Highlanders

Highlanders
Unlocking Identity Through History

James MacKillop

McFarland & Company, Inc., Publishers
Jefferson, North Carolina

LIBRARY OF CONGRESS CATALOGUING-IN-PUBLICATION DATA

Names: MacKillop, James, author.
Title: Highlanders : unlocking identity through history / James MacKillop.
Other titles: Unlocking identity through history
Description: Jefferson, North Carolina : McFarland & Company Inc., Publishers, 2023 | Includes bibliographical references and index.
Identifiers: LCCN 2023039046 | ISBN 9781476693125 (print) | ISBN 9781476650609 (ebook) ∞
Subjects: LCSH: Highlands (Scotland)—History. | Celts—Scotland—Highlands—History. | Clans—Scotland—Highlands—History. | Scottish Gaelic language.
Classification: LCC DA880.H6 M26 2023 | DDC 941.1/5004916—dc23/eng/20230906
LC record available at https://lccn.loc.gov/2023039046

BRITISH LIBRARY CATALOGUING DATA ARE AVAILABLE

ISBN (print) 978-1-4766-9312-5
ISBN (ebook) 978-1-4766-5060-9

© 2023 James MacKillop. All rights reserved

No part of this book may be reproduced or transmitted in any form or by any means, electronic or mechanical, including photocopying or recording, or by any information storage and retrieval system, without permission in writing from the publisher.

Front cover image and frontispiece: a stone monument or stele for seventeenth-century poet Iain Lom at Cille Choirill near Roybridge, Lochaber (photograph by Ronaldcameron, August 11, 2015; Wikipedia); MacKillop family tartan

Printed in the United States of America

McFarland & Company, Inc., Publishers
Box 611, Jefferson, North Carolina 28640
www.mcfarlandpub.com

Acknowledgments

Richard Marsh of Dublin read the entire manuscript, making countless, invaluable improvements, including the deletion of howlers. Effie Rankin and John Shaw gave good counsel at the very beginning of the project. My late teachers of things Gaelic, Charles W. Dunn and Ken Nilsen, set standards I tried to reach. Karen Bakke gave constant support during the long haul.

Table of Contents

Acknowledgments   v
Preface   1
   The Limits of Genealogy   7
A Note on the Words "Celt" and "Celtic"   8

1. The Foundations   13
      Where Are the "Highlands"?   13
      Peopling the Landscape   18
      Prehistoric Testimony   23
      The Scots/Gaels: Ethnogenesis   25
      The Picts   32
      Ireland and the Highlands   36
      The Norse in the Highlands   44
      The Scottish Gaelic Language   49

2. Medieval Highlands and Islands   54
      The Hammer of the Norse   54
      The Lordship of the Isles   58
      The Rise of the Clans   68
      Enumeration, Rivalries, an Alliance   82
      Feuds and Forays   86

3. The Seventeenth Century   89
      One King, Two Kingdoms   89
      Wars of the Three Kingdoms, 1639–1651   97
      A "Bald" Poet   105
      Departure of the Stuarts: The First Three Decades   108

Table of Contents

4. The Dreary Eighteenth Century 119
   Highland Society Before Culloden 119
   The Jacobites, 1745–1746 127
   Misery and Emigration 139

5. Romantic Amelioration 155
   Imposture in Badenoch 155
   Indigenous Voices 162
   Poetic Admirers from the Outside 164
   Abbotsford 170
   The Sett That Expresses 177
   A Royal Patroness 180
   Away from Balmoral 185

6. After Romance 189
   Sheep Over People 189
   The Blight of the Tubers 202
   The Great Disruption of 1843 206
   Mightier Than a Lord 209
   The Comic Highlander 213
   Suas Leis a' Ghàidhlig 216

Coda: Known Up Close Then Seen from Afar 220
Glossary: Persons, Places, Vocabulary 227
Bibliography 235
Index 251

Preface

Contempt, sympathy and romance. Three emotions rarely juxtaposed in sequence. They are the first words in the title of Krisztina Fenyo's study (published 2000) of Lowland perceptions of the Scottish Highlands during a decade of intense misery, 1845–1855. Just as thousands of impoverished tenants were being driven from their cottages, to be replaced by more profitable sheep, the potato famine struck. Tenants and their families who had escaped eviction were starving and begging on the roads. Contempt had indeed been the default view for centuries of well-mannered Lowlanders for their often rough-hewn Gaelic-speaking co-nationals. Lowlanders are "low" because they live on rolling fertile, green land, but their self-esteem has long been high. They control the largest cities and ports, and have dominated the Scottish nation for centuries. Lowland views may prefigure those of the wider world but are not identical with them. Highlanders are "high" because most have lived in mountains with meager soil or on offshore rocky islands. Earlier they were called *Scoti sylvestres* or wild Scots. Scattered across a wide area, they are fewer than the Lowlanders, but they are the Scots most often romanticized.

Following the boom in both popular and academic studies of Highland history after 1960, many previously obscure or dimly lit corners of the Highland story are now illuminated. Keeping up with all that has been said, let alone what interpretations have changed since 1960, would fill several lifetimes. There is a selective sample of titles in the bibliography. What this volume proposes to do is pick and choose from dozens of volumes for those details sketching out who Highlanders were thought to be and how they looked upon themselves. Decades, centuries and epochs have been reduced to a slender narrative with abundant markers to those persons and causes who played prominent roles even though they are only being outlined. As a book on Highland history this is a fairly short one, little more than 120,000 words. But its reach is long, from pre-history through the end of the twentieth century. It could be seen as a skeleton key: a device to open every door. In each chapter there is an overview of leading figures and themes with discreet mention of sources, usually only an author's name, a title, and a date, for consultation in the bibliography. No notes: the reader is free to move on without distraction.

Your author grew up in a cosmopolitan industrial city without a Highland enclave before genealogy became a popular passion for families beyond the privileged few of the Daughters of the American Revolution. I am four generations from emigration, and both of my parents could speak Gaelic because they were born on

Cape Breton Island, Nova Scotia, where Highlanders had resisted assimilation. In most other regards, I was only a few steps beyond the readers who know only that they have Highland names or at least one Highland ancestor. There was no mention at home about great battles or great outrages, or even what ships had brought us to the New World. In my parents' generation all that was to be discarded and forgotten. Those "few steps" include some details my parents passed along reluctantly and a self-published genealogy.

At the same time, I respect the genealogical hunger to find something of one's self in past records. An issue I return to repeatedly is whether a reader in the diaspora, possibly living in a vastly different culture, could ever trace a bit of himself or herself in some of the early populations, like the Picts or the Norse, or what roles ancestors might have played in the decades of clan wars. Are we really descended from them?

It was once my hope that I could extend genealogical lines into the larger history of the Highlands, including the prominent families like the Campbells, the Clan Donald, the MacKenzies and the Curries. I would start with the family names in my genealogy, each of them quite different. From these certain names we could leap into the currents of Highland history, as one might do in other European countries like England, the Netherlands or Italy. This cannot be done in the Highlands for a half-dozen reasons. Chief among them is that Highland family names originate in Gaelic and are reformed, sometimes irregularly, into English, and the individual families can be reshaped or subsumed by larger and more powerful clans. Tracing family lines with unreliable documentation is to enter a briar patch.

The model for the point of view I am taking here is Michael Arlen's *Passage to Ararat* (1975), a personal history of the Armenian people as seen from the diaspora, readers who know their ethnicity but do not know much about a far-off country not usually studied in school. Arlen made a strong claim for using the first person because he was then a celebrity writer for the *New Yorker*, where some chapters first appeared. Further, he was the son of a once well-known, bestselling popular novelist. His unstated questions seemed to be "Who are we? And how do we find ourselves in the lives of distant, obscure people?" As British Isles people, some knowledge of Highlanders, tartan, and whisky is widespread, but key figures in Highland history like Colkitto or Somerled, or celebrated episodes like the two battles of Inverlochy or the bloodbath of Harlaw, could never be currency on *Jeopardy!*

My aspiration is close to Arlen's, despite the contrasts in our subjects. There have always been far fewer Highlanders than Armenians, only about 400,000 at the apogee in the census of 1841. Smaller than that of modest Onondaga County, the fifth largest metropolitan area in New York State, where I reside. The Gaels who form the core of the Highland population have been distinct from the four other components of the Scottish nation, the Picts, Britons, Angles and later the Norse, from as early as the sixth century. Powerful and dominant in the early Scottish kingdom, the Gaelic Highlands receded from hegemony and became one of the poorest portions not only of Scotland but of the entire British Isles, from the eighteenth century until late in the twentieth. These include the repression of Gaelic language and culture along with the forced removal of defenseless people from their homes, leading to a worldwide diaspora, assimilation and forgetting.

Preface

I often meet people in the United States with prominent Highland names, like Rankin, Chisholm, Cameron, Beaton, or Gillis, not to mention the Mac/Mc, who are barely aware those are Scottish, let alone Highland. A recent episode in Scotland depicted this dispersal from another point of view. I spoke about a shared Jacobite heritage with a well-dressed gentleman at high tea in the five-star Inverlochy Castle Hotel near Fort William in Scotland. Our forebears had fought in the last land battle in the British Isles, Culloden. His ancestor had been an officer in the rebel army, who barely avoided execution when captured; mine were foot soldiers. On a warm autumn day, my correspondent was preparing to attend a celebration commemorating the escape of the Young Pretender, Prince Charles, in late September 1746. Although deeply schooled in his heritage, he was taken aback with the report from one of those recreational genetics kits advertised on television. He found that he indeed had many relatives all over Scotland and Britain and more than sixty in Canada. More startling, he reported unsmilingly, is that he had several hundred genetic kin in the United States. It was a moment of shared epiphany. The relationship of the Highlands and the wider world is the dispersal of Highland people. I expect many readers will be among the dispersed.

If immigrant lore had pretty much faded from my family, I did have a written record. A.D. MacDonald's *Mabou Pioneers*, an 880-page tome tracing all the families that emigrated from Scotland to the village on the west coast of Cape Breton Island, where my father was born. The author completed this heroic enterprise without institutional support and long before the Internet made recondite documents widely accessible. It was privately printed, the place of publication not given, about 1950 to 1952. A copy showed up in our home, somehow, where it was treated as curiosity rather than as a revered document. Although I was named on page 717, I found it initially incomprehensible, but it soon found its way to my personal library. Certainly, it instilled the notion that the remote past could be explored. It was not until I first visited Scotland in 1984, however, that I began to read it closely and compared it with more reliable sources. These told me told me that my great-great grandfather, Alexander MacKillop, had emigrated from Murlaggan, east of Roybridge, in the uplands of Lochaber, known as Brae Lochaber.

Other records, found later and more reliable than *Mabou Pioneers*, determined that my mother's family, the Gillises, landless farmers, were evicted from Loch Arkaig in Lochaber, west of the Great Glen.

Although both my mother's and father's families emigrated from identifiable points in the *Gàidhealtachd*, the name for Gaelic-speaking regions, in the early nineteenth century, their ancestors in the previous century could have drifted in from any of several regions, not all adjacent. If the names of persons that can be known are mostly cyphers, the rest are historically invisible. Both of my parents' families were part of a large migration of mostly Gaelic speakers and Jacobites to Nova Scotia in the eighty years following 1773. There were four Jacobite rebellions, the last culminating in the catastrophe of Culloden Moor, 1746, which led to the brutal repression of any persons thought to have anything to do with the cause. The families were usually poor and predominantly illiterate, in both Scotland and Nova Scotia, until the nineteenth century. Letters and diaries do not survive. When Dr. Samuel Johnson walked the Highlands in 1773, it seemed such an unknown wilderness that he likened the experience to visiting Sumatra or Borneo.

In part because so many people emigrated from the north of Scotland, artifacts of Highland culture are widely known: tartans or plaids, bagpipes and marching kiltie bands. The names of the two most powerful families, Campbell and MacDonald, are ubiquitous, and shorn of their roots somewhat banal. In the absence of actual knowledge of the hardscrabble life that Highlanders lived, most readers in the multicultural, urban, contemporary world are unaware that other Scots have long disdained the Celtic-speaking people of the north as thieves or "sheep-stealers." The once common insult was *teuchter* (pronounced "CHOOK-ter"), roughly the equivalent of "hillbilly." At one time Highland identity was something to be shed, and the name MacDonald might become Donaldson, MacSween, or Swanson, and MacKillop either Phillipson or Killop.

They were not, however, completely deracinated. They were both born while Queen Victoria was Canada's sovereign, my father Colin near the village of Mabou, 1900, where the post office is cited officially in Gaelic today, *Tigh Litrichean*, "house of letters," and my mother in 1902 about fifteen miles south near the town of Port Hood in a community then known as Harbour View, now Hawthorne. They both knew that their families had come from Lochaber, a storied region in what was known until 1974 as Inverness-shire. Neither knew a date of arrival for immigrants nor any identifying placenames in Lochaber. Despite being unable to find Lochaber on a map, they were aware that Badenoch was adjacent. My father knew that the family was a sept of prominent family, MacDonell (accent on last syllable), and could recite in Gaelic the names of his three grandfathers who preceded him in Cape Breton, implying immigration in the early nineteenth century. The English word "sept" appears to derive from the Latin *saeptum*, meaning "enclosure" or "fold." Septs are families that follow another family's chief, part of the extended family, but holding a different surname. Forty-two family names are cited septs attached to the MacDonells of Keppoch, some of them, e.g., MacGilp, Phillipson, clearly variants of MacKillop.

Both parents' families considered the dialect of Gaelic they spoke, *Gàidhlig Abrach*, pronounced "apprich," to be of higher status than that of my father's mother, *Gàidhlig Strathghlais*, pronounced "strai-wash," from Strathglass, and much higher than that of the MacNeill family, *Gàildhig Bharraidh*, from the Isle of Barra. They never gave any indication that they knew where Strathglass or the remote Isle of Barra in the Outer Hebrides were, only that they were removed from the Lochaber homeland.

My parents were of contrasting physical types. Tall and fair-haired, my father resembled some of his siblings and favored his mother, born Annie Belle Chisholm. Her somewhat Scandinavian appearance prompted teasing from my shorter grandfather Finlay, who died twelve years before I was born. I know today that the Chisholms migrated from Strathglass some distance from Lochaber, an area of extensive Norse settlement, very likely the explanation of why her Gaelic, *Strathglais*, sounded different though comprehensible to *Abrach* speakers. My mother, born Margaret Gillis, and all but one of her siblings were short and dark, almost

Mediterranean in appearance; some cousins on that side might be described as Levantine. Other Gillises on the same road, mostly descended from the same grandfather, Angus Bàn (fair) Gillis, were generally shorter than the MacKillops. She thought the Mediterranean coloring came from her mother's family, the MacInneses, few of whom I ever met. From the get-go, then, I knew Highlanders were not a single physical type, supporting findings of the genome studies that began about 1995.

On that first visit one could not overlook the reduced circumstances that had driven my parents out and to prefer assimilation and cosmopolitanism over heritage. Not that I was blind to this, but as a six-year-old I found some of it an adventure, especially horse-drawn carriages and wild blueberries. Fiddlers would come to a house after dinner to play tunes with a wild, almost feral beat. It was immediate and seductive and though nothing like anything I heard before, somehow accessible. The musicians' arrival was spontaneous and not necessarily prompted by our visit. This was, of course, a *ceilidh*, now recognized as a distinctive feature of the local culture, so that the highway past my parents' residences, Route 19, is now called the "Ceilidh Trail." I don't recall anyone using the term then. A child can easily put aside questions of comfort or status. It was thrilling to be there, and I found something of myself in what had been strange and unprecedented. My siblings, eight and nine years my senior, visiting by automobile the following year, readily inherited my parents' dismissal.

My parents' willful discarding of their heritage and eagerness to assimilate into the United States was not true of everyone in Cape Breton in their generation. Funds raised in the Nova Scotia *Gàidhealtachd* went to help restore the fifteenth-century Catholic church of Cille Choirill in Brae Lochaber east of Roybridge in the depression year of 1932. For many along Route 19 in Cape Breton, including my father's family, this would have been their parish church had they not emigrated, and unbeknownst to us, quite a few others knew this. If my parents had remained in Nova Scotia and I was raised there, or if none had ever immigrated, I might never have undertaken this project. So much of what has taken sustained effort for me to uncover could have been quotidian knowledge. A fuller first-hand knowledge would have guided many perspectives and perhaps spared me from howlers. Perhaps being removed from a tradition can give a curious author more motivation. Michael Arlen lived in New York, not Yerevan. Additionally, I note that John Prebble (1915–2001), who created the market for popular histories of the Highlands, was born in Sussex and spent part of his youth in Saskatchewan before returning to Britain. Similarly, Alistair MacLeod (1936–2014), the most distinguished fiction writer to treat with Gaelic Cape Breton, was born in Saskatchewan and spent most of his adult life in Windsor, Ontario. We who are farther from the *Gàidhealtachd* crave to know it in ways that the natives do not.

An explanation of how Gaelic family names were hammered into Anglicized equivalents requires a review of recondite subjects, like Gaelic phonetics, too lengthy and distracting to be included here.

Perhaps the most confounding difference in Highland naming for readers unfamiliar with the *Gàidhealtachd* is the preference for the patronymic or *sloinneadh*.

Generically a patronymic is a name or expression crediting paternity to another name. In that limited sense they may be found around the world in unrelated languages, e.g., English, Wilson: son of Will; Swedish, Johanson: son of Johan; Armenian, Hagopian: son of Hagop. In that sense, the clan names MacDonald and MacLeod are both patronymics but ones that became fixed to different families. Using the word *sloinneadh*, unfamiliar to most readers, denotes a patronymic that may be used in preference to a family name. This convention would have been dominant in the Highlands through early modern times. Readers of Russian novels understand how this works in practice. A character may have an esteemed family name, like Bolkonsky, Bezukhov or Rostov, but he will be addressed by his given name and patronymic, such as Sergei Sergeivitch or Alexei Ivanovitch, rather than as Mr. Rostov. This practice has persisted in the Cape Breton *Gàidhealtachd*. The first group genealogy of my father's village, A.D. MacDonald's *Mabou Pioneers* (c. 1951), is filled with such documentation. If a man was officially named John Beaton, among the commonest of names, *Pioneers* would cite him as his neighbors would, as Dhomhnaill Sheumais, viz. John son of Donald son of James. Often in Cape Breton a *sloinneadh* would effectively displace the official family name, a source of trauma for young children entering school. A five-year-old might learn that he would not be Dòmhnaill Lagain as at home and would now be Donald MacDonell. A child born out of wedlock would be linked to his or her mother, Dòmhnaill aig Màire, viz. Donald at Mary. The dominance of English over Gaelic did not obliterate this identity. In the twenty-first century people in the Mabou area might be known as Donald Johnny Murdoch (Murdoch as a given rather than a family name) or Angus Archie Donald Archie. In his 1997 study of Gaelic languages revivals, led by educated young people, Jonathan Dembling cites a representative old native speaker with the name "Joe Jimmy Alec." Over time, it seems very likely, a *sloinneadh* might be entered into an official record instead of a family name.

There is no fixed date when this would happen. The familiar narrative explaining the transition from the *sloinneadh* tells of the need to fill a clerkship in Speyside, 1531, in which the office holder was required to have the family name of Grant. As none of the locals was used to being addressed by his family name, no one applied. Thirty-eight years later in 1569 when the position was open again, more than forty tenants would answer to the family name Grant. Often the transition is driven by interaction with a government agency, such as joining the army or navy.

This was the case with persons of elevated status and not just tenants. Consider the well-born, seventeenth-century Royalist warrior usually known as Alasdair Mac Colla (c. 1610–1647). His entry in most references, including Wikipedia, employs Mac Colla. His full *sloinneadh* is Mac Colla Chiotaich MacDhòmhnaill, which translates as "son of Coll the Left-handed MacDhòmhnaill." English observers and scribes, unaware of the significance of the *sloinneadh* and contemptuous of heeding Gaelic phonetics, shortened this to "Colkitto," merging "Colla" and "Chiotaich," by which he is often known, even in academic histories. The English equivalent of his name is Alexander MacDonald, an admittedly common Highland name, by which he may never have been referred to in his lifetime.

The task of finding the recorded name 350 years ago, as the Cromwell family might expect, is even more daunting for a Highland family. When the *sloinneadh* was dominant, a person might be indifferent about an official family name. Persons living in the area of a powerful chief could take on his name for protection when there was no family connection. No record would survive. In the late nineteenth century (1887) the 8th Duke of Argyll, George Campbell, observed that recruits would readily drop what he knew to be their family names when enlisting in a regiment dominated by another clan.

The Limits of Genealogy

The number 2 to the twentieth power is 1,200,000. That means if any of us could trace our lines back twenty generations we could be descended from as many as 1,200,000 persons. The date for that could be the seventeenth century, during the career of Highland hero Alasdair Mac Colla or Colkitto. Tracing one family name, a father's, describes a smaller percentage of inheritance in each generation. Taken from the other direction, 2 to the twentieth power can yield 1,200,000 persons in descent from a powerful figure, especially when a man was not confined to the limits of bourgeois marriage and might take advantage of every woman in a household. Geneticist David Reich speculated in *Who We Are and How We Got Here* (2018) that almost any European might claim Charlemagne (fl. 800 CE) among his ancestors.

At the beginning of this study, I am assuming that most of my ancestors, as well as those of readers claiming Highland ancestry, could be found in any part of the Gàidhealtachd of the mainland or islands. We cannot know their names. Their lives were filled, no doubt, with quiet and sometimes strident desperation. This is an attempt to make that accessible to their many descendants.

A Note on the Words "Celt" and "Celtic"

The origin of the English words "Celt" and "Celtic" is clear and easy to trace. Many other questions dealing with the languages and their speakers, however, are in flux, some of them in contention. That is because there are now so many more scholarly workers in the field, scrutinizing every shard of information, and also because of unanticipated scientific advances, such as the DNA analysis of ancient populations. Much of what passed as conventional wisdom in, say, 1965, is under challenge or has been upended.

The Greek *Keltoí* appears in documents as early as 560 to 50 BCE. "Tall persons" might be a translation. It referred to the languages the Greeks observed along the Mediterranean. Centuries later the Romans observed speakers to the north and west speaking comparable languages; they called them *Celtae*. Celtic speakers did not name themselves as Celts or report a link between their disparate selves. From the beginning, then, Celticity was observed from the outside. No Celtic language had a word denoting that it might be part of a family of related languages. As Julius Caesar's Gallic Wars, which employs the word *Celtae*, was a common school text from the Renaissance and after, a sliver of educated European people would have known that "Celtic" denoted some ancient language. John Milton employs it in *Paradise Lost* (1667). And although he was ignored, as early as 1582 historian George Buchanan asserted that Scottish Gaelic was derived from ancient Celtic.

Ancient Celtic languages were spread across Europe from what is now France, northern parts of Iberia, the Low Countries, Britain, Germany, Switzerland, northern Italy and Austria to the Czech Republic, Hungary, Slovenia and beyond. Often the name people held for themselves in the ancient Celtic languages included the phoneme "gal," such as the Galatians in Asia Minor evangelized by St. Paul. Modern scholarship has added languages for which little documentation has survived, including Lusitanian in Portugal and Ligurian on the French-Italian border.

Celtic is a smaller branch in the Indo-European family of languages, along with Germanic, Romance and Slavic. Arguing where the Celtic languages might have originated has long been a forum for speculation, starting with being the tongue of the Lost Tribe of Israel from ill-informed commentators at the end of the eighteenth century. Since then, many authoritative scholars have outlined plausible origin stories, usually by trying to reconcile the disparate evidence from philology and archaeology, i.e., words vs. artifacts. Some of those proved as ephemeral as the rooting in the Lost Tribe. For most of the twentieth century the dominant view was that Celtic languages were first recorded in the Danube Valley, supported by the large site excavated at Hallstatt, Austria, with abundant material culture. Confidence is this view was undercut by discoveries of even older Celtic language inscriptions in distant regions like the north Italian lakes and in what was later called Celtiberia in northeastern Spain.

In the twenty-first century two different theories, both proposed by top scholars Barry Cunliffe and J.T. Koch (2019), argued that Celtic languages were already current in the "Atlantic Zone," including the British Isles, northwestern France and western Iberia by 300 BCE and spread to the east. Patrick Sims-Williams (2020) critiqued all other theories and favored an origin in the middle, Gaul or France. Evaluating such claims requires rigorous preparation.

Returning to the discussion of three centuries ago, Edward Lhuyd (or Lloyd), the Welsh-born keeper of the Ashmolean Museum at Oxford, revised the definition of "Celtic" with *Archæologia Britannica* (1707) when he argued that six languages spoken by marginalized modern populations were indeed survivors of the ancient Celtic languages. Working concurrently with Lhuyd in French was Paul-Yves Pezron making the same case in *Antiquité de la nation et de la Langue des Celtes* (1703). The languages were Irish, Scottish Gaelic, Manx from the Isle of Man, Welsh, Cornish and Breton. At that time all had large numbers of speakers, generally living less affluently than the rest of the population of hegemonic Britain and France. Cornish lost its last native speaker in 1777, Manx in 1974, but both are still spoken by enthusiasts who struggle to keep them alive.

The six are customary filed in two categories, the Goidelic embracing Irish, Scottish Gaelic and Manx, and the Brythonic, with Welsh, Cornish and Breton. A signal distinction between them is the hard "q" sound in Goidelic is replaced by "p" in Brittonic. Consider the Irish patronymic "mac-" as against the Welsh "ap-" and "ab-" from the Welsh "mab" meaning "son." Or the Irish "ceann" versus the Welsh "pen" for "head."

How and when the six formed two columns is a matter of some dispute far too complicated to be discussed well here. Many commentators feel the deeper split in the Celtic languages is between Continental, like Gaulish, Lepontic (in what is now Switzerland) and Galatian, now all extinct, and Insular, as found in the Britain and Ireland. Breton, though spoken in continental France, is Insular as it is derived from settlers who emigrated from Britain as the name "Brittany" (little Britain) implies. Some commentators argue that Irish, and thus Scottish Gaelic as well, exhibiting archaic characteristics, split off very early from Proto-Celtic. The rival schema depicts the P/Q split coming after Insular languages were separated from Continental. These divisions could have occurred in 900 BCE or as early as 3200 BCE.

Edward Lhuyd entered the new definition of the word "Celtic" in the discrete aerie of learned discourse at a time when the majority of English speakers were still illiterate. It would be decades, even centuries before many common people encountered the word, most likely in print rather than in speech. Thus, the default tendency to pronounce it with a soft -c-, "SELL-tic," rather than the hard -c-, "KELL-tic," to reflect its origin in Greek as well as the dominance of German scholars in the nineteenth century, who spelled the word Keltic. At one time pronunciation was a marker separating those who had given some thought to the subject from those encountering it for the first time. Significantly, since 1965 with the rising prestige of all things Celtic, in jewelry-making and music as well as literature, "KELL-tic" appears to have become the preferred.

Unusual for the name of a language or family of languages, the word "Celtic" has long enjoyed a favorable resonance, often for bogus reasons. Perhaps because speakers of living Celtic languages were dominated by the powerful nation states of Britain and France, "Celtic" through wish acquired heroic, irredentist even bellicose associations, warriors with a pedigree. Such is implied in naming the basketball team in Boston and the soccer team in Glasgow. The word "Celtic" is, of course, an adjective being used as a noun, e.g., "the Celtics." Demotically, some people still might cite "Celtics" as speakers of Celtic languages.

As the living Celtic languages were difficult to learn, infrequently taught in any school, and the ancient Celtic languages dead and unknowable, they became an empty stage on which the imagined and wished for might be made manifest. If the contemporary urban world were thought to be rationalist and soulless, then Celtic writing would be seen to bring the mystical and soulful. If the daily world were seen as pedestrian and dull, then the realm of the Celtic might bring magic. In addition came exploitive frauds. James Macpherson's *The Poems of Ossian* (1760–1763), posited an ancient epic literature, a peer of the Iliad and the Odyssey, that somehow survived in the Scottish Highlands and had escaped attention until his time. He offered the "translations," but the Celtic originals would take some time to produce. A fuller examination of Macpherson and Ossianism is found in Chapter 5.

Until now we have avoided denoting speakers of the Celtic languages as "Celts," although that was once conventional. From the widespread genome testing after 1990 we no longer assume that speaking a certain language over decades, even in a fixed place, confirms a physical identity. Vanished is the notion dominant from the nineteenth century until the end of World War II that a person speaking a European language, such as German, had a different physical (and implicitly moral) character from someone speaking a Semitic language, such as Hebrew, originating in southwest Asia. Instead, we know today that large numbers of early farmers from southwest Asia migrated to Europe before Semitic languages were spoken and also before the advent of Indo-European languages. The notion that language is ethnicity dies hard, however, and persists colloquially.

In 1920 the Irish historian Eoin MacNeill argued that there was no such thing as a Celtic race. A nationalist, MacNeill criticized the excesses of romantic nationalism and had opposed the bloody Easter Rising at the Dublin General Post Office in April 1916. As that failed shoot-out sparked the movement that led to the establishment of an independent Irish state in 1922, MacNeill is sometimes judged to have been on the wrong side of history. On the question of there not being a unified genetic community, or "race," called the "Celts," the conscientious research of recent decades supports MacNeill.

Since the beginning of the study of things Celtic in the nineteenth century, first in Germany, later in France, Britain and Ireland, there has been a wealth of physical evidence to scrutinize. Along with surviving artifacts captured by the Romans were the discoveries of extensive archaeological sites, filled with skillfully made weapons and jewelry, artistically sophisticated, dramatically unlike the classicism of the Mediterranean. The first great find of the nineteenth century came in 1846 with the uncovering of Hallstatt in the salt-mining regions east of Salzburg in Austria. It had flourished from 800 BCE to 450 BCE. Eleven years later came the discoveries at La Tène at the eastern end of Lake Neuchâtel in western Switzerland. Civilization here overlapped a bit with Hallstatt, blooming from c. 450 BCE though the first century BCE. Both sites also included human remains. As mentioned earlier, discoveries of Celtic inscriptions distant from those two sites has undermined the confidence that either might mark the origin of the Celtic languages. In the short run, however the continental finds support Lhuyd's thesis of 1707. Irish, Gaelic and Welsh can be linked to the ancient languages. Motifs from La Tène art could easily be traced in the Celtic art masterpiece of the late dark ages, The Book of Kells, compiled on the Isle of Iona, adjacent to the Isle of Mull, about 800 CE.

From this it was assumed that Celtic-speaking peoples must have invaded Britain and Ireland, perhaps about 500 BCE. This notion still existed in popular accounts of Celtic culture, such as television documentaries, as late as the 1980s. No physical evidence for any such invasion has ever been found, and the conventional wisdom today decrees that anyone speaking of it is marked as uninformed and out-of-date.

More importantly, the human remains, often bones and teeth, of ancient Celtic speakers revealed that they were not a unified tribe. This might have been startling in the 1990s, but by the time of this writing the observation is hardly surprising. Millions of people of different ethnicities have swabbed the inside of their cheeks to send off a sample of saliva for DNA testing. Excepting some Asian populations, such as the Japanese, most other people, certainly in North America but also in Europe, find they are descended from groups they had never guessed. Why should it have been different in ancient times when populations might flee war, famine and pestilence without regard for passports or visas? Some genetic markers from Celtic-speaking areas might show up in Britain, Ireland and northwestern France, but there is no evidence to support the notion of a mass migration from Hallstatt and La Tène to Scotland, Ireland, Wales or Brittany.

Continuing field work often undermines accepted assumptions. Some ancient regions populated by speakers of Celtic languages have not left jewelry, metal and stone artifacts of Celtic design. Further, some Celtic artifacts survive in regions where we assume there were few or no speakers of Celtic languages.

Tracing the genetic markers of early populations of any nation, or any language area, is both a complex and a contentious question. Gilbert Márkus (2017) labels as "ethnic fallacy" the notion that clear-cut ethnic communities existed as stable and well-defined entities in the ancient world. Perhaps because the issues pertain so deeply to cultural and personal identities, discourse can frequently become heated. Some commentators have taken dismissive positions, arguing that Celticism in the British Isles is merely a product of the romantic imagination. Consider Simon James's *The Atlantic Celts: Ancient People or Modern Invention?* (1999). The subtitle projects his thesis. As might be expected, *Atlantic Celts* was reviled in some quarters, savaged for errors in detail, as well as solecisms and omissions. Before this publication James had been a popularizer of Celtic culture, *Exploring the World of the Celts* (1993), as well as the chic host of a British television documentary on the Celts. James was hardly alone; consider John Collis, *The Celts: Origins, Myths and Inventions* (2003).

As several books have been written about the ethnic identity of ancient migrations, many contending with one another, the subject is too demanding to be dealt with here. We will give attention to the identity of populations of the Scottish Highlands in the first chapter. The citation of one densely written five-page article in the British journal *Nature* (2015) will suffice for the moment. The sixteen-person team compiling the article was led by Stephen Leslie and Peter Donnelly. Such a modest title as "Fine-Scale Genetic Structure of the British Population" does not signal how explosive many would find its results. A news account from the BBC summarized it this way, "Celts not a Unique Genetic Group." A centuries-old genetic identity may indeed persist, but it does not link the Cornish, Welsh, Scots and Irish. The people of Cornwall have an identity distinct from their neighbors in Devon, but it does not link them to the Welsh, who are divided into two groups. Instead, the Cornish resemble people elsewhere in England. As might have been expected, the population of Lowland Scotland, even though it once spoke Gaelic when it was imposed upon them in the early years of the Scottish kingdom, more closely resembles that of the English population immediately south of the border than it does the population of the Highlands. That Highland population, taken as a whole, does indeed resemble the more northerly of the two genetic communities found in Ireland. The Highland and Irish interface will call for much discussion in the first chapter.

1

The Foundations

Where Are the "Highlands"?

Like "the Lake Country" or "the Cotswolds," "the Scottish Highlands" are a non-national region of the British Isles most readers have heard of, even if they could not quickly identify them on the map. Certainly they would embrace Loch Ness, Ben Nevis and the storied Isle of Skye, but how much else? On close examination it is not immediately clear that "Highlands" is defined more by geology or by culture. The now-dated phrase "culture province" is commonly deployed to categorize the Highlands as an entity, but it may invite ambiguity. The "high" in "Highlands" implies that geology must also be part of its definition, but not all locales in the "Highlands" are mountainous or even elevated. "Culture province" is a translation of the German *Kulturkreis,* evoking a region set apart by language, religion and habitat—"an ethnic and cultural unity." Given that the Highlands have been divided by religion—Episcopalianism, Catholicism and different factions of Calvinism—the definition is already blurred. In German scholarship *Kulturkreis* would denote Gaelic Ireland and Scotland as a continuum, as they sometime are portrayed. While the two are related, as we shall consider in this chapter, they remain distinct. The Irish-speaking realm in Ireland is the called *Gaeltacht* while Scots Gaelic dominates what is called the *Gàidhealtachd*. Before 1500 Gaelic was also spoken in areas of the Lowlands, such as Carrick and Galloway, but in later centuries the term is nearly coextensive with "Highlands," except that many inhabitants of the Highlands have not been Gaelic-speakers for a long while.

The territories designated by the term "Highlands" have not always been fixed, and, further, the Highland/Lowland dichotomy was not noted at all in the first five centuries of the Scottish kingdom. There exist no words in Gaelic, even today, for the Highlands or Lowlands, only words for where Gaelic is or is not spoken. What we think of as the Highlands occupies only the westerly portion of the land above the Forth-Clyde slash across the middle of the nation and visible at first glance at the map. Figuring out just where the "Highlands" begin takes more definition and more scrutiny.

As soon as Highlanders emerge in Lowland commentary, they are viewed with deep disdain but are not defined geographically. This implies that culture was more determining than land forms from the beginning. In the first Scottish history, *Chronica gentis Scotorum* (c. 1370), Johannis de Fordun wrote in Latin of his

14   Highlanders

contempt for the northern population. Translations of his words would resonate down the centuries. After praising the refined, well-ordered people in the south and east, he proclaims: "The highlanders and people of the islands, on the other hand, are a savage and untamed nation, rude and independent, given to rapine and ease-loving, of a docile and warm disposition, comely in person, but unsightly in dress, hostile to the English people and language, and, owning to a diversity of speech, even

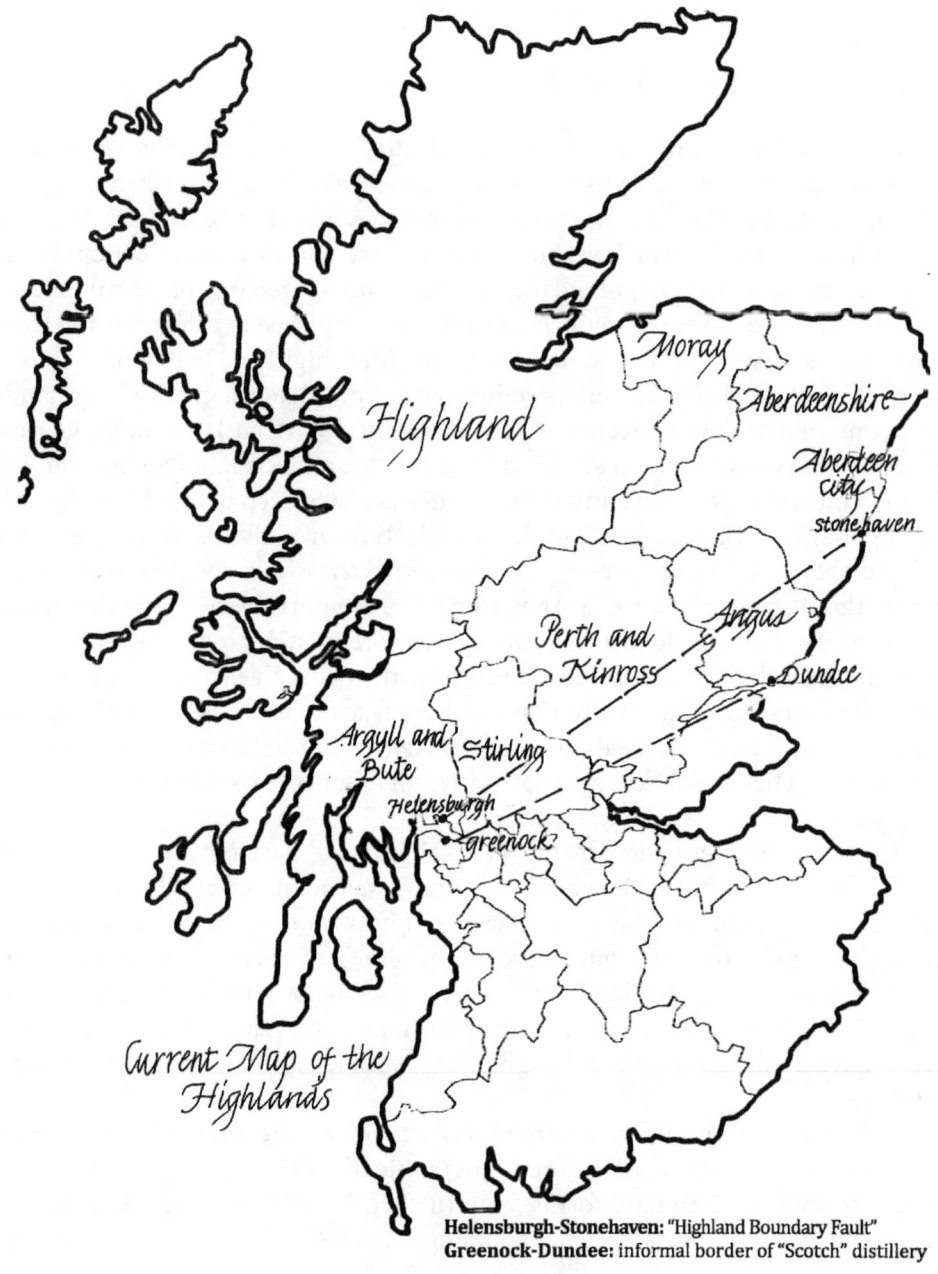

Current map of the Highlands.

to their own nation, and exceedingly cruel. They are, however, faithful and obedient to their king and country, easily made to submit to law, if properly governed." (W.F. Skene translation, 1871). During the fifty-year period when Fordun flourished, 1350–1400, the discrete principality known as the "Lordship of the Isles," *Dominiatus Insularum,* was showing sometimes strident independence from the Scottish Crown. Gaelic was ceasing to be spoken in the Lothians south of Edinburgh.

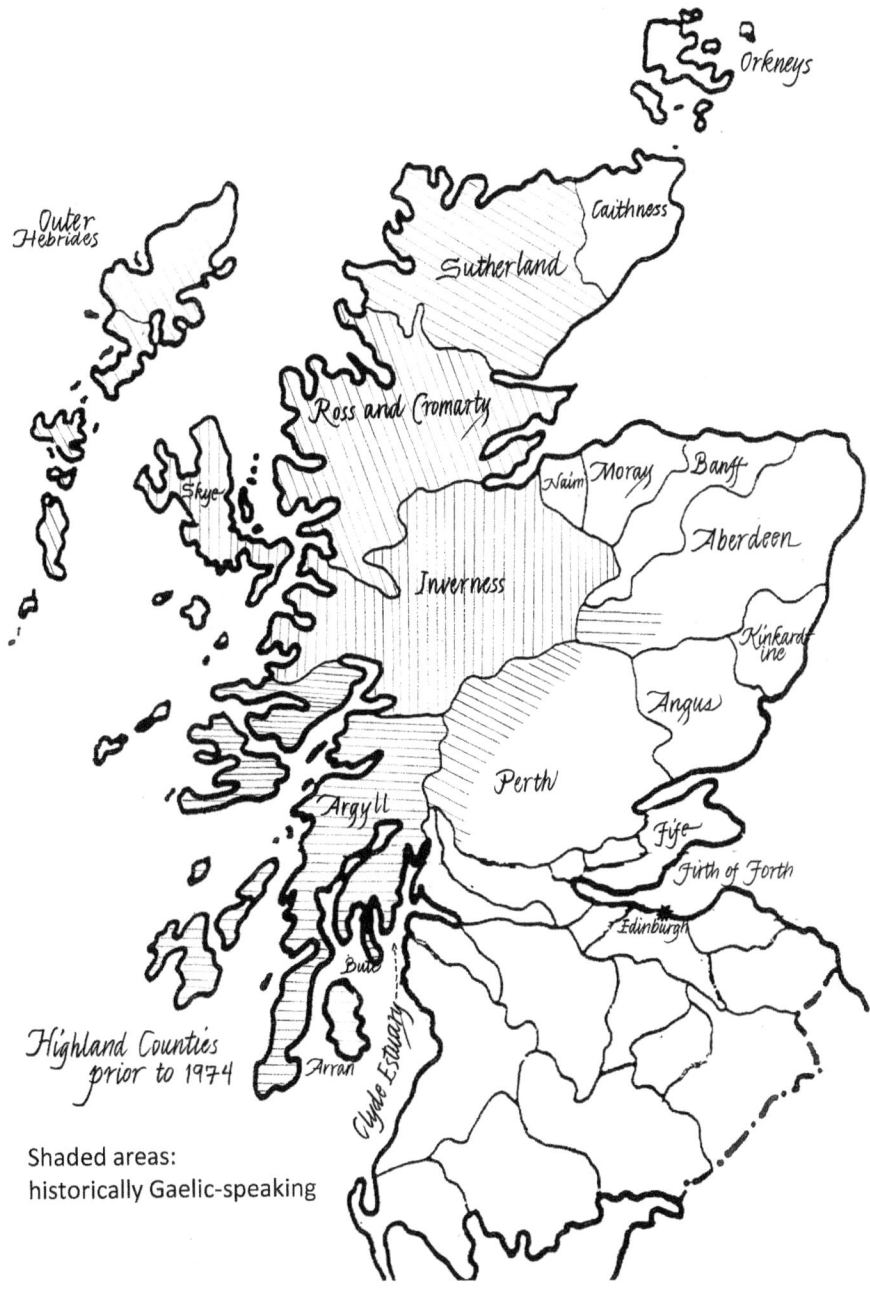

Highland counties prior to 1974.

Fifteen decades after Fordun, historian John Major in *Historia Majoris Britanniae* (1521) would draw sharper distinctions in pithier language. In the south he saw the well-behaved and productive *domestic,* householding Scots, or Lowlanders. To the north he observed an indolent population given to the chase and following worthless and savage chiefs, the *Scoti sylvestres,* "wild Scots."

From the founding of the Scottish kingdom, then called Alba, in c. 844, Gaelic was the language of the royal family and other persons in power. In later centuries it also was spoken in some southern areas of the country closer to the English border. The perception of the Highlands as an "other," separate from the centers of power in Edinburgh, grew as Gaelic was displaced by the Scottish or Scots language, the Germanic-based sibling of English. Competition also came from Norman French among the pre-modern elite and also from Norse-derived dialects. Gaelic persisted and persists in lands poorly suited for agriculture, colloquially thought to be north and west of the "Grampian line," the peaks of the low-lying Grampian Mountains. "North of the Tay" is another shorthand designation, which is useful in the east, but lands to the west, like the Kintyre Peninsula, lie farther south. Language, culture and clan organization may extend from the mainland to the westerly and northern islands, the Inner and Outer Hebrides, or they may be cited distinctly as in "Highlands and Islands." The Norse-influenced Orkneys and Shetlands to the north and northeast, however, do not share the same language and culture as the "Highlands."

In the three hundred years between the seventeenth century and the 1970s, the "Highlands" would have been thought of as embracing several shires or counties, Argyll with the Isle of Bute, Inverness, Ross & Cromarty, and Sutherland. The Norse-influenced Caithness, almost to the Orkneys, would not have been "Highland." The eastern border was uneven and contended. Adjacent portions of Perthshire and Aberdeenshire were usually thought of as "Highland," and possibly also parts of Angus-shire. Excluded were the low-lying, fertile counties just to the east of Inverness, Nairn, Moray and Banff.

Some geographers speak of a Highland Boundary Fault, a nearly straight line running from Helensburgh and the Isle of Arran in the former Argyll to Stonehaven in Aberdeenshire in the east. Other commentators place the western end of the division at Dumbarton. Such a line would include non–Gaelic Nairn, Moray and Banff. The Scotch whisky industry, more expansively, places the "Highlands" in an area north of a line drawn between Greenock (in the former Renfrewshire, and near Glasgow) in the west to Dundee, south of Aberdeen. Such a demarcation puts one of the centers of whisky production in Speyside, home to Glenlivit and Glenfiddich, labels now securely in the Highlands, even though the Spey stretches into the former Morayshire.

Since 1996 local government services have been administered by the Highland Council area, excluding large sections to the south and east as well as the western islands but including the non–Gaelic Caithness, Orkneys and Shetlands. In a challenge to English idiom, this means that the adjective "Highland" is used as a singular noun in addresses, e.g., "Spean Bridge, Highland."

The electoral district for the Scottish Parliament is named "Highlands and Islands." It overlaps with the Highland Council area, and thus includes

Norse-influenced Caithness, the Orkneys and Shetlands, and also the Western Isles, Argyll and Bute.

That district must necessarily encompass much land because it is so sparsely populated: 9.1 persons per square kilometer or 23.6 per square mile in 2012. This density, or lack of it, is comparable to what is found in Bolivia or Chad. In total, the Highlands are about a third of Scottish territory, perhaps 25,277 square kilometers, 10,030 square miles, smaller than Belgium but bigger than Maryland. The expanse is also comparable to that of Sicily.

Just what is denoted by the word "Highlands" is determined by who is speaking and when.

The cultural component in the definition of "Highlands" begins in the fourteenth century, but the physical, geological, is of course fixed. The cliché image of the Highlands as being filled with heather blooming on treeless hillsides is a reminder that the shrub is one of the few forms of vegetation that can thrive in such an unpromising environment. In *The Scottish Clearances* (2018), T.M. Devine estimates that only 9 percent of the land is suitable for cultivation. Earlier commentators cite even lower figures. Entirely uncultivatable are such distinctive landscapes as the Cairngorms and the Ben Nevis *massif,* an extensive alpine plateau at a height of three and a half to four thousand feet, solid ground but cold and granite. Almost as forbidding is the Moine Overthrust, a barren strip of rocky, chaotic country running from the Isle of Skye to Loch Eriboll in Sutherland. Elsewhere the vistas are filled with steep gneiss hills.

There was nothing in northern Scotland or Caledonia (Latin: wooded heights) to entice the Romans. In addition to the weak soil, the potential for Highland agriculture was dealt a cataclysmic blow by the explosion of the Icelandic volcano of Hekla in 1159 BCE. The residue from clouds of ash is still with us.

Such prospects have set the romantic heart aflutter since the mid-nineteenth century, but it was not always so. In premodern times the barrenness and darkness of the Highlands filled some observers with dread. In his *The Sacred Theory of the Earth* (1681), Thomas Burnet argued that such mountains were debris of the Flood, not a primordial part of Creation but rather ruinous memorials of divine anger. Early travelers found them uncouth and horrible. Daniel Defoe in this three-volume *A Tour Thro' the Whole Island of Great Britain* (1727) depicted the Highlands as ugly and "frightful." In one of the first volumes to focus on the Highland landscape, Edmund Burt's *Letters from a Gentlemen …* (written late 1720s), the author complains of the "horrid gloom" of the mountains and the "dirty yellowish" color of mountain streams. In Burt's view, the rugged terrain offers nothing but visual repulsion. He reviles "huge naked rocks [that] produced the disagreeable appearance of a scabbed head." They are "monstrous excrescences." Even Dr. Samuel Johnson, the person who invited the educated classes to know the Highlands, was repelled by the "wide expanse of hopeless sterility." Of the peaks so beloved today by tourists, he observed, "Beyond them were the rocks sometimes covered with verdure, and sometimes towering in horrid nakedness."

The abrupt inversion of earlier disdain for mountains and wilderness fostered by the romantic movement is a well-known story, retold with precision by Simon

Schama in *Landscape and Memory* (1996). More frequent travelers, many of them from the privileged classes, observed that Highland mountains were accessible. The highest peak, Ben Nevis, could be climbed. Even before the revelations of modern geology in the nineteenth century, anyone could see that the Highlands have a distinctive look. Mountains there are older, appearing before the age of dinosaurs, hundreds of millions of years before the emergence of any life form on earth. They lack the jagged peaks of later ranges like the Alps, Rockies or Andes. They are gnarled and worn down, a weathering that began long before the glaciers of ten thousand years ago.

Even older than the mountains is the single most dramatic aspect of the Highland landscape, what immediately catches your eye in a first glance at a map. This is the long slash running from the lower left toward the mid- to upper right, what is usually known as the Great Glen. So prominent in Highland discourse, it has many names, such as *An Gleann Mòr,* anglicized as Glen More, *Glenn Albainn* (Glen of Scotland), and anglicized as Glen Albyn. It is an ancient fault line running 62 miles, 100 kilometers, and partially filled by a series of bodies of water, the Firth of Lorne, Loch Linnhe and Loch Ness, all connected by the Caledonian Canal in 1822. The great shift of land, possibly as much as sixty miles, creating the Great Glen, occurred before continental drift had completed, before what would become what we know as the arrangement of great land masses, possibly 200 million years ago. Resonance from this cataclysm can be measured as far afield as the Baltics and Newfoundland. It is also visible in the long straight coastline of the Black Isle and the Tain Peninsula, whose rocks could have formed the north shore of Loch Ness. Because it is on an ancient fault line, Loch Ness is extraordinarily deep, 755 feet, 230 meters, or 126 fathoms. Add dark peat to the water, and little wonder the depths could provoke fantastical speculation of aquatic beasts.

First-time visitors to the Highlands often remark on an evocation of Scandinavian landscapes, how sea lochs resemble fjords. Early Norse invaders certainly found the Highlands congenial, though not as much as they did flat Normandy. This is not a subject to be explored here, except that Scotland was once connected to the Continent by a land mass known as Doggerland, which disappeared below the North Sea 6500–6000 BCE. Thus, many wild plants known in the Highlands are also found in Denmark.

Lastly, Highland weather is often remarked upon for good reason. It is one of the wettest regions not only in the British Isles but in the world. The annual rainfall is 180 inches (4,577 mm). This contrasts with the rain in Dunbar, southeast of Edinburgh: 22.05 inches (560.18 mm), lower than in sunny Barcelona. Sunshine on the northwest coast reaches between 711 and 1,140 hours annually, as opposed to 1,471–1,540 on the east coast or even the southwest Lowlands.

Peopling the Landscape

Of all the epochs of Highland experience, the scholarship of matters from before the time of the dynastic founder Somerled (c. 1100–1164) is the most volatile. Where there were once few workers in the fields, there are now many. The researchers of

1. The Foundations

recent generations have been equipped with recondite skills, especially in genetics, that produced startling results unanticipated by previous approaches. News flashes from the recent past have been so frequent and breathtaking that I am wary of putting some of these matters in print today for fear that what looks like reliable information might be superseded by the time this text reaches an intended reader. For the most part I will report what I see as the informed consensus of the third decade of the twenty-first century, and will provide rival versions where there is dispute.

We think that Homo sapiens were in the Highlands some millennia after the retreat of the ice cap, perhaps 10,000 BCE. We call these genetically distinct people the western hunter-gatherers, sometimes known by the acronym WHG. Their arrival in the north of Scotland came late, as they are recorded in other parts of Europe as early as 45,000 BCE. We also name this earliest age for the crudity of handmade tools, thus the Paleolithic or Old Stone Age. In the Highlands the WHG were fond of shellfish and left quantities of shells along the rugged coast of the still verdant islands and mainland. In this Scotland is parallel to Scandinavia where the WHG early favored the much harsher, fjord-riven western coast of what is now Norway.

This period was succeeded by the Mesolithic or Middle Stone Age, continuing from about 8000 BCE to 4000 BCE, populated by early European farmers, or EEF. Earlier scholarship had long known that skills required to move from hunting to farming had been imported from the Middle East. What we know now is that actual farmers from the Middle East brought the technology with them, not in a violent invasion like the later Vandals or Huns but dribbling in to unoccupied lands suitable for cultivation. Otherwise informed readers reading of this migration, still not widely known, for the first time will note how the evidence completely annihilates the dangerous follies of nineteenth-century ethnography, when language was thought to confer ethnic identity. The migration began before the introduction of a known language. The EEF also spread to the Highlands, more hospitable to farming before the eruption of Hekla in 1159 BCE.

Last came the Neolithic or New Stone Age, c. 3500–2500, BC, during which the British Isles lagged behind advances elsewhere in Europe. Although the concept of the Neolithic Age was proposed in the nineteenth century, and school children have learned the term for more than a century, our understanding of the character of that millennium has changed substantially. A key feature is now seen as the introduction of language. From the beginning study of comparative linguistics, when the British realized that the many languages of India were related to many of those in Europe, there was a default understanding that speaking words in syntax to communicate with others did not spring up spontaneously. Instead, certain groups led the way, teaching others who followed. Western scholars borrowed the word "Aryan" for a population group cited in the Sanskrit text, the *Upanishads,* because these fair-haired invaders appeared to resemble Europeans, at least northern ones; they are depicted as the founders of the family of languages bridging the east and west. "Aryan," needless to say, became problematic and was replaced by Indo-European, a term still in use to denote the language family. Gradually it became questionable if any such people who could be called the original Indo-Europeans actually existed, and, if so, where they lived. In the later twentieth century, the term "Indo-European," denoting the speculative Ur-language, was replaced by the abbreviation "IE," connoting the tentativeness of the entire matter. That was succeeded by the more favored PIE, for Proto Indo-European. The larger population groups might have formed earlier, but from internal evidence PIE is thought not to have originated before the invention of the wheel, about 3500 BCE.

Today the first speakers have a name and a geographic trajectory. They are the Yamnaya, nomadic sheepherders who evolved between the Volga and Don valleys but spreading into western Russia and Ukraine, who began to move into Europe after 4500 BCE. They are the dominant population in the group referred to generically as the ancestral north Eurasians, or ANE. They did not spread all over Europe, and today their DNA survives most often in the east and north, but their language spread far and wide. From them derive many of the languages of India, the more exotic Asian Tocharian, Iranian or Persian and relatives. Foremost, of course, are the major languages of Europe from the Romance, Germanic and Balto-Slavic families, sturdy independent lines like Georgian, Greek and Armenian, but excluding the outliers, Basque, Hungarian, Finnish and also Saami, spoken elsewhere in Scandinavia. In short, the newcomers taught language to the populations that preceded them. Among these were the P-Celtic languages of Welsh, Cornish and Breton, and the Q-Celtic, Irish, Manx and Scottish Gaelic.

In the contemporary understanding, the Yamnaya or ANE are the ancestors of relatively few Europeans. The languages deriving from PIE were learned by populations from several millennia earlier. Even the hunter-gatherers, the WHG, who had survived in discrete pockets in the advance of agriculture, adapted to the new languages as they merged in the larger population. Some commentators argue that the Basques are their unmixed descendants.

The three Stone Ages are succeeded by three named for metals of increasingly sophisticated technology, names we all learned in school: the Copper (or Chalcolithic Period), the Bronze and the Iron Age. These terms have been used by curators to classify artifacts and cannot always be dated accurately for different areas of the Middle East and Europe. They also overlap with the Stone Ages and each other. Further, they are not accompanied by massive migrations of population. Evidence for the beginnings of the Copper Age can be found as early as the sixth millennium BC. The addition of the hardening alloy tin gave us the Bronze Age from as early as 2000 to 800 BCE in much of Europe. Superior technology produced the Iron Age, noted in Anatolia (modern Turkey) by 1200 BCE, ushering in recorded history. The term "Iron Age," not incidentally, was coined by the Greek writer Hesiod (c. 700 BCE), with disfavor as he found iron to be a grim and unpoetic material.

Celtic languages and Celtic artefacts, not always found in the same places, are products of the Iron Age on the continent and in the British Isles. The origins of the Celtic languages are still unknown and much disputed, a topic not to be touched here. But just as there was no Celtic "invasion" of the British Isles, neither does it appear that there was a discrete Celtic invasion of Europe from the east. People speaking the Celtic languages appear to have resided, by and large, in areas before they learned the languages.

This also means that the many stone monuments that have survived more in areas of Celtic speakers than elsewhere, mostly built in the Mesolithic and Neolithic ages, do not appear to be Celtic expressions. We shall deal with those found in the Highlands briefly below.

These half-dozen or so paragraphs are a minimalist caricature of an immense subject whose study has exploded since 1990. It has its own serial publication, *The Journal of Genetic Genealogy* (2004–). These revelations are so recent that they have only begun to influence Highland self-perception. The notion that the DNA studies have upended the narratives of antique documents is widespread, but few know that the origins of the Indo-Europeans, now the PIE, have been identified and traced. These matters have already been dealt with in available publications, written for the most part by specialists. To treat with the phenomenon further would take more space than this entire volume. Readers wishing to know more might consult Stephen Leslie, *et al.,* "The Fine-Scale Genetic Structure of the British Population," *Nature* (2015); Jean Manco, *Blood of the Celts* (London, 2015); Alistair Moffat & James F. Wilson, *The Scots: a Genetic Journey* (Edinburgh, 2011); J.P. Mallory, *The Origins of the Irish* (London, 2013); and Alistair Moffat, *Before Scotland: The Story of Scotland Before History* (London, 2005). These are popular studies accessible to readers without specialized vocabularies. They do not agree with one another, and indeed, they often contend.

We do, however, have genetic markers both for Highlanders and speakers of Celtic languages, but they fall into different categories and must be seen in historical context. A genome is an organism's complete set of DNA (deoxyribonucleic acid), including all of its genes, containing all the information needed to build and maintain that organism. It gives rise to the cell's architecture and functional machinery. The nucleic acid sequences are encoded as DNA within the 23 chromosome pairs in cell nuclei. A copy of the entire genome is contained in all cells that have a nucleus, even teeth and fingernails. The recovery and examination of hundreds of early human body parts, especially by Harvard University and the University of Copenhagen, is what allows scholars to track migration in lawless, turbulent early Europe.

Among the first categories of genetic identity is the haplogroup, defining a population who share a common ancestor on the patriline or matriline. Some of these appear to have originated centuries earlier than our measurements of tool making, 20,000 BCE and before. There are four divisions of haplogroups: the African, the European, the Asian and the Native American. Conventionally, haplogroups are cited by letters of the alphabet. Immediately we can see how genetic research can run counter to our intuitions and previous experience. For example, the most common haplogroup in Europe is H, according to some sources, shared by about 40 percent of the population. But it is also found in the Middle East, central and northern Asia, northern and eastern Africa as far south as Madagascar. Needless to say, these are people who do not resemble one another and are otherwise not to be related racially or culturally.

My first encounter with the word "haplogroup" came in 2001 with the publication of Brian Sykes's *The Seven Daughters of Eve*, which brought this previously recondite subject into wider discourse, at least among educated people. Seven "daughters" = seven haplogroups for early Europe. Not coincidentally, this was also the year the Human Genome Project was completed. Desultorily, I got around to finding my personal stake in the question when the first of several companies I employed told me I belonged to group R1b. More precisely, the haplogroup should be named R, the additional digits implying narrower focus. R1a for Eastern Europe, R1b for Western, are termed subclades. The analysis sounded scientific and authoritative. Mine was a late entry to this subject, coming two years after Stephen Oppenheimer's iconoclastic *Origins of the British*, which had much to say about R1b. But I came a few years before the mass-market boom in DNA testing. In subsequent years the reliability of the tests has been challenged, and definitions of "haplogroup" have been adjusted. Additionally, the subject of genetic inheritance is profoundly complex, comparable to the usual touchstone of rocket science.

Although R1b is indeed prominent in Scotland and Ireland, it is also dominant in paternal lineage all over western Europe, especially in the Iberian Peninsula and France. Easily found information in popular sources report that it originated along the Caspian Sea before 12,000 BCE, and thus before the initiation of PIE languages. R1b can also be found as far away as western China and in Bahrain. Narrowing the focus, the subclade R1b1a2a1a2 finds its densest concentration in those areas of the British Isles where the Celtic languages persisted the longest as well as in Brittany.

A fuller genetic report will include a host of other alphabetized markers for specific identities. Alistair Moffat & James F. Wilson's *The Scots: a Genetic Journey* (2011) identifies many of them. M269 is not only common elsewhere in Europe but is characteristic of the main portion of the Clan Donald, other than the chiefs. I have it. Other markers signal migration from unexpected locations, such as M26 pointing to Sardinia. This is found fairly widely in the Highlands, and is also in my profile. The report from 23andMe says I am .5 percent Sardinian. That does not mean descent from the Italianate people now living there but rather migration from the substantial prehistoric population on the island. Others indicate more recent migration, such as M222, a link to the famed Irish king, Niall of the Nine Hostages (fl. 450 CE), once thought legendary though cited in many early genealogies. One of the most newsworthy items of this genetic research is that up to a third of the population of Ireland, especially in the north, and up to three million men worldwide, can claim descent from Niall. Some of his children are in the Highlands, and 23andMe says I am one of them. Authorities, some self-appointed, do not always reach consensus. 23andMe described my subclade, R-L21, as common among Gaelic speakers, while S145 is the "quintessential marker," according to Moffat & Wilson, for speakers of Scottish Gaelic. I did not have the second number in my report, however, even though all four of my grandparents most assuredly spoke Gaelic as a first language.

What appears to drive the boom for DNA testing is the understandable desire to find a sure, "scientific" reassurance of the self in the distant past. I confess to such a delight when I discovered I was R1b, which turns out to be not much of a distinction. Most of the writers arguing for a genetic identity of any Celtic-speaking group, including the Highlanders, are popularizers of the work of arcane specialists, most without prestige academic addresses. Celtic language specialists, who are not geneticists, have been less keen. The formidable Celticist Patrick Sims-Williams of

Aberystwyth, spoke for many when he said he did not find the evidence compelling in "Genetics, Linguistics and Pre-History: Thinking Big and Thinking Straight," *Antiquity,* 72 (1998), 505–527.

Prehistoric Testimony

The northern half of the isle of Britain is as well-endowed in ancient monuments as any region in Europe. The mysterious Callanish/Callernish on the Isle of Lewis are as photogenic as any ancient stone edifices on earth. For the most part, however, they have not become cultural signifiers the way Stonehenge is in England or Newgrange/Brú na Bóinne is in Ireland. Part of the reason for this is that the stones were raised in the Bronze, Neolithic and Mesolithic ages well before the 1159 BCE Hekla eruption and such names as Scotia or even Caledonia were affixed to the map. They may have been constructed by the ancestors of the people we call Scottish, but they are not always seen as Scottish expressions.

Benefiting from better care are the many standing stones at Callanish or Callernish on the west coast of the Isle of Lewis in the Outer Hebrides. Quarried from local gneiss, there are nineteen sites in little over the stretch of a mile above the waters of Loch Roag, of which the most prominent is Callanish I, a cruciform arrangement of five rows of standing stones. The biggest one from the rows stands 11' 6" (3.5 meters) at the west, and nearby is the central monolith at 15' 8" (4.8 meters). Despite their Gaelic name, taken from a nearby village, the stones were erected sometime after 3000 BCE, well before the advance of spoken Gaelic. We cannot know for what purpose the stones were erected, but as with other ancient monuments, careful scrutiny supports a theory of alignment of the stones with heavenly bodies, tracking the paths or stars and constellations. Recent archaeology has discovered many tiny pieces of pottery, indicating that Callanish I was in use for centuries and not abandoned for at least a millennium and a half after its erection.

Observed by such early travelers as Martin Martin (1695) and antiquarians as John Toland (1726), the stones were claimed early for Celtic culture when William Stukeley declared that they were "druid circles." Generous with this assertion, Stukeley described any number of early megaliths, including Stonehenge (built more than 1000 years after Callanish), to be "druid circles." Entirely without evidence, the notion has persisted in the popular mind and has been difficult to shake.

The 10,000 or so square miles, variously demarcated, that make up the Highlands, contain more than a thousand prehistoric monuments, many of them variants of those found elsewhere in the British Isles and western Europe. These include chambered tombs, cairns, hillforts and duns, as well as examples of the still mysterious cup-and-ring markings. Given that our definition of "Highlands" includes language and culture, it is not possible to argue that these edifices are characteristic of the populations who settled there, with the possible exception of the broch, built much later, from 390 BCE to 200 CE.

Along with disagreement over etymology and definition, there is no consensus over the broch's purpose and function. Several recurrent physical details suggest the broch might have been a defensive structure, an early form of the castle. Consider the thick walls, narrow openings or doors, and (in many) spiral staircases and the placement of scarcements (ledges), on which wooden platforms may have been built. This was the explanation of the eminent V. Gordon Childe in the early twentieth century. In his view, the broch was a residence where local landowners held sway over the local population. As further investigation continued, the thesis shifted from fortress to "stately home."

Toward the south end of the glen, about four miles south of Kilmartin Village lies a rocky crag, Dunadd, which played a continuing role in Highland history. Its Gaelic name, *Dùn Ad,* means only that it is a hill by the small river Add. It was probably once seen as an island as it was previously surrounded by a huge bog, *Mòine Mhòr* (Great Moss), now reclaimed, which could have served as part of the crag's defense. Repeated archaeological investigations, 1904–1905, 1929 and 1980, support the view that although it was occupied in the Iron Age, the busiest human activity came during recorded history when it served as a capital of the early Gaelic kingdom, Dál Riada. It is cited in the *Annals of Ulster* through the 600s and 700s. Indeed, it was visited by many notable people. Not only are there inscriptions in the early Irish script, ogham, but there is also an incised figure of a boar in Pictish style. Investigations have uncovered quern stones for grinding grain, tools, weapons, imported pottery and molds for the manufacture of fine metalwork, including jewelry. The best-known feature of Dunadd is the so-called "footprint of fealty," which may (or may not) have played a role in kingly ritual. Perhaps it was a Cinderella-like challenge for an aspirant, or a symbolic marriage of a new ruler and his subjects. When I first visited Dunadd in 1984, the only person there for over an hour, the foot-shaped slot in the stone looked as though it might have originated in nature and was later augmented by helpful patriots. From reports it appears that so many feet have been inserted in the crevice that the original has been replaced by a replica.

Dunadd was occupied for at least two centuries after Dál Riada was subsumed into the proto-Scottish kingdom of Alba in the 840s. As late as 1506, James IV of Scotland sent a commission, including the earl and bishop of Argyll, to meet at Dunadd to collect rents and to resolve feuds. Today it is an official Ancient Monument, under the care of Historic Scotland, but open to the public without charge.

Evidence for the ways people lived in the prehistoric Highlands has required more careful attention. During the unusually dry summer of 1976 an aerial orography expedition sponsored by the Royal Commission on the Ancient and Historical Monuments was scouring the landscape. Near Balbridie, east of Banchory, on the south shore of the River Dee, Aberdeenshire, they noted previously undetected cropmarks implying the existence of a large structure under the soil. Subsequent digging at the site, 1977–1980, allowed for the conceptual reconstruction of an enormous timber structure. Some of the outline of the building was plotted from the identification of large timber postholes. The long house constructed on the site is 85' (26 meters) long, 43' (13 meters) wide, covering an area of 3,546 sq. ft. (329.6 sq. meters).

Balbridie is one of the earliest known Neolithic settlements in Scotland, 4000–3400 BCE, and the largest Neolithic long house in Britain. Although the Dee Valley might be claimed as an eastern portion of the Highlands, as it is close to the Elsick

Mounth trackway, a route inland through the lower Grampian Mountains. The long house was built before the arrival of either Gaelic or Pictish. It is not unique. Postholes and rectangular outlines comparable to Balbridie have been found at Dreghorn, Ayrshire, and in Cambridgeshire.

Little discussed is the evidence of how poorer folk fared in the Bronze Age. They lived in an underground dwelling that was accessed by a passage, uncomfortable and unhealthy, but possibly warm in the winter. Not a cave but a man-made retreat. The English word for this disheartening reminder of a difficult past is "weem," from the Gaelic *uamh*: cavern, den, grave.

Unlike the experience of the other Celtic countries, ancient monuments in the Highlands are not magnets for lore and fanciful names. In Brittany almost every dolmen or menhir comes with a story, as do some stones in Cornwall. In Ireland the passage grave of Newgrange was thought to be the residence of the Apollo-like patron of poetry, Angus Óg. An exception to that pattern appears to be the name of a Highland natural feature, but turns out to be a solecism in translating Gaelic. That would be the celebrated (but still difficult to access) colonnaded basalt cavern on the island of Staffa in the Inner Hebrides, known as Fingal's Cave. John Keats and Queen Victoria were both ecstatic visitors, but none could match the joy of composer Felix Mendelssohn (1809–1847), who subtitled his orchestral jewel, *The Hebrides Overture,* "Fingal's Cave." Fingal was an occasional variant name for the old Gaelic hero Fionn mac Cumhaill/Finn MacCool. Not necessarily Scottish, it had been employed in James Macpherson's notorious forgeries, *The Poems of Ossian* (1760), about which more in Chapter 5. At the time of Mendelssohn's composition, 1829, most educated people would know it. Local Gaelic speakers knew the cave long before the advent of Macpherson or Mendelssohn, however. Perceiving that they heard a kind of music from waves washing against the side of the opening, they referred the place as *Un Uaimh Bhinn:* the melodious cave. This was mistranscribed as *Un Uaimh Finn,* which is gibberish in Gaelic. But the credulous, seizing upon the Gaelic spelling *Finn*, extrapolated it to Fingal.

The Scots/Gaels: Ethnogenesis

The Latin terms *Scotti, Scoti,* and their translation, "Scots," have not always denoted the people who live in Scotland. The etymology is disputed but seems to have been derived from an earlier word for "pirates." In early Latin texts it carries negative connotations. It would denote speakers of Old Irish, ancestor both of Modern Irish and Scottish Gaelic. Those people referred to themselves as *Goídel,* Gaels. As both Christianity and literacy came to Ireland before they reached the Highlands, *Scotia* became a name for Ireland, also called Hibernia in Latin. Consider that the name of the most learned man in the post–Charlemagne Carolingian court, Johannes Scotus Eriugena (c. 805–877), is usually translated as "John the Irishman." Not only was he born and educated in Ireland, but he flourished contemporary with the founding of the kingdom of Alba before it was known as Scotia/Scotland.

The realm of the Gael, far from being a nation-state, extended into what we now call Scotland, especially the Hebrides. As Irish Christianity spread, spiritual leader Colum Cille or Columba (c. 521–593), a descendant of the famed leader Niall of the Nine Hostages and a member of the powerful Uí Néill dynasty, established a monastery in 543 on Iona, off the west coast of the Isle of Mull in the Inner Hebrides. His life record and dates are testified in carefully preserved manuscripts. The evangelization of all of Scotland spread from here. In the first centuries, however, Iona was in effect still a part of Ireland. The most celebrated work of early Irish art, *The Book of Kells,* was compiled on Iona about the year 800. The Hebridean location is almost a footnote; no one ever refers to the *Book of Kells* as a Scottish masterpiece.

Iona and the adjacent Isle of Mull are off the coast of what was long called Argyll. Argyllshire was one of the most Gaelic counties of the Highlands until its borders were erased in 1974 and redrawn in 1996. Its name in Old Irish is *Airer Goídel,* country of the Gael, and in Scottish Gaelic, *Erra Ghaidheal,* coastland of the Gael. Its borders were not fixed and extended far beyond those of the former Argyllshire. "Coastland" implies that this might have been a route of entry for the Gaels, and the Irish word denotes that Argyll is the land of the Goídel, the word they use for themselves, i.e., "our land." Early written records support these semantics. The Benedictine monk known as the Venerable Bede (c. 673–735), "the father of English history," wrote in his *Ecclesiastical History of the English People* that "Britain received a third tribe, ... namely the Irish (*Scotti*). These came from Ireland under their leader Reuda, and won lands from the Picts ... they are still called Dalreudini after this leader." Bede does not suggest dates, but he was writing of events that would have taken place centuries earlier. He altered the brief account from the Breton scribe Gildas (fl. 560–570), who thought the Scots/Gaels had arrived coextensively with the Picts; together, in his telling, they would have displaced the Romano-British population. In suggesting that the Picts are already in Scotland Bede is endorsed by modern research and understanding. How the Picts nonetheless contributed to Highland identity will call for more attention later.

Our normative name for the realm Bede calls Dalredini, an extension of a petty kingdom from northern Ireland, is Dál Riada or Dál Riata; it derives from an imagined ancestor Eochu Riata, whose name may or may not be related to Dalredini. Modern historiography has employed accounts of the *Annals of Tigernach,* in Latin, Old and Middle Irish, compiled at the famed monastery of Clonmacnoise on the Shannon River, and unavailable to Gildas or Bede. Concurring with Gildas and Bede, these *Annals* portray Dál Riada as an extension of families from Ulster into Argyll and adjoining territories, since 1996 called Argyll and Bute, with different boundaries. The *Annals* further cite names of important leaders accepted as historical in modern references until recently. Áedán mac Gabráin, baptized by Colum Cille, was named as leader of the migration, establishing a capital on the mountain top of Dunadd. An early king Fergus mac Eirc or Fergus Mór, was thought to have brought over the fabled Lia Fáil (Ir. Stone of Destiny) to Scotland. Later tradition asserted that the Stone of Scone, placed under the throne of a new monarch at coronation, was identical with the Lia Fáil. In this narrative the narrow extension of the Irish Sea known today as the North Channel is known poetically as Sruth na Maoile, the Sea of Moyle.

Well before a new generation of researchers began to undermine the Bede version of an eastward migration across the Sea of Moyle, the notion of it had begun to appear implausible to commentators. One opined that the Ulstermen seemed to have brought no baggage with them. Ulster has always been one of the most fertile portions of Ireland, home to extensive ancient early civilization, whereas Argyll is rocky and unpromising, with few beaches or low coastal areas where invaders might wade ashore or transport possessions. Toward the end of the twentieth century, it was established that although the stonewalled ringfort was the commonest form of settlement in early Ulster, it is not known in early Argyll, although there are suitable locations for them. This was a small enclosure with earthen banks used for keeping cattle as well as for living accommodations. A comparable Scottish development was the dun, usually found on a hilltop. Even more unsettling is the data from the study of the crannóg, a distinctive feature of early Scotland and Ireland, not found in England.

In early Christian Ireland, fifth to seventh centuries, a common feature of the landscape was what we call now the ogham pillar: a standing stone with incised inscriptions in the pre–Roman alphabet known as ogham, codified slashes, containing the name of who was to be commemorated. Several hundred of these survive in different parts of Ireland, but there are only two in Argyll.

Surviving jewelry also implies two different aesthetic standards. Both Irish and Scottish Gaels were skilled makers of gold, silver and bronze brooches and pins, works that both identified a person's tribe and social rank. In Dál Riada the most widely known brooch had rectangular terminals with beveled edges, while the counterpart in Ireland had animal heads. Pins with spiral rings, in the manner of key rings, were common in Ireland but nearly unknown in Scotland.

With these and even more extensive findings, Bede's narrative of migration came to be called a pseudo-history in the twenty-first century, even though it is still cited in encyclopedias and reference books. There has been no shortage of theories to replace Bede, but not one has been anointed the most authoritative.

In 2001 Ewan Campbell proposed one of the most provocative of these in the widely read journal *Antiquity*. His thesis is announced in the title of a seven-page article, "Were the Scots Irish?" As both Irish and Scottish Gaelic derive from Old Irish, Campbell refers to populations on both sides of the Sea of Moyle as Goidels, a Q-Celtic language. In his view, not only was there no migration east, but the Goidels share an identity that separates them from the P-Celts of what is now Scotland, the Brittonic speakers and the Picts. Campbell cites as the interface between Q-Celts and P-Celts the *Druimm Albin* (also *Druim Albin, Drum Albyn*, Drumalban, etc.) the "Spine of Britain," sometimes identified as the indistinct "Grampian Line" cited above as the isobar distinguishing the Highlands from Lowlands. Culturally, it was once thought to be the line dividing Picts to the east and Dál Riada to the west. Even in the modern world trekkers and bikers can testify that it is indeed physically demanding to get one's self from Aberdeen to Fort William, whereas small craft can easily traverse the water between the Isle of Iona and County Antrim in Ireland. Thus, Campbell would see a single linguistic identity, with many regional variants, between the Druimm Albin and the Aran Islands. And the Scots would be "Irish," per his title.

An immediate problem with the thesis is that at different times Q-Celtic Scottish Gaelic was spoken to the east of the Druimm Albin just as P-Celtic languages were spoken both west of the line and in Ireland.

Historian James E. Fraser addresses the state of indecision in *From Caledonia to Pictland: Scotland to 795* (2009), the revised Volume One in *The New Edinburgh History of Scotland*. He cites Ewan Campbell in his bibliography and a footnote but does not discuss him in the text. Instead, Fraser borrows the word "diphyletic" from paleontology to describe the kingdom of Dál Riada that encompassed Kintyre and Cowal in southern Argyll and extended into Antrim in the north of Ireland. More simply, he posits a single unit derived from two lines of evolutionary descent. Medieval origin stories, he observes, were steeped in political significance at the time of writing and were not necessarily scrupulous about "historical accuracy." There is no clear evidence that the first half of the millennium saw the dedicated colonization of Argyll by a single Irish people. It seems more likely that there were gradual piecemeal movements of colonists across the Sea of Moyle in both directions, who have "gone native" in material terms upon their arrival and settlement. Movement between what became known as Argyll and Antrim appears to have begun in the Stone Age and continued for more than a thousand years, including the medieval centuries of the rising of the Scottish clans. Population transfers between Scotland, the Lowlands and Argyll, and Ireland, fostered by the English Crown, were transforming for the Plantations of Ulster in the seventeenth century.

Fraser also points out that identity, culture and the Gaelic language in Atlantic Scotland would not have developed as a single package. Each would have developed as a result of a multiplicity of factors and phenomena, at different times and for different reasons. Elsewhere Fraser touches on the issue of ethnogenesis, how disparate groups can be forged into a perceived single identity. The architect of this theory is Reinhard Wenskus of Vienna, where academics contended over makeup of such ancient groups as the Goths and Franks. One group saw identity made by the givens of birth, territory, language, religion and culture, while the other saw ethnicity rising primarily as a function of political interests with accommodations made to changes in those interests. Wenskus championed the role of the *Traditionskern*, "kernel of tradition," an elite group at the head of every new ethnic identity.

Whatever the origins of Dál Riada, surviving documents tell us much about the leaders of the petty kingdom and its organization. Key among them is *Senchus fer nAlban,* The History of the Men of Scotland, an Old Irish text believed to have been compiled in the tenth century, derived from earlier Latin sources. At that date Scottish Gaelic was not yet separate from Old Irish. A relatively short document, seventy to eighty lines in different manuscripts, its esteem was so high that several copies survive, both as a single text at Trinity College Dublin and also in medieval codices, the *Book of Ballymote* and the *Book of Lecan* (before 1418). Among other things, it portrays a Dál Riada that was anything but an impoverished backwater, with an organized bureaucracy as advanced as any in northern Europe. The *Senchus* also gives us glimpses of the lives of ordinary people, usually nameless in any other European record of the same time. In assessing the numbers of fighting men available in different areas, it is the closest thing to a census in Britain before the *Domesday Book* in the eleventh century. Up to 2000 men could be mustered for combat on land and sea.

The name of the early king cited in the Irish *Annals*, Fergus Mór, appears as well in the *Senchus*. Ewan Campbell argues that the text was altered to incorporate him. The first named kings of Dál Riada are Comgall and Gabrán, who died about 550. Cited but not explored are four founders of four kinships, or *cenéla*, singular *cenél*. People saw themselves as belonging to large extended families, which included all the descendants of a person's great, great grandfather; the Irish term for this is *derbfhine*. Having children, both male and female, fostered within the kingship helped to forge a network of social and familial ties. The word *Cenél* was widely used in early Ireland and appears to be similar in meaning to the more widely known *Tuath*. It would not have denoted the binding familial relationship denoted by the late Scottish term "clan." It would not occupy a territory with precise borders, but among the more northerly of these was Cenél Loairn above Loch Fyne, coextensive with what is called Lorn today. More easterly, below Loch Fyne, was Cenél Comgaill on the Cowal Peninsula, whose name preserves a variant of the seventh century. To the south and west lay Cenél nGabráin on what is now the Kintyre (*cinn-tìre*: headland) Peninsula; Fergus Mór's descendants settled here. West and offshore lay Cenél nOengusa on the Isle of Islay.

Along with upending Bede's thesis of Irish settlement of Dál Riada, recent archaeological digs have affirmed that the kingdom was more affluent than previously thought, more of a crossroads than a backwater. It owned larger quantities of continental pottery than any other region in Britain during the centuries of its flourishing. Harassed and sometimes overrun by hostile invaders like the Picts and the Norse, Dál Riada managed to use such moments for cultural appropriation. It was in Dál Riada and the nearby Irish monastery of Iona that the Insular Style emerged, borrowing also from Anglo-Saxon art and even farther afield. A jewelry workshop at Dunadd produced a bronze foil stamped with animal designs, fusing disparate aesthetics, similar to those found in the illuminated *Book of Durrow,* an early art treasure, also compiled on Iona. A notable masterpiece of such jewelry-making is the Hunterston Brooch, admittedly similar to brooches found in Ireland, but now displayed at the National Museum of Scotland.

The presumed capital of Dál Riada, the *caput regionis,* is usually thought to be Dunadd, a stronghold on the River Add. It lies in the archaeologically rich Kilmartin Glen, about four miles north of the modern town of Lochgilphead, as mentioned above. Undercutting this idyllic narrative of Dunadd is the assertion that the *caput regionis* might instead have been the highly photogenic Dunollie Castle, offshore, near the regional center of Oban. It was later occupied by the Clan MacDougall.

Despite the later fall in esteem of the Gaels in Scottish history, Dál Riada has long been a valorized reference in national discourse. Many families, not just Highland ones, have inflated their genealogies by claiming descent from ancestors of sixth-to-eighth-century Argyll. Pulled out of historical context, the name often has positive associations. Some years ago, I saw a Dál Riada nursery school in Edinburgh. In the ninth century, however, as the Gaels of the west began to unite, 844–868, with peoples to the east speaking other languages, the identity of Dál Riada was subsumed in an emerging nation. Centers of power also moved to the east, especially Scone and Dunkeld, and the center of learning moved from Iona to St. Andrews, out of what we would call the Highlands.

Our understanding of how the Gaels of Dál Riada came to be merged with neighboring populations is distorted by the self-confidence of nineteenth-century historians and educators who willfully misread obscure and ambiguous documents. Their views have entered discourse. Generations of Scottish schoolchildren were drilled that Scotland was launched as a nation in 844 when Kenneth MacAlpin (sometimes MacAlpine) united the Scots and the Picts. Some sources cite him as King Kenneth I. Otherwise reputable encyclopedias published before 1960 repeat the names and date.

By the beginning of the twenty-first century all of these "facts" had become undone, in part because of closer scrutiny of original sources and the examination of contemporary manuscripts. First to come loose was the date, which might have been any year between 843 and 848. Secondly, the name "Scotland," or Latin *Scotia*, did not appear until many years later. At first the entity was known as Alba, pronounced "al-uh-ba," with a schwa after the l, which is still found in Modern Scottish Gaelic. Also appearing much later is the English name "Kenneth," a transliteration of Cináed mac Ailpín or mac Alpín (Modern Scottish Gaelic Coinneach mac Ailpein). His name is certainly appropriate for a Gael, but whether he was actually a Scot or a Pict is a matter of some debate.

Cináed/Kenneth entered modern Scottish historiography from the unprepossessing-sounding *Poppleton Manuscript,* a document of questionable provenience that appears to have survived by mere chance. A monk named Robert of Poppleton in York commissioned its composition in the middle of the fourteenth century, approximately five hundred years after Cináed. Within *Poppleton* is the "Chronicle of the Kings of Alba," which cites twelve kings, beginning with Cináed, called here Kinadius. For perhaps three hundred years *Poppleton* may have been lost, but it was purchased by a French courtier, who knew nothing of its value, toward the end of the seventeenth century. He took it to France, where it still resides.

Citation of Cináed evidently persisted, but not in documents we can examine. Andrew of Wyntoun's Middle English *Orygynale Cronykil of Scotland* (before 1430) speaks of a Kyned, son of Alpyne. A century and a half later the early historian George Buchanan in *Rerum Scoticarum Historia* added unsupported lurid detail about how the father of the first Scottish king, now called Kenneth, had been murdered by Picts and his son sought vengeance against them.

The ninth is one of those centuries we used to call "dark," but in recent years more light has been cast upon it. Old Irish documents, such as the *Annals of Ulster,* are now translated and widely available; they often speak of matters in what became Alba, at the eastern reaches of spoken Irish dominance. The *Annals* record that in 839 the Norse ("heathen") destroyed Northumbria before raging north to inflict a serious defeat on the people of Pictland. The massacre of the local aristocracy included petty kings of two regions of the confederacy. Thus, the Picts were at a disadvantage just when Cináed and his retinue became more assertive.

Cináed appears indeed to have been a potent warlord, as Scottish schoolbooks instructed, and he led the merging of the Gaelic and Pictish hegemonies. He probably had stakes in both camps. Whatever his status in what remained to the Pictish hierarchy, becoming king of the fused entity of Alba defined his status, although he still might be cited as *Rex Pictorum*, King of the Picts. Further, scribes no longer speak of a king of Dál Riada. Shortly after this time annalists cease to speak of the Picts at all because they had become *fir Alban,* "men of Alba." *Alba* remains the Modern Gaelic word for Scotland, but from context we can see that the first usage of Alba did not denote what we mean by Scotland today but rather only the union of Gaels and Picts. As such it differed from territorial and kinship designations, as Dál Riada had been or *Ulaid* for Ulster in Ireland.

Perhaps centripetal forces might have encouraged the joining of rivals, even if Cináed had not appeared. In these same decades persons living on the island of Ireland were depicted in the Annals as *fir Éirenn*, "men of Ireland," for the first time, rather than identified as men of Ulster, Leinster or Connacht. Within the next century the residents of Gwynedd, Powys and Dyfed could greet each other as *Cymro,* "fellow Welshman."

The Scotland that appeared by the twelfth century is a hybrid kingdom, an amalgam of different peoples. Many nations of Europe and Asia are built on the unification of peoples from different invasions, speaking different dialects, sometimes in earlier smaller states or principalities, Gascony and Burgundy or Saxony and Bavaria. In most instances the regional differences are familial, the different dialects are related. Not so Scotland. Alba brought together the Q-Celtic Gaels and the Picts whose languages might be distantly related (more about that shortly), but that were mutually incomprehensible at the ascent of Cináed. Later would come the P-Celtic Britons of Strathclyde in the south west, with a language incomprehensible to Gaels, and the Germanic Angles of Bernicia in the south east. A fifth group was the Norse who settled widely in what would become Scotland, deeply influencing the basically Germanic Scots language spoken in the Lowlands. Small in numbers but enormous in influence were the Norman nobles, counterparts of the Normans in England and Ireland after 1066. Representative Scotsmen such as Robert the Bruce arose from Norman antecedents. The initially dominant Gaels became the principal component population of the Highlands. The loss of status for the Highlanders within the kingdom, a frequent theme in this study, may derive in part from the linguistic isolation of the *Gàidhealtachd* against the other groups, with connections to England, Wales and Scandinavia, as well as the dearth of natural resources.

The family Cináed established continued to rule Alba, as his successors' patronymics signal. He was followed by his brother, Dòmhnall mac Ailpín (858–862) and then by his grandson, Constantín mac Cináeda (862–877). Rulers were selected through what we now call tanistry or thanistry (as in "thane"), where one would be selected from a large pool of candidates with a claim to the throne based on ancestry or marriage. The succession was a formula for disorder rather than stability. Six kings were killed by their successors or in feuds. The most notable interruption came from a usurper who would become the most famous Scotsman of the era, Macbethad mac Findlaích (1040–1057), known to Shakespeare and to us as Macbeth. Shakespeare had shown scant interest in Scotland before the ascent of James I (James VI of Scotland) in 1603, and he never visited the northern kingdom. His attempt to please the new monarch drew from his reading of Raphael Holinshed's *Chronicles of England, Scotland and Ireland* (1577), which had taken materials from Hector Boece's *Scotorum Historiae* (1527).

The playwright felt no need to search out the meagre details of the historical Macbethad, which we have come to know only through generations of determined scholarship. The historical king was descended from the family group the Cenél Loairn of Dál Riada and was son of the *mormaer* (great steward) of Moray in the northwest; he was thus a man with a Gaelic name who lived in the more Pictish-derived area of Alba. His predecessor Donnchad (Duncan) had expanded Alba to embrace Caithness to the north and Strathclyde. He was killed in battle, possibly at Bothnagoune (now Pitgaveny) near Elgin. Macbethad did not murder him, but one account has them together at the time of Donnchad's death, and as in the play, he drove out Donnchad's sons. The new king reigned at Scone, in what was long Aberdeenshire, like his predecessors. His grip on power was so secure that he felt he could make a pilgrimage to Rome. After a seventeen-year delay a son of Donnchad named Máel-Caluim (Malcolm) did indeed kill Macbethad in what would later be Aberdeenshire, but did not seize the throne immediately. A stepson named Lulach ruled for a year until he too was dispatched by Máel-Caluim, who then became ruler of Alba.

In a reign lasting until 1093, the new king, Máel-Caluim III, usually known by the anglicized form Malcolm Canmore (*ceann mór*: great head/chief), established a dynasty that ruled for two centuries. He also made two important political marriages, first to Ingibiorg, widow of the ruler of Orkney, and the English noble, Margaret of Wessex, who had fled the Normans. A hater of all things Celtic, about which more later, Margaret discouraged the use of Gaelic. A rigorously pious and observant woman, Margaret was canonized shortly after death and remains on the Church's calendar of the saints.

Composing *Macbeth* in 1605–1606, Shakespeare could not know the locales scholarship has identified, but all of the placenames he cites are north of the Forth-Clyde lateral division of Scotland and close by the earlier realm of Alba. Cawder Castle, built long after Macbethad's time, is in the former Nairnshire, whereas Glamis is in Angus. The "blasted heath" where Macbeth encounters the witches is at Forres, in the former Morayshire, and Dunsinane may still be visited in Perthshire. Banquo is cited in the drama as the Thane of Lochaber, linking him to the region that would become the heartland of the surviving Gàidhealtachd as spoken Gaelic retreated.

It was in the century following Malcolm Canmore's time that the kingdom became more involved with its non–Gaelic regions south of Forth-Clyde to the Tweed and Solway, and the whole came to be perceived as *Scotia,* deriving from the early Gaelic rulers. The entity was first cited as the "Kingdom of the Scots" in 1161–1162, a term that had become common by the 1190s. The center of national gravity would remain in the north, however; Edinburgh did not become the capital until 1437.

The Picts

They are a people "garlanded with an air of mystery," to quote the Bryan Sykes (2006) phrasing. Almost no records in their language survive, we do not know what they called themselves, and they seem to have disappeared from history. Better yet, they left dozens of art works, often prudently cut into the hardest stone to ensure preservation, presciently executed in a style that would delight aestheticians centuries later. The title of the best-known book on them from the mid-twentieth century, F.T. Wainwright's *The Problem of the Picts* (1955), amplified the allure. "Problems" beg to be solved. Further, they appear to have gained their Latin name for sporting tattoos, like Maori warriors or the denizens of an Amsterdam "coffee shop."

For these and other reasons, the Picts represent the one aspect of this study that I can expect a person with a minimal acquaintance with early Scotland is likely to recognize, well ahead of the historical Macbeth or the Jacobite Rebellion with its vast romantic literature. At the same time, "problems," called *lacunae* in academia, also attract researchers employing empirical methods to determine answers. Demotic speculation about the Picts excites readers, but a wave of responsible investigation from about 1965 brings the Picts back to earth.

Consult any search engine for the Internet for what the words "Puzzle of the Picts" can yield, and one encounters a cornucopia of rich fantasy. I conducted such a search at the time of writing and found arguments for Pictish origin among the Finno-Ugric Estonians and other Baltic peoples, as well as the Basques, the Turks, the Arabs and the ancient Scythians of what is now Ukraine. Another day and speculation can go farther afield. Some assertions come with physical evidence, while others cite Classical documents. None of these has made much headway with perhaps pedestrian academics publishing heavy-handed articles in juried learned journals. They feel that the Picts were far less exotic and inexplicable as once thought.

The Picts were a confederation of as many as seven petty kingdoms that lived mostly in eastern and northern Scotland during the Late British Iron Age and early medieval periods. Their Latin name *Picti* appears in written records from at least 297 CE to the tenth century. It comes from *pingere*: to paint. As there is no Latin word for what we call a tattoo, the assumption has long been that *picti* would have served that purpose. But *Picti* appears to be a demeaning term for people above the Forth-Clyde divide, without specific reference to a language or identifiable ethnicity. Bear in mind that *Scoti, Scotti* translated as "thieves" and was applied to populations in Ireland, later acquiring more definite references. Apparent cognates of *Picti* that can be found in Old Norse, Old English, Welsh and Scots are probably borrowed from Latin. Some have speculated, without evidence, that *Picti* might have been adapted from a Pictish name for themselves. Another disputed suggestion for a native name is *Albidosi* from the tenth-century document.

Meanwhile, references to the people we call Picts were frequent in Old Irish, the ancestor of Scottish Gaelic as well as a written language in several annals in Ireland. The Irish word is recorded in several spellings, *Cruthin, Cruithini, Cruthni,* etc., and denotes not only populations in eastern and northern Scotland but also a group in eastern Ulster, which may or may not be an offshoot from what is now Scotland. Given that Irish is a Q-Celtic language that substitutes the Q sound for the P in P-Celtic languages, informed opinion now posits that the Irish word derives from a putative form, *Qritani,* a Goidelic form for the Britonnic *Pritani,* the name the early

Britons had for themselves. From that form the Romans derived their name for the native population, *Britanni*.

Not a single sentence in the Pictish language has so far been identified, and all speculation, learned and popular, draws on fragments found in personal and placenames. There is agreement, for example, that the prefix *pit-* found in such names as Pitlochry, Pitmedden and Pitcairn is certainly Pictish. The Venerable Bede proposed in the eighth century that the placename *Peanfahal* on the Firth of Forth (the modern village of Kinneil) appears to mix Pictish and Gaelic terminology. These are minuscule bases on which to construct a theory. In the mid-twentieth century the estimable authority Kenneth H. Jackson, a name we will hear again, argued that Pictish derived from prehistoric, i.e., pre–Indo-European languages, while a rival scholar, W.H. Chadwick, proposed that Pictish was fundamentally a British language that had coexisted with Gaelic from Roman times. Although he was a highly regarded eminence, Chadwick's view was undercut by being based on archaeological evidence, rather than linguistic, which diminished under scrutiny. By the end of the twentieth century, with Kathryn Forsyth's destruction of the non–Indo-European origin thesis (1997), learned sentiment moved more in Chadwick's way.

In the third decade of the twenty-first century informed consensus now favors the theory that Pictish was first a P-Celtic language close to what was spoken elsewhere in Britain, and it was changed by accommodation with Gaelic. This should not seem implausible. Early Ireland was invaded by several P-Celtic populations that were eventually subsumed into the Q-Celtic majority. Additionally, the Q-Celtic populations of early Wales folded into the P-Celtic principality. The P-Celtic south western portion of Scotland accommodated itself to the brief, medieval dominance of Gaelic. Further, when the Irish annals describe the *Cruthin, Cruithini*, etc., they do not depict an alien population vastly different in appearance or culture from those living elsewhere in the British Isles. Such is the view of James E. Fraser in *From Caledonia to Pictland: Scotland to 795*, the first volume of the New Edinburgh History of Scotland (2009).

It should also be noted that the Irish annals never comment on the *Cruthin/Cruithini* being distinguished by any body decorations or having exotic appearance. Neither are there any instances in Pictish art of human figures with any decorations suggesting tattoos. The widely reprinted somewhat racy illustrations of an unclothed Pictish man and woman covered head-to-toe in tattoos were produced by the Elizabethan artist and explorer John White (c. 1585). He had read Classical sources such as Dio Cassius (2nd century CE) but had recently traveled among the Roanoke Indians, adapting configurations never seen in early Europe.

Whether they were tattooed or not, the Picts readily accepted the Latin word *Picti* for themselves. Their realm, a confederation, never a nation, was sometimes called Pictavia in Latin. We can never be sure of the borders, but it lay mostly east of the line referred to earlier as Druimm Albin, "the spine of Britain," but also north of what we have been calling the Highlands. The confederacy linked seven parcels of land, not all of which are known to be kingdoms. Their names and putative regions sometimes leave a shadow on the map, although the ancient outlines of the seven come from learned guesswork. Farthest south was Fib, whose name is evoked in

Fife, sometimes still called "the kingdom of Fife." Above it to the north and west, coextensive with much of Perth, was Fotla, whose name survives in Atholl (*Ath-Fotla*). An earlier etymology positing that Atholl derived from *Ath Fhotla*: New Ireland, thus staking an eastern stake for Irish penetration, is under challenge. One of the most important of the seven was Fortriu, cognate with the Verturiones, partially coextensive with Moray in the northeast. The home of the historical Macbethad, Moray did not have defining natural boundaries but retained much the same outline until the abolition of the shires in 1974. To the far north lay Cait or Cat, unmistakably coextensive with Caithness, later dominated by Norsemen, and extending into parts of Sutherland. Among the parcels more difficult to define was Fidach, which some commentators would link with Inverness, in the heart of what would become the *Gàidhealtachd*.

Surviving physical evidence suggests that Pictish influence if not settlement was much wider than the seven entities in the confederation, sometimes called Pictavia, and spread far to the west of the Druimm Albin. As noted above, a Pictish styled boar can be found in the rock of the Gaelic fortress of Dunadd in Argyll. Anthony Jackson's modest but useful pamphlet, *The Pictish Trail: A Travellers Guide to the Old Pictish Kingdoms* (1989), provides hundreds of examples north and west. The finest and largest monument is the red sandstone Sueno's Stone (23', 7 meters) north east of Forres, in the former Morayshire. Sandstone means, however, that it is not the best preserved; it is now encased in armored glass. Dating from somewhere between 600 and 1000 CE, the stone shows how elusive discrete Pictish expression can be. Its name comes from a corruption of the Norse Sweyn Forkbeard, from a now-discredited association. Although covered with characteristic Pictish interwoven vine symbols, the stone's west face features a large Celtic cross with elaborately interlaced decoration. Figures appearing in sequentially a battle, a parade and a decapitation have been interpreted as depicting Cináed mac Ailpín's uniting the Gaels and Picts in the 840s. As has long been noted, Forres is also where Shakespeare has Macbeth encounter the three weird sisters. Jackson concatenates the most accessible Pictish monuments into eleven "trails." Ten begin south of the Forth-Clyde line and accumulate heavily east of the Druimm Albin line, but the eleventh begins in Inverness and extends to the west and north into the former Highland counties of Ross and Sutherland. Beyond his trails, Jackson also lists a hundred or so inaccessible sites, with many in territories usually thought to be Gaelic, such as the Isles of Raasay and Skye as well as Inverness, Ross and Sutherland shires.

Late twentieth-century archaeology pushed west the boundaries of Pictland from what conventional wisdom previously assumed. Between 1994 and 2007 Martin Carver led one of the most extensive recent digs in Scotland. This took place at what is now called Portmahomack on the Tarbat Peninsula in Easter Ross or eastern Ross-shire. The current placename may be from the Gaelic, *Port Mo Chalmaig*: the haven of a saint named Colmóc, given in diminutive form, but the site had been Pictish for centuries. After being Christianized, the Picts built a monastery here about 550 CE that was destroyed by fire about 800. Excavation yielded more than two hundred pieces of sculpture, four monumental stone crosses and evidence of workshops and burial cists. An attractive location by the sea, with beaches, Portmahomack is popular with tourists today and has been a favored destination for a long while. Not only are there remains of an Iron Age broch nearby, but it also appears to have entertained a Roman encampment, the farthest north of any such settlement, however brief. Raiding Vikings burned the Pictish monastery and occupied the surrounding area.

To resolve one more mystery, we now know that the Picts did not disappear. Rather, their name did. *Picti*, to repeat, is a Latin name. When Latin was abandoned as the language of annalists and chroniclers, *Picti* vanished with it. The Gaels had taken the upper hand in the new kingdom of Alba, which was sometimes known as *Albania* in the tenth century. As the Picts became Gaelicized, their P-Celtic language was forgotten, as were P-Celtic languages in Ireland. Gaelicism, along with Christianity (which had preceded the uniting with the Gaelic), also diminished distinctive Pictish art work.

Some Highlanders may feel that there is a wisp of glamour in claiming that some distant ancestors spoke Pictish. Mathematically, the idea is inescapable, but not one that can be demonstrated with a certain "look" or in a name. Pictish dissolved before the advent of clan names, let alone family names. In *The Scots: A Genetic Journey* (2011), Alistair Moffat and James W. Wilson propose that the Y chromosome group S145-str47 is a Pictish marker. In pie-charts on the map of the British Isles, without regard to other boundaries they find substantial numbers of people with S145-str47 across Scotland above the Forth-Clyde, with the greatest concentrations in Argyll and on the Isle of Skye. They find substantial numbers in the Orkneys and Shetlands, with traces through England, Wales and Ireland. Another marker, essentially unique to Scotland is R1b-str47 or R1b-Pict at least 3000 years old and pre-dating the Pictish language. Around 10 percent of Scottish men carry it.

Ireland and the Highlands

In the first paragraph of this chapter, we cited the concept of the "culture province," a translation of the German *Kulturkreis*. In German academic discourse the Highlands and Ireland would fit in the same *Kulturkreis* with comparable language and family organization, if not religion. At one time they were indeed a single unit linguistically. Old Irish is the ancestor of Scottish Gaelic just as it is of Modern Irish. The conventional wisdom used to accede to the views of Kenneth H. Jackson (1951) that Scottish Gaelic did not diverge from Irish until the twelfth century, although younger scholars see indications as early as the ninth; this will be a subject for further analysis later. In early Latin documents written in Scotland the phrase *lingua Hiberniae* clearly links the local language to the island to the west, not Caledonia. When the seventeenth-century Statutes of Iona began the centuries-long assault on Gaelic culture, the local tongue was referred to as "the Irishe language." Samuel Johnson and James Boswell speak of the language of the Highlands as Irish. An old name for Scottish Gaelic is "Erse" or "Earse," which means Irish, but does not denote the language of Ireland itself. 23andMe, one of the leading recreational DNA firms tells me that I am of Irish ancestry, despite documents tracing my line back to Lochaber in Inverness-shire.

1. The Foundations

In the centuries when the Venerable Bede's assertion that Gaelic Highlanders had migrated from Ireland was the uncontested assertion, the subject of Irish-Highland relations did not invite much discussion. Nonetheless, the most eminent nineteenth-century scholar William Forbes Skene (1809–1892) thought that the Irish and Scottish Gaels were two different peoples. In recent decades when new research has not supported Bede's narrative, we have come to see the links between the two entities as much more complex. The two books that have influenced my views are *The Irish-Scottish World in the Middle Ages* (2020), comprising thirteen papers from the Trinity College Medieval Symposium, edited by Seán Duffy, et al, and Wilson McLeod's *Divided Gaels: Gaelic Cultural Identities in Scotland and Ireland 1200–1650* (2004).

One can easily see Ireland from Scotland. The distance between the southernmost point on the Kintyre Peninsula, called the Mull, and the coast of Country Antrim is a mere ten miles (16 km). Islay, seat of the medieval Lordship of the Isles, is closer to Belfast than it is to Edinburgh. Even before the development of highly seaworthy craft, communication across such a narrow strait was inevitable. The crannog, the early lake dwelling on raised timbers, is found in both Ireland and Scotland, but from the excavations thus far, the oldest examples are on the Scottish side. The enigmatic ornamentations of rock faces known as cup-and-ring markings are found in both Ireland and Scotland, but also in England. The early settlement-fortifications known as hillforts, as well as the more defensible duns look much the same in Ireland and Scotland. All these take place before Colum Cille came to Iona or the "invasion" Bede depicted could have taken place. Between 200 BCE and 100 CE there were numerous exchanges between what became the Highlands and Ireland of the so-called "door-knob" spear butts and bone sword pommels, light materials that could be carried in a person's effects.

Larger enterprises tend to be more particular to location. The great passage-grave known as Newgrange in Ireland's Boyne Valley has no counterpart in Scotland. This is the huge, man-made mound, dating from 3200 BCE, that can be entered by a long, stone-lined passage, leading to an inner chamber—and illuminated by sunlight at the winter solstice. A smaller passage-grave (164', 50 m), very similar to Newgrange (279', 85m), can be found on the island of Gavrinis off the south coast of Brittany. But no evidence survives of any attempt to construct a passage-grave anywhere in Scotland. And the large, circular stone structures known as brochs, which resemble cooling stations for atomic power generators, are unique to northern Scotland and offshore islands. Not one can be found in Ireland. On the evidence of ancient stones, Ireland and the Highlands shared similarities before the advent of Old Irish and Christianity, but were not two halves of the same whole.

The lengthy study of British Isles DNA led by Stephen Leslie and published in *Nature* (2015) demolished the idea of a single, unified genetic identity for peoples speaking Celtic languages, as reported earlier. Leslie's work did allow, however, for close relationships between certain Celtic-speaking populations. Among the most assured of these was the genetic link between the Highlands and western Scotland with one of two groups in the north of Ireland. Sampling living people does not necessarily indicate how old—or ancient—the link might be. As we shall see, repeated communication between the Highlands and Ireland, in the north especially, could have enhanced the original genetic legacy.

The early centuries of the Christianization of Scotland meant a continuing stream of Irish clerics and their entourages crossing the water. Many have left their names on the map. St. Donnán (c. 580–617) founded a monastery on an island near the Kyle of Lochalsh, later fortified. He is the Donnán commemorated in Eilean Donan, rebuilt in the twentieth century to become Scotland's most photographed castle. Sometimes called Donnán of Eigg, he is thought to have been martyred on that Hebridean island 17 April 617. A later contemporary was Caorruill (sometimes Anglicized as Cairill or Kerrill but to be distinguished from Cyril) who founded several churches, the best known of which is on a high knoll, a former druidical site known as *Tom Aingeal,* in Brae Lochaber, Inverness-shire, later in the bailiwick of MacDonell of Keppoch. The stone church standing now on the knoll, known as Cille Choirill (formerly Anglicized as Killechyrille, etc.), was built in the fifteenth century. In its cemetery are memorials to leading poets, such as the seventeenth-century Iain Lom. Máel Ruba, or Máelrubai (642–722), who claimed descent from Niall of the Nine Hostages, established a network of monasteries, including Aporcrosan/Apurchrosan in 673, now known as Applecross in the former Ross-shire.

Meanwhile, in Irish and heroic literature, compiled by learned scribes, the core of what is sometimes called "Celtic mythology," action moves from specific Irish locations to Scottish ones without the sense that a border has been crossed. Cúchulainn, the great hero of the epic *Táin Bó Cuailnge* ("Cattle Raid of Cooley") in the Ulster Cycle, is trained in martial arts by the female warrior Scáthach, who, in most texts, lives on the Isle of Skye. In such a version she gives her name to the island as Dún Scáthaige, perhaps an attempt to etiologize or rationalize an existing name. The Irish hero's connection to Skye lives on in popular fancy. There is today a flourishing restaurant called "Cuchulain" in the prime tourist town of Portree, pronounced in an approximation of what it would be in Irish. In another well-known story from the Ulster Cycle, the tragic heroine Deirdre flees with her lover Naoise to Loch Etive in the former Argyllshire.

The Irish narratives of the Ulster Cycle, Fenian Cycle, and Cycles of the Kings, were put into great vellum codices in Ireland but not in Scotland. Some, not all, of the same characters and themes appear in later oral tradition, of what came to be called folklore. Admittedly, many of the motifs of oral tradition are international and may appear in distant societies speaking unrelated languages. Nonetheless, dozens of characters in Irish folklore also appear in Scottish Gaelic folklore. The Irish hero Fionn mac Cumhaill, found both in manuscript and oral traditions, was highly popular in Scotland, where he was sometimes known as Fingal. Although the attribution of Fingal's Cave on the Isle of Staffa to him is based on a solecism, he is cited widely elsewhere. The "parallel roads," markers from glacial-era lakes in Glen Roy, were thought to be blazed by him.

According to the American-born Wilson McLeod now at Edinburgh, for all that the Highlands and Ireland shared, they did not form a cultural unit. His *Divided Gaels* (2004) examines bardic poetry, c. 1200–1650. Scottish Gaeldom might have viewed Ireland as a wellspring of cultural and historical prestige, but it did not keep pace with Irish examples. Compared to Ireland, very few families patronized bards. The one existing volume of Scottish Gaelic poetry is minuscule compared to what was produced in Ireland. Almost half of the surviving Gaelic corpus can be found in one nearly impossible-to-read volume. *The Book of the Dean of Lismore* (compiled 1512–1526) includes materials in Latin and Lowlands Scots, with much more from Gaelic but in contrived orthography. Instead of employing the alphabet of Irish, all texts appear in a phonetic rendering, as Gaelic would have sounded to a Lowland Scots speaker of that time. The compilers, James and Duncan MacGregor, evidently assumed that few people could read written Scottish Gaelic, whereas Irish with its own orthography had been written since the sixth century.

McLeod's reluctant conclusion is that the culturally dominant Irish *litterateurs* looked upon Gaelic Scotland as distant and peripheral. This was concurrent with the rise of the Scottish kingdom in the east of the nation, with increasing disdain for all things Gaelic.

Simultaneously, however, there began a migration from Gaelic Scotland, especially Argyll and the Inner Hebrides, to Ireland: that of armed mercenary fighters and their families. These were the gallowglasses, or galloglasses, Highlanders whose service was sold to Irish chieftains and later defending native Irish interests against first Norman and later English aggressions. Our spelling comes from the Irish *gall óglaich*: foreign volunteers, or possibly young mercenaries. The first record of gallowglass service dates from 1259, when Aedh Ó Conchobair, a regional "king" of Connacht in the west of Ireland, received 160 Scottish warriors in a dowry when he married the daughter of Dubgall mac Ruaidri, a "king" in the Hebrides.

More gallowglasses came, employed by both Gaelic Irish and Hiberno-Norman lords. They may have come with entourages, but after having been given land, they also intermarried with the local population. In 1512 there were reported to be fifty-nine such groups throughout Ireland under the control of the Irish lords. In 1569 another 1200 arrived in a dowry of the daughter of Colin Campbell, 3rd Earl of Argyll. Gallowglasses supported the native cause in the Desmond wars during the reign of Elizabeth I, and in 1571 about 700 of them were executed. The renown of these fighting men spread beyond the British Isles. The five "Irish" soldiers in Albrecht Dürer's famous 1521 woodcut are conventionally presumed to be gallowglass immigrants. Their employment redounded to the Highlands in several ways. No one ever took a census of the gallowglasses, but David Stevenson (1980) estimated the number to be in the thousands. Remissions sent back from then-more affluent Ireland benefited Scottish chieftains. And the professionalism of mercenary service contributed to the martial esprit of Highland clans.

Submersion into the Irish nation did not mean the gallowglass origins were forgotten. Some names could be identified as gallowglass if family members wished so, as in MacCabe, MacSweeney, MacSorley and MacDonnell (not O'Donnell). The admired Irish fiction writer John McGahern (1934–2006) always identified the origin of his uncommon name as gallowglass, derived from Mac Eachráin. And in the late twentieth century, the gallowglass was rediscovered in popular romantic-adventure fiction.

Another migration of Scottish soldiers was far less well received in Ireland.

How many of these were Gaelic Highlanders or fighters from other portions of the kingdom we cannot be sure. After his momentous victory over the English at Bannockburn, June 24, 1314, Robert the Bruce set his sights on Ireland. Also known as Robert I of Scotland (1274–1329), he should be distinguished from a half-dozen other notables bearing the same name, especially his grandfather (1215–1295), the 4th Lord of Annandale, libeled through an odious misreading of history in Mel Gibson's film *Braveheart* (1995). His designation "the Bruce" echoes the Scoto-Norman name by which he was known in life, le Brus. Despite the French name, he would have been conversant in Gaelic, not yet subject to the disesteem described by Boece later in the century. He may also have claimed Irish ancestry on his mother's side.

Bruce's best-known story in modern popular culture also links him to Ireland. This is the try-try-again fable of Bruce's watching a spider fail in six attempts to rise and succeeding on the seventh. In some versions the episode is given a specific date, 1307, and set on Rathlin Island off Antrim, where several prominent Scots did indeed find refuge. Upon scrutiny, however, we cannot find mention of the story before Sir Walter Scott's *Tales of a Grandfather* (1828), who may have taken it from an episode about Bruce's comrade Sir James Douglas. The motif of the discouraged leader finding resolution in observing an insect is world-wide, noted among other places in Jewish non–Biblical legends of King David.

Historians suggest a welter of motivations for Robert's coveting of Ireland, starting with the heady confidence of having trounced the English against odds, as well as the sting of the loss of the Isle of Man to Norman-backed Scots not in his kingdom. His wife was an Ulster woman. Several Irish leaders invited Robert to the island with the hope that he might help them dislodge onerous Anglo-Norman settlers, and if he were successful, would crown his younger brother Edward as king. Additionally, as the English drew resources and taxes from Ireland, an invasion there would drain his richer southern foes. Another reason, implied by Robert's words in a 1314 letter to Irish chiefs, has been attractive to modern readers. After declaring that the Irish had been free since ancient times, the victory at Bannockburn would result in "permanently strengthening and maintaining inviolate the friendship between us and you, so that with God's will our nation may be able to recover her ancient liberty." "Our nation" certainly sounds as though he thought that Highland and Irish Gaels are one. Even without such precocious ethnic nationalism, the Scottish king recognized the English as the permanent adversary and that a military campaign in Ireland would unite the two smaller nations, one Gaelic the other part-Gaelic, against the hated Sassenach. Such pan-Gaelicism would not be seen again in political leaders until modern times.

Edward the Bruce landed with a force of 5000 men, a staggering number given the technology of the time, on 26 May 1315 near Larne on the Antrim coast. After overcoming considerable resistance, within a month Edward took the town of Carrickfergus and was proclaimed king of Ireland. Together with Irish allies, the Scottish army raged over large swathes of the Irish map. Edward II, then king of England was apprised of the threat to his hegemony. He ordered an assembly of the Anglo-Irish in Dublin, who failed to take action. This emboldened the Scottish dynasty to send a remonstrance to Pope John XXII to revoke the *Laudabiliter* of 1155 supporting the claim of the Plantagenet dynasty to control Ireland. This had given legitimacy to the Anglo-Norman take-over of Ireland by Strongbow, Richard de Clare, in summer, 1170, on orders of Henry II of England. The Pope, who had his mind on new crusades to the Middle East, ignored the request. As Ireland, along with the rest of Europe, was reeling from a famine, Scottish fortunes on the island declined, and Edward the Bruce was killed in the defeat of the Battle of Faughart in County Louth toward the end of 1318. The Irish adventures were retold in a sequence of books, 14 to 18, of John Barbour's epic poem *The Brus/The Bruce* written six decades later. Completed in 1375, *The Brus/The Bruce* is composed of 14,000 octosyllabic lines in Lowland Scots, the first great narrative in that language. Little-read today, it forged a seminal and glamorous national narrative and served as a resource for Sir Walter Scott and other romanticizers of history.

More than two centuries later yet another Scottish incursion swept into the north of Ireland but from newly powerful Highland clans, not the Crown in Edinburgh. It tracked some of the same names as those found in the steady stream of gallowglasses, but these Scotsmen had no intention of service in Ireland. How the clans achieved such power along with independence from the Crown is a subject for the next chapter. Descending from the Lord of the Isles, the Clan Donald, including the Mac Domhnaill/MacDonald and related families, became a power in the Highlands for centuries. The Clan reach was so wide that it split into different branches, with discrete regions centering on formidable castles. Mac Domhnaill South is also known as MacDonald Dunnyveg and the Clann Iain Mòr, historically occupying the Isle of Islay and the nearby Kintyre Peninsula. The ruins of their seat still stand, usually known as Dunyvaig (normalized differently from the family name) today, three miles east of Port Ellen on Islay.

Retaining some of the independence of the Lordship of the Isles, despite its union with the Scottish Crown in the previous century, the Clan Donald could maintain its own communications with the English Crown. Although generally hostile to the English, the Clan was open to alliances that might serve its immediate interests.

Controlling lands on the island of Islay and a nearby peninsula, the Mac Domhnaill South were necessarily seamen, crossing the waters in a nimble vessel known as the birlinn or berling, a flat-bottomed barge with both oars and sails. This meant Co. Antrim in Ireland was closer to Dunyvaig than was the Isle of Skye. As spoken Irish and Scottish Gaelic were still tolerably comprehensible to one another in the fourteenth and fifteenth centuries, the Mac Domhnaills and certain leading Antrim families might inter-marry, with exchanges of dowries and the making of promises. Antrim would prove to be a haven for survivors of duels or for men accused of treasonous crimes. By 1500 quite a number of Mac Domhnaills had settled in Ireland singly or in handfuls. They became so much of the local social fabric that the leader who would enforce Mac Domhnaill claim on Antrim and Rathlin Island, Somhairle Buidhe (1505–1590), was himself born at Dunanynie Castle near what is today Ballycastle in Antrim.

The Mac Domhnaill coveting of Antrim, therefore, was not merely another instance of a powerful war-making body seeking to dominate a weaker neighbor, or an echo of Robert the Bruce's ambitions. Instead, the Mac Domhnaills had engaged in their own alliances and intrigues with powerful Irish families and sought to strengthen their position by bringing in as many as 5000 troops from the Hebrides in one wave. They remained in Ireland and drifted from speaking Scottish Gaelic to Irish. This appears to be reflected in the switch from the preferred Anglicization of Mac Donald and occasionally MacDonell in Scotland, to MacDonnell as the default Anglicization in Ulster.

The sixteenth-century Ireland into which Somhairle Buidhe asserted Clan Donald authority was a cockpit of warring factions speaking both Irish and English. In the years since the Anglo-Normans laid claim to the island, England had failed to turn it into an orderly colony, an annoyance the Tudors hoped to address. To advance his cause Somhairle Buidhe led the MacDonnells against such Irish families as the MacQuillans and the O'Neills as well as the English. These were followed by alliances and betrayals. Somhairle was married to the half-sister of the notable Irish chief, Shane O'Neill. When Elizabeth ascended to the throne in 1559, Somhairle Buidhe submitted to her authority, serving his interests of that moment. He remained Catholic, however, even when Scotland became officially Protestant the next year, 1560.

Because he was also depicted by contemporary English scribes, he is known most often today, even in learned commentary, by the Anglicized form of his name, Sorley Boy MacDonnell, that partially erases his Highland identity. *Somhairle* is still a common Gaelic given name, adapting a Norse antecedent, and an echo of the first notable Highlander, Somhairle Mòr MacGhillebhride, known as Somerled, to be examined in the next chapter. The cognomen *Buidhe*, pronounced roughly "bwee," means yellow, implicitly his hair. It is unrelated to the English "boy" and does not imply youth or subservience.

For forty years, 1550–1590, Sorley Boy was a warring presence in eastern Ulster, with more recorded changes of fortune and alliances than can be detailed here. He came to dominate an area on the north coast of Antrim, centering on Dunluce Castle, near Portrush. Sorley Boy captured the fortifications begun as early as the thirteenth century and added what he described as Scottish embellishments. A scenic ruin today on a high promontory, Dunluce (Ir. *Dún Libhse*), esteemed by photographers and a major tourist attraction of the Six Counties of Northern Ireland.

The lasting contribution to Irish life of the MacDonnells of Antrim speaks to the peculiarities of clan life. Sorley Boy and the clan might have remained Scottish, and returned to Islay for additional troops when needed, but theirs was not a national intrusion into the life of the neighboring island. Their efforts were of no benefit to the Scottish Crown in Edinburgh. Instead, the MacDonnells of Antrim were proudly a sept of the Clan Donald, the only sept not in Scotland. In their entourage came many other families of the Clan Donald bearing different family names, my own among them. Thus, in researching any Highland family, one often finds that the name also appears in Northern Ireland, sometimes—not always—with a slightly different spelling. There were, of course, other opportunities for Highlanders to cross over the short passage to Ireland, starting with the gallowglasses, and with even greater movements of population in the century after Sorley Boy.

Tens of thousands of immigrants came from England and Scotland to occupy vast tracts of land, up to half a million acres, mostly in the north of Ireland, during the early seventeenth century. This movement is known today as the Plantation of Ulster. At the end of a seven-year war against English rule in 1607, large numbers of Irish chiefs fled the country, forfeiting their lands. In Irish history this is known as the "Flight of the Earls." Gaelic-loathing James I (James VI of Scotland) authorized the Plantation in 1609, although many individual adventurers sought to exploit Ireland's distress before that date. This continued for decades. Into Ireland poured thousands of farmers schooled in recently improved standards of agriculture. Nearly 100 percent Protestant, they were divided between the Anglicans of the north of England and Presbyterians from Lowland Scotland. The profound effect on Ireland, although well known, cannot be overestimated. The island became *de facto* two nations, culminating in the division of the thirty-two counties at the time of the Anglo-Irish War Treaty in 1922, with six remaining in the United Kingdom and twenty-six going their own way, first as the Free State, becoming the Republic in 1949.

Traumatic as the Plantation of Ulster may have been, it little affected Highland history and so does not merit much discussion here. What should be mentioned, however, is that the heritage of it in immigration misleads some readers on the subject before us, the links between Gaelic Scotland and Ireland. Specifically, who are the "Scots-Irish"? This is a term of American coinage with little meaning in Ireland or Scotland. Many of the Planters of Ulster experienced a surge in prosperity on their new farms on confiscated lands. This led to a phenomenal rise in the birthrate, with families producing more children than their holdings could sustain. Those surplus children migrated to the American colonies, speaking with a strange accent and rougher manners than the colonists who preceded them. Thus, they sought land on the frontier of settlement and in the Appalachian Mountains, especially in Tennessee and what is now West Virginia, but also Pennsylvania and the Carolinas. In Ireland they might have been Ulster Presbyterians, but in America they were neither like other Irish, often Catholic, or other Scottish people, often from the Lowlands. That prompted the term "Scotch-Irish" or "Scots-Irish." Fabled frontiersmen like Daniel Boone or Kit Carson often have Ulster Protestant names. Rediscovered as a submerged ethnicity of the United States in the late twentieth century, there is now a shelfful of studies on their cultural contributions, most notably "country music," focused on the Scots-Irish city of Nashville. Thirteen presidents of the United States have been of Scots-Irish heritage, the first of whom was Andrew Jackson, whose family emigrated from County Tyrone.

As late as the sixteenth century, William Gillis (1994) has reported, Highland families concerned that their family trees were insufficiently impressive sent genealogists in search of more high-status ancestors. They found what they were looking for in the twelfth-century *Lebor Gabála Érenn* (The Book of Invasions/Conquests of Ireland), five volumes long. Classed as a pseudo-history, the *Lebor Gabála* coordinates early myth, legend and saga with Biblical history, to explain how purported successive waves of invasion created the Irish people. Within its pages lay a cast of thousands available for plucking and replanting in Inverness or Argyll.

In the following century clerics from Ireland saved beleaguered Catholicism in the Highlands. Scotland's emphatic embrace of Calvinism under John Knox culminated in *The Confession of Faith of the Kirk of Scotland*, 1560 (henceforth called *The Scots Confession* to differentiate it from the *Westminster Confession* of 1690), which began the destruction of papal authority in the country. Attending a Catholic Mass brought severe punishment, and the celebration of Christmas and Easter was abolished. By 1600 there were no more than eighteen priests in all of Scotland, none who spoke Gaelic. To address this loss a group of Irish Franciscan clergy in Louvain, in what is now Belgium, repositioned to a friary in Ballycastle, Co. Antrim, for a mission to the Highlands. The mission lasted thirty years, 1619–1649, and had to be supported from Ireland and the continent. Scotland was too poor to provide alms. Many of the monks spoke Ulster Irish, which, with effort, could be understood. Surviving letters indicate the Franciscans found the Highlanders to be "half pagan," and living a life of greater hardship than they knew in Ireland or at Louvain.

Although Roman Catholics would become a despised and oppressed minority, the thirty-year Irish Franciscan mission had a lasting impact on the Highlands. It was in the Catholic areas that music, dance and storytelling would flourish, when those arts often languished in Calvinist areas. Catholic Highlanders would also become the most ardent Jacobites in successive rebellions. Essays collected by the eminent historian T.M. Devine examine the persistence of anti–Catholicism into modern times in *Scotland's Shame?* (2000).

The Norse in the Highlands

Repeated in several of the thorough studies of Scandinavian influence upon Scotland is an arresting perspective on relative distances that deserves to be repeated here. From the isolated but bustling capital of the Shetlands, Lerwick, a straight line drawn east to the warm-water port of Bergen, Norway, is under 210 miles (333 kilometers), shorter than to the northern Scottish city of Aberdeen. Ferry service today connects Lerwick to Bergen (Nor. Bryggen) just as it connects Lerwick to Aberdeen. Further, that 210 miles from Bergen to Lerwick is less than the distance from Bergen to Stockholm. While this feels counterintuitive after the domination of the nation state when the automobile is a prime form of transportation, it would have been an invitation to the Norsemen who led the world in the development of fast-moving ships capable of navigating long distances as early as the seventh century.

The preference for "Norse" over "Viking" is an indication of the widespread rise in esteem these people have enjoyed beginning about 1960. For figurative use, "Viking" is still with us, implying an implacable, brutish predator, which is indeed how the Norse were once perceived. From its roots in Old Norse and Icelandic, the word denotes only a person who has come ashore through a *vík*: an inlet or stream. Preferring "Norse" here denotes speakers of the Old Norse language, spoken in all the lands that became Norway, Sweden and Denmark, and subsequently Iceland, without differentiating among them. Abundant evidence, confirmed by recent scholarship, tells us that invaders who came to what we now call Scotland were more often from what is now Norway. When those pagan Norse first came to the British Isles, they headed for soft targets, monasteries and churches, where they indeed behaved abominably. They burned, they pillaged, and they carted off gentle, literate monks as slaves. Churchmen, however, were nearly the only people who could write, and so they vilified their tormentors.

Re-examination points to the dazzling logistical and tactical accomplishments of the Norsemen, spreading their influence as far afield as Newfoundland and Baghdad, founding cities as diverse as York and Kyiv (previously Kiev), as well as producing subtle and delicate art. The Norseman were not anticipations of the nineteenth-century European imperialists, subjugating the natives, as they instead settled in with and intermarried local populations. Thus, Normandy became a French-speaking province and integral part of France. When the genome study of Iceland was completed, the data showed a high percentage of Scottish and Irish heritage from women who were taken there instead of Scandinavian wives.

Not imperialistic and not coordinated. Their motivation is still under discussion, but sometime in the eighth century Scandinavia appears to have experienced a population boom that could not be sustained with meager agricultural resources. This meant a surplus of men who had no employment or demands to keep them home. They went forth in spurts continuously from about 790 CE until nearly 1100, and remained a presence, declining and eventually marginalized in the British Isles until the Norse-dominated Orkneys were ceded to the Scottish Crown in 1468.

Early Scottish records do not speak directly of the Norse, and we must rely on English and Irish sources. The *Anglo-Saxon Chronicle* reports the first Norse sighting in 789. Four years later, Norse invaders sacked the Irish monastery on Lindisfarne, a tidal island off the northeast coast of Great Britain. In 795 they raided the Isle of Skye and attacked the key Christian center at Iona in the Inner Hebrides. They returned in 802, 806 and 825. Surviving monks took Iona's prominent treasure, a magnificently illuminated manuscript of the Gospels, to the safe monastery at Kells in Ireland; thenceforward the volume would be known as *The Book of Kells*, for its sanctuary. Eventually invaders came inland to kill and to loot, inflicting continuous catastrophe upon the Picts east of Druimm Albin, climaxing with a massive slaughter of aristocrats, 839, as described in the *Annals of Ulster* and cited above. This led to Picts' merger with the Gaels of Alba under the rule of Cináed mac Ailpín.

As invincible maritime aggressors, the Norse targeted islands, the Orkneys and the Shetlands, or lands near water, such as Caithness. Later came the Hebrides, the Isle of Man, and Ireland, where they established a base of power in what is now Dublin. In the Orkneys, which have not been seen as affluent in modern history, they built finer residences than they had seen in Scandinavia. Blessed with richer and more abundant soil than either Scandinavia or mainland Scotland, the Orkneys were not merely a prize but an attractive alternative to living in the homeland. Invaders also broke into the Neolithic chambered cairn called Maeshowe and left graffiti in the Norse alphabet, runic.

From several Icelandic sources, corroborated in the *Annals of Ulster*, we learn that the Norse asserted their authority over the Hebrides about 850, within ten years of the union creating Alba. Widely read histories have favored attributing this conquest to Ketill or Ketil Björnsson, who bears the incomparable nickname of Flatnose (ON *Flatnefr*). Rival historians argue that sources favor Harald Fairhair, in part because Ketill was a common name without a standard spelling, and we cannot be sure he is the same person in different documents. And those documents come with a determinable chronology.

Ketill's name, however, has so lodged itself in discourse that he has been borrowed as a character in popular culture. According to the Icelandic *Saga of the Laxdalers*, Ketill said that he preferred to go west to Scotland because the living was good there. He knew the country well, having raided it extensively. Under the Norse, whom perhaps he led, the populations of the Hebrides gained a mixed cultural identity, the *Gallgáedil* for the foreigners, *gall*, who had become Gaelicized. Such a population did not have a fixed geographic location. *Gallgáedil* is also the root of the name "Galloway," a former county in the western Lowlands.

According to Icelandic sources one Thursteinn the Red, possibly a grandson of Ketill, pushed Norse influence inland, expanding through what is now Sutherland and Ross to as far east as Moray. These texts are of later composition, or at least revision of earlier records, as they speak of *Írland* and *Skotland*, terms not current until the mid-twelfth century. In modern times archaeological investigation has found meager evidence of Norse settlement in mainland Scotland beyond Caithness and Sutherland: a few graves and coin hoards. Plundering raids and other depredations faced little resistance. Neither would there be defense against the capture of nubile lassies for service in the Norse colony of Iceland. Evidence supports widespread Norse settlement in the previously Gaelic Hebrides, especially in the outer Islands, Lewis and Harris, and portions of the Inner Hebrides.

The settlements north of Gaelic Scotland grew richer and more powerful. There were six important centers, two on the Shetlands, three in the Orkneys, and one in what is now Caithness. Although these six lacked the disciplined administration of nineteenth-century imperial powers, they did have a collective identity as the *Northryars* or *Nordryars*: the northerlies, Anglicized as Nordreys. It is from their point of view that Norse names were affixed to the map. The farthest northwesterly point on mainland Scotland, in the former shire of Sutherland, is called Cape Wrath as the Norse *hvarf*: turning point. The frequent storms allowed later generations of sailors to think it a placename of English origin. Sutherland, meanwhile, is the most northerly of Gaelic-speaking areas but south of Northryars.

Raiders from the Northryars joined their compatriots from Scandinavia in the assaults upon Gaelic Ireland. Irish Gaels had not been seafaring people, and so the Norse came ashore at will, founding what would become that nation's port cities, such as the future Waterford and Limerick. Although the Gaels had settled along the Liffey River, it was the Norse who established Dublin about 840, not only as a *longphort*, ship camp, but as a citadel of power in the west, and a slave-trading emporium. The Irish name for Dublin, *Baile Átha Cliath*: town of the ford of the wattles, does not imply it is a port for maritime commerce. As in Scotland, the Norse would linger in Ireland. The native Irish organizing under the semi-legendary king Brian Boru defeated them at Clontarf in 1014, a site between the settlement and the coastline. Irish annals record that one of the most significant deaths among Norse forces was Earl Sigurd of Orkney. He was succeeded in Orkney by Thorfinnr the Mighty, a scourge of northern Scotland whose forays extended as far to the south as Fife. The Sigurd-Thorfinnr line continued for another four generations.

The second team of Norse-controlled islands was the *Suthreyjars*: the southerlies, Anglicized as Sudreys. These included the Outer and Inner Hebrides, Arran and Bute in the Firth of Clyde, as well as the somewhat distant Isle of Man, the center of power. During the twelfth century someone on the Isle of Lewis possessed what are now seen as some of the most beloved figures of "Scottish" art, the several dozen Lewis Chessmen, carved from walrus tusks and whale teeth. Two queens hold their hands next to their cheeks in a gesture variously interpreted as exasperation, contemplation or toothache. Leading contemporary scholars, alas, such as Alex Woolf of St. Andrews, believe they were carved elsewhere, perhaps Norway, and brought to Lewis.

A Victorian holiday destination and a tax-haven today, the Isle of Man, 221 square miles (572 square kilometers), is not usually perceived as instrumental in Scottish fortunes. Although Man is culturally closer to Ireland, fifty miles to the west, its long-extinct language, Manx, is a bridge between Irish and Scottish Gaelic, sharing many properties of the latter. During the era of Norse domination, 800 CE, busy sea lanes brought it into closer communication with the north and to Scandinavia. Plundering sea raids continued for a century and a half until Man fell under the Norse king of Dublin in 990, and so it remained for nine decades. In 1079 one Godred Crovan brought the island under the rule of the powerful earls of Orkney. Godred had just subdued the Norse king of Dublin and was more assertive over the Scots of the Hebrides. He created the Kingdom of Man, collecting the islands of the Suthreyjars as part of his realm. At a later date his successors took the Latin title, *Rex Manniae et Insularum*: King of Man and the Isles. By 1154 the Church of Rome appointed a bishop to Man with a title linking the see to the Hebrides. It is retained today in the city of Peel as the Diocese of Sodor and Man.

The king of Man remained nominally under the suzerainty of the king of Norway at the de facto capital of Nidaros (modern Trondheim). "Suzerain" is a word of modern coinage to describe medieval lines of power that do not have exact counterparts in modern bureaucracy. The Kingdom of Man had to pay fealty to Trondheim, often a logistical challenge. Both ends of the bargain spoke the same language, Norse. At the very least Trondheim would control international affairs while Man had autonomy over all local affairs. Only occasionally would the Norse exert much control over the Suthreyjars. Meanwhile, kings of Man might deal with authorities in England as well as the emerging kingdom of Scotland.

Most memorable of those interferences was the bloody intrusion of a terrifying king of Norway with a disarmingly informal nickname of Magnus Barefoot or Barelegs (1073–1103). In Norwegian his name is Magnus Olafsson, or Magnus III, with the sobriquet *Berfœttr* or *Berrføtt*. It may have come from his having adopted the short tunic worn by Gaels in Scotland and Ireland, presumably of lower status, making "Barelegs" the more apt translation, or that he actually rode barefoot as the Irish did, fleeing a Swedish attack.

At the very least Magnus sought to re-establish Norwegian influence around the Irish Sea, beginning with a naval assault on the Orkneys, taking the reigning earls prisoner, and installing his son Sigurd (possibly eight years old) as earl. Historians today disagree whether he sought to establish a proto-empire; the contemporary English chronicler, William of Malmesbury, thought Magnus's ultimate goal was to capture the throne of William II in London. Scottish and Norwegian historians believe his reach was more modest. Tamping down aspirations for independence in the Suthreyjars could have been sufficient. Once the Orkneys were in his hands, he raided mainland Scotland and islands without significant opposition. The distant Scottish king, Malcolm III, was attacking northern England. Magnus pillaged the islands of Lewis and Uist in the Outer Hebrides, followed by assaults on Skye, Tiree and Mull of the Inner Hebrides, as well as the peninsula of Kintyre. He visited but spared the holy isle of Iona.

About 1100, the rebellious Somerled Mòr MacGhillebhride, "the Hammer of the Norse," was born. He would launch powerful Highland families and become the first "Lord of the Isles," following the template of the Suthreyjars, with Fealty to Trondheim. The recurrent plundering of the Gaels of Scotland by the warlike Norse along the northern and western periphery inevitably produced a reaction from the natives. Magnus Barelegs would be the last Norwegian monarch to visit the Norse territories in the British Isles for one hundred fifty years. By that time the resurgent Gaels, a portion of the Scottish Kingdom, had become a more formidable power.

As contributors to Highland identity, the Norse usually rank third after the Gaels and the Picts, eventually blending in to become part of the dominant culture, as with other segments of the British Isles. A good comparison is the former Danelaw of northeastern England, home to characteristically Norse family names with the suffixes "–by" (from *byr*: farm, village, hamlet) or "–thorpe." The Irish name "MacLoughlin" means "son of the Norseman." Certainly, Norse DNA can be found throughout the British Isles, perhaps unevenly distributed.

Echoes of Norse intrusions to the Gaelic realm resound in spoken language and in placenames. Spoken Scottish Gaelic sounds quite different from spoken Irish, even with words of identical spelling. One of the most important is a kind of a voiceless -h-sound called pre-aspiration. It is found in Norse languages and Scottish Gaelic, but not in Irish. The subject of Norse loan words is the focus of Roderick W. McDonald's unpublished Australian dissertation, *Scandinavians and the Celtic West* (2009). He finds no more than 460 in Irish, Scottish Gaelic and Manx combined, and dismisses as inflated the ambitious claims of Norwegian linguist Magne Oftedal (1962).

Lingering in learned consciousness is the notion that the Norse were not merely present but once dominant. Neil Gunn, the best-informed of Highland historical novelists, alluded to this in a passage from his *Highland River* (1937), set in the small fishing village of Dunbeath on the east coast of Sutherland. "On one side of the harbor mouth the placename was Gaelic, on the other side it was Norse," he wrote. "Where the lower valley broadened out to flat, fertile land the name was Norse, but in the braes beyond it were [sic] Gaelic."

The Scottish Gaelic Language

Sharing the same Goidelic origins, both the languages of the Highlands and of Ireland are sometimes referred to as "Gaelic." With the coming of the Irish Free State in 1922 and the establishment of the Republic in 1949, the preferred term for the native language in Ireland has become "Irish," signifying that it is first of recognized national languages, followed by English.

Political semantics were quite different before independence; the revivalist Gaelic League was founded 1893. That distinction is generally honored by linguists and lexicographers and will be employed here, although it has not completely won out in popular consciousness. In English the word is usually pronounced "GAY-lik." Scottish Gaelic is pronounced "GAL-ik" in all of the Highlands, often idiomatically with the definite article, "the Gaelic." To pronounce "the Gaelic" as "GAY-lik" in a tourist town like Fort William is to invite an immediate rebuke. To imply that Scottish Gaelic is not distinct from Irish is, colloquially, considered bad manners. Issues or identity, status and esteem suffuse many discussions of both languages.

Both Irish and Scottish Gaelic survive in different dialects, often quite different from one another. That is because they were not the languages of nation states where one prestige dialect came to dominate all the others, as is the case with English and French. They are to a degree analogous with Italian and German, spoken in countries that did not become nation states until the nineteenth century. We know that the Italian of Milan is vastly different from that of Palermo, so also the German of Bremen and Munich. There are three main dialects of Irish: Ulster, Connacht and Munster. Ulster Irish, especially as spoken in Co. Donegal, is the closest to Scottish Gaelic.

Regional differences in Scottish Gaelic are exacerbated by a challenging geography, deep glens and remote islands, as well as bitter and unrelenting clan rivalries. These differences survived the migration to the Gaelic-speaking cultural colony of Cape Breton Island. In the early twentieth century both my parents were raised speaking the *Abrach* dialect from Lochaber, dominant in the neighborhood. They had difficulty understanding, as well as having some disdain for, the *Barrach* dialect from the Isle of Barra in the Outer Hebrides, even one hundred years after immigration.

We shall not revisit the still unresolved question of the different claims for historical origins of peoples in Ireland and the Highlands, or, for that matter, at what date Celtic languages, P- and Q-, might have been introduced. From the time of Colum Cille's founding of the monastery at Iona, c. 563, both sides spoke Old Irish and continued to do so for centuries. The Scottish portion did not go its separate way for some time, the date of which is uncertain. In 1951, Kenneth H. Jackson, perhaps the then-greatest eminence in the field, argued that the two could not have diverged before the year 1200. This has been the received wisdom for decades and is still cited. We are more aware today of the absorption of Pictish speakers and influence of lengthy predations from the Norse. More than a generation after Jackson, Colm Ó Baoill (1997) could point to evidence that Scottish Gaelic had begun to diverge from Irish before 900 CE. At any rate, the process took many centuries. As we note above,

Scottish invaders could pretty well make themselves understood in Ireland during the Bruce invasion in the early fourteenth century.

At a time when the vast majority of the population was unlettered, the prominent divergence came in spoken Irish and Scottish Gaelic. Both languages contain a multitude of sounds not heard in English, like the slender coronal stop versus the affricated stop, that can only be expressed in the International Phonetic Alphabet (IPA). A traveler today from Gaelic-speaking Lewis finds it next to impossible to be understood in Connemara, Co. Galway, one of the greatest concentrations of native Irish speakers. A student switching from the study of Irish to Scottish Gaelic, or vice versa, learns this immediately. A listener who has studied neither language can hear the difference between the two without much coaching, in part because of the Scottish pre-aspiration apparently borrowed from the Norse.

Another feature of spoken Scottish Gaelic never indicated in writing is what linguists call ingressive pulmonic speech, or IPS, defined by linguists only in recent decades. In this act the speaker appears almost to gasp, or suck in breath suddenly, when pronouncing an affirmation, such as "aye" or "yes." As it has no counterpart in English, IPS can be startling to listeners of spoken Scottish Gaelic. While receding in practice in the twenty-first century, it was commonplace in Gaelic Scotland and Canada as late as the mid-twentieth century, but was found rarely among Irish speakers, mostly in Ulster counties like Cavan.

On the printed page, however, Irish and Scottish Gaelic are more closely aligned, but far from identical. Scottish Gaelic orthography is more conservative than that of Irish. It retains, to give a prominent example, the digraph (paired letters, single sound) *éu* from Classical Irish that has disappeared from Modern Irish, except for certain regionalisms. A major distinction is that written Scottish Gaelic today uses only the grave accent (a left-leaning slash over a vowel) to indicate length, while Irish has only the acute right-leaning fada: Scottish Gaelic *làmh*, Irish *lámh*, for "hand." Both languages insert linkers, the consonants *n-* or *t-*, or the aspirate *h-*, to prevent a vowel at the end an article from eliding with a vowel beginning the next word. This is a paradigm we also see in French. In Irish the linker is flush against the noun, even if capitalized, e.g., *Tír na nÓg* (Land of Youth), but in Scottish Gaelic the linker calls for a hyphen, *Gàidhlig na h-Alba* (Scottish Gaelic language).

Quite a few cognates have slightly different spellings in the two languages, even while they remain recognizable.

English	*Irish*	*Scottish Gaelic*
Gael	*Gael*	*Gàidheal*
inside	*isteach*	*a-steach*
office	*Oifig*	*oifis*
island	*oileán, inis*	*eilean, inis*
bridge	*droichead*	*drochaid*
water	*uisce*	*uisge*

With the coming of the kingdom of Alba in the 840s, at the fusion of Dál Riada and Pictland, the Irish language-in-Scotland was on the rise, reaching its zenith in the eleventh century. Just as it was diverging into Scottish Gaelic, it was the language of the court and government, and of the aristocracy, clergy and intelligentsia. It spread throughout the kingdom as the borders expanded, even to the far southwest, where it persisted for centuries. That is why we have Gaelic placenames in regions where it was later despised and has not been spoken for centuries. Despite Gaelic's momentary prestige, not all subjects spoke it, and some regions had very few Gaelic speakers.

Movement against Irish-in-Scotland began at this moment from the very pinnacle of society, the royal court itself, a queen of English birth. Máel-Caluim/ Malcolm III (1031–1093) founded a powerful dynasty, known to history as the Canmores (*Ceann Mòr*: great head/chief). He is also the Malcolm cited by Shakespeare as the successor to Macbeth. His second wife was Margaret (1045–1093), a member of the Saxon royal family, to be displaced by the Normans, and quite a considerable figure on her own. Also known as St. Margaret of Scotland, she is the only royal Scottish saint, commemorated in many churches, such as St. Margaret's Chapel in Edinburgh Castle. Mary Queen of Scots kept her severed head in a venerated box. She refused to learn what was becoming Scottish Gaelic and gave her children English names. As records show, she also favored the appointment of English-speaking officers and retainers. These details on top of her prominence have made St. Margaret the proverbial enemy of Gaelic among champions of the language. Novelist Compton Mackenzie (1936), came to her defense, claiming many other forces militated against Gaelic, and that her negative influence has been exaggerated. Even as Gaelic began its retreat, it retained some official status. At the coronation of Alexander III in 1249 a traditional Gaelic storyteller recited the king's genealogy back to Dál Riada. King James IV (1473–1513), though he would also end the Lordship of the Isles, learned Gaelic as a second language and was the last Scottish monarch to speak it. He fell in the Scottish humiliation of Flodden Field, September 9, 1513.

Charles W.J. Withers in *Gaelic in Scotland, 1698–1981* (1984) devotes a volume, profusely filled with graphs and maps, to all the forces, economic, religious, social and political that were pushing against Gaelic. In earlier centuries the native Gaels were rivaled by Scoto-Normans, such as the Bruces. Foreign diplomats were unwilling to learn the Gaelic language. Trade began to flourish in port cities, and it was conducted in English. Improved agriculture burgeoned in the green Lowlands, not the heather-covered mountains. Gradually the royal court and the legal system shifted to Lowland Scots, or Broad Scots, officially a sibling of English, although many English-speakers find it difficult going. In Gaelic no distinction is made between English and Scots as both are called *Beurla* or *Inglis*. The realm of the Scots speakers is called *Galldacht* in Gaelic, which means "land of the foreigners," not the "Lowlands."

Two notes mentioned early in this chapter bear repeating here. The forbidding soils of the Highlands mean that no more than 9 percent of the land can be cultivated. Secondly, about 1375 John Fordun spoke of the first difference between the Highlands and the rest of Scotland by expressing his contempt for the population there. The Lowlands or *Galldacht* grew richer, and the Highlands lagged behind. As the clans developed tighter command structures, they prized the ability to move quickly on foot over trackless land. They did not have horses, and anyone pursuing them on horseback was at a disadvantage. A Highland raiding party might plunder Lowland treasure, but they were difficult to track down. Some of the motivation of the plunderers was the memory that so much of the rest of Scotland had once been Gaelic speaking.

John MacInnes (1989) finds expression of this sense of entitlement in an otherwise "beautiful" Perthshire song, *Bothan Airigh am Bràigh Raithneach*, in which one couplet reads:

> Why should we be without stock/
> Seeing that the foreigners have cattle?

Undeterred by the conspicuous differences in standard of living, many Highland chiefs maintained a sense of their own superiority. Praise poetry for them portrays a warrior class in an aristocratic game of war, priding themselves on prowess with weapons, especially the sword, and clad in bright tartans. Looking aside from the misery of the lowest reaches of Highland society, the poets serving different powerful chiefs dismissed the drudgery of Lowland farmers dressed in dull hodden (homespun) breeches. They were lowly peasants who ate kale, while the northerners dined on venison.

When the Scottish Crown finally moved to rein in the Highlanders, it was entirely on the basis of language. King James VI (James I of England, 1566–1625), the son of Mary Queen of Scots, had a deep and abiding loathing of everything Gaelic. Upon taking effective personal rule in Scotland at age seventeen he moved on a policy of pacification and "civilizing" the Highlands. Precursing his Plantation of Ulster, he and the Scottish Parliament "planted" hundreds of Lowland Scots settlers from Fife onto the Isle of Lewis in the Outer Hebrides in the 1590s on land confiscated from the MacLeods, to be repeated in the first decades of the 1600s. As the obedient Parliament had declared the Isle of Lewis to be beyond the bounds of civilization, the Fife Adventurers, addled with misinformation about non-existent riches, set about to plunder the territory in 1598 as if it were in in the Indies. Multiform disaster followed, starting with mass hunger and dysentery among the Adventurers. Eventually the islanders slaughtered the defenders of the newly built garrison at Stornoway.

James had more ambitious and far-reaching plans in mind. Through his agent, Andrew Knox, Anglican Bishop of the Isles, James demanded to meet with twelve prominent Gaelic chiefs, whom he then kept prisoner in Lowland castles. In August 1609, he offered them release if they would meet with him on the hallowed Isle of Iona, off the west coast of Mull. Nine relented, including an assortment of MacDonalds, MacLeans, a MacLeod, a MacKinnon and a MacQuarrie. Many did not attend, conspicuously the Campbells. To them he presented nine demands to be known in history as the Statutes of Iona, without offer of compensation for chiefly compliance. Some seemed inoffensive and unrelated to James's assault on the language, such as having inns constructed throughout the Highlands and the Protestant demand that the sale of wine and whisky be banned. Also Protestant was the request that the Established Church and its regular disciplines be maintained, such as having marriages performed in churches. This would forbid the supposed Gaelic custom of a trial marriage for a fixed period, a practice that did not in fact exist.

Three statutes limited the powers of the chieftains. Their retinues would be strictly limited. They were forbidden from carrying firearms. Sorning, exacting hospitality by force or threats, would be abolished.

Humiliating, even emasculating as the others may have been, the most irksome were those pertaining to language, arguably James's highest priority. Gaelic bards, authors of the praise poetry cited above, would be proscribed. Chiefs and leading clansmen should educate their sons, or even their daughters if they had no male heirs, in the Lowlands. Henceforward, clan leadership would be obliged to be able to speak with powers in the south. We may cite the language of the south, the *Galldacht,* as "Scots"; in the Statutes it is named as "English."

To romantic champions of the Gaelic language, many of whom did not find a voice until the nineteenth century, the Statutes are a signal outrage. Gaelic champions sometimes refer to them as the "Statutes of Icolmkill," to underscore the status of Iona in Celtic Christianity. Not all the Statutes were uniformly enforced, but the rule on obliging sons to be educated outside the Gàidhealtachd had an immediate and lasting effect. Within a short time the Gaelic elite was bilingual, while the great mass of the population was not. Eventually this would allow the elite to leave their traditional holdings and live with urban blandishments in Edinburgh and, eventually, London, and to see themselves as the counterparts of the holders of inherited titles elsewhere. Arguing that the vilification of the Statutes is misplaced, historian Julian Goodare (1998) sees them as markers in a long process. Instead, he would focus on the 1616 Act of the Privy Council of Scotland that declared no heir of a Gaelic chief could inherit unless he could write, read, and speak English. Also in 1609 another act of the Privy Council decreed that at least one English language school be established in every parish so that "the Irish language, which is one of the chief and principal causes of the barbarity and incivility among the Isles and Highlands, may be abolished and removed." The Privy Council spelled out what James had only implied.

Enforcement of some of the Statutes may have been lax, but in 1626 James's successor, Charles I, ordered the construction of an English-language school in every parish of the Highlands and Islands. More pernicious than James, Charles contemplated the wholesale removal of the Gaelic population in 1630, ethnic cleansing *avant la lettre.*

The efforts of King James and Charles were hardly death blows to Gaelic culture, but they were the first official actions whose stance would be repeated. Under the guise of religious education, getting young people to read the Bible, the Society in Scotland for Promoting Christian Knowledge (SSPCK), built its own intuitions. For starters instruction was English-only, and eventually Gaelic was banned from the schoolyard.

Politically, Gaelic speakers gained during the civil wars of the seventeenth century by being on the winning side, with charismatic leaders. In the several iterations of the Jacobite cause, except the first, the defeats would deliver the fate that James Stuart had wished upon his subjects.

2

Medieval Highlands and Islands

The Hammer of the Norse

Often in this study we speak of the "Highlands and Islands," the mainland of Scotland and the Hebrides, as if they were a cultural continuity, parts of the same whole. Certainly, both are in the Gaelic-speaking realm, the *Gàidhealtachd*, the islands more securely than the mainland during the past century. For the most part they share the same flora and fauna as well as a similar rocky terrain, except for outliers like Tiree, as flat as Kansas or Manitoba. When the great clans ruled the north, from roughly the fifteenth through the eighteenth centuries, names like MacLeod or MacDonald would link properties separated by expanses of water. The coupling of Highlands and Islands began as the kingdom of Scotland was becoming a nation state from 1500 and after the Lordship of the Isles lost independence in 1493 during the reign of James IV, the last king who could speak Gaelic.

This was not always so, however.

Before 1500, water transportation had a great advantage over travel on land, even more in Scotland, which did not inherit roads from Roman occupation. The Highlands had no roads at all until the eighteenth century. The islands, although set in frequently rough seas, were in constant communication with one another, and also with Scandinavia. As mentioned in Chapter 1, the Norse referred to these islands as the Sudreys, a term implying more places than the three hundred or so signified by the terms Outer and Inner Hebrides. The two first additions, Arran and Bute, are tucked under Argyll in the Firth of Clyde. Others today are not considered part of Scotland at all, such as Rathlin Island, above the northern tip of County Antrim, a frequent refuge for Scotsmen such as Robert the Bruce. Most important of all was the Isle of Man, despite being closer to Ireland. In the early Middle Ages, it was strengthened by Norse settlement, enjoyed wealth, power and influence over all the islands closer to Scottish shores.

The Norse had begun to arrive in the islands in the eighth century, eventually dominating them politically. Not only did they settle on Gaelic-speaking islands, but they intermarried with the local population, producing a hybrid culture, the *Gall Gàidheal*, under Norse rulers still paying fealty to the king of Norway. All this took place as the fragile Gaelic-speaking kingdom of Alba in the east was growing stronger, bringing the Gaelic language to farther reaches of what would be called

Scotland after its Gaelic origins. Neither entity could ignore the other; regular communication including intermarriage crossed borders. The Norse were too firmly entrenched in the islands to be removed and would retain a grip on them until 1263, even as Gaelic reasserted itself as the language of the original population. But the Gaels, while hardly an oppressed underclass, needed their own spokesman. This was Somerled.

Unquestionably historical, Somerled (c. 1100–1164), can also accurately be called legendary. More has been said and written about him than can be supported by records. Although his name remains unknown to many generally educated people, to Gaelic nationalists he is the first great hero, the "hammer of the Norse." In some ways the perception of his reputation resembles that of near contemporary Rodrigo Díaz de Vivar (c. 1043–1099) of Spain, known as El Cid, a warrior and smiter of national enemies before there was a nation. El Cid's memory benefits by being the focus of a flattering 3730-verse epic poem composed a hundred years after his death. Gaelic literary tradition was not up to such a task. But as the patrilineal ancestor of several important Highland families, Somerled's renown has grown by being inflated and polished in numerous clan histories and genealogies. Closer scrutiny of what records we have reveals some ambiguity about just how Gaelic he was, and also the apparent anomaly that he died fighting the Scots rather than the Norse.

He will always be referred to here as Somerled, a form he may not have known in life. In the *Chronicles of Mann* compiled a century after his death, he is *Sumerledo*. In Gaelic he was known as *Somhairle*, which remains a common given name in the Highlands. The Anglicization "Sorley" reflects what *Somhairle* sounds like to English ears. One of the families claiming descent from him is *mac Somhairle*, or MacSorley, not *mac Somerled*.

The solution has been a kind of procrustean Anglicization when dealing with Somerled and the Lordship of the Isles established by his descendants on the islands he dominated. It appears that an interest in such a heroic—and possibly flattering to the reader—ancestor as Somerled began before the wider study of early Scottish history. The same was true of William Wallace and Robert the Bruce, who are now always known by their English rather than their actual names (Uilleam Uallas/William le Waleys; Robert le Brus). The lost principality founded by Somerled's progeny was introduced in Sir Walter Scott's romantic poem, *The Lord of the Isles* (1815). The title character there is named Lord Ronald, the author's invention, instead of bearing a Gaelic name. This would be the first that many English speakers had heard of the Lordship. In Irish medieval history, with many more native surviving documents and Irish being the national language of an independent state, the Irish form was preferred over the Anglicization. Thus we speak of Somerled's early contemporary, the regional king who gave the Rock of Cashel to the Church, as Muircertach Ua Briain not Murtagh O'Brien. And so we cited king Cináed mac Ailpín not Kenneth MacAlpine, in the first chapter, which is also the preference of Wikipedia.

With discussion of Somerled and his legacy, however, Anglicization is too entrenched to be dislodged, even when it is misleading. It will take some explaining why there is first a "king" of the Isles and later a "lord." Most learned commentary on Somerled and his progeny speaks of noblemen named "John," when they were called "Iain" in life. In his Preface to *The Kingdom of the Isles* (1997), R. Andrew McDonald speaks of his "agony" in deciding to use English forms instead of Gaelic ones but does so "to be consistent with other standard works." We follow his lead reluctantly, and inconsistent with a preference for Gaelic forms elsewhere.

The desire to make Somerled more Gaelic than his name might suggest began early. No contemporary pedigree exists to outline his ancestry, but as many as twelve later genealogies for him, beginning in the twelfth century, filled in the gaps. Some link him with the court of Cináed mac Ailpín. The evidence supports what Somerled's name implied, that he was of mixed Gaelic and Norse heritage, a *Gall Gàidheal*. In 2004 a study traced the DNA of five Clan Donald chiefs who claimed descent from Somerled. Evidence demonstrated that they all did share a common ancestor who would have lived in the early twelfth century, and that person had patrilineal ancestry in Scandinavia. A 2011 study extended to 164 men with the name MacDonald confirmed the earlier results.

Little is known of Somerled's early life, except that the family holdings were in Morvern, in northern Argyll. Surrounded on three sides by water, just north of the Isle of Mull, in the twelfth century Morvern was a suitable location for launching campaigns via the shallow-drafted birlinn. The territory is thinly populated today and would not likely be seen as a prize itself. Somerled first asserted himself as a war leader when his father GilleBride faltered. Both father and grandfather GilleAdamnan had struggled with little success to displace Norsemen who had seized family properties. Despite the depredations of the ferocious Norseman Magnus Barelegs in the previous century, the Norse-Gaelic struggle over individual terrains remained unsettled. No date is given for Somerled's superseding of his father, but sometime after 1130 is a plausible speculation.

Somerled began to emerge as the greatest power in the region while others were looking away. Distant Norway was enduring a slow-motion civil war, 1130–1204, and did not extend its hand beyond its representatives in the Orkneys. The Isle of Man, with superior naval architecture, the forty-oared *skuta*, was co-opted. Somerled was cordial with Olaf, King of Man, and married his daughter Ragnhild (or Ragnhildis, Ragnhilde); with her he produced significant heirs, who rank ahead of offspring born to other women. Although one king, David I, claimed Argyll as his own, Somerled remained secure while the Crown sucked energy from other regional nobles. Beyond the Highlands David affected the character of Scottish life by introducing the elements of feudal order from the Continent when he planted Anglo-Norman knights and families on estates confiscated from Scottish landowners.

A local victory over the Norse attracted the admiration of other Gaelic leaders, and soon Somerled and allies were on their way to redeem individual properties from other local Norse warriors. No calendar records the dates of these acquisitions, but by 1140 Somerled dominated all the Hebrides south of Ardnamurchan, the westernmost point of land on the mainland: Coll, Tiree, Iona, Mull, Colonsay, Jura, Islay and the Kintyre Peninsula, often perceived as an island. To honor Somerled's rising status, David I of Alba/Scotland granted him sovereignty over the islands of Arran and Bute in 1136.

How deep Somerled's ambitions might have been has long been a subject of guesswork, beginning with seventeenth-century historians who wrote that he aspired to a Gaelic kingdom separate from Alba/Scotland. There is no contemporary evidence for such ambition, although he did see himself as an heir to the ancient hegemony of Dál Riada, partially coextensive with his domain. He early referred to himself as *rí*, a term widely used in both early Ireland and Gaelic Scotland. A cognate of the Latin *rex* (king), *rí* is nonetheless often translated in Ireland as "chief." In Scotland the term *rì* later devolved into the unique term mormaor (ScG *mòr maor*: great bailiff) and equated with the English "earl." In twelfth-century Alba/Scotland there were seven *rì*, all lesser than the *Ard-rìgh* (high king) at Dunfermline. These seven dominated mostly non–Gaelic regions of the east and north, but Somerled did not consider himself to be their counterpart. The *Chronicles of Melrose* describe Somerled as the *regulus* of Argyll, a translation of the Gaelic *rí airor Goidel*, which could mean "chief of the Gaels," but is conventionally translated as "king of Argyll." Neither Argyll nor the islands he controlled were kingdoms. He does, however, appear to have handled himself with a certain swagger. In any case, calling Somerled a "king" is to put him at odds, semantically, with the ruler who appeared a few generations later to be called the "lord of the Isles" (*Dominus Insularum, Rí Innse Gall*).

Even with Somerled's gains, Man still controlled the islands north of Ardnamurchan, namely Skye and the Outer Hebrides. During the benign forty-year reign of Olaf I, ending 1153 or 1154, this was tolerable co-existence. Murder and mayhem drove dynastic disputes that led to Somerled's defeat of Olaf's son Godred and declaring himself *Rex Insularum* in 1158 but still under the suzerainty of Norway as Man had been under Olaf. Before this confrontation Somerled had moved his center of operation to Islay, a shorter voyage to Man. At the apogee of his power, the Hammer of the Norse submitted to a Scandinavian monarch.

Islay, low-lying and boggy, would continue to play an important role in naval warfare and would become the home of the Lordship of the Isles, founded by Somerled's progeny.

Somerled was a builder who left lasting reminders of his era on the map. Through documentation or oral tradition his name is associated with more than a half-dozen castles; enthusiasts with shakier evidence would claim fourteen. A few today are intact, but most are in ruins. For whatever reasons their locations were chosen, all are visually striking to the contemporary eye. As befits a powerful ruler whose rise came from sea power, all the structures are near bodies of water, with four, Ardtornish, Salen, Aros and Mingary, close by Morvern, his first bailiwick. Finlaggan on Islay became not only Somerled's fortress but was later a citadel of the Lordship of the Isles as well as significant in the founding of the Clan Donald. Ardtornish, actually in Morvern on the Strait of Mull, would later play a continuing role in Highland history.

As Somerled's rule had no serious challengers until he had achieved stability with Godred, it is not clear why he should have led an invasion into the Scottish kingdom on the banks of the Clyde. The Crown had passed from the agreeable David I in 1153, to be taken by the weaker Malcolm IV (1153–1165) nicknamed "the Maiden" by historians because he left no heir. There has been no consensus on what drove Somerled, and some have suggested foolhardy vanity. R. Andrew McDonald (1997) freely admits that his interpretation is only a speculation. Somerled may have been a "conservative" resisting the cultural and social change by the Norman barons first under David and assertively under Malcolm the Maiden. The irony of describing Somerled as a conservative is that the mounted Normans were bringing a more feudal society with motte-and-bailey castles, what we are used to thinking of as one of the most archaic and repressive orders in recorded history. Instead, Somerled embodied an older social and political worldview that would lead to the development of the clans, quite different from feudalism, even though the clans are sometimes carelessly described as "feudal."

McDonald speculates further that Somerled would have dreaded most a Norman lordship that was moving westward into the shire once known as Renfrew, with potential design on Argyll and the Isles. If this is so, then the invasion of Renfrew by Somerled's Hebridean forces was a pre-emptive strike, with perhaps 160 vessels. It also led to a kind of land warfare the aging Somerled had not faced before. He was killed at the battle of Bargarran, 1164, in Renfrewshire, near what is now Glasgow International Airport.

Somerled had many children and appears in countless genealogies, but he did not found a dynasty. Within a short time, the southern half of his sea kingdom was claimed by Manx kings, led by his maternal uncle Ragnvald, who was overcome by the vengeful Godred. The northern half was divided among his warring descendants.

According to contemporary records, Somerled is thought to have had at least five sons and a daughter, some of them little more than cyphers. Little is known of Angus, but after five generations his descendants founded the Stewart/Stuart dynasty. The two most memorable sons were Dugald, who disappears from the record in 1175, and Ranald. From Dugald came the thirteenth-century Lords of Argyll and the Clan MacDougall. Ranald's legacy will later occupy much more of our attention. From his line descended the Lords of the Isles, the Clan Donald, Clan MacRory and Clan MacAlister, destined to play important roles in Highland history for centuries.

The Lordship of the Isles

The entity we know as the Lord of the Isles, centered in the Gaelic west, could never have flourished without the weakness and remoteness of the crown of Alba/Scotland. The English phrase was not known to the lords in life, and has more resonance in Latin, *Dominus Insularum* and *Dominus Inchegal,* or in Gaelic, *Triath nan Eilean* and *Rìgh Innse Gall.* There is no analogy to the Lordship in any modern nation-state, which did not appear in Europe until about 1500.

A notion that the Hebrides would have their own administration based on rapid water transportation was a legacy of successive Norse invasions that dubbed the island the Sudreys and made them answerable to Trondheim. Post-Somerled Scottish nobles harassed Norse settlements, and kings Alexander II and Alexander III offered to buy them. Provoked, the Norwegian king Haakon responded in folly, sending a fleet of 120 large ships to invade Alba/Scotland, landing in the Clyde Estuary. His defeat at Largs, October 2, 1263, while thought a stalemate by modern historians, is hailed by Scottish nationalists as the end of five centuries of Norse aggression.

Three years later Alexander III of Scotland negotiated with Haakon's successor, Magnus VI, to end conflict in the Hebrides with the Treaty of Perth, July 2, 1266. Norway would recognize Scottish sovereignty over the disputed territories for the lump sum of 4,000 marks and a subsequent annual payment of 100 marks. Scotland honored this obligation for decades. The Treaty also confirmed Norwegian sovereignty over the Orkneys and Shetlands, which would continue for two more centuries, until 1468 and 1472.

The Lordship did not simply secede from Scotland, like the Confederate States of America, although it engaged in battles with the Scottish kingdom, just as Somerled had at his death. Key to relative independence of the Lordship was the many-oared, light, high-speed Highland galley, the birlinn. Fittingly, two representations of the birlinn are known to us, on the Lordship escutcheon, and a similar one on the coat of arms of the Clan Donald, which derived from the Lordship.

How could the Alba/Scotland bear such insubordination?

In the 329 years between the death of Somerled in 1164 and end of the Lordship of the Isles in 1493, the kingdom of Alba/Scotland was less like a stone and more like a leaf in the wind. We have much documentation for the fifteen monarchs, one of whom was a seven-year-old girl, Margaret, Maid of Norway (1290). Along with recurrent English interference, there were two interregnums, 1290–1292 and 1296–1306, which invited one of the most celebrated episodes in Scottish history, the rebellion of the knight Sir William Wallace in the Second Interregnum, launching the First War of Scottish Independence. This *ne plus ultra* of Scottish patriotism may have been of English or Welsh origin, but he was part of the Normanized lesser nobility. The Norman form of his name is William le Waleys, and he was known in Gaelic as Uilleam Uallas. He was by no means a Gael himself, despite recent popular accounts to put him in Highland dress. His great victory at Stirling Bridge, September 1297, was followed by defeat at Falkirk ten months later. He was famously hanged, drawn and quartered in August 1305. And there are constant themes: English domination and humiliation of the Scots along with unspeakable and repeated cruelty. The nearly surreal sadism, as with the newly installed bishop Adam roasted alive in Caithness, September 11, 1222, might have been widespread, but we shall ignore most of it except when it affects policy or important decisions.

Many schoolchildren can identify the early capital of Alba/Scotland as Scone, now a small village 2 miles/3 kilometers from Perth. But that is a little like calling *Cináed mac Ailpín* by the name Kenneth MacAlpine, giving a modern identity to a pre-medieval simulacrum. By tradition Cináed chose Scone (Gaelic *Sgàin*, Scots *Scuin*), a site with both Pictish and Gaelic associations, and brought with him a coronation stone. Not until the passage of two and half centuries is there is a record of an edifice there, an Augustinian priory of 1114, long since disappeared. Nonetheless, Scone was unquestionably where Scottish kings would be crowned and remained so through the reign of James IV in 1488. Further, Scottish kings assembled an advisory council there called the Parliament of Scone, which lacked the authority of later parliaments.

Scone, however, was not a place to hold court. When Malcolm III (also Máel Chaluim) married the Gaelic-hating St. Margaret in 1070, the ceremony took place in Dunfermline, closer to the Firth of Forth. As they preferred to live there, the town was designated a "royal burgh," a title reconfirmed by their son David I in 1128. Other kings preferred to live in Perth, almost adjacent to Scone. Sometime after 1200 William I, the Lion, certified Perth a "royal burgh." For more than the next two centuries Scottish royals might live in either Dunfermline or Perth after coronation at Scone. During the William Wallace rebellion, when no monarch sat on the throne, Stirling was the de facto capital, 1296–1306. This ambiguity was resolved in 1437 when James I was assassinated in Perth, and the capital was moved to heavily fortified Edinburgh, a fortress of great antiquity, predating the establishment of Alba.

The zenith of early Scottish royal power came in the era of Robert the Bruce, or Robert I, the victor of Bannockburn, 1314, and the sponsor of the Declaration of Arbroath, 1320, as well as the magnet for some charming fables. The lengthy reign of his son and successor David II, 1329–1371, mixed fecklessness, bad luck and incompetence. He was challenged by a Balliol family pretender to the throne, egged on by the English. Worse, he honored the "Auld Alliance" with France by invading England disastrously, landing himself in the Tower of London for eleven years, 1346–1357.

David's misfortunes affected the larger concerns of this study. It was while David was in the Tower that the Hebridean leader John of Islay sought to be recognized as the Lord of the Isles.

Serving as regent in all but name during David's absences was a nobleman a few years older who would succeed him as Robert II. He is the first bring the name Stewart to the throne. The family originated in Brittany and came to Scotland with the Normans. The first local form of the name was Steward (Latin *Senescalli*), after a title created by David I two hundred year earlier and held by the family, but Scottified to Stewart and Gaelicized as Stiùbhairt in the era of Robert I, the previous king. Two centuries later the name would also be spelled Stuart to accommodate French orthography. To strengthen Robert II's connections to the Gaelic west, and also for a personal congeniality, he encouraged his daughter to marry the same John of Islay who was to declare himself the Lord of Isles.

The deed which established the Lordship of Isles, and allowed it to hold the third court in the British Isles, after England and Scotland, was not victory in battle or even an advantageous marriage, but rather only a citation in a letter from the Pope. John of Islay, son-in-law of the future Robert II of Scotland, had been calling himself *Dominus Insularum* for some time. He used it in a signature of the letter to the Pope, who used it as an address in return. Mail was slow, and the timing has been disputed, but 1353 seems to be most likely for the pope's response. Two centuries earlier Somerled had called himself *Rex Insularum,* but was never recognized as a "king" by the Pope.

There was no constitution, no declaration of independence. How the Lordship would define itself was determined by different holders of the title, some complaisant, others bellicose. At its zenith, the Lordship made its own laws, separate from those of Scotland, and collected its own taxes. Laws were written by judges called *britheamh*, hereditary posts on each island. Few of these tracts survive, but from second-hand reports the brieves favored Gaelic custom, more concerned with reparation than prevention, than the feudal, French-influenced practice of the Lowlands. Among the most contentious legal decisions of the Lordship was the awarding title for lands to favored magnates or families, without concurrence from the Scottish kingdom. These would be the bases of some later clan wars.

Tax revenues for the Lordship appear to have been bounteous. The statelet was divided into units of tax assessment called merklands, after the Norse silver coin *merk* or mark. Each merkland was required to deliver the equivalent of one merk, in silver or in kind, each year. We are not sure how many merklands there were, but Islay (239 sq.mi, 620 sq. km) alone had 360. Additionally, each merkland was required to support one gentleman "who does no labour," presumably a member of the chief's train or household.

The standard of living in castles in the west and islands was generally lower than what one would find in the residences of the most powerful in Perth and Dunfermline. The Lordship was so named about thirty years before John Fordun declared the people of the north and west to be the lesser sort. Local leaders in the Gàidhealtachd, whom contemporary historians dub "magnates," rose to higher status through the accumulation of properties, through useful marriages and sometimes through force of arms. Quite a few of them became self-declared lords of their islands or regions.

From heritage and fortuitous connections, **John of Islay** (c. 1320–1386), was better positioned than many others. He is also often known as John the Good, presumably for his generosity to the church rather than his munificence or sinless conduct. In life he was known as Eòin or Iain Mac Dòmhnuill, or Eòin/Iain mac Aonghais Mac Dhòmhnuill. Like other island magnates, his dominions had been growing, but he was also a descendant of Somerled, five generations removed through Ranald, the most prominent son. But it was not from Somerled nor Ranald that he would take an inherited family name we know as MacDonald, borne by all the Lords of the Isles, but Ranald's son Dòmnhall/Donald, who died in 1250. Countless Gaelic-speaking men bore this name before and long after this time, but this is the one destined to be commemorated, if not immortalized.

The phrase Clan Donald is a much later coinage. At the time of the emergence of the Lordship the family referred to themselves as the *Dhòmhnullach*.

As his prominence rose, John became more closely affiliated with Robert Stewart, the designated heir to the Scottish throne who would become Robert II. He wanted John to marry his daughter Margaret, which would require a divorce authorized by the pope. This led to the correspondence in which Pope Innocent VI addressed John as *Dominus Insularum* and granted the dissolution of the marriage, a century and a half before Henry VIII's request was denied. Blameless Amie was cast aside, and their children together were passed over for the Lordship. Meanwhile, Margaret's dowry brought even larger sections of the mainland, and the MacDonalds of the Isles would be closely related to the Stewarts ruling the kingdom.

John of Islay's son and heir, **Donald of Islay** (c. 1362–1422/23), had a radically different relationship with the Scottish Crown, in part because of the greater power of the Lordship vis-à-vis the royal family. The second Lord of the Isles is also known as Donald of Harlaw after the disastrous battle he fought with Lowland and royal forces, and also to distinguish him from the many other men named Dòmhnall Mac Dòmhnuill, even on Islay. Unlike his predecessors, he was sent to study at the University of Oxford, returning in 1378. Donald's route to the Lordship was challenged by a rebellion of his younger brother John who resented his meager inheritance, with the support of the MacLean kindred from their homeland on Mull. In contrast to the reign of his father, Donald faced battle after battle against formidable foes, which seemed to foster his own aggressions.

Robert Stewart, Donald's grandfather, proved to be a wretched king once he assumed the throne as Robert II. While generally timid and incompetent as a monarch, Robert was a lusty lion in the bedchamber, siring four sons and six daughters from his first wife, Elizabeth Mure, and at least eight acknowledged illegitimate sons by different women. Whereas succession was previously impeded by a dearth of heirs, now there would be many contenders. Two of those sons, Robert, Duke of Albany, the ablest, and Alexander, Earl of Buchan, an infamous blackguard, would bring problems to Donald of Islay.

Twenty years older than Donald, Alexander is better known to history as the "Wolf of Badenoch," a sobriquet unknown in his life, but who is the subject of continuing bad press. Ronald Williams (1984) called him a "psychopath," and in 2017 the *Scotsman* named him "Scotland's vilest man." His most notorious deeds were the destruction of the town of Forres in May and the burning of Elgin Cathedral in June 1390. Neither of these affected matters in Finlaggan, and Alexander committed other offenses. His aggressions were often led by a new private fighting force known in English as cateran, from the Gaelic *ceatharnaich* (warriors). Rather than family members or the medieval equivalent of conscripts, these were often "broken men" dissociated from their families, who introduced new levels of brutality and answerable directly to Alexander.

The single most deadly encounter between the Lordship and the Crown occurred during Donald's tenure: the Battle of Harlaw, 1411. The cause did not arise from Donald's desire for independence from the crown, nor was it a civil war as that term came to be understood in later centuries. Complex dynastic disputes involving a web of shadowy figures had visited many abrasions on Donald's vanity. More to the moment he felt that the Lord of the Isles should also be the ruler of the Earldom of Ross, to which he had a plausible claim. The Crown and most of the rest of Scotland wanted to prevent this from happening.

Depictions of the onset of war feel epic, with reported massive movements of fighting men. Historians report the huge numbers traveling over mountainous, nearly untracked terrain without disclaimer. The principal source is Walter Bower's fifteenth-century *Scotichronicon*. From Bower and parallel sources, Donald called up to ten thousand men to the muster at Ardtornish, his preferred residence on the south shore of Morvern instead of Finlaggan, and a frequent focal point in the early Highlands. From them he chose 6,600 for an assault to the east by sea and land. The report includes details of eagle's plume and saffron war-coats. En route to Inverness to confront the Duke of Albany, the invaders succeeded in taking Dingwall Castle, seat of the earls of Ross, and the largest castle north of Stirling at that time.

From there Donald moved east over what were the shires of Nairn, Moray and Elgin into what was long known as Aberdeenshire. King James I again being imprisoned by the English, the Scottish Crown was championed by another family member, Alexander Stewart, the Earl of Mar, supported by the Normanized barons. His terrain, Mar, more prominent in earlier times, lay in western Aberdeenshire, adjacent to the modern Braemar. He bore the family name and the title although he was the illegitimate son of the Wolf of Badenoch. In battle he manifested all his father's lupine tenacity. By the time the invaders and defenders faced each other July 24, 1411, at Inverurie, fifteen miles from Aberdeen, Donald's army may have included more than 10,000 fighting men. Stewart numbers were smaller but included men of high rank in armor. Before the introduction of gunpowder, the invaders were equipped with swords, short knives, bows and axes and round targe shields. Defending Stewarts added cavalry, spears, maces and battle axes. Stewart infantrymen stood in closely packed arrays of spearmen: the schiltron or shield-wall. Killing called for exhausting labor.

The total dead may have been only 1500, 600 for the defenders and 900 for the invaders, but they included well-born leaders from prominent families. No reliable accounts of the battle survive, but popular perception cited the familiar trope of slain bodies stacked in heaps, which served as history for a non-literate society. Further perception of the battlefield was so traumatic that mere citation of the place-name as "Red Harlaw" evoked dread. The ballad tradition was on the rise at that time, and the battle was replayed in both Gaelic, where it was known as *Cath Gairbheach* and in Broad Scots as *Reid Harlaw*. It has never been forgotten, even six hundred years later, and a 40-foot (12 m) memorial commemorates the site of the battle as remembered in song, poetry and popular memory.

Highland and Lowland memories contradict one another. The Earl of Mar and the Stewarts saw themselves the victors in that the MacDonald advance was halted, but Gaelic bards hailed Harlaw as the greatest Highland victory over a Lowland army.

For the MacDonalds, Harlaw was at most a temporary set-back. Far from being crushed, the Lordship would rebound and deliver vengeance within a generation.

In Broad Scots balladry Harlaw is also portrayed as a resistance to a rougher class of people. War propaganda always vilifies the other side, no matter the cultural and linguistic difference, but the Scots tone has prompted a long debate among historians. If the *Scotichronicon* is to be believed, Donald of Islay did indeed command the largest Highland army in history, greater than the Jacobite force under Prince Charles Edward in 1745–1746.

In his final years Donald retreated to a life of religious seclusion, not uncommon in that century. He had four surviving legitimate children, a daughter who married well, a son Angus who became Bishop of the Isles, another a monk, and Alexander who succeeded him, displaying even greater ambition. Donald died in 1423 and in buried on Islay.

That successor, **Alexander of Islay, Earl of Ross** (c. 1389–1449), known in life as Alasdair MacDòmhnaill, is the most storied of all holders of the Lordship, despite knowing many reversals and humiliations. A seventeenth-century history of the MacDonald family lamented that Alexander was "a man born to much trouble all his lifetime." As with the other lords, Alexander's struggles often pitted him against the Scottish kingdom, and under him the principality achieved significant victories, reaching arguably the apogee of power for the Gaelic Isles. He also returned the seat of the Lordship to Finlaggan.

Shortly after Alexander assumed the Lordship, James I returned from captivity to take the throne in 1424. The new Lord inherited from his father an alliance with the Crown against the Albany Stewarts.

For the next ten years their relationship was the stuff of florid drama with personal cruelties, betrayals and reversals of fortune. In a brazen act to flex his power, James marched north with an army and occupied the castle at Inverness, on which he had no claim. The king invited Alexander and allied magnates to the seized castle and imprisoned them. Most arbitrarily he murdered two kinsmen and openly toyed with the idea of supporting a pretender to the Lordship, a good-for-nothing cousin.

At his release, Alexander's desire for vengeance was at the least smoldering, but it was fanned into a raging fire by two uncles, who also flared against James I. They were Donald Ballach ("the freckled") and Alexander Carrach, Lord of Lochaber, also the two most prominent nobles in the Lordship. Their march against the king met some early successes but faltered through reckless planning. They advanced against Inverness, whose castle was then in the hands of the MacKintosh (Mac an Tóisich) kindred, not a party in the dispute between the Lordship and the throne. Malcolm MacKintosh, custodian of the castle, thwarted the invaders, prompting Alexander and allies to burn down the burgh. As Alexander and the Lordship allies looked formidable, they were joined by both the MacKintosh and Cameron kindreds whose home territories were nearby. Giddy with the thought of smashing James, Alexander entertained pretender claimants who might possibly replace the Stewart king. MacDonalds and Stewarts confronted each other at some field in Lochaber, perhaps the Braes, toward the end of June 1429. There may have been 10,000 men engaged. As soon as the royal standard was unfurled, alas, the MacKintoshes and Camerons bolted, allowing the king's forces to pummel the Lordship's men. Not content to overrun the Lordship armies, the royal forces moved west, seizing such MacDonald prizes as Dingwall in Ross and Urquhart on Loch Ness.

Alexander escaped immediate capture but not ignominy. He may have fled to Islay. Apparently, he surrendered, as he was taken to Holyrood, where he was stripped to his underclothes in front of James I, made to drop to his knees and hand over his sword, title and lands. To secure his imprisonment, Alexander was carted off to the mighty fortress of Tantallon Castle on the south shore of the Firth of Forth.

Within two years of the Battle of Lochaber, the Lordship and royal forces met again, September 1431, a few miles to the west at a celebrated site, Inverlochy, just north of the modern town of Fort William. Neither James I nor the confined Alexander of Islay were present, but their armies bounded forth with vigorous leadership. The Stewart Earl of Mar sought to make his claim to be Lord of Lochaber a reality, heightening the resistance of Alexander Carrach, the reigning Lochaber noble, and Donald Ballach, Alexander of Islay's redoubtable uncles. The results were a resounding victory of the Island Lordship over the Scottish throne, a repayment for continuing humiliations as well as the pain of Harlaw and the Braes of Lochaber.

The confluence of waterways and trails made Inverlochy an inviting spot for military confrontation. A second battle was fought there in the Scottish Civil War, February 1645, with Montrose, one of the most glamorous of all Highland warriors. The 1431 slaughter was celebrated in two poems by Sir Walter Scott, while 1645 is retold in detail by Gaelic poet Iain Lom, a work later widely known in translation.

As he lived until 1449 Alexander succeeded more effectively in shaping Highland history than did other Lords, also because of his skill in placing his many illegitimate sons in influential positions, Hugh (Ùisdean) at Sleat on the Isle of Skye, and Celestine (Gilleasbaig) at Lochalsh. The MacDonalds of Sleat would prosper and become one of the most prominent branches of the family. Today the Clan Donald Centre and Museum of the Isles is housed in the Sleat estate at Armadale.

Alexander's successor, the fourth and last Lord of the Isles, was **John of Islay, Earl of Ross** (1434–1503). The Gaelic form of his name is Iain or Eòin Mac Dòmhnaill, but by his reign some Lordship records were kept in English, so that he may have been known in life as John of the Isles. Some commentators refer to him as John II to distinguish him from John, also Lord of Islay, but who did not claim the title of Ross. No one has suggested a sobriquet to counter "the Good" attached to the first John, but "John the Bungler" would not be misleading. It was partially because of his misrule that the Lordship came to an end.

Early commentators, such as Hugh MacDonald, the seventeenth-century historian of the Clan Donald, remarked on John's absence of derring-do and dash. They depict a person of meek and modest demeanor, more suited for the clergy or scholarship. He allowed a Scottish king, James II, to bully him into marrying a woman he loathed, with whom he would produce no legitimate heirs. Whatever restraint he displayed in conversation was no deterrence from acts of breath-taking hubris.

John ascended to the Lordship at age fifteen in 1449. The concurrent rapid succession of Scottish kings should have been an asset for the Lordship. Two, James II, reigning 1437–1460, and James III, 1460–1488, became king as minors and went to early deaths. The throne, recently moved to Edinburgh, was in a virtual civil war with the Douglases, a powerful family from southern, non–Gaelic Scotland.

An actual civil war we know as the War of the Roses, between the Yorkists and Lancastrians, was then raging south of the border. James II looked upon this as an opportunity to regain Roxburgh Castle on the Tweed seized by the English ninety-eight years earlier. Maladroitly, James's capture destroyed the edifice. Sensing advantage for the Lordship. On the winning side this time, John of the Isles joined the royal forces in this encounter, giving him a fatal taste for bargaining with the English.

Recognizing that the Scottish throne would be slow to act during a regency, John flirted with the anti-royal Douglases. They encouraged the mischief of John's attacking the Norse-speaking Orkneys, a gratuitous aggression with no cost. After declining as a sea power, Norway had joined the Kalmar Union of the three Nordic kingdoms in 1397. That Union was ruled from Copenhagen, an impoverished court with no resources to defend distant possessions. Edinburgh paid no attention.

Success emboldened John for wilder schemes. Concurrently, Lancastrian forces suffered defeats in England, sending Henry VI to seek asylum in Scotland where he hoped to plot regaining power. The border so easily crossed, the Yorkist Edward sent a commission of five, headed by the new Earl of Douglas, to make a common cause with the most prominent Scottish noble, John of the Isles. What followed was called the Treaty of Westminster, which John signed secretly at Ardtornish February 13, 1462; it is thus sometimes referred to as the Ardtornish-Westminster Treaty. It called for nothing less than the end of the Scottish kingdom, a long-time English goal. The lands north of the Forth-Clyde line would be divided among three Scotsmen, John of the Isles, his MacDonald ally Donald Balloch and the Earl of Douglas. Douglas would regain his forfeited lands south of the Forth, but everything else south of the Forth-Clyde line would go to England. Further, the three Scotsmen would forever become sworn vassals of England and would assist the English crown with its wars in Ireland and elsewhere. In exchange John of the Isles would receive a salary of £200 in times of war, but only 100 merks (the price of 14 horses) in times of peace. Donald Ballach would receive £40 a year in time of war and half in times of peace.

As the Treaty was not proclaimed, John could move stealthily before his betrayal of the nation began to unravel. Unexpectedly, fortunes shifted in the War of the Roses, and Edward IV signed a peace treaty with Edinburgh, thus flummoxing the plot to carve up Scotland. The Scottish Parliament asked that John appear to explain his actions, which he refused, meeting instead with young James III a year later. For ten years the follies of Westminster-Ardtornish distracted and sullied the Lordship.

The king established a commission to decide what should be done with the erring Lord of the Isles. It was headed by the Earl of Argyll, known in English as Colin Campbell, a family that had long supported the Crown against the Lordship. Campbell, in Gaelic *Na Caimbeulaich*, is a name cited here for the first time. The family added the silent "p" about 1470 to appear more Norman. The shared enmity between the Campbells and MacDonalds is a given in Highland history. Colin, Gaelic *Cailean*, etc., is a common name among the Campbells, with thousands in the historical record. That familial antagonism, however, did not prevent the Earl of Argyll from having his daughter marry Angus Òg, John's son. In acting against his daughter's future father-in-law, then, the Earl of Argyll recommended the forfeiture of John's title, and when he failed to appear, death sentence *in absentia*. A delegation of Earls was sent to the Isles with this news, at which John submitted and returned to Edinburgh to face the consequences. In yet another reversal of fortune, James III, "with wonderful moderation," decided to pardon the reckless Lord.

In discussion with Parliament, the royal mercy came with conditions. The long-standing claims of an independent Lordship of the Isles was now exchanged for a feudal title. It would not be inherited but instead would be granted by the Scottish Crown. For the moment, the Crown preferred that the title be given to John's bastard son Angus Òg, son-in-law of the Earl of Argyll.

Some histories misleadingly describe Angus as the last independent Lord of the Isles, but his father outlived him. His name requires a moment of comment. It has long been common in Gaelic Scotland as well as being the name of a centuries-old (until 1974) shire northeast of Perthshire. Its very commonness is one of the reasons it is readily Anglicized, although some historians unaccountably use a Gaelic form, Aonghas, for this son of John of the Isles. The father and grandfather of Somerled were both named Angus. In that instance, the elder is called Angus Mòr. The word *mòr* literally means "big," but it is translated as "the elder," "great," or even "fat," depending on the context. When Somerled's father is called Angus Òg in that context it means young Angus as opposed to an older Angus. But Angus Óg [Irish diacritical] is also the name of an Apollo-like deity of poetry in Celtic mythology, thought to live in the passage grave of Newgrange at the Bend of the Boyne. It is as common in early Irish and Scottish records as Ali and Hussein are in Muslim discourse.

Angus Òg did rule as Lord of the Isles, and although most of the MacDonalds preferred him to his disgraced father, he exhibited an unsettling streak of instability and possibly madness. Shifts of allegiances did not move swiftly, but it was clear that the Lordship of the Isles was headed toward its own civil war pitting son against father. John of the Isles attracted support from outside the Clan Donald, with the MacLean (Mac Gill'Eain) kindred of Duart on the Isle of Mull, the MacLeod (MacLeoid) kindred of Skye, Lewis and Harris, and the MacNeill kindred from the far island of Barra, as well as the Stewart Earl of Atholl.

There were several encounters, the greatest of which was at sea at an inlet near Tobermoray, in 1481, at the north of Mull and called the Battle of Bloody Bay. Angus's forces were victorious, but John of the Isle was not killed, only disempowered. Most of the Clan Donald rallied around Angus, but the power of the Lordship appeared diminished, leading to a revolt of the magnates in 1488. Two years later while Angus was sleeping, an Irish harper named Diarmaid Ó Cairbre stole into his room and slit his throat.

As the father-son drama was playing out in the Hebrides, there was a concurrent succession of kings named James Stewart in Edinburgh. James III, so generous to John of the Isles, had enlarged the Scottish kingdom through marriage.

For James IV (1473–1513) then only twenty, a chief concern was John of the Isles' inability to control the MacDonald mayhem. The island confederacy had to be dissolved if order was to be maintained in the remoter districts. When the Scottish Parliament met in May 1493, John, fourth and last Lord of the Isles, was deprived of his title and estates. The next year John appeared before James IV, making a formal voluntary resignation and surrender of the Lordship. After a period of rest in the royal household, he spent the remainder of his days in a monastery at Paisley near Glasgow.

James IV also took the title Lord of the Isles for himself, and it remained with the Scottish crown after his death. When James VI of Scotland became James I of England, it passed to the English Crown and still exists. At this writing the Lord of the Isles is Prince William Windsor-Mountbatten (b. 1982), who is also Prince of Wales.

James IV is often described by historians as the ablest and most attractive of all the Stewart kings of Scotland, capable of speaking eight languages. He made a politically astute marriage to Margaret Tudor, daughter of Henry VII. This "union of the thistle and the rose" produced six offspring. In a century a Stuart king would sit on the throne of England. Significantly, he demanded that all the children of nobles be educated. More than any of his predecessors, he made a study of Scottish geography and ethnography. He established what we call Scots or Broad Scots as the language of the nation. To confuse matters, he and his court referred to the language as "English," just as they frequently denoted Gaelic as "Irish." Linguists have always seen Scots as a sibling of English, related but distinct, as Swedish is from Danish, but this has not penetrated the popular mind in North America and elsewhere, where it is often referred to as "Scots Dialect."

For people living within the Lordship life may have been little different in 1494 than it had been in 1492, but for Gaelic nationalists 1493 is a date to be cited with outrage. In ballad literature the preceding decades came to be known as *Linn an Àigh*, the Age of Prosperity, although the phrase was not coined until sometime later. The decades succeeding the Lordship came to be known as *Linn nan Creach*, the Age of Forays, for the disorder and clan wars that followed. This phrase is contemporary with events and is more widely known, but recent scholarship has argued that bloodshed and destruction may not have been as extensive as once portrayed.

Ever the man of action, James IV traveled west to claim the fealty of all the nobles and magnates who had previously been vassals to John of the Isles. As mentioned before, he concerned himself with the old Highland seat of Dunadd, and he was the last Scottish king to speak Gaelic, which he learned as a second language. This took two years of negotiations, the granting of pardons and the awarding of further titles, but by 1494 the king had the authority he wished. There would be further conflicts with other clans, and that led to his undoing: ignominious defeat and death at Flodden Field in 1513.

The actual record of the Lord of the Isles cannot diminish its stature in the Highland imagination. Highland Gaels are an indigenous ethnic minority who have occupied the poorest quarters of the kingdom to which they gave their name. The other minorities within the British Isles, the more numerous Irish and Welsh, have their own hegemony: for the Irish a separate island and later a sovereign state and for the Welsh a principality. The less numerous Manx and Cornish lost their languages and assimilated. For Highland Gaels the Lordship of the Isles was when they ruled.

The Rise of the Clans

Few topics in this study engender more heated discussion than anything else having to do with the nature of the clans. On one side we have the generations of new scholars who emerged about 1960, many from families who are the first to have a university education and who have mastered recondite languages, like Old Norse, Norn, Old Irish, early Scots and early Gaelic, as well as paleography to decipher early manuscripts. This is at a time when there is wider access to rare documents; items previously under lock and key are now on-line. On the other side is a larger, more popular audience whose informed reading begins in the generation of Sir Walter Scott. They turn to clan histories, venerated, prestige texts of considerable antiquity, even though they may have been composed long after events depicted. Some readers rely on clan histories for a sense of personal identity, reveling in tales of heroic deeds on the battlefield, vanquishing traditional foes. A man of such a disposition is likely to have several dress ties of the clan tartan, which is also true of the present author.

Most contemporary Scottish historians would concur with a statement something like this: "The notion that a clan is group of men all possessing the same surname and all descended from a common ancestor is completely erroneous" (my phrasing). The word "clan" from *clann* "children," is late coinage in Gaelic and an even later borrowing in English, not recorded in English until about 1425. Its usage is now so widespread, usually with no allusion to matters Scottish—*cf. Clan of the Cave Bear* (1980), Jean M. Auel's prehistoric fiction, or the hip-hop group Wu-Tang Clan—that we have to struggle to remember that it is not merely a synonym for "family." The word was coined in Gaelic and borrowed in English because it incorporated unique features that existing words could not convey for that epoch, the conflict between the Hebrides, first headed by the Norse and later the Lord of the Isles, and the Scottish Crown. In early Ireland and in the well-remembered proto-kingdom of Argyll in the sixth to eight centuries there were a number of terms for kin-groups. First was *tuath* denoting a large group or a whole people, such as the divines who follow Danu of Celtic mythology, the Tuatha Dé Danann. In Dál Riada all the Gaels would be in the tuath. More definite was the family group that included all the members descended from a common great-grandfather, the *derbfhine*, *derbfine* (from OIr *derb*: certain) who might inherit property or power. The early Irish and Scottish Gaels did not follow the primogeniture of the Mediterranean, assuring succession to the first-born male. Among the Gaels a successor was chosen from the derbfhine, the cue for endless disputes. Between the wide tuath and the narrow derbfhine was the *cenél*, *cenéla* (pl.) a "kindred." The cenél is recorded in Irish history several centuries before the appearance of the clan as with the Cenél Conaill of what would later be Donegal or the Cenél Eógain of what would later be Tyrone and was a signifier of an aristocratic pedigree. This also appears to be the meaning when the word appears in the records of Dál Riada of Argyll from the sixth or eighth centuries. Here we have Cenél Loairn (after Lorn) and Cenél nÓengusa (after Angus). Membership in the cenél conferred status but did not call for service in combat.

As we saw in the discussion above of the emergence of the Clan Donald from among the descendants of Somerled in the Lordship of the Isles, it was political turmoil rather than mere ethnicity that prompted the launching of several of the biggest and oldest clans. Alba, the predecessor to "Scotland," was a small regional power that embraced the Gaels of the northwest and Isles. Through weak leadership, the influence of the Scottish kingdom was intermittent but had to define itself against two adversaries: the ever-present threat of the English to the south, but also the frequently predatory Norse in the Hebrides, not quieted until the Battle of Largs in 1263. When a strong, dominating Scottish monarch emerged it was during the reign of Robert I, the Bruce (1306–1329), which brought with it Norman ideas of feudal allegiances and tenures. When the leader of a kinship, a cenél, swore his support to King Robert, it gained a feudal charter that made the leader a tenant-in-chief, the head of a feudal court. This gave him an advantage over the leader of a neighboring cenél who lacked such authority. Vassalage, ironically, enhanced authority. He could dispense justice and establish primogeniture, pushing aside the old Celtic derbfhine or tanistry, in which a leader was chosen from a larger pool. Swearing fealty to the Lord of the Isles, the rival of the Scottish king, also raised a chief's profile.

The earliest citations of the word *clan* in Gaelic appeared before it was defined by the emergence of several groups calling themselves clans. These come in the twelfth-century marginal notes of a ninth-century Gospel, speaking of a Clan Canan and a Clan Morgan, about which we know nothing else. The descendants of Somerled (d.1064) are referred to figuratively as Clan Somhairle by historians, but it is not clear that the term was in contemporary use. *Clann* may have been a synonym for *cenél* for a while and evolved into something more particular. In a widely cited quotation, I.F. Grant (1935) says that the clan was "a hybrid institution, a mixture of tribal tradition clustering around the *ipso facto* landholder of the soil—whether he held possession by feudal charter, lease or feu, or by mere sword right—and the chiefs largely because of the inefficiency of the Lowland authorities continued to fulfill functions of a tribal leader."

The clan is not feudal as that term is understood in most of Europe. The Highland clans never had such trappings of feudalism as a sheriff, justiciars, etc. Under feudalism the king holds power by allodial—not subject to any superior—right, and is accountable only to God. A feudal ruler is defined by how much land he controls, a fixed place on the map. The status of clan chief may have been raised by the association with Scoto-Norman feudalism, but he was a patriarchal figure. The people he ruled may have been tenants who bonded with him by taking his surname even though they were not blood relatives. Unattached freemen might join the clan thus taking the clan name. A clan chief might reside in a fortress, but he was not as rooted as was the feudal lord. The MacDonalds did not have to remain at Finlaggan on Islay. In a thinly populated land with migrating herds of cattle, where clan leaders were also devoted to hunting deer in remote glens, demarcated borders were not as fixed as with agricultural feudalism.

Clan histories, many of them not written until the seventeenth century or later, often postulate the most ancient of origins, in heroic Ireland or Dál Riada. Given the paucity of medieval records and the unreliability of those we have, it is a conundrum to determine which, if any, came before the others. Undaunted, spokespeople for the Clan Robertson claimed the title of "oldest certifiable ancestry" in a *Scotsman* news article of January 2016. This was based on the evidence of links to Niall of the Nine Hostages (fourth-century Ireland), as in marker M222 among clan chiefs (hardly unique) and associations with the mormaers of Atholl contemporary with the rise of Alba. Early cited as the *Donnachaidh* (of Duncan), the clan did not assume the name Clan Robertson (an Anglicized form) until a hundred years after Bannockburn, by which time the Lordship of the Isles and the MacDonalds were flourishing.

Part of the difficulty is knowing when a group we know to be a clan started referring to itself as such. As we considered above, what we now know as the Clan Donald, denoting itself as the *Dhómhnullach,* emerged during the tenure of the first

Lord of the Isles, John of Islay, 1326–1386. Near the end of that century in the parliament of 1390, at the beginning of the reign of Robert III, the second Stewart king, members' associations with different clans were made most conspicuous.

Not all clans are of solely Gaelic origin. The MacDonalds and the MacLeods were mixed Norse-Gaelic, the first Stewart immigrated from Brittany, the first Chisholm and Beaton chiefs were Norman, those of the Frasers, Cameron and Grants Anglo-Norman. Although in fact persons of different family lines may have joined a clan and taken its name, many clans do have generalized genetic profiles that would include a multitude of members. Today their official structure is recognized by the Court of the Lord Lyon, which regulates heraldry and coats of arms. Most clan surnames, passed from generation to generation, as distinguished from the *sloinneachach* or patronymics, originated in the sixteenth and seventeenth centuries and did not become prime to a person's identity until later. Many clan names clearly were adapted from patronymics, MacDonald, MacLeod, MacLean, but many more were not: Campbell, Cameron, Beaton. Tartans, carelessly called "plaids" by the uninitiated, sometimes claim fourteenth-century origins, but most were codified and regularized in the nineteenth century, or even later.

To enhance the patriarchal character of the clans, many claim to be the offspring—*síol* (seed, sperm)—of a distant male ancestor, fanciful or historical. As mentioned in Chapter 1, Clan Campbell was much taken with the story of Diarmait and the boar in the Old Irish Fenian Cycle. Not only did they put the boar in their coat of arms but also referred to themselves as *Síol Diarmait, Dhiarmaid*, etc., the Seed of Diarmait. Clans MacKinnon and MacGregor assumed themselves to be descended from Cináed mac Ailpín, the founder of Alba, and so styled themselves *Síol Alpín*. The desire to be linked to Niall of the Nine Hostages was widespread, and the clans MacSween, Lamont, MacLean, MacLachlan and MacNeill assigned themselves the honor of *Síol Niall*.

The longevity and many transformations of the clans tend to obscure what they were like at the beginning and in their first centuries. Today, for example, clans with recognized chiefs are considered a "noble community" under Scots law. Much protocol is written and codified. It was not always so. After the recriminations following the failure of the Jacobite rebellions in the eighteenth century, clan chiefs moved away from traditional clan territories and began to live in cities, keeping company with nobles of Lowland and English society. This cleansed them of a martial dimension, so much of a clan's character, especially in the decades after the forfeiture of the Lordship of the Isles in 1493, the so-called *Linn nan Creach*, the Age of Forays. The last great clan battle—not concerned with religion or royal succession—was at Mulroy in Glen Roy, Lochaber, in August 1688.

Clans arose in territories where the power of the central authority was weak. At the beginning, a clan was composed of everyone who lived in the chief's territory or from territories owing allegiance to the chief. The Highlands tend to be divided into discrete parcels of islands, peninsulas, and narrow glens, but limits of a chief's territory were not precisely defined as a modern surveyor would demarcate. The boundaries could also change with shifting fortunes. When a clan was launched a chief might embrace everyone in his territories, even if they were clearly not blood relatives or actually bore different surnames. Taking the chief's surname made them part of the clan. At the same time, a chief might expel or outlaw certain persons from the clan, including blood relatives, who then could not use his name. Surnames passed only from the father, *not* the mother. In more recent centuries claimants to a chieftainship have been able to take their posts through a maternal line but by changing their surnames to accommodate the requirements of the office.

Not everyone adjacent to a chief's territory joined the clan. Some people retained their own surnames while being affiliated with or perhaps even related to a larger, more powerful clan. The name for such a subsidiary clan is the "sept," possibly derived from the Latin *saeptum*, meaning "enclosure" or "fold." It may also be a variation of the English "sect." The word "sept" is also found in Irish history, with the same meaning. Confusingly, a sept of one large clan might have the same surname as a sept belonging to a different clan, as happens in the instance of your author's family. Further, a sept might change allegiances, being attached to one great clan for decades and shifting to another, for whatever reason. If the chief of a major clan went to war, the members of the sept would be there with him. In the nineteenth century through the influence of the British Army and the enthusiasm for all things Highland, sept families sometimes acquired their own tartans.

A sept must be distinguished from a "cadet branch" of a great clan. The cadet branch consists of the male-line descendants of a patriarch's younger sons (cadets). Such a branch would retain the same surname of a great clan, but in contrast to the septs might pursue interests separate from those of the principal chief.

Although the founding of a clan may have been an *ad hoc* response to an immediate circumstance, most eventually began to fall into patterns of administration and interaction as if following a template, although none was ever written. In the long run membership in a clan would put many demands on the person, especially males, but joining was attractive and offered rewards. Prime was a sense of belonging, of collective heritage in an impoverished, lawless land. The word for that identity is *dùthchas*, which books on the clans denote as almost untranslatable, even as it is essential. In the Edward Dwelly *Gaelic-English Dictionary* (1911) it is assigned four definitions: "1. Place of one's birth. 2. Heredity, native or hereditary temper. 3. Visage, countenance. 4. Hereditary right." These could be summarized as the belief that clan members are entitled to a permanent stake in the territories pertaining to their clan. With this sense of belonging comes an obligation to recognize the personal authority of the chiefs and leading gentry as trustees for the clan. From a distance this may sound like the pledge to a fraternal organization, but much more binding. In folk narratives the word is spoken with affection and reverence, something to be respected, never resented. Through the warmth of *dùthchas*, it is understandable that members began to think of themselves as *clanna*, children of one family.

As the chiefs maintained a stable authority and could negotiate with the Scottish Crown, the concept of *oighreachd* ran parallel with *dùthchas* and gradually displaced it. Dwelly has an easier time with it: "1. Heirship. 2. Inheritance, possession, freehold estate, landed property." The word signals the clansman's willingness to support a chieftain's authority to negotiate charter with the Crown and to be a landed proprietor as well as a trustee. *Oighreachd* denotes land owned by the clan elite, when the territory stretched beyond shared living space. In short, although the clan system still differed from feudalism, the chief moved from being a patriarch to resembling a lord, as the introduction of the Scots term "laird" implies.

Two features of clan life that were uncommon in other parts of Britain helped to tighten the social ties of the clan. The more familiar is known in English as "fosterage," and had been practiced in Europe from ancient times and was common in pre–Conquest Ireland. The child of one family would be taken in infancy to be raised by a different family, always retaining the identity of the birth parents. Hard as this may have been on mother and child, it could forge strong links between the families as the child, in adulthood, could claim to be in both. Whereas fosterage might bridge great distances elsewhere, in the Highlands it existed only between certain families in a clan's gentry.

Harder to grasp is the unique concept of "manrent," which also sounds unattractive to modern readers. The first citation of manrent appears at the beginning of the clan system in 1442, and the Scottish parliament made the first attempts to abolish it, unsuccessfully, in 1457. They persisted through the seventeenth century. Manrent might appear to approach vassalage or indentured servitude, but without the opprobrium. A person or an entire clan would pledge to serve the chief of another clan, "to be friend to all his friends, and foe to all his foes." A weaker man or clan, not necessarily a sept or a cadet, pledged to serve a stronger lord, often in the form of a covenant. These covenants might be bonds of friendship between parties of equal rank or power, often in treaties of defensive or offensive alliance, and usually did not continue much further than the occasion on which they were formed. On the positive side for those being "rented," smaller clans retained their surname and colors without being swallowed up by larger ones. And as with fosterage, manrent helped to forge bonds transcending the borders of a clan in its glen or on its island. In the short run the strengthening of one clan against rivals might help to maintain a balance of power, but more often the strengthening of fighting strength with manrent appears to have encouraged a turbulent and warlike spirit.

Clan chiefs and most of the clan gentry devoted themselves to such masculine enterprises as hunting and to becoming fit for conflict and often gave less attention to the management of the clan's resources. That task went to what were initially lesser gentry usually known by the English term "tacksmen." Much of the time the role was what in England would be called "estate managers." They managed rents and assigned strips of arable land to tenants in a system called *runrig*. Their income and status rose and the clans slowly moved from payment in kind—barter—to currency. They might lend corn seed and tools and later arrange for the droving of cattle to markets in the Lowlands, being rewarded with a minor share of the profits, making them incipient entrepreneurs. T

As Gaelic-speaking Highlanders interacted less and less with Scots-speaking Lowlanders, the very word "clan" was what others in the nation disdained or feared about the Gàidhealtachd. As R.G. Nicholson (1974) wrote: "'clan' became a bad word in Lowland mouths; clans did wicked things."

As the clans were increasingly removed from life in the rest of Scotland, which was growing more and more like other European nations, they preserved manners and relationships from earlier centuries. Among the most startling of these are relationships within marriage. The reader may have noticed the high incidence of what modern historians call "illegitimacy" in the families of the Lords of the Isles. What we today describe as the birth of a child conceived with a woman not a man's lawful wife, was not always perceived as scandal or misfortune, nor was the child disdained as a "bastard" among early clans. The word "clan," after all, comes from *clann*, meaning children, not parents or parents and children. As the marriage practices of medieval and early modern Highlands were often at variance with Christian canon law, the authors of flattering clan histories written from the seventeenth century and on tend either to ignore irregularity in marriage or to downplay its prevalence and significance. John Major's 1521 diatribes against the "wild Scots" includes an indictment of immorality, and the punitive Statutes of Iona (1609) addressed questions of marriage customs that James VI disdained. It has taken modern scholarship a while to articulate what the complaints against marriage in the heyday of the clans were. W.D.H. Sellar's landmark essay, "Marriage, Divorce and Concubinage in Gaelic Scotland" (1981), puts the issues into a larger context while dismissing lesser charges of clannish irregularity.

Even though Highland life was *terra incognita* for most educated people, many had heard of the somewhat racy notion that the mountain people engaged in a kind of trial marriage called "handfasting." It had been mentioned in Martin Martin's *Description of the Western Isles of Scotland* (written c. 1695), the only book about the *Gàidhealtachd* that anyone read before Boswell and Johnson and long in print. Sir Walter Scott speaks of it. Highland handfasting was such a widely known given that it is the mode of marriage in Alan Jay Lerner and Frederick Loewe's Broadway fantasy, *Brigadoon* (1946). Sellar argues that emphasis on the practice distracts us from looking at larger and older issues.

As spelled out by Martin, "handfasting," literally a handshake, described the agreement of two chiefs that the heir of the one should live with the daughter of the other as her husband for twelve months and a day. If at the end of that time the lady had brought forth a child, he would marry her and claim the offspring as his own. If she had not produced, or if he had come to disdain her company, the contract was considered at an end and each party was at liberty to marry or handfast with any other. Twenty years before Sellar, A.E. Anton dismissed the entire question. He said "handfasting" was a north of England and Lowland term for betrothal. The limited instances of its occurrence were more common in the Lowlands than Highlands. And he berated the two most authoritative nineteenth-century historians, Donald Gregory (1836) and W.F. Skene, as being so "inept" as to repeat such a libel of Highland probity. Seller grants that Anton is on the mark for Gregory's and Skene's misuse of the term, but he concurs that there were many peculiarities in the marriage customs of earlier centuries. To deal with those issues calls for a knowledge of Old Irish and access to early Irish documents.

Not only was Old Irish the parent language of Scottish Gaelic, but many documents were written in it before the first word of Scottish Gaelic appeared on parchment. Important among those is an extensive body of traditional laws greatly unlike Roman law adapted by the Church as Canon Law. The usual name for them is *Brehon*

(Old Irish, *breithem*), although Sellar does not use it. Brehon laws have not influenced statutes of any modern state, but most law school libraries will include books on them, often Fergus Kelly's *A Guide to Early Irish Law* (Dublin, 1988), as more than a cultural curiosity. The early Irish church, in its laws as well as many practices, was so widely at variance with the rest of Christendom that the papacy gladly endorsed Henry II's conquest of Ireland in 1170 to bring the island in line. In the mid- to late twentieth century, as many students became aware that early Ireland was vastly different from modern Ireland, and there was a fashion for all things "Celtic," many feminists were delighted to learn that under Brehon law women could make contracts, inherit property in their own name, and initiate divorce. A closer examination, however, would prove that pre–Conquest Ireland and apparently early Gaelic Scotland were societies no modern woman would find inviting.

Brehon law recognized many types of sexual union, some lasting, some temporary and some merely transient. It is now universally accepted by Irish scholars that Brehon law allowed for polygamy, concubinage and divorce, and these views persisted long after the introduction of Christianity in the sixth century. Much less so after the Anglo-Norman conquest of the late twelfth century. A first or principal wife was known as a *cétmuinter*, implying that there would be other wives. The usual purpose of a second wife was to produce sons. The term for her status was *adaltrach*, literally "adulteress," clearly reflecting the Church's disapproval. Various types of concubines of inferior status were also recognized. Children of such a union would be considered legitimate for the purposes of succession. The *adaltrach*'s position was not secure; if she failed to produce a male heir she could be dismissed. In the midst of this, women had some surprising rights. A *cétmuinter* could divorce her husband on several grounds, if he became insane, mistreated her, was not a sexual performer, either impotent or homosexual, or indeed if he took an *adaltrach* she found objectionable.

Outside any law, of course, powerful men, especially if they were landowners, might take sexual advantage of dependent and bondswomen under them. Long true and widespread. Such routine exploitation was one of St. Augustine's criticisms of slavery. Brehon law did not go so far as to license predatory magnates. It did allow a man of some station to have more than one mate and to legitimize their offspring. Implicit also in the laws is that the women would be of comparable station, not servants or the legally disadvantaged. Reliable records detail the private life of a High King (*Ard Rí*), an esteemed but honorary title, not yet the head of a nation state as the Scottish king was. Tairrdelbach Mór ua Conchobhair (Turlough O'Connor, 1088-1156), also King of Connaught, fathered seventeen sons by four wives. His term, 1120-1156, ended before the Anglo-Norman conquest. But even in the sixteenth century, when Elizabeth I was trying to tighten her grip on Ireland, the second earl of Clanrickard (d. 1582) was said to have been married six times, with five wives living at the same time.

Sellar argues confidently that early Irish practice continued in the early years of the Gàidhealtachd. As mentioned, he does not use the term Brehon Law, but in the years of the Lordship of the Isles the term for a judge was *britheamh*, clearly derived from the Old Irish *breithem* and comparable to the Modern Irish *breitheamh*.

Instead, Sellar prefers the phrase "Celtic secular marriage," not only because it was in defiance of canon law but also because it declined outside the Highlands after the twelfth century. Genealogies support that Highland magnates and clan chiefs readily married Irish noble women from as early as the thirteenth century and extensively from the time of the Bruce incursion in Ulster in the fourteenth century and the MacDonald settlements. The Scotsmen considered Irish marriage arrangement to be compatible with their own. Sellar laments that the history of early Highland law has not been written, and there is a dearth of documentation, perhaps attributable to the relative poverty and thinner population of the Highlands, as opposed to Ireland. What records we have may be misleading, Sellar adds. It was not that difficult to present relationships resulting from Celtic secular marriage in Canon law guise, and it was often politic to do so.

Hugh (Ùisdean) MacDomhnaill, a son of Alexander, the third Lord of the Isles in the fifteenth century, is usually described as an "illegitimate" son in that he was not a child of his father's *cétmuinter*. This caused him no loss of status as he became the founder of the Sleat branch of the Clan Donald in the south of the Isle of Skye. When he died, he left six sons and heirs, each by a different mother.

After reviewing more evidence, Sellar concludes: "One cannot doubt Celtic secular marriage survived late in Gaelic Scotland as in Gaelic Ireland." He suggests no date for the end of plural marriages in the Highlands, but the advance of strict Calvinism in many glens and islands, as well as the Statutes of Iona, certainly contributed. During the decline of the old order Christianized record-keeping reflected the values preferred by the Scottish Crown. The notable Clanranald chief John Móideartach was born "illegitimate," possibly from a mother of low status. The clan history described him of being of natural birth but "without doubt ... a man truly worthy of preferment." He succeeded his father in 1530 and was legitimized by the Crown in 1532.

Regardless of one's status within an individual family unit, to live in a clan from the thirteenth to the eighteenth century was to live in an "absolute patriarchy," in the words of the Rev. John MacInnes. To live in any European kingdom in the centuries before John Locke and the Enlightenment was to be denied the personal freedom modern citizens take as entitlement. In MacInnes's insightful and illuminating essay, "Clan Unity and Individual Freedom" (1972), men and women were both caught in an authoritarian vise grip more limiting than anything befalling contemporary denizens of London or Edinburgh. Such hardships are ignored by the authors of later Highland romances. The will of the chief was absolute, even though it had no foundation in Scottish law. MacInnes seconds the debunking views of the 8th Duke of Argyll, George Campbell, in his *Scotland as it was and as it is* (1887): "the people of the Isles were absolutely at the disposal of their chiefs." There was probably no sin, except possibly sacrilege, which earned a heartier condemnation from the clans folk than disloyalty to parents or to the chief, the father of his people. The adage was that the bond between people and the chief was as close as a man's flesh to his frame.

This did not mean that a chief was necessarily an ogre, or that a chief would characteristically exploit his position with petty cruelties. The chief stood in several relations with the clan: he could be a landlord, leader and judge. He might also be a matchmaker. In his *A Description of the Western Islands of Scotland* (1703), Martin Martin observed that if a Barra man lost his wife, or a wife her husband, each could apply to the MacNeill for replacement, and that his selection was reported to be satisfactory.

Unlike medieval rulers in other parts of Europe, clan chiefs did not employ jesters, who might be impudent with impunity. The sole person who might speak of something other than obeisance was the poet, of whom more found a station in clan society by the seventeenth century. One of the most-often cited examples of this independence comes from the prolific Iain Lom ("bald John"), sustained by MacDonell of Keppoch. Much of his extensive output survives and be discussed further in the next chapter. Better known for depictions of the Civil War, he did not shrink from condemning a murder of two young men within the Chief's family, indicting other members lusting for the chieftainship as the perpetrators. The episode in known as *Murt na Ceapaich,* the Keppoch Murders. His denunciation of the shame brought upon the clan was widely circulated. Nonetheless, he escaped physical punishment but was forced into exile with the MacDonalds at Sleat, where he had a half-brother.

The deadliest loss of freedom is what in modern terms might be called universal conscription. If the chief was bent on war, which was frequent, his men must serve. A conscientious objector was inconceivable. As most clansmen were illiterate, no battle diaries survive, but clearly the individual conscience could not be stifled. After the failure of the 1715 Jacobite rising one John Mackintosh was captured at Preston by government troops. He pleaded for his life by saying that as a Mackintosh he was officially a Jacobite, but his own sentiments were different from those of his clan and his countrymen. In the much larger 1745–1746 rising, it was rumored that many clansmen would prefer to do battle with their chiefs than the opposing Hanoverians, and indeed massive numbers deserted.

No matter how onerous the demands of clan membership, people paid them gladly to join. Rewards exceeded costs. It was a distinction and an honor to be a member. No one was ever abducted and made a member against his/her will. Not to be a member was to be a "broken man," a vagrant. Not least among the benefits of membership was safety, protection from predators and thieves. Like nearly all of Europe before the eighteenth century, there was no constabulary in the trackless Highlands. There was a sheriff in Inverness, who never sent deputies on patrol. Laws might have been written, but their enforcement was haphazard. The armed men of the clan, who entertained themselves with display of martial skills, could resemble a default police force, just as it could resemble a militia if not an army. The clan, of course, was neither and always prioritized its own interests. Long before the English-speaking world romanticized clan life as manly and heroic, there was a collective apprehension of how a clan behaved, as is reflected in the history of several words in widespread use. Take for example "henchman," a word of Old English rather than Gaelic origin and carrying no suggestion of Scottish associations. The second definition in the *Oxford English Dictionary,* however, is "the chief personal attendant of a Highland chief." It carries far weightier connotations than its genteel, classical synonym, "myrmidon" for a "faithful follower … who carries out orders without question." Similarly, "blackmail" is also a word of English origin, but the first definition in *Oxford* is "a tribute levied by freebooting Scottish chiefs in return for protection or immunity from plunder." A closer examination of the subject reveals that demands from tributes are recorded in the Lowlands and along the Borders as well as in the Highlands. But the *OED* specifies "chiefs," i.e., heads of clans, not impoverished noblemen or bandits.

The structure and conduct of the clans went through many shifts and adjustments in the five centuries between their emergence in the thirteenth century and their destruction (though not annihilation) after Culloden Moor in the eighteenth. They were frequently in armed conflict with one another, first in the century of conflict after the forfeiture of the Lord of the Isles in 1493, and later more conspicuously during the Civil War of the 1640s. The meager economy of the Highlands would not allow the clans to live in a constant state of warfare, even if they were prepared. Meanwhile, fractious clans found ways to torment and provoke one another short of armed combat.

Cattle are mobile wealth. They don't have to be stolen but can be stampeded with little expense of labor. As we have all been exposed to popular American literature about great cattle herds on the western plains, we are likely to think of the word "rustle"—driving cattle from their owner—to be a synonym of "theft" and to carry some opprobrium. Not so the Scottish Gaelic word *creach*, which has several meanings, one of which is to lift cattle from their owners. "Cattle-lifting," the default translation, implies some lightness in the moral implications.

In Old Irish, spoken in Scotland until Gaelic evolved from it, stealing cattle and driving them great distances might be portrayed heroically. Not only does the great epic *Táin Bó Cuailnge*, "the Cattle Raid of Cooley," valorize the theft of a great bull from one province of Ireland to be driven a distance to another, but that is not the only such narrative. *Táin* means story of a cattle raid, and under literary conventions of early Ireland narratives are categorized by the first words in their titles; thus there are several *Táin*s.

Dwelly translates *creach* as "plunder, booty, pillage," although it is frequently translated as "foray," which means to make a sudden raid, often for plunder. As Ross Crawford described it in his 2016 dissertation, "Warfare in the West Highlands and Isles of Scotland," a creach is the greatest aggression a clan can inflict on another without escalating tensions to hand-to-hand combat. Patricia M. Menzies (2001) described it as "a laudable method of displaying enterprise" and training for the more serious business of feuding. Its counterpart in Broad Scots is "reiver," denoting mischievous cattle-raiders along the border with England, no more villainous than a company of Robin Hoods. The Scots word "reiver" migrated to the U.S. South and remains in regional usage denoting a "thief" but carrying a lighter implication something like "rascal." William Faulkner used it as the title of his last work, *The Reivers* (1962), a rare comedy.

Stuart McHardy's popular history *School of the Moon: The Highland Cattle-Raiding Tradition* (2004) speaks of a "tradition" of Highland cattle-raiding, but his attention is focused on the eighteenth century.

The century of disorder following the end of the Lordship of the Isles, the oft-cited *Linn nan Creach,* has offered a feast to Gaelophobes, mostly noisily by John Major, whose *A history of Greater Britain as well England as Scotland* (1521) coined the distinction for "wild Scots." Major's essentialist ravings about the fundamental bellicosity of Highlanders fed a robust tradition of ethnic and cultural antagonism that would clearly infect the Scottish royal family. The reign of James VI (James I of England) brought the Gaelic-suppressing Statutes of Iona (1609) and the first attempts to extirpate Highlanders from their glens. Surviving glamorizing of Highland identity by James Macpherson and Sir Walter Scott, the dour, polemical works of Major (sometimes spelled Mair) (1760), were reprinted for the last time in 1892. The notion that the era of clan dominance was an epoch of grotesque barbarism never completely disappeared, of course. John L. Roberts' *Feuds, Forays and Rebellions: History of the Highland Clans 1475–1625* (1999), comes close to titillation in recounting coarse brutality on all sides. The publisher's blurb on the cover describes the text as "dramatic and entertaining history." Roberts, who evinces no knowledge of Scottish Gaelic, previously taught geology at the University of Newcastle-upon-Tyne.

The new generation of historians emerging in the twentieth-first century has found the charges against the clans to be less severe than received wisdom would have had it. Two such works with these views are Maureen Meikle's *The Scottish People 1490–1625* (2015) and Ross M. Crawford's Glasgow dissertation, "Warfare in the West Highlands and Isles of Scotland, c. 1544–1615" (2016) cited above. Crawford is the more polemical, constantly belittling historian John Major, whom he names "Mair." There is more, however. An unashamedly scurrilous attack on Highland barbarism appeared in the anonymous 1764 tract, much reprinted, that Crawford does not dignify with mention. The abbreviated title is *A history of the feuds and conflicts among the clans ... from the year 1031 unto 1619*. Neither Meikle nor Crawford denies that some very uncivil behavior unquestionably took place, but they interpret episodes in context. Recent research had already established that written records do not support the vision of constant warfare. In his study of Scottish blood feuds (1986), Keith Brown had argued in his examination of the years 1573–1625 that there were fewer than half as many fracases of any extent in Gaelic Scotland as in non–Gaelic. Elsewhere in Scotland, the Crown suffered a horrendous defeat to the English at Pinkie Clough, September 10, 1547, east of Edinburgh, with a reported 15,000 killed. And for that matter, what was happening elsewhere in Europe in this century, including among the highly civilized city states of the Italian peninsula?

Along with the continuing harassment of the feuds and forays, there were really only a handful of serious clan battles in one hundred twenty-five years examined here, none yielding the kinds of body counts from Bloody Harlaw (1411), between the Lordship of the Isles and supporters of the Crown, or large scale encounters in the Scottish Civil War, or for that matter, the Jacobite Rebellion of the 1740s. Part of the reason for that is that religion was not yet a contributor to clan rivalries, even though the Reformation was coming to Scotland at this time. The *Confession of Faith,* August 17, 1560, committed the Scottish nation to the destruction of Papal authority with severe punishments for participating in Catholic worship; it also abolished the reputedly "pagan" celebrations of Christmas and Easter. Of far greater incentive to fractiousness were land and succession disputes as well as presumed insults to the honor of the clan or its chief. Crawford advises that disputes over land were not simply control of an economic resource but rather the essential foundation of all noble power. Clans would raise their swords over lands that yielded very little of use.

It was only a question of succession, not ideology, religion or greater ambition, that led to the most notorious combat of the era often known in English as the Battle of the Shirts at the north end of Loch Lochy in the Great Glen, July 1544. A key feature in the story of the battle is that the day was so hot (uncommon in the Highlands) that the warriors from both sides threw off their chainmail hauberks and continued the fight in their shirts, or undershirts. Whatever charm that motif may have had in giving the battle high place in oral tradition is coupled with a horror at the near total devastation of the belligerents. On one side was Clan Fraser of Lovat, assisted by Clan Grant and Clan MacKintosh with 300 men in the field, and on the other was Clan MacDonald of Clanranald, assisted by Clan Cameron, with 500. At the end of the day only five of the Clan Fraser side survived, as opposed to only eight for the MacDonalds, a total of 787 killed. The chieftainship of Clan MacDonald of Clanranald was at stake, and Hugh Fraser, 3rd Lord Lovat, favored one of claimants, his nephew, Ranald Galda or Gualda, also supported by the Scottish Crown. Tensions grew over a period of months with much jockeying with different clans, involving for a while the Earl of Huntly, who withdrew before the battle.

The mass shedding of blood did not alter Highland history greatly, except to diminish the prominence of the Frasers. MacDonald and Cameron allies from Lochaber, Glengarry and Glencoe sacked Fraser lands near Urquhart Castle on Loch Ness and destroyed what they could not carry home.

The greatest horror story from this era, consistently retold to visitors from James Boswell and Samuel Johnson to *New Yorker* scribe John McPhee in *The Crofter and the Laird* (1969), is the slaughter of the MacDonald innocents, men, women and children of the Isle of Eigg in 1577. One of the Small Isles in the Inner Hebrides, 5.5 miles (9 km) by 3 miles (5 km), north of Ardnamurchan, Eigg was then populated by Clanranald MacDonalds and found itself in the line of fire of an undeclared war with Clan MacLeod. According to oral tradition, a group of MacLeods, despite tensions, were being hosted on the island when some of the men made unwanted amorous advances to local women. Island men bundled off the visitors and cast them adrift in the Minch, until they were rescued by other MacLeods. Hot for revenge they returned to the island where they were spotted by scouts, prompting the natives to hide in a cave on the south shore, *Uaimh Fhraing* (Cave of Francis) with a narrow entrance obscured by moss, undergrowth and a small waterfall. The MacLeods searched for three to five days before they found a tell-tale footprint near the entrance. They then covered the entrance with thatch and roof timbers and set fire to them, dampened with water from nearby. The smoke asphyxiated everyone inside, reputedly 395 souls; the sole survivor and tale-teller was an old woman who had resisted seeking refuge.

Doubts about the veracity of the story had lingered for some time, even though Sir Walter Scott reported seeing bones at the site in the early nineteenth century. In his dissertation (2016), Ross M. Crawford is openly skeptical, finding it to be an all-too-convenient anti–Highland calumny. A BBC expedition the following year, 2017, went to Eigg, now a popular tourist destination where the cave story is always on the agenda, and undermined Crawford's hopes. Quite plausibly, many of the bones have disappeared in more than four centuries. But focused scrutiny and sustained physical examination does indeed provide much evidence to support the oral tradition.

What is certain, however, is that the MacDonalds and MacLeods were locked in a lethal embrace for another generation, with breath-stopping savagery. Although both clans occupied territories on the mainland, most of the fighting took place on islands, Skye and the Uists. According to several popular histories of the Highlands, though not documented by Crawford, a marauding force of MacDonalds sought revenge the next year (some accounts say three years). They were of the Clanranald branch but sailed in from the Uists. After surprising people at worship in the Trumpan Church on the Waternish Peninsula in north Skye, they set its thatched roof alight and then barred the doors. It was a fiery replay of the cave on Eigg, with one survivor to tell the tale, this time a small girl burned badly in the conflagration. Her words enraged the MacLeods, who set off for Ardmore Bay, where the invaders were departing. MacLeods slaughtered MacDonalds almost to a man. Their bodies were dragged to a turf dike, giving the massacre a folkloric name of *Blàr Millieadh a' Ghàraidh Milligearaidh,* The Battle of the Spoiling or Spoiled Dike.

The struggle between the MacLeods and MacDonalds continued for five years, during which time both sides attracted allies and the Gàidhealtachd was plunged into even deeper misery with plague and famine. In 1601 came the denouement in *Blàr Coire na Creiche* (the Battle of Corrie of the Spoil) in the Cuillin Hills of Skye, sometime in June. According to oral tradition, the battle was the last between clans to employ only medieval weapons, swords, bows and arrows. Then again, the same claim is made for the Battle of Mulroy in Lochaber, 1688, eight decades later. The results were devastating for the MacLeods. Whatever the casualties, they were perceived to be so egregious that the Crown became involved, demanding that both sides dissolve their forces and observe the "King's Peace," August 22. Although the specifics are not spelled out, the documents make clear that Màiri MacLeod was at the center of the dispute.

Popular histories recount tit-for-tat atrocities following the murders at Ardmore Bay, fueling the argument depicting Highland barbarism. Such atrocities burn in clan histories and may be marked with commemorative stones, even when their documentation is shaky. The Glengarry MacDonells have been charged with burning a congregation of MacKenzie worshippers in the church of Kilchrist, Easter Ross, in 1603. MacDonald histories are adamant that the church at Kilchrist had been abandoned and was a ruin by that year. Afterwards James VI of Scotland, always an enemy of the MacDonalds, awarded the Isle of Islay, one seat of the Lord of the Isles, to the Clan Campbell.

The final encounter of *Linn na Creach*, the Battle of Glen Fruin, 1603, inspired even more atrocity-filled oral tradition, and brought together two clans not seen in the earlier encounters, Clan MacGregor and Clan Colquhoun. It is better discussed in the next section.

Enumeration, Rivalries, an Alliance

Lochcarron ties of Scotland offers tartans for 450 Scottish names, all selling well enough to keep the sett or pattern in the catalogue. Depending on who is doing the counting, there may be as many as 600 Scottish names, nearly all of whom call themselves a "clan," even when a single name might have belonged to different septs and might denote quite different families. We have referred on previous pages to well-known, large clans like the MacDonalds, MacLeods and Campbells. We have neglected clans in other parts of Scotland. About 1384, when the Scottish Parliament gave legal status to existing clans, and Gaelic was still a language allowed in legal discourse, other large families had themselves assigned this official recognition. Characteristically, these clans may have a Gaelic motto, but they do not have Gaelic names, nor did many of their members ever speak Gaelic. Among these are clans with names like Armstrong, Johnstone, Maxwell, Wemyss and Turnbull.

Just spelling out the names of all these contenders, Highland and Lowland, and allowing a few lines for identification, their terrain and traditional allies and adversaries, would require a volume larger than the extent of this study. Further, several such works already exist and are listed in the bibliography. Two of the most often consulted are George Way (of Plean) and Romilly Squire's *Collins Scottish Clan & Family Encyclopedia* (1994) and Sir Iain Moncrieffe's *The Highland Clans* (1967), republished often in both the U.K. and U.S. under different imprints.

Similarly, the shifting alliances, betrayals and enduring enmities of the clans could fill another volume and will be touched on here when they pertain to larger questions such as the Civil War or the successive Jacobite rebellions from 1689 to 1746. For the moment there are only a handful of clans whose presence is so ubiquitous that we cannot proceed without having a handle on them. There are the two conspicuous rivals, the Clan Donald and the Clan Campbell. To them we add the proscribed or outlaw family, the Clan MacGregor, and the sole alliance of families known as the Clan Chattan (discussed below).

We have already seen how the Clan Donald, initially a family of Norse-Gaelic origins, was linked to Somerled, the first self-described monarch of the Hebrides, and how his descendants became the Lords of the Isles for a century and a half. The clan was one of the most significant players in Highland life up until the catastrophe of Culloden, 1746, in which it played a leading role. Territories where the Clan has been dominant are widespread, from the Uists in the Outer Hebrides to the Mull of Kintyre in the south and Lochaber in the east, but they are not continuous. Many are in the former shire of Inverness, including those on Skye, but interspersed among other powerful clans, such as the MacLeans, Frasers, Camerons and MacPhersons.

The discontinuity of Clan Donald holdings partially explains why it has split into so many branches. Clans, being more than families or fraternal organizations, are recognized by the Crown through the Lord Lyon King of Arms, who regulates heraldry and determines which chiefs are recognized to merit coats of arms, thus classed as armigerous. These would include MacDonald of Sleat, in southern Skye, host to the Clan Donald Museum; Clan MacDonald of Clanranald, whose original seat was at the now ruined Castle Tioram, 50 miles (80 km) west of Fort William;

Clan MacDonell of Glengarry in a dramatic landform renowned for its beauty, running due west of the Great Glen; Clan MacDonell of Keppoch, in Lochaber east of the modern towns of Spean Bridge and Roybridge; the Clan MacAlister, in south Argyll and Kintyre. MacDonald of Clanranald is possibly the most numerous of all branches.

Those not meriting coats of arms from the Lord Lyon have nonetheless played important roles in Highland history: Clan MacDonald of Dunnyveg, once centered on Castle Dunyvaig (yes, different spelling) on Islay; Clan MacDonald of Lochalsh in a mainland area opposite Skye; the Clan MacDonald of Glencoe, for the famed area near the shifting borders of Lochaber and Argyll, adjacent to where the River Coe empties into Loch Leven; the Clan MacDonald of Ardnamurchan, after the thinly-populated peninsula that is also the western-most point of the mainland, dividing the Inner Hebrides. The MacDonells of Antrim cited in Chapter 1 were once a cadet branch of the MacDonalds of Dunnyveg but do not belong to Scottish associations.

For 450 years the constant adversary of the Clan Donald was the Clan Campbell, whose lands in Argyll were generally to the south and east but close enough for raiding parties. The Gaelic name is *Na Caimbeulaich*, usually translated as *cam*, "crooked," possibly figurative for wry or sassy, and *beul*, mouth. As mentioned above, the silent "p" was added during Scoto-Norman ascendancy and a fashion for all things French to give the name a gallic flair. The folk etymology that the name derives from *camp belle*, beautiful field, is a flattering fabrication. The roots of the family appear not to be in Normandy but rather among the P-Celtic ancient Britons of Strathclyde in east central Scotland who migrated north to Argyll through fortuitous marriages. Early seats were either on Loch Awe or Loch Avich. Eventually the clan settled at Inveraray on the west shore of Loch Fyne, the longest sea loch in Scotland. Construction on the current imposing castle began in 1743, replacing foundations from the fifteenth century. Nonetheless, freshwater Loch Awe, running northeast to southwest, was long perceived to be the heart of the Campbell realm.

From earliest days Clan Campbell favored the Scottish Crown, being firm supporters of Robert the Bruce, and exchanging marriage partners with the royal family. They were prominent on the battlefield at the Bannockburn victory over the English in 1314. Property taken from Clan MacDougall, enemies of the Bruces but allies of the MacDonalds, was granted to the Campbells. The clan's fortunes were still tied to the Crown when the Stewarts came to power in 1371. Thus, Clan Campbell became the main instrument for royal authority in the Gàidhealtachd. When the Lordship of the Isles ascended to hegemony the first member of the clan, Donnchadh (or Duncan) was elevated to the rank of lord, 1445. The next was the rank of Earl of Argyll bestowed upon Cailean (or Colin) in 1457. His is a preferred given name in Clan Campbell; there have been thousands of Colin Campbells. After the forfeiture of the Lordship of the Isles in 1493, Clan Campbell had good reason to consider itself the natural successor to Clan Donald in terms of the leadership of the Gaels of the Hebrides and western Highlands. The Campbell lordship also became a bastion of Gaelic learning and culture as well as armed strength. These early decades laid the foundation for the heated rivalry with the MacDonald heirs of the Lordship of the Isles, later magnified by battles in the Civil War, the Massacre at Glencoe, and the Jacobite Rebellions.

In his popular history, *The Great Feud: The Campbells and the MacDonalds* (Stroud, UK, 2000), Oliver Thomson views most of Highland history through this contentious interface.

The name "Campbell" is today the most numerous clan-derived surname in Scotland, after Smith, Brown and Wilson, and in the years before census-taking the Campbells appear to have been more numerous than the MacDonalds, even under different spellings. Further, their territories are more adjacent to one another, many in Argyll, with an outlier in the former Ayrshire, and the differences between different branches are less pronounced than among the MacDonalds. Only four branches have their own tartans, Campbell of Argyll in the grand residence at Inveraray, Campbell of Breadalbane in the watershed of Loch Tay, Campbell of Cawdor, who held the former MacDonald stronghold of Islay from 1621 to 1726, but whose name comes from distant Nairnshire, and Campbell of Loudon, whose name comes from a barony in the former Ayrshire in the Lowlands. Others who have competing claims for which might be the oldest division within Clan Campbell also resided in Argyll castles: Auchinbreck, Craignish and Strachur. The branch once known as Campbell of Possil became Carter-Campbell of Possil in the eighteenth century when it merged with an Irish family.

Except for some missteps during the Cromwellian interlude in the seventeenth century, the several Earls of Argyll played their hands well and became the most prominent family in the Highlands. For services to William of Orange, latterly William III, the 10th Earl of Argyll, Archibald Campbell, became the first Duke of Argyll on June 21, 1701. Within a short time he was garlanded with a dozen more titles, Marquess of Kintyre and Lorne, Viscount of Lochow and Glenyla, Lord Inveraray, etc., boosting his status even higher. Although the estate at Inveraray includes 75,000 acres, successive Dukes of Argyll have lived in metropolitan areas, usually London, where different residences have been commemorated in Argyll Streets. Always the most visible of Scotsmen, successive Dukes of Argyll have been persons of accomplishment, including the 8th Duke, cited above, who wrote a two-volume history of Scotland. Torquhil Campbell (b. 1968) became the 13th Duke in 2001.

Although never as powerful or numerous as the Clan Donald or Clan Campbell, Clan MacGregor figures prominently in narratives of Highland history because of its many misfortunes. Part of that record of adversity may have arisen from having original homelands, Glen Orchy, Glenlochy and Glenstrae in eastern Argyll, so close to Campbell hegemony. Those glens, visually stunning, are today largely uninhabited. Like many clans, MacGregor (*Clann Ghriogar, na Griogalach*) makes claims to an early foundation not supported by surviving record: one assertation states that the original Gregor was a sibling of Cináed mac Ailpín, founder of Alba in the ninth century. Instead, Clan MacGregor entered written records in 1390. It first laid claim to territory on Loch Awe, which included lands that had been granted to Clan Campbell by Robert the Bruce. The MacGregors and Campbells were united with the Crown against the English at the catastrophe of Pinkie Clough, 1547, but the larger clan continued to harass and persecute the smaller. A description of its plight introduced the resonant phrase "Children of the Mist," which has caromed through Scottish history for centuries, applied first to the MacGregors then to others. It was picked up by Sir Walter Scott and has been used as the title of a dozen works of historical and fantasy fiction, even a ballet, its connection to Clan MacGregor mostly sundered.

Still, Clan MacGregor could be a puissant force and responded sharply to insults and affronts. In early 1603 the Clan Colquhoun, who had been granted a royal commission to suppress the MacGregors, executed two clansmen. The Colquhouns had been allied with the Campbells and were close with the Crown. When over 400 MacGregors marched into Colquhoun territory, they were met with a force of 500 foot and 300 horse at Glen Fruin near Loch Lomond, February 7. It was a rout, with the MacGregors displaying superior tactics and greater stamina in the field. This reversal of fortune would have been sufficient to make the battle a sensation, but narratives about it quickly attracted a bogus strand, viz. that the MacGregors had wantonly killed students who had come to watch the encounter. An account of the battle appears in the introduction to Sir Walter Scott's *Rob Roy* (1817), about the later historical figure (1671–1734) from the clan. A 1967 archaeological investigation into what had long been thought to be a mass grave of Colquhouns revealed a mound of Bronze Age origin. In his 2016 dissertation, Ross Crawford argues that the reported atrocities at the Battle of Glen Fruin, as well as the supposed burning of the congregation at Kilchrist, both 1603, are prime examples of poisonous anti–Highland agit-prop.

Within two months, reports of the Glen Fruin bloodshed, presumably with embellishments, infuriated King James VI (James I of England), who issued an edict abolishing the very name MacGregor. Anyone bearing the name must renounce it or face death. In 1604 the chief of the MacGregors and eleven of his most important men were hanged at Mercat Cross, Edinburgh. Survivors were hunted like animals, and many changed their names to such as Murray or Grant. The proscription lasted until 1774 with interruptions; Charles II repealed it at the Restoration, but William of Orange reimposed it. The name never disappeared, of course, and appeared in records during the seventeenth-century Civil War and until the repeal of proscription.

Through intermarriage and geography, some clans may have felt a certain affinity with another, and could make ad hoc alliances to achieve short-term goals, such as the defeat of a common enemy. These were usually not lasting. The prime exception to this pattern is the confederacy known as the Clan Chattan (*Na Catanaich, Clann Chatain*), whose origins are cloudy and disputed but may date to the reign of Malcolm II (1005–1034). Initially Chattan was a conventional clan possessing lands in Glenloy and Loch Arkaig in eastern Lochaber, today nearly uninhabited. Later its seat was at Tor Castle, today a ruin near the city of Fort William. The clan's continued fortunes lay elsewhere, primarily in the former shire of Inverness, often overlapping or juxtaposed with Clan Donald territories but mostly to the north and east of Campbell power centers. In the fourteenth century through a fortuitous marriage to a daughter, Eva, of Clan Mackintosh (*Clann Mhic an Tòisich*: clan of the leader, thane), it grew until it reached the confederation of twelve clans. Historian Charles Fraser-Mackintosh (1898) said the total was once up to sixteen.

The obscure etymology of "Chattan" is disputed but may incorporate the word "cat," as signaled by the cat on the clan coat of arms and the motto, now in English, "Touch not the cat but (except with) a glove." A cat and the same motto are also found on the Mackintosh coat of arms. It is surely no coincidence that the British wild cat, the felid, was long associated with Rothiemurchus, a clan property. The forest of Rothiemurchus is one of the last standing portions of the great Caledonian Forest, and wild cats are still sighted there.

Clan Chattan has long been linked to the Mackintoshes, and the current chief is a Mackintosh, but a different Mackintosh would head the clan of that name. Despite this, the Mackintoshes would not be the "blood" of the original clan, a distinction that falls to Clans MacPherson, MacBean and MacPhail. Second would be the Clan Mackintosh, with all their cadets and septs. And third would be the families not related but confederated nonetheless: Clan MacGillivray, MacIntyre in Badenoch, MacLean of Dochgarroch (i.e., MacLeans of the North), Clan MacQueen of Strathdearn, Clan MacThomas, Clan Shaw of Tordarroch, Clan Davidson, Clan Farquharson. These had been growing together over decades and forged a Band of Union in 1609, the same year as the Gaelic-repressive Statutes of Iona imposed by James VI (James I of England).

The Clan's action of 1609 might have been titled the Band of Union, but all historians refer to it as a *con*federation, or looser order. It lacked a central authority to enforce a single political line on every one of its members and septs. The twelve confederated clans did not present a challenge to Clan Campbell. And no other confederation ever arose to counterbalance it.

Beyond Feuds and Forays

The continuing hardships of *Linn nan Creach*, the Age of Forays, included unending warfare with heavy casualties, famine, plague, and the restrictions on personal freedom in the clans. Clan chiefs may have been occasionally benevolent, but they were not patrons of the arts, like the contemporary princes of the Italian peninsula. A tradition of sculpture fostered by Iona and other ecclesiastical centers had withered over the centuries. As the bagpipe was enjoying wider use, a distinctive, subtle musical form known as the *pibroch* (*ceòl mòr*, "big music") was developing and would flourish in the next century. Achievements with the written word, as mentioned in the previous chapter, were quite meager compared with what one finds in contemporary Ireland, a much larger population. Most Gaelic-speakers, including most poets, were illiterate. Who would be their scribes? This makes it all the more astounding that one of the most admired and studied of all Gaelic poems, 46-verse, 184-line *Òran na Comhachaig*, The Song of the Owl (once known in English only as "The Owl"), appears to have been composed about 1585. We assume this from internal references to Raghnall or Ranald Òg, chief of the MacDonells of Keppoch, whose death is recorded as 1587.

A much darker voice associated with the later *Linn nan Creach* arises from a Nostradamus-like figure usually known as the Brahan Seer. His cognomen comes from a castle fifteen miles northwest of Inverness, where he may have been a workman. Some sources boldly assert that his family name in English would have been Kenneth MacKenzie. In abundant folk literature from many corners of the Highlands, he is known as *Coinneach Odhar Fiosaiche* (Somber Kenneth of the Prophesies), whose Anglicized pronunciation is "Kenneth Oaur" or "Owir." There are no citations of Coinneach Odhar Fiosaiche's name in print before Thomas Pennant's *A Tour in Scotland* (1769), but his many enthusiasts, scouring records for plausible shards to support his existence have seized upon the citation of a "Kennoch Owir" who was prosecuted for witchcraft on January 23, 1577, on the Isle of Lewis in the Outer Hebrides. This would make him contemporary with some of the era's signal outrages, such as the mass suffocation of the MacDonalds on the Isle of Eigg, also 1577. But it is not supported by internal evidence. The earliest date for his pronouncements is an accusation that the Earl of Seaforth committed adultery during a sojourn in Paris, 1663, which Coinneach had learned through second sight, *dà sheallach*, presumably as a contemporary.

The Brahan Seer's widely circulated prophecies began to appear in newspapers in the 1850s and were collected and published by Alexander Mackenzie in Inverness, 1877, often reprinted and still available on-line, along with a cluster of items by other authors. While much of his language is gnomic, as with Nostradamus, open to generous interpretation, some statements are daringly specific, such as family tragedies among the Seaforths or the dredging of the Caledonian Canal linking Loch Ness and the sea. His contemporary admirers proclaim that he said, "When the ninth bridge cross the Ness, there will be fire blood calamity." That ninth bridge was built in 1987. Within two years there was a disastrous fire: the Piper Alpha oil rig exploded in the North Sea, killing 167 workers. This was followed by flood when the 127-year-old rail bridge was washed away. And, lastly calamity: Pan Am flight 103 crashed on Lockerbie, Scotland, killing 279, December 1988, and burning portions of the town. Other predictions are more benign if no less remarkable. "When men in horseless carriages go under the sea to France, then Scotia shall rise anew from oppression." The tunnel under the English Channel opened in spring, 1994. And the Scottish Parliament, closed for nearly 300 years, reopened in July 1999.

The gloom of the Brahan Seer is hardly unique in early Scotland, and has been traced to Norse antecedents as well as the thirteenth-century Scottish poet called Thomas the Rhymer. What makes his prophesies individual is the vision of an emptied landscape. "The Highland people will become so effeminate as to flee their native country before an army of sheep." The depopulation of the Highlands was, of course, the central tragedy of Gaelic history. And while the calamity of Culloden could eventually be romanticized, the departure of whole families from a once warlike people, not always through the forced Clearances, evoked only bitterness and shame.

Much as the Brehon Seer still thrives on the Internet, academic acceptance of the entire phenomenon has withered. Historian William Matheson (1969) has charged that much of what Alexander Mackenzie assembled about a member of his own clan does not stand up to close study. Several "facts" are simply inaccurate. Coinneach Odhar appears to have been a catch-all persona to whom dark sentiments might be attributed with no more reality than the skeptical workman Murphy of Murphy's Law. Scottish history is filled with apocryphal figures thought to be historical, like the riotous Jenny Geddes cited in the next chapter. Much of the rest is Mackenzie's hammering together of disparate materials.

Our dissolution of the Brahan Seer persona does not mark as gulls the many authors who have cited him over the last century. They serve as a counterweight to the Technicolor romantic fantasies that run from Sir Walter Scott to Diana Gabaldon. His "prophecies," if they may be called that, concur with the frequent catastrophes that scattered Highland sons and daughters.

3

The Seventeenth Century

One King, Two Kingdoms

When Mary Queen of Scots was forced to abdicate in 1566, her thirteen-month-old son was named King James VI of Scotland. Reflecting the increasing cosmopolitanism of the dynasty, he would take the French spelling of the family name, Stuart, that his mother had acquired before reaching the throne. Four regents would serve him in youth. At age thirty-four, with the death of Elizabeth I in 1603, he also became James I, king of Great Britain and Ireland. The United Kingdom would not follow for a century, in 1707. Of all the ground covered thus far in this enterprise, this is probably the most familiar to readers.

James's reign in Great Britain, 1603–1626, was filled with signal accomplishments: the colonization of Virginia at Jamestown, 1607, and the King James translation of the Bible, 1611. The king's arrival prompted Shakespeare to write *Macbeth* (c. 1606), the first dramatic exploration of Scottish history. Theaters flourished, and Jacobean drama became a more florid, but distinguished extension of the Elizabethan. It was the era of John Donne and Sir Francis Bacon.

Content to leave a capital of inferior cuisine and increasing Calvinist opposition to the episcopacy, James was initially satisfied to relocate in London. He famously remarked that he had traded a stony couch for a deep feather bed. While he personally could embrace many Calvinist attitudes, he bristled at the egalitarianism that gave authority to assemblies, presbyters in place of clerics appointed by a monarch. Succinctly, he remarked, "No bishops, no kings." Among his many publications was *Basilikon Doron* (Royal Gift, 1599), in which he argued that monarchs were ordained by God, not men: literally the divine right of kings. Still, there were adjustments to be made in London. He did not understand the English political order, and was put off by the enthusiasm of crowds, so unlike those in Edinburgh that kept their distance. A peculiar popular belief of the time was that simply being near the king or actually touching him brought curative powers.

What was clear to both nobles and the common folk was that a deep gulf separated the two kingdoms, and that Scotland was a much poorer country. As many folklorists have testified, the notion that Scotsmen, more insultingly as "Scotchmen," were parsimonious, especially ungenerous in entertaining with a fevered pursuit of the cheapest goods, derives from this time. It was untoward to make fun of

Scottish courtiers for their shabby dress, and so the target instead became their reputation for being unwilling to part with a penny. The Calvinist unease with luxury and refinement that became dominant in Scotland contributed to the long life of the demeaning stereotype.

Few if any Highlanders would have accompanied James to London, but the status of the Highlands changed by being a portion of Great Britain rather than only of Scotland. Always the scourge of the Gaels, James as King of Scotland commissioned the Fife Adventurers to civilize the Isle of Lewis in 1598, ending in catastrophe, as mentioned in Chapter 1. He was much more effective eleven years later when acting as King of Great Britain and Ireland in a second act of ethnic cleansing. His loathing of the Irish Gael led to the massive Plantation of Ulster, which transformed Irish culture, and the effects were still very much with us in the twenty-first century. He unquestionably learned from his failure with the Adventurers, and ordered an invasion too large to fail. His depredations against the native Irish aristocracy, before the Plantation, led to the departure of Hugh O'Neill, Rory O'Donnell and others for safe harbor in Catholic countries, 1607, the fabled "Flight of the Earls." Seen against the Irish narratives, we view the punitive and humiliating Statutes of Iona, 1609, somewhat differently than we did in Chapter 1, where they appeared to be the most successful of many efforts to stifle and degrade Gaelic culture. The Highland nobles may have been forcibly Anglicized, but they retained their rank and residences. For some clans supporting the Crown, notably the Campbells, first the Earl, later Duke, of Argyll, this was to be expected. But others, such as Cameron of Lochiel, who followed different courses, also retained secure titles. The presence of the nobles would have a continuing effect on the political future of the Gàidhealtachd, but was far from a benefit to the common people. Reports from the Irish Franciscans in the Highlands in the first half of the seventeenth century depict lower standards of living than they were used to in their homeland.

As a portion of the Kingdom of Great Britain and Ireland, the Highlands would now be drawn into disputes that originated far beyond its borders. Clan tensions and feuding did not diminish but rather became aligned with forces across the Kingdom, culminating in the Civil War of mid-century. Even before James went to London, profound change had come to Scotland from distant lands in the Reformation and often bloody conflicts between competing faiths and confessions.

Talk about religion in Scottish history is still contentious, even when the Church of Scotland, the Kirk, the principal player in the narrative, is in precipitous decline, and most of academia is secular. That is probably because religious disputes were for a long time far more bitter than they were in England, or later in the United States and Canada, and religious choices of families could be as much a part of a person's identity as a clan name, and persist among people who no longer regularly attended services. In his mass-market *Highlanders: A History of the Gaels* (1996), journalist John Macleod candidly champions the point of view of the Free Church of Scotland, and speaks with contempt of Moderate Calvinists. Episcopalians, Catholics and Jacobites are dismissed as "bigots."

Consider the widely varying portrayals of John Knox (c. 1514–1572), founder of the Reformation in Scotland, a champion of democracy, literacy and industry, and a towering figure in the history of Edinburgh. He is commemorated at several sites, and his reputed house on the Royal Mile is a major tourist destination. He also contended with the youthful Mary Stuart, who retained the Catholicism of her French childhood, a religion repressed after 1560. In the many portrayals of Mary's life, often by Roman Catholic or secular authors, Knox is often seen as more of a villain than Mary's executioner, Elizabeth.

As mentioned briefly in the previous chapter, the Reformation came to Scotland with stark force in the *Confession of Faith*, August 17, 1560. The Church of Scotland would more often be known by its Scots name, the Kirk. This a full generation after Henry VIII's split with Rome launched the Church of England in 1534, a story every school person knows. Whereas the Church of England, Anglicanism or Episcopalianism, did not initially make a sharp break with Catholicism, the case in Scotland was strikingly different. John Knox had two consecutive residences with Jean Calvin in Geneva, 1554–1559, and he returned to Scotland on fire with reformist zeal, and was met with powerful support. Within months the celebration of the Mass was outlawed as idolatrous and Catholicism itself was illegal. This was impossible to administer completely, and Catholicism survived here and there, more in the Highlands than in the Lowlands. The Earl of Huntly in the northeast was Catholic as was Clanranald in the west. An English report of 1600 surmised that perhaps a third of nobles and gentry remained Catholic, but for the most part it was an underground faith. Under Knox's guidance the Kirk occupied existing Catholic structures and assets. Adherents of Mary Stuart mustered armed resistance that fizzled in the 1570s.

The Kirk was Calvinist in spirit, beginning with the abolition of "pagan" celebrations for Christmas and Easter. The harp, long a favored instrument in Celtic countries, was soon banned. Hundreds of harps were rounded up and burned in the market square as tools of the devil. Traveling entertainers were suppressed, as were beggars. Adultery was punishable by death. Clergymen who proselytized to have believers return to Catholicism were executed publicly, the fate of Scottish Jesuit John Ogilvie, who was hanged February 28, 1615. These interpretations of the Gospels were administered in the Lowlands and growing urban centers but, once again, were not always enforced in far glens and islands of the Gàidhealtachd. The Kirk was one with the Crown, or as we would say today, the state. Thus, late-arriving Protestant denominations like the Quakers and Congregationalists, who preached separation of church and state, were unwelcome in Scotland. Contained within the Kirk, however, were many faithful who had been Catholics a few decades before and might have been more at home in what the Church of England was becoming. Many of these were in the Highlands.

The Kirk, however, had not yet become Presbyterian, the name by which we often know it today. "Presbyterian" denotes a religious organization in which committees of members, the presbyters, elect the leadership. James reviled Presbyterianism, as mentioned above, and relished the right to appoint bishops, a task he studied intently. This rankled the dominant Calvinist strain within the Kirk because they looked upon the office of the bishop as a noxious inheritance from Romanism and not sanctioned by Scottish Christianity going back to St. Columba on Iona.

Nonetheless, the Scottish faithful remained with the Kirk, even with appointed bishops, in part a tribute to James's skills as a diplomat and tactician.

James's son Charles I (1600–1649) lacked his father's political judgment. He also made a poor physical appearance, standing much less than middle height and speaking with a heavy stammer. First-hand reports do not support the flattering Van Dyke triptych portraits, so often reprinted. Perhaps because he was the only English monarch to be executed, he has enjoyed undeserved good press over the centuries, as in Mr. Dick's memorable obsession with his head in Dickens' *David Copperfield* (1850). Seen from a Scottish point of view, many of his problems were of his own making. Heedless that the Kirk was growing stricter and more severe, he disapproved of the "plainness" of Scottish services. When he was crowned king of Scotland at Holyrood in 1632, he flouted the Calvinist consensus in Edinburgh and demanded an Anglican ceremony brought in from London. Together with the Archbishop of Canterbury, William Laud, he promoted the Anglican *Book of Common Prayer* in 1637, codifying belief and practice. Scottish bishops contributed to the writing, which Charles insisted be composed in secret and be adopted sight unseen.

Reaching Edinburgh in summer, this was the prayer book that sparked a riot, immediately. The reputed leader was a street vendor named Jenny Geddes, whose name would long resonate in Scottish history. Many Scots looked upon the *Book of Common Prayer* not only as an assault on their faith but more their national identity. At the Kirk General Assembly in Glasgow the next year thousands of the faithful signed the Solemn League and Covenant to resist all the changes that Charles wished to introduce, and banish the hated royally appointed bishops as well. "Covenant" is a biblical word for bond or agreement with God. In the short term this upsurge is what made the Kirk Presbyterian, but in the long term "Covenant" and "Covenanter" were the prominent words. When Charles moved to repress those who opposed him in the small-scale forerunners of civil wars known to historians as the Bishops' Wars, 1639, 1640, the combatants were the Royalists versus the Covenanters. Ferocious fighters, the Covenanters went into battle under the banner of "Jesus and No Quarter." Not only did they transform the Kirk into a largely Calvinist church, but they took over most of Scotland as well.

The word "Covenanter," not always familiar to non–Scots, is a counterpart to "Roundhead" in England from about the same time, as well as "Puritan" in New England. The committed were armed and ready for civil wars coming to both Scotland and England by mid-century. The historical Covenanters eventually lost power with the restoration of the Stuarts in 1660 and became an oppressed group themselves, but their designation has lived long as a metaphor for a person of strict and uncompromising religious views, just as "Puritan" does in the United States, and so also to a lesser extent "Roundhead" may still be used.

Because Calvinism in general believed that a "well-ordered" monarchy was part of God's plan, the majority of Covenanters initially went along with Charles I, even with his backsliding into what they increasingly viewed as pagan residue from the past. Gritting their teeth, they could even support the king's ultimate authority in clerical affairs, until he tested their allegiance.

Events in Continental Europe promoted more discussion of theology and sharpened tensions between competing points of view. The Thirty Years' War, 1618–1648, fought mostly in what is today Germany, began between Catholics and Protestants, but as bloodshed increased it engulfed a panoply of barely related issues. That war also attracted volunteers from England and Scotland, who returned home to champion what some of them saw as an embattled Protestantism. It was not long before the more determined Calvinist elements within the Kirk felt they should make common cause with like-minded forces within the Church of England, six decades before the Act of Union forged a United Kingdom. Within a parallel but more complex political narrative, the Calvinists of the Church of England were more bellicose than those in Scotland. Their anger went on the march as they became the Parliamentarians with the outbreak of the nine-year English Civil War, August 22, 1642. The fortunes of war may have zigzagged but clearly favored Parliamentarians. The execution of Charles I and dictatorship of Oliver Cromwell in the Commonwealth were on the horizon.

The tone was thus both militant and confident when 121 Scottish and English Calvinist clergy met to define their beliefs in the *Westminster Confession of Faith* in 1646. It is a systematic exposition in thirty-three chapters of Calvinist orthodoxy (which neo-orthodox scholars call "scholastic Calvinism"). Much of the *Confession* specifies what could be shared with many Christian traditions, such as acceptance of the paradox of the Trinity and, more importantly, the primacy of Jesus's sacrificial death and resurrection. In common with much of Protestantism, the *Confession* proclaims that the Scriptures, Old and New Testament, are the inspired, written Word of God, and that they possess infallible truth, which implicitly demeans the status of royally appointed bishops. The Latin name for this doctrine is *sola scriptura*. It also proclaimed *sola fide*: it is by faith alone that one is saved.

Very early in the text, the *Confession* states that the Pope is the Antichrist, and that the Roman Catholic Mass is a form of idolatry. And as there is no separation of church and state, civil magistrates have divine authority to punish heresy and may forbid marriage with non–Christians, implicitly Catholics as well.

The Kirk adopted the *Confession* the next year, 1647, without amendment. Acceptance in England came more slowly and would follow a different trajectory, especially as Oliver Cromwell was a Congregationalist. In Scotland, our concern here, the *Confession* became the dominant document of the faith, still honored in the many fractures, splinterings and permutations that were to come, and is still part of the inheritance of many Presbyterian groups in North America. In the third decade of the twenty-first century the Kirk has fallen on hard times. From 1966 to 2006 enrolled members fell by more than half, from 1,230,000 to 504,000, and down to 352,912 by 2015. In 2019 it was thought that only 137,000 were attending weekly services. Many commentators assume the Kirk as it has been known will be unrecognizable before the end of century. The *Westminster Confession,* with some modifications, is central in the Kirk's many descendants. One of the most vigorous non–Kirk denominations, the Free Church of Scotland, founded in 1843 and incorporating many Evangelical believers, with a conspicuous presence in the Highlands, is emphatic in its veneration of the *Confession*.

Laymen and clergymen whose convictions led them to be Episcopalians, with a service that resembled the Roman Catholic Mass, found themselves marginalized and put-upon. Calvinist conviction was stronger in the Lowlands than Highlands and well-nigh universal south of the Clyde-Forth divide. Clergy with Episcopal sentiments were hounded from their pulpits. The Episcopal linkage with the Stuarts, however, served those faithful well at the Restoration of Charles II in 1660. The king was appointing bishops in Scotland by 1662, and all office holders were asked to denounce the 1638 Covenant. Before long the Covenanters found themselves marginalized and persecuted. Episcopalians thrived under Charles II and the short reign of James II, 1685–1688. They could not recognize the Calvinist William of Orange, who ruled with his wife as William and Mary. After the Act of Union, 1707, the Episcopalians broke from the Kirk and formed their own unit, first called the Episcopal Church in Scotland, in the Act of Toleration, 1712, later the Scottish Episcopal Church. The often-heard phrase "English Kirk" was pejorative. Always smaller in number than the many Calvinist groups, the Episcopalians were more widespread in the Highlands than Lowlands, including such prominent families as Cameron of Lochiel. The non–Campbell portions of the former shire of Argyll have often been perceived as Episcopal. The church was destined to play a decisive role in the history of the Highlands over the next century and a half.

Suppressed and despised, Roman Catholics receded from much of Scottish life, with a few privileged and protected families remaining in the Lowlands and isolated pockets on the mainland and islands of the Highlands. The oft-cited Irish Franciscans were critical to Catholicism's very existence in the first half of the seventeenth century. Clergy had to be trained abroad. An attempt to establish a Catholic seminary at Glenlivet had to be abandoned when the building was repeatedly burned to the ground. Embattled Catholic areas often found themselves in conflict with Calvinist neighbors. In the remote Outer Hebrides, Barra was Roman Catholic, as was South Uist, but North Uist was Calvinist.

Although there were many rigorously observant Calvinists in the Highlands, the long-term result of the *Westminster Confession* was to embitter the divide between the Gàidhealtachd and the rest of Scotland.

The age of disorder and constant danger known as *linn nan creach*, the time of feuds and forays that characterized the previous century from the fall of the Lord of the Isles, might have dissipated by the early seventeenth century and Stuart ascendance in London, but the lot of ordinary Highland people was not significantly improved. As Allan I. Macinnes details in a scrupulously researched and insightful essay, "Lochaber—the Last Bandit Country, c. 1600–1750" (published 2000), the common scourge was lawlessness. It was not found in every region, and initially it did not flourish under a religious or political aegis, but as the decades passed, many bandits found that their ungovernable actions could be put in service of a cause.

Cattle rustling, or "lifting" as *creach* is often translated, might be sanctioned by a clan and so cannot always be described as "banditry." In some clans participation by young men approaching maturity was considered a rite of passage, proving who among the gentry had the virility and fitness to lead. As late as 1670 the MacDonells of Keppoch in Lochaber ranged as far as the northeast to remove cattle from the Moray estates of the Roses of Kilravock as part of a wedding celebration for a leading member of the clan gentry. This was so open that bribes—protection money—might be invited to avoid such a raid, one of several Highland instances that prompted the English word "blackmail" in its original but now obsolete meaning. Or the injured owners might pay a *rascal,* a fee perhaps half the value of the property, to get it back.

More feared were the bandits who did not negotiate, the subclass known as the caterans, or "broken men," men not part of a clan who might temporarily offer services to a chief and then move on. The word for them has appeared here before, but it acquired more negative connotations in the seventeenth century, almost a synonym for thief or bandit. As early as 1587 the Scottish Parliament canvassed landlords in the Highlands and Islands to see how many controlled lands on which caterans dwelt; there were 95 so afflicted throughout the Gàidhealtachd. Leading chiefs within Lochaber, however, were not cited as they did not possess feudal title, as conveyed by the charters, to the lands on which their clans were settled. After two more surveys the Parliament learned that 45 clans were involved in theft and other banditry. At least eleven, mostly in areas adjacent to Lochaber, were unable to prevent their clansmen engaging in thievery. In the eyes of the central government, not surprisingly, banditry was seen as a distinctively Highland problem, of which Lochaber was the epicenter.

Macinnes thinks there are two reasons for this. Even in the Highlands' meager agricultural terrains, Lochaber was one of the few places in the seventeenth century that might attract seasonal labor. Displaced clans, such as the proscribed MacGregors and the MacPhees of Colonsay, could be migrants. Secondly, the mountains riven by long, deep glens offered refuge for lawbreakers.

So feared were rovers from Lochaber that landlords as far away as the Lowlands were willing to hire potential thieves in an early form of the protection racket. Macinnes describes this as "rent-a-thug." The reputation of Lochaber men for rough behavior contributed to the fearsomeness of Royalist troops of Alasdair Mac Colla (Colkitto) in the Scottish Civil War, 1644–1645 discussed below. And the tolerance for lawlessness by chiefs and others in power called down the condemnation of Iain Lom, the major poet of the century.

Usually diffuse and resistant to strong leaders, the many bandits would occasionally settle differences and unite. During the 1650s the most prominent of these gathered around one Iain Mac Dòmhnaill (the commonest of names), usually known as Iain Dubh. He was never cited in English as Black John but rather in the Anglicized pronunciation, Ewen Dhubh. They fashioned themselves as their own clan, Clann Iain Dubh, and because of Iain's family name they were thought to be linked to the MacDonalds of Glencoe, but author Macinnes proudly proclaims that most of them were MacInneses, his own ancestors. Their base centered in Laroch, on Loch Leven, now absorbed into the modern town of Ballachulish. Their periodic cattle raids, however, ranged as far as the Braes of Angus on the eastern shore.

The threat to everyday commerce continued in the region through the Civil War and changes in regime. The Restoration of the Stuarts, 1660, the dynasty that later Highlanders would die to defend, led to repression and exploitation under James Maitland, Duke of Lauderdale, seeking "to impose absolutism on the cheap," in Macinnes's words. The reputation for banditry replaced religious non-conformity as the justification for an increased military presence, turning the Highlands into a training ground for unremitting repression.

Decades later, the narrative of endemic disorder was demolished by the Commission on Pacifying the Highlands, 1682–1684. Instituted by James, Duke of York (later James VII & II, father of the "Old Pretender"), the Commission brought together representatives of seventy landowners, as well as gentry and nobles from the Lowlands. The Commission expected to find ubiquitous thieving but quickly explained away the low number of convictions as being due to the efficacy of arbitration between the clans rather than to a high incidence of fugitives from justice. Pressing on, determined to root out wrongdoers, the Commission after two years pretty much exonerated the clan elite, praising them for cooperation in suppressing cattle lifting and other thievery. Ensuring further that he would have a warm place in the hearts of the MacDonalds, James threw the weight of the Crown to their side in repressing Campbell attempts to acquire more land and power.

The Lowland and English surety that the Highlands were populated by warlike thieves speaking a barbarous language made them an "other" in the language of post-colonialism. Silke Stroh has argued in *Gaelic Scotland in the Colonial Imagination, Anglophone Writing from 1600 to 1900* (2017) that the Highlands fulfilled the template for colonies even before contemporary settlements in North America (Jamestown, 1607; Plymouth 1621), dependent extensions of the motherland, or conquests of warlike, non–Western states in Asia (British East India Company, 1612; Conquest of India, 1757). She is partially anticipated by Michael Hechter's *Internal Colonialism* (1977). Samuel Johnson's oft-cited remark that the Highlands were as remote and unknown as Borneo can be read as an implicit endorsement of such a view. The imposition of the humiliating Statutes of Iona (1609) and the forced Anglicization of the chiefs and privileged families sounds like the act of a hostile colonial power, when the result was the further degradation of the status of the mass Gaelic-speaking population on the isles and in the glens. Dismal events of the following two centuries, the failure of the Jacobite cause and the Clearances, strengthen Hechter and Stroh's analyses. Iain Mackinnon (2017), however, disputes this view.

Accounts of Highland life in the seventeenth century feel different because of our sharpened perception of life in these decades. The volume of documentation increases many times over. Even without mass literacy in either English (Scots) or Gaelic, many more observers had pens at this time, and their records were preserved. Whereas earlier Highland military encounters, "bloody Harlaw" or the Battle of the Shirts, might indeed have had high casualties, they retain an almost legendary quality. Those in the seventeenth century, such outrages as the sack of Aberdeen or the (second) battle of Inverlochy, come to us with depictions of atrocities and unbridled viciousness that anticipate what we so often see in modern warfare.

The personae of leading figures, such as the Marquis of Montrose, are drawn in telling and humanizing detail so that we feel we can "know" them, in a way that we cannot grasp such shadowy early persons like Somerled or John the Good, First Lord of the Isles. Such documented attention to character raises the profile of the person. That is why Montrose's illustrious ally known by many names, Alasdair Mac Colla, Colkitto, etc., can be shown to be the first prominent Highland commander, so conspicuous that he attracts enhancing oral traditions, or legends. We now have the evidence to know what is historical and what is embellishment.

As most non–Scottish Anglophones learn the history of England before that of Scotland, we can easily succumb to a default position of seeing civil war in Scotland as an extension of widely studied events south of the border. The warring sides there are almost a paradigm: high-living, well-dressed Cavaliers vs. the sour, dour Roundhead Parliamentarians, or doomed Charles I beheaded by incipient dictator Oliver Cromwell. Along with these being misrepresentations of English history, such notions are best discarded before examining how all the bloodletting affected life in the Highlands. While the Scottish Civil War, 1644–1645, was fought on Scottish ground with Scottish protagonists, it was linked with less well-known combats in Ireland as well as the cataclysms in England.

A more practical way to outline the relationship between Scottish battles and those elsewhere is to adopt a term suggested by recent historians that is not yet in widespread use: the Wars of the Three Kingdoms: England, Scotland and Ireland. Semantically, it may seem inappropriate to call Ireland a "kingdom" as it had no king, but the monarchs of England had dubbed their Irish territory a kingdom, displacing the Lordship of Ireland, as early as 1541. The king of England was simultaneously king of Ireland, without a separate coronation as in Scotland. Wales, integrated into England since the time of Henry VII, was and is a principality. As the focus here is on Scotland, there is no space to examine issues behind fighting elsewhere, but in an outline, we can at least name the other conflicts.

Wars of the Three Kingdoms, 1639–1651

Scotland:
The Bishops' Wars, 1639–1640
The Scottish Civil War, 1644–1645

England:
First Civil War, 1642–1646
Second Civil War, 1648–1649
Third Civil War, 1650–1651

Ireland:
The Irish Rebellion, 1641
Confederation Wars in Ireland, 1642–1649
Cromwellian Conquest of Ireland, 1649

Put in this context we can see that the Scottish Civil War, 1644–1645, much of it fought in the Highlands, was not merely an outrunner of the English Civil War, but rather a localized chapter of a much larger narrative that indeed began in Scotland with the two in-tandem Bishops' Wars, 1639, 1640, cited above in this chapter. At issue was a struggle between the Covenanters, formed the year before and full of fire, and King Charles, fatally rigid, over the administration of the Kirk, the Church of Scotland. After they had expelled Charles's bishops, the Covenanters declared that they, not the King, would select the new canons of the Kirk. The nominal premise for the outbreak of war might initially look trifling: the timing of the meeting to appoint the new canons—either the fixed date when the Covenanter Assembly met annually, or the unfixed date when the king agreed to attend. For an absolute monarch the Scotsmen were making an intolerable challenge to his authority. Relying on his own resources, he sent an army of 20,000 toward Edinburgh.

Strategies were grandiose and complex with much marching about, but before the year was over there was almost no fighting in the Highlands and few casualties anywhere. A Royalist Irish force under the Earl of Antrim was to depart from Carrickfergus in Ulster to be joined by Catholic clans, notably the MacDonalds, upon its arrival, but this was thwarted at Dumbarton on the Firth of Clyde. As he neared the Scottish border, Charles realized to his dismay that many of his troops were ill-trained conscripts, and declared that he would not cross the line if the Covenanters stayed ten miles beyond, which they did. This led to a truce. Meanwhile a smaller group of Royalists under Viscount Aboyne arose south of Aberdeen. A larger Covenanter force under General Alexander Leslie defeated them at Brig of Dee. Accompanying Leslie was a dashing 28-year-old nobleman, James Graham, the 1st Marquis of Montrose (1612–1650), destined to be one of the most prominent figures of the century, often cited as the "Great Montrose."

In the interlude between the two Bishops' Wars, the Kirk's General Assembly reasserted its right to appoint the executives of the church and, further, made Covenanting compulsory for all office holders, civic or ecclesiastical. These were too much for Charles, who launched the second war, paid for from his own resources when the English Parliament would not support him. This time the cause of the invasion was unambiguously religious, sectarian, and against the Covenanters rather than against Scotland. In anticipation of troops crossing the border, the Covenanters seized Aberdeen and surrounding territories, a perceived (perhaps wrongly) Royalist stronghold. In June the Covenanter Scottish Parliament granted the Marquis of Argyll, Archibald Campbell, a commission of "fire and sword" against Royalist areas in Lochaber, Badenoch and Rannoch, leading to a campaign of burning, brutality and looting over a large area. Although nominally Covenanter vs. Royalist, as well as Campbell vs. MacDonald, this was also the first instance in Scotland of organized sectarian violence, as the victims of Argyll were exclusively Roman Catholic, regardless of whether they were in the Clan Donald. This included the vandalizing of Cille Choirill, the two-hundred-year-old hilltop church where Dòmhnall, poet of *Òran na Comhachaig* was buried. Although both sides had been militating against each other for decades, the issue, again, was not clan or territory, but religious faith, for the first time. As several commentators have noted, the Scots here were following the template of religious violence from the Thirty Years' War, still flaming in the mini-states co-extensive with modern Germany. Numbers of Covenanters had volunteered to fight for Protestants there.

Buoyed by continuing success in Scotland beyond the Highlands, the Covenanters crossed the border to invade England, the Marquis of Montrose taking a leading role. They reached as far as Durham when the Presbyterian-dominated Parliament, implicitly friendly to the Covenanters, forced Charles to make peace.

The King was shortly to be occupied by the rebellion in Ireland. In other circumstances, Scotland would have been of greater concern than Ireland, but the rebellion there in 1641 concerned a larger population and greater tracts of land, as well as the public humiliation and slaughter of Protestants who had settled in Ireland after the Plantations earlier in the century. The English defeat of the rebellion in Ireland led to the widespread seizure of Catholic lands as well as the mass eviction of rebels and their families to the New World, both the American colonies and the islands of the West Indies. The extirpation of despised, unwanted Gaels from Ireland foreshadowed schemes for the depopulation of the Highlands. A lower-keyed war commenced the next year in Ireland and continued for another seven years.

It would be another two years, until 1644, for fighting to begin anew in the country with the Scottish Civil War, during which time the Marquis of Montrose dramatically switched his affiliation from Covenanter to Royalist. This would lead to his becoming a hero in Highland memory, although he was not a Gael himself. The site of his castle in what used to be Angus-shire in the east of Scotland lies in what is usually classed as the Lowlands, even though its Norman-sounding name, Montrose, has a Gaelic equivalent (*monadh rois,* perhaps of Pictish origin). As a Scottish patriot, he bridled when Charles I (though a Stuart) imposed bishops upon the Church of Scotland along with the Episcopal *Book of Common Prayer* and signed the National Covenant. At no time, however, was there anything puritanical in Montrose's character, although he was Presbyterian. He was open to the values and tastes of the Royalist cause, pushed along by his meeting Charles in the parley after the Second Bishops' War. His unhappiness with the royal appointment of bishops was less than his unease at making Presbyterians masters of the state. The ascendancy of the sour Marquis of Argyll, Archibald Campbell, who had jailed Montrose after a challenge to his authority, to lead the Presbyterian and national party exacerbated matters. Argyll drove Montrose more toward the King's cause, no matter how maladroit he might be. In the two years following the Second Bishops' War, Charles assigned the marquessate to Montrose and appointed him Lord Lieutenant of Scotland, the prime Royal and soon Royalist commander.

Scotland may have been nominally at peace for those two years, 1642–1643, but the English Civil War had begun in 1642 between Charles and the Parliamentarians while fighting raged without cease in Confederation Ireland. As the Scottish troops in Ireland had a well-earned reputation for ferocity and effectiveness, the Calvinist Parliamentarians sought their alliance in the field, the first time English and Scottish would have shared the same cause. The Scottish price for this support would be that the Church of England would have to adopt the *Solemn League and Covenant for Reformation and Defence of Religion,* i.e., that the Anglican Church should become a replica of the Kirk, a Scottish Presbyterian take-over of England.

The Scots quite visibly strengthened the Parliamentarian cause in England, alerting Montrose that turmoil and bloodshed might be inescapable in Scotland. There is no single date for the commencement of the undeclared Scottish Civil War, but Montrose was gearing for combat from the beginning of 1644. Both sides were Scottish, with English and Irish assistance, and much fighting in the Highlands. The Civil War was distinct from the clan wars of the previous one hundred fifty years, but Montrose constructed a mostly Highland Royalist army by exploiting burning grievances and resentments, renewed by Argyll's gratuitous destruction of Catholic properties in the Second Bishops' War. Not everyone in Montrose's army was Catholic, but many of the MacDonalds who joined were. From early 1644 Montrose was in communication with Lord Antrim in Ireland, who promised 10,000 troops for the Royalist cause, a portion of whom would go against the Covenanters in Scotland. In late March an invasion force of Highland and Irish troops under Clan Donald commander Alasdair Mac Colla departed Ireland for Scotland. After sporadic resistance and diversions, it landed on Ardnamurchan in Argyll and captured Mangar Castle in July. From there they would march east to Blair Castle in the Grampian Mountains, Perthshire, to be joined by Montrose.

Both Montrose and Alasdair Mac Colla (c. 1610–1647) would be lionized in later literature, the former in English the latter in Gaelic. We shall refer to the Highland hero as Alasdair Mac Colla, although he is cited under a multitude of names. He lived in a Gaelic milieu, was recorded by English historians and later was celebrated in Gaelic, Scots and English oral traditions. Although many earlier Highland figures are known under different names, his is almost a worst-case scenario, including Anglophone misunderstandings of Gaelic colloquialisms. In his study of Mac Colla, *Highland Warrior: Alasdair MacColla and the Civil Wars* (1980), David Stevenson devotes five pages to sorting them out, and we allowed a paragraph to the issue as a template of difficulty in the Preface. At birth his name would have been Alasdair MacDhòmhnaill, one of the most common in the Gàidhealtachd. At a time when historians thought it unnecessary to know Gaelic, he was cited as Alexander MacDonald or MacDonell, forms he may never have heard in his lifetime. Instead, he would have been known by his *sloinneadh* or patronymic, mac Coll or Mac Colla. Coll was also a common name then, but Alasdair's father was famous; he was distinguished by a cognomen Ciotach, meaning "left-handed" but probably suggestive of "cunning" or "deviousness." The full *sloinneadh,* mac Colla Chiotaich, was incomprehensible to English ears, and thus was rendered Colkitto. Gaels apparently did not find the designation insulting and adopted it in Gaelic contexts, a language lacking the letter k.

Well-born and trained for battle, Mac Colla enjoyed a background and status comparable to those of Montrose, although he is usually cited second in accounts of the War. His father had been the lord of the Inner Hebrides island of Colonsay, from which the family had been expelled by the Campbells in 1639. He was proudly a member of what he called the Clann Iain Mòr (Big John), what we have called elsewhere the Clan Donald South or the MacDonalds of Dunnyveg. The domain extended from the Hebrides, notably Islay, into large portions of Ulster; this extension of clan hegemony was discussed in Chapter 1. Mac Colla sought to repair the division and disunity of Clann Iain Mòr and to restore it to power. With the deportment of the gentry, young Mac Colla, possibly thirty, joined the Catholic Confederate rebellion in Ireland and was quickly made a commander. Not only did he distinguish himself in battle, but he introduced a new tactic to be known as the "Highland charge" or *a' dol sìos* (going down). At the Battle of Laney, February 11, 1641, while the Protestants were slowly and laboriously reloading their muskets,

Mac Colla ordered his men to drop their firearms after the first round had been fired. They should then pick up their swords and targes (the small, round distinctive shield), and scream their war cries at the opposing army while running toward it before musketeers could reload. From reports of the Battle of Laney, this was an effective maneuver: more than seven hundred Protestants were killed. The notoriety of the Highland charge spread quickly, and when Mac Colla commanded the tactic again, opposing forces ran in fear, increasing its usefulness. Highland armies continued to employ it after Mac Colla's passing, down to the time of Culloden.

The Innovation of the charge adhered tightly to Mac Colla's legend and separated him from the more Anglicized Montrose in popular memory. Appearing undisciplined, bordering on the barbaric, the tactic embodied features of Gaelophobia in non–Highlanders. It also added to unflattering portraits of Mac Colla in Protestant accounts of the Civil War. Dark-browed, much taller than average height (at least 6', perhaps 7'), Mac Colla was the perfect ogre for Covenanters, a perception magnified by events in the Civil War, where he earned the nickname *fear thollaidh nan tighean* (destroyer of houses).

To return to the progress of Mac Colla's Highland and Irish forces across Scotland, they reached Blair Castle within a month, August, to find the garrison abandoned. Shortly Montrose appeared in Highland dress for the first time. Despairing of the Royalist cause, he had crossed into England hoping for recruits, and, failing, returned to join the formidable Highlander. Together they forged a renewed Loyalist army. The implications of that term should not mislead us. Portraits and caricatures of Montrose do indeed present the image of chic Cavalier, but most of the fighting men were rough rural people unable to write English or Gaelic. They wore no uniforms and were distinguishable in combat by attaching a sheaf of oats to their persons. There was no Royal purse to support the Royalists, who regularly looted conquered properties, especially if they were taken from the Campbells. Neither were soldiers contracted in their service; after any battle, won or lost, they might choose to return to their homes. Their priorities under the Royal Standard were resistance to the Covenanters, antagonism to Clan Campbell, protection of Catholic populations, and yes, ultimately, support of Charles I against the Puritan Parliamentarians.

Within days came jubilant victories. On September 1 Montrose and Mac Colla crushed a Covenanter force at the Battle of Tippermuir (also Tippermore, etc.) three miles from Perth. Regardless of which standards were flying, this was the first encounter between a mostly Highland army and a Lowland army in more than two centuries. Three thousand Royalists overcame 7000 Covenanters under the hapless Lord Elcho. Strategic deployment of the Highland charge was decisive. Reports of the triumph made for thrilling news across the Gàidhealtachd. In Covenanter eyes, however, the Royalists were tarnished by the pillaging and looting of the town of Perth, but worse would follow.

Within two weeks Montrose and Mac Colla led a somewhat smaller army, speedier for being slimmer, against again a large Covenanter force under poor leadership, to enter and ravage Aberdeen. As it was only a short time since Montrose had breached the gates of Aberdeen as a Covenanter himself, local Royalists such as the

Earl of Huntly, were reluctant to embrace him. Once in the city the Royalist forces lost all restraint in looting and rioting. Non-combatants were harassed and humiliated, men stripped of their clothes while robbed and women raped. Such atrocities may well have always occurred in war time, and much worse was happening concurrently in the Thirty Years' War. What made this brutality significant is that it was recorded from eye-witness accounts and widely circulated. It heightened Lowland disdain for Highland "barbarism," and meant that few non–Highlanders would join Montrose and Mac Colla.

The victories against superior numbers were to be savored, and led to the army's increasing numbers from the Highland population: men of different clans forgot rivalries when attracted to Mac Colla's share of glory. After some indecisive skirmishes, like that of Fyvie Castle, Mac Colla led punitive raids into Campbell country, killing stray men and burning houses, a riposte for what the Campbells had done on Lochaber three years earlier but earning the commander his reputation as a destroyer. This understandably provoked the Covenanters, who increased their numbers, spoiling for a confrontation in the spring. Montrose and Mac Colla withdrew to Lochaber, near the modern towns of Spean Bridge and Roybridge. It was a relatively mild winter, but snow could be deep at higher elevations.

Fired up by Mac Colla, the Royalists were ready for battle as soon as possible. What followed was the most cinematic moment of the Scottish Civil War in which the Royalist army, all on foot with the tiny cavalry elsewhere, marched up deep Glen Roy and then trudged through the trackless snow in an unexpected flanking movement to meet Argyll and the Covenanters at Inverlochy, near the modern town of Fort William, February 1–2, 1645. It was a Hannibal-over-the-Alps moment long proclaimed in Gaelic lore. While not completely taken by surprise—the Covenanters thought they were facing only a regiment of Royalists—they were overwhelmed and humiliated when Montrose's entire army fell upon them. The Royalists may have been fighting under Charles I's standard, but the heat of the attackers was clearly driven by clan and religious grievances. Impartial observers recorded that Gaelic, or Campbell, Covenanters suffered a higher casualty rate than those from the Lowlands. The most influential observers were anything but impartial, and most prominent was the Clan Donald poet known as Iain Lom, then in late adolescence, who was to become the most admired Gaelic literary figure of the century. He observed the battle while sitting in a tree and narrated it in a treasure of the Gaelic language, *Là Inbhir Lochaid* (Day of Inverlochy). More about him later. Iain Lom's account of the battle is a hymn to heroism in which Alasdair Mac Colla is the dominant figure and Montrose is marginalized. The poet's written words are still with us, but at a time when many Gaels were illiterate, they were recited and memorized and became the foundation of innumerable legends and songs.

The Covenanter leader Archibald Campbell, the Marquis of Argyll, watched in horror from his barge and fled in disgrace, his stature rudely diminished. In Anglophone Scotland Montrose was on his way to legend. But much as Charles was jubilant to hear of Inverlochy, triumph could not secure the king's place on the throne in London. Within weeks the English Parliamentarians launched the New Model Army and defeated the Royalists at Shrewsbury.

From spring through early summer, the Scottish Royalists under Montrose drove to one decisive victory after another, often against even greater odds than at Inverlochy, each a devastating blow to the Covenanters. All took place north of the Forth-Clyde line. They looted the town of Dundee April 3–4 with impunity, but spared it the indiscriminate killing visited upon Aberdeen the year before. The Battle of Auldearn in the former Nairnshire, northeast of Inverness, is credited by commentators as an example of Montrose's strategic brilliance.

Far from being tempted by euphoria over battlefield success, Scottish Royalists must have been suffering a sense of futility as Charles' cause was shrinking in England. His army virtually collapsed at the Battle of Naseby, June 14, with only a "rump" escaping. Yet Montrose triumphed again at Alford in Aberdeenshire on July 2, the only one of his six victories without Mac Colla by his side. Reunited with Mac Colla he scored his largest-scale victory, 5000 Royalists over 7000 Covenanters, at Kilsyth near Stirling, August 16.

The Calvinist Lowlands trembled at the mention of the names Montrose and Mac Colla. With Charles's fortunes in decline, this would have been the moment for the Royalists to march into Edinburgh. The Covenanter government was in near diminishment, and the Marquis of Argyll, Archibald Campbell, had fled the country. Historians have long speculated, although we have no evidence, that Montrose harbored ambitions to take the capital. But a Royalist government in Edinburgh, with Montrose as a regent or viceroy, certainly would have changed the course of the English Civil War, despite the failures of Charles's army.

This was not to happen. Instead of one of the great what-ifs of Scottish history, Montrose and Mac Colla split their alliance, even though Montrose had knighted him. The Gaelic partner wanted to wreak more vengeance on the Campbells. As David Stevenson, Mac Colla's biographer and champion, wrote, "The story of Alasdair's [Mac Colla's] stay in Argyll in 1647 is one of plunder, destruction and atrocity." He continued until the hated Argyll raised fresh forces and was able to corner Mac Colla in Kintyre, and he escaped to Ireland. Accompanied by both Highland and Irish forces, he continued to do battle with the Irish confederacy for another two years before he was captured at the Battle of Cnoc na nOs (Knocknanuss: Hill of the Deer) in Co. Cork. He had been promised quarter if he surrendered, but was betrayed. The date and means of his execution are disputed. He was either thirty-six or thirty-seven.

Without Mac Colla the Royalist army was much depleted and went to catastrophic defeat at Philiphaugh near Selkirk in September 1645, barely a month after the triumph of Kilsyth. This was an opportunity for Covenanters to slaughter all the Royalists they could find, including non-combatants, as retribution for all that they had suffered. Concurrently, the inept Charles I had thrown himself on the mercies of Scottish forces in England, who demanded that the remaining Royalist forces in Scotland be disbanded. Montrose complied, eventually landing in the Netherlands, where he remained until after Charles was executed, January 30, 1649.

As he was still the Stuart Lord Lieutenant of Scotland, Montrose resolved to avenge Charles's death and place his son, Charles II, then in exile, on the thrones of Scotland and England. This prompted his last adventure, foolhardy and ill-advised.

He sailed to Orkney in March to raise a small force, aiming to invade Scotland from the far northwest. After ignominious defeat in Ross-shire in April, he wandered the Highlands for a few weeks before being captured and taken to Edinburgh. The following year, 1650, the Scottish parliament convicted him on May 20, and he was executed as a common criminal May 21: hanged, drawn and quartered. Most of his corpse was left to rot on the gallows, and his severed head was placed on a pike before the Tolbooth, the city's most prominent public building. The mangled body and severed head remained in place until the actual restoration of Charles II, and were not removed until January 7, 1660. He was thirty-eight at death. His battered remains were later honored at Holyrood Castle.

Concurrent with the deaths of Charles I and Montrose, Cromwell was leading a blitzkrieg and a campaign of genocide in Ireland, and the Wars of the Three Kingdoms would roil for four more years. Scotland, however, would no longer be a theater of combat.

Before coming to these pages, some readers may have been barely familiar with the names Montrose and Alasdair Mac Colla or may never have heard of them at all. For many centuries, however, their memories loomed large in the Scottish and even more in the Highland imaginations. The events of 1644–1645 are a century before the Jacobite catastrophe of Culloden Moor, 1746, the best-known event of Highland history. For readers outside Scotland the phrase "Scottish Civil War" barely strikes a chord, or can be mistaken as an appendix of the English Civil War, whereas in Scotland the names Montrose and Mac Colla, or Colkitto, conjure up six great victories, Inverlochy being the sweetest. A martyr's death before age forty, one in betrayal the other in humiliation, burnish their myths.

Mac Colla's acclaim in Gaelic began even before his death in the poetry of Iain Lom and Diorbhail Nic a'Bhriuthainn (Dorothy Brown), who marginalized Montrose's role and ignored Mac Colla's vindictiveness. Linked to these was a substantial body of encomium in prose and verse, intended to be memorized and recited. Above that there are innumerable songs, in some of which Mac Colla is cited only as a presence, that continued in both Scottish Gaelic and Irish traditions until the present. "Gol na mBan san Ár" ("Lament for the Women of the Massacre") was composed to commemorate Mac Colla and his female followers, portraying him as a kind of fertility figure as well as a warrior. The famed Irish traditional music group the Chieftains included it in their *Boil the Breakfast Early* (1980). The proliferation of citations of Mac Colla in popular tradition accounts for the high number of variations in the forms and spellings of his name. In 1958 Angus Matheson devoted 84 pages to studying traditions accruing to Mac Colla's persona. Mac Colla was and still is commemorated in Ireland with songs and harp tunes, including a 1991 composition for harps and uillean pipes by Irish harper Janet Harbison, "Battle of Alasdair," on his death at the Battle of Cnoc na nOs.

The generation of Montrose's legend began two years before his death. A companion named George Wishart compiled a lengthy record of the Marquis's successes and insights in *Memoirs of the Most Renowned James Graham, Marquis of Montrose* in Latin by 1647. The immediate intention was that the document would help the Marquis secure a position on the continent should the entire Royalist cause come to naught. It succeeded. Ferdinand III of the Holy Roman Empire offered an appointment with the rank of field marshal, but Montrose remained devoted to the Stuarts, Charles I and II. A copy of the *Memoirs* was attached to his person at his execution. The Wishart text would later serve as a source for Sir Walter Scott's novel, *A Legend of Montrose* (1819), which renewed interest in the legend in post–Jacobite Scotland. The twentieth-century Scottish adventure novelist John Buchan (*The 39 Steps*) took a profound interest in the Marquis and his campaigns, but his erudite study *Montrose: A History* (1928) does not invite the popular reader. Instead, Buchan allowed Montrose a short guest appearance in his popular novel of the previous year, *Witch Wood* (1927). Other popular historical novels depicting his story include Maurice Walsh, *And No Quarter* (1937), and Nigel Tranter, *The Young Montrose* (1972) and *Montrose: The Captain General* (1973).

A "Bald" Poet

As mentioned above, part of Alasdair Mac Colla's heroic reputation began with his portrayal in a long narrative poem, *Là Inbhir Lochaid* (Day of Inverlochy), by a poet usually known as Iain Lom (Bald John), the greatest of the century and one of the most admired in the language. As with Alasdair Mac Colla, when we deal with a personage who not only spoke Gaelic but was known primarily in Gaelic documents, we often find it awkward to speak of him in English. "Iain Lom" sounds like a nickname, and the little-mindedly consistent compilers of some references insist on calling him "John MacDonald," which would have been his name in English but is not useful because he might never have answered to it, and it was borne by so many men. His full name in Gaelic, with patronymic, is Iain mac Dhòmhnaill mhic Iain mhic Dhòmhnaill mhic Iain Alainn; this virtual pedigree will not be used here. The seeming familiarity of just "Iain Lom" should not be seen as signaling his low status but rather how widely he was cited in oral tradition. He was a member of the MacDonells of Keppoch, the most powerful family in the area, and through his full name claims descent from the first Lord of the Isles, making him a person of privilege by the standards of his society. Despite that and being the racy persona of caustic wit emerging in his poetry, he is an enigma. We are not sure of his vital dates, possibly 1624 to 1707; his death date has to be after his denunciation of the Act of Union with England. Neither are we sure of the implication of *Lom*. It may actually have signaled a hairless pate, or chin, or perhaps a tonsure. We have no depictions of his person. Or the sobriquet may be figurative implying plain-spokenness or resistance to insincere ingratiation. He may or may not also have been known as *Iain Manntach* (stammering John). Some sources describe his having a mild limp. We know nothing certain about his life, but he was thought to have studied at Valladolid, Spain, which is plausible as Catholics of his generation had to leave the country to get an education. He was on good terms with a sister and is sometimes attributed a son with no mention of a wife.

In his work he may be titled *Bàrd na Ceapaich* (Bard of Keppoch), as his modern editor dubs him. Unmistakably informed by the classical tradition inherited from

Ireland, Iain Lom embraced the colloquial language of his time and would have been as accessible as if writing for a mass market serial of later centuries. Indeed, much of his poetry is about current events. His tendentiousness and partisanship are qualities that academic criticism of the last centuries have thought diminish a poet's stature. Further, he was a champion of Roman Catholicism and the Jacobite cause, views not shared by the majority of Gaelic scholars. On the other hand, his fierce opposition to English Puritanism and his late-in-life patriotic assault on the Act of Union still strike favorable chords.

Iain Lom's literary eminence means that we could not have mentioned the second Battle of Inverlochy without citing him, and he will later witness the first sparks of Jacobitism with the departure of King James VII & II. More to the moment, there are jarring episodes in clan history that might have remained local and parochial if Iain Lom had not spoken of them and taken a shocking role in them. The best known is the 1663 episode of the inter-family Keppoch murders, *Murt na Ceapaich*, now often included in any history of the Highlands, and was cited briefly in the previous chapter.

The murder victims were Alasdair Mòr and Raghnall Òg, sons of Dòmhnall Glas (gray, pale), the eleventh Chief of Keppoch, who had fought with Montrose at Inverlochy and had just died. The young men had been in Rome, completing their education. The elder of the brothers, Alasdair, gave a celebration for his accession to the chiefship of the clan. Invited was his uncle, Alasdair Buidhe (yellow, golden), who had commanded the clan in his absence. While murderous covetousness over succession is commonplace in Scottish history, this transition came with an additional moral tension. Local men feared that the youngsters with their fancy foreign education would want to clamp down on the unchecked lawlessness and banditry for which Lochaber had become infamous.

Suspicion immediately fell on an uncle, Alasdair Buidhe (yellow, or golden-haired), but no evidence was ever brought against him. Instead, the culprits were another branch of the Keppoch MacDonells known as *Siol Dughaill* (seed, brood of Dougal), who secretly lusted after the chieftainship: Alasdair of Inverlair and his six sons.

Outraged, Iain Lom himself sought out other Clan Donald chiefs for revenge against what had been done to his kinsmen. He first reached out to the chief of Glengarry of Invergarry, who responded that what looked like a murder might have been an accident. A more congenial Sir Seumas Mac Domhnail of Sleat on Skye first responded with a witty exchange of literary allusions. He stalled Iain Lom's powers of persuasion for two years before relenting, when he obtained a state commission to avenge the murders. Seumas sent fifty men to the mainland, where they were met and guided by Iain Lom to the killers' strongly barricaded residence at Inverlair House, east of Keppoch. The invaders from Sleat broke through and slaughtered the seven miscreants. His vengeance unsatisfied, himself decapitated each of the seven using the same dirk from the murder of the two young men, and buried their bodies in a nearby knoll, even though the blackguards' father was thought to be married to the poet's sister. Making a rope of heather, he threaded it through the seven heads, and slinging the grisly burden over his shoulder set out for Invergarry to show the trophies to the first chief who refused him. Passing by Loch Oich he washed the heads in a well near the shore, long known in local lore as *Tobar-nan-Ceann* (Well of the Heads). Pressing on, Iain Lom insisted that the heads be shown to both Sleat and Glengarry, the latter requiring a walk of nearly nineteen miles. As compensation for having refused Iain Lom, a later Glengarry heir erected a monument to the seven heads, which still stands west of the Caledonian Canal.

In 1818 a Dr. Smith of Fort William, along with a few friends, excavated a knoll at Inverlair and found seven headless skeletons, giving further credence to the story just recounted.

Gaelic discourse was in decline in Iain Lom's lifetime, and relatively few speakers could also read, which makes the poet's acclaim all the more remarkable. At the time of the Restoration, Charles II named him Poet Laureate. He continued to comment on public events, the fall-out from the Glorious Revolution, 1688, and the much-hated Act of Union. But later in the century, his was one of many voices, not the dominant one.

Along with our not knowing the date of his death, we cannot know its circumstances or consequences. Neither do we know the fate of his body or where it might actually be buried. His attributed burial place, however, is much photographed and fairly well known. It is in the churchyard of the fifteenth-century Cille Choirill in Brae Lochaber, atop a high promontory known as Dùn of Tom Aingeal (hill of fire or light), a name evoking druidical resonances. In the late nineteenth century, businessman Charles Fraser-Mackintosh erected an ornately carved memorial stone to mark the spot. Nearby is a modest, more recent stone for Dòmhnall, the hunter-poet of *Òran na Comhachaig*.

Simultaneous with the fault lines drawn over sectarian differences, Calvinist vs. Catholic vs. Episcopal, or political issues Royalist vs. Parliamentarian, the bilious clan hatreds over land issues never disappeared and could erupt into bloodshed at any time. In the very year that the last Stuart king was driven from the throne in a bloodless coup, the last clan battle to be fought in the Highlands erupted in Lochaber only walking distance from Keppoch House, scene of the murders, and Iain Lom's supposed burial place at Cille Choirill. It was called *Maol Ruadh, Maoile Ruaidh* (reddish hill), or Mulroy, August 4, 1688. The poet, as far as we know, never spoke of it, although an attributed son did. If the conflict appears to be archaic, many combatants armed only with bows and arrows, the issues driving each side had been simmering, sometimes boiling, for more than two hundred and fifty years.

At the first Battle of Inverlochy, 1431, the first chief of the MacDonells of Keppoch, Alexander Carrach, supported his brother Donald Ballach, against the Crown forces under the Earl of Mar and suffered a humiliating defeat. As a penalty for his participation Alasdair forfeited his lands, which were conveyed by feudal charter to the Chief of the Mackintoshes. Tightening their grip on the territory, the Macintoshes obtained a Crown charter from James III in 1476. It was confirmed by James IV in 1493, and by Mary Queen of Scots in 1562. The MacDonells never budged from the area but paid rent under what we would call revocable lease. Meanwhile, the Macintoshes had become a part of the Clan Chattan, discussed in the previous chapter, as the only federation of clans. Thus, when the MacDonells stopped paying rents—what they saw as tribute—in the 1650s they had become egregiously in arrears by 1688. When the Macintoshes decided to collect on what was due, from what they perceived as a tribe of thieves, they drew on their allies. Clan MacKenzie, also a part of Clan Chattan, clearly reluctantly, delivered 500 men. MacDonell of Keppoch began with only 200 but quickly drew eager allies from other branches of the Clan Donald in Glengarry and Glencoe as well as the nearby Clan Cameron.

As the invading force, the Macintoshes and Clan Chattan advanced toward Keppoch House in lower terrain, next to where the modern A86 passes. In a deft maneuver, the MacDonells lured the Mackintoshes and allies into Glen Roy, then well inhabited. Taking the high ground on Maol Ruadh, Keppoch and allies descended with a variation of the feared Highland Charge. An observer from the Crown later wrote of the scene of terror: hundreds of screaming men, swords held high, and many barefoot. This was a rout, killing the chief of the MacKenzies and many of the gentry. When the slaughter of defeated forces continued, the Crown sent trained forces to attack the MacDonells, most of whom immediately fled, and to burn their houses and barns. The late arrival of the Crown troops caused some commentators to argue that Maol Ruadh should not qualify as the "last clan battle," an issue we shall ignore.

Bloody as Maol Ruadh was, it has not lived in the popular imagination as vibrantly as two other conflicts in the next three years, Killiecrankie and Glencoe. That may be because Iain Lom neglected it. The modest marker, a cairn on a single-track road going into Glen Roy, much smaller than for the Seven Heads, is little visited by tourists. In 2012 Scottish violinist Donald Grant composed "The Lament for Mulroy," surprisingly often played for a contemporary work in the rarefied world of chamber music.

Departure of the Stuarts: The First Three Decades

The episode sometimes known as the "Glorious Revolution" is among the most widely known in English history, nearly as familiar as the animosity between Elizabeth I and Mary Queen of Scots. Even the most laggard student will know of it, so we can treat it briefly. James II of England (VII of Scotland), the last Stuart king, made himself unpopular and was taken from the scene in a bloodless coup and replaced by his younger sister and her Dutch husband, who reigned as William and Mary. The English historians who called the passage "glorious" were Protestants. The change of persons on the thrones of England and Scotland was greeted with horror in the Highlands. The wrenching response to the end of the Stuarts would eventually lead to the central catastrophe of Highland life.

James, the second son of Charles I, became king at age 51, February 6, 1685. He lived most of his life as the Duke of York, under which title he was immortalized in an accident of fate. When the former New Amsterdam was taken from the Dutch in 1664, it was renamed New York in his honor. Apart from that his career has suffered bad press from later historians, but he was revered in the Highlands for his role in the Commission on Pacifying the Highlands, 1682–1684, mentioned above. He converted to Roman Catholicism in 1668 and was renowned for his devotion. This did not limit his private life, as he produced a brood of illegitimate children, including four with the eminent Arabella Churchill. Apart from this, his reign was challenged from the beginning with attempts to topple him, the most formidable by James Scott, illegitimate son of Charles II, known as the Duke of Monmouth. As the King became more unpopular, these challenges to his rule convinced Parliamentary elders that he was vulnerable.

A failed challenge to his rule by Archibald Campbell, 9th Earl of Argyll, worked in James's favor. The King had Campbell executed for treason, upending that increasingly powerful family. This delighted the Campbell enemies such as the Camerons, MacLeans and certain branches of the Clan Donald.

It was not simply that James II, head of the Church of England, was a Roman Catholic, but more that he sought to introduce favorable treatment for Catholics, a disparaged minority since the time of Henry VIII, a century and a half earlier. He also attacked the established church, putting disobedient bishops in the Tower of London. This was not done under enlightened tolerance but rather from the divine right authority of the monarch. His playful brother Charles II had not concerned himself much with divine right, but James II was a throwback to his father, Charles I. When James's second wife, Mary of Modena, a Protestant in her forties, produced a son, James Francis Edward on June 10, 1688, and promised to raise him as Roman Catholic, it was more than non-royal people in power could bear.

James's daughter Mary from his first wife would have assumed the throne at her father's death if Prince James Francis Edward had not been born. William of Orange, despite speaking Dutch, was close to the royal family, being both James's son-in-law and his nephew. An appeal was soon sent to William; he responded quickly but took a few weeks to raise an army. When the winds allowed, he landed with 70,000 men at Torbay, Devon. James's reign ended legally December 11, when he fled, was captured, and later escaped to France. William and Mary were proclaimed joint monarchs of England in February, and of Scotland in March.

From France, James went to Ireland to continue to fight there, with baleful consequences. William crushed James and his Irish hosts at the Battle of the Boyne, July 1690. This forever linked the name of William's dynasty, the House of Orange, with Irish Protestantism. And James's name was reviled by generations of Irish poets, e.g., the proverbial *Séamus an chaca*: James the shit.

As just mentioned, William and Mary began their joint rule in Scotland, March 1689, without a shot being fired locally. Before the month was over the commander of the King's forces in Scotland, John Graham, 7th Laird of Claverhouse (c. 1648–1689), found himself denounced as a traitor because of his uninterrupted support of the Stuart dynasty. Then about forty-one, Graham was descended from a distinguished family with a royal pedigree and was related to James Graham, the Great Montrose. An Episcopalian, he could handle a few Gaelic phrases as he had commanded Highland forces while serving as a kind of Royal policeman in the challenges to James's rule. As he had also been named the Viscount Dundee, he traveled to that city April 13 to raise the Scottish Royal Standard for King James and the Jacobite cause. From the Latin *Jacob* for James, this was the first instance of the word's use; it would later point to Prince James Francis Edward. The city, however, was strongly Williamite and despite a personal affection for Graham, would not be a source of recruits for his cause.

Paradoxically, it is for his association with Dundee that Graham would be remembered because of later celebrations of his life. This happened twice in the works of Sir Walter Scott, as a character in *Old Mortality* (1816) and the poem "The Bonnets o' Bonnie Dundee" (1828), but much more the insertion of Scott's words in an existing melody, universally known as "Bonnie Dundee." The tune is a jaunty earworm, one of the most loved expressions of Highland nationalism, inspired by Jacobitism's smashing victory. Their presence in popular memory makes it feel awkward to refer to the first Jacobite as Graham rather than Dundee.

It is from poetry of the time that we know how Graham/Dundee gathered his troops and went into battle. Iain Lom, then in his sixties and walking with Dundee's forces, composed *Cath Raon Ruairidh* (The Battle of Killiecrankie) on the spot. We learn much more, however, from an epic composed in Latin by James Philip of Almerieclose, the *Grameid* (1691), which includes practical along with poetic considerations. Dundee moved to Lochaber to raise his army, much to be expected when we consider how often the region has been mentioned in this chapter. Some came from Kintyre and the Isles, implying wider support. Among the recruits were Catholic Gaels and non-juring Episcopalians along with a handful of Presbyterians. The Episcopalians, who gravitated to the officers' ranks, were called non-juring because they would not acknowledge the Kirk as the established church until their own confession was recognized after the Act of Union (1707). The chief of the Keppoch MacDonells did not join the forces as they moved east for a confrontation with the Williamite army. Dundee had no funds to pay wages, and the army would have to support itself on plunder. An early discouragement was Dundee's finding that Highlanders would not respond to the orders of continental discipline he had employed with the Scottish army in support of the Crown. They did understand, however, Mac Colla's initiation of the Highland charge.

Battle was entered at the pass of Killiecrankie three miles south of Blair Castle, with the Williamites under General MacKay enjoying numerical advantage, perhaps 4000. Dundee started with 2000, joined by Irish Jacobites handicapped by having either few weapons or none at all. That made the Jacobite victory, July 27, all the sweeter. Not to be savored long as the tone turned to tragedy when Dundee himself was killed in the battle. Deprived of skilled and charismatic leadership, Jacobite forces were crushed in the next month at Dunkeld, silencing the Jacobite cause in Scotland for more than two decades. Just as the name "Killiecrankie" was evocative of joy and high spirits in Gaelic proverbs, "Dunkeld" meant defeat, conclusion. Although it did not enter popular imagination, there was yet another humiliation. About 600 die-hard supporters wintered in Lochaber for one last effort. They were defeated at Cromdale in May 1690.

Killiecrankie and Dunkeld were concurrent with the 105-day Siege of Derry in Ireland, in which James II himself participated. It ended August 1, 1689, with relief by the Royal Navy, another cause commemorated by Orangemen in Ireland.

Highland sentiment against the regime remained toxic. Iain Lom railed against William as a "borrowed king" and condemned Mary for her disloyalty to her father. Taking positive, preventative measures, the Scottish government in the person of the Secretary of State, John Dalrymple, Master of Stair, offered a total of £12,000 to Highland chiefs for swearing an oath of allegiance to William. The offer was made in the Declaration of Achallader, June 1691, one month before the Battle of Aughrim in Ireland, July, ended any prospect of a second Stuart restoration. That is nowadays overshadowed by annual commemorations of an earlier Williamite victory, the Battle of the Boyne July 1690, known as Orangemen's Day and the Glorious Twelfth. Lord Stair included an irksome proviso. A pardon would be issued to any chief with Jacobite sympathies if he signed by January 1, 1692, with severe reprisals for those who did not meet the deadline.

The events that followed in the three months of December 1691 to February 1692 have been much studied and are indeed the subject of several books, many taking advantage of private sources not known until much later. We have an omniscient view not available to seventeenth-century observers. Today we know, for example, that Lord Stair rejoiced that some clans were laggard in signing, and he appeared to salivate at the thought of destroying such Roman Catholics ("Papists") as the Glengarry MacDonells. Only one clan failed to meet the deadline, the Episcopal MacDonalds of Glencoe, whom Stair also reviled as thieves. A series of missteps allowed Stair's malign wishes to be fulfilled. On December 30, before the deadline, one MacIain of the Glencoe household trudged to the newly built Fort William to sign the oath, but was turned away by Lieutenant John Hill, who said he was not authorized to accept it. Confirming that MacIain had arrived on time, Hill sent him on a long slog overland to Inveraray on Loch Fyne, where the local magistrate, a Campbell, administered the oath on January 6, after which MacIain returned to Glencoe. Some chiefs signed by proxy instead of in person, and the reviled Glengarry did not swear until February 4—a bold violation of the deadline—but Scottish Privy Council ruled that only MacIain and Glencoe would be excluded from indemnity, despite the tardy attempt to comply.

In late January, two companies of approximately 120 arrived from the north under the command of Robert Campbell of Glenlyon, a local landowner whose niece was married to one of MacIain's sons. They were from the Earl of Argyll's Regiment of Foot, entitling them to "free quarter." Host families submitted to this as an alternative to paying taxes in a largely non-cash society. The traditional enmity of the clans was overlooked, as Glencoe MacDonalds themselves had been billeted on the Campbells thirteen years previously. For two weeks, the quartering of the Campbell troops passed without incident.

On February 12 Campbell of Glenlyon received orders from a Major Duncanson of the Argyll regiment that the time had come deliver the necessary punishment "without feud or favour." The tone of the order implies that Duncanson doubted that Campbell might lack the stomach to carry out the order, and dispatched another Argyll officer, Captain Thomas Drummond; he out-ranked Campbell and had no compunctions. He killed two people who asked for mercy. MacIain the emissary was killed but his sons escaped. Although accounts vary, this is no indication the slaughter was disciplined and systematic. Even today there is no agreement on the total number of dead, long thought to have been 38, but according to different scholars, maybe as few as 25 or perhaps 30. Popular histories, unvetted by authorities, had added lurid details of torture and humiliation. One alleges that MacDonald's wife was stripped naked by the murderous guests and driven out in the snow, her body found the next day. At least three books still in print repeat this calumny, but it is not supported by the most reliable authorities.

Whatever the total death count, it is almost trifling when compared to recent encounters at Killiecrankie and Maol Ruadh, but the infamy surrounding Glencoe is easy to understand. The outrage of killing hosts on a signal after accepting their hospitality for two weeks is indeed stupefying. And it is magnified when we learn that the MacDonalds tried to comply before the deadline. In the longstanding antagonism of the Campbells vs. the MacDonalds, Glencoe appears from a distance to be an egregious instance of Campbell villainy. The occasion of the massacre, however, was not a clan battle like Maol Ruadh, but the triumphant Williamites dominating the weakened Jacobites. It was Lord Stair, not a Campbell, who wanted the MacDonalds exterminated. Whereas Robert Campbell of the Argyll (i.e., Campbell) regiment sought the billeting, not all the perpetrators were named Campbell, nor was each victim named MacDonald. The heat that the massacre invites does not allow for much nuance.

Iain Lom's short diatribe *Murt Ghlinne Comhann* (The Massacre of Glencoe) appeared almost immediately, with non–Gaelic accounts following quickly. A copy of the orders to kill given to Campbell of Glenlyon made their way to France, where they were published in the *Paris Gazette*, April 12. The account criticized the government but also portrayed the MacDonalds negatively. Jacobite activist Charles Leslie followed with an inflammatory pamphlet, *Gallienus Redivivus, or Murther Will Out* (1695) citing Glencoe as but one iteration of government malfeasance. Later Jacobites made sure that the Leslie pamphlet was widely read over the next century and the "Glencoe Massacre" was a phrase everyone knew. More than two dozen poets and fiction writers have treated with or adapted it, from Sir Walter Scott to the twenty-first century prestige fantasist George R.R. Martin. The Glen itself is blessed with some of the most luscious Highland scenery, including a waterfall, and has become a major tourist attraction, just off the A-828/A-82 highway between Oban and Fort William.

William's consolidation of power and authority quieted the Scottish countryside, but the nation as a whole suffered an increasing misery index in successive crop failures. At a time when poor records were kept, millions died all across northern Europe. Counter-intuitively, these were also years for innovations that greatly changed Scottish life. In 1696 the Scots Parliament passed the Act for Setting Schools, which launched public schools and a drive for universal literacy. In the Highlands schools were only for students who spoke English.

The year of 1696 also saw the establishment of the Bank of Scotland, one year after the Bank of England. The driving force behind the Scottish enterprise was a mercurial businessman with a huge capacity for persuasion named William Paterson from Dumfries. Contemporary accounts depict a man we might call charismatic before that word was current outside religious contexts. He sensed that his countrymen resented being the poor relation of their southern neighbor. The Sassenach benefited from the riches of colonies in which Scotsmen played subsidiary roles. He argued that the Scots could tap into foreign largesse if they established their own colonies, without English participation. The idea was not as far-fetched as it sounds today, because other Scotsmen had fostered their own colonies already. James Drummond, the 4th Earl of Perth, had launched New Perth within the English colony of New Jersey, 1683. Its site is still alluded to in the modern town of Perth Amboy. After the Plantation of Ulster early in the century, portions of the north of Ireland were in effect Scottish colonies.

Paterson was not thinking only of English paradigms but also of the Dutch, a smaller nation than England. Amsterdam had become one of the richest cities in the world, learning how to regulate capital trading, well before London. Much of Dutch wealth arose from a trading company reaching around the world. Together with an East Lothian landowner, Andrew Fletcher, Paterson aimed for a Scottish trading company, a seemingly logical step up from the founding of the Bank of Scotland. That would provoke the English to be rivals instead of allies. The first attempt was a company for trading with Africa and the Indies. Protectionist English merchants made sure that any ships from a new Scottish company would be blocked from distant ports they controlled. So Paterson and Fletcher turned to the New World, where lands ruled by the Spanish were thinly populated, notably what is now Panama. Instead of trading with the natives, they would send hard-working industrious Scotsmen to settle in a colony to be known as New Caledonia. This would be under the auspices of the Darien Company, named for the existing Spanish province to be occupied. The name for the enterprise in history is Darien Scheme, a phrase of dread for Scottish nationalists.

Peterson and Fletcher fired up a get-rich-quick fever, raising hundreds of thousands of pounds from both the wealthy and what would be called today small investors. Historians disagree on the total, but it was arguably somewhere in excess of a quarter of the liquid capital in the kingdom. Prospective settlers also signed up to sail into the unknown, a blighted swamp swarming with insects already claimed by Spain, who had no interest in sharing it with strangers. Up to 1200 sailed away the first year with no knowledge of where they were going, arriving in November 1698. One of the leaders was a Thomas Drummond, a key executioner of the Glencoe Massacre. A second expedition of up to 1200, unaware of how the previous fleet had fared, arrived in November 1699. Panama suffered heat and humidity never imagined in Scotland. The settlers brought along the finest Scottish goods, such as powdered wigs, woolen hose, and bright new tartans, that they hoped to trade.

Not only were there no takers, but every aspect of the Scheme led to disaster. Crops failed. Previously unknown diseases ravaged. The Spanish were threatening, and the natives, although hostile to the Spanish, could offer only gifts of fruits and vegetables. King William was unsupportive, as he had no wish to soil relations with Spain. An unceasing rain began to rot the clothes on the settlers' backs. Death was rampant, and by March 1700, only about 250 of all would-be colonists were left to limp back to Scotland in shame. Conspicuous fecklessness was as hard to bear as approximately 2000 painful and humiliating deaths.

Within a short time, it was clear that the financial ruin was even more significant for the nation than the humans involved.. Sensing that its northern neighbor was in grave need, the English Parliament passed the Alien Act in 1705, banning Scotsmen from inheriting land in England, a gratuitous insult. Although the Darien Scheme is prominent in popular memory for the extinction of Scottish independence, there were other liabilities, not particular to the Highlands. By 1705 the Scottish parliament drew plans for the eventual union of the kingdoms. Scottish representatives would be a minority in a new entity to be called the British Parliament. The Scottish legal system and Scottish schools would be locally controlled. There was much public debate over such a momentous turn of events, a refutation of Bannockburn and William Wallace. Unquestionably the most inflammatory provision in the Act of Union was that prominent Scottish investors in the Darien Scheme would be reimbursed for their losses. Several prominent persons not involved with Darien argued for the abandonment of a national cause and the acceptance of a comforting embrace from Britannia, with the promise of a higher standard of living to come. Prominent among them was John Dalrymple, Lord Stair, responsible for the massacre at Glencoe.

On January 16, 1707, the Scottish parliament voted itself out of existence. The white saltire cross of St. Andrew was merged with the cross of St. George and the red saltire for Ireland to form the Union Jack, flag of the United Kingdom. That splendid design had emerged a century earlier and effectively if not officially became the national flag 1801 at the Act of Union of Ireland.

While the movement of Scottish King James to London 104 years earlier was looked upon favorably, the actual Union of the two kingdoms was seen as a disgrace in Scotland. There was rioting in the streets across Scotland, with special vehemence in Glasgow. Iain Lom, then possibly in his eighties, spoke with as much anger as he ever mustered in *Òran an Aghaidh an Aonaidh* (A Song Against the Union). Distaste for the Union became party policy for the Tories, who proposed ending it in 1713. The Union remained a sore point for Scottish nationalist just as Glencoe was for Highlanders, and remained so until at least 1999 when the Scottish parliament reopened. Anger was still livid in 1791 when Robert Burns penned "Such a Parcel of Rogues in a Nation," taking aim at Scottish malefactors who sought to pay off their foolishly acquired debts by promoting the Union. The musical version was always popular with the parochial audience of Scottish nationalists, but its fame went worldwide when the traditional rock group Steeleye Span made it the title number of a top-selling album in 1973.

Jacobitism, which had flourished in the brief burst of the Bonnie Dundee, was not heard from in public discourse during the first seven years of the new century, but it was by no means dead. In 1700 the still sovereign Scottish parliament passed the Penal Act to discourage the growth of "Popery." This was not simply bigotry, but a measure against a Catholic return to the throne. King James's heir, Prince James Francis Edward, was reaching maturity and living in Catholic countries. In its several iterations, Jacobitism was dominated by the Episcopal faithful, with Roman Catholics in smaller numbers. Yet many Catholics were indeed Jacobites, as was Iain Lom. The poet's diatribe against it notwithstanding, many Jacobites found themselves pleased with the Act of Union. It often happened that what irked the Lowlands brought smiles in the Highlands.

When King James II & VII died September 16, 1701, his son and putative heir was living in luxury at the Palace of St. Germain-en-Laye outside Paris, fully supported by the French Crown. Louis XIV declared him King James III & VIII *prétendant*. The word should have been translated as "claimant," but was strongarmed into the English false cognate as "pretender," which could never shake the negative semantics. At the Act of Union, the prince was nineteen, but because of the greater prominence of his son Charles Edward Stuart in history, we usually cite him as the "Old Pretender."

Together with French allies, James Francis Edward plotted what was to be the first Jacobite restoration in 1708. French intelligence reported the massive Scottish dismay at the Act of Union but also observed strong Episcopal support on both sides of the border, which the Prince, now twenty, duly noted. Not until the Act of Tolerance, 1712, would the Episcopal church gain legal status in Scotland, and even afterward it bridled under Calvinist domination. Louis would supply a fleet of warships and privateers for an invasion, along with a company of French troops. The plan was to land on the east coast of Scotland, ignore Edinburgh but instead seize Stirling as quickly as possible and make it a capital. With Scotland secured, a force would be sent to the northeast of England to take control of the Tyne-Tees coal resources, the fuel upon which Britain was becoming dependent.

Bad weather, bad health and bad luck thwarted the invasion. On the way to the invasion, the Prince was stricken with measles, then looked upon as one step short of small pox. This kept him marooned in the port of Dunkirk. In the wait for his recovery, the Channel was struck by a furious storm and many of the French ships did not sail, and those that did were manned with seasick crews. One of the ships landed in the Firth of Forth at Burntisland, where it found eager Jacobites ready to join the campaign to Stirling. Only one ship arrived, however, without reinforcements or the Pretender.

The 1708 venture is often overlooked by historians and dismissed as a fiasco when it is discussed at all, but unmistakably the presence of French support and Scottish population ready to respond to a royal signal were lessons to be valued.

William had been replaced on the throne by the hapless Queen Anne, one of the melancholiest of all British monarchs. As a Protestant daughter of James II & VII from his first marriage, she was indeed a Stuart. The last of her eighteen children had died by 1700, raising concern about her succession. The Tories might have accepted James Francis Edward if he would turn Protestant, a proposal he would not entertain. To find a suitable Protestant claimant, Parliament sought out the family of Anne's younger sister, Elizabeth, who had married into the Bohemian royals, well-connected to several German petty kingdoms. Elizabeth had long since died, and her heir Sophia, Electress of Hanover, was in her seventies, thought unsuitable for the British throne. But she had a Protestant son named Georg Ludwig then in his forties. He was willing to Anglicize his name to George Louis and to move to London. These machinations took place distastefully while Anne was still alive, incurring her disgust. She loathed any mention of the Bohemians and would not allow them to set foot in the Kingdom. Nonetheless, at Anne's death in 1714 the "Bohemian" prince was crowned George I, founding the House of Hanover. His thirteen-year reign, greeted with riots as with the Act of Union, remained wildly unpopular. Given that he returned to Germany as often as he could, it was widely thought he could not speak English at all, a libel refuted by recent historians. His discomfort in England, coupled with the role of Parliament in his selection, meant that during his reign power drifted each year from the throne to the representative body. He never visited Scotland, and there is no indication he had any opinion of it.

Scotland had never forgotten the Stuarts, nor had Tories on either side of the border. James Francis Edward was now a dashing young man of twenty-seven, free of visible illnesses. His cause was taken up by unhappy Scottish nobles led by John Erskine, the 6th Earl of Mar. In 1713 they put forth a Quixotic bill in Parliament calling for the end of the Union. Erskine was not a Gael, but as mentioned in the previous chapter, his bailiwick, once prominent in Scottish discourse, lay in western Aberdeenshire adjacent to Braemar. He has been known to history by the uninspiring nickname of "Bobbing John" after his propensity for changing sides, as he had once been a champion of the Union. He was once Secretary of State for Scotland. The ascension of George I, however, steadied his resolution. When he tried to approach the new king at a function in the summer of 1715, the German-born king turned away so as to snub him in the most public of manners. By September 6 Erskine had mustered about 5000 men, mostly Highlanders, and raised the Jacobite standard at Braemar and seized both Inverness and Perth. Then began a march toward Edinburgh. Even without modern communications, the response across Scotland was electric. Shortly the rebel numbers more than doubled. Many of the new troops came from the Lowlands and were put under the command of Brigadier William Mackintosh, who aimed to cross the border to England and link up with Jacobites there.

The Earl of Mar's, Erskine's, army, possibly numbering 7000 to 8000, met a government force of fewer than 4000 under the command of John Campbell, 2nd Duke of Argyll, at Sheriffmuir, not far from Stirling, November 13. There was much see-sawing back and forth, and for a while it looked as though the Jacobites would be victorious. Government forces suffered higher casualties. But the ambiguity of the conclusion was resolved when the Earl of Mar left the field to retreat to Perth, and later to leave the country. Argyll, while bloodied, had stopped the Jacobite advance.

Concurrently a second Jacobite force of 4000, mostly Scottish with some English, moved against Preston in Lancashire, occupying it in November. This lasted only five days, as Government forced the Jacobites to surrender on November 14. It is sometimes cited as the last battle fought on English soil.

Giving the entire venture a tone of fatuousness, Prince James Francis Edward did not arrive in Scotland, at Peterhead in Aberdeenshire, until December 22. Nonetheless, 1715 should not be dismissed as a pop-gun worthless enterprise. The Earl of Mar's numbers at Sheriffmuir, once mistakenly inflated to 12,000, were certainly larger than those in the Jacobite forces at Culloden Moor, April 16, 1746. They took Preston without a fight.

The aftermath was painful for supporters of the cause. Several supposed leaders were executed, including the Englishman James Radclyffe, 3rd Earl of Derwentwater, while many clan chiefs, such as Sir Ewen Cameron of the Clan Cameron, went into exile. Huge fines were imposed and lands forfeited. Pro-Hanoverian clans such as the Presbyterian Campbells, Munros and Sutherlands grew more powerful and wealthy. James Francis Edward and his entourage were no longer welcome in France and would have to seek exile in Rome, capital of the Papal States.

With yet another armed attempt to restore the Stuart monarchy coming only four years after Sheriffmuir, the 1719 rising can easily be mistaken as just another iteration of the same story. But 1719 has quite a different character from 1715; it was fought on ground more deeply in the Gàidhealtachd and embroiled many more foreign players, including Spain and Sweden. Indeed, some historians now argue that the Jacobite cause was exploited by non–British nations whose interest in who was king of Scotland was incidental.

Looming in the background was Spain's grievance at the loss of its Italian possessions of Sicily and Sardinia in 1713, and Britain's subsequent interference. When Spanish troops landed in Sicily in July 1718, the Royal Navy destroyed the Spanish fleet, beginning the War of the Quadruple Alliance. This pitted Spain against Britain, France, Austria and the Dutch Republic: tall odds. Enter an exiled dissident Irish Protestant noble, the Duke of Ormonde, who encouraged the Spanish to take more ambitious initiatives. He envisioned an invasion of southwest England with the help of famed strategist Charles XII of Sweden, and a march to London to place Prince James Francis Edward on the throne. King Charles had his own frictions with the House of Hanover, but died in 1718 before the launch of such a massive invasion.

Undaunted, Ormonde and the Spanish thought that any scheme to unsettle Britain by restoring the Stuarts should run through Scotland. They made common cause with some leading Scottish Jacobites, approving of the Earl of Mar's efforts in 1715, but were not allied directly with him. Among them was George Keith, who went to Spain to guide the Spanish Marines. He was joined by his brother James Keith, the Earl of Seaforth, and Jacobite exiles in France, such as Cameron of Lochiel. The invasion force of two frigates and about 300 marines landed on the Isle of Lewis in the Outer Hebrides by March 1719, and occupied the port of Stornoway. Although news of this landing rallied a number of potential fighters among Scottish Jacobites, plans to march on the mainland stalled when word was received that Ormonde and other Spaniards would not be joining them. By the time the invaders reached Lochalsh their numbers were about 1000, including 400 MacKenzies and 150 Camerons, but much smaller than the Earl of Mar's forces four years earlier. With Spanish backing, however, they had arms and ammunition for twice as many. As they moved east, they decided on May 10 to store the excess in Eilean Donan Castle, a site with thousand-year-old antecedents, on the north side of Loch Duich. Forty Spaniards would guard it. Alerted to the invasion, the Royal Navy bombarded the castle and sent ashore government troops. Using the invaders' own gunpowder, they spent two days in leveling it to the best of their ability.

The castle lay in ruins for two centuries until John MacRae-Gilstrap restored it, 1919–1932, to give us Scotland's most photographed edifice.

Despite this loss, the Jacobites marched east toward Inverness, while a government force under Joseph Wightman headed west on June 5 to meet them. Battle commenced June 10 in the narrow confines of Glen Shiel (often Glenshiel), with the invaders having a slight advantage in numbers, c.1440 to 1100. This time the invaders suffered liabilities not borne by the Earl of Mar four years earlier. Wightman's government forces put them on the defensive on low ground, and so there was no opportunity to deploy the much-feared Highland charge. Much worse, the government forces brought with them a new weapon, the mortar, not seen before by the Spanish or the Highlanders. It struck terror.

The year of 1719 seriously damaged the Jacobite cause, even though casualties were not as high as they might have been (invaders 100 killed and wounded; government 140), and repercussions were mild. The Spanish were treated as professionals and were repatriated. Jacobite nobles were given more lenience than in 1715. The brothers James and George Keith took service elsewhere, both becoming Prussian generals. Those to suffer the most were Episcopalians, as they were perceived to be the majority of the Highland volunteers. Tolerance granted toward them in 1712 was diminished, and Episcopalians, especially if non-juring (not accepting the legitimacy of Williamite and Hanoverian succession), would grow into the major religious faction of the Jacobites in the next generation.

Prince James Francis Edward, now thirty-one, had resided in Spain, never to join the invasion. The year of 1719 was an important year for him nonetheless. He took as a bride the seventeen-year-old Polish princess Maria Clementina Sobieska, grand-daughter of king Jan Sobieski, the Christian hero who had saved Europe from the Turks at Vienna, 1683. She brought with her a huge dowry of more than a million sovereigns and a famous collection of jewelry, allowing the court of the Pretender to have some of the accoutrements of one heading a nation-state. On December 31, 1720, she delivered a son and heir, Charles Edward Louis Silvester Severino Maria Stuart.

4

The Dreary Eighteenth Century

Highland Society Before Culloden

In the late seventeenth and early eighteenth centuries the British government was present in the Highlands through the military. One of the principal towns, still second in population after Inverness, was Fort William. The name is resonant of a frontier, as in the North American west, like Hollywood's Fort Apache, or Fort Frances, Ontario. Oliver Cromwell initiated the idea for an armed camp to be adjacent to the battlefield of Inverlochy to be called Gordonsburgh in 1654, but it took General MacKay to build an actual fortress and name it after the new king in 1690. The local Jacobite population found both halves of the name irksome and so referred to it as *Gearasdan* (the Garrison) in Gaelic; that name is found on bilingual signs currently in place.

Two motions of the British government in 1725 affected Highland life deeply. One was the Disarming Act, prompted by the failed Jacobite invasion of 1719, banning weapons for both loyal and rebellious clans. In a society that esteemed military prowess and hunting so highly, such laws could not be fully effective. In that same year Major-General George Wade accepted the commission to blaze roads through the territory. In the next fifteen years he supervised the building of 250 miles of roads linking Fort William up the Great Glen to Fort Augustus (previously *Cille Chuimein* or Kiliwhimin) to Inverness, and thence south eighty miles to Dunkeld. This called for the building of high bridges over rushing mountain streams, preserved in many placenames today.

To protect this enterprise, especially during construction, Wade recruited a Highland militia drawn from loyal clans, mostly Campbell, but also Fraser, Munro and Grant. They were to be called the Black Watch, probably after the now familiar dark tartan compiled for them. A revisionist explanation is that they were a "watch," i.e., a guard against the protection racket of raiders, a practice that has entered English as "blackmail." Recruiting Highlanders to serve the government was a novelty so soon after the two failed Jacobite uprisings of 1715 and 1719. The militia would cease when Wade departed, but its tartan and identity were assigned to a new infantry regiment formed in March 1743, for service in Flanders. Later, in an affront to nationalist memory, the Black Watch Regiment was deployed with Hanoverian forces in 1745–1746 but not sent to Scotland. Successive regiments went through several transformations in service to the Empire, but the Black Watch rightly claims to be the oldest of its kind.

During this time the Gaelic Highlands remained an uninviting space for other peoples in the British Isles. Along with the banditry and a forbiddingly difficult language that few non-Gaels could speak, there were few opportunities for profit. There were no burghs or trading centers to foster a middle class. Almost completely absent were large tracts of arable land as found in the Lowlands and most European countries. Highlanders produced very little for sale, although immense herds of cattle might be driven across borders for exchange. Their well-worn tracks, called "drove roads," became the templates for later thoroughfares. The only raw materials for sale were slate and lime. The laborious harvesting of kelp would come later in the century. Inverness, dominated by non-Gaels, had the largest population, but it did not compare with Lowland urban centers like Roxburgh, Dundee or Aberdeen. Nonetheless, travelers taking notes on what they beheld continued to enter the territory, some of them driven by agendas. In 1709 the Society in Scotland for the Propagating of Christian Knowledge (SSPCK) had the dual goals of suppressing the Gaelic language and Roman Catholicism. It is from the observations of non-Gaels and outsiders, rather than from Gaelic sources, that we learn more about the habits and manners of common people and how they perceived each other.

It would be anachronistic to describe these many reports as condescending or demeaning, but there is a kind of early *National Geographic* sense of wonder that the people being described are profoundly different from the observer or presumed reader. In his *A Late Voyage to St. Kilda* (1697), the Skye-born Martin Martin, with a medical degree from Leiden, reported that the islanders were flabbergasted to encounter literacy for the first time. Ink markings on paper could record what people said; the markings could be viewed and exact words repeated. St. Kilda was the most remote speck of the Gàidhealtachd, forcibly evacuated as uneconomic in the twentieth century, but the report fed the perception that speaking Gaelic discouraged participation in contemporary life. Edmund (sometimes Edward) Burt recorded in 1726 when most of the Highlands were still bartering that he gave a poor woman a shilling which she held up in contempt and surprise, saying, "What must I do with this? My children cannot eat it." Others prefigured the missionaries a century later departing to relieve the suffering of the non-Western world. Sir Robert Sibbald wrote in *Provision for the Poor in Time of Dearth and Scarcity* (1699) that "everyone may see death on the face of the poor ... their ghostly looks, their feebleness." Admittedly the horrible weather and crop failure of the 1690s, which also prompted the catastrophic Darien Scheme, was an especially low period.

The authoritative Scottish historian T.M. Devine (2018) has argued that the endemic poverty of the western Highlands is the great reality for centuries of Scottish history. It was poverty, not fierce warriors with claymores, that made the Scottish government so reluctant to impose its authority throughout the territory. Interrupting that region of want were occasional pockets of affluence, such as clan chiefs and their families as well as the possessors of cattle ready for market.

Some of the travelers were writers of distinction, such as novelist Daniel Defoe, publishing 1724–1727, who wrote quite ill of what he found. A bit more even-handed was Edmund Burt, whose *Letters from a Gentlemen, c. 1730* is a prime source for what we are saying here; his observations are coordinated with the findings of contemporary historians. Burt was the first to report many instances of what we now think of as commonplaces of Highland life. The first appearance of the word "kilt" in English comes from his pages. His work is often juxtaposed with post–Culloden travelers, such as naturalist Thomas Pennant, 1774–1776, and Thomas Thornton, 1804.

No society, of course, can remain stationary, but our attention here is given to the first half of the eighteenth century in a kind of default portrait, as everything worsened with the repressions after the defeat of 1746. That year is more than a political landmark. Independent of the rebellion, the Highlands began to move toward a cash economy about 1745. Previously transaction took place in barter, meaning that the lowest ranks of society might own no currency. The movement to cash was ultimately a hardship for the poorest farmers because they became subject to market price for goods set elsewhere by means they could not comprehend. A falling price for a bushel of oats in London and Amsterdam could mean catastrophe for a hardworking farmer in Argyll or Ross.

By 1700 the power of the clans had diminished from the height a century or two earlier. Nonetheless, the chief was at the pinnacle of a regional society. A sacred oath was to be sworn by the hand of a chief. Edmund Burt was put off by the slavish deference shown the chief, much as John Major had been in 1521. Every man in the clan still wished to be thought of as the chief's soldier. The chief was also the proprietor of clan holdings, but he did not manage them. As the head of the clan, nominally a family, the chief initially did not wish to be thought of as a landlord. Those duties were turned over to a strata of lease holders known as tacksmen. Excluding the chiefs and their families above, and landless servants and further below them, caterans or "broken men" in the sub-strata, there were three levels of Highland society: tacksmen, tenants, and subtenants. Since the nineteenth century we have denoted tenants by the English term "crofter." Subtenants came to be denoted by the Scots term "cottar," possibly because of its celebration in the poetry of Robert Burns. Whereas the subtenants, with tiny possessions of land, were by far the majority of the population, they were little noted in official records or bardic poetry praising chiefs before the arrival of English-speaking travelers and reporters. Some commentators have argued that their humble position with a secure place on the land was superior to that of the landless farm laborers who were hired seasonally. In many ways, their status was worse, as they lacked the freedom to decide their movement. If the tenant to whom they were obliged were to decide to move and connect with a different tacksman, the cottar had no choice but to abandon what had been home and to follow. Martin Martin records a subtenant woman who had given birth to twins and was ordered to deliver one of them to a superior status household. Lower still were landless male and female servants, small in number, and found mostly in southern counties. Folks from outside Gaeldom looking for Highland ancestors at such glorious victories as Inverlochy or Killiecrankie are mathematically most likely to be descended from subtenants or servants whose names are absent from surviving documents. Subtenants who fought in those battles are not noted. Combatants of the lowest social order at Culloden, however, are recorded in Livingstone and Aikman's *No Quarter Given* (1984), but not their families.

The tacksmen, unique to Highland society, are likely to be the most unfamiliar to readers. Their dominance rose with the decline of clan warfare in the early seventeenth century, when they assured social stability. Their departure in the late eighteenth century compounded post–Culloden Moor misery.

Put most simply, the tacksmen signed leases for properties with their proprietors, the chiefs, frequently kinsmen. They lived as quasi landlords among the tenants profiting on the differences between the rents they collected and the payments made to the chiefs. The English word, used almost universally, may be an approximation of the Gaelic *fir-tacsa*. However, *tacsa* translates as "support, substance or solidity" and may mean "buttress" or "comfort" rather than "lease," as we understand it in commercial discourse. It may possibly come from the Scots *tack*: seizure, hold, bail, security. The tacksmen may look like incipient bourgeois, but the older term for gentry, *daoine uaisle*, came to imply them. They usually avoided manual labor. To the charge that the tacksmen were nothing more than parasitical middlemen, Samuel Johnson gave an impassioned response. He felt that without them the tenantry, to say nothing of the subtenants, would be given up to grossness and ignorance. He saw the tacksmen as teaching skills and imparting knowledge and civility. From the distance of three centuries this may sound like a more attractive life than those whose hands were in the soil, but it was also a life of constant tension. The chief and his family could be willful and indulgent, hungry for extra comforts, whereas the tenants may literally have been starving when the rent was due. Leases were not for fixed terms and could be arbitrarily and of erratically different lengths, with those of tenants generally shorter. Additionally, if the chief was intent on war, it was the tacksman who had to line up the troops. It is now thought to have been a strategic mistake for Archibald Campbell, the 3rd Duke of Argyll, a Hanoverian, to have opened the post of tacksman to the highest bidder, dispossessing older, more established lease holders. This weakened his position in 1745, whereas his rival, Donald Cameron of Lochiel, a Jacobite, was in a stronger position for keeping his tacksmen close.

The tacksmen's closeness in blood and social rank to the chief meant there was a deep gulf between them and the tenants. If a farm's income was from twenty to fifty-five pounds a year or its equivalent in barter, the tenants' possessions would be from five to twenty pounds per annum. The subtenants were allowed small parcels of land from the tenant, with the agreement of the tacksman, worth perhaps fifteen to forty shillings. In addition to payment, subtenants and even tenants might be subject to thirlage, imposed bonds of servitude, such as the unpaid performance of certain tasks, or restrictions of movement according to the wishes of the chief or the tacksman.

One farm earning thirty pounds a year was inhabited by seventy-one persons, including the tacksman and his wife and children plus eight men servants, six women, and two boys and ten subtenants and families. Such a number of people subsisting on a small parcel of land would be unknown elsewhere in Europe. Despite the Highlands' being thinly populated, living space was congested.

4. The Dreary Eighteenth Century

Very few of the living quarters for non-privileged persons survive from before 1800. Powerful chiefs, a handful of people, lived in castles. Those in ruins imply a most insalubrious living, and the others have been remodeled constantly over the centuries, e.g., Achnacarry, rebuilt in 1802 for Cameron of Lochiel. Either way, portrayals of how the Highland elite lived before Culloden has been erased. For the lowest social orders, we may see the ruins of the *clachan*, a hamlet of small stone cubicles, usually near a spring, without a church or commercial or official building of any kind. In some instances, only the stone outline of residences survives. The stone shells of abandoned houses on lonely moors or along the lochs that make such poignant photographs were built either by tacksmen or more prosperous tenants in the eighteenth century. Neither they nor the clachans indicate the way most people lived. Burt and other commentators depict poor people living in dwellings made of perishable organic materials such as turf, straw, heather and ferns, not only for roofing but for walling. Burt also remarked that many dwellings seen from a distance were as so many heaps of mud, cottages made of turf and heather of one room only, divided by a wicker curtain.

The most commented-upon dwelling was the so-called "blackhouse," a colloquial term with a fluid definition. It could describe any residence perhaps a hundred years or older and in ruinous condition, and "black," i.e., caked with earth or turf, when seen from a distance. These were more common in the windy Outer Hebrides with a shortage of trees, but were also found far inland. Recent research suggests this vernacular architecture was probably adapted from Norse antecedents. Most often the blackhouse was constructed of double-thick drystone walls and thatched roof. Usually, they did not have windows or a chimney. A turf fire burned on a hearth with the expectation that smoke would escape through a smoke hole in the roof, meaning the residence usually had some smoke present. Turf or peat, the near universal fuel, released many more particles than either soft or hard wood, or, later, than coal. Another reason to call the residences "black" houses. They did, however, have rounded corners to deflect outside winds. Most were rectangular in plan with interior spaces divided into activity areas. Furniture was almost nonexistent. Little soap was used, and there were few candles. What little lighting there was came from burning the split roots of fir trees. Some, but by no means all, incorporated a cow byre beneath the same roof. The notion of people living side-by-side with cattle, while hardly true of every Highlander, was an occasion for derision when people left the Gàidhealtachd for the wider world, such as joining the British Army or Navy. Some residences deemed "blackhouses" survived until the twentieth century, on the testimony of B&B owners until the 1950s.

In the Highlands, unlike the Lowlands or elsewhere, usable farmland was separated by ridges, moor, bog and waterlogged areas. These disadvantages, topped by a harsh climate, called for a different plan of land allotment, usually called by the Middle English term "runrig" (from "run," an enclosed area, and "ridge"; elsewhere "rundale" or "runridge"). Under this procedure the shares of each tenant were scattered across what was arable in intermixed strips, which were often regularly subject to reallocation in order to ensure reasonable fair access to good and bad soils. Rarely, perhaps only in favored sections of the southern or eastern Highlands, would the strips be configured into compact blocks. Modern commentators observe that with no individual leases or ownership of plots of land, there was little incentive to improve it, for instance by drainage or crop rotation systems. Along with this, with common grazing an individual owner had no incentive to improve the quality of his stock. Whatever its influence on the economy or social movement, the runrig system is remembered as so distinctively Highland that the word was taken as the name of a Celtic folk group that flourished from 1973 to 2018, known for Gaelic lyrics. Based on the Isle of Skye, performers came from different parts of the Gaelic world, including Cape Breton Island, Nova Scotia.

Many commentators, especially the "improvers" fostered by the Whig Party in the late eighteenth century, argued that the system described here, from the lease by the tacksmen down to the subtenants on runrig land, made it impossible for a richer class of peasants to emerge, and the potential for capital accumulation was limited. According to T.M. Devine (2018), however, the effects of kinship and the use of land in return for labor services meant that the precious asset had to be distributed and not settled on a small number of dominant peasant families. There is no evidence of social striving within one's rank, tenant or subtenant. Except in times of famine (regrettably frequent), there was enough to eat. And despite the squalor, Highlanders were praised by outsiders for their generosity and hospitality to visitors.

Uneasy with the generous welcome, many visitors can be seen holding their noses. Although the streets of any metropolis would have had an abundance of horse manure, Edmund Burt complained that what he found in towns and near Highland settlements was higher than his shoe. When he asked why it was not cleaned, he was told, "It will not be long before we have a shower." Increasing his disdain was the likelihood of so many people to go barefoot in all weather, in frost or snow, including most children. Most women of lower station walked barefoot, as did many men of comparable station. Women and men of high station might walk barefoot while having servants, also barefoot, carrying shoes—thought a luxury—for them, to be put on upon arrival.

Those women with dirty feet washed their laundry while stomping on clothes in a tub, sometimes holding each other. With their dirty bare feet, the women would also hull barley. If they should do their laundry in an icy loch or stream, their feet would turn blood red in the cold.

Although nutrition had not yet become a subject of disciplined study, Burt sensed that most Highlanders, especially children, ate poorly. He describes many as suffering distemper and enduring "the itch," as likely a sign of poor hygiene as inferior diet. The suggestion that a persistent itch was a marker of Highlanders' inferiority spread to Lowlands and beyond with outmigration. In one of the first-ever slurring, anti–Highland cartoons of 1764 there's a depiction of a "scrubbing post," against which suffering wretches would rub their backs, as much animal as human. In his study *Improvement and Romance: Constructing the Myth of the Highlands* (1989), Peter Womack argues that the unseemly penchant for scratching was as much a part of the early derisive caricature of the Highlander as a kilt and a scraggly beard.

Introduced to Europe from South America in the sixteenth century, potatoes were not grown in the Highlands and Islands until the 1740s, when they quickly became universal. They displaced the cereals oats and barley. Being less prone to storm damage and more tolerant of damp soils, they grew well and could support four times as many people as any available cereal. This, in turn, promoted a rise in population, as it did in Ireland. It was not uncommon in the decades preceding Culloden for poor women to produce as many as twenty children, who then suffered a high mortality rate. This was one of the few items of Highland life noted by Adam Smith in *The Wealth of Nations* (1776). As in Ireland, the ubiquitous reliance on a single crop would bring catastrophe in the 1840s.

Burt added, however, that Highland diet was not always monotonous. Even poor tables might be graced with food thought rare luxury in Edinburgh or London, such as salmon and trout freshly taken from the river. The limited means of preserving food made it difficult to ship them any distance. With the presence of so many arms among Highland men, many were indeed hunters limited to a region or season. Thus partridge, grouse, hare, duck, mallard, woodcock and snipe might appear in the Highland household of even the lowest social orders. But observers were appalled that routine might be interrupted with wafers of dried cow blood, and even more distressing coagulated blood served on a bannock, the unleavened griddle cake made of oats (usually), barley or wheat. Unaccountably, it survives to the twenty-first century as "black pudding." A genuine treat was to have honey on the bannock.

Sources disagree about the status of women and attitudes toward sexual morality. Edmund Burt reported, "A stranger might think there was but little occasion for strict laws about fornication." Before him Martin Martin was disgusted by what he saw as trial marriages, in which a rejected wife might be returned to her family. He contributed to the notion of the "handfast marriage," which as we considered in an earlier chapter was overblown and never a universal practice. In some places couples engaging in intercourse before marriage would be subject to public shaming. In the Lowlands Robert Burns wrote, "Address to the Unco Guid, Or, The Rigidly Righteous," based on his own experience of this. Illegitimate birth was not usually a reason for obloquy or exclusion from the community. If a mother could plausibly argue that the child was the result of a liaison with a man of high rank, or the chief, the child would be well treated. One of the long-term results of the Statutes of Iona (1609), obliging the chief and his family to learn English, is that the top stratum of clan society was increasingly Anglicized, even if resident in the area. An elevated cultural status could be license for exploitation. Some lived in Edinburgh or even London supported by rents from the Gàidhealtachd.

As for the character of Highland people, observers are divided. Educated Gaels had noted as long ago as John Fordun at the end of the fourteenth century the readiness of other Scotsmen to speak the worst of them. The phrase in Gaelic was *Mìoran mòr nan Gall*: the great malice of the Lowlander. Literally, a proverbial sentiment. A poem attributed to Alexander Montgomerie of Ayrshire (c. 1540–1611) begins with this couplet:

> How the first Helandman, of God was maid
> Of an horss turd, in Argylle, as is said.

One stream of invective united a calumny of Gaelic idleness and lawlessness. When Calvinist preachers railed against Episcopalians and Catholics, those were cited as prime failings. The early visiting commentators found little reason to challenge this libel. The growing of potatoes, as well as hunting and fishing, was not especially labor intensive, and both tenants and subtenants saw no reason to make excuses if there was little to occupy them between sessions in the fields. When Burt asked women how they felt about their husbands sitting idly for long periods, they responded that the men were "gentlemen." Many husbands felt that some chores were beneath them as fit only as "women's work," to which their wives acceded. This might include weaving or helping during a harvest.

As for crime, we have already considered that the *creach* or cattle raid, or deer-stealing, were indeed considered little more than sport and as honorable as warfare. A satirical sixteenth-century poem in Scots depicts a Highlander as a cattle thief from the moment of creation. While cattle might be fair game, the theft of personal belongings in a society of few creature comforts appears to be unknown. Burt reported that the theft of a chicken or a sheep (before the introduction of large flocks) was thought reprehensible. In any case, there was no shame at having run afoul the law. Burt reported on a conversation with an old woman who said she had married three times. Her first two husbands had been kind men, but they had "died for the law," a euphemism for having been hanged. In his view, she shrugged off their crimes and execution.

The culmination of all this ethnic disdain is a shabby polemic published anonymously and titled *A History of the feuds and conflicts among the clans in the northern parts of Scotland and the Western Isles from the year M.XXXI.* [1031] *unto M.DC. XIX* [1619], (1764), eighteen years after Culloden. It purports to treat of the malign behavior of the Gaels in a "catalogue of atrocities" with much attention given to the Lord of the Isles. Peter Womack (1989) thinks that the immediate purpose of the book was to channel the innate bellicosity and "unrestrained butchery" of Highland men into the British Army. It was an implicit refutation of Whiggish notions of "improvement," through which the Gaels could be dragged into the lower reaches of the emerging commercial and industrial economy. A letter to the *Westminster Gazette* opined that no one should concern themselves with education of the children of savages: "better they should work in the scandalously neglected herring industry." When scrutinized by modern scholars, many of the book's assertions and projections collapse. But when there was no other history of the Highlands available, it was deemed authoritative and cited extensively for the next sixty years.

Despite the poverty and insults, Highlanders were by no means a pariah class or *Dalits* (untouchables). The other side of the common people's fealty and veneration of the clan chief, is that they might bear a proud name. They felt (wrongly) that they were one family if they shared the same name. Illiterate people could recite lengthy (probably unreliable) genealogies, up to twenty generations, of illustrious ancestors, whose magnificence was inflated by the boastful clan histories that began to be compiled in the seventeenth century. As several commentators observed, Highland men, even if idle and unwashed, walked with pride.

Quite a few visitors praised the Gaels they met. Daniel Defoe in the 1720s, although critical of much of what he found, said that the Highlander could be as fine a gentleman as one could find in any country. Distinguished engineer Thomas

Telford (1757–1834), the builder of bridges and canals, might rank first among English admirers of things Highland. And Samuel Johnson, despite his lengthy iteration of all that he found to be disappointing or disgusting, allowed that "civility seems a part of the national character of the Highlanders." To this he added another line projecting his Tory philosophy, favoring authority: "Every chieftain is a monarch, and politeness, the natural production of royal government."

There are few comments on the mental state of people living with unrelieved toil in physical discomfort, but we can deduce mass unhappiness from surviving proverbs. Consider Michael Newton's evidence (2009). *Feumaidh an talamh a chuid fhèin*: "The earth, i.e., the grave, will get its own." Or *Am fear a gheibh gach latha bàs, 's e as fheàrr a bhitheas boò*: "The man who finds death each day is the man who lives best." Suicide, however, was rare. Highlanders were observed to have lacked the lighthearted nature of their Gaelic brothers in Ireland. At one level this is an ethnic cliché barely worth mentioning, but the Irish indeed more quickly embraced comic and satirical themes, often directed at the clergy, appearing in poetry of the Middle Ages. Comic Highland figures began to appear in English stage plays a few decades after Culloden, but people who are objects of comic scorn do not produce that so readily themselves. With the exception of Iain Lom's pointed derision, there are few reasons to smile in Scottish Gaelic poetry. And there would not be a Highland humorist until the end of the nineteenth century.

The Jacobites, 1745–1746

The one episode of Highland history any reader can be assumed to have heard of before beginning this volume is the failed Jacobite Uprising and ruinous defeat at Culloden Moor, April 16, 1746. From a distance it looks like a great folly, the Darien Scheme with better color: a headstrong Young Pretender leading under-equipped starry-eyed naïfs from the boondocks against the greatest military power in Europe. How could it end in anything but debacle? The actual battle was under an hour long, but it has been studied and re-interpreted constantly for good reasons. Many of the assumptions that come easily turn out to be misguided. Many of the portrayals, especially in popular, romantic literature are simply wrong. Judgments of earlier historians turn out to be heavily biased and neglectful of important evidence. One recent study, Jacqueline Riding's densely packed 502-page *Jacobites: A New History of the '45 Rebellion* (2016), promises to correct errors and fill in gaps. She has taken on a Herculean task that can only be evoked here, not repeated. In some ways Culloden can be seen as a larger edition of the Battle of the Little Big Horn in United States history. So much has been said, and there is so much to say, that every party, every political agenda can find evidence to make its own case for interpretation.

The failures of the 1715 and 1719 actions by no means ended Jacobitism, but what survived was transformed from a mere advocacy of the Stuart dynasty. The family, apart from individual members, retained some positive implications. Indeed, the Stuarts *had* been restored once in 1660, prying open the vise grip of puritanism and reopening the theaters. In England and Wales many Tories looked fondly on the Stuarts because they had favored mercantilist strategies protecting British trade, whereas the Whig government that grew stronger in Parliament under the Hanovers promoted land commitments seen as expensive. In Scotland mention the Jacobite cause became a magnet for anti-Treaty or anti-Union sentiment that grew bilious as the century wore on.

As late as February 1742, there was a Parliamentary crisis when long-serving Whig Prime Minister Robert Walpole was forced to resign by an alliance of defectors from his own party with some from the opposition. Angry Tories led by the Duke of Beaufort asked for French help in restoring Prince James Francis Edward to the throne. His name came readily to mind, and it was not absurd to assert his kingship.

Rather than being tarred by an association with Catholicism or rural populations, Jacobitism—or a non-committal defense of it—came to be considered chic among young urban sophisticates. The Hanovers were bores, and the Stuarts comparatively glamorous.

Concurrently Jacobitism was losing its religious identification, effectively decoupling from Roman Catholicism. James Francis Edward was not especially pious, declining the example of his observant but philandering father, but still residing in the Papal States. His son young Prince Charles Edward, was so little taken with the faith of his fathers that he jettisoned it for Protestantism four years after Culloden. The Rising of 1745–1746 was anything but a "Popish Plot," which its enemies claimed, a charge that might have been made against the Earl of Mar's 1715 rebellion. France's and Spain's antagonism to England was not rooted in religious faith. And once the rebellion was underway not only did many Catholic clans, such as the Clanranald MacDonalds and the MacNeills of Barra, refuse to support it, but the majority of Episcopalians were joined by a few Calvinists and even a Quaker.

After having lain dormant for two decades, the spark of Jacobitism could be fanned into flames in the 1740s for a number of reasons. Usually ignored is that the United Kingdom was distracted by an engagement in an extensive war on the Continent fought in different, disconnected theaters. The War of the Austrian Succession, 1740–1748, pitted the Bourbon dynasty against the Habsburg, with Britain allied with Maria Theresa and the Austrian cause. This was an invitation for France to favor any mischief that could be visited upon the island nation across the Channel.

Enter the Young Pretender. Prince Charles Edward has suffered such damning bad commentary over the centuries, including being vilified by Voltaire in *Candide* (1759), that we do well to remember that he was initially thought charismatic and has always had a handful of defenders. He was tall, handsome, effervescent and winning, speaking four languages: Italian, French, Spanish and English. Both his fair skin and commanding demeanor were thought inherited from the Sobieski dynasty. While it is commonly thought that his father, James, the Old Pretender, was too ancient and doddering to enter the fray again, that was not true. In 1745 he was fifty-seven, the same age as retired general George Washington when he became president of the United States in 1789, but he unmistakably enjoyed the safety and comfort of being a "royal" guest. Instead, it was a youngster who took his comfort for granted and itched for a kingdom that might have been his. Witnessing the French and Spanish siege of Gaeta south of Rome when he was but thirteen gave Charles

Edward the sensation that battle was not something to be dreaded. James Francis Edward implicitly egged his son on by naming him Prince Regent in December 1743. Charles's personal agenda, as most of his followers were unaware, was not simply to sweep away the Treaty of 1707 but to restore the divine right of kings as promoted by James I & VI and the taste for absolutism that lingered in the dynasty through his deposed grandfather.

When the French government gave renewed support to his father, James Francis Edward, in 1744, Prince Charles took this as an invitation. He traveled to France with the sole purpose of commanding a French army that he would lead in an invasion of England. Though twenty-three and inexperienced, not to mention untrained, he received a hearing. In the Treaty of Fontainebleau, the year before, 1743, Louis XV and his uncle, Philip V of Spain, agreed to cooperate against Britain, which could include an attempted restoration of the Stuarts. In February 1744, even before Charles arrived in Paris, the French had assembled 12,000 troops and transports, planning to invade the Thames Estuary. As with earlier attempts to invade Britain, such as the Spanish in 1719, the idea was to strike in winter when the winds would be unfavorable for the defenders. Once again, this backfired, and storms worked in Britain's defense. Louis cancelled the invasion in March but declared war on the United Kingdom.

Charles negotiated with the French Crown beginning in August 1744. He suggested an alternative plan: a landing in Scotland. As Charles did not realize, the notion had been proposed six years earlier by a noble named John Gordon of Glenbucket and dismissed by both the French and James Francis Edward himself. Further, Scottish informants in communication with the French were against such a plan unless there was substantial French support. Initially there was none. But after a French victory at Fontenoy in April 1745, authorities were willing to allow Charles two unpromising transport ships, the 16-gun privateer *Du Teillay* (in some accounts *Dutillet*) and an elderly 64-gun warship, *Elizabeth,* captured from the British in 1704. The warship also came with weapons and 100 volunteers from the French army's Irish Brigade. The French offered no financial support. To cover his expenses Charles pawned the Sobieski rubies, literally the family jewels.

(All dates cited are New Style or Gregorian, the calendar the United Kingdom did not adopt until 1752. At the moment, all dates were recorded Old Style, eleven days behind France, the Netherlands, etc.)

The force left Saint-Nazaire for the Western Isles in early July and ran into trouble quickly. Keeping a close eye on the coast, the *HMS Lion* engaged the *Elizabeth* in a four-hour battle, forcing Charles's larger resource to return to port with the weapons and the 100 fighting men. The *Du Teillay* forged on, landing at the small island of Eriskay between South Uist and Barra, July 23, 1745. He immediately declared that he was home and had no intention of returning to the place from where he came. Legend has it that when he first stepped on the land of his forefathers, he pulled from his pocket a handkerchief containing seeds of a flower called pink sea bindweed. He thought them Scottish, but they were not in fact native to the island. They thrived, nonetheless, and the (supposed) spot is today called *Coilleag a' Phrionnsa*: the Prince's Cockleshell Strand.

As Charles had done no reconnaissance of the kingdom he sought to conquer, he had no concept of how weak Scotland was in summer 1745. The abolition of the Scottish Privy Council in 1708 removed the only effective government executive as well as the main agency for intelligence gathering. Sir John Cope, the government commander in Scotland, had at his disposal a mere 3000 troops for the entire nation. Further, Clan Campbell, expected to be a bulwark of Honoverian hegemony in the western Highlands, had been weakened by fighting on the Duke of Argyll's estate seven years earlier.

In opposition in July, Charles had little to offer. He had 4000 French gold coins, a few weapons, and seven companions, known in Jacobite lore as the "Seven Men of Moidart," after a rugged region of the west coast, the first section of the mainland they touched. They were Scots, English and Irish.

1. The Marquis of Tullibardine, William Murray, brother of the chief strategist Lord George Murray, who will be properly introduced later. *2.* John William O'Sullivan, an Irish professional soldier in French service. After the failure of the rebellion Scottish Jacobites blamed him for "tactical ineptitude," probably unfairly. *3.* Sir Thomas Sheridan, an Anglo-Irish courtier, veteran of 1715. *4.* Sir John MacDonald/MacDonnell, French subject of Irish origin, from the Antrim branch of the Clan Donald. Led the cavalry at Culloden and often clashed with Lord George Murray. *5.* Francis Strickland, English Roman Catholic, veteran of the 1715 rising, reviled by James Francis Edward. *6.* The Rev. George Kelly, non-juring Protestant Irish clergyman, always a Jacobite, with a colorful career: escaped from the Tower of London. Managed Jacobite propaganda efforts and drafted the Manifesto issued early in the campaign. *7.* Aeneas MacDonald, Scottish banker who spent his adult life in Paris, aided Charles with finances; he survived to write a memoir of the rebellion.

All the seven were either well born or educated and about a generation older than Prince Charles; Thomas Sheridan may have been thirty-six years older. The number seven is always cited in Jacobite lore, perhaps to underscore the horrendous odds against the cause, but scrupulous recent scholarship identifies servants and others of lower social rank.

The invaders came ashore on the mainland and made their way to Glenfinnan at the northern tip of Loch Shiel, significantly adjacent to and evoking the defeat of 1719 at Glen Shiel. By August 19 the Jacobite marchers numbered 700, according to O'Sullivan's estimate. This called for the unfurling of the Royal Standard and the formal launch of the campaign to restore the Stuarts. Glenfinnan launched *Bliadhna na Thearlaic*: Charles's year. Defeat at Culloden would actually be 270 days off. The site is also a prime instance of gorgeous *echt*-Highland scenery, fifteen miles west of what is now the tourist center of Fort William. Mass tourism was two centuries off, but Charles and his team chose the ideal location for future Jacobite pilgrimage, even when disfigured with a lamentably designed nineteenth-century monument.

Even with most of his men on foot, Charles moved quickly. Fort William, then a garrison, was soon occupied. Then onward to the east on the new roads built by General Wade, put to a purpose he never intended. More sympathizers were joining en route as Charles had predicted. When the force reached Perth on September 4 the most significant of volunteers stepped forward, a local aristocrat named Lord George

Murray. Active in the 1715 and 1719 risings, for which he was pardoned, Murray was unquestionably dedicated to the cause. Well-informed about Highland military customs, his skills clearly outranked O'Sullivan's, and so he was made commander over him. This understandably rankled the Irishman, who was reduced to second-guessing. Murray's reputation among historians is divided. For all his training and experience, he was quick-tempered and unwilling to confer or to take advice. Murray immediately set about re-organizing the forces before an assault on the capital. Murray's many successes were gained despite the liability of the headstrong, groundless confidence of the Prince.

Defense against the rebels could not have been weaker. The senior government officer in Scotland, Lord President Duncan Forbes, was aware of the Prince's landing by August 9, before Glenfinnan. Forbes sought to keep clan leaders loyal to the Hanovers and succeeded with some but failed with Cameron of Lochiel and Lord Lovat, who joined the Jacobites. The word in English would be "Out" for supporters of the Prince as it has remained colloquially ever since. Meanwhile, luckless Sir John Cope, the government commander, was realizing that the majority of his 3000 men were untrained recruits. Further, he lacked information on Jacobite intentions, but the Prince was well-informed, now, about him. Lord George Murray had been one of Cope's advisors before defecting.

Prince Charles entered Edinburgh unopposed on September 17. James Francis Edward was proclaimed king of Scotland the next day with Charles as his regent. Edinburgh Castle itself remained in government hands. On September 21 the determined Jacobites intercepted and scattered Cope's army in less than twenty minutes at the Battle of Prestonpans, near Edinburgh. This was a cannon shot, less than a month after Glenfinnan, that would alarm all of Europe, starting with England. George II's son, the Duke of Cumberland, William Augustus (for whom Fort Augustus on Loch Ness was named), was called home from Flanders, along with 12,000 troops.

As regent, Charles issued two declarations in early October to consolidate his support in Scotland. The first was to dissolve the "pretend Union" between Scotland and England, and the second was to reject the 1701 Act of Settlement forbidding anyone but a Protestant from being monarch. He also requested that the *Caledonian Mercury* publish the Parliamentary enquiry into the Glencoe Massacre, fanning resentment against the oppression of the "Glorious Revolution." His proposal of the repeal of the 1725 malt tax was enthusiastically received, even when not enacted. Although Edinburgh was never Jacobite, merchants reported with relief that the occupiers were not predatory, the memory of brutal treatment from Alasdair Mac Colla and Montrose during the Civil War still in living memory.

Numbers in the Jacobite army ebbed and flowed, and what kind of men were in it changed from month to month. A popular notion, fostered by John Prebble's *Culloden* (1961) and Peter Watkins' quasi-documentary film adaptation (1964), is that the majority were unwilling tenants and subtenants, unlettered and Gaelic-speaking. The drama this promotes is irresistible, a ragtag semi-feudal troop in tartans and kilts pitted against the best-trained forces in Europe. Some men, called by historians "levies," from certain clans were forced into service and were indeed casualties in battle. Such combatants would have comprised most of the 700 accompanying the Prince at Glenfinnan, and are depicted on the left side of David Morier's oft-reprinted painting of Culloden fighters. As more volunteers joined the rebellion they became an ever-smaller fraction, never more than 49 percent of the total. Jacqueline Riding (2018) punctures the Highland romantic legend further by quoting contemporary sources that describe them as the most poorly equipped ("swords without guns, and guns without swords") of the Jacobites. All were infantry, never cavalry. So poorly dressed that many Highland fighting men were reduced to stealing shoes from passers-by to continue the march. At apparent turning points in the campaign, more often victories than defeats, they were prone to desert and walk home. Nonetheless, Highlanders in tartan were indeed in the front lines at Culloden. Of all the volunteers, however, they were the most likely to make the Stuart restoration a prime goal, especially with the promise of religious toleration and the relaxation or end of anti–Catholic laws put in place by the vanished Scottish Parliament.

There were in all eleven units of mostly Highland fighters, "out" for the Prince in 1745. They were: *1.* Cameron of Lochiel's Regiment. *2.* The Atholl Brigade composed of mostly Gaelic Perthshire men, nominally under the command of William Murray, the Marquis of Tullibardine. *3.* The Appin Regiment, tenants of the Stewarts. *4.* MacDonell of Keppoch's Regiment, incorporating some MacDonalds of Glencoe. *5.* MacKinnon's Regiment, mostly Skye tenants. *6.* MacDonald of Clanranald's Regiment, joining after initially refusing. *7.* MacDonell of Glengarry's Regiment, one of the largest. *8.* Lady Mackintosh's Regiment, raised by Lady Anne Farquharson-Macintosh in Inverness but consisting mostly of Clan Chattan men pressed into service. *9.* Lord Lovat's Regiment, raised from tenants of Simon Fraser, 11th Lord Lovat. *10.* Maclachlan's Regiment, raised mostly in Argyll by the Jacobite commissary general. *11.* Chisholm's Battalion, the smallest unit, made up of eight tenants from Strathglass. Other members of the Chisholm family fought on the government/Hanoverian side.

As mentioned before, ending the Union was more important to other volunteers, such as the nearly 500 Lowland gentlemen, some of them Presbyterians unused to making common cause with the barbaric Gaels, who formed the cavalry. Almost a quarter, at times, of the Jacobite army came from the non–Gaelic northeast, and perhaps a fifth came from Perthshire, which straddles the Highland line. Volunteers came from nearly all regions of Scotland except the highly Calvinist southwest and the largest cities, like Edinburgh, as cited above. Forces also came from outside Scotland, such as the 200 men led by Francis Towneley of the Manchester Regiment, and the perhaps 350 led by John Drummond of the *Royal-Ecossais*, made up of Scotsmen who had been in French service. Among the most important were the Irish Picquets, drawn from Irish units in the French army. A picquet (U.S. picket) is a small mobile force that characteristically advances before the larger main body of an army. Although they have receded from popular memory, the Irish Picquets suffered heavy casualties at Culloden and were critical in allowing Prince Charles's escape.

There was no single uniform for the army, and only the Highlanders wore tartans, kilts and distinctive bonnets. Many wore uniforms of previous service. As many as possible, however, wore the white cockade, *An Cnota Bàn*, first seen in the 1715. It is fixed in popular memory from citation in Robert Louis Stevenson's *Kidnapped* (1886), and a catchy late eighteenth-century melody still performed by traditional musicians.

The Jacobite occupation of Edinburgh stretched into October with the expectation that an English army would soon be dispatched to suppress the rebellion. French support had never materialized, despite promises from nobles who spoke without authority. Charles argued that the sure way, at last, to bring in French cooperation was to invade England. The Jacobite Council reluctantly agreed, accepting Charles's promise of French alliance, which he did not have grounds to make. Strategist Lord George Murray rejected the route of previous Scottish invasions at Berwick-upon-Tweed and opted instead for a route through Carlisle in the northwest, an area that had been Jacobite in 1715. Shortly after the last Jacobites left Edinburgh on November 4, the government forces under General Handasyde reoccupied it on November 14. The door back to central Scotland was now closed.

Progress into England was almost as giddy as the bolt from Glenfinnan to Edinburgh. Despite official disdain for the rebels, commentators at the time were impressed that the Jacobite army, 8000 strong, moved so rapidly. Part of the reason for this is that the army brought along so little baggage, often only what a soldier had on his back. What little artillery there was came from captured government weapons, some easily acquired. Carlisle, for example, had been a fortress before 1707 and was now fallen into disrepair. As it was perceived to face no immediate threat before now, it was defended only by eighty elderly veterans. The one fit body of government troops in northern England was at Newcastle in the east, under the command, ironically, of General Wade, the Highland road builder. His attempt to attack the Jacobites was thwarted by an unseasonable snowstorm in mid–November.

Entering Preston, a sizeable but Jacobite town, on November 26 was a heady experience and also invited volunteers from nearby Manchester. The government had still put up little resistance by the time the Jacobites reached Derby on December 4. London was within striking distance, but many in the Council began to feel the invasion had gone far enough. Despite the Scottish and Irish veterans from French service, the necessary French support kept being pulled back. Was there an invasion force forming in Dunkirk? Or was the port simply busy as usual? Worse, Prince Charles admitted he had not heard from English Jacobites since leaving France and had lied in making that claim. Most of the Council believed that the Hanoverian regime would not simply collapse if the Jacobites entered London. More reliable were the reports that General Wade had overcome the snows of the north, and the Duke of Cumberland was returning from Flanders with intentions of cutting off the Jacobite path of return home. He landed in Carlisle December 22. The Council was now overwhelmingly in favor of retreat.

Always quick on their feet, the Jacobites sped north, evading government patrols, crossing back into Scotland on December 20. The next goal was to take Stirling Castle, long a focus for different military campaigns. With the aid of French artillery, a token that was actually delivered, the Jacobites put Stirling under siege for two months. This was a task for a trained army. The Jacobites lacked the discipline and logistical agility to pull off such an enterprise. During the two-month interlude, on January 17, a portion of the rebel army defeated a government relief force at nearby Falkirk Muir, at which time many levies thought victory was occasion to walk home. It was to be the last Jacobite victory, and the siege was lifted February 1. The main force retreated north and west to Inverness, a government-supporting town in a Jacobite region. Not all Scotsmen welcomed them. A militia formed in Glasgow to harass the retreating army and later joined the red coats (*saighdearan dearg*) at Culloden. The Duke of Cumberland's force advanced north but to the east, reaching Aberdeen on February 27, a bit over 100 miles from Inverness. Both sides elected to halt operations until the weather improved.

The forces resisting the Jacobites can go under different names. Following the practice of different historians, we have called them the "government" up until Culloden. Given that those troops were now led by the Duke of Cumberland, Prince William August, third and youngest son and most-favored child of George II, many commentators favor "Hanoverian" at the battle and after; that is also the dynasty the Jacobites sought to displace. Either is preferable to calling them the "English," despite the red-coated uniforms. When Cumberland returned from the Continent, he brought with him five thousand Hessian mercenaries, who were not deployed at Culloden. On April 16 eleven of the sixteen infantry battalions on the field were indeed English, but three were Lowland Scots, one Highland, and one was Irish.

Cumberland was in his twenties, four months younger than Prince Charles. April 15 was his twenty-fifth birthday. In the many popular accounts of Culloden, the corpulent Duke is often portrayed as a cartoonish adversary of the matinee idol handsome Prince. Needless to say, his high military rank was a perquisite of being in the royal family. Unlike Prince Charles, however, Cumberland had undergone extensive training and was known as a no-nonsense officer uninterested in pomp. In the five-week interval between his arrival in Aberdeen and the march to meet the Jacobites, Cumberland put his men through constant exercises, while Prince Charles and his men relaxed in the winter respite.

Cumberland's move to the west signaled that the two armies would face each other. The weather had improved sufficiently by April 8 that the Hanoverians broke camp, reaching Culloden by the 11th, joined by six further battalions of infantry and two cavalry regiments. Then they easily dispatched 2000 Jacobites supposedly defending the Spey River, and moved on to Nairn, the last town on the route before Inverness.

The Jacobites named the proposed field of battle, chosen by John O'Sullivan, one of the original Seven of Moidart. We always refer to the site as Culloden Moor (Gaelic *Cùl Lodain, Cùil Lodair*: back of the small pond) because it is adjacent to Culloden House, a landmark with Jacobite associations, five miles (8 km) east of Inverness. Locally the relatively flat, boggy open pasture was known as Drumossie Moor. Chief strategist Lord George Murray, objecting to Drumossie, favored a nearby location that historians feel would have been even more disadvantageous.

Lord George's next suggestion was calamitous. The Jacobites' easy victory at Prestonpans had begun with a sneak attack on government forces the night before the expected battle. Knowing that the Hanoverians would be celebrating the Duke's birthday on the 15th in Nairn, Murray proposed a night march of thousands to go there. Not only was Nairn twelve miles (19 km) distant, but the force started after dark to avoid being seen by the Royal Navy and along unfamiliar roads. Realizing his folly too late, Murray canceled the raid, and attempted to return a third of his men, whom he misled on the way back to base. Two-thirds did not hear the cease command, continued forward and were lost, missing the battle. Others straggled back, exhausted, and either slept through the battle or went onto the Moor barely able to stand.

April in the Highlands does not mean spring weather. On the morning of the 16th the Moor was treated to a snow storm followed by sleet. Undeterred, Cumberland and the Hanoverians struck camp by 5:00 a.m., marching across country, to be sighted by the Jacobites by 10:00. The armies faced off, taking assigned positions—some squabbled over—on the Moor. The Jacobites would be facing into the snow and sleet. At approximately 1:00 p.m. the Jacobite artillery fired the first shot, and shortly afterwards the Prince gave the order to advance. The battle lasted about an hour, during which the Jacobite cannon were of little use.

As the battle has been contended over by interested parties for more than two and a half centuries, and more recently regularly re-enacted in costume, a modern author whose attention is really on the over-riding issue of Highland identity approaches the subject with trepidation. Interest in the battle remains intense and divided. Further, even after so much time, new information keeps coming to light. Since 2001, the site has undergone extensive geophysical, topographic and metal detector surveys in addition to archaeological surveys. We now know that the Jacobites used more muskets than pistols, and of French manufacture with slightly smaller caliber. On the other hand, we are not sure of the total Jacobite numbers or how many were deployed on the Moor, except that both numbers should be considerably smaller than the Earl of Mar's mostly Roman Catholic army of the 1715 uprising.

The total Jacobite force may have been as high as 8,000 with perhaps 5,000 on the Moor. Many fighters slept through muster, and all were poorly rested. Their pay, when it was delivered, was five pennies a day. We can be sure from government records of prisoners, that many would never have been placed in a modern army at all: 13.6 percent were 50 years old and upwards, while a further 8 percent were 16 and 17 years old. Quite a few were physically and mentally unfit, deaf mutes, the partially blind, and men hobbling along on club feet. Despite cliched popular portrayals, no more than a fifth carried swords. Refuting the notion that Highlanders are taller than Lowlanders, their average height was 5' 4".

Hanoverian numbers were certainly higher. Jacqueline Riding (2018) asserts that while the official count was 6,410 infantry with 787 cavalry on the Moor, other sources give Cumberland's full command as considerably higher. These men had received £6 if they enlisted by the previous September and £4 after that. They were better fed, warmly clothed in clean red coats with good shoes and despite a long march over rough country in previous weeks, better rested. The battle may well have been one-sided, but the contest was not simply a matter of numbers. By employing the feared Highland Charge, the Jacobites overwhelmed the Hanoverians a few times and did inflict some casualties. The Duke of Cumberland, however, had schooled himself on dealing with Charge on the advice of earlier government strategists. He instructed his men never to thrust a bayonet forward at an oncoming soldier, but instead go either to the right or left, everyone on the battle line in unison. Hanoverian artillery remained viable and effective during the entire encounter, but Riding feels it may have been less lethal than previously thought.

At the end of the day there were between 1200 and 1500 Jacobite dead, with 500 taken prisoner. As quite a number of Jacobites slept through the battle and expected to take up arms the next day, it took a while for the Hanoverians to round up all the combatants. It would be weeks before the number of captured reached 3471, to be disposed of in different ways, described below. The Hanoverians suffered 50 dead, 259 wounded.

The contrasting accounts of the battle of Prince Charles and the Duke of Cumberland during the battle illustrate the difficulties faced by a commentator dealing with the behaviors of different regiments and clans whose descendants remain deeply invested in the narrative of the campaign and its commemoration.

Prince Charles unquestionably left the field. Jacobite partisans like to cite the report that he vowed during the time of the battle, "They won't take me alive." In contrast, detractors of Charles quote the disaffected ally, Lord David Elcho, as crying out, "There you go for a damned cowardly Italian." Only the quote does not always have the same phrasing. In Peter Watkins's quasi-documentary *Culloden* (1964), the line has become, "Run, you cowardly Italian." Perhaps because it became a document of 1960s anti-war sentiment, the Watkins film was seen by millions and was broadcast continually on television, and is still shown to students. It portrays Charles as a clueless popinjay, an empty coat without charm. Anecdotally, when I speak to people of Culloden, I find that many can quote the jeer instantly, possibly as an implicit summation of Charles's character. Other sources tell us, however, that the notion of Lord Elcho's jeering Charles, in whatever phrasing, is an invention of Sir Walter Scott.

The Duke of Cumberland has been suggested as the nominal antecedent of the red flower known as "sweet William," but he was also denounced as "The Butcher" in his lifetime. The persistence of the flower folk etymology, even when refuted by *OED* citations of the name two centuries earlier, implies that many people were relieved to be rid of the Jacobites. Stories of Cumberland's brutality on the battlefield can withstand scrutiny. When a nearby officer refused to dispatch a wounded rebel lying before them and was dismissed, Cumberland is reported to have asked a second of lower rank to perform. Even if this narrative was contrived, Cumberland's treatment of the families of the defeated could justify the sobriquet. Such a libel did not trouble Londoners relieved at having avoided invasion. The following spring, April 1, 1747, less than a year after the battle, George Frideric Handel premiered the nominally Biblical oratorio *Judas Maccabeus* to celebrate the Hanoverian victory. It contains the refrain, "Hail the conquering hero, come."

Prince Charles escaped from Culloden and was on the run for five months. Erik Linklater traced all the places he passed by in Inverness, Ross-shire, Skye, up and down the Outer Hebrides and included pictures of what they looked like in the mid-twentieth century in a highly popular account, *The Prince in the Heather* (1965). Perhaps the best-known commemoration of the Prince's evasion of capture comes in Sir Harold Edwin Boulton's words to the traditional melody known either as "The Skye Boat Song" or "Over the Sea to Skye." The music was collected in the 1840s and the words added in the 1870s and so do not fit neatly into historical narrative. Charles did not escape the mainland to Skye but rather returned to it from Benbecula in the Outer Hebrides. It has been performed so often by such diverse artists as Paul Robeson and Rod Stewart, the Highland equivalent of the Irish "Danny Boy," that audiences forget its political rooting.

The Crown placed a £30,000 reward for assistance in his capture, but there was never a hint of betrayal. Of the many Highlanders who aided the Prince in his flight, by far the most celebrated is Flora MacDonald, a tacksman's daughter from the Isle of Skye, who disguised him as a servant named Betty Burke, in order to escape Skye for the mainland. Thus, the reverse of "The Skye Boat" song, confusing some listeners. For this relatively minor service, Flora MacDonald has become one of the best-known women in all of Highland history, honored in the naming of dozens of women, including a leading Canadian politician (1926–2015). On September 19 he reached Borrodale on Loch nan Uamh in Arisaig for deliverance the next day aboard the frigate *L'Heureux*, never to return, despite songs and poems yearning for him. A bronze marker commemorates the spot. And as late as the third decade of the twenty-first century, the faithful gathered in September to remember the departure.

With Charles departed from the scene, the remaining Jacobites spent a few days in disarray. Lowland regiments headed south but rallied at Ruthven Barracks before receiving orders to disperse. In one of the most intriguing digressions from the central narrative, Highland units were reported to have received £35,000 in gold from French sources and resolved to fight on. This ended in mid–May when Cumberland marched north to Fort Augustus on Loch Ness to stop them. The French gold was never found, and true believers were still searching for it in the third decade of the twenty-first century. A favored location for treasure-hunters is the western reach of Loch Arkaig.

What to do with so many prisoners became a challenge to military management. When Cumberland reached Inverness, he freed all the inmates that Charles's forces had imprisoned and stashed some of the Jacobites there. Other were taken to different sites in England to stand trial for high treason. Some were held in hulks on the Thames or in Tilbury Fort. In general, common soldiers fared better than ranking officers: 120 foot-soldiers were executed, about a third of them deserters from the Hanoverian army. Among the others, only one in twenty was put on trial, after drawing lots. Of those most had their sentences commuted to penal transportation to the colonies, the fate of 936. Two hundred twenty-two were banished, to find their fates outside Britain. Three hundred eighty-two were exchanged for prisoners of war held by France. What happened to 648 is not known, perhaps "lost." Any combatants who had previously been in French service were repatriated.

Officers designated "rebel lords" were dealt with harshly and in public, with hangings in Carlisle, York and at Tower Hill in London. The grisliest deaths were delivered to rebel lords at Kennington Common in London, where the hanged were also disemboweled. Jacobite lords Kilmarnock, Balerino and Lovat were beheaded; Lovat, named Simon Fraser, was the last person so executed in Britain, April 1747. Vengeance persisted. Archibald Cameron, betrayed by one of his own clansmen on his clandestine return, was hanged June 7, 1753. Severity was the Duke of Cumberland's policy, ensuring his sobriquet "butcher." A degree of backlash against him included condemnation by Robert Walpole and a rash of scurrilous caricatures.

One of Cumberland's wishes was unfulfilled. He would have preferred that rebels be extirpated from Scotland and transported to the colonies. Such a notion, however, once raised, did not disappear from elite discourse.

When Cumberland's proclamation that all rebel weapons should be surrendered, and only one clan complied, he felt free to wreak retribution on the countryside. Any rebel found armed would be killed on sight. Stately homes of chiefs and chieftains were ransacked and fired. Achnacarry, Cameron of Lochiel's residence, perhaps the finest of any Jacobite, was leveled (later to be rebuilt with the same name). The impoverished abodes of tenants and subtenants offered little to a punishing vandal, but they had tools and utensils to be looted and cattle to be driven off. While Cumberland's men were on the way to burn Keppoch House of the MacDonells, they hanged three Highlanders with the rope of a salmon net. Hamlets that had been occupied for centuries were burned, never to be reoccupied. And so it was in presumed Jacobite areas like Morar, Moidart and Arisaig. Islands could not escape; Eigg was laid waste. Raasay, which had sheltered Prince Charles for two nights, was "pacified" with determined zeal. Civilians, if they were thought to have aided the rebellion, were not spared. At Strathbogie, Elizabeth Williams was convicted of trying to "inveigle" men into French service. For this she was seated in a cart facing backward toward her accomplice, Peter McConachy who was stripped to the waist and tied in the rear of the cart and flogged as she watched. The charge against him was tied around his neck, and then the cart was trundled through the town.

Parliamentary measures would change the Highlands more than the depredations of vengeful troops. Their purpose was not nominally punitive but rather to integrate Scotland and the Highlands more thoroughly into the rest of Britain. One was to oblige all members of the Episcopal clergy to give oaths of allegiance to the reigning Hanover dynasty. Non-juring clergy had been even more significant to the Jacobite clause than had been Catholics. More transformative was the Heritable Jurisdictions (Scotland) Act of 1746, ending the right of landowners to govern justice on their estates through barony courts. This meant that the old clan system was effectively dismantled. All clan chiefs, regardless of their affiliation, could no longer call their men to arms, even though only a portion of the clans had risen in support of the Stuart cause. This would choke off the possibility of another rising in the Gàidhealtachd. Lords who had remained loyal to the Hanoverians were greatly compensated for the loss of their traditional powers. The Duke of Argyll, of Clan Campbell, received £21,000. In contrast, lords and clan chiefs supporting the Jacobites, when not executed, were stripped of their estates, which were then sold, the profits devoted to trade and agriculture.

The third ruling was intended to humiliate, as the previously cited Michael Hechter (1977) and Silke Stroh (2017) point out in the asserting that the Highlands were a suppressed colony within Britain. This was the Act of Proscription, in two parts, that chronologically preceded the end of Heritable Jurisdictions, coming into force August 1, 1746. The first half was the Disarming Art, which ordered the removal—confiscation—of every weapon in a Highland household, a society where hunting for game had long been esteemed. On his tour of the Highlands with James Boswell, Samuel Johnson found this law especially noxious as it left the natives "despoiled of defence." Even more resented was the second half, the Dress Act. "Highland Dress" was now banned, except in the army, where the Black Watch Regiment had supported the Hanovers. To be specific, now forbidden were: the plaid (garment), the kilt as well as the philibeg or little kilt, trowse, shoulder belts or any part whatever of what peculiarly belongs to the Highland garb. Not only all tartan but also "parti-coloured plaid or stuff to be used for great coats or upper coats."

By the time the law was repealed in 1782, kilts and tartans were no longer quotidian Highland wear. The long-term consequences of the Dress Act were just the opposite of what the legislators intended. Banning gave tartan a recognition and prestige it had lacked before. What had been the culture of a reputedly "barbaric" underclass would eventually come to represent the nation. Tartan, gracelessly called "plaid" by non–Scots, achieved royal recognition when the Hanoverian George IV wore a tartan kilt on a visit to Edinburgh in 1822. A few decades later the Highlands-loving Victoria would help make it a world fashion.

The repression of Jacobitism and everything Highland apparently fostered clandestine codes. The West Highland Museum of Fort William displays an almost nonsensical blotch of painting that reveals Prince Charles's portrait when seen in a cylindrical mirror. This was composed when possession of a conventional likeness might have meant jail time. Holding a wee dram for a toast over a glass of water was thought to salute the "king over the water." As I bear a name perceived as Jacobite I have been presented with this little ritual, an invitation to camaraderie rather than a trivia quiz, on several occasions in the Highlands. A degree of sentimental Jacobitism has spread widely in Scottish popular culture. The song of sweet farewell, a rival of "Auld Lang Syne," titled "Will Ye No' Come Back Again," is sometimes called "Charlie's Song" and includes some verses about Prince Charles, inviting the listener to think it has been handed down from the time when tartan was banned. The author of "Will Ye No' Come Back Again" and "Charlie Is My Darling," Cornelia Oliphant, Lady Nairne (1766–1845), flourished after Prince Charles had died.

Misery and Emigration

Many readers will approach the period of more than seven decades from Culloden Moor in 1746 to George's IV's arrival in Edinburgh wearing a kilt in 1822 with the sense that they already know the guideposts. Many common people of those days were suffering and were departing from Highland glens and islands. These expectations derive from two widely read works published centuries apart.

The first, of course, is the one-volume edition combining Samuel Johnson's *A Journey to the Western Islands of Scotland* (1775) and James Boswell's *A Journal of a Tour to the Hebrides* (1785), which report on their walk through the Gàidhealtachd in 1773. It is the one book of Highland history most readers are likely to have heard of if not read, a delight that rewards return visits. As scrutiny of the late eighteenth century, however, many other travelers came both before and after. Johnson and Boswell might have been shocked and dismayed from time to time, but other observers were far harsher and more detailed.

The second is John Prebble's *The Highland Clearances* (1963), the biggest-selling book on Scottish history from the last two centuries. His most derisive detractor, Michael Fry (2005), allows that he single-handedly created contemporary Highland historiography. Prebble, born in England and raised in Canada, spent part of his adult career in British television. He wrote scripts for the prestige drama series known on U.S. Public Television as *Masterpiece Theatre*. His prose is blessed with an infectious lucidity rarely found in academic writing. It is through his influence that the word "clearance" is now familiar to all of us, as the issue of tenants being forced from their land had been marginalized by historians. It was a word favored by the nineteenth-century polemicist Alexander Mackenzie, an important source for Prebble. *The Highland Clearances*, along with a string of others, including *Culloden* (1961)—also the basis for Peter Watkins's film (1964)—and *Glencoe* (1966), focused attention on the actual as opposed to romantic Highlands as nothing had before. T.M. Devine (2018) reports that before Prebble there was scant interest in the Highlands in Scottish academia, but after him they became a prominent subject in the discipline with additional course offerings and in dissertations written.

Many historians, meanwhile, gnash their teeth at Prebble's egregious errors in dating as well as his vilification of landlords to the displacement of other issues in emigration. Through Prebble's influence, in learned discourse if not actual reading of his text, many people look to the forced eviction of helpless peasants from thatched cottages and their replacement by herds of Cheviot sheep as the *only* reason the Gaels emigrated. James Symonds (1999) remarked that many people of Highland descent in the Atlantic provinces of Canada assume that all their ancestors were "impoverished sheep thieves" hounded out by unforgiving landlords. Certainly, such things happened, but more in the nineteenth century than the eighteenth and for economic reasons rather than retribution for Jacobitism. Eric Richards' book, also titled *The Highland Clearances* (year 2000) corrects Prebble's errors and places his argument beside others, such as the financial distress of the landlords, but does not refute the central argument. Authoritative historian T.M. Devine, especially in *The Scottish Clearances* (2018), reminds us that the departure of surplus rural population was European-wide in the same period, especially in the Lowlands. Only Thatcherite journalist and gadfly Michael Fry, *Wild Scots* (2005), refutes and actually ridicules Prebble. He sees traditional Highland culture and economy as stifling if not imprisoning, and says that the Clearances, painful in the short run, should be seen as liberating, allowing former crofters to participate in the free market economy. Fry, a graduate of Oxford and Hamburg, is also the author of *Adam Smith's Legacy* (1992) and *How the Scots Made America* (2005). His *Wild Scots* was issued by a major publisher, John Murray, and is available in paperback, but appears to have had little traction against Prebble.

Through these decades run four narrative strands, to be discussed below, and above them stands an imposing reality that was shrugged off at the time and is not always recognized today. The four are (a) the magnitude of human suffering that increased in the glens and islands after Culloden; (b) the widespread motivation to leave the Gàidhealtachd and all that was familiar and fought for by seeking strange and often unwelcoming refuge elsewhere; (c) the unexpected launch of a fascination with all things Highland at the publication of James Macpherson's *The Poems of Ossian* (1760–1763); and (d) the concurrent denigration of all things Highland that preceded Macpherson and persisted after his decline. The first two of these will occupy our attention in the next section of this chapter and can be spoken of together. The outrages of the Clearances are to be considered, but the depths of poverty and want are profitable discussion with any effort to emigrate. *Ossian* and its effects will occupy the first part of the next chapter. And the increased berating of Highlanders, not just as "wild Scots" but as a socially inferior people incapable of playing a significant role in modern life, is a subject threaded through the remainder of this chapter and much of the sixth, two chapters away.

What is overlooked, almost the proverbial elephant in the room, is the counter-intuitive rise in population. As T.M. Devine writes, "A rapid and sustained increase in the population is the critical and dominating factor in the social history in the century after c. 1750, though often ignored in popular accounts of clearance." Along with the chronic poverty, noted by Edmund Burt, there were two severe crop failures in which livestock also perished. The first was 1770–1771, and the second and far worse was 1782–1783. Hollow-eyed, starving waifs came down from the hills and crowded the roads. The government and charity of private individuals prevented the multitudes from dying of starvation. Still, more babies were born, and the total population continued its steady climb. The peak in Highland population, as cited in the first chapter, was found in the census of 1841, a statistic with more baleful resonance in this context.

Individuals who learned Scots could always migrate to the Lowlands, and after 1603 with English they could move south of the border. Mass Highland emigration to British colonies in America appears to have begun about 1760. A pamphlet published in 1784 stated that between the years of 1763 and 1775, before the American Revolution, more than 20,000 Highlanders left their homes to settle on the other side of the Atlantic. According to the old *Statistical Account of North Uist,* between 1771 and 1775, a space of only four years, several thousand emigrated from the Western Highlands and Islands alone. These made no dent in the total number of residents.

Devine gives no specific reasons for Highland fertility, but the population was rising all over Scotland. Between 1750 and 1821 the total numbers went from 1.265 million to two million, an increase of two-thirds in sixty-five years. We cannot measure a cause and effect relative to numbers, but the introduction of small pox inoculation in the 1760s appears to have contributed. As mentioned earlier, the introduction of the potato also allowed a small farm plot to sustain more people. The first potato plot, a small garden, not a complete farm field, was near Stirling in 1739 and more soon appeared in nearby areas. The larger more nourishing potato cultivated in Ireland was introduced to South Uist in 1743 and soon was planted on adjacent islands, not reaching universal cultivation for decades. In the short run this was an advantage, but within a century would become an invitation to catastrophe.

The Lowlands with their many fertile fields, modern agriculture, and in time nascent industries, were prepared to absorb a growing population, turning people into assets for economic growth. In the Highlands, whereas we said that less than 9 percent of the land can be cultivated (today), there were no occupations to fill.

Although there would be dozens of accounts of physical distress in Highland populations in coming years, one of the oldest surviving documents from post–Culloden times emphasizes the emotional climate. *A Full and Particular Description of the Highlands* (1752) by a John Campbell laments that so many common people suffered from the unkindness of their superiors at home and should want to take up service in foreign lands. This often meant fighting in armies pitted against their fellow-countrymen. He does not mention what must have been continual verbal retribution against Jacobitism, nor does he cite the American colonies. Although Campbell does not acknowledge the episode, many subtenants and servants would remember the tawdry prefiguration of the Clearances known as *lang nan daoine* (the treachery of the people) from 1739. MacLeod of Dunvegan and MacDonald of Sleat, lords from the Isle of Skye, rounded up more than one hundred of their own people from Skye and Harris (pulled from their beds in oral tradition) and packed them off for America. The lords had accepted payment for the tenants to be indentured servants, condemning them to the same social stratum as slaves rather than as freemen. Their ship wrecked off Donaghadee, Ireland, from where they escaped.

Lamentably, many in Scotland's intellectual elite were not friends of the Highland poor. Edinburgh in the mid-eighteenth century was relishing the Scottish Enlightenment, in which Scottish thinkers such as Adam Smith and David Hume were some of the most admired minds in the west. But a perversion of enlightenment thinking in Scotland also produced what we would later call scientific racism. This was already the era of the anonymous and scurrilous *History of the feuds and conflicts among the Northern Parts of Scotland …* (1764), cited earlier, arguing with louche documentation that the Gaels were irredeemably violent and warlike. New were works like John Pinkerton's *A Dissertation on the Origin and Progress of the Scythians or Goths* (1787) arguing that the Celts were the inferior aborigines of Europe, already driven to impoverished corners of the continent and destined to be displaced by the superior Anglo-Saxon Teuton people. The Highland Celts, as he saw it, were a "weak and dispirited people" as evidenced by the "wholly melancholic" nature of their poetry and song. Such views were restated in Pinkerton's two-volume history of Scotland (1789), which Hugh Trever-Roper described as being filled with "pathological hatred." James Hunter (2005) quotes a contemporary Lowland newspaper repeating such views to a wider audience: "Ethnologically the Celtic race is an inferior one and, attempt to disguise it as we may, there is … no getting rid of the great cosmical fact that it is destined to give way … before the higher capabilities of the Anglo-Saxon." As shall see in the next chapter, everything "Celtic" was to gain a romantic patina in the early nineteenth century, but race-haters were not deterred. Notorious Edinburgh–based doctor Robert Knox wrote in his *The Races of Men* (1850), "The Celtic race must be forced from this soil." "Notorious" is not a gratuitous slur for Dr. Knox, as he is also remembered for his association with the scandalous Burke and Hare "body snatcher" murders in Edinburgh, 1828. His *Races of Men* was published in Philadelphia because scientific racism had gained a wide readership in the United States.

Of the many writers giving first-hand accounts of the Highlands, excluding Johnson and Boswell, Thomas Pennant (1726–1798), is the most thorough and the most-often cited. An offspring of the Welsh gentry, Pennant was one of Britain's leading men of science, or "naturalists" as they were then called, and an antiquarian. Among his other works are *British Zoology* and *A History of Quadrupeds*. His two works, *A Tour in Scotland, 1769* (1771) and *Voyage to the Hebrides* (1774), were big sellers and well-received. Johnson and Boswell praise them and acknowledge their influence. If Pennant has fewer readers today it may be because his view of the Highlands is far bleaker. His overall view is a portrayal of famine and wretchedness from beginning to end.

As he saw it, what little agriculture there was rarely produced enough grain to supply the inhabitants, and in many places "the isles annually experience a temporary famine." The Isle of Islay has some of the most arable land in the Hebrides, and was once the seat of the storied Lord of the Isles. Even here, he observed, residents had to import a thousand pounds worth of meal annually to ward off starvation. For Pennant the normal state of the Western Highlands appears to be one bordering on famine, or what would have been considered so in a less wretched country; periodically many will die from absolute want of food.

Pennant never appears to be comparing notes with Burt from four decades earlier, but when he is put side by side with the earlier writer, his view is more damning. "The houses of the common people in these parts are shocking to humanity, formed of loose stones, and covered with clods, which they call *devots*, or with heath, broom or branches of fir: they look, at a distance, like so many black mole-hills. The inhabitants live very poorly, on oatmeal, barley-cakes, and potatoes; their drink whisky, sweetened with honey."

Unlike other observers, Pennant separates his feelings toward the sexes, often being more sympathetic to women's lot. "The men are thin, but strong; idle and lazy, except when employed in the chace [sic], or anything that looks like amusement; are content with their hard fare, and will not exert themselves farther than to get what they deem necessaries." (cf. John Lane Buchanan, below, on their near bondage of some subtenants.) "The women are more industrious, spin their own husbands' cloaths [sic], and get money by knitting stockings, the great trade of the country. The common women are in general most remarkably plain, and soon acquire an old look, and by being much exposed to the weather without hats, such a grin, and contraction of the muscles, as heightens greatly their natural hardness of features."

Agreeing with modern historians, Pennant saw the end of barter and the introduction of cash as detrimental to the poor, in part because it measured how little they had as well as making them subject to prices set elsewhere. "Tenants pay their rent generally in this country in money, except when they pay in poultry, which is done to promote the breed, as the gentry are so remote from any market. ... Labour is here very cheap, the usual pay being fifty shillings a year, and two pecks of oatmeal a week."

Cattle were the only article upon the farm which affords money to the tenant, and payment to the tenant and payment to the landlord. Any luxury that came to the Highlands was from an exchange of what livestock could be sent to the south or to Ireland. Transport from the islands was obviously difficult, but Pennant reported that 4000 animals crossed the Kyle Rhea annually, from Skye and the other islands.

Pennant's discourse is not all written in the same tone. He was delighted, for example, to discover the delicious Arctic char.

As for Skye, today a magnet for tourists and one of the most-loved tracts of land in the Gàidhealtachd, Pennant wrote: "The poor are left to Providence's care; they prowl like other animals along the shores to pick up limpets and other shellfish, the casual repasts of hundreds during the year in these unhappy islands. Hundreds thus annually drag through the season a wretched life; and numbers, unknown, in all parts of the Western Highlands, fall beneath the pressure, some of hunger, more of the putrid fever, the epidemic of the coasts, originating from unwholesome food, the dire effects of necessity." Johnson and Boswell, having read Pennant shortly afterwards, visited the same areas and took a different tone. They felt that the Highlanders did not realize their wretched condition and did not appear to be unhappy.

Visiting Skye about ten years later, the missionary John Lane Buchanan (published 1793) was even more severe than Pennant, as well as giving a more damning portrait of the tacksmen than we have seen elsewhere. He argued that poverty allowed the tacksmen to treat the subtenants, although "descended by ancient and honourable families," as beasts of burden and in some respects as slaves attached to the soil, bound into forced labor. Among the most degrading of that labor was the harvesting of kelp offshore. It was not the kind of seaweed that is thrown up on a beach by the tide but is instead a vegetation that must be searched out.

Kelp, producing an alkaline extract from seaweed, grows abundantly in Scottish waters and had been exploited for local purposes starting in the previous century. The first commercial development was in the Orkneys, 1722, and had spread to the Western Isles by the 1760s. At first it was used in the making of soap and glass and the bleaching of linen, but its price shot up with increasing use of gunpower and armaments in warfare. The ingredients in Spanish barilla were superior for manufacture, but an import tax on that commodity, as well as salt, raised the demand for kelp. That would peak when Napoleon's invasion of the Iberian Peninsula shut off barilla entirely.

Twenty tons of wet seaweed were needed to produce one ton of calcined ashes; the process was highly labor intensive during the season when the weed was either raked in or washed by the sea onto the shore where it was dried and burned. The harvesting, from which both Pennant and Buchanan recoil, required the kelper to wade into the sea at low tide and, with the help of saw-toothed sickles, harvest ton after ton of the weed. The purest form of the weed was found near underwater rocks, requiring the laborer to be partially submerged in often icy water.

As the kelp trade was profitable for a period, the kelpers might have made a decent living if they were paid employees. Some populations shifted to the shore while the demand for kelpers' labor expanded, often to the neglect of farmsteads. As tenants and subtenants, however, the kelpers worked as part of their arrangement with the tacksman or lord. The profits flowed upward. In one special sore point with Highland nationalists of the twentieth century, kelping profits paid for the once grand Armadale Castle, now in ruins, residence of Lord MacDonald of Sleat. The grounds are also home to the Clan Donald Museum.

Kelping came to a crashing halt at the end of the Napoleonic wars, and Spanish barilla, chemically superior, returned to the market without a tariff. As many as 20,000 kelpers found themselves unemployed, and their farm plots too neglected to revive. Emigration was the only solution.

We shall see in the next chapter that some travelers were attracted to the Highlands by the strangeness and what is now recognized as the dramatic beauty of the landscape. Conspicuously, the romantic poets William Wordsworth and John Keats made a pilgrimage to the Gàidhealtachd. Coeval with them a poet of humble background, the "Ettrick Shepherd," James Hogg (1770–1835), was repelled by what he found. In his *Highland Tours* (1804), with an introduction by Sir Walter Scott, Hogg assumed the voice of a letter-writer, arguing against building the Caledonian Canal, asking how the lot of the poor could be improved by canal traffic. "My dear sir, you are not aware of what prodigious numbers of poor people drag on a wretched existence in those distant glens and islands, who are scarcely privileged, as we would think, with one of the comforts or conveniences of life. As for instance, what do you think of upwards of ten thousand people subsisting on the dreary and distant island of Lewis, which with the exception of one very inconsiderable part, is one extensive morass; while the whole rent of the island, although lately advanced, does not reach to a thousand pounds. This is but one instance of many, and it may well be supposed, nay, I am *certain*, that there are many thousands in these counties, that cannot be *worsed* unless they are starving to death."

The Ettrick Shepherd was entertained in the elegant Cameron residence of Achnacarry, rebuilt from its post–Jacobite destruction, when his comments directly influenced several of your author's ancestors. Hogg thought the sublime view of Loch Arkaig was ruined by landless and scruffy peasants who had taken up temporary residence there. Heeding the poet's complaint, Cameron had the families of squatters driven off, packed on to ships, and sent to Nova Scotia. It was thus that my mother's family, the Gille Íosa arrived in Pictou, Nova Scotia, on the *Dove* of Aberdeen in 1802, where their name became Gillis. Technically, this was not a clearance because the Gillises were not tenants, nor were they replaced with sheep.

Some observers were more empathetic with the common people, but most were appalled. The French visitors in 1786, Francois and Alexandre de La Rochefoucauld (heirs of the aphorist) and Maximilian Lazowski, were more defensive of Highland women, finding them attractive and "well-built." Alexandre (quoted 2001), however, also supplied a shocker, a description of women spreading manure with their bare hands, even loading a cart by hand instead of using a shovel.

Summarizing all the doleful reports, T.M. Devine used modern phrasing: to outsiders the Highlands looked like "a great rural slum."

In the midst of this squalid disorder, decision-makers within the British government realized that the mass of underutilized and desperate young men could be put to good use. New initiatives could exploit the fabled Highland military ardor, whose repute was undiminished by the defeat at Culloden. The Army, if not in red coats, put them in their own uniforms. As mentioned above, the famed Black Watch Regiment was formed to protect General Wade's road-building and preceded the 1745–1746 rebellion. In anticipation of fighting on the Continent, the government mobilized six regiments of the line between 1753 and 1763, including Fraser's and Montgomery's Highlanders. When the Seven Years' War expanded into North America as the French and Indian War, a further ten regiments came forward, for a total of 12,000 men, equal to the Jacobite forces under the Earl of Mar in 1715 and many more than had followed Prince Charles Edward in 1745–1746. The Secretary of War in 1751, Lord Barrington, strongly favored Highland recruitment, vigorously endorsed by William Pitt when he became prime minister in 1756. Paradoxically, as the clans were dwindling into extinction, the Highlands reached a level of militarization they had not known since the Civil War and Inverlochy.

Highland units were soon to distinguish themselves as fighting men, but also prompting the stinging and best-remembered slur of centuries, a dusky Koh-i-noor of disdain. The British had put Quebec under siege and confronted French regular troops on the Plains of Abraham, September 1759, when General James Wolfe, a Hanoverian veteran of Culloden, learned that Highland regiments would be sent into battle. He allowed that they might prove an asset for his efforts because "they are hardy, intrepid, accustomed to a rough country, and no great mischief if they fall." The phrase has had a life of its own and is sometimes attributed to other occasions. Alastair MacLeod employed it as the title of his admired novel, *No Great Mischief* (1999), depicting the Highland diaspora in Canada.

Rising from the Seven Years' War to Napoleonic times, the numbers according to the most recent estimates reached from 37,000 to 48,000 in regular, fencible and volunteer units from a Highland population ranging from 250,000 to 300,000. Unlike other colonial recruitments, Highland soldiers were not confined to the lower ranks, and as many as twenty-one achieved the ranks of lieutenant-general or major-general, with forty-eight becoming lieutenant-colonel. Achieving glory for the Crown, some soldiers never returned. At the prestige retirement home, the Chelsea Pensioners in London, veterans with Highland backgrounds became the largest proportion.

Small remissions might be sent home, but the men were missed. As T.M. Devine reports (2018), the parish of Gairloch in Wester Ross had been nearly stripped of all its menfolk by 1799. A survey for the Lord Lieutenant of Ross-shire arrived at the conclusion that hardly any adult males could be found there, and for the most part the population consisted mainly of children, women and old men because of the sheer scale of recruitment. In the extensive territories of the Earl of Breadalbane, straddling Argyllshire and Perthshire, as many as three farm tenancies out of every five had experienced some form of recruitment by the 1790s. Many Highland troops trained at Fort George at Ardersier, east of Inverness, a formidable bastion built to control the clans after Culloden. Now it was "the great drill square," where Highland levies prepared for war overseas.

Jacobite militarism was, in effect, co-opted for imperial service. The success of this maneuver served as a model for the exploitation of subjugated people with martial traditions, such as the Gurkhas, Sikhs and Pathans of Nepal and India. Unexpectedly, the thinly populated Highlands turned out to be exhaustible, not only because of over-recruitment, but also from death in battle, disease, discharges, natural attrition, and increasingly, emigration. Even regiments with the foremost esprit and reputations were obliged to extend the territorial range of their recruitment. Records show that at least a third of the famed Black Watch Regiment fighting at Waterloo were drawn from other parts of Scotland and even England. Later, some regiments shed the kilts and sporrans as more non–Gaels were enlisted. After the potato famine of the 1840s some regiments would have only a minority of men from the glens and islands.

The acclaim and esteem accorded Highland regiments contributed to a limited elevation of Highland Gaels when juxtaposed with the other Gaels on the western shore of the Irish sea. So argues Robert Clyde in *From Rebel to Hero: The Image of the Highlander, 1745–1830* (1995). Whereas the Irish had always been troublesome with extensive rural violence, such as the White Boys, etc., the wild Scots, possibly more noisome, had marched across England and threatened London. It is no less than surprising that in such a short time after Culloden, the former rebels were to be regimented in distinctive and coherent units, officered by clan gentlemen, permitted to wear the once-proscribed Highland dress, and encouraged to develop their own ethnic esprit de corps. Such privileges were not accorded to the Irish, who vastly outnumbered Highlanders in the military, or to battalions drawn from the Scottish Lowlands.

We have little evidence, e.g., letters or works of fiction, to measure changing public attitudes, but it seems evident Britons in positions of power no longer considered a Stuart counter-revolution to be viable, and the Highlands, unlike Ireland, were no longer an internal threat. A bellwether of this shift can be seen in the later career of Flora MacDonald, Prince Charles's fabled Isle of Skye rescuer. Once settled in North Carolina, she and her family supported George III against the American rebels in 1776. All the same, Highland troops were not allowed to linger long in Scotland after training but were rapidly dispatched overseas.

It would an error to say that Highland units were "favored," because they were often given more dangerous assignments than other units, and they suffered high casualties. But they soon came to be publicly acknowledged as crack troops of imperial warfare, winning praise for their bravery in North America, the West Indies and India, enduring long and arduous tours of duty in forbidding climes over several years. T.M. Devine opines that they may have been willing to stay abroad rather than return to rack-renting and clearances at home. Whether their valorization helped prepare the way for the coming romanticism of the Highlands is impossible to say. At the very least, their marching in different British cities made a sign of brightly colored tartans familiar to more people, now dissociated with rebellion.

As we have said, the term "clearance" was not in widespread use when tenants and subtenants were forced off their property by landlords. It was not until the polemicist Alexander Mackenzie in the 1870s that its current definition was established. That and the explosive semantic implications of the word make it treacherous to say just when the practice began. The "clearance" as we understand the word now resembles what was called "enclosure" for a century before, in both Scotland and England, in which subsistence pick-and-shovel farmers were driven off land to make room for more profitable grazing cattle.

Post-Prebble historians tend to see the clearances coming in two phases: one from perhaps 1760 until c. 1815, and the second from 1815 to 1820 until 1850. Prebble spent more time on the second period, in which human suffering was more outrageous and villains crueler and more unrepentant.

Both clearances ran concurrently with other forms of emigration as well as enlistment in the British Army. A cleared family was not criminal and suffered no stigma other than poverty and a lack of spoken English. Those suffering eviction from a clearance might mix easily with other Highlanders in industrial Scotland, especially Glasgow, or in England. The one exception would be Nova Scotia, where the surging numbers of poor, unskilled immigrants were so unwelcome as briefly to have invited a poll tax to enter the province. Recent historiography has argued that not all Highlanders in the Maritime Provinces were the destitute, expelled from Scotland.

The first phase of clearances came as a part of the Scottish agricultural revolution that struck the Highlands after it had come to the Lowlands and England. The engine behind this was the growing demand for food by industrial cities. In the Highlands the effect was more traumatic because, as few tenants knew, landlords were facing crippling debt and the likely prospect of bankruptcy. The runrig system, which always discouraged improvement, became unsustainable. When insecure landlords put properties out for bid, this gravely damaged those middlemen, the tacksmen, often driving them from the *baile* or township. This did not happen simultaneously across the map, as the missionary Buchanan observed of still-exploitive tacksmen in Skye, cited above. Displaced and departing tacksmen do not fit tightly into the template for clearance victim, but they suffered a fate imposed upon them. The tacksmen might have a few pennies in their pockets, but the tenants and subtenants, often dependent on tacksmen's managerial skills, were left helpless. The Society in Scotland for the Propagating of Christian Knowledge reported that after 1772 no fewer than sixteen vessels filled with emigrants had sailed from the western parts of the counties of Inverness and Ross alone containing perhaps 6,400 souls, carrying with them at least £38,000 sterling. This contrasts with the want of second-phase clearance victims, who would be fortunate to have one penny in pocket.

The SSPCK, by its very inception, was hostile to Roman Catholicism and Catholic leaders. Roman Catholic lords and tacksmen considered it their obligation to guide tenants and subtenants to new lands. John MacDonald of Glenaladale, from the cadet branch of the great MacDonalds of Clanranald, was stubbornly Catholic and Jacobite in convictions. Grieving for the passing of the tacksman's old position and honor, he said his friends (or tenants) were facing ruin unless "some other path was struck out for them." That path was to settle on the land he bought on the island of St. John in the unexpectedly temperate Gulf of St. Lawrence in 1772. The island was recently taken from the French and later renamed Prince Edward Island, now called Canada's "Garden Province." MacDonald sought out oppressed people, tacksmen and tenants, from South Uist, Moidart, and Arisaig, and they sailed aboard the *Alexander*. He wrote before he departed from Greenock that emigration would demolish Highland lords, who deserved such a fate. This was one year before the Highland influx to nearby Nova Scotia, a much longer story. The island was not to become a Catholic colony, however, as the first settlers were followed by the anti-papist Calvinists Glenaladale hoped to escape, causing some of the first wave to cross the Northumberland Strait to friendlier environs in Nova Scotia. Glenaladale's benevolence together with the relatively benign ending makes this unlike other clearance stories, but Prebble includes it early in his history.

Highland settlement of Nova Scotia began in September of the following year with the landing of the fabled *Hector* at Pictou, across the Northumberland Strait from Prince Edward Island. Tens of thousands would follow to a province which bore the Latin name for "New Scotland" before they arrived. Sectarian differences were foremost on immigrants' minds, with Protestants going to the right of the harbor or west, Pictou County, and Catholics to the left or east, Antigonish County.

Anti-Catholicism down to post–Culloden times was not simply an extension of doctrinal disputes seen in John Knox's excoriation of Mary Queen of Scots or the *Confession of Faith* (1560) that called for the execution of Jesuits and other priests. Instead, the Glorious Revolution of 1688, removing James II from the throne, led to a spate of anti–Catholic laws in 1704 and 1708 ostensibly on political grounds. Because William and Mary had guaranteed Protestant succession, Roman Catholics were, on the face of it, potential threats to the government, if not specifically called Jacobite. There is some question how thoroughly these laws were enforced, but they stayed on the books until 1778; in Scotland, where they enjoyed support from the Calvinist majority, they remained in force until 1793.

From the 1560s Catholics could be neither governors, schoolmasters, guardians nor factors, and a fine of a thousand merks (then the approximate price of 140 horses) was imposed upon those who employed them in such capacities. Heavy fines were imposed on noblemen or others sending their sons abroad to be educated in foreign seminaries. Catholics were incapable of acquiring real property, either by purchase or by deed of gift made in their favor, or in trust on their behalf, such deeds being by law absolutely null and void. They were also incapable, after the age of fifteen, of inheriting estates. A Protestant turning Catholic forfeited his whole inheritance to his nearest Protestant heir. After Culloden Moor, Gaeldom's first bishop, Hugh MacDonald of Morar, was hunted incessantly for ten years. When captured and tried he was banished from the realm and threatened with death should he ever return. For thirty years most Catholic districts of the Highlands did not have a priest or lay worker.

Antagonism toward Catholics remained a conspicuous feature of Scottish life long after the repeal of anti–Catholic laws in 1793, more in the Lowlands than Highlands. T.M. Devine and others address the issue in *Scotland's Shame? Bigotry and Sectarianism in Modern Scotland* (year 2000). In the third decade of the twenty-first century, press reports give a much higher incidence of hate crimes against Catholics than for Jews or Muslims.

Lord Colin MacDonald of Boisdale was born a Roman Catholic and converted to the Church of Scotland. With the zeal of a convert often lacking in cradle Calvinists, he determined that his mostly Catholic tenants of the island of South Uist should change their ways to his. He began with strong-arm tactics, like forcing children to eat meat during the fasting of Lent. Catholics suffering under such treatment referred to it as *creideamh a' bhata-bhuidhe* (yellow-stick belief), which sources solemnly explain is a phrase deriving from Boisdale's actual punishing yellow cane. The *OED* confirms that "yellow stick" does indeed denote the harassment of Catholic tenants by Protestant lairds in the Hebrides, but records it as early as 1715 on the Isle of Rùm. It is attached here to MacDonald because he used it to introduce another form of clearance. In 1771, thirty-six families, out of 300 tenant families, did not have their leases renewed. Eleven of those emigrated the next year with financial assistance from the Roman Catholic Church.

Before the American War of Independence, substantial groups of Gaelic-speaking settlers left for colonies north and south. Devine estimates their number to be above 10,000, which alarmed some landlords. They were usually led by displaced tacksmen and families, such as that of Flora MacDonald, cited above, who settled in the Cape Fear region of North Carolina. Although she returned to Skye, other Scottish people, Lowland and Highland, preferred North Carolina, and it today has a more visible Scottish presence than any other U.S. State; not to say that Scottish names, Highland games, kiltie bands, etc., are not found everywhere. Substantial Gaelic-speaking, pre–Revolutionary settlements were also found in Georgia and New York, focusing on the Mohawk Valley and the eastern Adirondacks. As with Flora MacDonald, the other Gaelic settlements (not all Jacobite) tended to support the Hanoverian George III against the American rebels, 1776–1783. This prompted some of the New York Gaels, most of them Clan Donald, to become Loyalist refugees across the border in Canada, settling in some of the Anglophone territories west of Quebec, or "Upstream" on the Saint Lawrence, soon to be called Upper Canada (in Gaelic *Canada Ard*), later Ontario. They called the county Glengarry.

News of this Gael-friendly, unoccupied Glengarry territory reached the lairds of the MacDonells of Glengarry, rulers of mostly Catholic tenants. The decision-maker in this instance was a woman, Marjorie, wife of weak-willed Duncan MacDonell. History has given her a pejorative nickname, *Marsailidh Bhinneach* (Light-headed Marjorie), but she was as decisive and heedless as a Dickens villain. Disappointed that the rents returned by their impoverished tenants did not compare with her plush dowry, in 1782 she accepted the offer of wily entrepreneurs named Thomas Gillespie and Henry Gibson to take a lease on a sheep walk along remote Loch Quoich. This required the removal of the five hundred people living there. They were packed off three years later to Canada aboard a ship appropriately named *Macdonald*: nineteen tacksmen and families in cabins and 520 subtenants and cottars, all below decks. More evicted tenants and subtenants followed later in 1785, 1787, and 1788, until there were more people living in the Canadian Glengarry than the one in Inverness. Unlike the smaller settlements in the now American former colonies of North Carolina, Georgia, and New York, Glengarry of Upper Canada tended to resist assimilation, and the Highland presence is manifest there today. Canada, of course, was part of the British Empire, later Commonwealth, where ties to the British Isles were viable. But the concentration of large numbers in Nova Scotia and Manitoba kept spoken Gaelic as a living language for generations.

Until this point, we have made scant mention of sheep because the preferred livestock in the pre–Culloden Highlands had been cattle, the prizes in so much rustling, called "lifting," and one of the few commodities to earn income through export to the Lowlands and England. The model of tenants-out/sheep-in trumpeted by John Prebble did not become widespread until late in the eighteenth century, and not dominant until after the Napoleonic wars in the nineteenth. Before the sheep-for-tenant transaction could begin there had to be changes in both livestock and the market for new products.

There had always been sheep in the Highlands before 1760 as there had been in other parts of Europe. Christians understood shepherd-and-flock metaphors from first-hand experience. They were as small as dogs, and although their flesh could be eaten it was found to be so meager it was consigned to the very poor. The hair taken from their backs, not so lush as to be called fleece, could be woven into thin garments that did not provide the insulation we now expect of woolen fabric. One farmer sensed that sturdier breeds were available elsewhere in Britain and might thrive in northern climes. Sir John Lockhart-Ross of Balnagown returned from twenty-five years at sea in 1762 to inherit a broad swath of mountain, loch and glen running from the Dornoch Firth to the western coast, much of it barren hillsides. Starting a new career at age forty-two, he sought to improve the estate that visibly fell short of its potential. He drained and reclaimed marshy valleys. He did not renew leases of those tenants nominally resident on the estate but living in the Lowlands, and raised the rate for the immobile subtenants. These were measures any landlord might have taken. Then he noticed herds of black-faced Linton sheep in Perthshire in the east, straddling the Highland-Lowland line. Not only could they survive killing northern winters, but they produced three times as much meat as cattle raised on the same amount of land.

To assure his own command in transforming his land, Sir John took over the management of one of the farms on his property and invited Lowlander Thomas Geddes to bring him herds of black-faced Lintons. Ross-shire, although north of Inverness, turned out to enjoy milder winters, with less snow, as well as warmer summers, than some southern counties. Former subtenants who had been removed from upland pasture accurately perceived the new flocks as a threat to their way of life. They shot the sheep at night, drove them into the lochs, and terrorized the shepherds. Their verbal threats and curses, made in incomprehensible Gaelic, went unheeded. And to tenants' baleful regret, Sir John and Thomas had a good year, with bountiful yields of both wool and mutton, and set their sights higher.

Vibrant as the Lintons had been, Sir John and Thomas Geddes were looking for stronger, hardier breeds, less subject to disease, that would give a greater yield of mutton and wool in proportion to the high acreage of pasture needed. Several candidates suggested themselves—Merino, Leicester and Forest, who made appearances—but far and away the most formidable was the Cheviot or True Mountain or Long Hill breed, developed over centuries in the Cheviot Hills of the north of

England and already present elsewhere in Scotland. The beast comes with short, thick wool, suitable for a coarse twill weave to make warm blankets and coats. Pleasing to herd owners and distressing for threatened subtenants, the Cheviot makes an almost cinematic entrance. It could have been assembled by a genetic designer, with little variation in size or weight. An early agronomist, John Naismyth, observed that they look so much like one another that any two ewes taken from hundreds might be assumed to be twin sisters. Naismyth further praised the Cheviot stature and temperament: "mild and pleasant." An early Cheviot farmer named Robson called the breed "the four-footed clansman of the Highlands." Actual clansmen, subtenants and Gaelic-speaking, were wary. They dubbed the Cheviot *Na Caoraich Mòra*: the Big Sheep.

Unmistakably, the introduction of the Cheviot at Balnagown was a prefiguration of things to come, but Sir John Lockhart-Ross and Thomas Geddes did not reach the craven heartlessness of the most infamous clearances in the nineteenth century. Their thought was that the new herds could co-exist with the subtenants, many of whom raised black cattle instead of growing crops. As more and more landowners turned to the Cheviot the two economies clashed. Pastoralism was most efficient when practiced on a large scale, which raised insurmountable barriers for most tenants. The size of the flocks also called for more managerial expertise. Trained graziers from outside the Highlands could guarantee proprietors regular and rising incomes in a single payment, whereas the hard-pressed tenants, a larger number on the whole, were much less reliable and their payments might arrive in dribbles, subject to the weather and the volatility of the market.

Simultaneously, the price of wool began to rise faster than other commodities from the 1780s and following, driven by new enterprises in industrial Britain. Thus, a landowner in the Highland was faced with choosing between the meager rents of tenants who had been there for centuries, sometimes bearing his name, and two commodities, wool and mutton, for which there was an ever-increasing demand.

Two landowners to take Lockhart-Ross's lead lay to the north of his property, both great champions of what was then known as "Improvement," a word of conflicting implications. How it came to be dreaded is discussed in Chapter 6. Taken by itself, of course, it sounds like something desirable, to be sought. In the misery of the late eighteenth century, it quickly came to be associated with discomfort and the destruction of the old order. One was Sir John Sinclair of Ulbster in non–Gaelic Caithness. In the naïve hope of benefiting his people, he brought the Cheviot north to an estate that he and his family had purchased from the Earl of Caithness. He had no intention of driving away the current inhabitants of his estate, Langwell. Instead, he recommended that small tenants should be continued in their possession, persuaded to join their holdings and capital, to hire a common herdsman, and purchase a small flock of perhaps 300 sheep. Part of their rents could be taken in kind, in wool and mutton. Such a generous and altruistic plan could rightly be called "enlightened," but had to compete in a grasping, even rapacious economy. Small-scale evictions of tenants, not so massive as to be called "clearances," were beginning.

John Sinclair of Ulbster became, in time, the Chairman of the British Wool Society, a voice of wide influence. Aside from his benign recommendations, his listeners were impressed that thin soil of the Highland landscape could indeed support the greater carcass weight and wool-carrying capacity of the mighty Cheviot, and that the beast flourished farther north than conventional wisdom had assumed.

Perhaps even more influential than Sinclair was Sir George Mackenzie of Coul, a man of science given to reckless experiment, and a proficient author, as in his *General View of the Agriculture of the Counties of Ross and Cromarty*, published later. Prebble calls it "A Landlord's View." Despite having a Gaelic name himself, Sir George thought Highlanders should happily accept their future as servants of servants. He also recommended ways of increasing the yield of the flocks of the field.

What Sir John Lockhart-Ross, Sir John Sinclair and Sir George Mackenzie all had in common is that while landowners, they were not clan chiefs, the kind of person more often the holder of titles to large tracts of land. Their tenants might be honorifically "their people," but they made no presumption of a familial tie to the landlord.

All this led to the climactic moment of the first phase of the Clearances in 1792, after the streaming of Cheviots in the Highlands became an inundation, a torrent. It was known in Gaelic as *Bliadhna nan Caorach*: the Year of the Sheep, or in English as the "Ross-shire Sheep Riot." The force that brought diffuse anger and tension was the Cameron brothers, Captain Allan and Alexander, who were leasing (i.e., were intruders from Lochaber) the property of Kildermorie from Hector Munro, 8th Laird of Novar, a colonel in the Black Watch. The property was free of human inhabitants. Without license to do so, the Camerons had in May taken the cattle of the people of the neighboring village of Strathrusdale in Easter Ross, ostensibly to make way for the entering flocks of sheep. For weeks there was no reaction. At a wedding in Strathrusdale, July 27, the local celebrants without political affiliations devised a plot to drive away the sheep farmers as well as all the sheep.

Together with reinforcements from nearby Ardross, they marched to Kildermorie where they found their cattle guarded by the Camerons. The men of Strathrusdale were led by Alexander Wallace, known as "Big Wallace," who threatened the Camerons, also sizeable men but outnumbered. One of the Camerons produced a loaded gun and a foot-long dirk, but Big Wallace grappled with and disarmed him, allowing the Strathrusdale men to recover their cattle. A week after the wedding-day confrontation, about 400 men from surrounding districts were driving 6000 sheep from the counties of Ross and Sutherland south toward Beauly, Inverness-shire. Affronted farmers and herders of the area had lifted the sheep from Kildermorie and were driving them back to whence they came. None of the rustlers injured the sheep nor did they filch one for themselves. It was, however, an act of open rebellion. Sheriff Donald MacLeod of Inverness found his constabulary not up to the task of rounding up so many men and beasts and so called up the Black Watch (42nd) Regiment. He also condemned the rustlers as a violent and seditious mob. The majority of the sheep-lifters scattered and returned to their crofts.

Punishments for rustling were meted out only to six standing in for many. All were venerated as the clearances increased in outrage and viciousness, their names repeatedly invoked.

Two, Hugh Breck MacKenzie and John Aird, were ordered to be transported for seven years "beyond seas to such places as His majesty shall appoint," and that if they returned to Britain within those seven years that they would be sentenced to death. Inequity was the rule. Malcolm Ross was held in prison for one month and fined £50, while William Cunningham was imprisoned for three years. Donald Munro and Alexander MacKay received the severest punishments: banishment from Scotland for the rest of their lives.

That the *Bliadhna nan Caorach,* Year of the Sheep, should burn in popular memory was also a cautionary tale. The "riot" itself was a minor, seemingly parochial event, without casualties, but it persisted as a sore point for good reason. In the coming contest between man and sheep, it was clear which would be the expected victor. A few enlightened members of the gentry would speak on behalf of the threatened crofters, but to little effect. The constabulary, law, courts and army were not on their side.

5

Romantic Amelioration

Imposture in Badenoch

Seventeen sixty looked to be yet another dolorous year in the impoverished Highlands. The humiliating Act of Proscription, banning Highland dress—even tartan—was very much in effect. A year earlier General James Wolfe lightly shrugged off the suggestion that Gaelic-speaking troops under his command might be slaughtered in the assault on French-held Quebec. In two years, a new landlord, Sir John Lockhart-Ross, would introduce black-faced Linton sheep to his estate at Balnagown, changing—changing utterly in the long run—the life of Highland tenants and subtenants. In 1760 a twenty-four-year-old schoolmaster from Badenoch, without position, wealth or connections, published a pamphlet of fifteen prose pieces, all laments for fallen warriors, translated, he claimed, from the Scottish Gaelic. He titled the pamphlet *Fragments of Ancient Poetry collected in the Highlands of Scotland, and Translated from the Galic [sic] or Erse Language*. His name was James Macpherson. Almost immediately extracts were published in *The Scots Magazine* and *The Gentleman's Magazine*, reaching a wide swath of the best-educated people in the kingdom. Though they were titled "Fragments," each item was complete, a cautionary contradiction that no one heeded. The sensational reception given to fairly modest works would change utterly how Scotsmen, and eventually all Europeans and Americans, looked upon the Scottish Highlands.

Macpherson gained an important admirer, Hugh Blair, who would become a benefactor and life-long champion; some have suggested he might have been a silent collaborator. Blair was a professor of rhetoric at the University, connected to the city's leading intellectuals, such as David Hume, and unusual for an academic had a flowing purse. Blair raised a subscription to sponsor Macpherson's further researching of materials in western Inverness-shire, including the isles of Skye, North Uist, South Uist, and Benbecula. There he alleged to have found new manuscripts, which he would translate with assistance of recognized authorities. Later he made an expedition to the Isle of Mull, uncovering yet more manuscripts. In 1761 he announced the discovery of an epic in six books on the third-century hero Fingal. Later that year he published *Fingal, an Ancient Epic Poem in Six Books, together with Several Other Poems composed by Ossian, Son of Fingal, translated from the Gaelic Language*. The name Ossian had not appeared in *Fragments*. The following year he followed with another epic, *Temora*. The three were reissued in one volume as *The Works of Ossian* 1765; this was later known as *The Poems of Ossian*, although all are in prose.

Given that news traveled more slowly in the mid-eighteenth century, *Ossian* was an ostentatious hit. Skepticism about *Ossian*'s authenticity regarding something so unexpected was immediate, but who had the authority to evaluate the "original" materials, which, incidentally, were not at hand? Quite a few people could read Scottish Gaelic, but there was no such thing as a Scottish Gaelic scholar. In Ireland, however, despite efforts to repress the native language, there were quite a few men deeply informed about the island's literary history. Chief among them was Charles O'Conor the Elder (1710–1791), from an esteemed learned family and well-connected to counterparts in Scotland and England. He found errors in chronology, the formation of Gaelic names and the fundamental implausibility of Macpherson's claims, which the author could not substantiate.

From a reading of Macpherson's texts, the critical reaction was divided. Thomas Gray (1716–1771), known for "Elegy Written in a Country Church Yard" and the most popular English poet of the day, was rapturous. His welcome to *Ossian* was anticipated by his own ode *The Bard* (1757), drawn from Welsh sources. For the first half century after publication, those accepting Macpherson's "translation" outnumbered the doubters and included some of the leading minds of the era, such as Sir Walter Scott, Denis Diderot, Voltaire, Johann Goethe and Thomas Jefferson. As late as 1844 Henry David Thoreau juxtaposed *Ossian* with Homer and Chaucer in the pages of *The Dial*, the premier American journal for the intellectual elite of the time. Skeptics were championed by the vociferous Samuel Johnson, a critic of incomparable stature, in some of the most scathing literary invective of all time. He declared that Macpherson was "a mountebank, a liar, and a fraud and that the poems were forgeries." When asked if any man today could write such poetry, his immortal reply was, "Yes. Many men. Many women. And many children." Not done yet, he called *Ossian* "as gross an imposition as ever the world was troubled with." Johnson's diatribe was weakened, however, by his patronizing contempt for the Gaelic language and his ignorance of it. He thought it a rude, barbarous language, unworthy of sublime poetry, such as found in *Òran na Comhachaig* (c. 1585), and blustered that there were no manuscripts in it more than one hundred years old. In rapid support of Macpherson, the Advocates Library presented a Gaelic text 500 years old, and later another one even older.

Macpherson was born at Ruthven in the Gaelic-speaking parish of Kingussie, and an uncle had served in the Jacobite army of 1745, going into hiding for nine years as a result. At the most superficial level, he looked as though he might be what he claimed to be. Careful observers, however, had noted him as a dissembler from the get-go. In an episode brought to light by the authoritative modern folklorist and linguist John Lorne Campbell (1933), Macpherson revealed his limitations in a flagrant solecism when encountering Iain Mac Fhearchair (John MacCodrum), official Bard to the Chief of Clan MacDonald of Sleat, on North Uist in 1760. He asked, "*A bheil dad agaibh air an Fheinne?*" Presumably he meant to ask, "Do you know anything of the Fianna?" Without knowing it he had asked, "Do the Fianna owe you anything?"

The bard quipped in reply, "*Cha n-eil agus ge do bhiodh cha ruiginn a leas iarraidh a nis*," or in English, "No, if they did it would be useless to ask for it now." Bard Mac Fhearchair continued the dialogue with politeness, and Macpherson seemed unaware he had been exposed. Along with being a quick wit, Mac Fhearchair was a poet of stature.

Ever wary, Macpherson would go on to a life in politics, elected to Parliament in 1780 where he remained for the rest of his life. A pen for hire, he wrote the Parliamentary response to the American Declaration of Independence, which had been mostly written by his admirer Thomas Jefferson. Never married, he acknowledged five illegitimate children by different women. He succeeded in being buried in the Poets' Corner of Westminster Abbey. In life his imperfect knowledge of Gaelic was never confronted.

At his death he left copies of the Gaelic "originals" for the *Poems of Ossian*. These were published in 1807 and proved to be nothing more than translations of Macpherson's words into modern Scottish Gaelic.

Undeterred, Macpherson's champions continued the authenticity debate for more than a century. As late as 1896 the upmarket Edinburgh publisher Patrick Geddes issued a deckled-edge edition of *The Poems of Ossian* with credulous, assertive, even pious annotations and notes from William Sharp, who also wrote Celtic Revival poetry and fiction under the pseudonym "Fiona MacLeod." More than a million words were published on Macpherson's behalf, summarized by George Black in *Macpherson's Ossian and the Ossianic Controversy* (1926).

Informed opinion today concurs with the analyses of Derick S. Thomson, a leading twentieth-century authority on the language, in his *Gaelic Sources of Macpherson's Ossian* (1952). Much as the author misrepresented himself, he did draw on oral traditions that neither he nor anybody else understood at that time. Thomson allows that from the beginning Macpherson might honestly have thought he was collecting the *disjecta membra* of a forgotten epic. Ballads and other narrative traditions had existed continuously in dominantly illiterate societies since the Middle Ages, including Gaelic Scotland. At one time such oral tradition was designated "popular antiquities" under the misapprehension that they descended from classical models. Claiming, groundlessly, that they originated in the third century was the first of several prevarications. We have records from Dál Riada from three centuries after that, but not such narratives with recurrent characters and themes. Thomson allows that Macpherson sometimes followed actual Scottish Gaelic ballads, employing scribes to record from oral tradition and manuscripts that he was incapable of dealing with himself. Then he altered the original characters and introduced a great deal of his own. *Fingal* can be traced to sources, but the second epic, *Temora*, is largely his own creation. In sum, Thomson wrote, "Macpherson was neither as honest as he claimed nor as inventive as his opponents implied."

What made Scottish Gaelic and Irish oral traditions different is that the Irish material was connected with a huge body of written narrative recorded by Irish ecclesiastics in large codices, like *Lebor na hUidre*, The Book of the Dun Cow (compiled before 1106). These narratives fall into four inter-connecting cycles that have been named by more recent scholars: (a) The Mythological Cycle, (b) The Ulster Cycle, (c) The Fenian Cycle and (d) The Cycles of the Kings. Of these the Ulster

Cycle, centering on the hero Cúchulainn and containing the epic *Táin Bó Cuailnge*, has enjoyed the most prestige. The Fenian, centered on the hero Fionn mac Cumhaill and the warriors of the Fianna, while not lacking in its own distinctive poetry, was the most demotic and widely known. Lastly, the Cycles of the Kings, sometimes called the Historical, portrays dominating personalities thought to be actual, like Conn Cétchathach (of the Hundred Battles) and Niall Noígiallach (of the Nine Hostages). Within all four cycles action sometimes takes place in Gaelic Scotland, which appears to be an extension of Ireland. Cúchulainn, for example, takes lessons in martial arts from an Amazonian figure named Scáthach on the Isle of Skye. The Mythological Cycle lent itself to very little oral literature after the twelfth century, and the Ulster Cycle and the Cycles of the Kings to only a limited amount. The Fenian Cycle, on the other hand, encompasses a larger body of words recorded from oral tradition than in the earlier manuscripts inscribed by the monks. Not only were the oral narratives popular in Ireland but they also flourished in Gaelic Scotland. According to the twelfth-century *Book of Leinster*, every professional storyteller could recite at least 120 tales of the Fianna.

Many Fenian tales are cleverly assembled in the twelfth-century frame narrative *Acallam na Senórach,* The Colloquy of the Elders, regarded by scholars as an important compendium of the tradition. In the *Acallam* the great days of Fionn and the Fianna are past, and Fionn's son Oisín is telling of them to a skeptical listener, often an imagined St. Patrick. Thus, in oral tradition Oisín (pronounced uh-SHEEN) is the default narrator, speaking of both of his father as well as his Galahad-like son Oscar. The reader has no doubt already assumed the leap that Macpherson made. Recognizing the difficulty a non–Gaelic speaker might have with the name, Macpherson invented the name "Ossian." He presumed that the conventional narrator must have been the long-lost author, incalculably old. The Gaelic name *Oisín* is the diminutive of *os*, deer, which Macpherson gives no evidence of knowing.

A name for the heroic father was another matter. The form "Fionn" now favored in learned commentary is actually the Modern Irish version, a reflection that so many oral narratives were recorded in Modern Irish. In Old Irish the character's name did not always have a standard spelling and might be *Finn*, *Find*, *Fin*, *Feunn*, etc. The name translates as "fair," as Macpherson may have known. In *Fingal* (1762) Macpherson invents the woman's name "Fiona," originally "Fióna," a feminization of Fionn. The common anglicization of Fionn is Finn MacCool. "Fingal," or *fionn gall*, Fair Foreigner, existed in Scottish tradition before 1760. The placename Fingal (for "fair foreigners," i.e., Norwegians?), appears twice on the map of Ireland. Many readers appear to have found "Fingal" to be euphonic before Macpherson's expropriation. It is curious, though, that Macpherson should have made the central hero of a putative national epic a man whose name translates as "foreigner."

The immense popularity of Macpherson's coinage was so great that for a while in the nineteen century it appeared to displace the authentic Oisín. When a group of scholars banded together in Dublin, 1853, to preserve the perishable manuscripts of the Fenian Cycle, they called themselves the Ossianic Society. In some contexts, "Ossianic" might indicate any traditional lore from Ireland or Gaelic Scotland.

The Oscar in Macpherson comes over from Gaelic tradition pretty much unscathed. Fingal's father Comhall looks like Fionn's father Cumall but pronounced differently. Macpherson's Morven, which appears to denote all of Gaelic Scotland, is not identical with the actual Morvern in north Argyll. With others one has to read the full of the narrative to see that Dar-thula is derived from Deirdre, and the place name Temora has been wrested from Tara, which in Gaelic is *Temair*. From the beginning of the enterprise, however, Macpherson favored his own creations, such as the star-crossed lovers in the first of the *Fragments*, Shilric and Vinvela, or Oscar's great love, Malvina. Many of his coinages have enjoyed a long life after *Ossian*, such as Selma, Fingal's palace or capital, now affixed to the map of the United States. Not one of the Gaelic Fenian narratives depicts any maritime adventures, but Macpherson puts his heroes on a ship named Balclutha, commemorated in the name of a New Zealand town and elsewhere.

Admittedly, Macpherson was dismissed as an "exploitive fraud" in the Preface to this volume, but that does not diminish his depth, significance or influence. His calculations, which appear aimed at amassing fame and wealth, may not have included a cultural self-definition for the Gàidhealtachd, but in elevating the narratives of the mostly illiterate underside of an impoverished society he was forging a "national" narrative where none had existed. The great nations of Europe had produced national stories for themselves, some qualifying as "epic," in the Middle Ages that became centerpieces of national identity. For Spain it was *El Cid*, for Russia *Prince Igor*, for France *The Song of Roland*, for England and France, *Beowulf* and the Arthurian legends, for Ireland the *Táin Bó Cuailnge*, and for Lowland Scotland *The Bruce*. Whereas informed speakers and writers of Scottish Gaelic had known that the language was derived from Old Irish, clear to seventeenth-century writers like Iain Lom and the clan genealogists, Macpherson attempted a declaration of linguistic independence by arguing that Ossian and Fingal lived in third-century Scotland before the fall of the Roman Empire. Yes, "bogus," but self-flattering.

Narratives from the peasantry, so "racy of the soil," became the focus of sustained academic study, led by the Brothers Grimm, Jakob (1785–1863) and Wilhelm (1786–1859). The more the subject was studied, the weaker were Macpherson's claims for great antiquity. The term "folklore" was not coined until 1846 by antiquarian William John Thoms, displacing "popular antiquities." They were also seen as intensely national. Symphonies and operas were composed on themes recorded from poor, marginalized populations with distinctive voices for a nation.

Macpherson also inspired imitation, much of it inferior to what he had done, some of it winning lasting acclaim and prestige. About a half-dozen fellow Scotsmen tried to cut in on Macpherson's success using different translation strategies, like including bogus Gaelic "originals," and either complimenting or rebuking the author of *Ossian*. Among these are John Clark's *Works of the Caledonian Bards*, etc. (1778), Dr. John Smith, *Sean Dana le Oisian, Orran, Ulann*, etc. (1787), and the MacCallum brothers, Hugh and John, *Original Collection of Poems of Ossian, Orran, Ulin, and other Bards*, etc. (1816). Some knew Gaelic better and wrote better prose than Macpherson, but were less adroit marketers. Their works were not widely circulated, had little impact, and today are hard to find in libraries. Much more accomplished is the so-called "Welsh Macpherson," Edward Williams (1747–1828), who is better known in his created persona of Iolo Morganwg. He unquestionably knew

Welsh much better than Macpherson knew Gaelic, and reference books elevate him to "charlatan" rather than a mere fraud. He created a body of literature in medieval Welsh and ascribed them to the actual fourteenth-century poet Dafydd ap Gwilym; they were convincing enough to be included in a 1789 edition of the poet, and the imposture was not uncovered for decades. Morganwg also founded the society of Welsh poets known as the Gorsedd, an esteemed body still with us. It sponsors the annual festival of Welsh culture known as the Eisteddfod.

The name of Finnish scholar Elias Lönnrot (1802–1884) offers a corrective narrative of what James Macpherson might have been. Finland was a Grand Duchy of Imperial Russia in the early nineteenth century, having been dominated by Sweden for centuries before that. The non–Indo-European Finnish language, like Scottish Gaelic, was one that foreigners were reluctant to learn. It was a land with a rich traditional popular culture but no national epic. Lönnrot collected ballads and other popular literature of unknown antiquity and concatenated them into a volume of 12,078 verses titled *The Kalevala* (1835), expanded to nearly double the length fourteen years later. Not only was he proficient in Finnish, but he never presented his results as anything other than what they were. It became in effect the national epic, although readers were fully aware that some words in it had been in the mouths of peasants only recently. Prominently, it was celebrated by Finnish composer Jan Sibelius, where most non–Finns first hear of it.

Most contemporary readers attempting to consume even a few pages of the *Poems of Ossian* will find incomprehensible the ecstatic acclaim accorded to it from some of the finest minds and artists of the day. Samuel Johnson, though a Scotophobe, had Macpherson's number. He was a dreadful wordsmith who produced groan-inviting prose, and a hackneyed plotter where characters are given to killing loved ones by mistake, and dying of grief, or joy. I had to flog myself to get through the 416 pages of the 1896 Patrick Geddes edition, not one of which delivered the slightest suggestion of delight. One possible exception was locating the work's most famous quote, "They came forth to war, but they always fell," in Duan Second of "Cath-Loda: a Poem." I have never met a living person who reported even fleeting pleasure in reading *Ossian*, and few who would claim to have finished it.

This mercifully short example repeats an exchange of two corners of a love triangle in *Fingal*, suggested by critic Dafydd Moore (2004):

> From the hills I return, O Morna, from the hill of the dark-brown hinds. There I have slain with my bended yew. There with my long bounding dogs of the chace [*sic*]. I have slain one stately deer for thee.—High was his branchy head, and fleet his feet of wind.
>
> DUCHOMAR! calm the maid replied. I love thee not, thou gloomy man.—Hard is thy heart of rock, and dark thy terrible brow. But Cathbat, thou son of Torman, thou are the love of Morna.

Where to begin? "Thee," "thou" and "thy" English had disappeared from usage before the eighteenth century and is a puerile attempt at archaicism, as are the outmoded syntax and discarded spellings, "chace" for "chase." Prolix, pseudo-Homeric locutions, "dogs of the chace" for hunting dogs, "bended yew" for bow, "branchy head" for antlers just take up space. Inverted word order cannot disguise a shopworn cliché, "Hard is thy heart of rock."

Unbearable as we may find the *Poems of Ossian,* their initial reception in Britain can be explained with an eye toward contemporary literary fashion. During the 1750s and 1760s there was a short-term vogue for morbidity and the gloom of cemeteries. Lamentation and mourning are everywhere in *Ossian.* Lines like, "She is as fair as the ghost of the hill, when it moves in a sunbeam at noon, over the silence of the Morven," won him swooning applause. Early responses to the texts made favorable comparisons with sentimental portrayal of nature in *The Seasons* (1726–1730) by Scottish writer James Thomson (1700–1748). We now assume Macpherson was a stealthy admirer and maladroit imitator of his countryman.

Macpherson's weakness as a stylist proved to be an unexpected asset for his international reputation. His prose was unidiomatic, a gift to translators, just the opposite of what was presented by his countryman Robert Burns.

Translations into French appeared in 1762, before *Ossian* was complete. The full corpus was available in 1777. Other nations came more quickly to the fray. Clergyman Melchiorre Cesarotti began an Italian translation in 1763, completed 1772. Universally considered superior to Macpherson's originals, it helped to launch the Romantic movement in Italy, and was the version Napoleon especially admired and recommended. Michael Denis completed the full translation into German 1768–1769, attracting some of the most esteemed writers in that language, like the proto-nationalist Friedrich Gottlieb Klopstock. The most admired of them all, Johann von Goethe, included a passage from Macpherson in the masterwork of his early career, *The Sorrows of a Young Werther* (1774), which he translated himself. And soon *Ossian* made its way into Spanish, Russian, Dutch, Polish, Czech and Hungarian.

Nowhere was *Ossian* more popular than in Scandinavia, even though it did not appear in Danish until 1790 and Swedish in 1794–1800. There the Scottish roots seemed to disappear, and local readers began to think of Ossian and Fingal as Nordic figures symbolic of nationalist aspirations. The French general Jean-Baptiste Bernadotte settled in Sweden, where he named his only son Oscar on the recommendation of Napoleon his ally. Bernadotte later became king of a united Sweden and Norway, and when he died that son became King Oscar I, the first of several rulers of that name. From the prominence of the royal family, Oscar became a popular name in Scandinavia and on the continent, its Gaelic roots forgotten, Oscar Wilde notwithstanding.

The translations were the basis of hundreds of paintings, sculptures and musical works by leading figures like Franz Schubert, Jean-François Le Seuer, Johannes Brahms, and Jean-August-Dominique Ingre. Often, as with the Scandinavian royal family, artists overlooked that the source material was Scottish. A notable exception was composer Felix Mendelssohn's *Hebrides Overture* (1829), alternatively titled *Fingal's Cave.*

In English artists had to contend with Macpherson's lamentable prose and the growing apprehension that he was a crook. Those detriments did not deter William Blake, Samuel Taylor Coleridge, Matthew Arnold, Elizabeth Barrett Browning, and in America Thomas Jefferson and Henry David Thoreau, as mentioned before, and painter Frederic Edwin Church of the Hudson River School. The English-language writer most directly influenced by Macpherson appears to be James Fenimore

Cooper. On the testimony of Barrie Hayne, "*Ossian*, Scott and Cooper's Indians" (1969), many of the woodland heroes in *Leatherstocking Tales* are Ossian and Fingal transmogrified in the new continent.

As we have said in a previous chapter, while Macpherson was making a career for himself and conquering the world, impoverished subtenants were standing in icy cold water harvesting kelp. The mighty Cheviot was giving landlords new opportunities to maximize profits. A year after the completion of *Ossian,* one of the most trenchant of all anti–Highland calumnies appeared; the anonymous *History of the Feuds and Conflicts Among the Clans* argued that Gaelic-speakers were impossibly barbaric, irredeemable. In 1772, as Macpherson's fortune took a precipitous upward trajectory, playwright Richard Cumberland premiered *The Fashionable Lover*, in which the reliable comic character was Colin MacLeod from the Isle of Skye. Gaels streamed out of the north to make their way in the metropolis; this is how they were greeted.

Nonetheless, Macpherson had appeared to prove that a people as coarse and uncouth as the Highland Gaels inherited a grand epic to be compared with the works of Homer. The esteem for Ossian and Fingal eventually redounded to native turf. The Highland Society of London was formed in 1778 to preserve the dress, music and "martial spirit" of the Gaels. The admiration for Highland regiments no doubt contributed to the sentiment for the Society. The Act of Proscription against native dress would not be repealed until 1782, a measure the Society promoted. The immediate priority was to promote bagpiping and the composition of Gaelic poetry, whose innate worth Macpherson had incidentally elevated. The means to accomplish this was an annual gathering, the first being called the Falkirk Tryst in October 1781. Falkirk is about twenty miles northwest of Edinburgh with unique national resonance as the site of both William Wallace's defeat (1298) and the Jacobites' last victory (1746).

Indigenous Voices

Poor people may produce poetry at next to no expense. The Highlands lagged behind other quarters of Europe in the production of fine and applied arts. Native musical tradition awarded high status to piping calling for subtle, measured composition and performance, but it is often an acquired taste for non–Gaels. Calvinist Scotland had repressed the playing of the harp, and there were no Highland symphony or chamber players. Neither were there Highland painters, tapestry-makers, jewelers or sculptors. Visually stunning castles, but no distinguished architects. For a person with restless energy and an artistic temperament, the surest way to achieve excellence was in poetry, as had been the case back to the time of *Òran na Comhachaig* (c. 1585).

A lively, sophisticated tradition of Gaelic poetry had existed long before the time of Iain Lom in the previous century and was flourishing in Macpherson's time despite his ignorance of it. Appreciating it fully requires a reading knowledge of Gaelic, and it is too extensive for close examination. Poets of both low and high rank in the Gaelic social order might contribute. Among the most colorful was the Villon-like thief and a murderer, Dòmhnall Donn (d. 1691), introduced candidly by D.S. Thomson in a reference work (1983) as a "cattle-lifter and poet."

He is distinguished from the hundreds of Highland men named Dòmhnall Donn by his residence in the hamlet of Bohuntin in Glen Roy, fast by the site of the last clan battle of Mulroy (1688), where cattle rustling was rife.

Iain Mac Fhearchair, John MacCodrum (1693–1779), stood far higher in clan society, though illiterate, because of renowned friends and also the ready display of his fabled wit. He was called a bard, an honorific position, and a *seanchaidh*, the name for a storyteller who is credited with accurate and erudite history. The chief of MacDonald of Sleat, whose tenant the poet was, testified that he could recite for hours on end. He was the poet of North Uist who James Macpherson was led to in order to learn of the Fenian Cycle, where a solecism revealed the author of *Ossian*'s ignorance, cited above.

The poet with the greatest stature in this era is usually known in critical commentary as Alasdair mac Mhaighstir Alasdair [Alexander, son of the Reverend Alexander] (c. 1698–1770), who was born of privilege and attempted to tutor Prince Charles Edward in Gaelic. His father was a non-juring Episcopalian, and in maturity Alasdair converted to Roman Catholicism. In a court of law, he would have been known as Alexander MacDonald, one of thousands of men holding that name. The Gaelic form of his name not only links him with an extensive body of work in the language, but also reminds us that he was born the son of an educated man, a graduate of the University of Glasgow, which Alasdair apparently attended as well. He is the only poet in this generation who could cite Catullus.

Much humbler were the circumstances of the poet usually known only as Rob Donn (1714–1778), sometimes known as the "Burns of the North." Part of that ascription is based on his social station as the son of a subtenant and life of hardship (much grimmer than Burns), and another on the thickets presented by reading his work in an obscure regional dialect. "Rob Donn" (brown-haired Bob) takes the same form in Gaelic and English and is not usually accompanied by a family or clan name but is often claimed by the Clan MacKay. The other golden age poets composed in mutually comprehensible language, but Rob Donn's Gaelic would have presented problems for them. And, as with Burns, much of his word play is dependent on his native idiom, much reduced when the language is standardized and flattened. Illiterate in Gaelic, Rob Donn knew no English yet was directly influenced by Alexander Pope, whose witty verses were translated into Gaelic and recited to him. Astoundingly, he achieved a formidable body of work first composed mentally, memorized, and then recited to scribe. In *The World of Rob Donn* (1979), a twentieth-century admirer, Ian Grimble, studied all the poems to outline a portrait of Gaelic Society in its last moments before vanishing.

Although Dùghall Bochanan (1716–1768) spoke Gaelic as a first language and published in Gaelic, it seems more apt to call him by the English form, Dugald Buchanan, because he became an important translator and also published poetry in Scots, the sibling of English.

Employing more refined language than his contemporaries, Buchanan is often noted as the "Gaelic Cowper," after the English poet William Cowper (1731–1800), fifteen years his junior. Much of that elegance was based on earlier Gaelic models studied in works of the bards of both Scotland and Ireland. Trending more toward Cowper, Buchanan was knowledgeable of Shakespeare and admired English Puritans, whom he translated into Gaelic. Contradictory as it sounds, Buchanan was also hoodwinked by James Macpherson's *Ossian* and remained innocent of that author's chicanery. Together with the Rev. James Stuart of Killin, Buchanan worked on the Gaelic translation of the *New Testament*, 1755–1767. Also in 1767, he published his *Laoidhean Spioradail*, Spiritual Hymns, following the example of Alasdair mac Mhaighstir Alasdair, with a strikingly different reception. Not only was it immediately embraced, but the volume was constantly reprinted for 108 years, at a time when many Gaelic speakers either left the country or were forced to learn English.

Paradoxically, the imposture of such a poor Gaelic scholar as Macpherson spurred in interest in native poetry. Public esteem for the language led to the founding of the Highland Society, which sponsored a competition, called the Falkirk Tryst, in 1781 attracting a host of participants. The first winner was an already established (though illiterate) poet, who had left the Gàidhealtachd for Scots-speaking Edinburgh, where he was a member of the City Guard (i.e., police). He was readily known by both the English and Gaelic forms of his name, Duncan Bàn MacIntyre and Donnchadh Bàn Mac-an-t-Saoir (1724–1812). In the next eight years he would win five more times. This made him, briefly, something unanticipated: a Gaelic-speaking minor celebrity in the Scots/English-speaking world. Applause, however, proved a detriment to his art and his person. In hopes of ingratiating himself to the judges as a cheerful and convivial fellow, his poetry turned to patriotic mush, when he had supported the Hanoverian forces in the Jacobite campaign of 1745–1746. He began to make risibly vain statements about the popularity of Gaelic south of the border, apparently conflating Macpherson's reputation with his own.

Poetic Admirers from the Outside

The Scottish poet of the age was of course a Lowlander, Robert Burns (1759–1796), the man who thrust Scottish subjects more surely into British discourse than anyone before him. It was inevitable that critics would compare Gaelic poets with him, even if they did not read him, nor he them. Without his making the Highlands a priority, however, he did much to brighten the vision of the Highlands of many British readers, and not simply because of his artistic excellence and charm. Burns had grown up in Ayrshire, one of the corners of the Lowlands most antagonistic to the Highlands and Gaelic culture; he rose above parochialism. In 1787, the year he also turned from recited poetry to songs, he made a tour of the Highlands that included a visit to the battlefield of Culloden. The Jacobite threat had vanished, and the Boswell-Johnson tour of Scotland was already well known. He wrote "The Chevalier's Lament" the next year, giving a more naively positive portrait of Prince Charles Edward than any evidence can support. He has the Young Pretender on the run those months after the catastrophe, far more concerned about the fates of his "gallant" Highland supporters than for his own skin. The legend-makers of Bonnie Prince Charlie could not have asked for more.

Burns' knowledge of Jacobitism was not profound. He certainly never embraced the autocratic whims of the Stuarts. This nominal attraction to Jacobitism extended back to the 1715 rebellion led by the Earl of Mar. His "The Battle of Sherramuir" blurs the name "Sheriffmuir," but he is more exact in "The Braes O' Killiecrankie" and "Bonie Dundee" [sic] of 1689. A member of the Masonic Order, he seemed unaware that the Earl of Mar and the 1715 attempt was the most Roman Catholic of Jacobite enterprises. Instead, the defiance of the Whigs and the Covenanting "true blues" was in line with his rejection of the reactionary and repressive ministers and elders in Ayrshire.

Other titles speaking well of the Highlands include, "The Birks of Aberfeldy," "Farewell to the Highlands"—best known by its oft-quoted first line, "My Heart's in the Highlands," "Highland Mary," and "The Humble Petition of Bruar Water to the Noble Duke of Athole," in which the personified water begs the nobleman to plant more trees.

Slowly, almost imperceptibly, a vogue for the Highlands began to appear among people with advanced ideas, including most of the English romantic poets. There were other elements in the zeitgeist, to be considered later, but the role of Burns cannot be overplayed. John Keats is candid in giving credit in "Lines Written in the Highlands after a Visit to Burns Country." He took a walking tour of the Highlands very different from that of Johnson and Boswell, when meals and accommodations were hard to come by. Despite being characterized by his weak health, Keats climbed the heather-covered mountains, producing "Sonnet. Written Upon the Top of Ben Nevis." His "Staffa," the island containing Fingal's Cave, indicates Macpherson's influence.

George Gordon, Lord Byron, despite being London-born, was the most Scottish of the romantics and required no cues from Burns to enter the Highlands. His mother, Catherine Gordon, claimed descent from James I of Scotland (1394–1437) and inherited property in Aberdeen, where the poet spent much of his childhood. Before becoming famous, he still spoke with a Scottish accent, a liability he labored to shed. When he was eight years old, 1796, the poet developed scarlet fever. For his health, Byron's mother took him out of the city to a retreat near the peak of Lochnagar, in the Dee River Valley of the Grampian foothills. It is near the site of Balmoral, later the Highland home of the royal family. Thus, the characteristic Highland landscape is lovingly presented in one of his earliest published poems, "Lachin y Gair" (1807):

> Yet, Caledonia, beloved are thy mountains,
> Round their white summits though elements war;
> Though cataracts foam 'stead of smooth flowing fountains,
> I sigh for the valley of dark Loch na Garr.

Given what he knew first-hand, it is dismaying that some of his view is clouded by the Macpherson imposture, which he never challenged. So he also produced "Ossian's Address to the Sun" and included Ossianic place names along a Dee Valley setting in "When I Roved a Young Highlander."

William Wordsworth, Byron's older contemporary, knew that Macpherson was a fraud and imposter, but he could not shake his attraction to the premise of *Ossian*, as John Robert Moore (1925) pointed out. It was partially the lure of Macpherson that prompted William to lead his sister Dorothy and their esteemed friend Samuel Taylor Coleridge on a tour of the Highlands in 1803. They entered through the Trossachs, today a major tourist region, and were immediately enthralled with what they saw. In one of his first poems from the journey, "Glen-Almain; or, the Narrow Glen," he dismissed the question of authenticity as unimportant:

> Does then the Bard sleep here indeed?
> Or is it but a groundless creed?
> What matters it?

We can know much about how the journey went from Dorothy's florid memoir, *Recollections of a Tour Made in Scotland, AD 1803*, marking her as first of a long line of awe-struck tourists, given the vapors by the "excessive beautifulness" of what they found. Her eyes were not closed to the poverty of the inhabitants or the wretched housing, but all were overcome by the poetry of "water, rocks, heather and bare mountains above." Her heart was filled with awe of a boy tending cattle approaching Tarbet, at Loch Lomond. Spoken Gaelic might be incomprehensible—she called it "half-articulate"—but she assumed he was calling home the cattle for the day. "His appearance was in the highest degree moving to the imagination; mists were on the hillsides, darkness shutting in on the huge avenue of mountains, torrents roaring, no house in sight to which the child might belong." Putting aside the special case of Burns, however, she was the first literary visitor to smile on what she beheld, a *volte face* from Pennant, Boswell, Johnson, La Rochefoucauld, et al.

Dorothy Wordsworth could find no publisher for her *Recollections* in her lifetime, and she was no doubt going to market too early, a decade before Sir Walter Scott's *Waverley* (1814). Her words had to wait for publication until 1874, after her death. As romantic sentiment swept over the educated classes in the nineteenth century, her loving but patronizing view of a sanitized and picturesque peasantry would become commonplace, with thousands of examples. The adorable shepherdesses in the paintings of French academic painter William-Adolphe Bouguereau (1825–1905) might be the apex of this sentiment.

Her brother William, meanwhile, more than a tourist, studied what could be known of Highland history and politics, subjects not readily accessible in England. Although he knew that Rob Roy MacGregor had been thought an infamous outlaw and his entire clan proscribed, he wrote "Rob Roy's Grave" after a visit to the Balquhidder churchyard. In Hanoverian circles, Rob Roy's name still evoked dread, but Wordsworth was ready to see him as a Scottish equivalent of Robin Hood, before that bandit's legend had been regenerated in the nineteenth century. More to the moment, Wordsworth also projected Rob Roy as an embodiment of the promise of the French Revolution long before the storming of the Bastille. The last stanza reads:

> For Thou, although with some wild thoughts,
> Wild Chieftain of a Savage Clan!
> Hadst this to boast of; thou didst love
> The *liberty* of Man

Elsewhere, as in his "Sonnet in the Pass of Killicranky," Wordsworth signaled that his reading of the Jacobites had forgiven them their reactionary values and instead their fey insurrection now looked like a place to invest romantic values. As commentator Robert Clyde (1995) points out, Jacobites were not to be confused with Jacobins, and Rob Roy, a law unto himself, never sought to liberate his people, let alone Scotland or mankind. Undeterred by this, Walter Scott, a conservative appalled by events in France, cited Wordsworth on the title page of his novel *Rob Roy* (1817).

Two Wordsworth poems more directly affected the elevated view of the Highlands educated readers would soon be assuming. They are "To a Highland Girl" and "The Solitary Reaper," both among the most admired in his lengthy output but also the most often anthologized and most often studied by later generations. Like his sister, the thirty-three-year-old poet was smitten with the scene—in his case, by two young women working in the fields. To the first, the Highland girl at Inversneyde (now Inversaid), upon Loch Lomond, he croons:

> Sweet Highland Girl, a very shower
> Of beauty is thy earthy dower!
> Twice seven consenting years have shed
> Their utmost beauty on thy head!

Unlike Dorothy, however, William saw the Solitary Reaper as an "other," separated from him by a language he cannot comprehend. He concludes the poem with two stanzas confessing that she is an unknowable stranger, and that his attraction for her gives him no insight to who she is or what she thinks, an unprecedented enlightened perception:

> Will no one tell me what she sings?—
> Perhaps the plaintive numbers flow
> For old, unhappy, far-off things,
> And battles long ago;
> Or is it some more humble lay,
> Familiar matter of today?
> Some natural sorrow, loss or pain,
> That has been, and may be again?
>
> Whate'er the theme, the Maiden sang
> As if her song could have no ending;
> I saw her singing at her work,
> And o'er the sickle bending;—
> I listened motionless and still;
> And, as I mounted up the hill,
> The music in my heart I bore,
> Long after it was heard no more.

Not all romantic poets were of one mind, as we should expect. Robert Southey, whose critical status has fallen in modern times, was named Poet Laureate in 1813, although four years younger than Wordsworth, who succeeded him thirty years later. As Scott was launching what would be a mania for the Highlands in later Regency years, 1814–1820, Southey spoke with the authority of his appointment and was resistant to trends. He did not get to the Highlands until 1819, fifteen years after the two Wordsworths and Coleridge, and then was with the famed engineer Thomas Telford. Their goal was scientific; Southey gave priority to agriculture, and the scenery was incidental. All the same, he could speak well of several sites in the Great Glen, focusing his praise on Ballachulish and Loch Linnhe, still cherished by tourists today. But he marked the stone huts inhabited by tenants and subtenants to be the worst housing he had ever seen in the coinage, "men-sties." Perhaps because this was after Highland regiments had won glory on the battlefield, Southey thought Highland Gaels deserved better as they were to be preferred over their Celtic cousins across the Irish Sea, the "ignorant and ferocious barbarians" of Hibernia. Reckoning Highland Gaelic to be worthy of "improvement," he favored their removal to more salubrious environments, an attitude not far from endorsing the Clearances. He would remain skeptical of the rising fashion for what would eventually be called tartanism, and was quick to find fault when opportunity allowed.

Percy Bysshe Shelley eloped to Scotland with his first wife, the child-bride Harriet Westbrook, but never roamed as far as the Gàidhealtachd.

Whereas the Wordsworths, Coleridge and certainly Southey knew that Macpherson was an imposter, *Ossian*'s faithful defenders were also prepared to find beauty and cultural value beneath the sometimes-sordid face of the Highlands. Chief among them was a popular poet and essayist from a privileged background who went to live in Laggan along the Great Glen, where she learned Gaelic and succumbed to the rough glamor of local life. Anne Grant (1755–1838) was born in Glasgow of an educated family with a Gaelic name, MacVicar. More than one commentator has dubbed her a "white settler," on analogy with the imperial experience in Africa. In Grant's girlhood her father accepted an army commission in the colony of New York, where she learned Dutch from the local gentry and admired the dignity of the Mohawks. On the family's return her father took an appointment at Fort Augustus in Inverness-shire, where she married a refined clergyman, James Grant, a fine gentleman with barely any income. They remained there for twenty-one years until James's early death, 1801, which unexpectedly spurred her literary output. Her career rests on a series of paradoxes. In a life filled with want and hardship, she was mother to twelve children, only one of whom outlived her, and she was a prodigious reader and writer. Far from any metropolis, but a demon letter-writer, Grant became conversant with the literary lights of the day. Without financial means, she attracted the attentions of the cream of society, such as the Duke and Duchess of Gordon, who not only provided stipends but rounded up three thousand subscribers to back her work.

Her first collection, *Poems on Various Subjects* (1803), appeared two years after her husband's death and coeval with the Wordsworth-Coleridge tour. Three years later, inserting her Gaelic name MacVicar, she produced the three-volume *Letters from the Mountains* (1806) achieving sales unimaginable today. This was followed by a work of scholarship, the two-volume *Essays on the Superstitions of the Highlanders of Scotland* (1811)

Her dogged defense of Macpherson, even after the damning "originals" were published in 1807, is the key to her vision. It is through Anne Grant that the fantasized, noble Highlander of *Ossian* is presented as a person one might actually encounter in the glens. Taking her as a guide, a passel of popular novelists spelled out what they would look like such as: Susan Ferriter, *Marriage* (1818), *The Inheritance* (1824), and *Destiny, or the Chief's Daughter* (1830); Mary Brunton, *Self-Control* (1811) and *Discipline* (1814). These appeared concurrently with Walter Scott's burgeoning output, but took quite different views. Forgotten, such books are hard to find today, but their views have remained persistent in popular, romantic fiction set in the Highlands.

In his account of her, Robert Clyde (1995) suggests that some of Anne Grant's sensitivity about the authenticity of *Ossian* was that some questioned *her* poems. Specifically, some readers doubted whether her depiction of idyllic scenes and simple goodness of the Gaels could exist in an area well-known for its deprivation. She replied in high dudgeon that indeed Utopian scenes and Arcadian virtues could be found in her alpine region, and that her eyes were open: "I have always represented the country as wild and barren to the last degree, and the inhabitants as living in a great state of poverty and hardship." On her dominant view she doubled down, "—when I impute to the natives tenderness of sentiment, ardour of genius and gentleness of manners beyond their equals in other countries,—every one that knows anything of them must know that these have always characterized them."

As must be implicit from this context, the historical novel set in the Highlands was not simply the creation of Walter Scott, as is often attributed to him. Instead, another woman novelist anticipated him by a few years but is far less known. She was Jane Porter (1776–1850), born to a cultivated family in Durham, later to move to Edinburgh after her father's death while she was still young. Scott was a regular visitor to her home. Her literary career did not blossom until the family returned to London, where she was encouraged by a coterie of women writers. Scholars who have given her any attention perceive more influence from Lord Byron and the Byronic hero than what is found in Scott. She was innocent of any suggestions from the popularity of Anne Grant.

The first of her considerable output was *Scottish Chiefs* (1810), based on the medieval patriot William Wallace. The historical Wallace, a Scoto-Norman lesser noble, was remote and difficult to know, but she did not simply conjure up a narrative. Instead, she relied on the fifteenth-century poem known by the short title, *The Wallace* (c. 1477), attributed to "Blind Harry," as a source for most of the Wallace legend. It was written 172 years after the subject's death. Nothing in Wallace's life records, which we know better than Porter could, suggested that the warrior was a Gael, and neither did "Harry." Yet Porter portrays the Highlands as the essence of Scotland. Although Porter has a fraction of the fame of Walter Scott, many modern readers would find her work easier going than say, *Waverley* (1814), the break-through work. Somehow *Scottish Chiefs* came to be thought of as a children's or young boy's novel. It has never been out of print and currently exists in eight different editions. A landmark early twentieth-century edition was illustrated by American artist N.C. Wyeth. "Blind Harry" was also a source for Randall Wallace's filmscript of *Braveheart* (1995), directed by Mel Gibson, where far more outrageous liberties were taken with the Wallace legend than Jane Porter attempted.

Abbotsford

At 220' 6" (61.11 meters), the Scott Monument dominates Princes Street in Edinburgh and is the most massive for any English-speaking author, second only worldwide to the monument for José Martí in Havana. A second Scott monument dominates George Square, the main public space in Glasgow. Scott's readership may have fallen in the past one hundred years, but no other English-speaking nation has found itself expressed so thoroughly in a single author, not America in Mark Twain, Ireland in James Joyce, or even England in William Shakespeare. The most patriotic of any prestige author, Sir Walter Scott (1771–1832) gave us the oft-quoted lines:

> Breathes there the man, with soul so dead,
> Who never to himself hath said,
> This is my own, my native land!

The author of *Lady of the Lake*, *Waverley* and *The Bride of Lammermoor* was no jingoist, however. He arose after the Edinburgh intellectual golden age of philosopher David Hume and economist Adam Smith, who were content to think of themselves as "north Britons," and found much of Scotland a bit uncouth. His first goal was to have educated people simply know that Scotland had a dramatic history, and secondly to venerate the most decisive figures and moments. The third goal that Lowland and Highland cultures be bound up as one came later, after his thirty-fifth birthday. By his own word he knew little of anything Gaelic in his youth, and his first visit to the Highlands came when he was a law clerk directing an eviction.

The ninth child of a well-to-do lawyer, Walter Scott suffered from childhood polio which left him lame, but he nonetheless grew up in comfort. His early education with the strictest elements of the Church of Scotland, emphasizing the history of the Covenanters, was displaced when he joined the Scottish Episcopal Church and also became a member of the Masonic Lodge. He never veered from his family political views as a property-defending and royalty-supporting Tory. Appalled by the French Revolution, he instinctively opposed street demonstrations by the rabble and railed on his deathbed against the onset of the Reform Act of 1832. He was also an unabashed snob and social climber.

As a youth Scott had been an enthusiastic reader of Macpherson's *Ossian* and by his own testimony committed lengthy passages to memory. But in a preview of his discernment as a critic and book reviewer, he turned against the imposter's prose even as he could recite it. "The tawdry repetitions of the Ossianic phraseology disgusted me rather sooner than might have been expected from my age." He did not need an official refutation of authenticity, but he also recognized that learned Gaels of his acquaintance clung to Macpherson's premise as if it were a scriptural absolute. Out of courtesy, he would not speak of the matter with them. What appears to have stayed with Scott was Macpherson's assumption that ancient Scotland, even the barbaric and violent Highlands, could not be equaled as a setting for the romantic imagination, more appealing than the classicism of Rome and Greece.

An ambitious young man, Scott thought first to seek his fortune as an advocate, judge and legal administrator before turning to literature. Handsome despite his limp and articulate, Scott was also a man of public affairs and was at ease before crowds when not at the writing desk. It was not until he was thirty-four that he began to publish his own work, at first long narrative poems, beginning with *The Lay of the Last Minstrel* (1805), followed by *Marmion: A Tale of Flodden Field* (1808), *The Lady of the Lake* (1810), *Rokeby* (1813) and *The Lord of the Isles* (1815). The first of these was a medieval romance drawing on the numerous, anonymous Border Ballads of the Scottish-English border. This immediately put him ahead of Macpherson just in knowing what a ballad was. He had worked with John Leyden on the two-volume collection *Minstrelsy of the Scottish Border* (1802), containing forty-eight ballads, more than half seen for the first time. This was also a tip-off to his favorite Scottish terrain: the far south. When he built his neo-gothic mansion, Abbotsford, it was in the former border county of Roxburgh. All five of the poems had Scottish historical settings, but it was not until the third, *Lady of the Lake*, that he ventured into the Highlands. With trepidation. He confessed in a letter to Lady Abercorn, "My great deficiency is that being born and bred not only a lowlander but a borderer I do not in the least understand the Gaelic language and am therefore at a loss to find authentic materials for my undertaking."

Those fears proved unjustified. *The Lady of the Lake* was the most successful of the five, selling more than 20,000 copies. The lengthy narrative, told in six cantos, is costume romance rather than historical fiction, set in the dreamy time of James V in the early sixteenth century. Included are a specific locale, Stirling, an outlawed noble, duels and fraught love affairs. As will no doubt sound incredible to a contemporary reader, poetry made Scott both rich and famous. Rivaled only by Lord Byron, whose first two cantos of *Childe Harold's Pilgrimage* (1812) allowed him to wake up one day and find himself famous, Scott was otherwise the most admired poet of the day. Some of his verses, like "O what a tangled web we weave, / When first we practise [sic] to deceive!" (*Marmion*) have become so proverbial they are commonly attributed to Shakespeare. In 1813 he was offered and refused the poet laureateship, deferring to his friend Robert Southey.

Following the custom of the time, when Scott turned to fiction-writing at age forty-three, he published anonymously, not revealing his identity for a dozen years. His contemporary Jane Austen did the same. Financially secure, his name deleted, Scott could take a risk in writing the first Jacobite novel. The moment was most apt. Napoleon had just been defeated at Leipzig, with Highland regiments playing a prominent role. If the Jacobites, rebellious, violent and perhaps unhygienic, were to be united with the industrious and orderly Lowlanders, this was Scott's moment. Appearing in three volumes with the full title of *Waverley; or, 'Tis Sixty Years Since*, the novel presents thirty-six characters. And a brief summary of the action is confessedly a distortion.

Scott employs reliable strategies to engage and persuade the open-minded. His protagonist, Edward Waverley, is an English visitor to Scotland, inviting the identification of the reader. In learning about both sides of the Jacobite rebellion, he is attracted to two beautiful women, Flora and Rose, allied with rival forces.

Edward starts life with no political affiliation for himself, but learns about the parties from his admired uncle Sir Everard, with whom he lives in aristocratic refinement. Everard keeps the family tradition as a Tory, the party that had been friendlier to the Jacobites. His father, a widower, is a Whig who works for the Hanoverian government in nearby Westminster. Edward's innate sense of honor leads him to think of public service, and through his father he is given a commission in the Hanoverian army and posted to Dundee. After some training suited for his rank, he takes leave to visit a friend of his uncle, Baron Bradwardine, whose household includes the lovely unattached daughter Rose.

Some wild Highlanders come to visit Bradwardine's castle, and instead of being repelled, Edward is intrigued. He goes to the mountain lair of the Clan Mac-Ivor [sic], where he meets the chieftain Fergus and his unattached sister Flora, again a lovely young woman whose wild beauty contrasts with that of Rose. Fergus and Flora are active Jacobites, preparing for the rebellion, which does not cause Edward to flee. Instead, as he has overstayed his leave he is accused of desertion, then arrested, something the reader feels to be an injustice. Just then the Highlanders, including Flora, rescue him and take him to the Jacobite stronghold at Doune Castle. The insurrection now underway, the Jacobites hold Holyrood Palace in Edinburgh, where they take Edward to meet Prince Charles Edward himself. Edward is charmed.

Entreaties of the comely Flora Mac-Ivor are not to be resisted. He has fallen in love with her, and her devotion to the cause appeals to his disposition. Edward goes over to the Jacobite cause and takes part in the dramatic victory at Prestonpans, September 1745, a combat Scott describes in detail from army records. In the heat of battle, Edward has the good fortune to save from death Colonel Talbot, a distinguished English officer and a friend of his family. Soon afterwards Edward is separated from Fergus and the Mac-Ivors during a battle that the Hanoverians are winning. Local people take Edward in until he can leave in safety. Then he reads in a newspaper that his father has died and so heads for London. The debacle of Culloden Moor does not appear in the pages of *Waverley*.

Once the Jacobite cause collapses in 1746, the grateful Colonel Talbot intervenes to win Edward a pardon for joining the rebels. Edward heads north to the imperiled estate of Baron Bradwardine and asks for the hand of his daughter Rose in marriage. The Baron is also pardoned, but the Mac-Ivors do not fare as well. Fergus is to face trial in Carlisle, which Edward resolves to attend. While there Edward meets Flora for the last time, who tells him that she will join a convent in France. Found guilty of treason, Fergus bravely goes to his execution.

Scott's concluding concerns are with property. In continuing gratitude, Colonel Talbot returns Baron Bradwardine's estate, taken from him in the rebellion, and pays to restore it to original appearance, complete with the family crest. Edward Waverley, with funds from selling his late father's house, makes all well with the estate in the north, where he will live with Rose.

The usual defense of the historical novel made by its champions is that a compelling narrative from a well-informed author can provide the newcomer with deeper insights into past events than might be given by dusty but accurate scholarship with documentation. Alas, as one of the first historical novels in English, *Waverley* offers a poor trot for the laggard student seeking to know of the events of 1745–1746. We never learn just what motivated the Jacobites or what distinguished them from their

Tory friends, not to mention the absolutist tendencies of many Stuarts themselves. Absent is the centuries-old enmity of the clans, specifically Clan Campbell vs. Clan Donald. The key concept of *dùthchas,* or hereditary trusteeship, an integral tie that bound a chief to pursue the clan's interest above his own, was beyond the author's ken. The actual MacIvor or MacIver (Gaelic *Maciomhair*) clan was frequently allied with the Clan Campbell and Clan MacKenzie, and not inclined to Jacobitism. Gone are all religious questions, with Episcopalians and Catholics on one side and Calvinists on the other. With so much action set in castles or outlaw camps, one would never guess that most Jacobite combatants were impoverished tenants and subtenants. The one battle most thoroughly depicted, Prestonpans, shows Jacobite strategists at their finest. Wretched humiliating defeat occurs off the page. The final and greatest omission is that the Duke of Cumberland's brutal suppression of rebels and supposed rebels, horrors that infuriated a pious conservative like Dugald Buchanan, are simply excised. Edward Waverley ends the narrative living in a restored castle with a beautiful and empathetic damsel at his side.

Exuberant readers of 1814 closed their eyes to such shortcomings. Reception for *Waverley* exceeded all expectations, both in Britain and on the Continent. Composer Hector Berlioz wrote an overture to epitomize his admiration for it. Perhaps the omen was in Scott's subtitle, "sixty years since," as no one alive could remember the fear that unkempt Highlanders might be foraging in their property. The author was never primarily a propagandist, despite championing several agendas, but *Waverley* accomplished what no polemic, tract or pamphlet could. Highlanders, Jacobites, could now be spoken of in the parlors of respectable folk.

Already middle-aged, Scott now set a furious pace with his pen. He would produce twenty-seven novels in the next seventeen years, three volumes of poetry, four works for the stage, a two-volume history of Scotland, a life of Napoleon, five volumes of popular history for children, *Tales of a Grandfather* and more. Although *Waverley* is one of Scott's less-read works today, far short of *Ivanhoe* (1820) set in medieval England, it was his ticket at the time. Scott was officially anonymous for twelve years, although many guessed his identity, until financial reversals forced him to blow his cover. Thus, as successive novels kept rolling off the presses, they were described as being by the "Author of *Waverley*," and all of them were known as the "The *Waverley* Novels," regardless of locale, even *The Talisman* (1825) set in Syria.

Scott revisited the Highlands only occasionally in post–*Waverley* works. Despite the promise of some titles, the long poem *The Lord of the Isles* (1815), the novels *A Legend of Montrose* (1819) and *The Fair Maid of Perth* (1828), he has little to say about the still unassimilated Gaels. His most significant words appear in *Rob Roy* (1817), partially set in Northumberlandshire but also near Loch Lomond, and two little-read short stories, "The Highland Widow" and "Two Drovers" (both 1827).

In plot structure *Rob Roy* resembles *Waverley* in that the protagonist is an Englishman, Frank Osbaldistone, who goes north of the border and becomes involved with Jacobitism, the 1715 rebellion, partially because of a beautiful well-born woman, Diana Vernon. The famous proscribed outlaw, Rob Roy MacGregor, cited in the title, is a supporting character. Comments on the perceptions of and defense of Highlands come in asides and in the speeches of supporting characters, though not Rob Roy himself. As much of the narrative concerns cattle-dealing, Scott speaks in bovine metaphors. A Lowlander confronts, "hordes of wild shaggy, dwarfish cattle and ponies, conducted by Highlanders, as wild, as shaggy, and sometimes as dwarfish, as the animals they had in charge...." Strangers are surprised by the antique and fantastic dress and cannot comprehend the unknown and dissonant language. The Gaels, called here "mountaineers," are armed with musket, pistol, sword, dagger and shield even in such peaceful occupation. They stare with amazement at windows of luxury goods whose use they do not know.

Scott allows his English narrator Osbaldistone to indulge shopworn anti–Highland calumnies, that these are lazy people, easily given to crime, who live in a society without laws. But he is reproved by a Lowland magistrate, Bailie Nicol Jarvie, one of the author's best comic creations. In dismissing the charge of a penchant for crime, Jarvie, speaking in broad Scots, presents an argument later associated with liberal enlightenment. There is not enough work to employ "even one moiety of the population." Jarvie informs the Englishman of Highland hardships, of scarcity and overcrowding against resources (in a thinly populated landscape).

More deeply, he chides Osbaldistone for his ignorance and presumption: "Ye ken naething about our hill country, or Hielands, as we ca' them." If the court system with baileys and magistrates little penetrates into clan hegemony, that does not mean that Gaelic-speakers are lawless? Jarvie (clearly Scott's mouthpiece) then praises the absolute authority of the local laird. Just his command and "the loon maun loup," i.e., the lad must jump to attention. There is no need for jails when order is enforced with dirk and broadsword.

Unfortunately, Scott surrenders to anti–Gaelic prejudice, and betrays his own ignorance, in having Jarvie speak of the sensitive subject of Highland cattle raids on Lowland flocks. Whatever had happened in earlier, wilder centuries, the clans were not crime families by the time of the action of the novel, c. 1715. We know from recent research unavailable to Scott, that the Highlands had also produced a criminal element outside the clan system, disapproved of but unrestrained by the lairds.

The two short stories differ from most of the novels in two ways. Both deal with common people instead of Scott's preferred aristocrats, and both are set in post–1746 Scotland, or the recent past. "The Highland Widow" portrays generational change, implying that increased integration into Lowland Scotland and the United Kingdom is loosening the tightly held dogmas of the most determined rebels. Elspat, the widow of the title, who was married to an old Jacobite and infamous cateran, Hamish MacTavish Mhor (cf. *mòr*: big), is distressed to learn that her son, Hamish Bean, has enlisted in a Highland regiment headed for America. Ignorant and isolated from the world, she is a caricature of the "old order" in the Highlands, not only Jacobitism but implicitly barbarism and cattle-stealing. She resents the substitution of civil order over the laird's commands. In contrast, the son (another mouthpiece for the author) praises all the Highland heroes of the past but adds that all the more recent chiefs are either dead or in exile. "We may mourn for it, but we cannot help it. Bonnet, broadsword, and sporran—power, strength and wealth—were all lost on Drummossie-muir [Great Hill of Shame, i.e., Culloden]."

Despite such argument, the widow is able to detain her son beyond the time he was to report for duty, and as a result, he is taken prisoner by his fellow Highlanders and executed for desertion.

Less tendentious is the better-known "The Two Drovers," a story he claimed to have heard long before in outline, lingering in his mind until he wrote it.

Narrated at the opening and closing by a clerk, the action begins as Robin Oig M'Combich, a Highland cattle-drover, rather short and well-liked, is about to leave for England. His aunt Janet of Tomahourich, delays him so that she can perform the *deasil*, a traditional ceremony to protect the herd and the drover from harm. With the second sight of a Highland seer, she sees English blood on his dirk, the dagger that every Highlander carries for protection. She asks that he leave it behind. Although proud of his heritage, his name taken from the outlaw Rob Roy, his grandfather's friend, Robin is less a believer in superstition. At Doune Fair he joins his friend from previous droves, Harry Wakefield, a large, strong, pugnacious Yorkshireman, and they agree to travel together, with their herds, to the cattle markets in England.

The reader soon understands that the two men are not only characters, but types. Robin is "as light and alert as one of the deer of his mountains." Harry is a contemporary iteration of old England's "merry yeoman." In a gesture of camaraderie, Robin tries unsuccessfully to teach Harry the Gaelic word for calf. Reaching a town, they break up to find grazing lands for their cattle, and by some incredible misfortune, they pay rent for the same patch of land. This forces Harry to poorer pasture. Learning of the mistake, Robin immediately tries to make amends and heal the rift between them, but Harry is incensed and storms off. Later when they meet again in a pub Robin offers his hand in friendship, Harry scoffs and challenges the Scotsman to a fist fight and knocks him down. Recognizing that Harry is much bigger, Robin withdraws and goes for the dirk he left behind, hearing Harry's taunt of "Coward!"

Two hours later, after walking six miles in each direction, Robin returns with his dirk and stabs Harry, killing him, recovering his honor. He then turns himself over to the law. An English judge in Carlisle rules that if Robin has used his dirk in the fist fight he would have been charged with manslaughter. As this killing was premeditated, the judge is compelled to demand the death penalty.

Uncomprehending of the legal distinctions, Robin accepts the natural conclusion to his destiny. "I give a life for the life I took," he says, "and what can I do more?"

"The Two Drovers" is often cited as the first of many Saxon vs. Celt narratives of the nineteenth century, which might substitute the Welsh or the Irish in place of the Highlander. It did not require much work to wrest the author's intentions. No subtle allegory was intended. The milieu of the Celt included magical or pagan elements. His honor code has no standing in a court of law. And much though the narrator makes Robin the more sympathetic of the two drovers, his diminished stature leaves him at a disadvantage against a more powerful adversary.

Scott's patriotic campaign to see Lowlanders and Highlanders united as a single nation never implied that he was an advocate for the Gaels. As a public figure, he was careful to appear non-committal on contentious issues. In his letters, however, he seemed untroubled by the kinds of clearances that so inflamed John Prebble a century and a half later. He praised the "improvements" (explosive word) of his friend the Countess of Sutherland when she moved tenants from their residences and replaced them with sheep. Nor was he concerned by the mass migrations that were depeopling the glens and islands. In what may be a libel, his later critics note how familiar he was with anti–Gaelic slurs. In *Waverley* one character speaks of children in the north as "Gillie wet-foots." He has been accused of being casual with the phrase, "bare-arsed Highlanders," also attributed to philosopher David Hume and no doubt familiar to many privileged Lowlanders.

It was off the page that Scott burnished the image of the Highlander and made Highland dress a signifier for the nation. King George IV visited Edinburgh in mid-August 1822, and in a moment both comic and epoch-making, he wore a kilt revealing his plump bare legs, establishing tartan's semiotic definition that has been with us ever since.

As the stage manager of this extravaganza, Scott knew he had found a mark in George IV (1762–1830), sixty years old at his arrival in Edinburgh, seriously overweight, wearing years of dissolute indulgence on his face. Compensating but not disguising powder and rouge on his pudgy cheeks were visible to the crowd. On his head Scott placed a feathered bonnet as "chief of chiefs." In the previous decade during the decline of his father, George III, he had been the high-living Prince Regent, pal of uber-fop Beau Brummell, and progenitor of innumerable illegitimate children. No British monarch had gone north of the border since 1650, and there was no precedent for a royal visit since the Union, 1707. Scott had prepared for this opportunity, flaunting the title Master of Ceremonies, not only with his literary pre-eminence but through his efforts to locate the Honours of Scotland (now called the Crown Jewels, of the pre–1603 monarchy), and putting them on display.

The tartan kilt, today ubiquitous, was largely Scott's innovation for the occasion. Traditional Highland dress, worn by some Jacobite soldiers, had indeed been banned to great chagrin, 1746–1782, but had been re-adopted widely. Travelers from the 1780s and 1790s reported a few kilts in the countryside of Inverness-shire, but not in the city of Inverness, and no reputable gentleman in the capital would be seen in one. Scott's confidence that he knew what tradition had been came from his reading of the research David Stewart of Garth, whose *Sketches of the Character, Manners and Present State of the Highlanders* (MS available 1819; published 1823) purported to give accurate pictures. Today, with hundreds of surviving garments catalogued in museums, we see that his theses do not withstand scrutiny. Scott, nonetheless, made them the standard. Any local luminaries who wished to attend the Grand Ball, August 19, 1822, had to dress following the king's example. The invitation read that except for those in uniform, "no Gentleman is allowed to appear in anything but the ancient Highland costume."

Some guests were allowed to deviate from Stewart of Garth's prescriptions, men who already owned their own "ancient" costumes. Scott wrote to certain Highland chiefs so that they might participate in the "gathering of the clans" (his phrase), not only for the King's benefit but for the elite of Edinburgh. One he wrote to was John Norman MacLeod, 24th chief of the clan, asking him to come to Edinburgh and "and bring half-a-dozen clansmen, so as to look like an Island Chief as you are…."

The upper crust of Edinburgh, who still often spoke of lazy, violent and drunken Highlanders in slurs, certainly did not think of themselves as Gaels but complied anyway. Twelve hundred people met the king within seventy-five minutes. Their unhappiness is noted in letters and diaries. Even well-born Highlanders, Scott's default allies, wrote privately of their unhappiness.

Scott won the day, and the nay-sayers have been pushed aside. His retelling of events remains dominant. Today a statue of the king in costume stands prominently in the New Town, and George IV Bridge, an elevated road despite the name, is the address of many important buildings.

The route of Highland tartan becoming the national signifier, unlikely as it was, had more than one enabler. Scott may not have read it, but during the Napoleonic wars Johann Wolfgang von Goethe had written about how much he liked seeing brightly colored Highland regiments on the march. Within the Scott household, George IV's appearance, August 1822, was looked upon as a family victory. The novelist's son-in-law John Lockhart boasted that the royal visit had certified "Sir Walter's Celtification of Scotland." In another phrase Lockhart proclaimed that Scott had pulled off a "plaided panorama," a realm of mist, lochs and mountain draped in tartan. Giving Scott's notions more urgency was James Logan's *The Scottish Gaël, or Celtic Manners, as Preserved Among the Highlanders* (1831), whose subtitle presents his argument. It's a mistake to think of Highlanders as backward when they *preserve* the heritage of the nation. Logan's research was worthless as history, but it launched the mania for tartan, something Scott had only anticipated. Logan's later book, *The Clans of the Scottish Highlands* (1845), with color plates by R.R. MacIan, remains in print, a gift "coffee table book" found in many homes today. At the very least tartan's brilliant colors make a striking contrast with the dark and dun hues favored by a Calvinist nation.

The Sett That Expresses

Many people outside the Gàidhealtachd use the word "plaid" most readily and look upon "tartan" as an alternative. Within the Highlands the visitor who confuses the two is berated as having committed a *faux pas* and scolded in mock dudgeon (not always so mock). "Tartan" is the word for distinctive crisscrossed, horizontal bands of multiple colors that originated on the loom and may be found anywhere. "Plaid" is the word for a large piece of tartan cloth, worn as a kind of kilt or large shawl and often slung over the shoulder; a man sleeping in the rough might use a plaid as bedding. To avoid confusion, your author has avoided the word "plaid" in its Highland meaning. "Sett," a word unfamiliar to general readers, is the distinctive pattern in the tartan. Counter-intuitively, "tartan" appears to be derived from the French *tartarin* or *tiretaine*, whose etymologies are disputed, possibly "Tartar cloth." The Scottish Gaelic word that pertains, *breacan*, is rarely borrowed in English. There are also Irish tartans, cited in a near-identical word *breacán*, but they indicate a region rather than a clan.

Anyone with a loom can vary the colored threads in a weave, even serendipitously, so we can find vague anticipations of tartan everywhere, including China.

Something with a closer resemblance to a tartan was found at the Iron Age Celtic settlement of Hallstatt, Austria, and something even closer stuffed into a third-century earthenware pot found at Falkirk. George Buchanan spoke of the Gaels wearing a distinctive "marled" material in his *History of Scotland* (1582); "marled" may be a Scots equivalent of the Gaelic *breacan*. All of these are as so many will-o'-the-wisps. Descriptions of Jacobite forces at the Battle of Killiecrankie indicate that some of the rebels wore leather or plain clothing, while others had distinctive white, black and green garments, not noted as "tartan." Martin Martin in his *A Description of the Western Islands of Scotland* (published 1703) observed that residents of different regions and islands wore different colors, but did not yet attribute them to clans. Dòmhnall Bàn MacNeacail's 1716 poem, *Laoidh an Tàilleir* (Ballad of the Tailor), has recently been explained as a satire on Gaelic worthies who wished to abandon traditional dress, anything approaching tartan, to look more British (Sumner, 2013). When the Black Watch Regiment was formalized (1739), it took the pattern it is still known for so as to be distinguished from the different clans members had been drawn from and whose setts had not yet been regularized. The favoring of tartans, regularized or not, by combatants in the 1745–1746 rebellion, as depicted in the famous Morier painting, associated them with bellicose Gaeldom and led to their being banned, 1746–1782. From reports, however, we know that men in the field were not known by their various tartans, different within a single clan, but by wearing a white cockade, usually on a hat or bonnet. Forbidding, in effect damning, tartan no doubt led to its lasting identification with Highlanders and with Scotland.

If Scott and Logan had presented tartan as a baton, two skilled charlatans ran with it. They were not natives of the British Isles and may have been Polish adventurers. Usually known as the Sobieski Stuarts, John Sobieski Stolberg Stuart and Charles Edward Stuart (aka Charles Allen Hay) claimed to be grandsons of Prince Charles Edward Stuart himself and his wife, Princess Louise Stolberg, through their legitimate but unnamed son. This met an immediate challenge and was impossible to prove, and today is thought to be bogus. Without any blood ties, however, they appear to be more adroit heirs of James Macpherson. Wherever they came from, they were in Scotland from at least 1822, when the visit of George IV also provided a redemption for Jacobitism. Claiming a link to Bonnie Prince Charlie allowed them a warm welcome from some prominent families, and if they did speak with a Polish accent, Prince Charles's mother was a Sobieski, one of Poland's finest families. Among the people they visited were the Grants of Rothiemurchus, the family of admired author Elizabeth Grant (unrelated to "white settler" Anne Grant), whose two-volume *Memoirs of a Highland Lady* is an oft-cited source of details of the very few privileged Highlanders. Elizabeth Grant had dismissed *Waverley* as "utterly at variance with truth," but she was completely taken with the Sobieski Stuarts as were so many others. Sir Walter Scott, however, took a strong dislike to the brothers, intensified by their conversion to Roman Catholicism. As they began their rise in commodifying tartanism, the novelist was bankrupt and in failing health, and could not be a brake on their commerce.

The Sobieski Stuarts' pretended lineage and their claim to forgotten, possibly esoteric knowledge of the origin of different tartans, were the basis of a growing enterprise. For a long period, they resisted calls to produce the source of their esteemed "knowledge," and eventually published something called the *Vestiarium Scoticum* (1842) based on the purported rare, ancient manuscript. Only they were never able to display the "original" from which all their patterns and setts had come. With a more modest claim, they published *The Costume of the Clans* (1844), which failed to meet the experiences of people who had been familiar with tartans all along, although not manufacturing them for sale in large numbers. Soon other merchants and self-anointed experts produced other volumes on the origin and classification of tartans, of which James Logan's *The Clans of the Scottish Highlands*, cited above, has had the longest shelf life.

The levels of chicanery in the foundation of tartan fashion have invited an amount of snickering from Scotophobes over the years. The most trenchant of those was the prestigious English historian Hugh Trevor-Roper's "Invented Tradition: The Highland Tradition of Scotland" in a widely read iconoclastic volume *The Invention of Tradition* (1983), edited by Eric Hobsbawm and Terence Ranger. He iterated some of the names and dates just recounted, but went further, puncturing the balloon of nearly *all* Highland tradition. He was refuted by two well-informed historians, Howard Gaskill (1986) and Donald Meek (1991) in little-read scholarly journals. Their views parallel what Derick S. Thomson had to say about James Macpherson: the Sobieski Stuart brothers and others were not as honest as they presented themselves but not as inventive as their detractors charged. Given Trevor-Roper's eminence and status, his views have persisted, just as John Prebble's have on the Clearances. He was so taken with the idea of fabrication that he later published *The Invention of Scotland: Myth and History* (2008), charging that the penchant for fabulizing the past runs through all of Scottish history, not just in the Highlands. Trevor-Roper's humiliation at having authenticated (later repudiated) the bogus *Hitler Diaries*, also in 1983, did not dull the sting of his Scottish critiques.

Well before George IV's bare calves were seen in Edinburgh or the Sobieski Stuart brothers arrived in town, the Highland Society of London set out to name and register official clan tartans on April 8, 1815. Founded in 1778, the Society had an admirable record for integrity, and should be distinguished from the Edinburgh Highland Society founded a decade later, or Scott's Edinburgh Celtic Society, 1820, established to add luster to the royal visit. The Society had fostered public readings of poetry in Gaelic and called for the "originals" of Macpherson's *Ossian*. It "respectfully solicited" examples of clan tartans from the most responsible spokesmen, often the chiefs themselves. Quite a few had no idea of what their tartan might be, but professed great interest in what could be determined. A communication survives from Alexander MacDonald, 2nd Baron MacDonald, who apologized for being so far removed from his Highland heritage and wrote, "Being really ignorant of what is exactly the MacDonald Tartan, I request that you have the goodness to exert every means in your power to obtain a genuine Pattern, such as will warrant me in authenticating it with my arms."

In some cases, with recognition from the clan chief, the clan tartan is recorded and registered by the Lord Lyon King of Arms, the same agency that certifies claims of selected families to be recognized clans. Once approved by the Lord Lyon, after recommendation by the Advisory Committee on Tartan, the clan tartan is then recorded in the Lyon Court Books. Non-Highland entities may also be recorded in the Lyon Court Books in other Gaelic and Celtic countries. The Irish surname Fitzpatrick has registered two tartans. Whether "official" or not, almost all Scottish clans claim more than one tartan. Beyond the official, families may claim what they wish. Your author's surname, MacKillop, is a sept of the MacDonells of Keppoch, but some one claimed a tartan for us in 1908, which is in fact the MacDonell tartan. The MacKillop tartan is available for sale in blankets, scarves and and ties as well as being found on the cover of this volume. In February 2009, the Scottish Parliament passed the Scottish Register of Tartans Act, which established the Scottish Register of Tartans, the SRT. Previous to this several competing voices, all of them private, sought establish authority over rival claims. The Scottish Tartans Society, STS, founded 1963, launched a register of Publicly Known Tartans that evolved into the Scottish Tartans World Register, with up to 3000 setts; it ceased operation in 2008. The Scottish Tartans Authority, the STA, founded 1995, claimed to have details of 10,000 tartans. Every Canadian province has a tartan as do several U.S. states. Given the vanity of jurisdictions where Scottish people have settled, as well as the aspirations of commercial entities like Burberry, there may well be as many as 14,000 tartans.

Industrialization, of course, drove the boom in Tartan marketing, with improved dyes as well as mechanized looms. Some patterns or setts were favored over others. The most popular is arguably the Royal Stewart, dominantly red, recorded by enthusiast James Logan in *The Scottish Gael* (1831), the book that nudged along the Sobieski Stuarts. It was the personal tartan of Elizabeth II, and is the mostly likely to appear on wrapping paper and biscuit tins. In 1853 Prince Albert designed a tartan called the "Balmoral" for his wife Queen Victoria. Only the royal family was allowed to wear it, and it never became popular. The second best-known is the Black Watch, as discussed in a previous chapter, which predates George IV's visit.

A Royal Patroness

Balmoral, about 50 miles (80 km) west of Aberdeen and near the village of Crathie in the Dee Valley, has been a Royal residence since 1852. Its antecedents go back to Robert II (1316–1390), and quite a number of edifices had been on the site over the centuries. Victoria and Albert had visited Scotland as newlyweds and searched the glens and islands before settling on Balmoral, culturally at the edge of the Highlands. With Albert taking a hand in design, a new castle appeared in an idealized "Scottish baronial" style in the next four years and remains the personal property of the Royal family and is not a part of the Crown Estate.

Whereas it was closed to the public, what happened in Balmoral was news, extensively reported in expanded mass communications. Under Victoria, the castle—really a country home—became a shrine of real and presumed Highland culture, including extensive displays of tartan. It may never have been planned, like Scott's exploitation of her uncle George IV, but Victoria became the most effective publicist for tartan in the century, the driver of its ubiquity. Under Victoria's championing of tartan, it was first thought appropriate clothing for children, especially girls. It also tended to shed an unstated political message. In the first decades after Scott, a strident Tory, wearing tartan in Scotland often signaled conservative nationalism. Over the decades, even into the twenty-first century, tartan has without plan been used for bifurcated messaging. On one hand comfortable bourgeois complacence, and on the other a muted impudence. The efforts of both Scott and the 1745 lads have not been expunged from collective memory.

Being in a wooded region, Balmoral did not present an opportunity for the royal family or visitors to see much of the local economy, no shabby housing, unsightly poverty, or forced evictions of tenants and subtenants, subject of the next chapter. The full estate today extends to 50,000 acres (20,000 hectares), allowing plenty of room for Albert to hunt deer, and for Victoria to take extended walks. Speaking often of her Stuart ancestry, Victoria could indeed depict herself as a Scot; she studied Scottish history extensively and declared herself a Jacobite. While she attended the Highland games in nearby Braemar, her meeting with actual Highlanders was not common and on her own terms. Once on a carriage ride from Fort William along what is today the A86, she was hailed by her subjects in the towns. In her diary she lamented that the children in Roybridge, once the habitat of poet Iain Lom, waved to her with unwashed faces. Then there is her much speculated-upon relationship with Highlander John Brown. He was a personal attendant, nearly always in Highland dress when photographed with her and clearly a favorite. Anything beyond that is an inexhaustible subject for romance writers.

Among the many guests invited to Balmoral was a steady procession of painters, especially landscape painters. The romantic potential in visualizing the wild scenery of the north was nothing new, having preceded Victoria by two generations. Alexander Runciman (1736–1785), prompted by Macpherson, produced his most famous work *The Hall of Ossian* in 1772. Putting aside Macpherson's pedestrian prose, Runciman knew the intensity of authentic native poetry in Gaelic. He produced twelve large subjects subsequently on Ossianic themes, without placing them specifically on passages in the texts. The most eminent British painter of the age, J.M.W. Turner (1775–1851) visited Loch Fyne, Argyllshire (1815), venue for several paintings, even before Scott had discovered the Gaels. His works were in with line the growing fascination that had brought Wordsworth and Keats to the Highlands. Victoria was looking for something gentler and idealized, what would later be called "Balmoralism." The Bavarian-born watercolorist Carl Haag (1820–1915) spoke to the queen's heart in works like *Evening in Balmoral (*1858) and *Morning in the Highlands—the Royal Family Ascending Lochnagar* (1859), with the family in formal wear near the top of the mountain cited by Lord Byron.

The artist most associated with Balmoralism was London-born Sir Edwin Landseer (1802–1873), an extraordinarily popular figure in his day. Starting in his teens with portrayals of St. Bernard dogs rescuing the stranded in the Alps, he was applauded for his depictions, in painting and sculpture, of animals, particularly horses, dogs and stags. His best-known works, the lions at the base of Nelson's Column in Trafalgar Square, are photographed many times each day. Attracted to the

Highlands well before Victoria was, his visits to Balmoral were occasions of considerable joy. He attempted to teach both Victoria and Albert to sketch. In his portraits of the royal children as babies, each was usually in the company of a dog. Earlier, in the year before her marriage, Victoria commissioned a portrait of herself as a present to Prince Albert. Other commissions include two portraits of Victoria and Albert dressed for costume balls, at which he was a guest himself. One of his works was an equestrian portrait of Victoria, unfinished at his death because of crippling depression and his being institutionalized.

Landseer's Highland output is so extensive that it is a bit unfair to have him epitomize Balmoralism, as we have. In his youth he produced *An Illicit Still in the Highlands* (1826–1829), and later in life he painted the pessimistic *Flood in the Highlands* (1864). But the painting for which he is best known is *The Monarch of the Glen* (1851), a heroic frontal portrait of a stag, widely distributed in steel engravings at the time, and now housed in the Scottish National Gallery in Edinburgh. Whether it is *echt*-Balmoralism or not, *Monarch* is the most widely known depiction of the Highlands (distinctive peaks in the background, the word "glen" in the title). Novelist Compton Mackenzie expected readers to know of it in titling his comic novel *Monarch of the Glen* (1940), about innkeeping in the Highlands, later a successful British television series. Its imagery is persistent. When Stephen Frears in directing *The Queen* (2006) has an unresolved Elizabeth II (Helen Mirren) try to find a way out of a dilemma on responding to the death of Princess Diana, she drives her own Land Rover on the grounds of Balmoral and encounters a stag evoking the *Monarch*.

Just as there had been Highland landscape painters before Landseer, so there were contemporaries who saw things differently, like William Wyld and William Henry Fisk. Further, as Landseer was anathematized by the modernists for his sentiment and flattery of patrons, many critics today would rank Horatio MacCulloch (1805–1867) much higher. His visions were darker and brooding, like *The Ruins of Inverlochy Castle* (1857) or *Glencoe, Argyllshire* (1864), but increased the allure of the Highlands all the same.

It would be glib to cite Victoria as a force in the development of the Highland tourist industry, because tourism grew everywhere in nineteenth-century Europe with more abundant leisure for the rising bourgeois and vastly improved transportation. Balmoral was remote, and the public could not set foot through the gate until 1931. Yet the Royal family had given examples of what to do in a region with generally poor roads and a still impoverished population: admire the scenery and hunt. As it was not industrialized, the Highland region contained the largest remaining wilderness in Western Europe with abundant game as there had been in the time of *Òran na Comhachaig* in the sixteenth century, only now it was managed. For the most affluent 5 percent of the British population, a mention of the word "Highlands" was coming to mean hunting deer and grouse. The notion long preceded Victoria. As early as 1784 a wealthy Yorkshire landowner, Col. Thomas Thornton, established a hunting camp on the Speyside. His love affair with the Highlands treated the landscape as if it were uninhabited. When more bourgeois hunters came north, they would take trains, thus avoiding unsettling confrontations with beggars still found in towns and along narrow country roads.

The most celebrated Highland route, the "Road to the Isles," did not come into use until the end of Victoria's reign in 1901, with the completion of the curved Glenfinnan Viaduct, with its twenty-one semicircular arches. It is such a source of national pride, that the Viaduct appeared on a £10 note issued by the Bank of Scotland in 2007. Famed engineer Thomas Telford blazed the route in the early nineteenth century, forty-two miles from Fort William to Mallaig, where a ferry takes the traveler to the Isle of Skye. One may also drive an automobile to Mallaig on a highway, finally widened to allow two vehicles to pass in 2007, but the train gets all the attention. It is one of the most famed train routes on earth and has long been on the "must-see" list of train buffs. Further, the phrase "Road to the Isles" strikes such a chord in the hearts of Highland nationalists that it inspired a song by Pipe Major John McLellan, published in 1917. The lyrics are lovingly festooned with Highland placenames, not all of them on the route.

The train route has always been a tourist attraction and has appeared in innumerable films and television programs, including those in the Harry Potter franchise. Fans of those films are so numerous and passionate, they have in effect rewritten history. Today the train employs an anachronistic steam engine, as it does in the Harry Potter films, and is called the Jacobite Steam Train, with a stop at the village of Glenfinnan, where Prince Charles raised his standard in 1745.

She may not have been known as a tippler, but Victoria and Balmoral radiated the gravitas that allowed a discriminating knowledge of Scotch whisky to be seen as a badge of connoisseurship. Whisky distillation in Scotland was noted in the *Exchequer Rolls* as early as 1494, but it was not until late in Victoria's reign that it was favored by European privileged classes.

There's a semantic kerfuffle in calling the whisky "Scotch," as is standard usage. It is a word that does not appear often in these pages. From the time of James I and his impecunious courtiers in 1603, "Scotch" was a patronizing if not insulting term, just as "Chinaman" is for a Chinese. That opprobrium was erased when referring to whisky, a tip-off to the beverage's rocketing prestige while Victoria was at Balmoral. The early history of the liquor is obscure and contended, with rival claims for Ireland and Scotland, studiously ignored here. The Irish *uisce beatha* and the Scottish Gaelic *uisge-beatha* both mean "water of life," equivalent of the Latin *aqua vitae*, all originally general terms for distilled spirits. Both the Scottish and Irish terms had earlier transliterations, *usquebaugh* and *iska baha,* appearing to suggest that the words have separate if parallel histories. This may justify the orthographic convention that Scotch is spelled without the -e-, "whisky," and Irish with, "whiskey," with both spellings found in North America.

James IV, who died at Flodden Field, 1513, was known to be a champion of whisky, but for the most part it was the drink of the poor in remote regions, its manufacture clandestine. The first taxation of whisky in 1644 was a boon for illicit distilling. In 1782, more than 1,000 illegal stills were seized in the Highlands, probably only a fraction of the total in operation. As mentioned above, painter J.M.W. Turner observed that raids on illegal stills were a feature of the landscape. Highland magistrates, themselves members of the landowning classes, were reluctant to crack down on law-breaking tenants, as they used ill-gotten income to pay their rent. Whisky's social status took a step up with the Excise Act of 1823, effectively suppressing the illegals but also encouraging professional distilling, producing a standardized but less intense and smoother product. The next year a farmer, George Smith, working for the Duke of Gordon, took out a license to found Glenlivet Distillery, to make single malt Scotch.

French misfortune changed the status of Scotch whisky. The episode, well-known to vinophiles, is today called the Great French Wine Blight, for the invasion of the grape *phylloxera* bug, first noted in the former French province of Languedoc in 1863. In the next twenty years it devastated perhaps 40 percent of French vineyards, an economic as well as gastronomical catastrophe. The Blight is remembered in America for the opportunity it presented to the nascent California wine industry. Its effect was arguably even greater for the smaller Scotch enterprise. Whisky was too potent to replace wine on a large scale, but the subtle, layered textures of single malt Scotch, for which there were now several firms, could compete well in the brandy market. A prudent tax policy raised the price of Scotch, marking its consumption as more upmarket. Consider the recognition in the town of Beaune, capital of the Burgundy wine culture. The streets are flush with merchants vending the pricey local vintage. In their midst one shop is selling Scotch, its flat façade blazoned with tartan. The Irish whiskey industry, lacking the cachet of Balmoral, became a distant second choice. Prestige forged in a moment of crisis has proved remarkably sturdy.

Victoria and Albert may have attended the Highland Games in nearby Braemar (1844), but it is a claim too far to assert the Queen and Balmoral promoted the revival of the games. The competition at Braemar had only begun in 1826, but the site carried weighty significance. Not only was the area still Gaelic speaking, but Braemar Castle had been the residence of the Earl of Mar, leader of the 1715 Jacobite rising. Instead, the spontaneous popular fascination with the games rode on the mid-nineteenth-century tide of tartan mania, inspired by Victoria, supplemented by the admiration for Highland regiments. To some degree the cultural face of the games is what Walter Scott had hoped for. Displays of tartan have always been signifiers, along with Highland dress, dance competitions and bagpipes. The Lonach Games at Strathdon claim to date from 1823, but other dating is difficult to chart, as the organizers were usually local and saw no need to keep strict records. Individual contests, such as the caber toss, might indeed be centuries old, and Máel Coluim (Malcolm, 1031–1093) sponsored athletic competitions, but the games as we know them, with several contests juxtaposed in a kind of festival, is the product of Victorian times. As the popularity of the games spread south across the border to England and beyond, the distinction between "Highland" and "Scottish" came to be blurred, perhaps a step beyond what Scott hoped for. In the third decade of the twenty-first century, there are at least 135 games world-wide, more in Canada and the United States than in Britain, but including Hungary, Brazil and Indonesia.

The several competitions, such as the caber toss, stone put, the hammer throw, sheaf toss, etc., provide reliable theater and are not seen elsewhere. It is often noted that Baron Pierre de Coubertin was favorably impressed by the Highland games displayed at the Paris Exposition of 1889 before he planned the revival of Olympic

Games in Greece. As entertainment the games can take themselves seriously, with conspicuous attention to protocol, but they do not intend to teach. Attendees may leave with fond feelings for the heather and the hills but little more. On other hand, the games are egalitarian and ecumenical. Ancient enmities, Campbell vs. MacDonald, Highland vs. Lowland, have vanished. Participants and attendees can find the games occasions of ethnic pride, insurance against the memories of poverty and the Clearances. At the same time the games do not herald ethnic chauvinism and are anything but exclusive. Similarly, the games have avoided acquiring any political or religious taints for the most part.

Away from Balmoral

No matter how depleted our taste for Walter Scott fiction may be in the twenty-first century, the Waverley novels continued to sell well all though the nineteenth century, throughout the English-speaking world and beyond. A complete set with lavish binding, displayed in the parlor or drawing room, would have been an asset for a bourgeois family asserting credentials for refinement. Tartanism notwithstanding, as mentioned above, Scott had little to say about actual Gaels as they lived their lives; that remained to be seen. The Highlands, with a failed rebellion and so beloved of landscape painters, became a mecca for costume romance, often influenced by Anne Grant, as mentioned: lovable, naïve peasants, perhaps given to superstition but unsoiled by the grime of the commercial world. Borrowed from Scott were bold warriors, only now with Gaelic names, and the lassies were always beautiful, often red-haired.

Seduced by this bogus allure was American abolitionist and novelist Harriet Beecher Stowe (1811–1896), forever associated with the trenchant *Uncle Tom's Cabin* (1852), depicting the inhumanity of chattel slavery. On visiting the romantic Highlands as a guest of well-to-do-landlords, the Duke and Duchess of Sutherland, her eyes became filled with stars. Her *Sunny Memories of Foreign Lands* (1854), gives a stunningly addled defense of the Clearances, completely oblivious to any human suffering. Donald Macleod's smoldering riposte *Gloomy Memories in the Highlands of Scotland*, published in Canada (1857; republished 1892), can stand at the beginning of a tradition of anti-romantic realism, not continued until the twentieth century. Macleod had earlier attacked the Sutherlands in twenty-one letters to an Edinburgh newspaper. The suffering of common people in the glens and on the isles was known to journalists, and would be reported in official documents, recounted in the next chapter.

Following the success of *Waverley*, as well as *Scottish Chiefs*, the romanticized Highlands became a top theme in popular fiction. This provoked an early angry rebuke from a London-based author who claimed to know the truth about the Gaelic north. Sarah Green's two-volume *Scotch Novel Reading: or, Modern Quackery, by a Cockney* (1824) is an angry polemic arguing that the Gaels are an impoverished, uncouth population given to violence, never to be prettified. Many of the titles she damns were ephemeral, however, not recorded elsewhere and impossible to find today. One of her points is valid, admittedly, a knowledge of Gaelic or a sure-footed familiarity with regional geography were not required to get into print. Alma Randall Emmons' workmanlike Cornell University dissertation, "The Highlander in Scottish Prose Fiction" (1941), labors to sort out all the materials. Her evaluations are more considered and generous than what you are reading here. From her work, however, we can see that there are really only two pieces of fiction worth mentioning from before 1900, Robert Louis Stevenson's justly famous *Kidnapped* (1886) and its little-read sequel *Catriona* (1893). A third Highland fiction, *The Master of Ballantrae* (1889), begins with the contrived premise that two brothers, Jamie and Henry Durie, should take opposite sides in the Jacobite Rebellion so that, win or lose, the family estate can be retained by one of them. When the defeat at Culloden comes early, the rest of the action is set outside Scotland, including North America. There was a time when Edinburgh-born Stevenson (1850–1894) was dismissed as a man who picked up Scott's lead and wrote adventure books for boys. Just as continuing critical comment has sent Scott's reputation into steady decline, Stevenson's has been on the rise. To read *Kidnapped* juxtaposed with any Waverley tome today is to find it superior on every count, both his facility with the subject matter and his skills as novelist. His descriptions of actual places, like the Isle of Mull and the region called Appin in Argyll, sound as though he had been there. Characters in the action are based on historical figures pretty much the way the surviving records portray them. Not that he was hidebound to his research. He sets the action in 1751 when the key events actually took place in 1752.

Kidnapped was serialized in *Young Folks* magazine before it was published, and it pulses with fast-moving action told by a youthful narrator. Why not see it as a sibling of *Treasure Island*, one of the great boys' books of all time? More tellingly, it appeared the same year as the short fiction "The Strange Case of Dr. Jekyll and Mr. Hyde," now recognized as much more than a tale of horror. Critics who have returned to *Kidnapped* as adults see subtler characterizations instead of mere types so usual in the genre, and meditations on justice and the justice system, along with narrative delight. The novel's champions have included Henry James, Argentine Nobel Laureate Jorge Luis Borges, and twenty-first-century historical fiction doyenne Hilary Mantel.

Because of his prestige, composer and Scotophile Felix Mendelssohn's tribute to Gaelic Scotland in *The Hebrides Overture* (*Fingal's Cave*) would be heard in concert halls all through the nineteenth century, as well as today. Not so any Highland music, as frequently as it was performed by the musicians of the many tartan-wearing regiments. The Scottish romantic composer, Hamish (born James) MacCunn (1868–1916), was a Lowlander from Greenock, despite his Gaelic name. He came to maturity when Sir Walter Scott still defined Scottishness, and Richard Wagner was the charismatic new force in the concert hall. The delicacy of Highland music was alien to his taste. His best-known, still widely performed work, *The Land of the Mountain and the Flood* (1887), took its title from Scott's *Lay of the Last Minstrel* and evoked the Scottish-English border. His best-known opera, *Jeannie Deans* (1894), was based on Scott's *The Heart of Mid-Lothian*. A second opera *Diarmid* (1897), is based on the tragic love story of Diarmait and Gráinne from the Fenian Cycle, known both in Ireland and Gaelic Scotland. MacCunn's libretto makes him Scottish.

Analyses of MacCunn's work describe *Diarmid* as an evocation of Wagner's *Tristan und Isolde*. One contemporary review gave the composer the back-handed compliment of liberating his nation from the dominance of folksongs and bagpipes. The other works with promising titles, the *Cior Mhor* overture (1885) and the *Highland Memories* suite (1897), give no indication of drawing on Gaelic musical sources.

It was not until late in the nineteenth century running into the twentieth that Scottish Gaelic music could be known as something other than the culture of peasants. Individual initiative was built on two phenomena not considered before, both arising from elite niches in the population. The first was the growth of academic knowledge of Gaelic, and the second was the fashion for things "Celtic" among artists who set themselves apart from the bourgeois and mass markets.

Inspired by the Brothers Grimm's studies of traditional culture, and even more extensive field work in Scandinavia, an aristocrat named John Francis Campbell of Islay (1822–1885) decided to sponsor something comparable in Gaelic Scotland. Along with his privileges from birth, he was highly cultivated in the arts and brought considerable financial resources. When he could not accomplish a task himself, he sought the most skilled persons and paid what they asked. The results were *Popular Tales of the West Highlands* in four volumes (1862), followed by a single volume of Fenian tales, *Leabhar na Féinne: Heroic Gaelic Ballads Collected in Scotland* (1872), what Macpherson had purported to employ but in fact barely knew. These could never have the sales of a Scott or Stevenson novel, but they brought to a wider learned readership the argument that the Gaels had a substantial body of narrative literature that stood comparison to what was found in more affluent and sovereign societies. In 1882 the first Chair of Celtic was established at the University of Edinburgh, held by a Gael, Donald Mackinnon. More collections of literature in translation would follow, such as *Waifs and Strays of Celtic Tradition*, 4 vols. (1889–1891), edited by Lord Archibald Campbell (not closely related to J.F. Campbell) and others.

The Campbells and their compatriots paid no attention to music, presenting an opportunity for Marjory Kennedy-Fraser (1857–1930), again from a family of manifest artistic cultivation. She was born in Perth, just beyond the limits of the Gàidhealtachd, but she traveled widely with her father, a well-known singer in a family of musicians. She began to study Gaelic music as early as 1882, and took instruction in the language from poet Mary Mackellar. Widowed with two children at thirty-six, she did not have substantial resources but was well-connected to changing fashions and artistic trends. Through a close relationship with painter John Duncan and publisher Patrick Geddes, she was enchanted by the Celtic Renaissance developing in Dublin around poet-playwright William Butler Yeats and the women of the Dun Emer, later Cuala Press. Geddes of Edinburgh was also the publisher of the 1896 *Poems of Ossian* with defiantly credulous notes of authenticity. Duncan led her to the Gaelic-speaking island of Eriskay, where he did a portrait of her against the landscape.

Witnessing the emigration from the island and all the Hebrides, as well as the displacement of Gaelic by English, she took it upon herself to transcribe, eventually to record, all the music of a vanishing but still living tradition. She was anticipated by and drew from an earlier collector from the Isle of Skye, Frances Tolmie

(1840–1926). She also worked with a bilingual minister, Kenneth Macleod, who also—independent of Kennedy-Fraser—produced "The Road to the Isles," cited above. Work proceeded slowly with first results not published until 1909, with the full *Songs of the Hebrides*, giving credit to Macleod, in 1922.

What distinguished Kennedy-Fraser from the Campbells of *Popular Tales* and *Waifs and Strays* is that she was a performer first and a collector second. She wanted material for herself, something suitable for the concert hall, an art song, not an item for a fireside or encampment. Her phrase for her efforts was "to blend traditional melody with appropriate harmonic setting." To this end she was highly successful. Her concerts were well attended, and she was awarded a CBE (1928) and an honorary doctorate of music from the University of Edinburgh (1930), in the year of her death.

The most admired of her efforts is "An Eriskay Love Lilt," an elegant and captivating piece of music, which is constantly performed and available in multiple recordings as well as on-line in the third decade of the twenty-first century. Usually classed as "traditional," it is far from that. Kennedy-Fraser based her "Lilt" on the folk song known as *Gràdh Geal mo Chridhe*, "fair/dear/bright love of my heart," which she collected from Mary MacInnes on the Isle of Eriskay. When they are performed side-by-side, as I have witnessed several times, one can hear some thematic parallels. The Gaelic song might be sung by a barefoot lassie of the islands, but the "An Eriskay Love Lilt" was written by someone conversant with Franz Schubert and Robert Schumann.

A chapter that begins with a discussion of James Macpherson and ends with Marjory Kennedy-Fraser should not imply that the two are comparable. Kennedy-Fraser is incontestably more admirable, a diligent worker not given to misrepresentation who left us more than one work of lasting beauty. What she shares with Macpherson, as well as Sir Walter Scott, Edwin Landseer and Robert Louis Stevenson, is the assumption that the Gaelic Highlands, what Thomas Pennant had depicted as a vast tract of rural poverty, is better seen through their eyes or heard with their ears.

Only 2.75 square miles (703 hectares), tucked under the much larger South Uist in the Outer Hebrides, Eriskay has played an outsized role in the Highland story. Each appearance links disparate episodes of contrasting tone. Prince Charles Edward's ship *Du Teillay* landed here in 1745 before he went to the mainland to unfurl his standard at Glenfinnan. Moving from the heroic to the comic, the freighter *Politician*, loaded with booze, was stranded on Eriskay in 1941, allowing the islanders an unanticipated bounty. This maritime "disaster" prompted Compton Mackenzie (1883–1960) to write *Whisky Galore* (1947), one of the most hilarious comedies written with a Gaelic setting. It was filmed in 1949 and 2016, sometimes marketed under the title *Tight Little Island*. These are to say nothing of the Eriskay pony or Eriskay jersey (distinctively seamless). The residents of Eriskay, about 150 at the time of this writing, are better served by Marjory Kennedy-Fraser's romantic evocation.

6

After Romance

Sheep Over People

T.M. Devine cites a fuller version of the following quotation at the beginning of his *The Scottish Clearances* (2018):

> The chatter and gossip of half the salons and drawing-rooms of European intellectualism hang over the antique Scottish scene like a malarial fog through which peer the fictitious faces of heroic Highlanders, hardy Norsemen, lovely Stewart queens, and dashing Jacobite rebels.
> Those stage-ghosts shamble amidst the dimness, and mope and mow in their ancient parts with an idiotic vacuity but a maddening persistence.
> —Lewis Grassic Gibbon & Hugh MacDiarmid
> *Scottish Scene; or, The Intelligent Man's Guide to Albyn* (1934)

Neither Gibbon (born James Leslie Mitchell, 1901–1935) nor MacDiarmid (born Christopher Murray Grieve, 1892–1978) ever claimed Highland antecedents, but they strove to find an obscured Scotland under the "malarial fog" of the "persistent" appeal of the romantic Highland mythology. Grassic wrote novels of poetic realism set in the Lowland county of Mearns/Kincardine. MacDiarmid, in spite of his Gaelic pseudonym, was an eccentric left-wing intellectual who became the patriarch of Scottish literary nationalism by raising the status of Lallans or Broad Scots. Also hidden by the myth, the actual Highlands remained the rural slum depicted by Thomas Pennant for several generations. Some of the most degrading and infuriating episodes in Highland history took place after scenes from Macpherson's *Ossian* were sung in operas on the European stage, and even more after tartan became an international fashion. Although John Prebble barely cites the "romantic attachment to kilt and tartan," it is not hard to see how his *The Highland Clearances* (1963) became an angry polemic in reaction to it.

At the beginning of the nineteenth century, the Highlands were still suffering from all the blights described at the end of the fourth chapter. Entry into the cash economy meant the subtenants were subject to price fluctuations set in distant markets they could not comprehend. Rural population continued to boom, partially because of the potato, more than the meager arable land could support. The price of wool was rising faster than that of other commodities the Highlands produced. As long as war raged with France, kelp would maintain a good price, but that was doomed to collapse soon.

Out-migration continued on the upswing, first to the Lowlands and the rest of Britain, but increasingly to the New World, and eventually the Antipodes. Most trans-oceanic transportation came aboard cargo vessels that imported raw materials, especially timber, from Canada. They were cruelly unsuited to be passenger ships, uncomfortable, squalid and dangerous for a short voyage, unimaginable for one lasting weeks in rough seas. Of some 700 passengers aboard the *Sarah* in 1801, 49 died en route to Canada. Passengers had to be inoculated for small pox, and there were Crown rules for the numbers of people packed in. Unscrupulous captains flouted such protections by counting two children as one passenger, or worse, three smaller children as one adult. This might still have been before the era of mass communication, but the treatment of emigrating Highland poor came to be seen as an intolerable moral failure. To address the suffering, in 1803 Parliament passed the Passenger Vessels Act, often cited as the Ships' Passenger Act. It would address questions of hygiene, food and comfort, but notably failed to deal with the continuing threat of typhus. It also raised fares. Whereas an Atlantic crossing to Canada in 1802 was £3–£4, the fare now jumped to £10—possibly £ 825 today—forbidding to many subtenants with only pennies to their name.

For the moment the Passenger Vessels Act looked like a gesture of enlightened benevolence, but gimlet-eyed observers reminded the public that landlords supported its passage vigorously. They clearly did not wish to see the draining of such a large pool of cheap labor. Mention of this comes early in this chapter to qualify dominance of the poverty/eviction/sheep replacement paradigm so widely publicized that will be demonstrated in subsequent pages. The fuller story has divergences from the norm.

Among those who immediately denounced the Act was the benevolent nobleman, the 5th Earl of Selkirk, Thomas Douglas (1771–1820). Born the same year and into the same class as Walter Scott, he also attended the same schools as the Tory novelist. Selkirk's responses to the world they both inherited could hardly have differed more. While still a law student he was shocked to see poor crofters displaced by their arrogant landlords. When he inherited both his title and considerable wealth unexpectedly, he set about to address human suffering as a personal mission. First, he helped support the migration of poor Scottish farmers, not all of them Highland, to Prince Edward Island, and following that to support movement to a colony called Baldoon (now Wallaceburg) on the shore of Lake St. Clair in southwest Ontario.

Galled by the hypocrisy of the Passenger Vessels Act, Selkirk published his own analysis of matters with his own recommendations, *Observations on the Present State of the Highlands of Scotland* (1805). Instead of keeping Highlanders home in near starvation, he argued, the British government should be seizing upon this tremendous opportunity to establish in the colonies a set of people who were demonstrably well suited to pioneering and whose military antecedents could make them useful in foiling ambitions of the United States against the imperial domain to the north. Not only had Selkirk traveled widely in still untracked British North America, but he became conversant with colorful explorer, Stornoway-born Sir Alexander Mackenzie (1764–1820), the man who charted Canada's longest river in the far northwest, named for himself. After much maneuvering, legal and personal, Selkirk married Jean Wedderburn, a member of the family running the Hudson's Bay Company, and thought about new lands opening west of the Great Lakes.

This led to the most improbable and reckless of Highland settlements abroad, when 128 men led by Miles Macdonell sailed in 1812 to Hudsons Bay and trekked overland to the Red River of Rupert's Land, in what is now Manitoba. The understanding was that they would not compete in the fur trade, but they arrived too late for a planting and so became dependent on the indigenous population, the Métis, who were allied with the North West Company, Hudson's Bay's rival. The colony never thrived. Tensions with the Métis increased, culminating in the Battle of Seven Oaks, 1816, in which twenty-one of Selkirk's men, including the new governor, were killed, but only one Métis. His legal and financial problems multiplying, Selkirk was nearly broke at his death in 1820. Nonetheless, Highland settlement continued, with Gaelic being widely spoken in Manitoba until the late twentieth century. The Earl's name is commemorated in several locations, starting with the City of Selkirk.

The intermingling and intermarriage of the Gaels with indigenous populations was not common elsewhere in Anglophone colonies (putting aside the history of Ulster Protestants or the U.S. western frontier). Word of this cultural interface brought forth a memorable insult from Patrick Sellar, one of the ogres of the Clearances narrative to be discussed later in this chapter. As he was trying to drive families from their residences in Sutherland, he wrote that "the aborigines of Britain" occupied much the same sort of position as the "aborigines of America." Both "live in turf cabins in common with the brutes" and both "were shut out from the general stream of knowledge and cultivation flowing in upon the commonwealth of Europe from the remotest fountain of antiquity." So, it followed from his point of view, if the cause of civilization was advanced by expelling aborigines from their ancestral lands to make way for productive settlement, including sheep-farming, so too the expulsion of the shiftless Gaels was a benefit for the common good.

On a sunnier note, the award-winning Manitoba playwright Ian Ross (b. 1968) sets the action of many of his works among the Métis. Just as he has a Scottish name, so do many of his characters.

Most observers would perceive the Earl of Selkirk as a benign and enlightened figure, notwithstanding his pecuniary interests in the Hudson's Bay Company, and the unhappy fates of many of his colonists. He certainly saw himself acting for the benefit of mankind. So, strange to say, did many of the persons, men and women, who were responsible for removing poor Highlanders against their wills from the environs where they and their families had lived for generations. Although most from afar look like so many Scrooges in tartan or Marxist caricatures of heartless exploitation, many of them saw themselves as aiding the poor. The key word is "Improvement," widely used in the mid-eighteenth century, in England and Wales even more than in Scotland. It might mean tearing down stone cottages with thatched roofs and replacing them with dwellings protected by non-flammable materials. Any of a thousand actions might contribute to "Improvement." In time the word's implications came to parallel those of "urban renewal" in the mid-twentieth century. When imposed from above or the outside, "Improvement" could be destructive to intangible human relations. The semantic shift in association of the word "improvement" can be dated to 1820 in the response to the publication of the unctuously self-congratulatory *An Account of the Improvements on the Estate of the Earl of Sutherland* by James Loch. As the commissioner of the Earl's (later Duke's) estates in both Sutherland and in England, he was the creator of the Policy of Improvement and thus its apologist, although Patrick Sellar is the more familiar *bête noire* of the narrative. Commentators removed from the scene, the "liberal media" of the day, could deride the moral self-congratulation of the "Improvers." English journalist Thomas Bakewell wrote in 1820, when the Clearances were still on the rise, that "Improvements" he had observed meant taking a man, his wife and their six small children from a humble abode and leaving them "encamped in the open air like gipsies." From this point the word "Improvement" gained an ill odor. We may use the word "Clearance" as the default term, though it did not become current with its present implications until about 1880.

Initially the citation of "Improvement" may not have been so hypocritical. In Chapter 4 we considered the case of Marjory Grant MacDonell of Glengarry, who assisted the local crofters, doubly hard-pressed as Jacobites and Roman Catholics, to migrate to the new, open land of Glengarry County in Upper Canada, now Ontario. True, she filled the emptied lands in Scotland with sheep, for her profit, but she might stand company that included the Earl of Selkirk, even with John Prebble's lengthy list of her sins.

No so her daughter Elizabeth, who married the 24th chief of Chisholms of Strathglass in 1795, when her husband was an ailing old man. Strathglass, as the name signals, is a wide, shallow valley west of Loch Ness, about twenty-five miles (42 km) west-south-west of the city of Inverness. As in Glengarry, the crofters were both Roman Catholic and Jacobite, serving in the battlefield at Culloden Moor. Elizabeth was in Strathglass more than five years before she decided she was surrounded by too many unsightly crofters, kinsmen of her ailing husband. Egged on by the factor, or estate manager, Thomas Gillespie, Elizabeth began to feel that the clan tenants and subtenants were worth more to her and her husband if they were out of sight. Many young men were mustered into the British Army, not such an attractive choice when there was a concurrent war with France. Many more would be cleared from the land and put on ships for Pictou, Nova Scotia, less salubrious than Glengarry County on the St. Lawrence. Ships' records are not complete, but in 1801 and 1802, the last years before the Passenger Vessels Act, 5000 people left Fort William, mostly for Pictou and fewer for Upper Canada. The death rate from fever was horrendously high. Among those who survived the passage, though old and frail, was the Gaelic poet Donald Chisholm, "Donald the Blacksmith." Before departure he had written verses giving his companions hope for the new life awaiting them across the ocean. More convincingly, he denounced The Chisholm for the treatment of his own people: "Our chief is losing his kin! He prefers sheep in his glens, and his young men away in the Army!"

The Chisholm holdings in Strathglass were so extensive that Elizabeth and Thomas Gillespie did not empty all the properties at the time of the 24th chief's death in 1817. Some of the finest fields were still in cropland, tended by tenants. So the 25th chief, Alexander Chisholm, continued the family policy toward the tenants, with some new cruelties. He had the factor invite all the remaining men of the valley to meet at the inn in the principal town of Crannich for the purpose of learning what would happen to their leases. After they waited for some hours, his carriage arrived—empty. The Chisholm would not appear, and in his stead was the factor, who had no instructions to enter into any arrangements with them. There was no alternative for them but the emigrant ship. The best lands in Strathglass were let without knowledge of the longtime tenants to shepherds from other counties, many of them in the Lowlands.

Seen from our point in time, the passive submission of the misused previous tenants looks startling. How this should have become an expected reaction will be a subject for further discussion after we have reviewed other clearances. Not only did the Chisholms cause no disorder of any kind, but after many of the evicted had settled in Canada, 1832, they sent word back to Strathglass affirming their loyalty to the clan. They hailed the chief even though they no longer lived in their homeland. Did they bear no grudge? Was this an admirable but naïve testimony that they went willingly, even gratefully, to the filthy and dangerous emigrant ships? Some observers suggest that this was rhetorical irony meant to shame the chief over the betrayal of the noble clan ideal of *ceann-cinnidh*, binding the leader with his "children," the clan.

Patrick Sellar (1780–1851), the most vilified figure in the story of the Clearances, claimed that "improvement" was paramount in his mind. Not without reason has his name been tarred. His demeaning quote on the worthlessness of "aborigines" such as the Gaels and the Métis was quoted above. Almost an evangelical for the removal of crofters, Sellar was educated at Edinburgh and considered himself to be a creature of the Scottish enlightenment as a student of the likes of Adam Smith and Dugald Stewart. In the days before mass communications, he wrote highly emphatic letters advocating Improvement, employing the rhetoric that made him fearsome in the courtroom. Together with an older partner, William Young, his services were for hire to landlords who lacked the managerial skills or stomach to do the job themselves. Significantly, Sellar was the grandson of a tenant farmer who had been cleared from his property in non–Gaelic Morayshire in the northeast of Scotland. Rather than being embittered, Patrick Sellar said this family's upward mobility arose from the foresight of an improving landlord. Patrick's father, the first generation out of the croft, had been educated and became a prosperous lawyer.

Sellar and Young's services were employed often, but their biggest assignment, and most deserving of attention, was with Lord and Lady Stafford, who would become the Duke and Duchess of Sutherland as they are often known, possibly the richest couple in Britain at that moment. Confusingly, the couple are known under different names at different times. George Granville Leveson-Gower married the former Elizabeth Gordon, daughter of the last Earl of Sutherland. George was Marquis of Stafford, and his wife the Marchioness, the term Prebble prefers for her. James Loch's apologia for Improvement refers to George as the Earl. He was elevated to the rank of Duke and thus Elizabeth the Duchess. Sutherland was generally a thinly populated, poor and remote county, not often cited in this study. The Lord's holdings increased through inheritance while Sellar was working with him, and he claimed title to 63 percent of the total land in the shire. Overland transportation within the shire was difficult and slow, but the Duke and Duchess's castle at Dunrobin in the far southeast of the county was but fifty miles from the town of Inverness.

Visiting Sutherland first in 1809, Sellar was appalled by the backwardness of what he found: antiquated farming techniques and ineffective drainage of swamps. He and Young approached George and Elizabeth, then known as the Staffords, suggesting their services, and she was readier to accept the offer as she had improving ideas of her own. As with the Chisholms of Strathglass, the lady of the estate, then known as Lady Stafford, was the prime decision-maker. She had already wanted to eliminate the tacksmen, whose role had been diminishing in the previous decades, and she was keen on introducing sheep. In 1807 she had ordered ninety families removed from the parishes of Farr and Lairg. Once Sellar and Young were appointed factors in 1810, the first improvements were technological and logistical rather than human. Although they were not Sellar's or Lady Stafford's first concern, 213 out of 253 tenants found themselves evicted.

It took years before Sellar and Young would apply their harshest improvement plans, and that in one of the remotest corners of the dukedom at Assynt on the rugged Atlantic coast. Arriving circumspectly, the two first secured the support of the tacksman (still on the job) and ministers, who then advised their people to go without protest. With this urging was the warning that their departure was the wish of Lady Stafford herself, who expected them to obey her agents. The tacksman who went along with the edict, of course, found himself removed from his home. Even before the homes could be flattened or the crofters crowded upon ships, the white waves of Cheviot sheep swept into the croplands. There was no unrest, no resistance of any kind, but angry verses with rhetorical raised fists have survived.

In the next year, 1813, Sellar and Young struck again, in territory removed from Dunrobin, the Strath of Kildonan to the north coast, bordering with Caithness (to be distinguished from other, larger Kildonans elsewhere in Scotland). Things did not go well for the pair from the beginning. The strath was the bailiwick of the Clan Gunn, known to be fractious and intractable, and well supported by income from illegal distilleries. They and others were alert to what had happened in Assynt and so greeted the first inspections of Sellar and Young with affronting hostility. News of this setback reached Lady Stafford in London, who thought Scotland might be too irksome for a summer visit but reaffirmed her confidence in her factors. Tensions rose further when an improving associate, a Mr. Reid, the Northumbrian manager of a southern sheep combine, arrived in Kildonan with his notebook, asking many questions. He beat a quick retreat, and when he reached Golspie, near Dunrobin Castle, he claimed that he had been attacked by a mob of mad Gaels and feared for his life; no witnesses corroborated. But rumor flared, including the charge that the men of Strath of Kildonan intended to march on Dunrobin Castle to burn the place, expel all sheep farmers and hang Young and Sellar. They did, at least, wish to make a petition. The threat was enough to call up the Sheriff and the constables, who read, in no figure of speech, the Riot Act. It was in English, however, and not understood by the Gunns and other Highlanders.

As the Gunns and people of Kildonan returned home, they were pursued by a detachment of red coats, the 21st Foot, some artillery and wagons loaded with ammunition. In response to the Sheriff's urgent plea, they had been force-marched from Fort George. Their armed presence was enough to dishearten the crofters, now resigned to wait for their writs of removal. The troops arrested a few suspicious-looking sorts, but they were soon released. This was enough to encourage the estate to make a few concessions, such as paying more for the cattle of those cleared, and also allowing some of the uprooted to relocate nearby or become herring fishers rather than to emigrate. The whole process was a severe shock to Lady Stafford and her team, who were "genuinely astonished at this response to plans which they regarded as wise and benevolent," according to Eric Richards (1999). She had established a refuge for the displaced in a town on the north coast, named for herself, Bettyhill.

Ninety-six men and women proudly chose exile and sailed from Stromness, joining the Earl of Selkirk's risky venture to head through icy Hudson Bay to the Red River Valley of what is now Manitoba, cited above. That party was destined to be well remembered because their descendants included a prime minister of Canada, John Dieffenbaker (1895–1979). During his term in office, 1957–1963, he made a well-publicized visit to the Strath of Kildonan, marking a headstone, drawing world attention to the Clearances a few years before the Prebble book appeared.

A third clearance in as many years was scheduled for Whitsun, May 15, in 1814, in Strathnaver, north and west of Kildonan. If one were to believe in omens, the venture did indeed begin badly, increasing in misfortune as events unfolded. Through the indignation of a humble but articulate observer, the names of the factors and the landlords, a century and a half later, were destined to be blackened in Scottish history because of it.

At the end of the previous year, December 1813, Patrick Sellar bid on a lease for one of the sheep farms to rest on land that he as factor was about to clear. It would have been usual practice for an incoming sheep farmer to burn heather on the hillsides to prepare for the grass he would plant for grazing. Only as he was also the clearing factor, he was aggrieving the cattle-raising tenants he was about to evict. Exacerbating matters, some of Sellar's sheep began to die off, not being able to graze, and his partner Young delayed in organizing coastal lots for ejected tenants to find respite.

After Sellar convinced the local clergyman, the Rev. David Mackenzie, to threaten the crofters with hellfire and damnation for the slightest disobedience, he commenced the evictions. When houses had been emptied, he would stay to watch as the walls and roofs were torn off and the roof timbers were set ablaze. The stoneman and articulate reporter Donald Macleod was taking notes on all that he saw and dubbed Sellar's actions *Bliadhna an Losgaith*, the Year of the Burnings. He reported being present at the pulling down and burning of the house of William Chisholm. In it was lying his wife's mother, Margaret Mackay, nearly one hundred years old. According to Macleod's record, Sellar then said, "Damn her, the old witch; she has lived too long. Let her burn!" Flames engulfed the house and caught some of the woman's bedclothes, but she was removed and died five days later. Recent historian Eric Richards has disputed Macleod's account, arguing that the woman was carried to an outbuilding before the house was destroyed.

More than two decades later, Macleod, the burnings still vivid in his mind, wrote of them in twenty-one letters to the *Edinburgh Weekly Chronicle*. They were published in a single-volume *History of the Destitution in Sutherlandshire* (1841), but not widely circulated. This was before his *Gloomy Memories*, his rebuke of Harriet Beecher Stowe's cooption by the Duke. Alexander Mackenzie republished *Destitution* in his *History of the Highland Clearances* (1883), a major source for John Prebble's *The Highland Clearances*, assuring that Macleod's reports have become the best-known narrative since 1963.

Sellar's abrasive interpersonal manner guaranteed him many enemies. Prominent among them was the sheriff-substitute for Sutherland, Robert MacKid, a Gaelic-speaking Highlander. Although he was a lawman, Sellar had caught him poaching on the Sutherland properties a few years earlier. Ready to pounce, MacKid charged Sellar with culpable homicide and arson. The prosecution, however, was up against the established power, and Sellar was acquitted April 23, 1816, but forbidden to take part in any further clearances. That mattered little because he became the Staffords' most substantial tenant. Famine struck all over the northern hemisphere that year, the so-called "green winter," with frost in July, resulting from the explosion of the Sumbawa Volcano in the south Pacific, allowing Sellar to polish his reputation by supporting famine relief, as well as further emigration. He died a wealthy man in 1851.

The 2nd Duke and Duchess of Sutherland, a second George and his wife Harriet, successors to the earlier George and Elizabeth, were greatly relieved at Sellar's acquittal, taking this as a justification of their clearance policies. They hired a new factor and related to Sellar only as a prosperous leaseholder after that. Their fortunes continued to rise. In 1835 the estate began an ambitious remodeling of Dunrobin for the next fifteen years, eventually reaching 189 rooms, visually more dominating than Balmoral.

Meanwhile the reputation of the Sutherlands, especially George Jr. and Harriet, has succumbed to the calumnies of Donald Macleod as amplified by John Prebble and by Ian Grimble in *The Trial of Patrick Sellar* (1962). In recent years there has been a campaign to tear down the massive statue of the First Duke of Sutherland in nearby Golspie because it is a "Murderer's Monument." The 100-foot memorial to the Duke, known locally as "Mannie," has had graffiti sprayed on it along with the word "monster" in green paint. Local police believe there is an ongoing campaign to topple Mannie, also mockingly known as "Wee Mannie," once and for all.

Eighteen fourteen, the Year of the Burnings, *Bliadhna an Losgaith*, also saw the publication of Walter Scott's *Waverley*.

The Clearances continued in the Highlands through the first half of the nineteenth century, becoming subsumed into the horrors of the potato famine of the 1840s. They were but one of several parallel unfolding trajectories. Foremost, despite all adversity, the population continued to increase, hitting a peak in the census of 1841, a statistic gaining new resonance in this context. This meant striking contrasts across the landscape of the Gàidhealtachd, with glens and islands almost entirely emptied of people while not far away one would find congestion. Steady economic, non-clearance, voluntary emigration continued through the nineteenth century and into the twentieth. The prevalence of destitute Highland men seeking work in rainy

Glasgow prompted the nicknaming of the canopy adjacent to the train station as "the teuchters' umbrella." Continuing discrimination against Roman Catholics after that ceased to be public policy, but a higher percentage of departures for people of that faith remained constant.

Unreported by John Prebble and his allies was the ongoing problem of landowner indebtedness. Far from the conspicuous wealth of such as the Duke of Argyll or the Duke of Sutherland, dozens of families living in elegant homes confronted the financial wolves at their gates. Eric Richards' *The Highland Clearances* (year 2000) speaks of the financial suicide of an entire class of people. The threat of losing their lands convinced many landowners to displace crofters, even those bearing the same family name, despite professions of regret and misgivings. Even without going that far, the perception of economic insecurity was enough to send some crofters on their way.

Selected citations from the doleful list of further clearances can point to trends.

1820. Strath Oykel, on the far western coast of Sutherland, not in the Duke's domain. Hugh Munro, the Laird of Novar, having raised rents to the limit, decided to evict tenants, many of whom had lost family members in the Napoleonic wars, and replace them with sheep. A riot followed at Culrain, with the militia firing on crofters armed with stones. Defeated, the tenants departed. The area is almost uninhabited today but famed for salmon fishing.

1821. Gruids, Sutherland, five miles to the north of Culrain. This time tenants were pro-active. Seeing the sheriff-officers coming with writs of removal, they stripped the men of their clothing, whipped them and burned their documents. Sensing a greater threat, authorities called in the red coats from Fort George. Defenseless, the crofters took to the hills to watch, and, resigned, walked across Sutherland to seek employment at Brora.

1822. George IV wears kilt in Edinburgh, launching the fashion for tartan.

1825. Isle of Rùm (also Rum, Rhum), Inner Hebrides. Leaseholder Dr. Lachlan Maclean decided that 450 were too many people for such a small island and told them they had to leave. He dispatched and paid the fare for 300 tenants on two overcrowded ships for Cape Breton Island, Nova Scotia, the next year, with others to follow. When he imported 8000 blackface sheep, he also had to search for shepherds. The collapse of mutton prices in 1839 bankrupted Maclean. Population today, c. 20–30.

1841. Census puts Highland population at all-time high, above 400,000. Henry Baillie, Member for Inverness, formed a committee to investigate the welfare of the area and concluded that there were too many people living in the Gàidhealtachd. Recommendation: establish a course of aggressive emigration.

1841 September. Durness. James Anderson, a Lowland leaseholder of Keneabin farm near Durness, in the far north of Sutherland sought to rid himself of tenants behind in their rent. Most were fisher-folk, for herring and some deep-sea species. Writs for removal were greeted with violent crowds, who chased the sheriff and his men for twenty miles. The mere threat of calling out the red coats crushed the tenants' resolve, and by autumn 1842 their land was filled with sheep.

1842. Strathconon, remote glen in Ross-shire. James Falconer Gillanders drove out 400 people, who took shelter on the Black Isle. By October of that year, Gillanders drove them from there as well. These continued in following years.

1845. Glencalvie, southern Sutherland. Absentee landlord William Robertson, after telling his tenants they were safe, allowed his factor James Gillanders to evict ninety. Denied shelter at a church in Glencalvie (no longer on the map), they sought refuge in the church at nearby Croick, where they scratched messages in the glass. With messages still visible, the windows are a place of pilgrimage for people commemorating the pathos of the Clearances. In this instance the ministers publicly stood with their parishioners against the landlords.

1845–1846. Potato blight hits Ireland, the Highlands, and also Gaelic Nova Scotia. Crop failure begins in central farms and spreads to distant peninsulas and islands.

1847. James Bruce, a writer for *The Scotsman*, declares Highlanders' problems stem from their own laziness. A good solution would be to remove them from the vicious influence of the idleness in which their fathers have been brought up.

1849. Glenelg, Wester Ross, port for one of three Skye ferries. Bristol-born sheep farmer James Baillie wants 500 small tenants shipped to Quebec, although 40 to 50 families could not find a place on the first ship. When Baillie boasts of his support of £2000, plus £500 from the Destitution Board, he is attacked by journalist Thomas Mulock, who also directs ire at other landlords. Threatened with the charge of libel, Mulock flees the country.

1849. North Uist, Outer Hebrides. Lord Macdonald decides to evict 110 families, more than 600 people, from Sollas in North Uist, provoking some rioting. Mulock attacks Lord Macdonald along with Baillie.

1850–1853. Isle of Skye, Inner Hebrides. Lord Macdonald drives hundreds from Strathaird District, Suisnish and Boreraig.

1851. South Uist and Barra, Outer Hebrides. Colonel Gordon of Cluny summons his tenant farmers with a fine if they do not attend a meeting to discuss rents. Once there, over 1,500 men are overpowered, bound, and loaded on to ships bound for Canada. Those who resist are truncheoned and handcuffed. Many historians class Gordon's actions as a response the famine rather than a Clearance parallel to others. Discussed further below.

1853. Knoydart, a peninsula in west Lochaber, Inverness-shire. The widow of the 16th Chief of Glengarry orders the sudden eviction of her last 400 subtenants, including women in labor and the elderly. Their houses are torched, with no provision for land or sea transportation. When they try to return to their burned properties, they are chased off.

1854. Strathconon, Ross-shire. Completion of the Clearances begun in 1842

As this abbreviated summary notes, the Clearances may have been occurring all over the Gàidhealtachd, glens, straths and islands, but not everywhere. None in Argyllshire, a central county with a substantial population, but nevertheless the crofters departed and the sheep came in. More evictions were in remote areas, like the peripheries of Sutherlandshire and the Outer Hebrides. Also note: tenants and subtenants may have been overpowered, but they were not always compliant, nor were they apathetic and passive. Michael Lynch in *Scotland: A New History* (1991) suggests that there were more than fifty major acts of resistance against the Clearances. Poaching on large estates, commonplace before the evictions, could be seen as taking on a political aggression when increased. While some clergymen went so far as to preach to crofters that their suffering was punishment for their sins, it was also true that many more favored the property rights of landowners over the plight of the evicted. After a dispute in the Kirk, the established church, in 1843, known as The Great Disruption, the break-away Presbyterian Free Church refused to accept donations and was critical of donors. This is the subject of further discussion later in this chapter.

Matters in the remote Highlands were usually parochial and commanded little widespread attention. The Gàidhealtachd was the poorest quarter of the United Kingdom—then including Ireland—until well into the twentieth century. It is seemingly counter-intuitive that one of the best-known poems lamenting Highland depopulation should have appeared in the prestige *Blackwood's Magazine*, in September 1829. Other contributors to the journal in this era included Samuel Taylor Coleridge, Thomas de Quincey, and Edgar Allan Poe. The title is "The Canadian Boat Song," also used a decade earlier (to confuse matters) by Irish poet Thomas Moore for an item of a very different order. This "Boat Song" is anonymous, and after much time has been squandered on speculating about the true author, there is no satisfactory candidate to credit with authorship.

The first three verses sound the vital themes:

Canadian Boat Song

> Listen to me, as when ye heard our father
> Sing long ago the song of other shores—
> Listen to me, and then in chorus gather
> All your deep voices as ye pull the oars;
>
> Fair these broad meads—these hoary woods are grand;
> But we are exiles from our fathers' land.
>
> From the lone shieling of the misty island
> Mountains divide us, and the waste of seas-
> Yet the blood is strong, the heart is Highland,
> And we in dreams behold the Hebrides.

The word "Clearance," not yet current at time of publication, does not appear, nor does "eviction." But in the seventh verse the author adds,

> No seer foretold the children would be banished,
> That a degenerate lord might boast his sheep.

The poem might have been a lament rather than a polemic, but any reader could easily discern than the pathos of emigration came with a political edge and a designated villain. Responding to the poignant image of the "lone shieling" cited in the first line of the third verse, some readers prefer the title "The Lone Shieling," for the poem. The shieling or shepherd's hut is a distinctive feature of the Highland landscape. Commemorating this title, the Cape Breton Highlands National Park in Nova Scotia built a stone and thatched shieling in 1942, long a tourist destination and photo opportunity. The full text of the "Boat Song" appears on a plaque along with the statement that the edifice is intended to commemorate the Clearances.

As the "Boat Song" is anonymous, it has not been assigned a place in the literary canon, but somehow it was judged to be so sonorous that it should be included in collections of poetry to be memorized and read aloud, alongside more expected choices like Thomas Gray's "Elegy Written in a Country Churchyard." I have met at least two dozen people in the U.S. and in Canada, born before 1960, who will respond with "We in dreams behold the Hebrides" if I happen to cite the islands.

People who know the poem as a recitation piece are unlikely to know its political context or even to have heard of the Clearances.

Within Scottish Gaelic discourse, spoken by a decreasing population and read by an even smaller number, the Clearances were an occasion of rage during much of the nineteenth century. These included songwriters like Ewen Henderson, "the bard of the Clearances," author of *Dùthaich Mhic Aoidh* (about Mackay country, north Sutherland), the lawbreaker poet Mary MacPherson, the nostalgic Niall MacLeòid, and the well-born doctor Iain MacLachlainn. Their works, filled with mockery of the Duke of Sutherland, James Loch and Patrick Sellar, are much in line with the views of Donald Macleod's *Gloomy Memories* published in English in far-off Canada in the 1850s.

The Clearances, sometimes known as improvements or evictions, have remained a theme in Scottish Gaelic writing, even though the number of Gaelic monoglot authors has steeply declined. Outside the Highlands Gaelic literary tradition may appear to be a minuscule, archaic minority, but occasionally an exceptional voice commands attention beyond the Gàidhealtachd. The most prominent of those by universal agreement was Sorley MacLean (1911–1996), or Somhairle MacGill-Eain, who was once short-listed for the Nobel Prize. Born into a Gaelic-speaking family on the isle of Raasay, just east of Skye, the poet knew of the Clearances from hosts of different relatives. His best-known work, *Hallaig*, published in the Gaelic journal *Gairm* (1954), focuses on one deserted township in the southeast corner of his native island. Although not one of the more outrageous instances (Prebble gives it less than a sentence), between 1852 and 1854, a landlord named George Rainy removed all the people living there, including the poet's family.

Some of the imagery and phrasing of *Hallaig* evokes earlier Gaelic poetry and song, such as Duncan Ban MacIntyre's *Beinn Dorain*. These resonances cannot be translated, even when the English text is by the poet himself or, in another, by Irish Nobel Laureate Seamus Heaney. A first-person narrator employs several tree metaphors, such as the hardwood birch, something alive but rooted in the nature and the history of the place. Contrasted with the birch is the softer pine, planted by the intruders and intended for an earlier harvest and profit. Defying the canard that Gaelic poetry has little effect beyond a tiny coterie, *Hallaig* has inspired an organ work by William Sweeney, and words from it are quoted in Peter Maxwell Davies' opera, *The Jacobite Rising* (1997).

The citation of a Clearance verse in a Jacobite opera raises the question of how events are modified in memory. The catastrophe of Culloden Moor is the one event from Highland history that everyone knows, even though the numbers killed in the rebellion and subsequent repression are much smaller than those uprooted in evictions, both by force and economic depredation. Since *Waverley* (1814), elements of the 1745–1746 Rising narrative have been retold constantly, generally becoming more romantic. It has also been trivialized and commodified. Jacobite Cruises take tourists to the sights of Loch Ness. In contrast, for many decades the Clearances were too dreadful to speak of, or, in the diaspora, were forgotten. The famed English prose work on the Clearances is, of course, John Prebble's Penguin history

(1963), for which the detraction "a novel" is not entirely a liability. There are, however, also three historical novels on the Clearances, all by writers of stature who seek to humanize recorded events with passionate conviction.

They are Neil Gunn's *The Butcher's Broom* (1934), Fionn MacColla's *And the Cock Crew* (1945), and Iain Crichton Smith's *Consider the Lilies* (1968). While each of the three sets action in a different location, all three appear to be based on the Sutherland Clearances of the early 1820s run by the Staffords, James Loch and Patrick Sellar. Further, each author appears to be familiar with the two volumes by Donald Macleod, especially *Gloomy Memories*. All three are derisive of ecclesiastical authorities, more than Prebble is.

Neil Gunn (1891–1973) was praised earlier in these pages as the most conscientious of Highland historical novelists. His *Butcher's Broom* is set in a place called Riasgan where the Sellar-like villain is named Mr. Heller. Fionn MacColla (Thomas Douglas MacDonald, 1906–1975) was a colleague of the 1930s Scottish Renaissance along with Hugh MacDiarmid. He shifts more blame to the English and redraws Sellar as the "Black Foreigner." Iain Crichton Smith (1928–1998) has stature as a Gaelic poet only a few notches below Sorley MacLean and is also known for exquisite ironic short stories in English. His *Consider the Lilies*, where action is seen through the eyes of an aging uncomprehending woman, appears at first glance to be happening in the present. Donald Macleod, in life a stonemason, is fictionalized and made an atheist. Patrick Sellar appears under his own name. Smith is sharply critical of organized religion, having one of the book's ministers tell the evicted crofters that they are being punished for their sins. Neil Gunn concurs. In *Butcher's Broom* he writes: "The Church will help the law in the matter.... Every minister will threaten their people with the fires of hell, if they don't go peaceably." MacColla has his minister tell his flock they cannot resist God's judgment and must submit before a worse fate befalls them.

None of these three became a huge seller to compare with, for example, a middling romantic fiction like D.K. Broster's *Jacobite Trilogy* (1925), but they have a persistent if niche readership. Gunn's *Broom* and Smith's *Lilies* have long been available on both sides of the Atlantic and at the time of this writing remain in print, both on paper and electronically. Used copies of MacColla's *And the Cock Crew*, out of print, command three-digit prices on both sides of the Atlantic.

As his title signals, anger over the Clearances is a prime issue in left-wing nationalist playwright John McGrath's choleric stage work *The Cheviot, the Stag and the Black, Black Oil* (produced 1972, published 1974). Causing much comment at its premiere, the drama depicts the evictions as the template of all later misfortunes to afflict the Highlands. In one speech a voice cries out that the Clearances would go forth without resistance, and only organized militance can stop them.

All poets, fiction writers and playwrights, in Gaelic and English, from the political right or left, depict the Clearances as an outrageous ordeal of human suffering. Not one, thus far, has taken up the neoliberal banner of Michael Fry (2005) to see the evictions as temporarily painful liberation from the strictures of medievalism and a welcome entry into the free market. Some poets in Gaelic Nova Scotia refuted the sentiment of "Canadian Boat Song," preferring the democratic freedom of the world, even in continuing poverty, over what was left behind.

In the years since the re-establishment of the Scottish Parliament in 1999, there has been renewed effort to commemorate the generations of forced evictions in the Gàidhealtachd. In 2007 Scottish-Canadian mining magnate Dennis MacLeod funded the erection of a three-meter (10') bronze monument titled *Exiles*, designed by Gerald Laing. It consists of three figures, male and female, on a spiral plinth on top of Creag Bun-Ullidh in Helmsdale, 600 feet above sea level. Close enough to be evoked by the location is Kildonan, site of the eviction that produced so many emigrants in Selkirk's adventure across Hudson Bay to the Red River Valley. This also explains why Dennis MacLeod erected a duplicate of *Exiles* in Winnipeg, Manitoba. It was hoped by Dennis MacLeod, as well as Scottish First Minister Alex Salmond at the unveiling, that *Exiles* would be a counterforce to the self-congratulatory monument, Mannie, to the Duke of Sutherland in Golspie, 16.7 miles (27 km) away. In 2014, the last year for which there are accessible records, *Exiles* drew 35,000 visitors.

One of the first acts of the new Scottish Parliament was to denounce the Clearances and extend the embrace of the nation to the dispersed:

"Expressing regret for the occurrence of the Highland Clearances and extends its hand in friendship and welcome to the descendants of the cleared people who now reside outwith our shores. 27 September 2000"

The Blight of the Tubers

Juxtaposing the words "potato" and "famine" so quickly prompts the national modifier "Irish," that we have to step back for a moment to remember that this was an international scourge afflicting several nations during the 1840s. In Ireland the successive annual failures of the potato crop affected millions of people, a singular national trauma in West European history. The misfortunes in the Scottish Highlands were smaller by many measures but nonetheless catastrophic. Together with the Clearances, the potato famine drove about a third of the total population of the western Highlands to emigrate between 1841 and 1861.

As mentioned earlier, although the potato had been introduced from South America centuries before, it did not become universal in the Highlands and Islands until about the 1740s, the decade of the final Jacobite rising. The famously infertile Highland soil was not as hospitable to the potato as that in Ireland had been, possibly reducing the human damage when the crop failed. Farmers had to construct a narrower rig or ridge called a *feannag*, often on land so intractable as to have never previously been cropped. In a clumsy irony, intended to demean cottars and crofters, this was known in English as a "lazy-bed," despite requiring continuing strenuous and exacting labor. The *feannag* would not lie close to a crofter house, where some other items might flourish in a garden. Thus, the potato, especially the succulent species known as the lumper, served with butter, might be the principal source of nutrition for a poor family, but it was not a monocrop.

The fungus-like micro-organism killing the potato is known as *Phytophthora infestans* and was first noted in North America, cited in Illinois, 1842, then spreading as widely as Virginia, Ontario and Nova Scotia. Nothing would be visible to the farmer as he was working the crop. When he dug up the tuber, instead of the firm white flesh there would be a brownish mush, robbed of all nutrients and gag-inducing to eat. Gaelic Nova Scotia experienced a smaller version in July and August 1845, of what soon blighted Ireland and the Highlands. From the British Isles it spread to the Continent and beyond, causing considerable damage in Belgium.

Phytophthora infestans struck both Ireland and the Highlands in 1846, devastating about three-quarters of the harvest that year. Increasing the suffering, the following winter was especially cold and snowy. The first agency to address the widespread hunger was the Free Church of Scotland, split from the Established Church, the Kirk, three years earlier (a subject of further discussion below). The Free Church was strongly represented in the affected areas. Acting promptly, it raised alarms and organized relief, regardless of the denomination of the stricken. It organized transport for over 3,000 men from the famine-stricken regions to work on the Lowland railways. Not only did this mean fewer mouths to feed, but also a ready source of remittance payments to provide for families left behind.

As was the case in the widely studied concurrent famine in Ireland, government action was limited by unwavering adherence to free-market dogmas. Sir Charles Trevelyan, effectively the senior civil servant in the Treasury, rebuffed all requests from distraught landowners and absolutely ruled out direct subsidies. Trevelyan, customary vilified in accounts of the Irish famine, argued against upsetting the free play of normal market forces. He did allow, however, in a letter of September 1846, that "the people cannot, *under any circumstances*, be allowed to starve." The government's first action was to put pressure on the landlords to meet their responsibilities. Some had the resources and willingness to respond, but others, especially among the remaining hereditary landowners, were in strapped financial straits and were either in denial of their shortfall or unwilling to speak of it publicly.

As in Ireland, the pro-free market law allowed for the sale of foodstuffs from blighted areas to foreign markets willing to meet a higher price. This provoked demonstrations by the hungry in such remote ports as Wick in far Caithness along with Cromarty and Invergordon in Ross-shire. Troops were sent in to quell all disturbances, with no acknowledgment of what had prompted them.

The death toll in the Highlands and Islands was minuscule when placed next to Ireland, and modern historians estimate that the crop failure directly affected up to 200,000 people, including those suffering from prolonged starvation with such afflictions as dysentery, scurvy and typhus. The government official who delivered heroic labors on behalf of the Scottish Gaels was the Devon-born military man with an inauspicious quasi-Dickensian name, Sir Edward Pine Coffin. By employing naval craft Coffin was able to distribute oatmeal and other supplies from depots he established at Tobermory in the Outer Hebrides and Portree on Skye. Coffin was also a scrupulous observer of actors on the scene, including landlords and ecclesiastics. The crop failure of 1847 was less extensive, but followed by another severe winter. Death rates returned to something close to normal.

With the perception that the worst had passed, the government left any further famine assistance to the Central Board of Management for Highland Relief, which had been launched by the Free Church but attracted donations from the Highland diaspora in England and in North America. From this flowed what was called "Eleemosynary Relief": direct assistance to the distressed from funds raised from widespread alms and gifts rather than taxes or the largess of the wealthy. This continued from 1847 to 1850, and had no counterpart in Ireland, further explaining the lower Scottish death toll. Central Board relief came with strictures, however. Relief was not available to anyone with disposable capital, such as owning a single cow. As the Board had a dread of "pauperizing" the poor, i.e., making them dependent on payments, all relief came with work requirements, always at rock-bottom wages. Some commentators argued that any other course promoted the innate laziness of the Gaels. Workers who had fended off the Grim Reaper for three years were more determined to leave the Highlands when Eleemosynary Relief ended, and there were continuing though lesser crop failures. Furthering the drive to emigrate were the Scottish poor laws. Unlike those in England, relief could only be given to the sick and infirm, never to the able-bodied.

Recognizing that a large portion of the population was in distress, the government asked Sir John McNeill, chairman of the Board of Supervisors of the Scottish Poor Law Boards, to investigate matters and recommend remedies. He toured and studied for two months in the spring of 1851. Despite a Gaelic name, much associated with the Isle of Barra, McNeill was a far less empathetic observer than Sir Edward Pine Coffin had been. His analysis outlined both structural and cultural liabilities. The subdivision of a single croft between tenant and subtenants was a prescription for failure. Worse was the "insularity" of the Highlanders. Inheriting themes first pronounced by James VI & I more than two hundred years earlier, McNeill found that the social identity inherited from the clan structure, and even more the Gaelic language, were heavy liabilities. As an example, he cited the labor paralysis after the collapse of the kelp industry. Because of their work habits and language, unemployed crofters and cottars were slow to seek work in the rest of the kingdom, which they regarded as a foreign country. (Although many starving subtenants had done just that.)

In McNeill's view the well-intentioned programs to aid the able-bodied had been deleterious, although he recommended no changes in the Scottish Poor Law, allowing parochial boards to give discretionary relief. He was also skeptical of various schemes attempted locally to relieve destitution as they had been applied without much attention paid to the severity of local destitution or the relative mobility of the unemployed. Instead, together with his committee McNeill agreed that in the short term, prompt and widespread emigration was necessary to the well-being of the population and to their extrication from their current difficulties. With the population reduced, the remaining crofters would have greater opportunities for employment, economic improvement and access to further education.

Official action followed quickly. In January 1852, McNeill and Sir Charles Trevelyan created the Highland and Island Emigration Society. Thus, in addition to the evictions of individual landowners and factors, there was now an agency, funded by donations, to encourage Gaelic crofters, especially the many who were distressed, to leave the Kingdom for destinations overseas. These were usually in British North America, but the Society also sponsored around 5000 former tenants for passage to Australia.

The year of 1852 was also the year that the Royal Family took up residence in the idyllic retreat of Balmoral, at the eastern edge of the Gàidhealtachd.

The diminution of the death toll and the establishment of a society hurrying emigration did not, of course, stamp out the persistence of the potato blight. It continued through the 1850s but increasingly in farther corners of the Highlands and Islands. During this decade the persistent blight drove out more than 40 percent of the population on the rocky peninsula of Ardnamurchan, the westernmost point of the mainland, often cited as the dividing mark between the upper and lower Inner Hebrides. As it happens, that unhappy emigration, not strictly speaking a Clearance, included the ancestors of Canadian novelist Hugh MacLennan (1907–1990). Born on Cape Breton Island, he readily called himself a "Scotchman," in the Canadian idiom. But after a visit to Ardnamurchan, and learning the often-ignored history, he wrote in *Scotchman's Return* (1960) that he found it difficult to embrace his Highland, rather than his Canadian, heritage and did not respond to the romance of tartanism.

Harder hit were the islands of the Outer Hebrides, both large and small. On Lewis, Sir James Matheson, one of the most heroic figures in this part of the story, had spent £33,000 in six years to support his tenants and followed that with more help in six of the next thirty years. Elsewhere more skittish landlords dreaded that Poor Law-sponsored relief for the destitute would levy taxes on them, further encouraging assistance from the Emigration Society.

The polar opposite of Sir James Matheson was John Gordon of Cluny, the wealthiest commoner in Scotland, worth £2 million at his death in 1858, when one pound was worth £60 in today's money. Known for his parsimonious habits and vanity, he liked to be called "colonel" but held that rank in the Aberdeen militia rather than the Army. In the gallery of villains of the exploitation of the Gaelic peasantry, Gordon occupies a perch near that of Patrick Sellar and the First Duke of Sutherland. He had, in 1840 at a fire sale fee, obtained ownership of the entire island of Barra in the Outer Hebrides, traditionally the home of the MacNeills. Despite its remoteness and the Roman Catholic faith of many islanders, Barra had long played a role in mainland clan alliances. The last MacNeill proprietor was a spectacularly poor manager, inviting crofters to move there during the short-lived kelp boom, and then ran his properties at a loss despite high rents. While the islanders still raised some cereal crops, they were dependent on the potato harvest. The blight hit later but harder. Gordon first responded with makeshift managerial approaches, like consolidating smaller crofts into larger holdings better able to support their tenants (his apologia) or to reduce the number of destitute islanders dependent on him (the view of his detractors). Gordon never actually evicted tenants, and his factor denied them any assistance in leaving the island. Instead, Gordon and his team simply made life miserable, offering inferior and unpalatable meal. The tenants began to scatter, taking any advantage or assistance they might find.

Gordon of Cluny's unsavory reputation was first written in Sir Edward Pine Coffin's damning commentaries, which were not widely circulated. "Unsavory" expanded to infamous in heartrending and inflammatory newspaper reports of penniless, ragged Barra refugees on the streets of Glasgow, unable to speak English, before Christmas, 1850. These were amplified by further reports from Canada when refugees arrived at different ports in Quebec and Ontario. The Vice-President of the Scottish Benevolent Society in Hamilton (then still Upper Canada) wrote, "The emigrants from Barra and South Uist, amounting to between two and three thousand, were the most destitute I ever saw coming into this country." Many were in rags, and some children, having outgrown their garments, were actually in a state of nudity.

The Great Disruption of 1843

Conservative commentator Michael Fry has argued that the 1843 schism in the Kirk was the most significant domestic event in Victorian Scotland. At the same time, the announced issue of the "Disruption" hardly seems to be a fighting matter to a twenty-first-century readership: who should make clerical appointments? The patrons of a congregation or its members? Readers of Max Weber will understand that religious disputes, whether doctrinal or administrative, rarely become heated without relationship to economic, social or political issues that lie nearby.

Religious faith, including attendance at services, heeding the authority of the clergy, strict attention to dogmas, and latterly unflinching sabbatarian observance, has long been paramount in Highland identity, perhaps even more than in Lowland identity. Until this point in the narrative, however, we may have made more references to the Episcopal and Roman Catholic faiths, both minority populations. They were the core of Jacobitism and contributed more than their share of poets and musicians. The dominant faith of the Highlands from the sixteenth century, however, has been Calvinism, first in the body of the established church, the Kirk. Its founding was an analogy with Anglicanism, the established Church of England, but in practice the two were highly different. To be "established" means to be authorized by and interacting with the state. From the beginning the Kirk always bridled at the influence of civil law and reacted strongly to appointments originating with the Crown or other secular actors. Further, Calvinism was not confined to the central stream of the Kirk. Many of the Covenanters, key players in the mid-seventeenth-century Civil War, were unhappy that the Glorious Revolution of Protestant monarchs William and Mary did not acknowledge their National Covenant and so refused to rejoin the Kirk. They founded the Reformed Presbyterian Church of Scotland in 1690. Other splinter groups would follow, like the Relief Church and the Original Secession Church.

The Parliament in Westminster, never a friend of Calvinism, pretended to solve the problem with the Patronage Act, 1712, again on analogy with Anglicanism in England. This ordered that ministers had to be chosen by lay patrons, the inheritors or landowners of a parish, as they were in England. The General Assembly accepted this grudgingly. In an ineffective expression of their discontent, they passed an annual protest against the Patronage Act. Like the Kirk itself, the General Assembly had a national significance beyond strictly religious matters, especially after the Act of Union. It became the substitute national forum in the absence of a parliament. The ruling party of the General Assembly was usually called the Moderates, who were most accommodating to the Patronage Act.

Over the first decades of the nineteenth century the Kirk began to develop evangelical cadres within the ranks, given to an agenda of reviving Calvinist orthodoxy, biblical instruction and fiery sermons while working toward a more vigorous Christian social ethic. While not promoting the term "fundamentalist," they were hostile to interpretive Biblical scholarship examining the authorship of the Gospels. Increasingly, also, they came to revile the designation "Moderate," a term often with anodyne connotations elsewhere. In the Kirk's General Assembly, the "Moderates" came to be portrayed as get-along, go-along sell-outs without fixed principles.

Influencing the General Assembly in unanticipated ways was the Reform Act of 1832, a thunderclap in British political attitudes. It created for the first time in Scotland a popular parliamentary electorate. If voters could elect their Members of Parliament, why could they not elect their ministers? The Moderates, still more affluent and powerful, lost their majority in the General Assembly to the evangelicals in 1834. One of the new majority's first measures was the Veto Act, giving parishioners the right to reject a minister nominated by a patron.

In the twenty-first century we expect evangelicals or fundamentalists to be people of the political right, but in 1830s and 1840s Scotland, the more evangelical clergy in the Kirk favored what we have to see as left-wing policies. At issue were the Clearances. The more evangelical clergy sympathized with put-upon crofters and began to refuse donations from evicting landlords. Those same landlords were the patrons of the congregation that the Patronage Act of 1712 gave the power of appointment.

On May 18, 1843, 121 ministers and 73 elders left the General Assembly at the Church of St. Andrew on George Street in Edinburgh, to form the Free Protesting Church or Church of Scotland Free, which would eventually be called the Free Church of Scotland. In another five days a rump version of the General Assembly, the Disruption Assembly (thus the name for the schism) met with 474 ministers out of a total of 1,200 joining the Free Church. Eventually up to 40 percent of the clergy adhered to the new Church. Perhaps because the evangelicals had spoken up for the crofters in the Clearances, the Free Church had even more impact on the Highlands than the Lowlands. This was three years before the advent of the potato famine, which would heighten the influence of the break-aways.

Within Free Church history, the Great Disruption is seen as basically a spiritual phenomenon, in direct line with the Reformation and the National Covenant. Part of the lore of the Free Church is the personal price defectors from the Kirk paid: those who left forfeited livings, manses and pulpits. Additionally, by separating from the established church, the Free Church also turned off the spigot of public funding and had to scramble for volunteer donations. On this matter the fervor and zeal of Free Church laymen proved an asset. Within three years Free Church leaders, clergy and lay, had become skilled in raising donations from the faithful, even the impecunious. As was noted above, when the potato famine hit, the Free Church led Eleemosynary Relief projects. An additional strand in the Free Church's vision of its own history is grievance for the disdain it suffered from the established and powerful, not all of them in the Kirk. Again and again, property owners all over Scotland sought to deny the defectors land to build new houses of worship when the edifices of the Kirk were closed to them. An oft-repeated outrage concerns the Episcopalian Cameron of Lochiel, who controlled much property near the crossroads town of Fort William. After long delays, he allowed the Free Church some of the worst land in Lochaber, a bog near Corpach so swampy that people used to trap wild horses in it. The building there was never durable and had to be demolished in 1976.

As evangelicals, committed to preaching to people in their own language, the Free Church's embrace of Gaelic helped to make it more popular in the Highlands and Islands. Previously the Kirk and the Moderates had been indifferent to Gaelic. Within a short time virtually all of the Highland lay people in the Kirk went over to the Free Church, except for some parishes on Skye. Soon the remnant of the established church was referred to as the "Auld (old) Kirk." The entire Free Church message, the intensity of conviction, the volunteerism, the commitment to the poor and the perception that the established comfortable and moderate were suspicious and probably worthy of damnation, was deeply appealing to Highland Calvinists. In the view of Michael Fry, sympathetic to the Free Church, the shift from the Kirk deepened the division between the Highlands and Lowlands. The Calvinist Gàidhealtachd retreated into a "spiritual laager," driving the Gaels into "a redoubt of an oppressed, introverted culture estranged from the Lowlands." The Free Church nonetheless had a scattered presence in the Lowlands.

Although other faiths may have assisted with the emigration of their members, especially Catholics, only the Free Church sought to establish a distant colony where the religion could flourish without contaminations from backsliding creeds. This led to the spreading of a Scottish presence on the South Island of New Zealand, where the Dunedin colony attracted up to 12,000 settlers, many from the industrial Lowlands along with Highlanders, in its first dozen years.

As mentioned earlier, large numbers of the Highland poor settled in the thirteen colonies before independence, and later in Canada and Australia, but New Zealand had been a destination for small farmers and their families and people with some negotiable skills. No convicts were sent to New Zealand, and no poor houses emptied to fill its fields. Neither were the Scots who went there disadvantaged. When the Lay Association of the Free Church of Scotland, through a company called the Otago Association, founded Dunedin in 1848, the links to Scotland were most conspicuous. Dunedin is the Anglicization of the Gaelic name—*Dùn Èideann*—for Edinburgh. The city's first surveyor, Charles Kettle, attempted to follow instructions to emulate characteristics of the Scottish capital, a "romantic" urban vision with grand avenues and quirky streets. Much as the Free Church dominated the early decades, they were not exclusive, either for faith or ethnicity. When gold was discovered nearby at Gabriel's Gully, the expected "rush" followed, making the population highly cosmopolitan. Arriving first, the Scots maintained an advantage. New

Zealand's only castle, Larnach Castle, 9 miles (14 km) west of Dunedin on the Otago Peninsula, was built in 1871 in the Scottish baronial style. The city has long been known as the "Edinburgh of the South." With a population today of about 106,000, Dunedin may be the most Scottish city outside the British Isles, without looking very much like any place in Scotland.

The Dunedin colony should not be confused with the widely publicized wanderings of maverick clergyman Norman McLeod (1780–1866), who was not a member of the Free Church. His many adherents, though nominally Calvinist, were called "Normanites," and followed him first to Nova Scotia for nearly two decades, then to Adelaide, Australia, and finally on to Waipu, North Island, New Zealand. By 1859, 883 people had arrived, dominantly Highland, representing 19 clans, continuing to flourish until McLeod's death in 1866. McLeod had a dominating presence on Cape Breton Island, Nova Scotia, and is fondly remembered in New Zealand, but his followers intermarried with the locals, their religious and ethnic identity dissipating.

Meanwhile in Scotland, the potato famine, in which the Free Church had played a heroic role, was ebbing, and the Church was becoming more proficient in the fund-raising required to build houses of worship. The defining act of the Great Disruption might have been from spiritual motivations, but thwarting the authority of the landed classes had inescapable political consequences. Similarly, assisting the starving in famine times might have been genuine Christian charity. When coupled with resisting landlords, the charity nudged the Free Church to the left, especially when the Liberal Party was founding in 1859. That party bound together the former Whigs, free-trade Tories known as Peelites, and radicals deriving from the Chartist movement. An issue in coming decades would be land reform, in the Highlands and elsewhere, and the Liberals looked upon the Free Church as a natural ally. As such they were often classed with the radicals, though most Church members were abstemious, Bible-believing Christians of strictest moral observance. Radical liberalism was indeed popular in the Highlands in mid-century, and one wag remarked that the Free Church was "the radical Liberal Party at Prayer."

Mightier Than a Lord

In the decades following mid-century of the Victorian era, as remarked upon in the previous chapter, flattering allusions to the Highlands ran high in national and even international discourse. Balmoralism gave a certain chic to Highland styles, especially tartan. Idealized portrayals of Highland landscapes, by Landseer and others, were in high demand. For the most affluent there was no finer holiday to be had than hunting or fishing in the Highlands. All this overlooked the reality that most of the remaining crofters, Gaelic-speaking or not, were still living in a huge rural slum more fetid that those found in smoke-covered industrial centers like Glasgow and Dundee. The contrast between the chimerical ideal and sordid reality could not go unremarked forever.

True, recurrence of the potato blight abated, especially when new species were introduced. Landlords might have been less inclined to evict against a tenant's wishes, but the renter remained insecure because rental contracts were usually year-to-year, almost never for a decade or more. We know about the discontent and sense of grievance of the peasantry from the findings of the Napier Commission, beginning in 1883, whose origin is discussed below. The 5000 pages of testimony there gave voice to crofters who were either illiterate or had no outlets for their sentiments.

Prominent was the deep psychic wound of the Clearances, nominally evicted by one's own people or factors authorized by them. Rubbing the wound was the perception that sheep herders, strangers from different shires, were living higher than the tenants still struggling with crops in infertile soil. Worse, when some sheep farms failed through mismanagement or loss to competition from New Zealand and Australia, those properties were turned over to sporting preserves where the wealthy played, often within view of a destitute blackhouse. As anti-landlord agitation was becoming violent in Ireland during the same period, some observers have questioned why the Highland Gaels seemed relatively quiescent: the same people thought innately belligerent during the dominance of the clans, who also were such effective warriors for the Empire while serving in Highland regiments.

The Irish experiences would ultimately have great influence on Highland crofters, but the circumstances between the two Gaelic lands were significantly different. Irish landlords since Elizabethan and Cromwellian times had been composed of an alien strain, the often disdainful Anglo-Irish who did not share the language, culture or religion of the tenants. In Gaelic Scotland the landlords were often chiefs of the clan, Anglicized since the time of James I, but nominally the same people as the tenants. At the same time, the Napier Commission reported that many tenants felt the insult of the Clearances more acutely with the sense that the clan ethic of *dùthchas* had been sundered by clan-affiliated landlords.

Although poverty was not always as acute in Ireland as in the Gàidhealtachd, militancy came more quickly to the surface there. Unassuaged by the Landlord and Tenant (Ireland) Act of 1870, peasant agitation became a mass movement. The Land League, founded in 1879, benefiting from charismatic leaders like Michael Davitt and the support of the Roman Catholic Church, became a power player in the land. The principal weapon was the rent strike by coordinated tenants under the aegis of the League, but also included the ostracism of Captain Charles Boycott in autumn, 1880, an international *cause célèbre*. The Gladstone administration, perhaps wary that all this energy might be directed toward a larger goal, Home Rule, had passed the Land Law (Ireland) Act in 1881.

Crofter agitation in Scotland began slowly, from the farthest reaches of Gaeldom and mostly in the Hebrides, where there were actually fewer sheep runs. The first shot was the "Bernera Riot" in 1874, on the island of Great Bernera off the west coast of Lewis in the Outer Hebrides. In one sense Bernera fits in at the end of the Clearance narrative, as the disturbance began with tenants giving an irate demonstration at the prospect of eviction, but "riot" goes in quotes because the aggrieved succeeded in taking their case to court, where they won.

Irish Land League champion Michael Davitt toured Scotland, where he was welcomed by journalist John Murdoch of the pro-crofter newspaper *The Highlander*. Even with further visits by lesser Irish luminaries, as well as the reports of Hebridean migrant workers in Ireland, the nature of agrarian protest in Scotland would be different. Highland population was more scattered, harder to assemble for a mass rally. There was no looming greater disruption to social order, like the appeal of Home Rule. Highland agrarian leaders were much taken with the social theories of American writer Henry George, whose *Progress and Poverty* (1879) was a world-wide best seller appealing deeply to Russian novelist Leo Tolstoy, among others. Read by both left and right, George was hardly a radical. Abrupt if not violent action was inevitable. The first attempt at an Irish model rent strike erupted at Kilmuir on the Isle of Skye, which succeeded in reducing tenants' rates by a quarter. A much more publicized action also took place on Skye, in a hamlet south of Portree known as Braes, no longer cited on the map. In early 1881 Lord Macdonald had transferred the rights to graze on a hill known as Ben Lee from the crofters to a sheep-farmer. These were years of bleak harvests, with some of the worst weather in thirty years. A first step for the tenants was to draw up a petition to have grazing rights restored, which was rejected. In November 1881, on the day the rents were due, the men of Braes marched into Portree to declare at the lord's office that the rents would not be paid unless the rights were restored. Lord Macdonald's response was quick: about a dozen tenants and their families would be evicted. Action was slower; it took until next spring for the sheriff-officer from Portree to be dispatched for the eviction. When they arrived April 7, 1882, they were greeted by about 150 people who forcibly seized the eviction orders and immediately burned them

This was a crime known as deforcement. At least five of the protesting crofters were known to authorities and warrants were issued for their arrest. In less than two weeks William Ivory, the Sheriff of Inverness of which Skye was a part, arrived together with fifty policemen called up from Glasgow. An icy April rain was falling, not unlike what drenched fighters at Culloden Moor in the third week of April. Knowing the lay of the land, the locals boxed off the Sheriff and his men at a tight passage on the road, pelting them with stones and missiles. The lawmen defended themselves, ineffectively, with truncheons. Heads were bloodied on both sides. Eventually, the Sheriff with five captives in tow slipped by the protestors. This would come to be known as the Battle of the Braes, April 19, 1882, for which a commemorative marker still stands. A smaller fracas erupted at Glendale the next year. Although not one firearm was discharged at either encounter, the reports of Gaelic crofters with fists raised standing their ground was a canon shot heard all across the United Kingdom.

Distressed crofters would learn that they had unanticipated friends beyond the Highland Line. The year of 1883 saw the establishment of the Highland Land Law Reform Association in London with limited but achievable goals within the parliamentary system. In the short term the Association would co-ordinate disparate and spontaneous groups to make sure their voices were heard. Tempers were rising, and more of the aggrieved, perhaps one thousand, were refusing to pay their rents. Gunboats filled with marines arrived to preserve order. Some crofters were attracted to the more radical Scottish Land Restoration League, headquartered in Glasgow, which aimed to take away land from the rich and redistribute it to the tenants.

The Gladstone government responded by launching a study before any action could be taken. Called the Napier Commission, it was no mere nostrum. The chair, Francis Napier, a Borders peer, had been Governor-General of India. All members were persons of substance, such as Cameron of Lochiel, the Liberal MP from Inverness, and the first Professor of Celtic at the University of Edinburgh, Donald Mackinnon. Half the members spoke Gaelic. They convened their first hearing in May 1883, most fittingly at Braes on the Isle of Skye. Interviews were held everywhere including the remotest corners of the Gàidhealtachd like St. Kilda, and the non–Gaelic Orkneys and Shetland. Brigades of interpreters produced crisp English texts from the Gaelic testimony of the unlettered. In a day before technological innovations, the Commission worked with head-spinning speed, delivering a five-volume, 50000-word report by April 24, 1884.

A statement to Parliament reduced the research to one ringing line: "a state of misery, of wrongdoing, and of patient longsuffering, without parallel in the history of our country."

The report, whose title begins, *Evidence Taken by Her Majesty's Commissioners ...*, is an incomparable anthropological document compiled long before there were field studies of the marginalized poor, allowing countless previously anonymous people to speak in their own voices, without fear of recrimination when outlining the causes of their disappointment and rage.

Within the report also were some recommendations, many from Lord Napier himself, that pleased neither the Highland Land Law Reform Association, now often referred to as the Highland Land League, or Prime Minister Gladstone. It called for a half-dozen modest changes, such as allowing each tenant the right to gather peats, heather, thatch and seaware (coarse seaweed used for fertilizer). A crofter must be compensated for all permanent improvement, should he relinquish or be evicted from his tenancy. But there was no defense against eviction, the Napier report recommended security of tenure only for crofters on large holdings, paying £6 annually in rent and holding a thirty-year lease, of whom there were very few.

More rapid change was coming along another avenue. Also in 1884 suffrage was extended to allow more successful crofters a voice at the ballot box. This led to election of five members of Parliament who fashioned themselves The Crofters' Party. Its slogan, *Is Treasa Tuath na Tighearna*, The People are Mightier than a Lord, had taken on a life of its own, emblematic of a rebellious movement, even if not affiliated with the five MPs in the Party.

Not that opposition to the crofters was cowering. Gladstone tried to pass a law granting Scottish crofters more rights, but it was defeated in May 1885. He left office shortly afterwards but returned as Prime Minister in January 1886, and the Crofters Holdings (Scotland) Act passed June 25, 1886. Many aspects of this Act were borrowed from the Irish Act of 1881 and adapted to Highland circumstances. In summary, these were the three F's: fixity of tenure, fair rents, and freedom to inherit. Such provisions were hugely more radical than anything the Napier Commission had advised and provided each and every crofter with a security the Highland Land League had set as goal. This rendered crofters immune from eviction, permitting them to transfer croft tenancies to their heirs. A crofter's house was even free of the rates, or property taxes, and it could not be seized for debt. All this felt like a modernized and legally enforceable equivalent of the *dùthchas* of clan hegemony. Crofting would continue, and tenants would not all be replaced by sheep.

Nothing was done for cottars nor for others with no crofts of their own.

In the short run the tenantry felt the flush of victory. With a general reduction on rents, the frequently squalid housing on large estates displayed small but encouraging signs of sprucing up. The radical rival to the Land League, the Scottish Land Restoration angrily proclaimed that the Act fell far short of what Highland people were entitled to expect—unrestricted ownership of land worked. Meanwhile, the surrogate for ownership, security of tenure, tended to slow or even halt the development of the crofting counties, suppressing what growth from resources might have been possible. Landlords, who suddenly found themselves in weaker positions when challenged in court, were worse off than ever. They were tacitly judged guilty of past abuses and stripped of many rights previously taken for granted. The Highland farming might now legally look more like the rest of Britain, but the Gàidhealtachd was still the poorest quarter of the United Kingdom. Unfairly, in the view of historians from both the left and right, the 1886 Act came to be judged more for its significant failures than its many successes.

In the next twenty years, into the new century, agrarian discontent continued, an annoyance for successive Liberal and Conservative governments. As might be expected the Conservatives favored landlords and were quicker to send in troops when disorder erupted. But both parties recognized the acute distress of Highland agriculture, perhaps a legacy of the Napier Commission, and agreed a number of Parliamentary remedies. The Crofters Commission, with no counterparts elsewhere in Scotland, created by the 1886 Act, was given real authority and, in effect, is still with us, having been succeeded by the Highland and Islands Development Board (HIDB), a development agency favored by Conservatives and, later, the Highlands and Islands Enterprise (HIE). Added to these were the Crofter Commission Delegation of Powers Act, 1888, the Crofters Common Grazing Regulation Act (1891), the Congested District Commission (1892), and the Small Landholders (Scotland) Act (1911). Eight more legislations would follow in the twentieth century. These together with enlightened government programs and the booming attraction of the Highlands and Islands as a tourist destination would integrate the Gàidhealtachd as a vital player in the United Kingdom economy.

The Comic Highlander

The hackneyed caricature of the Scotsman as obsessive penny-pincher has been with us for centuries. Conscientious research has traced this figure to the ridicule of impecunious courtiers who accompanied James I to London in 1603. As mentioned earlier, the stereotype was continually propped up by the perception that Scotland was a less affluent kingdom than England, a constant theme in the conversation of Samuel Johnson. In the nineteenth century the stingy Scotsman donned Highland dress, an unexpected consequence of George IV's 1822 visit to Edinburgh. Also cited in earlier chapters is the long-standing disdain for Highlanders, as expressed in the line *Mìoran mòr nan Gall*, the great malice of the Lowlander, a phrase from the esteemed eighteenth-century poet Alasdair mac Mhaighstir Alasdair. Condescension lies behind the once-familiar ethnic slur for a Highlander, teuchter, which carries no more venom than the American "hillbilly." Not an insult to provoke a duel or lawsuit.

The sneering or "malice" was not an effective driver of comedy, perhaps because Calvinist Scotland was not hospitable to theaters until the late nineteenth century. The first stage Highlander, Maclaymore of Lochaber, appeared in *The Reprisal: or, The Tars of Old England* (1757), by novelist Tobias Smollett (1721–1771). A more patronizing caricature was Colin MacLeod of Skye in Richard Cumberland's *The Fashionable Lover* (1772), produced in London. He's a country bumpkin with a unique accent. Comic and insulting portrayals of Highlanders certainly existed but did not get wide currency. Most of the examples in Peter Womack's *Improvement and Romance: Constructing the Myth of the Highlands* (1989), Robert Clyde's *From Rebel to Hero: The Image of the Highlander, 1745–1830* (1995) and Michael Newton's *Warriors of the Word: The World of the Scottish Highlanders* (2009), are pre–Clearances, but some themes persist. The libel that the Gaels were an unclean, even animal-like population is not common in written records, even letters and diaries, but seems evident in oral tradition. Womack reports that an one grossest caricature of the scratching Highlander appears on a post card as late as 1914, with the caption, "God bless the Duke of Argyll for this claw post."

The stage Scotsman, or "Scotchman," was nowhere near as ubiquitous as the stage Irishman, in part because Dublin was a venue for new productions that might travel all the British Isles, and Irish performers were frequent in Britain. Some Scottish figures appear in playwrights of distinction, such as W.S. Gilbert's non-musical comedy *Engaged* (1877). When costumed, the Scottish character was likely to attract one or more easily recognizable Highland accessories, even when identified as coming from the Lowlands or speaking with a broad Scots accent. A producer's goal was comedy, not cultural anthropology.

The master personality to emerge in such roles was Sir Harry Lauder (1870–1950), a singer, comedian, composer, music hall/vaudeville performer, who was the world's most highly paid person in show business in the years before World War I. Learning how to dial back his heavy Edinburgh accent at an early age, he was magnetic on stage and drew huge crowds wherever he went in the English-speaking world, with his own private train to tour North America, as well as to South Africa and Australia. He was knighted for his ability to raise millions for the allied effort in the First World War. His singing voice won praise from famed tenor Beniamino Gigli. Prolific, he wrote many of his own songs as well as more than a half-dozen books that went into multiple editions.

His public persona affected a Highland frame, starting with the ever-present kilt, sporran, tam o' shanter, and distinctive walking stick. He called it his "cromach," which Dwelly's dictionary spells *cromag*, for "crooked little thing." The Yiddish theatrical word for it would be "shtick," a device used as a reliable laugh-getter. As photographed hundreds of time, it appears to have been constructed by a stage carpenter, with twists and curls most unlikely to have appeared in nature. It was so well known in Lauder's day that "Harry Lauder's walking stick" is still an informal name for the corkscrew hazel ornamental cultivar of common hazel (*Corylus avellana* "Contorta"). For millions of people in popular audiences, this was a Highland artifact. The attributed "wildness" of the glens manifested in farce.

However, Harry Lauder was Edinburgh-born and not a Highlander. In the contentious academic jargon of the third decade of the twenty-first century, he was a cultural appropriator. To use an analogy more inflammatory than illuminating, what he acted out approached what white Al Jolson did when he sang "Mammy" in blackface. It was not parody or satire. By borrowing and adapting the signifiers of a group of lesser status, he freed himself from petit bourgeois restraint and allowed his character to be more of a cut-up. His jokes and songs were simply not as funny when delivered in Edinburgh Street clothes. On the surface all this looked benign, even fond. Lauder-as-showman was hardly the fusion of the two cultures that Walter Scott proposed, but in a circuitous route the figure can be traced to that source. At bottom Lauder was a patriot if not a nationalist, long before any anticipation of the Scottish National Party. No less a personage than Winston Churchill dubbed Lauder "Scotland's greatest ever ambassador." The Highland garnishes on an essentially Lowland voice made him lighter, more charming, without a hint of resentment or stridency for the poorer kingdom.

His best-known song containing a presumed Gaelic phrase is, "A Wee Deoch-an-Dorris." Context takes care of translation for an audience. The lyrics offer a last drink before departing, a convivial nightcap. It is an expression of Caledonian bonhomie to drive away any lingering notions of murderous Jacobites or, for that matter, scowling, fun-hating Calvinists. The first adjective in the title is the Scots "wee" and the rest is pidgin Gaelic. In school Gaelic the phrase would be *deoch an doruis*, "drink at door," and the final consonant would be pronounced "-sh." Coming at the end of the first decade of the twentieth century, the song's popular appeal could gain on the rising prestige of Scotch whisky, the age-old peasant liquor by then esteemed by the elite. Such notions were superseding the older perceptions of Highland poverty and rebellion, or, before those, of cattle rustling.

The phrase "deoch-an-dorris," however, lies safely in a Lowland context, as the next verses demonstrate:

> Just a wee deoch-an'-dorris
> Before we gang awa'....
> If y' can say
> It's a braw brecht moonlect necht,
> Yer a' recht, that's a.'..

The words are not only broad Scots, but music-hall comic Scots, transparent enough for the non–Scot to interpret upon hearing but rough enough to clang on English ears.

Before Lauder Highland dress was seen most often as a uniform for Highland regiments, known for toughness and bravery, "the ladies from hell." Bagpipe bands echo the military paradigm, with all musicians in stone-faced ardor, even the frequently flamboyant drum major not breaking character. After Lauder Highland dress also became a costume aiding a comic performer.

And so Highland dress, proscribed after Culloden Moor, became at last a comic costume, appearing in stage performances and in the cinema. The Anglo-American team of Stan Laurel and Oliver Hardy employed the Highland comic costume repeatedly, especially in the late silent film *Putting Pants on Philip* (1927) and the sound hit *Bonnie Scotland* (1935). The English-born Laurel had been raised near Glasgow and claimed to find Scottish humor most congenial. Further, he was a friend of Harry Lauder, who, according to the billing, donated a kilt and sporran to Laurel. After their film career ended, the team toured British Isles theaters, 1947, dressed in kilts.

Suas Leis a' Ghàidhlig

The Scottish Gaelic language has long suffered from the depredations of powerful enemies. Against them have been champions who have compensated for their smaller numbers and lower status with unwavering determination. Any number of books have plausibly predicted Gaelic's eventual demise; see Nancy Dorian, *Language Death: The Life Cycle of a Scottish Gaelic Dialect* (1981). It is useless in commerce and inadept in technology. There may be a Gaelic word for computer, *coimpiutair*, but where would one find Gaelic instructions for the use of the *coimpiutair*? In the third decade of the twenty-first century, however, the decline in the number of speakers in the United Kingdom has slowed, 57,602 at last count, while the number of students learning Gaelic is on the rise. Monolingual speakers in the U.K. have disappeared. Given the powerlessness of most Gaelic speakers, along with depopulation, the language might well have disappeared as well if not for professors of Celtic languages in the universities and Celtic societies in cities outside the Gàidhealtachd. Boosting these in unanticipated ways was devolution and the re-opening of the Scottish Parliament in 1999.

In 1872 the Education (Scotland) Act provided universal education in the kingdom, at a time when there might have been 50,000 Gaelic speakers. Following the wishes of the SSPCK (and earlier, King James VI & I), the Act completely ignored Gaelic. Accommodations were made piecemeal for the many monolingual students but administered by school boards reputed to be anti–Gaelic. It would take almost 130 years to reverse this injustice.

An unexpected force for change came from German universities, institutions like Bonn and Tübingen, who pioneered the study of early European languages. The connection between ancient and modern Celtic languages had been established about 1700 but was not widely known. The German linguists produced the first dictionaries and grammars of Old Irish and made clear that Scottish Gaelic was derived from it. Not only did Old Irish contain a richness and complexity to make it a peer of Classical languages, but it produced a large volume of literature centuries before the major European languages. The new prestige for the word "Celtic" (pronounced with a hard -c- as in German *Keltic*) had enormous impact in Ireland, Wales and Brittany, and eventually in Scotland as well. The first chair of Celtic (not "Gaelic") was established in 1882 at the University of Edinburgh, with Colonsay-born native speaker Donald Mackinnon taking the appointment. Few students would enroll for study, and only at the graduate level. Glasgow, St. Andrews and Aberdeen would follow with comparable appointments. A transformation in the status of Gaelic was not imminent, but Mackinnon was prepared to become a public figure, serving on the Napier Commission, as mentioned above. The Edinburgh chair followed eleven years after the founding of the first journal devoted to scholarship in Highland history and culture, *Transactions of the Gaelic Society of Inverness* (1871), with all articles written in English. Inverness, while often dubbed the "capital of the Highlands," was not a dominantly Gaelic town. Adjacent to the Gàidhealtachd, however, it had attracted a coterie of landowners and the well-heeled who drove the Society. It also promoted the advancement of the language and sought to restore its place in schools

While Highland advocacy societies had existed from the end of the eighteenth century, the first to promote the use of Gaelic was An Comunn Gàidhealach, or the Gaelic Association, founded in Oban, 1891. Perhaps because Gàidhealach was a challenge for beginning students to pronounce, it is usually known as "An Comunn" informally rather than by the translated English name. Originally modeled on the highly successful National Eisteddfod of Wales, An Comunn established a Highland counterpart to be known as The Royal National Mòd, hosting a wide array of activities in literature, history, art and music, especially dance competitions. It also featured three successive publications, all of which had ceased by 1970.

After twenty-five years lobbying, An Comunn was able to convince educational authorities that the Gaelic language was a sufficiently rigorous subject as to be worthy of certification, but it did not rank as a "foreign" or "modern" language for Civil Service or professional entrance requirements. A student might demonstrate a proficient command of the language, but such knowledge was merely an ornament that counted toward nothing until about 1960. In his survey of Gaelic language status, *The Lion's Tongue* (1974), Kenneth MacKinnon was critical of An Comunn methods: instruction "encouraged attitudes towards the native language that ran counter to its maintenance."

Attendance at the National Mòd was usually portrayed as a family affair, often with culturally conservative grandparents bringing their grandchildren along in the hopes that they might embrace their heritage. Underneath all this respectability was a strain of defiance and rebellion. The 1961 Mòd saw the premiere of a choral work titled *Suas Leis a' Ghàidhlig*, "Up with Gaelic," with lyrics by Donnchadh Mac Ille Ruaidh. Several videos of sober-looking older people in Highland dress singing the words are available on You Tube. The title is, however, a call to action. During my first tours of the Gàidhealtachd in the 1980s, I frequently came across the phrase as graffiti, in bright yellow or white paint from a small brush done with studied roughness. In visual rhetoric, the graffiti implied a voice of the suppressed and powerless against a dominant order.

An Comunn was two years ahead of its Irish counterpart, the Gaelic League, or Conradh na Gaeilge, founded by poet, translator and essayist Douglas Hyde, who was later the first president of an independent Ireland. The League's signal triumph, of course, was winning official status for the Irish language, even when as the Free State the nation was still in the Commonwealth. Compared with these, all Scottish victories shrunk a bit.

Meanwhile, the Scottish Government, even before devolution, had launched the Gaelic Development Agency, which sponsored a new office in 1984 under the name *Comunn na Gàidhlig*, or "CnaG" for short, to focus on language attainment for young people. The name invited confusion with the An Comunn, perhaps deliberately, but the two could hardly have been more different. Language proficiency was prime, not just an item on the agenda. CnaG fostered physical activity, especially in natural environments. One non–Gaelic feature is the John Muir Award, named for the Scottish naturalist active in the United States, prominent for advocating wilderness preservation.

The force helping Gaelic achieve academic status as well as increasing its speakers was a seemingly quixotic figure from an unanticipated quarter. He was Iain Noble (1935–2010), an Eton and Oxford graduate, a financier and merchant banker who was *not* a native speaker himself but the most effective Gaelic enthusiast of the past century. The final result of Noble's long efforts is that it is now possible for a student to earn a recognized university degree almost entirely through the medium of Gaelic. Today the institution founded by Noble in 1973 as Sabhal Mòr Ostaig is one of thirteen colleges and research centers of the University of the Highlands and Islands.

When the Edinburgh bank that the 34-year-old Noble ran was bought out in 1969, he used the windfall to purchase 20,000 acres mostly on the Sleat peninsula in southeast Skye, nearly all historically MacDonald lands. Much Highland activity had crisscrossed these territories, and the name MacDonald of Sleat has appeared often in this narrative. Noble's first thoughts were to develop enterprises pertinent to the area, two distilleries and a hotel. He wanted these to bear Gaelic names. His vatted malt whisky would be called *Poit Dhubh*, literally "black pot," but winkingly understood to mean "illicit still." He persuaded the Bank of Scotland to print bilingual Gaelic and English checks/cheques. (Spoiling this story a bit, the Clydesdale Bank had already begun this service without Noble's petition.) Next were street and road signs. When the Inverness-shire highways authority sought Noble's land to expand the road system, he said he would waive compensation for the property if he could give the roads Gaelic names. It agreed, a seemingly small victory, but the official recognition Noble knew would be useful. And from that he sought Gaelic signage for towns and railway stations, as was found in Ireland since the establishment of the Free State in 1922. He won his way once more.

Noble launched Sabhal Mòr Ostaig in 1973 with a modest mission: a venue for prospective teachers of Gaelic in primary schools to enhance their training. *Sabhal Mòr* means "big barn" or "big hall," the Gaelic name for an edifice inherited from the MacDonalds. Ostaig is a local placename. Significantly, Noble shunned a patriotic, heroic, romantic or religious name. His championing of the language would not be burdened with any extraneous agenda.

Once it was clear that Sabhal Mòr was not a folly or merely a rich man's indulgence, it began to attract favorable press attention. There was a major expansion of the college campus and a sizeable growth in student numbers. Eventually came an innovative language immersion program, *An Cùrsa Comais*, promising to enable Gaelic learners to attain comprehension and fluency within a year. By 1997 this had grown into a one-year certificate, followed the next year by university-level courses leading to a B.A. degree.

Influenced in no small part by the growth of Sabhal Mòr, people began to think of higher education north of the Highland Line. For centuries those seeking a university degree, or entrance to the professional and managerial class, understood they had to leave the Gàidhealtachd to achieve it. The move to make higher education accessible for more of the population in the United Kingdom began after World War II, first in England, but also in Scotland. The University of Strathclyde was founded 1964, University of Stirling 1967. Nineteen years after the launch of Sabhal Mòr, planning began in 1992 for a university of the Highlands and Islands, the "UHI Project." By 1998 Open University confirmed degree validation for the nascent institution. This was of course before devolution in 1999, which greatly speeded things along, but still in steps. It was not until 2011 that full recognition came to the University of the Highlands and Islands, to be known simultaneously by its Gaelic name, *Oilthigh na Gàidhealtachd agus nan Eilean*. It consists of thirteen individual colleges in multiple locations, some of them in regions where Gaelic was not dominant, like Caithness, the Orkneys and Shetland. The number of students enrolled at the time of writing was 9,905.

Although many more students attending UHI learn through the medium of English, the Gaelic students have more than kept pace. There are now two adjacent campuses in the Sleat Peninsula, and, since 2002, an associate campus on the Isle of Islay. Courses of instruction deal with Gaelic language, music and culture, Gaelic and media studies, and the Atlantic World. In adapting ever-changing new technology, Sabhal Mòr is au courant, with students employing the latest innovations at the same pace as those in North America and the rest of Europe and Britain.

It would be an error to attribute more influence to Sabhal Mòr Ostaig than it deserves. Some would argue that it has ridden the sea change in public opinion and is concurrent with new directions in public policy. In 2005 the Scottish Parliament passed the Gaelic Language Act to give the language greater protection and prominence as an official national language. It also established the Gaelic Language Board, Bòrd na Gàidhlig, advising ministers on matters pertaining to the language, culture and education.

Across the Highland landscape bilingual signage is universal, even—to local annoyance—in non–Gaelic areas like former Caithness (borders erased 1974), and instruction in the language continues to grow. It is a more secure component of the Highland identity than at any time since the Statutes of Iona in 1609.

Coda: Known Up Close
Then Seen from Afar

In the Preface I spoke of a conversation about the Highlands with a patrician gentleman I met at the five-star Inverlochy Castle Hotel near Fort William. Although I never knew his name, his words have lingered with me in writing the later chapters here. Descended from a Jacobite officer who escaped execution, he was in the area to attend a ceremony commemorating Prince Charles Edward's departure for France in September 1746. Without an overbearing display of erudition, he made frequent, casual references to Alastair Livingstone, Betty Stuart Hall and Christian Aikman's *No Quarter Given* (1984), a conscientious attempt to seek out the name of every person who participated in the Rebellion. It seemed he had all but memorized it. And how much else? I had never met any person so deeply invested in and knowledgeable about the matters in this book. He never tried to best me on details, although he easily could have. Instead, he wished to report his discovery in taking a DNA sample, "recreational genetics," to see to whom he might be related. As reported in the Preface, he was startled to see that most of his connections were outside Scotland and outside Britain, scattered to the winds: sixty in Canada and several hundred in the United States. If I did not know before, I now assumed that the potential reader of this volume is more likely to be one of those scattered hundreds rather than someone who lived in the Gàidhealtachd or visited it from time to time. I admit that anyone so well-informed as the Inverlochy gentleman would likely be displeased at my presumption to tell this anfractuous story in such a small space.

Without knowing anything of the "hundreds," around the world, I have also assumed that the majority of them (those in Canada and New Zealand excepted) are culturally assimilated and have forgotten that names like Cameron, Beaton or Forbes—to say nothing of MacDonald and Campbell—are of Highland origin. Quite a few, a number impossible to calculate, will know the general origin of their names, with family members affecting to be thrilled by bagpipe music and the men sporting family tartan ties. We can expect that most, however, and their neighbors, will be aware that the Highlands exist although the distinction between the "Highlands" and all of Scotland is not always immediately clear, as in the Scottish—or are they—Highland games, like tossing the caber.

This puts Highlanders way ahead of other European indigenous ethnic minorities, like the Sámi/Saami or the Bretons. A Finno-Ugric speaking minority, well under 100,000, in different Scandinavian countries, the Sámi were long badly treated by the famously egalitarian Norse majority surrounding them and are now nearly invisible. The two most prominent Sámi-descended immigrant, are singer-artist artist Joni Mitchell, and, actress Renée Zellweger, with a Swiss name, whose ethnicity is only perceived by other Sámi. Bretons are only slightly more visible, but the best-known Breton-named American, Jack Kerouac, is rarely cited for his ethnicity. Although the Bretons were one French group not celebrated for their cuisine, most educated people see a cultural distinction in the Breton crêpe and galette. Then again, in my experience the majority of women named Brittany, Britney, Britni, etc., are either unaware that there is a geographical space with that name or unable to tell you anything about it. An exception might be made for the Basques of the French and Spanish Pyrenees, who have maintained a higher standard of living than the majority around them. They have also been championed by Pablo Picasso and Ernest Hemingway. Much of their popular identity has been shaped by political violence, whose cause is not widely understood.

At the shallowest level, most associations with the Highlands are positive. There might have been a time that "Highlander" was a name given to a cheaper mode of something for sale, an allusion to Scottish clichéd penny-pinching, with possibly a lighter spin. That has passed. At present the more luxurious model of the Toyota Sports Utility Vehicle (SUV) is called the Highlander, apparently evoking strength or endurance. Scottish Gaelic prefixes and other elements put a positive luster on newly coined placenames in North America, implying a retreat from the pedestrian and humdrum, or perhaps also the industrial. An upper-middle-class neighborhood in Syracuse, New York, built in the 1920s, is called Strathmore. Scottish people did not develop the neighborhood, and the Scottish population in the area is slight. In North America T.M. Devine's judgment that the Highlands, at the beginning of the nineteenth century, were seen as a giant, rural slum seems to have been deleted. The notion of suburban Highland idyll, always implicit but never spelled out, is brutally mocked in David Mamet's play *Glengarry Glen Ross* (1984) depicting the bitter rivalries of four desperate, unscrupulous real estate salesmen. We never see the undesirable properties they are trying to unload on guileless buyers, but they come with stereotyped Highland names, now a stale trope.

Real estate aside, the allure of the Highlands as a dreamy, misty desirable place beyond the horizon persists. Consider that the title "My Heart's in the Highlands," taken from a line of Robert Burns, has been employed a dozen times, usually on romance novels. American playwright and novelist William Saroyan (1908–1981) used it three times, in fiction, memoir and stage drama. The most memorable dates from 1939, a short stage work about a Scotsman in some of California's shabbier environs longing for the dreamy mountains far away.

A thousand times more pervasive than Saroyan's whimsy and working-class wistfulness is the relentless inundation of the Highland romance novel, which began with Jane Porter in 1810. No attempt has been made here to number or categorize all the titles, but if we extrapolate from Alma Randall Emmons's 1941 dissertation, we can assume there must be several thousand, most of them no longer available even as their plot conventions and tropes linger. In November 2022, a search for "Highland Romance Fiction" yielded more than fifty titles on Amazon.com, while the same search in the catalogue of the Onondaga County Public Library delivered eighty-one. A hasty survey of cover art over the decades points to directions the genre has taken. For much of the twentieth century, from the time hardcovers had illustrated dust jackets and later paperbacks followed suit, we usually had male and female figures, fully clothed, in some semblance of eighteenth-century dress, lace collars, tricornered hats, etc. No more. Illustrations of recent decades have signaled a slide toward erotica, even soft porn. In a gender reversal of the "bodice-ripper" romantic fiction, the Highland romance customarily features a kilted Nordic-looking man, blond or red-haired, shirtless with a hairless torso at right, and a clothed damsel at the left of the frame. Consider the prolific Maddie MacKenna's *Seduced by a Highland Thief* (2020), whose subtitle is also the name of the author's series, "A Steamy Scottish Historical Romance Novel."

If some of our fellow mortals find respite from the toil and humiliations of the daily grind with tales of dashing Highlanders, they will receive no brickbats from this corner. The danger of distorting actual Highland narrative might once have existed, as Lewis Grassic Gibbon and Hugh MacDiarmid argued in 1934, cited at the beginning of Chapter 6, but that moment has passed. We can gain perspective from other fields of historical study preceded by a vast popular, romantic literature: (a) the settling of the American West vs. 140 years of cowboys and Indians, and (b) the opening of Africa vs. H. Rider Haggard, the great white hunter, etc. Unobtrusively, the truth of what was happening on the American "frontier" and in "darkest Africa" was conscientiously recorded at the time and now provides evidence for the revisionism speaking in harsh terms of "ethnic cleansing" and "genocide" that has triumphed in the last generation and half. Some of the current view comes from research by the descendants of formerly oppressed people who have entered the academy and energize discourse. We have a parallel in the educated grandchildren of put-upon teuchters, but also of the efforts of John Prebble, no matter how much he is disputed.

We can see the dominance of authentic Highland history over romantic aberration in the state-of-the-art Visitor Centre at Culloden Moor. The battlefield has been maintained fastidiously since the nineteenth century, with weather-worn cairns marking the positions of different clans and regiments on the field. Successive archaeological investigations have not been intrusive or disruptive. Before entering the cinematic presentation of the battle in the Centre, the visitor passes down narrow aisles of printed expositions and illustrations giving extensive information on the Stuarts, the Hanovers, leading personalities, and troop movements in advance of the battle. The information is in line with current informed scholarship. Taken as a whole it would equal a substantial lecture or a pamphlet, more than a hasty tourist might want to consume if not so cosseted. In viewing the data spread over some distance, interspersed with artifacts the visitor is assured of having been exposed to a solid orientation. The ensuing film presentation, projected on four walls of what could be a lecture hall, is fast-moving and gripping. The performers for both the Jacobite and Hanoverian forces are amateur re-enactors wearing authentic tartans and uniforms.

If our default expectation of the Highlands is romantic escape, it is not all the doing of the authors of popular fiction. Several governmental agencies, from both the left and the right, have zoned the area to resist the roadside blight of the American West, with billboards and junk food joints, or the exploitation of choice locations in the Irish Gaeltacht by wealthy foreigners. Such policies separate the Highlands from industrialization and commercialism.

Thus, in one of most admired films of Michael Powell and Emeric Pressburger, *I Know Where I'm Going!* (1945), a dignified young Englishwoman (Wendy Hiller) is about to enter into a passionless marriage for the affluence it provides, when her progress is interrupted in the Hebrides. Not only is the film shot on location, but the placenames are actual, e.g., the port of Oban, not fictionalized as in *Brigadoon* (repositioned from its German origin). There she meets a tweedy Scotsman, Torquil MacNeil (Roger Livesay), and chooses genuine love, unsullied by monetary concerns.

Only the natives portray the Highlands and Islands in a comic or unflattering tone. Topping the list are several works by Compton Mackenzie (1883–1972), notably *Hunting the Fairies* (1949) and *Whisky Galore* (1947), cited earlier, about the booze-filled freighter that capsized on the Hebridean isle of Eriskay and how the wily islanders accommodated this bounty with the law. Mackenzie was also a sage commentator on Highland history and culture. More recently the ambidextrous Oban-based Alan Warner has portrayed Argyllshire life in two unrelated genres, the thriller and broad comedy. His *Morvern Callar* (1995) assumes a tone of moral decay associated with *film noir*. His protagonist is a female retail clerk in a dead-end job in an unnamed seaside town, unmistakably Oban. We see it as a backwater to be escaped from. When her affectless lover commits suicide, she realizes he has left behind a completed novel. Cutting his body into small pieces, she disposes of incriminating evidence and claims his manuscript as her own. Upon publication, it achieves heady acclaim, and she leaves for adventures in the Mediterranean. This was filmed by Lynne Ramsay in 2001. In 1998 Warner published *The Sopranos*, depicting the mischievous coarse manners, and poverty, of a Catholic girls' choir from Oban. It was adapted for the stage by Lee Hall for the Edinburgh Festival as *Our Ladies of Perpetual Succour* (2015) and from there to London (2017). It was filmed as *Our Ladies* (2019) by Michael Caton-Jones.

The man at the Inverlochy with his grip on *No Quarter Given* already has his own vision of what Highland cultural identity can embrace: the glories, the pain and the degradation. No problem to accommodate a discordant voice, such as found in the verse from Alexander Montgomerie of Ayrshire (c. 1540–1611) alleging that God had fashioned the "Helandman" from "an horss turd." Anyone who has made a study of Culloden and its aftermath knows that acknowledgment of defeat and humiliation is part of what bolsters pride. The crudity and cruelty from one's detractors are means of enhancing the virtue and strength of our people. Black and Jewish intellectuals stiffen their group identity by iterating the verbal abuse thrown against them.

The farther one gets from Culloden, Inverlochy or the Isle of Skye the more any mention of the Gàidhealtachd is piecemeal and disconnected. There is no single cultural hero comparable to what the Finns have in Jean Sibelius. Irish pubs and taverns around the world are decorated with posters proclaiming political heroes, Robert Emmett and Daniel O'Connell, and dozens from literature: Brendan Behan,

Sean O'Casey, James Joyce, now joined by Seamus Heaney. Italian restaurants have many more, from Dante through Garibaldi and Frank Sinatra. There is no venue for a Highland heroes' gallery, and if there were, whom could we name? We have no portraits of the most likely poets, Rob Donn and Iain Lom. How many people have heard of the warriors Somerled, Colkitto, Montrose or the Bonnie Dundee? Heaven forfend that any pantheon includes two names appearing most prominently in this volume, Prince Charles Edward Stuart and James Macpherson. Meanwhile, the place of Highland culture is uncertain in the surviving celebrations of Scottishness, starting with the Burns Night dinners in late January. I have been asked to participate in these several times and can recite "Address to a Haggis" in authentic broad Scots. The presentation of the formulaic panegyric that must conclude with the toast "To the immortal memory" is the other program item. The first time I delivered one of those for a chapter of the St. Andrew's Society, a scowling older woman on a cane informed me later that it was the first time she had known of a Jacobite being so invited.

The proliferation of athletic competitions, the Games, cited in Chapter 5, are ambivalently called "Highland" or "Scottish." Admittedly they do include Highland dance contests, so named, in nineteenth-century versions of traditional costume. They are, however, a charming cultural fossil appearing nowhere else. Neither have they been adapted to create another contribution to contemporary culture the way Irish dance billowed into *Riverdance*, an international hit of lasting appeal. Worse, in Douglas McGrath's film adaptation of Dickens' *Nicholas Nickleby* (2002), Scottish actor Alan Cumming improvises a Highland fling for clownish comic effect.

Although they are a fraction of the diaspora, certain numbers of Highland-descended people retain a sense of connection to the Gàidhealtachd. It has been my assumption that some of them may wish to grasp the skeleton key I offer here. Quite a few have already claimed an aspect of Highland identity, taking widely different tones.

Consider the case of Nicola Fuller, the flamboyant, larger-than-life and alcoholic mother of Alexandra Fuller, who dominates two of her daughter's memoirs, the best-selling *Don't Let's Go to the Dogs Tonight* (2001) and *Cocktail Hour Under the Tree of Forgetfulness* (2011). The Fullers were embattled white settler farmers in three Black African countries when resentment of colonialism and white privilege was becoming violent. Alexandra had been born in England, with the family taking up a banana plantation in Rhodesia while she was a small child. For mother Nicola it was not whiteness or Englishness that she cherished as much as her Scottishness. A constant reader in a country where books were hard to come by, Nicola encouraged her daughter's literacy and stressed that she should know her rarefied heritage among the Highland Gaels. That would lead to a veneration of the myth-shrouded Isle of Skye and the MacDonalds of Clanranald. Their war cry, *A dh'aindeoin có theireadh e*, "Gainsay it who dares," strengthened the family's stubborn resolve to stick it out.

As the previous six chapters have sought to show, Highland Gaels also suffered victimhood and degradation. Most unexpectedly the world of *haute couture* became a theater in the mid–1990s to remember outrages in the Gàidhealtachd. Almost everything was unlikely about the career of Alexander McQueen (1969–2010), the most admired British designer of the last half century. Not only was he the chief at Givenchy who formed a partnership with Gucci, but the posthumous show of his work at New York's Metropolitan Museum was the second biggest draw in its history. In person McQueen dressed like the gauche working-class boy he was, the son of a taxi driver, born in greater London. He was still called an *enfant terrible* at forty. As his fame grew, however, he became more Scottish, with an attachment to the Isle of Skye quite different from Nicola Fuller's. He dropped his given name from birth, Lee, in favor of his middle name Alexander to sound more Caledonian.

The show that brought McQueen to the world's attention was titled "Highland Rape" in 1995. The title referred directly to the Clearances of the eighteenth and nineteenth century, but it was not the history lesson that made it controversial. Some models appeared to be attacked and abused, walking the runway with clothes that were slashed and torn, and in tatters of lace with spatters of fake blood. Not surprisingly, some reviewers interpreted the staging to be about women who were raped, and criticized what they saw as glamorizing rape and favoring misogyny. McQueen responded that the title referred to England's rape of Scotland and that he wished to refute the romantic depictions of Scotland.

We cannot know the total numbers of the Highland diaspora, how many millions of people worldwide share DNA with the Scottish Gaelic speakers of, say, 1746, or 1841. My assumption is that the majority have assimilated and forgotten their roots, and many could be unaware of that heritage. Or unaware if their families were Highland or Lowland. A considerable number do not have Scottish names. Yet thousands look to Scotland to find something of themselves, just as Nicola Fuller and Alexander McQueen did. Several publications are on the scene to serve them. One is the slick-paper, richly illustrated *Scotland* magazine published six times a year by Chelsea Magazine Company in London and distributed worldwide. Issue #115 appeared in 2021. In the back pages are sixty notices for clan societies, all but a handful Highland. And with them more than a dozen notices for non-clan organizations, chapters of the St. Andrew's Society, etc.

In the last half century or more, we have abandoned attempts to define the essentialist character of a nation or ethnicity. The notion is unsupportable, and when applied has proven to be detrimental, even as it lingers in demotic discourse: barroom talk. Once vivid pictures from the past, victory at Killiecrankie or the tenant's eviction from a ruined cottage, are amorphous in the long run and anything but immutable. They are rightfully remembered, even commemorated, but they do not define in absolute terms. Instead, we can consider the episode or person who happens along, unexpectedly, who embodies and expresses the aspirations and values shared by a wide swath of people from the same ethnicity. For Highland Gaels of the last half century, such a man would be Calum MacLeod, who constructed his own stretch of road pretty much by himself.

Crofter, assistant lighthouse keeper and part-time postman, Malcolm MacLeod (1911–1988), Calum for short, was born in Glasgow and taken to Raasay, the island of his forefathers, as a child. It is the land mass one sees from the harbor at Portree, and has become a tourist destination just recently, possibly because it is only reachable by ferry. Some of its stature within Gaelic culture comes from its being the setting for Sorley MacLean's masterwork *Hallaig* (1954), depicting the Clearances. Calum and his brother Charles, who lived at Arnish in the remote north of the island, took a commission of £35 a year from the local council to construct a nearby walking track during the winters, 1949–1952. This prompted a sense of urgent concern for the island's undeveloped roadways. After decades of unsuccessful community lobbying for a new road at the north of the island, Calum decided to build the road on his own.

Purchasing Thomas Aitkin's manual *Road Making & Maintenance: A Practical Treatise for Engineers, Surveyors and Others* (1900), for half a crown, he started to work replacing the old narrow footpath. The Department of Agriculture provided some of the heavy lifting, clearing land with a compressor, and explosives at a cost of £1,900. Calum set to work by himself. Over a period of approximately ten years (1964–1974), he constructed 1¾ miles (2.8 km) of road between Brochel Castle and Arnish, using little more than a shovel, a pick and a wheelbarrow. Several years after its completion, the road was adopted and surfaced by the local council. By that time Calum and his wife were the only inhabitants of Arnish. Despite the remoteness of north Raasay and Calum's hesitance to celebrate himself, recognition from the wider world was coming. In his last years he was awarded the British Empire Medal for "maintaining supplies to the Rona Light." The citation avoided making any mention of the road, a subject of continuing contention with local authorities.

Several artists were more forthright. In the year of Calum's death, 1988, the trad group Capercaillie produced an album titled *The Blood is Strong* (a note of muted patriotism) that included the song "Calum's Road." By that time the enterprise had become so well known the title needed no explanation. Employing different music, British circle dance choreographer Cindy Kelly opened a dance number also titled "Calum's Road," performed worldwide in that niche genre. Another trad group named Runrig released an album in 2001 titled *The Stamping Ground*, including the song "Wall of China/One Man" alluding again to the Raasay achievement.

Music and dance invited more words. In 2006 Roger Hutchinson published *Calum's Road*, a journalistic account that is the source of this passage. It also inspired playwright David Harrower to produce a stage play titled *Calum's Road* by the Communicado Theatre Company, directed by Gerry Mulgrew, at the National Theatre of Scotland in 2011. It toured the country in 2013. Colin MacDonald's radio adaptation was also broadcast in 2013. The rights to Hutchinson's book were sold to serve as the basis of a feature film, which has not yet appeared.

There is nothing in the tale of Calum MacLeod's solo roadbuilding that evokes any specific episode retold in this volume: not a victory and not a humiliation, not a rebellion and not a submission. He was not only a Gaelic speaker but a Gaelic writer, prolific in well-informed local histories as well as a frequent contributor to the journal *Gairm*. He knew where he lived. Lacking economic and political sway, his tenacity gave him power over the world he inhabited. Despite having fame thrust upon him, he was never driven by vanity. Paradoxically both proud and modest, he would have his way. Such a figure can excite Highlanders' sense of their own identity.

Glossary: Persons, Places, Vocabulary

Argyll. Old Irish, *Airer Goídel*, country of the Gael; Scottish Gaelic, *Erra Ghaidheal*, coastland of Gael. Name for an extensive region in the west Highlands whose borders and definition changed over centuries. For most of modern history the name denoted Argyllshire, a 3110-square-mile county south of Inverness-shire, erased from the map in 1974. Some of the territory was included in the new county of Argyll and Bute in 1996, with different borders. In medieval Scotland, Argyll might refer to large expanses of the west coast where Gaelic was spoken. Co-extensive with much of the proto-kingdom of Dál Riada. Much associated with Clan Campbell, whose chief is the Duke of Argyll. The usual leading town is Inveraray, on Loch Fyne, Scotland's longest sea loch, site of the Campbell seat, built 1743.

aoir. Although literally the Gaelic word for satire, it would be ribald and filled with vituperation and condemnation, leading to the venomous.

armigerous. In heraldry, entitled to bear arms.

Antrim. Easternmost county in Ulster, or what is now Northern Ireland. Not only closest to Scotland but dominated by the Clan Donald and frequently appearing to be an extension of the Scottish Highlands.

bagpipe. See *pìobaireachd*.

baile, bailtean. The basic farming unit in the Highlands before 1750, consisting of anything from four to twenty or more families working land on the runrig management system and raising grazing cattle on common land. Often translated as "township." The Irish cognate, also *baile*, Anglicized in so many town names, e.g., Ballyshannon, usually implies a town or bigger population.

Bald John. Translation of Iain Lom (q.v.), seventeenth-century poet, a MacDòmhnaill, usually known by his given name and sobriquet.

Ben Nevis. Gaelic: *Beinn Nibheis*. Highest mountain in the Highlands and in all of the British Isles, 4,413 feet, 1,345 meters. In Lochaber, not far from Fort William and the battlefield of Inverlochy.

birlinn, birling. ScG: *birlinn, beirlinn; birlinnean* (pl). Large rowing boat or barge, widely used in the eras of Somerled and the Lordship of the Isles. Smaller than the Norse and Manx *skuta*.

blackhouse. A colloquial English term with a fluid definition. Often it depicted a humble dwelling constructed of double-thick drystone walls with a thatched roof; usually without windows or chimney, in which smoke from a turf fire would escape through a hole in the roof. More common in the treeless Hebrides than the mainland, and thought to have Norse antecedents. Later might describe any older residence in ruinous condition. Translated to Gaelic, *taigh, tigh dubh*.

Bliadhna an Losgaidh. The year of the burnings, 1814, part of Patrick Sellar's campaign to drive tenants out in the Strathnaver Clearances.

Bliadhna nan Caorach. The Year of the Sheep, 1792, when crofters first rebelled at their displacement by livestock. Many more flocks would displace crofters in the nineteenth century.

broken clan. A clan without a claim to land.

broken man. An ex-clansman displaced from his original territory, cateran.

cadet branch. Male-line descendants of a patriarch's younger sons (called "cadets"). Cadet branches of a major clan might bear the same surname as the rest of the clan but inhabit different territories and make their own alliances. Cf. sept.

cas-chrom. *Cas*, foot; *chrom*, crooked. The ubiquitous, primitive hand- or foot-plow in the Highlands, requiring back-breaking labor. Its citation in poetry denotes the common folk.

cateran. Irregular fighting man in the Highlands. From *ceatharna* 1. troop, fighting band; 2. party of freebooters; 3. yeomanry (in the military sense); 4. group of well built, "manly men." In medieval times a cateran might be in service of a lord, but later had more negative connotations: a tough guy, a cattle-lifter, freebooter, or "broken man," i.e., displaced from original territory.

Ceann-cinnidh. Gaelic expression for the chief, chieftain, head of a clan. The Gaelic version implies more of an ideal bond between a leader and his people.

cenél, cenéla (pl). Old Irish and Gaelic word usually translated as "kindred." Dating from earlier written records, it precedes the use of *clann* and is not interchangeable with it.

ceòl beag, ceòl mòr. See *pìobaireachd.*

Cheviot. Known in Gaelic as *Na Caoraich Mòra*, the Big Sheep. Breed of sheep named for the hills in the north of England where it was bred. Known outside the Highlands for the excellence of its wool, the Cheviot was the favored breed in the Clearances, and thus in the minds of some is associated with dread.

Cille Chuimein. Gaelic name for site now occupied by Fort Augustus.

Cináed mac Ailpín, Cinaed. Shadowy ninth-century king (d. 858) who united Picts and Gaels to form Alba, the anticipation of what would become Scotland. Founder of a long-lived dynasty. Known in English as Kenneth Mac Alpine, a form not known until centuries after his death.

clann. Gaelic word for "children," yielding the word clan, a kinship group among Scottish people, first Highlanders and later also Lowlanders.

Clann Iain Dubh. Figurative name for a group of seventeenth-century bandits presumably led by Iain Mac Domhnaill but consisting mostly of MacInneses. Also known as Clan Ewen Dhuibh.

Clann Iain Mòr. Another name for the Clan Donald South or the MacDonalds of Dunnyveg.

còir a' claidhimh. "Sword right," a form of lordship based on sheer force of arms.

Conn of the Hundred Battles. Ir. Conn Cétchathach. Shadowy early Irish king (third century?), widely cited in early Irish literature. Claimed as an ultimate ancestor by the Lord of the Isles and the Clan Donald. Distinguish from the more likely historical Niall of the Nine Hostages.

cottar. Word common in Lowland usage made popular by poet Robert Burns for farm workers with no land of their own, sometimes sub-let a small patch of land by their employer or a crofter. A subtenant, of lower status than a crofter.

creach. Literally, pillage or plunder; foray. Often used to describe a cattle raid of limited scope.

crofter. Word of English origin used for tenants in the Highlands and Islands; of higher status than a cottar.

cromach. Non-standard spelling for *cromag*, a crooked walking-stick, employed by Harry Lauder.

cuid-oiche. The right of hospitality in a tenant's property. Men with only marginal associations with a chief might demand lodging and food from a person of lower status; often abused.

Dál Riada, Dál Riata, Dalriada. Proto-kingdom of sixth-to-eighth-century Argyll, connected to and perhaps an extension of the Dál Riada of Northern Ireland.

daoine uaisle. Gentlemen through manners

and training, often kin of the chief. In a fighting unit could imply the more skilled soldiers, not just the officers. In the eighteenth century this came to refer to the tacksmen (q.v.).

davach, davoch. OI: *dabach, dabhach*; ScG. *dabhach*. Early Scottish measure of land, dating from at least the eleventh century. In the east, 4 ploughshares consisting of 8 oxgangs, possibly larger in the poor soils of the west, as many as 416 acres. Tenpenny land, liable for an annual payment of 10 pennies as the tax called skat. Sufficient to support sixty head of cattle. A word of Danish origin, *skat* also gives us the "scot" in "scot-free."

Dòmhnall Donn. (brown Donald). Name borne by thousands of Highland men, most prominently the "cattle-lifter poet" of Bohuntin (d. 1691), discussed in Chapter 5.

Donald. Eponym of the Clan Donald and the MacDonald families. From the primitive Celtic forms *dubno*, world; *walos*, mighty. Old Irish: Domnall. Scottish Gaelic: Dòmhnall. The shadowy (d. c. 1250) grandson of Somerled, who in life would have borne the patronymic mac Raghnaill. The family was first known in Gaelic as *Clann Dòmhnaill*, later as *Mac Domhnaill*. Medieval spelling was not standardized, and the diacritical over the first vowel can vary, *Dòmh-* and *Dómh-*. Dòmhnall is nominative. The prefix Mac- puts the name in the genitive, thus Dòmhnaill, and sometimes Dhòmhnaill. Scribes do not always follow these conventions.

Druimm Albin, Druim Albin, Drum Albyn, Drumalban. (ScG: the spine of Scotland) A medieval geographical concept that has been drawn at different places at different times. Long thought to be synonymous with the "Grampian Line," i.e., the unofficial border of the Highlands. In 2001 Ewan Campbell revived the use of the term, arguing it was the invisible line along the split in the Celtic languages, with the P-Celts (Picts, Britons) to the right or east, and the Q-Celts (Gaels) to the left or west. At other times it has been thought to be the eastern border of Argyll, the view of R.A. McDonald (1997).

Drumossie Moor. Traditional name for the large, open field 5 miles (8 km) east of Inverness renamed Culloden Moor after the battle there, April 16, 1746.

Dunfermline. Town in Fife, a de facto capital of Scotland from c. 1070 to 1437, while kings were still being crowned in Scone; rivaled by Perth.

Dunadd, Dun Add. (ScG: fort of the Add [valley]). Rocky, isolated 276-foot hill in north Strathclyde (until 1974 Argyllshire), 4 miles (6 km) north of Lochgilphead, capital of the early kingdom of Dál Riada. Inhabited until the sixteenth century.

Dunyvaig. ScG. *Dùn Naomhaig*: Fort of the Galleys. Normalized spelling for the medieval castle, now in ruins, on the Isle of Islay. The branch of the MacDonalds that takes its name from the castle prefers the normalized spelling of Dunnyveg. Dunivaig is a lesser variant.

dùthchas, dùthcas. Almost untranslatable term that encapsulates a pervasive belief that clansfolk are entitled to a permanent stake in the territories pertaining to their clan. The collective heritage of the clan, and members' right to settle in territories where chiefs provided protection. With the sense of belonging comes the obligation to recognize the personal authority of the chiefs and leading gentry as trustees for the clan. Succeeded by *oighreachd*. Cf. Dwelly: "1. Place of one's birth. 2. Heredity, native or hereditary temper. 3. Visage, countenance. 4. Hereditary right."

factor. Word, always in English, for an estate manager or land agent with power over the more independent tacksman, whom they often displaced. Factors often decisively led the clearances of the early nineteenth century, giving the word threatening implications for crofters.

feannag, feannagan (pl). Narrow ridges or rigs constructed over previously intractable land for the cultivation of potatoes. Although the *feannag* demanded continuous arduous labor from crofters and cottars, the term was translated as lazybed, lazy-bed as an insult to the Gaelic worker.

Fenian Cycle. One of four bodies of interconnected narrative in early Irish literature, centering on the hero Fionn mac Cumhaill. Perceived as more popular than the Ulster Cycle. Recorded by medieval learned scribes, it continues in oral tradition to the present day in both Ireland and Scotland.

Fingal. Variant name for Old Irish hero Fionn mac Cumhaill. The ascription of the cave on the Hebridean island of Staffa comes from an error in copying from the Gaelic.

Fionn mac Cumhaill, Find mac Cumhal, Fingal, etc. Central hero of the Fenian Cycle of Old Irish literature. His stories were widely known in Gaelic Scotland. Thought to have blazed the "parallel roads" (actually of glacial origin) in Glen Roy, Lochaber.

Fortriu. A leading proto-kingdom of the Picts. In 2006 Alex North argued that it was much farther north, on the shores of the Moray Firth, than previously supposed.

Garmoran. Archaic name for a region in the west Highlands, including Knoydart, Morar, Moidart, Ardnamurchan and the Small Isles. John of Islay gained the title Lord of Garmoran when he married Amie mac Ruari in 1346.

Haakon, Hakon IV (1201–1263). Last Norwegian king to invade the mainland of Scotland, where he was defeated at Largs, 1263. Much-esteemed in Norway where his reign, 1217–1263, was a medieval golden age.

handfast. A handshake as a pledge. Commentators from c.1700 proposed that Highlanders engaged in a "handfast marriage," a trial union of a year and a day that could be terminated if the female had not produced a child. Once widely accepted, the term is now seen as a misrepresentation and a libel upon Highland moral behavior. Marriage in the time of clan domination, however, differed from the bourgeois monogamous norm of the last two centuries. See Chapter 2.

Hebrides. Etymology: spelling a corruption resulting from a misreading of the Latin *Ebudae*.

Iain Lom MacDòmhnaill (1624?–1707). Renowned seventeenth-century poet usually known only by his given name and sobriquet, Iain (John) Lom (bald).

Inverlochy. Site just north of the modern town of Fort William. Locale for two important battles: September 1431 between Lord of the Isles (Gaelic) forces and Royal forces; and February 1645 between Royalist (mostly Gaelic, this time) and Covenanter armies.

Iona. Small island, 3.5 by 1.5 miles, southwest of Mull in the Inner Hebrides. For more than a millennium, the most important Christian site in the Gàidhealtachd. Evangelized by Colum Cille in 563 CE, popularly thought to have established the monastery there, actually constructed sometime later. Initially an outpost of Irish Christianity, and culturally an outlier of Ireland. Connected to Roman Christianity by the Benedictines, 1203. Burial ground for four Irish, eight Norwegian and innumerable Scottish kings.

justiciar. Rank given to two supreme judges under early Scottish kings.

laird. A Scots term, equivalent to the English "lord," for the owner of a landed estate. When Gaelic clan chiefs adopted the term for themselves, the move signaled a claim to elevated status.

Largs. Small town in the former Ayrshire where the last Norse invasion of Scotland, under Haakon IV, was defeated in 1263.

lazybed, lazy-bed. See *feannag*.

Lebor Gabála Érenn. (OIr. Book of Invasions, literally the Book of the Taking of Ireland). Classed as a "pseudo-history," a twelfth-century text synchronizing myths, legends and genealogies, within a framework of Biblical exegesis, to chart the purported invasion and early history of Ireland. Widely known in the early Highlands. Consulted by scribes for certain clans seeking esteemed if contrived ancestors.

linn nan creach. The time of the forays, the period of disorder and clan warfare after the forfeiture of the Lord of the Isles, 1493, lasting through the early seventeenth century.

Lord of the Isles. Irish: *Rí Inse Gall* [lit. king

of the foreigners' isles, i.e., Hebrides]; *Triath nan Eilean*. Latin: *Dominus Insularum*. Also, *Dominus de Inchegal* [Lord of the Hebrides]. All the Lords of the Isles bore the clan name Mac Dòmhnaill, Anglicized as MacDonald.

Mac Alpine, Kenneth. See Cináed mac Ailpín

machair. A flat or low-lying coastal strip or arable or grassland, unique to Highlands and Islands; the calciferous sand requires continuous fertilization with animal manure or seaweed, and is vulnerable to erosion. A loan from the Gaelic *machair*.

manrent. The obligation or promise of a weaker person or clan to provide service or support to a patron faithfully.

marquis, marquess (UK). A word of French origin for a person of noble rank in Britain, and usually given English pronunciation; a rank below that of a duke but above that of an earl or count. Perhaps because its French etymology implies a noble from a frontier region, it was once favored for Highland nobles.

merkland, markland. The amount of land for the value of one mark, an Old Norse coinage. Under the Lord of the Isles this was a term for tax assessment, but it appears originally to have denoted a rental. The term survived until the eighteenth century where one traveler defined it as the amount of land that could support fourteen cows and one horse.

mormaor. ScG: *mòr maor*: great bailiff. In medieval Scotland, the high steward of a province; perhaps equated with the English earl.

Na Daoine. "The men," may indicate different men on different occasions. After the establishment of the Free Church of Scotland the phrase denoted select laymen, a spiritual elite with detailed knowledge of the scriptures who often wielded authority within a parish.

Napier Commission. Informal name of Parliamentary committee that investigated Highland agrarian unrest, 1883–1884. The five-volume, 5000-word report is a treasure trove of testimony of contemporary life. Conclusion: "a state of misery, or wrongdoing, and of patient longsuffering, without parallel in the history of our country."

Niall of the Nine Hostages. Ir. Niall Noígiallach. Ancestor and eponym of the powerful Uí Néill dynasty that dominated Ireland for six centuries. Uncertain dates, reigning 379–405 CE? Long thought legendary, his status changed with the genome studies beginning 1990. He is now identified with a hyper-fertile male who fathered enormous numbers of children in his ascribed era. His marker is M222. Fully one-third of Irish people appear to be descended from him, as do large numbers of Scottish Highlanders, and as many as three million men worldwide. Distinguish from the more shadowy Conn of the Hundred Battles.

Non-juring Episcopalians. Members of the faith who refused to acknowledge the ascendancy of William and Mary at the "Glorious Revolution" of 1688, and later refused to acknowledge of House of Hanover.

Nordreys. Anglicization of the Norse *Northryars, Nordryars*, meaning "northerlies." Norse-influenced islands north and east of Cape Wrath. Compare: Sudreys.

Norn. A form of Norwegian spoken in the Orkney and Shetland Islands and in Caithness. It was still the dominant language when the islands were ceded to Scotland, 1468–1469, and became extinct in Caithness about that time. It gave way to Scots gradually over centuries, with the last native speaker thought to have died in 1850.

oighreachd. Dwelly: "1. Heirship. 2 Inheritance; possession, freehold estate, landed property." Succeeds the older concept of *dùthchas*. The willingness of clansmen to accept a chief's or later laird's authority to negotiate charters with the Scottish Crown, allowing the leaders to be landed proprietors as well as trustees of the clan.

Òran na Comhachaig. Lengthy song, one of the oldest masterworks in Gaelic, c. 1585, whose title is usually cited in Gaelic but is sometimes translated as "The Owl Remembers" or "The Owl of Strone." Topographical and valedictory, it is usually attributed to Dòmhnall Mac Fhionnlaigh nan Dàn.

P-Celtic. The modern Brythonic languages of Welsh, Cornish and Breton, also ancient Gaulish. Cf. Q-Celtic.

patronymic. See *sloinneadh*.

pìobaireachd. The Gaelic word refers to all bagpipe music in general. Its borrowing into English in the eighteenth century, pibroch, more narrowly denotes a highly structured, subtle performance worthy of being called "classical." The Gaelic form for the more elevated expression is *ceòl mòr*, big music, as opposed to *ceòl beag*, small music, for dancing. The martial use of the bagpipe came after the growth of Highland regiments at the end of the eighteenth century.

plaid. ScGaelic, *plaide*. A rectangular woolen scarf or a checked cloth of tartan worn over one shoulder as a large shawl. It may be big enough to serve as bedding while sleeping in the rough. Substituting the word "plaid" when "tartan" is intended is a gross *faux pas* that marks one as uninformed.

Prionnsa Teàrlach. Prince Charles, i.e., Prince Charles Edward Stuart.

Q-Celtic. The Goidelic languages of Irish, Scottish Gaelic and Manx. Cf. P-Celtic.

redshank. Demeaning English term for rough-mannered Gaelic fighting men, purposely not distinguishing between Irish and Highland, mercenaries or clansmen.

Rob Donn, brown-haired Rod or Bob. Names borne by hundreds of Highland men, most famously by the illiterate Sutherland poet, 1714–1778, whose family name is uncertain, possibly MacAoidh/MacKay. Little used is the English name, Robert Calder Mackay, contrived for him by commentators.

Roybridge, Roy Bridge. Gaelic: *Drochaid Ruaid*: bridge over the Ruad (red) river. Small village in Lochaber, in the former Inverness-shire, 12.5 miles (20 km) northeast of Fort William on the A86. Includes Keppoch House, seat of the MacDonells of Keppoch. Nearby are the 15th-century church of Cille Choirill, reputed burial place of Iain Lom, and Mulroy, site of the last clan battle (1688).

runrig. Historical land tenure system in the Highlands. "A system in which land was divided into thin strips with a (not necessarily contiguous) number being occupied and cultivated by each of the chief holders (chiefly *in runrig*)." OED

Scoto-Norman. Name for Normans who came to Scotland in the eleventh century, generally assumed privileged positions in society, and became merged with the native population over centuries. Comparable to the Anglo-Normans of England and the Hiberno-Normans of Ireland.

sept. Gaelic and English term, possibly from the Latin *saeptum*, "enclosure," or "fold," or an errant variation of the English "sect." It denotes a family or clan with its own surname that is allied with a larger clan, often considered a part of it. Septs with the same surname, though not necessarily the same family, may be allied with different clans. In the nineteenth and twentieth centuries many septs acquired their own tartans.

sett. The distinctive patterns of colors in a tartan that indicate a clan.

skuta. The formidable, forty-oared warship of the Isle of Man during the time of Somerled and later the Lordship of the Isles. The name and design are of Norse origin

sloinneach. Gaelic for the patronymic, e.g., *mac Aonghais*, son of Angus, or *nic Aonghais*, daughter of Angus, a person would be known by in life but not passed to the next generation. Distinguish from the clan surname, also indicating paternity, *Mac Domhnaill*, Mac Donald, passed through generations but not always used informally. The prefix *mac* may not be capitalized in the *sloinneach* but often is with the surname of a great landed family, e.g., MacDonald, MacLeod. This distinction is not always followed.

Somhairle Buidhe. (1505–1590). Somhairle of the yellow hair, chief of a sept of the Clan Donald that extended dominance into Ireland during the sixteenth century. Name often Anglicized as Sorley Boy by historians of his Irish campaigns.

Sorley Boy. Anglicization of Somhairle Buidhe (q.v.).

sorn, sorning. The chief's claimed right to force tenants to provide free lodging and maintenance for armed clansmen.

Stewart. Normative Anglicization of the Gaelic Stiùbhart (q.v.). French spelling Stuart introduced while Mary Queen of Scots was in France.

Stiùbhart. Default Modern Gaelic spelling for the royal line of Stewart. Also the Gaelic word for steward, the occupation. In earlier historical records the spellings are Stiùbhairt and Stiùbhert.

Strathclyde. British or P-Celtic kingdom of early Scotland, fifth to eighth centuries, whose capital was the fortified rock of Dumbarton. Embraced the Clyde watershed, south of the Gàidhealtachd, extending perhaps as far south as the Anglo-Saxon kingdom of Mercia. Subsumed into Alba. The name was reborn in 1974 when a new jurisdiction encompassed some of the same territory.

Stuart. French spelling of Stewart (q.v.), adopted while Mary Queen of Scots was in France, sixteenth century

Sudreys. Anglicization of the Norse *Suthreyars*, meaning "southerlies." All the Norse-invaded islands west and south of Cape Wrath, e.g., both Outer and Inner Hebrides, Arran, Bute, Rathlin (north of Co. Antrim), and the Isle of Man. Compare: Nordreys.

tacksmen. Gaelic *fir tacsa*. Lease holders of land belonging to the clans, initially drawn from the lesser gentry. As payment changed from barter and in kind to cash, the status and influence of the office rose. In the eighteenth century the older term *daoine uaisle* expanded to refer to them. Cf. Scots *tack*: seizure, hold, bail, security. Also *fir taic*: supporting men.

tacsa. Gaelic word inexactly translated as lease. Dwelly prefers: "1. Support, substance, solidity. 2 Buttress. 3. Comfort."

tartan. A textile pattern of stripes of varying widths and colors crossing at right angles, forming a distinctive pattern identifying a certain clan. Distinguish from the garment plaid, featuring a tartan on it. The sett is the pattern within the tartan that indicates the clan.

tascal. Payment made by an injured party to thieves to recover stolen or "lifted" property, often cattle; usually half the presumed price of the stolen property.

teuchter. Lowland derisive term for a Highlander, especially if Gaelic-speaking, pronounced "TCHOOK-ter," with many variant spellings. Of disputed origin. The "teuchters' umbrella" is the canopy near the Glasgow train station.

thirlage. Scottish law. Servitude imposed upon tenants requiring that their grain must be ground by a certain mill, from which a portion is taken for recognized fees of multure.

tonnag, tonnac. A short square of tartan or any coarse material used as a loose covering over the shoulder; a kind of shawl; a short plaid.

Ulster Cycle. One of the three bodies of interconnected stories in early Irish literature, which includes the great epic, *Táin Bó Cuailnge*. Includes stories of Cúchulainn and Deirdre, some parts of which are set in Scottish locations. Enjoys more prestige than the more popular Fenian Cycle.

Wars of the Three Kingdoms. Historians' shorthand for eight interlocking conflicts in the mid-seventeenth century, culminating in the execution of Charles I and Cromwell's Directorate. The three kingdoms are England, Scotland and Ireland. They are: Bishops' Wars, 1639–1640; Irish Rebellion, 1641; Confederate Ireland, 1642–1649; Scottish Civil War, 1644–1645; Cromwellian Conquest of Ireland, 1649; English Civil Wars, First 1642–1646, Second 1648–1649, Third 1650–1651. The Scottish Civil War was fought extensively in the Highlands.

weem. (ScG. *uamh*: cave). Not a cave, despite the etymology, but a man-made, primitive underground dwelling inhabited by the medieval poor.

White Cockade, the. ScG. *An Cnota Bàn*. A

signifier worn by Jacobite soldiers in lieu of a common uniform, as early as 1715 and widespread in 1745–1746.

Citations:

Dwelly, Edward. *The Illustrated Gaelic-English Dictionary*. Herne Bay: E. Macdonald, 1902–1911. Rpt. Glasgow: Gairm, 1972

OED. *Oxford English Dictionary*. Oxford: Oxford University Press, updated constantly, 2023

Bibliography

Many writers in Gaelic preferred to be known by the Gaelic forms of their names, e.g., Iain Mac Fhearchair, but are referred to in commentary by English forms that do not resemble the Gaelic, e.g., John MacCodrum. Both forms are included here, with cross reference to the author's preference.

Adamnán [also Adomnan] of Iona. *Life of St. Columba*, ed. Richard Sharpe. Harmondsworth: Penguin Classics, 1991, 1995.

Adams, Ian, and Meredyth Somerville. *Cargoes of Despair and Hope: Scottish Emigration to North America, 1603-1803*. Edinburgh: John Donald, 1993.

Aitchison, Nicholas B. *The Picts and the Scots at War*. Stroud: Sutton, 2003.

Alcock, Leslie. *The Neighbours of the Picts: Angles, Britons and Scots at War and at Home*. [Rosemarkle]: Groam House Museum Trust, 1993.

Alcock, Leslie. "Was There an Irish-Sea Culture-Province in the Dark Ages?" in D. Moore, ed., *The Irish Sea Province in Archaeology and History*. Cardiff: Cambrian Archaeological Association, 1970, 55–65.

Anderson, Alan Orr. *Early Sources of Scottish History, A.D. 500 to 1286*. Edinburgh: Oliver & Boyd, 1922; rpt. with corrections, Stamford: Paul Watkins, 1990.

Anderson, Alan Orr. *Scottish Annals from English Chroniclers: A.D. 500 to 1286*. London: D. Nutt, 1908; rpt. Forgotten Books, 2015.

Anderson, George, and Peter Anderson. *Guide to the Highlands and Islands of Scotland*, etc. London: John Murray, 1834 [first Highland travel guide].

Anderson, Marjorie O. "Dalriada and the Creation of the Kingdom of the Scots," in Dorothy Whitelock, et al., eds., *Ireland in Early Medieval Europe: Studies in Memory of Kathleen Hughes*. Cambridge: Cambridge University Press, 1982, 106–132.

Anderson, Marjorie O. *Kings and Kingship in Early Scotland*. Edinburgh: Scottish Academic Press, 1980.

Anderson, Marjorie O. See *Chronicle of Holyrood*.

Anton, A.E. "'Handfasting' in Scotland." *Scottish Historical Review* 37 (1958): 89–102.

Argyll, George Douglas Campbell, 8th Duke of. *Scotland as It Was and as It Is*. 2 vols. London: D. Douglas; New York: Putnam's, 1887.

Armit, Ian. *Celtic Scotland*. London: Batsford; New York: Barnes & Noble, 1997.

Armit, Ian. *Scotland's Hidden History*. Stroud: Tempus, 1998.

Armit, Ian. *Towers of the North: The Brochs of Scotland*. Stroud: Tempus, 2002.

Bahaldy. See Drummond of Bahaldy, John.

Bannerman, John. "The Dal Riata and Northern Ireland in the Sixth and Seventh Centuries," in J. Carney and D. Greene, eds., *Celtic Studies*. London: Routledge & Kegan Paul, 1969, 1–11.

Bannerman, John. "Literacy in the Highlands," in Ian B. Cowan and Duncan Shaw, eds., *The Renaissance and Reformation in Scotland*. Edinburgh: Scottish Academic Press, 1983, 214–235.

Bannerman, John. "Notes on Scottish Entries in the Early Irish Annals." *Scottish Gaelic Studies* 11 (1968): 149–170.

Bannerman, John. *Studies in the History of Dal Riada*. Edinburgh: Scottish Academic Press, 1974.

Bannerman, John W.M. "The Lordship of the Isles," in Jennifer M. Brown, ed., *Scottish Society in the Fifteenth Century*. London: Edward Arnold, 1977, 209–240.

Barbour, John. *The Brus/The Bruce* [composed 1575], ed. W.W. Skeat. Scottish Texts Society, vols. 16 and 17. Edinburgh: W. Blackwood, 1894.

Barbour's Bruce. Ed. M.P. McDiarmid and J.A.C. Stevenson. 3 vols. Edinburgh: Scottish Texts Society, 1980–1985.

Barclay, Gordon. *Farmers, Temples and Tombs: Scotland in the Neolithic and Early Bronze Age*. Edinburgh: Canongate, 1998; rpt. Edinburgh: Birlinn, 2005.

Barclay, Gordon, ed. *The Peoples of Scotland: Picts, Vikings and Scots*. Edinburgh: Canongate, 1999. Contains Martin Carver, "Surviving in Symbols: A Visit to the Pictish Nation," 64 pages; Ewan Campbell, "Saints and Sea-Kings: The First Kingdom of the Scots," 63 pages; Chris Lowe, "Angels, Fools and Tyrants: Britons and

Anglo-Saxons in Southern Scotland, AD 470–750," 64 pages; Olwyn Owen, "The Sea Road: A Viking Voyage Through Scotland," 64 pages.

Basu, Paul. "Cairns in the Landscape: Migrant Stones and Migrant Stories in Scotland and Its Diaspora," in A. Árneson, et al., eds., *Landscapes Beyond*. Oxford: Berghahn, 2012, 116–138.

Basu, Paul. *Highland Homecomings: Genealogy and Heritage Tourism in the Scottish Diaspora*. London: Routledge, 2007.

Beattie, Alastair G., and Margaret H. Beattie, eds. *Pre-1855 Gravestone Inscriptions in Lochaber and Skye: a summary of, and index to, pre-1855 gravestone inscriptions found in burial grounds in the western part of the mainland portion of Invernessshire, the Small Isles, Skye and associated islands*. Edinburgh: Scottish Genealogy Society, 1990.

Bellesheim, Alphons. *History of the Catholic Church of Scotland; From the Introduction of Christianity to the Present Day*, trans. Sir David Oswald Hunter Blair. 4 vols. London: Blackwood, 1887–1890.

Bingham, Caroline. *Beyond the Highland Line: Highland History and Culture*. London: Constable, 1991.

Black, George F. *Macpherson's Ossian and the Ossianic Controversy*. New York: New York Public Library, 1926, 1927.

Black, George F. *The Surnames of Scotland: Their Origin, Meaning and History*. New York: New York Public Library, 1946.

Black, Ronald. *An Lasair: Anthology of 18th Century Scottish Gaelic Verse*. Edinburgh: Birlinn, 2001.

Blackie, John S. *The Language and Literature of the Scottish Highlands*. Edinburgh: Edmonston and Douglas, 1876.

Blundell, Dom Odo, O.S.B. *The Catholic Highlands of Scotland*. Vol. 1, Central Highlands. Vol. 2, Western Highlands. Edinburgh: Sands, 1909, 1917.

Blundell, Nigel. *Ancient Scotland*. Edison: Chartwell Books, 1996.

Blundell, Nigel. *Scotland*. New York: Barnes & Noble, 1999.

Bodmer, Walter F., Sir. "The Genetics of Celtic Populations." *Proceedings of the British Academy* 82 (1993): 37–57.

Boece, Hector. *Scotorum Historiae*, etc. 1527. Revised as *Scotorum Historia*, 1575. Dana F. Sutton of the University of California, Irvine, posted the 1575 text online, 2010. John Bellendon's 16th-century translation into Scots was published in Edinburgh, 1821.

Boileau, Ethel. *Clansmen*. New York: E.P. Dutton, 1936.

Book of Clanranald. Ed. Iain Lom MacVurich. Included in Cameron, Rev. Alexander.

Boswell, James. *The Journal of a Tour to the Hebrides with Samuel Johnson, LL.D.*, 3rd ed. London: Dilly, 1786; rpt., ed. R.W. Chapmen. Oxford: Oxford University Press, 1924.

Bower, Walter [1385–1449]. *Scotichronicon: In Latin and English*, ed. D.E.R. Watt. Aberdeen: Aberdeen University Press, 1987–1998.

Bowlus, C.R. "Ethnogenesis: The Tyranny of a Concept," in Andrew Gillett, ed., *On Barbarian Identity: Critical Approaches to Ethnicity in the Early Middle Ages*. Turnhout: Brepols, 2002, 241–256.

Bradley, Daniel R., et al. "Neolithic and Bronze Age Migration to Ireland and the Establishment of the Insular Atlantic Genome." *Proceedings of the National Academy of Sciences of the USA* 113, no. 2 (2015): 368–373.

Broderick, G. See *Chronicles of the Kings of Mann and the Isles*.

Broster, D.K. *The Flight of the Heron*. London: William Heinemann, 1925.

Broun, Dauvit. "*Alba*: Pictish Homeland or Irish Off-Shoot?" Paper delivered at the Fifth Australian Conference on Celtic Studies, University of Sydney, July 2004.

Broun, Dauvit. "Anglo-French Acculturation and the Irish Element in Scottish Identity," in Brendan Smith, ed., *Britain and Ireland, 900–1300*. Cambridge: Cambridge University Press, 1999, 135–153.

Broun, Dauvit. "Britain and the Beginning of Scotland." Sir John Rhŷs Lecture, British Academy, 5 December 2013. Unpublished.

Broun, Dauvit. "Dunkeld and the Origin of Scottish Identity." *The Innes Review* 48 (1997): 112–124.

Broun, Dauvit. *Image and Identity: The Making and Re-Making of Scotland Through the Ages*. Edinburgh: J. Donald, 1998.

Broun, Dauvit. *The Irish Identity of the Kingdom of the Scots*. Woodbridge: Boydell Press, 1999.

Broun, Dauvit. "The Origin of Scottish Identity," in Claus Bjørn, et al., eds., *Nations, Nationalism and Patriotism in the European Past*. Copenhagen: Academic Press, 1994, 35–55.

Broun, Dauvit, and Martin MacGregor, eds. *Mìorun mòr nan Gall: "The Great Ill-Will of the Lowlander?": Lowland Perceptions of the Highlands, Medieval and Modern*. Glasgow: University of Glasgow Press, 2007.

Brown, Daniel G. "The Highland Clearances and the Politics of Memory." Unpublished dissertation. University of Wisconsin–Milwaukee, 2014.

Brown, Jennifer M. See Wormald, Jenny, ed., *Scottish Society in the Fifteenth Century*.

[Bruce, Edmund?]. *The Highlands of Scotland in 1750*. See Lang, Andrew, ed., *The Highlands of Scotland in 1750*.

Bruford, Alan. "The Sea-Divided Gaels: Some Relationships Between Scottish Gaelic, Irish and English Traditional Songs." *Éigse Cheol Tire* I (1972–1973): 4–27.

Buchan, John. *Montrose: A History*. Boston: Houghton Mifflin, 1928.

Buchan, John. *Witch Wood*. London: Hodder and Stoughton, 1927.

Buchanan, John Lane. *Travels in the Western*

Hebrides: From 1782 to 1790. London: Robinson, 1793; rpt. Waternish: Maclean Press, 1997.

Bumsted, J.M. *The People's Clearance.* Edinburgh: Edinburgh University Press; Winnipeg: University of Manitoba Press, 1982.

Burnett, John A., ed. *The Making of the Modern Scottish Highlands, 1939-1965.* Dublin: Four Courts, 2011.

Burns, Robert. "The Battle of Sherramuir," "The Birks of Aberfeldy," "The Braes O' Killiecrankie," "Cameron Kant" [song], "The Chevalier's Lament," "Farewell to the Highlands" [also known by first line, "My Heart's in the Highlands," written 1790], "Highland Mary" [written, 1792], "The Humble Petition of Bruar Water to the Noble Duke of Athole," "Parcel of Rogues in a Nation" [1791]. *Poems and Songs of Robert Burns,* ed. James Kinsley. 3 vols. Oxford: Clarendon, 1968. See also *Selected Poems and Songs of Robert Burns,* ed. Robert P. Irvine. Oxford: Oxford University Press, 2013.

Burt, Captain Edmund [in some editions Edward]. *Letters from a Gentleman in the North of Scotland to His Friend in London,* etc. *(Written, c. 1730),* 5th ed. 2 vols. London: Gale, Curtis & Fenner, 1822. Ed. Andrew Simmons, Edinburgh: Berlinn, 1998.

Byrne, Kevin. *Colkitto! A Celebration of the Clan Donald of Colonsay (1540-1647).* Isle of Colonsay: House of Lochar, 1997.

Byron, Lord, George Gordon. "Lachin y Gair" [written 1807], "When I Roved a Young Highlander," "Ossian's Address to the Sun." *Complete Poetical Works of Byron,* ed. Paul Elmer More. Boston: Houghton Mifflin, 1905, 1903, 1975, 117, 135-136, 139-140.

Cairney, Christopher. "Gaelic Borderlines and Borderlands in the New Cultural Geography of Scotland," in L. Lunan, K.A. Macdonald, and C. Stassi, eds., *Re-Visioning Scotland: New Readings from the Cultural Canon.* New York: Peter Lang, 2008, 1-11.

Calloway, Colin G. *White People, Indians and Highlanders: Tribal People and Colonial Encounters in Scotland and America.* New York: Oxford University Press, 2008, 2010.

Cameron, Rev. Alexander. *Reliquiae Celticae; Texts, Papers and Studies in Gaelic Literature and Philology Left Behind the Late Rev. Alexander Cameron,* ed. Alexander MacBain and John Kennedy. 2 vols. Inverness: Northern Chronicle, 1892-1894. Contains proverbs, vol. 1, 151-159; vol. 2, 475-507.

Campbell, Alexander. "Traditions of Lochaber." *Transactions of the Gaelic Society of Inverness* 26 (1904-1907): 300, ff. [unpaginated, online, Electric Scotland].

Campbell, Archibald Fortrose. "The Keppoch Murders." *Transactions of the Gaelic Society of Inverness* XXXIX-XL (1948): 167-175.

Campbell, Archibald, Lord. *Highland Dress, Arms and Ornament.* London: Dawsons of Pall Mall, 1969.

Campbell, Archibald, ed. *Waifs and Strays in Celtic Tradition.* 4 vols. London: David Nutt, 1889-1891.

Campbell, Ewan. *Saints & Sea Kings.* One of four parts of Barclay, Gordon. *The Peoples of Scotland* (1999).

Campbell, Ewan. "Were the Scots Irish?" *Antiquity* 75 (2001): 285-292.

Campbell, George Douglas. See Argyll, George Douglas Campbell, 8th Duke of.

Campbell, John Francis. *Leabhar na Féinne: Heroic Gaelic Ballads.* London: Spottiswoode, 1872.

Campbell, John Francis, ed. *Popular Tales of the West Highlands, Orally Collected.* 4 vols. Paisley: Gardner, 1861; rpt. London: Gardner, 1890-1893. See 19 proverbs relating to the Feinne, vol. 4, 231-234.

Campbell, J[ohn] Gregorson. *Superstitions of the Highlands and Islands of Scotland, Collected Entirely from Oral Sources.* Glasgow: J. MacLehose, 1900; rpt. Detroit: Singing Tree, 1970.

Campbell, John Lorne. *Private Gaelic Census of 1932: Original Replies Sent to Clergy.* [Inverness Co., N.S.,] 1932.

Campbell, J[ohn] L[orne], ed. *A Collection of Highland Rites and Customes* [sic]. Ipswich: D.S. Brewer: Totowa: Rowman & Littlefield, 1975.

Campbell, J[ohn] L[orne], trans. and ed. *Highland Songs of the Forty-Five.* Scottish Gaelic Texts Society. Edinburgh: John Grant, 1933; rpt., Edinburgh: Scottish Academic Press, 1984.

Campbell, J[ohn] L[orne], and Derick S. Thomson. *Edward Lhuyd in the Scottish Highlands, 1699-1700.* Oxford: Clarendon Press, 1963.

Campbell, K.D. "Geographic Patterns of R1B in the British Isles: Deconstructing Oppenheimer." *Journal of Genetic Genealogy* 3, no. 2 (2007): 63-71.

Carmen de Morte Sumerledi. See Anderson, Alan Orr, *Early Sources of Scottish History, A.D. 500 to 1286.*

Carmichael, Alexander. *Carmina Gadelica* [published 1900], 2nd ed. Vols. 1 and 2. Rpt. Edinburgh: Oliver and Boyd, 1928.

Carmichael, Alexander. *Carmina Gadelica,* ed. J. Carmichael Watson. Vols. 3 and 4. Edinburgh: Oliver and Boyd, 1940-1941.

Carmichael, Alexander. *Carmina Gadelica,* ed. A. Matheson. Vol. 5. Edinburgh: Oliver and Boyd, 1954.

Carmichael, Alexander. *Carmina Gadelica,* ed. A. Matheson. Vol. 6. Edinburgh: Scottish Academic Press, 1971.

Carver, Martin O.H. *Portmahomack: Monastery of the Picts.* Edinburgh: Edinburgh University Press, 2008.

Chambers, Robert. *History of the Rebellion in Scotland under the Viscount Dundee and the Earl of Mar in 1745-1746.* 3 vols. Edinburgh: Constable, 1827, 1867, 1929.

Chapman, Malcolm. *The Gaelic Vision in Scottish Culture.* London: Croom Helm; Montreal: McGill-Queen's University Press, 1978.

Childe, V. Gordon. *Scotland Before the Scots: Being the Rhind Lectures for 1944*. London: Methuen, 1946.

[*Chronicle of Holyrood*]. Recte, *A Scottish Chronicle Known as the Chronicle of Holyrood*, ed. M.O. Anderson. Edinburgh: Scottish Historical Society, 1938.

Chronicle of Melrose: From the Cottonian Manuscript, etc. [covers years 1171–1263]. Ed. Alan Orr Anderson, et al. London: P. Lund Humphries, 1936.

Chronicle of the Kings of Alba. See Hudson, B.T., ed. and trans. "The Scottish Chronicle."

Chronicles of the Kings of Man and the Isles. Chronica regum Manniae et Insularum, 2nd ed. Ed. and trans. George Broderick. Douglas: Manx Museum and National Trust, 1995.

Clarke, Edward Daniel. *A Tour in Scotland in the Summer and Autumn of 1797*. Printed in vol. 1, pp. 277–429, of *The Life and Remains of Edward Daniel Clarke*, by Rev. William Otter. London: C. Cowie, 1825.

Clarke, Peter. "Who Needs the Gaelic." *Daily Telegraph* [London], February 4, 1995.

Clarkson, Tim. *The Makers of Scotland: Picts, Romans, Gaels and Vikings*. Edinburgh: John Donald, 2011.

Clyde, Robert. *From Rebel to Hero: The Image of the Highlander, 1745–1830*. East Linton: Tuckwell, 1995.

Collis, John. *The Celts: Origins, Myths and Inventions*. Stroud: History Press, 2010.

Copeland, Libby. *The Lost Family: How DNA Testing Is Upending Who We Are*. New York: Abrams, 2020.

Cowan, Edward J. "The Discovery of the Gàidhealtachd in Sixteenth Century Scotland." *Transactions of the Gaelic Society of Inverness* 60 (1997–1998): 259–284.

Cowan, Edward J., and R. Andrew McDonald, eds. *Alba: Celtic Scotland and the Medieval Era*. Edinburgh: John Donald, 2000, 2005.

Craig, David. *On the Crofter's Trail: In Search of the Clearance Highlanders*. London: Cape, 1990.

Crawford, Iain A., and Roy Switsur. "Sand Scaping and C14: The Udal, North Uist." *Antiquity* 51 (1977): 124–136.

Crawford, Ross Mackenzie. "The Massacre of Eigg in 1577." Unpublished paper, 2014. Available for download from Academia.com.

Crawford, Ross Mackenzie. "Warfare in the West Highlands and Isles of Scotland, c. 1544–1615." Unpublished dissertation. University of Glasgow, 2016. Theses:gla.ac.uk/7310/.

Crichton Smith, Iain. See Smith, Iain Crichton.

Crookston, Peter. *Voices from the Hill: Life on the Land Where a Highland Laird Saved his Crofters from the Clearances*. CreateSpace, 2018.

Cummins, W.A. *The Age of the Picts*. Far Thrup: Sutton, 1995; New York: Barnes & Noble, 1998.

Cunliffe, Barry. *Europe Between the Oceans: Themes and Variations, 9000 BC–AD 1000*. New Haven: Yale University Press, 2008.

Cunliffe, Barry, and John T. Koch, eds. *Exploring Celtic Origins: New Ways Forward in Archaeology, Linguistics and Genetics*. Oxford: Oxbow, 2019.

Darling, F. Fraser. *Natural History in the Highlands and Islands*. London: Collins, 1947.

Darling, F. Fraser. *West Highland Survey: An Essay in Human Ecology*. Oxford: Oxford University Press, 1955, 1956.

Davidson, Neil. "Marx and Engels on the Scottish Highlands." *Science & Society* 65, no. 3 (Fall 2001): 286–326.

The Dean of Lismore's Book. See MacLauchlan, Thomas, ed. and trans. *The Dean of Lismore's Book*.

Defoe, Daniel. *Tour thro' the Whole Island of Great Britain*. 3 vols. London, 1724–1727. Rpt., ed. Samuel Richardson, London: J. Osborn, 1738.

Dembling, Jonathan. "Joe Jimmy Alec Visits the Gaelic Mod and Escapes Unscathed." Unpublished M.A. Thesis. Halifax: St. Mary's University, 1997.

Devine, T.M. *Clanship to Crofters' War: The Social Transformation of the Scottish Highlands*. Manchester: Manchester University Press, 2013.

Devine, T.M. *The Great Highland Famine: Hunger, Emigration and the Scottish Highlands in the Nineteenth Century*. Edinburgh: John Donald, 1988; rpt. Edinburgh: Birlinn, 1995.

Devine, T.M. *The Scottish Clearances: A History of the Dispossessed, 1600–1900*. London: Allan Lane, 2018.

Devine, T.M. *The Scottish Nation: A History, 1700–2000*. New York: Viking, 1999.

Devine, T.M., ed. *Scotland's Shame? Bigotry and Sectarianism in Modern Scotland*. Edinburgh: Mainstream, 2000.

Dickinson, William Croft. *Scotland from the Earliest Times to 1603*. Oxford: Oxford University Press, 1977.

Dodgshon, Robert A. *The Age of the Clans: the Highlands from Somerled to the Clearances*. Edinburgh: Birlinn, 2002.

Dodgshon, Robert A. *From Chiefs to Landlords: Social and Economic Change in the Western Highlands and Islands, c. 1493–1820*. Edinburgh: Edinburgh University Press, 1998.

Dodgshon, Robert A. *No Stone Unturned: A History of Farming, Landscape and Environment in the Scottish Highlands and Islands*. Edinburgh: Edinburgh University Press, 2015.

Dorian, Nancy. *Language Death: The Life Cycle of a Scottish Gaelic Dialect*. Philadelphia: University of Pennsylvania Press, 1981.

Douglas, Thomas. See Selkirk, 5th Earl of, Thomas Douglas.

Dressler, Camille. *Eigg: The Story of an Island*. Edinburgh: Polygon, 1998.

Driscoll, Stephen T. *Alba: The Gaelic Kingdom of Scotland AD 800–1124*. Edinburgh: Birlinn, 2002.

Driscoll, Stephen T., J. Geddes, and M.A. Hall, eds. *Pictish Progress: New Studies on Northern*

Britain in the Early Middle Ages. Leiden: Brill, 2011.

Drummond Norie, W. *Loyal Lochaber and Its Associations, Historical Genealogy, and Traditionary.* Glasgow: Morison, 1898.

Drummond of Balhaldy, John. *Memoirs of Sir Ewen Cameron of Locheill* [sic], etc. Edinburgh: Abbotsford Club, 1842.

"Duan Albannach." Ed. Kenneth H. Jackson. *Scottish Historical Review* 36 (1957): 126–137.

Duffy, Christopher. *The '45: Bonnie Prince Charlie and the Untold Story of the Jacobite Rising.* London: Cassell, 2003.

Duffy, Seán. *Robert the Bruce's Irish Wars: The Invasions of Ireland 1306–1329.* Stroud: Tempus, 2001.

Duffy, Seán, David Ditchburn, and Peter Crooks, eds. *The Irish-Scottish World in the Middle Ages.* Dublin: Four Courts, 2020.

Dunbar, John Telfer. *Highland Costume.* Edinburgh: Blackwood, 1977; London: Batsford, 1981, 1989.

Dunbar, John Telfer. *History of Highland Dress: A Definitive Study of the History of Scottish Costume and Tartan*, etc. Edinburgh: Oliver & Boyd, 1962; Philadelphia: Dufour, 1962, 1964; London: Batsford, 1979.

Dunbar, John Telfer. "The Lordship of the Isles." See Loraine Maclean, ed., *The Middle Ages in the Highlands.*

Dunbar, Robert. "Poetry of the Emigrant Generation." *Transactions of the Gaelic Society of Inverness* 64 (2004–2006): 22–125.

Dunbar, William (c. 1460–c. 1520). "The Dance of the Sevin [sic] Deidly [sic] Synnis [sic]," in Charles W. Dunn and Edward T. Byrnes, eds., *Middle English Literature.* New York: Harcourt, Brace, Jovanovich, 1973.

Dunmore, Stuart. "Heritage, Ideology and Contrasting Gaelic Identities in Scotland and Nova Scotia." Third Celtic Sociolinguistics Symposium, NUI Galway, November 17, 2018.

Dunn, Charles W. "Gaelic Proverbs in Nova Scotia." *Journal of American Folklore* 72 (1959): 30–35.

Dunn, Charles W. *Highland Settler: A Portrait of the Scottish Gael in Nova Scotia.* Toronto: University of Toronto Press, 1953; rpt. Wreck Cove: Breton Books, 1991.

Dwelly, Edward. *The Illustrated Gaelic-English Dictionary.* Herne Bay: E. Macdonald, 1902–1911; rpt., 8th ed., Glasgow: Gairm, 1973.

Emmons, Alma Randall. "The Highlander in Scottish Prose Fiction." Unpublished dissertation, Cornell University, Ithaca, New York, 1941.

Feachem, Richard. *Guide to Prehistoric Scotland.* London: Batsford, 1963; 2nd ed., 1977, 1980.

Fenyo, Krisztina. *Contempt, Sympathy and Romance: Lowland Perceptions of the Highlands and the Clearances During the Famine Years, 1845–1855.* East Linton: Tuckwell Press, 2000.

Fforde, Catriona. *A Summer in Lochaber: The Jacobite Rising of 1689.* Isle of Colonsay: House of Lochar, 2002.

Forbes Leith, William, S.J. *Memoirs of Scottish Catholics, During the XVII and XVIII Centuries.* 2 vols. London: Longmans, Green, 1909.

Fordun, Johannis de. *Chronica gentis Scotorum.* Original, c. 1370. *Chronicle of the Scottish Nation*, ed. W.F. Skene. 2 vols. Edinburgh: Edmonston & Douglas, 1871–1872.

Forsyth, K. *Language in Pictland: The Case Against 'Non-Indo-European Pictish.'* Utrecht: de Keltische Draak, 1997.

Foster, Sally M. *Picts, Gaels and Scots.* Edinburgh: Historic Scotland, 1996.

Foster, Sally M., ed. *The St Andrews Sarcophagus: A Pictish Masterpiece and Its International Connections.* Dublin: Four Courts, 1998.

Fraser, Iain. *The Pictish Symbol Stones in Scotland.* Edinburgh: Royal Commission on the Ancient and Historical Monuments of Scotland, 2008.

Fraser-Mackintosh, Charles. *An Account of the Confederation of Clan Chattan, Its Kith and Kin.* Glasgow: John MacKay "Celtic Monthly" Office, 1898.

Fry, Michael. *Wild Scots: Four Hundred Years of Highland History.* London: John Murray, 2005. See review, "Clearing the Air," *The Economist* (September 3, 2005), 74.

Gaskill, Howard. "'Ossian' Macpherson: Towards a Rehabilitation," in E.D. Schaffer, ed., *Comparative Criticism* 8 (1986): 113–148. Refutes Trevor-Roper thesis, 1983.

Giblin, Cathaldus, ed. *Irish Franciscan Mission to Scotland, 1619–1646.* Dublin: Assisi Press, 1964.

Gibson, John G. *Traditional Gaelic Bagpiping, 1745–1945.* Montreal: McGill-Queens University Press, 1998.

Gibson, Rob. *The Highland Clearances Trail.* Edinburgh: Luath Press, 2007.

Gillies, William. "The Invention of History—Highland Style," in Alasdair A. MacDonald, Michael Lynch and Ian B. Cowan, eds., *The Renaissance in Scotland: Studies in Literature, Religion, History and Culture Offered to John Durkan.* London: E.J. Brill, 1994, 144–156.

Gillies, William, ed. *Gaelic and Scotland/Alba agus á Ghàdhlig.* Edinburgh: Edinburgh University Press, 1989.

Grant, Anne. *Poems on Various Subjects.* Edinburgh: J. Moir, 1803.

Grant, Anne Macvicar. *Letters from the Mountains: being the real correspondence of a Lady...* 3 vols. London: Longman, Hurst, Rees & Orme, 1806, 1807.

Grant, Donald. Violinist, born Roybridge. Linked to a lament for the battle of Mulroy, 1688. Composed c. 2012?

Grant, Elizabeth of Rothiemurchas. *Memoirs of a Highland Lady.* 2 vols. Edinburgh: J. Murray, 1889; rpt. Edinburgh: Canongate, 1988.

Grant, I.F. *Highland Folk Ways.* London: Routledge & Kegan Paul, 1961.

Grant, I.F. *In the Tracks of Montrose.* London: Maclehose, 1931.

Grant, I.F. *The Lordship of the Isles: Wanderings*

in the Lost Leadership. Edinburgh: The Moray Press, 1935.

Grant, I.F. *Social and Economic Development of Scotland Before 1603*. Edinburgh: Oliver and Boyd, 1930; rpt. Westport: Greenwood Press, 1971.

Grant, I.F., and Hugh Cheape. *Periods in Highland History*. London: Shepheard-Walwyn, 1987.

Gray, Malcolm. *The Highland Economy, 1750–1850*. Edinburgh: Oliver and Boyd, 1957.

Green, Sarah. *Scotch Novel Reading, or Modern Quackery*. 2 vols. London: Newman, 1824.

Gregory, Donald. *History of the Western Highlands and Isles of Scotland, 1493–1625*. Edinburgh: William Tait, 1836; rpt. London: Thomas D. Morrison, 1881; rpt. Edinburgh: Berlinn, 2008.

Grigor, Iain Fraser. *Mightier Than a Lord: The Highland Crofters' Struggle for the Land*. Stornoway: Acair, 1979.

Grimble, Ian. *Clans and Chiefs*. London: Blond & Briggs, New York: Barnes & Noble, 1980; rpt. Edinburgh: Birlinn, 2000.

Grimble, Ian. *Highland Man*. Edinburgh: Highlands and Islands Development Boards, 1980.

Grimble, Ian. *The Trial of Patrick Sellar: The Tragedy of Highland Evictions*. London: Routledge, 1962.

Grimble, Ian. *The World of Rob Donn*. Edinburgh: The Edina Press, 1979.

Grose, Francis. *Antiquities of Scotland*, etc. London: S. Hooper, 1797.

Growney, Eugene. "Scotland in Early Irish Literature." *Transactions of the Gaelic Society of Glasgow* (1891–1894): 239–275.

Gunn, Neil M. *Butcher's Broom*. Edinburgh: Porpoise; New York: Walker, 1934; rpt. New York: Walker, 1977; rpt. Edinburgh: Polygon, 2006.

Gunn, Neil M. *Highland River*. Edinburgh: Porpoise; London: Faber; Philadelphia: Lippincott, 1937, 1942; rpt. Edinburgh: Canongate, 1981, 1997.

Gunn, Neil M. *Silver Darlings*. London: Faber, 1941, 1945, 1968, 1978, 1986.

Gunn, Neil M. *Sun Circle*. Edinburgh: Porpoise, 1933; rpt. London: Souvenir, 1983, 1996; rpt. Edinburgh: Canongate, 1996, 2001.

Hayes-McCoy, G.A. *Scots Mercenary Forces in Ireland (1565–1603)*. Dublin: Burns, Oates & Washbourne, 1937.

Hayman, Jarvis. "Conflict in the Highlands, the Archaeology of the Scottish Highland Clearances." Unpublished dissertation. Canberra: Australian National University, 2010, 2015.

Hayne, Barrie. "*Ossian*, Scott and Cooper's Indians." *Journal of American Studies* 3 (1969): 73–87.

Hechter, Michael. *Internal Colonialism*. Berkeley: University of California Press, 1977.

Heimskringla. See Snorri Sturluson.

Henderson, Andrew. *A History of the Rebellion, 1745 and 1746. Containing a Full Account of Its Rise, Progress and Extinction; The Character of the Highlanders and their Chief-tains... By an Impartial Hand, who was an Eye-witness to most of the facts*, 2nd ed. London: R. Griffiths, 1748.

Henderson, Diana. *Highland Soldier: A Social Study of Highland Regiments, 1820–1920*. Edinburgh: John Donald, 1989.

Henderson, George. *The Norse Influence on Celtic Scotland*. Glasgow: Maclehose, 1910; rpt. Breinigsville: Andesite Press, 2015.

Herbert, Máire. "Sea-Divided Gaels? Constructing Relationships Between Irish and Scots, c. 800–1169," in Brendan Smith, ed., *Britain and Ireland, 900–1300: Insular Responses to Medieval European Change*. Cambridge: Cambridge University Press, 1999, 87–97.

Hill, James Michael. *Fire and Sword: Sorley Boy MacDonnell and the Rise of the Clan Ian Mor, 1538–1590*. London: Athlone Press, 1993.

Hill, James Michael. "The Origins and Development of the 'Highland Charge,' c. 1560 to 1645." *Militärgeschichtliche Mitteilungen* 53 (1994): 295–307.

The history of the feuds and conflicts among the clans in the northern parts of Scotland and in the western isles from the year M.XXXI [1031] unto M.DC.XIX [1619]. Now first published from a manuscript, wrote in the reign of King James VI. Glasgow: R & A Foulis, 1764. Often reprinted.

Hogg, James. *Highland Tours: The Ettrick Shepherd's Travels in the Scottish Highlands and Western Isles in 1802, 1803, and 1804*. Hawick: Byway Books, 1981.

Homer, Reverend Philip B. *Observations on a Short Tour Made in the Summer of 1803, to the Western Highlands of Scotland*. London: for the author by W. Nicholson, 1804.

Hopkins, Paul. *Glencoe and the End of the Highland War*. Edinburgh: John Donald, 1986.

Horsburgh, Davie. "When Was Gaelic Scottish? The Origins, Emergence and Development of Scottish Gaelic Identity 1440–1750." *Rannsachdh Na Gàidhlig 2000/Scottish Gaelic Studies Conference*, 2–4 August 2000, 231–242.

Houston, R.A., and W.W.J. Knox, eds. *The New Penguin History of Scotland: From Earliest Times to the Present Day*. London: Allen Lane/Penguin, 2001.

Hudson, B.T., ed. and trans. "The Scottish Chronicle." *Scottish Historical Review* 77 (1998): 129–161. Includes Chronicle of the Kings of Alba (also known as the Older Scottish Chronicle or the Scottish Chronicle from the Poppleton Manuscript).

Hughes, Kathleen. "Where are the Writings of Early Scotland?" in David Dumville, ed., *Celtic Britain in the Early Middle Ages: Studies in Scottish and Welsh Sources*. Woodbridge: Boydell Press, 1980, 1–21.

Hunter, James. *Culloden, and the Last Clansman*. Edinburgh: Mainstream, 1994.

Hunter, James. *A Dance Called America: The Scottish Highlands in the United States and Canada*. Edinburgh: Mainstream, 1994.

Hunter, James. "The Gaelic Connection: the

Highlands, Ireland and Nationalism, 1873–1922." *Scottish Historical Review* 54, no. 2 (1975): 178–204.
Hunter, James. *Glencoe and the Indians*. Edinburgh: Mainstream, 1996.
Hunter, James. *Insurrection: Scotland's Winter Famine*. Edinburgh: Birlinn, 2017.
Hunter, James. *Last of the Free: A Millennial History of the Highlands and Islands of Scotland*. Edinburgh: Mainstream, 1999.
Hunter, James. *The Making of a Crofting Community*. Edinburgh: John Donald, 1976.
Hunter, James. *On the Other Side of Sorrow: Nature and People in the Scottish Highlands*. Edinburgh: Mainstream, 1996.
Hunter, James. *Scottish Exodus: Travels Among the Worldwide Clan*. Edinburgh: Mainstream, 2005.
Hunter, James. *Scottish Highlanders: A People and Their Place*. Edinburgh: Mainstream, 1992.
Hunter, James. *Set Adrift Upon the World: The Sutherland Clearances*. Edinburgh: Birlinn, 2016.
Hutchinson, Roger. *Calum's Road*. Edinburgh: Berlinn, 2006.
Iain Lom [John MacDonald]. *Orain Iain Luim: Songs of John MacDonald, Bard of Keppoch*, ed. Annie M. MacKenzie. Scottish Gaelic Texts Society. Vol. 8. Edinburgh: Scottish Academic Press, 1965, 1973.
Innes of Learney, Thomas. *The Tartans of the Clans and Families of Scotland*, 8th ed. Edinburgh: Johnston and Bacon, 1971, 1975.
Jackson, Anthony. *The Pictish Trail: A Travellers Guide to the Old Pictish Kingdoms*. Kirkwall: Orkney Press, 1989.
Jackson, Kenneth H. "Common Gaelic: the Evolution of the Goidelic Languages." *Proceedings of the British Academy* 37 (1951): 71–97.
Jackson, Kenneth H. See *"Duan Albannach."*
James, Simon. *The Atlantic Celts: Ancient People or Modern Invention?* Madison: University of Wisconsin Press, 1999.
Jarvis, Robert C. *Collected Papers of the Jacobite Risings*. Manchester: Manchester University Press, 1971, 1972.
Johnson, Samuel. *A Journey to the Western Islands of Scotland*. London: W. Strahan, 1775; rpt. ed. R.W. Chapman, Oxford: Oxford University Press, 1924.
Johnstone, Chevalier de. *A Memoir of the 'Forty-five,'* ed. Brian Rawson. London: Folio Society, 1958.
Johnstone, James. *Memoirs of the Chevalier de Johnstone*. 3 vols. English translation, Aberdeen: P. Wylie, 1870–71; revised from the *Memoirs of the Rebellion of 1745 and 1746, etc.* London: Longman, 1820, 1822.
Keats, John. "Staffa," "Lines Written in the Highlands after a Visit to Burns Country, Sonnet. Written Upon the Top of Ben Nevis" [composed 1818].
Keay, John, and Julia Keay. *Collins Encyclopaedia of Scotland*. London: HarperCollins, 1994, 1995; rev. ed. London: Trafalgar, 2001.
Kennedy-Fraser, Marjory, with Kenneth MacLeod. *Songs of the Hebrides: Collected and Arranged for Voice and Pianoforte with Gaelic and English Words*. 3 vols. London: Boosey, 1922.
Kermack, W.R. *The Scottish Highlands: A Short History*. Edinburgh: Johnston & Bacon, 1957, 1967.
Kilgour, William T. *Lochaber in War and Peace. Being a Record of Historical Incidents, Legends, Traditions and Folk-Lore*. With notes of the topography and scenic beauties of the whole district. Paisley: Gardner, 1908.
Kincaid, Barbara. "Scottish Emigration to Cape Breton, 1758–1838." Unpublished dissertation. Halifax: Dalhousie University, 1964.
Kirk, Robert. *The Secret Commonwealth of Elves Fauns and Fairies*. First published, 1691. Rpt., ed. and introd. S.F. Sanderson, Cambridge: D.S. Brewer for the Folklore Society, 1976.
Knox, John. *A Tour through the Highlands of Scotland and the Hebride Isles in MDCCLXXXVI* [1786]. London: J. Walker, 1787, 1797.
Knox, John. *A View of the British Empire, more especially Scotland; with some proposals for the Improvement of that Country, Extension of the Fisheries, and the Relief of the People*, 3rd ed. London, 1785.
Knox, Robert. *The Races of Man*. Philadelphia: Lea and Blanchard, 1850.
Koch, John T. "Celts, Britons and Gaels—Names, Peoples, and Identities." Delivered Scoil na Gaeilge, National University of Ireland Galway, March 7, 2000; Society for Name Studies in Britain and Ireland, 9th conference, University of Wales Bangor, April 30, 2000.
Koch, John T., et al., eds. *Celtic Culture: A Historical Encyclopedia*. Vol, I [only published]. Santa Barbara: ABC-CLIO, 2006.
La Rochefoucauld, Alexandre de. See Scarfe, Norman, ed.
Laing, Lloyd, and Jennifer Laing. *The Picts and the Scots*. Stroud: Sutton, 2001.
Lane, Alan, and Ewan Campbell. *Dunadd: An Early Dalriadic Capital*. Oxford: Oxbow, 2000.
Lang, Andrew, ed. *The Highlands of Scotland in 1750*. Edinburgh: William Blackwood & Sons, 1898. Includes text attributed to Edmund Bruce.
Laoide, Seosamh. *Alasdair Mac Colla*. Dublin: Gaelic League, 1914.
Layne, Darren S. "Spines of the Thistle: The Popular Constituency of the Jacobite Rising in 1745–46." Dissertation. University of St. Andrews, 2015.
Lee, Henry James. *History of the Clan Donald, the Families of MacDonald, McDonald and McDonnell*. New York: R.L. Polk, 1920.
Lees, J. Cameron, Rev. *A History of the County Inverness (Mainland)*. Edinburgh: Blackwood, 1897. Extracts were published as *From Inverness-Shire's Story*. Blanefield: Lang Syne, c. 1980.
Lenman, Bruce. *The Jacobite Cause*. Glasgow: Richard Drew, 1986.
Lenman, Bruce. *Jacobite Clans of the Great Glen, 1650–1784*. London: Methuen, 1984.

Leslie, Stephen, et al. [16 persons] *The Fine-Scale Genetic Structure of the British Population*. Nature 519, no. 7543 (March 19, 2015): 309–314.

Leyden, John. *Journal of a Tour in the Highlands and Western Islands, 1800*, ed. James Sinton. Edinburgh: Blackwood, 1903.

Lismore, The Dean of's Book. See MacLauchlan, Thomas.

Livingstone, Alastair, Christian Aikman, and Betty Stuart Hart. *No Quarter Given: The Muster Roll of Prince Charles Edward Stuart's Army*. Aberdeen: Aberdeen University Press, 1984; rpt. Glasgow: Neil Wilson, 2001.

Livingstone, Colin. "Lochaber Placenames." *Transactions of the Gaelic Society of Inverness* 13 (1886–1887): 257–269.

Loch, James. *An Account of the Improvements on the Estates of the Marquess of Stafford, in the Counties of Stafford and Salop and on the Estate of Sutherland*. London: Longman, 1820.

Logan, James. *The Clans of the Scottish Highlands. The Costumes of the Clans*, illustrations by R.R. McIan. London: Ackerman, 1845, 1847; rpt. London: Webb & Bower; New York: Knopf, 1980.

Logan, James. *The Scottish Gaël or Celtic Manners as Preserved Among the Highlanders*, 2nd ed., Alexander Stewart. Edinburgh: Maclachlan and Stewart, 1876 [first ed., 1831].

Low, M. *Celtic Christianity and Nature: Early Irish and Hebridean Traditions*. Edinburgh: Edinburgh University Press, 1996.

Lumsden, Alison. "'Beyond the Dusky Barrier': Perceptions of the Highlands in the Waverly Novels," in Dauvit Broun and Martin MacGregor, eds. *Mìorun mòr nan Gall:"The Great Ill-Will of the Lowlander?": Lowland Perceptions of the Highlands, Medieval and Modern*. Glasgow: University of Glasgow Press, 2007

Lynch, Michael. *Oxford Companion to Scottish History*. Oxford: Oxford University Press, 2001.

Mac Fhearchair, Iain. See MacCodrum, John.

Mac Gill-eain, Somhairle. See [MacLean, Sorley].

MacAlpine, Neil, and John Mackenzie. *Gaelic-English and English-Gaelic Dictionary*. Glasgow: MacLaren, 1832; rpt. Glasgow: Gairm, 1971.

MacAoidh, MacKay. See Donn, Rob.

MacAulay, John. *Birlinn. Longships of the Hebrides*. Cambridge: The White Horse Press, 1996.

MacBain, Alexander. "Place Names of Inverness-shire." *Transactions of the Gaelic Society of Inverness* 25 (1907): 55–85.

MacBain, Alexander, and William J. Watson. *Place Names of the Highlands and Islands of Scotland*. Stirling: Eneas Mackay, 1922.

MacCaig, Norman. "A Man in Assynt." *The Poems of Norman MacCaig*. Edinburgh: Polygon, 2005.

MacCodrum, John [Iain Mac Fhearchair]. *The Songs of John MacCodrum*, ed. William Matheson. Scottish Gaelic Texts. Vol. II. Edinburgh: Oliver & Boyd, 1938.

MacCoinnich, Aonghas. *Plantation and Civility in the North Atlantic World. The Case of the Northern Hebrides, 1570–1637*. Leiden: Brill, 2015.

MacCoinnich, Aonghas. "Where and How Was Gaelic Written in Late Medieval and Early Modern Scotland? Orthographic Practices and Cultural Identities." *Scottish Gaelic Studies* 24 (2008): 309–356.

MacColla, Fionn. *And the Cock Crew*. Glasgow: T. Douglas-MacDonald, 1945.

MacCulloch, Donald Brown. *Romantic Lochaber*. Edinburgh: Moray Press, 1948; rpt. Inverness: Lines, 1996.

MacCulloch, John. *The Highlands and Western Isles of Scotland*. 4 vols. London: Longman, 1824.

MacDonald, A. "Two Major Early Monasteries of Scottish Dalriata: Lismore and Eigg." *Scottish Archaeological Forum* 5 (1973): 47–70.

MacDonald, A.D. *Mabou Pioneers: A genealogical tracing of some pioneer families who settled in Mabou and the District*. Publication place not given: privately printed, c. 1950, 1952? Rpt., Antigonish: Formac, 1977. Often cited in discourse as "Mabou I." See Rankin, Reginald, ed. *Mabou Pioneer II*. Mabou: Privately published, 1977.

[MacDonald, Alexander] (c. 1698–1770). See Mac Mhaistir, Alasdair.

MacDonald, Allan. *Bàrdachd Mhgr Ailein: the Gaelic Poem of Fr. Allan McDonald [sic] of Eriskay (1859–1905)*, ed. and trans. J.L. Campbell. London: Constable, 1965.

Macdonald, Donald J. of Castleton. *The Clan Donald*. Loanhead: MacDonald Publishers, 1978; rpt. Gretna: Pelican, 2008. Originally 3 vols., 1896–1904.

Macdonald, Keith Norman, ed. *MacDonald Bards From Medieval Times*. Glasgow: Norman MacLeod, 1900; rpt. Glasgow: Alexander MacLaren, 1929.

MacDonald, Norman H. *The Clan Ranald of Lochaber: A History of the MacDonalds or MacDonells of Keppoch*. Edinburgh: privately printed, 1972.

MacDonell, Ann, and Robert MacFarlane. *Cille Choirill, Brae Lochaber*. Spean Bridge: privately printed, 1986.

MacGowan, Douglas. *The Stone Mason: Donald Macleod's Chronicle of Scotland's Highland Clearances*. Westport: Praeger, 2001.

MacGregor, Martin. "Gaelic Barbarity and Scottish Identity in the Later Middle Ages." See Broun, Davit, and M. MacGregor, eds. *Mìorun mòr nan Gall: "The Great Ill-Will of the Lowlander?": Lowland Perceptions of the Highlands, Medieval and Modern*. Glasgow: University of Glasgow Press, 2007.

MacGregor, Martin. "'Làn-maràs mìle seòl': Gaelic Scotland and Gaelic Ireland in the Later Middle Ages," in *Congress 99: Cultural Contacts Within the Celtic Community*. Glasgow: Celtic Congress, 2000, 77–97.

MacGregor, Martin. "Warfare in Gaelic Scotland in the Later Middle Ages," in Edward M. Spiers, Jeremy Crang and Matthew Strickland, eds., *A Military History of Scotland*. Edinburgh: Edinburgh University Press, 2012, 209–231.

Macinnes, A.I. "Scottish Gaeldom: The First Phase of the Clearance," in T.M. Devine and Rosalind Mitchison, eds., *People and Society in Scotland*. Edinburgh: John Donald, 1988.

Macinnes, Allan I. "Lochaber—The Last Bandit Country, c. 1600–1750." *Transactions of the Gaelic Society of Inverness* 64 (2008): 1–21.

MacInnes, John. "Clan Sagas and Historical Legends." *Transactions of the Gaelic Society of Inverness* 57 (1990–1992): 377–394.

MacInnes, John. *Dùthchas nan Gàidheal: Collected Essays of John Macinnas*, ed. Michael Newton. Edinburgh: Birlinn, 2010.

MacInnes, John. "The Gaelic Perception of the Lowlands," in William Gillies, ed., *Gaelic and Scotland/Alba agus á Ghàdhlig*. Edinburgh: Edinburgh University Press, 1989, 89–100.

MacInnes, John. "Gaelic Poetry and Historical Tradition," in Loraine Maclean, ed., *The Middle Ages in the Highlands*.

MacInnes, John. "The Oral Tradition in Scottish Gaelic Poetry." *Scottish Studies* 12 (1968): 29–43.

MacInnes, John. "The Panegyric Code in Gaelic and Its Historical Background." *Transactions of the Gaelic Society of Inverness* 50 (1976–1978): 435–498.

MacInnes, John, Rev. "Clan Unity and Individual Freedom." *Transactions of the Gaelic Society of Inverness* 47 (1972): 338–373.

MacInnes, John, Rev. "West Highland Sea Power in the Middle Ages." *Transactions of the Gaelic Society of Inverness* 48 (1972–1974): 377–394.

Macintyre, Duncan Bàn. *The Songs of Duncan Bàn Macintyre*, ed. Angus MacLeod. Scottish Gaelic Texts Society. Edinburgh: Oliver & Boyd, 1952.

Macintyre, L.M. "Walter Scott and the Highlands." Unpublished Ph.D. thesis. University of Glasgow, 1976.

MacKay, J.G. *More West Highland Tales (transcribed and translated from the original Gaelic...)* London: Oliver and Boyd, 1940.

Mackellar, Mary. "Unknown Lochaber Bards." *Transactions of the Gaelic Society of Inverness* 12 (1886): 211–226.

MacKellar, Mary Cameron. *Poems and Songs, Gaelic and English*. Edinburgh: Maclachlan and Stewart, 1880.

Mackenzie, Alexander. *A History of the Highland Clearances*, etc. Inverness: A and W Mackenzie,1883; rpt. Glasgow: A. Maclaren, 1946; Edinburgh; Mercat, 1983, 1991, 1997. Includes text of Donald Macleod, *A History of the Destitution of Sutherlandshire*, 1841.

Mackenzie, Alexander. *The Prophecies of the Brahan Seer*, ed. Elizabeth Sutherland. Inverness: A and W Mackenzie, 1877, 1882, 1888; rpt. London: Constable, 1925, 1977.

Mackenzie, John, and John Logan. *Sàr-Obair nam Baird, the Beauties of Gaelic Poetry and the Lives of Highland Bards*, etc. Glasgow: MacGregor, Polson, 1841. Republished more than a dozen times, e.g., Edinburgh: John Grant, 1907; revised by Kaledon Naddair, Edinburgh: Keltia, 2001.

Mackenzie, Sir Compton. *Catholicism and Scotland*. London: Routledge, 1936; rpt., Port Washington: Kennikat Press, 1971.

Mackenzie, Sir Compton. *Hunting the Fairies*. London: Chatto and Windus, 1949.

Mackenzie, Sir Compton. *Whisky Galore*. London: Penguin, 1948.

Mackinnon, Iain. "Colonialism and the Highland Clearances" *Northern Scotland* 8, no. 1 (2017): 22–48.

MacKinnon, Kenneth. *The Lion's Tongue: The Story of the Original and Continuing Language of the Scottish People*. Inverness: Club Leabhar, 1974.

MacKinnon, Lachlan. *Place Names of Lochaber*. Fort William: Saltire Society, Lochaber Branch, 1973.

Mackintosh, Alexander M. *The Mackintoshes and Clan Chattan*. Edinburgh: Privately printed, 1903.

Maclaren, Archibald. *The Highland Drover; or, Domhnul Dubh M'Na-Beinn at Carlisle* [bi-lingual stage comedy]. Greenock, 1790.

MacLauchlan, Thomas, ed. and trans. *The Dean of Lismore's Book*, introd. W.F. Skene. Edinburgh: Edmonston & Douglas, 1862.

MacLean, Calum I. *The Scottish Highlands*. London: Batsford, 1959; rpt. Inverness: Club Leabhar, 1975.

Maclean, Fitzroy. *Highlanders: A History of the Scottish Clans*. London: David Campbell; New York: Viking Studio Books, 1995.

Maclean, Loraine, ed. *The Middle Ages in the Highlands*. Inverness: Inverness Field Club, 1981.

Maclean, Loraine, ed. *The Seventeenth Century in the Highlands*. Inverness: Inverness Field Club, 1986.

MacLean, Sorley. "The Poetry of the Clearances." *Transactions of the Gaelic Society of Inverness* 38 (1939): 293–324.

[MacLean, Sorley], Mac Gill-eain, Somhairle. *Dàin do Eimhir*. Glasgow: MacLellan, 1943. Translated into English, Iain Crichton Smith, as *Poems to Eimhir*. London: Gollancz, 1971; rpt., introd. Donald Meek. Stornoway: Acair, 1999.

[MacLean, Sorley], Mac Gill-eain, Somhairle. "Dòmhnall Donn of Bohuntin." *Transactions of the Gaelic Society of Inverness* 42 (1953): 91–110. Rpt. in *Ris á Bhruthaich*.

[MacLean, Sorley], Mac Gill-eain, Somhairle. *Ris á Bhruthaich: The Criticism and Prose Writings of Sorley MacLean*, ed. William Gillies. Stornoway: Acair, 1985. "Dòmhnall Donn," 211–234; "Poetry of the Clearances," 48.

MacLennan, Hugh. *Scotchman's Return and Other Essays*. New York: Scribner's, 1960.

MacLeod, Alistair. *No Great Mischief*. Toronto: McClelland & Stewart, 1999.

Macleod Donald. *History of the Destitution of Sutherlandshire*. 21 letters to the *Edinburgh Weekly Chronicle*, turned into one volume by an unknown binder, 1841; later published in Alexander Mackenzie, *History of the Highland Clearances*, 1883.

Macleod, Donald [also M'Leod]. *Gloomy Memories in the Highlands of Scotland: versus Mrs. Harriet Beecher Stowe's Sunny Memories in (England) A Foreign Land.* Toronto: Privately printed, 1857. Glasgow: A. Sinclair, 1892; rpt. Bettyhill: Strathnaver Museum, 1996.

Macleod, John. *Highlanders: A History of the Gaels.* London: Hodder & Stoughton, 1997.

MacLeod, Nigel. *The Literature of the Highlanders: Race, Language, Literature, Poetry and Music.* Stirling: Eneas Mackay, 1892; 2nd ed. and additions, ed. John MacMaster Campbell, Stirling: Eneas MacKay, 1929.

Mac Mhaister Alasdair, Alasdair [Alexander MacDonald]. *Alasdair mac Mhaighstir Alasdair: Selected Poems,* ed. Derick S. Thomson. Edinburgh: Scottish Academic Press for the Scottish Gaelic Texts Society, 1996.

MacNeill, Eoin, Niall Mac Muirdach, and Seosamh Laoide. *Alasdair Mac Colla: sain-eolus ar a gníomartaib gaisge.* Dublin: Gaelic League, 1914.

MacNeill, Nigel, ed. *The Literature of the Highlanders.* London: Lamley, 1892; 2nd ed. with additional chapter by John MacMaster Campbell, Stirling: Eneas MacKay, 1929.

MacNeill, Peter, and Ranald Nicholson. *Historical Atlas of Scotland, c. 400-1600.* St. Andrews: Conference of Scottish Medievalists, 1975.

MacNeill, Peter G.B. *Atlas of Scottish History to 1707,* ed. Hector L. MacQueen and Anna May Lyons. Edinburgh: The Scottish Medievalists and Department of Geography, University of Edinburgh, 2000.

MacPhee, Kathleen. *Somerled: Hammer of the Norse.* Castle Douglas: Neil Wilson, 2004; Castle Douglas: NWP, 2013.

Macpherson, James. *The Poems of Ossian.* Edinburgh: Geddes, 1896. Published serially under the title *Fragments of Antient Poetry collected in the Highlands of Scotland,* 1760-1763.

Major [also Mair], John. *Historia Majoris Britaniae* [1521], *A History of Greater Britain as well as England and Scotland,* Archibald Constable, et al., ed. and trans. Edinburgh: Scottish Historical Society, 1892.

Mallory, J.P. *The Origins of the Irish.* London: Thames & Hudson, 2013.

Manx Chronicle. See *Chronicles of the Kings of Mann and the Isles.*

Márkus, Gilbert. *Conceiving a Nation: Scotland to AD 900.* Edinburgh: Edinburgh University Press, 2017. Supersedes Smyth, Alfred P. *Warlords and Holy Men.* Edinburgh: Edinburgh University Press, 1984, in the New History of Scotland series.

Martin, Martin. *A Description of the Western Islands of Scotland, Circa 1695.* London: Andrew Bell, 1703. Stirling: Eneas Mackay, 1934. Ed. and introd. Donald J. Macleod, Edinburgh: Birlinn, 1994.

Martin, Martin. *A Late Voyage to St. Kilda, the Remotest of all the Hebrides.* London: Brown and Goodwin, 1696. Bound with *A Description of the Western Islands,* etc.

Martine, Roddy. *Scottish Clan and Family Names: Their Arms, Origins and Tartans,* rev. ed. Edinburgh: Mainstream, 1996.

Matheson, Angus. "Traditions of Alasdair Mac Colla." *Transactions of the Gaelic Society of Glasgo,* 5 (1958): 9-93.

Matheson, William. "The Historical Coinneach Odhar and Some Prophecies Attributed to Him." *Transactions of the Gaelic Society of Inverness* 46 (1969-1970): 66-88.

McDonald, R. Andrew. *The Kingdom of the Isles: Scotland's Western Seaboard, c. 1100-1336.* East Linton: Tuckwell Press, 1997.

McDonald, Roderick W. "Scandinavians in the Celtic West: Loanword Evidence and Social Impact." Unpublished dissertation. University of Sydney, 2009.

McGrath, John. *The Cheviot, the Stag and the Black, Black Oil.* [Stage work] Produced 1973. London: Methuen, 1974.

McHardy, Stuart. *School of the Moon: The Highland Cattle-Raiding Tradition.* Edinburgh: Birlinn, 2004.

McIan, R.R. *The Clans of the Scottish Highlands, the Costumes of the Clans.* Text by James Logan. London: Ackerman, 1845, 1847. Rpt. New York: A.A. Knopf, 1980.

McKerral, Andrew. "West Highland Mercenaries in Ireland." *Scottish Historical Review* 30 (1951): 1-14.

McLeod, Wilson. *Divided Gaels: Gaelic Cultural Identities in Scotland and Ireland, c. 1200-1650.* Oxford: Oxford University Press, 2004.

McLeod, Wilson. "*Rí Innsi Gall, Rí Fionnghal, Ceannas nan Gàidheal*: Sovereignty and Rhetoric in the Late Medieval Hebrides." *Cambrian Medieval Celtic Studies* 43 (2002): 201-213.

McLeod, Wilson, and Meg Bateman, eds. *Duanaire na Sracaire = Songbook of the Pillagers: Anthology of Scotland's Gaelic Verse to 1600.* Edinburgh: Birlinn, 2007.

McLynn, Frank. *Charles Edward Stuart: A Tragedy in Many Acts.* London: Routledge, 1988.

McNeil, Kenneth. *Scotland, Britain, Empire: Writing the Highlands 1769-1860.* Columbus: Ohio State University Press, 2007.

McPhee, John. *The Crofter and the Laird.* New York: Farrar, Straus and Giroux, 1969, 1981; rpt. New York: Noonday, 1992.

Meek, Donald E. "The Gaelic Ballads of Medieval Scotland: Creativity and Adaptation." *Transactions of the of Gaelic Society of Inverness* 55 (1986-1988): 47-72; rpt. *Ossian Revisited,* ed. Howard Gaskill. Edinburgh: Edinburgh University Press, 1991, 19-48. Refutes Trevor-Roper thesis, 1983.

Meek, Donald E. *Tuath Is Tighearna: Tenants and Landlords.* Scottish Gaelic Texts Society. Edinburgh: Scottish Academic Press, 1995.

Meikle, Maureen M. *The Scottish People 1490-1625.* Raleigh: Lulu.com, 2015.

Miller, Hugh. *Sutherland as it was and is, or how a country may be ruined.* Edinburgh: Johnstone,

1843. Also in electronic text [introduces the term "clearances"].

Moffat, Alistair. *Before Scotland: The Story of Scotland Before History*. London: Thames & Hudson, 2005, 2009.

Moffat, Alistair. *The Highland Clans*. London: Thames & Hudson, 2010.

Moffat, Alistair. *Scotland: A History from Earliest Times*. Edinburgh: Birlinn, 2017.

Moffat, Alistair, and James F. Wilson. *The Scots: A Genetic Journey*. Edinburgh: Birlinn, 2011.

Moncrieffe. Sir Iain. *The Highland Clans: The Dynastic Origins, Chiefs and Background of the Clans and of Some other Families*. New York: C.N. Potter; London: Barrie & Jenkins, 1977.

Monro, Donald J. ["Dean"]. *A Description of the Western Isles of Scotland* [sometime subtitle: *and the genealogies of the clans*]. [Compiled 1549–1553.] Edinburgh: Auld, 1774. Published with Martin Martin, *A Description of the Western Islands*, etc. Stirling: Eneas Mackay. 1934. Rpt. Edinburgh: Birlinn, 1994. Ed. R.W. Munro, Edinburgh: Oliver & Boyd, 1961. Baltimore: Clearfield, 1993.

Moore, Dafydd, ed. *Ossian and Ossianism*. 4 vols. London: Routledge, 2004.

Moore, John Robert. "Wordsworth's Unacknowledged Debt to Macpherson's Ossian." *PMLA* 40 (1923): 362–378.

Morrison, Hew. See Rob Donn.

Mulholland, James. "James Macpherson's Ossian Poems, Oral Traditions, and the Invention of Voice." *Oral Tradition* 24, no. 2 (2009): 393–414.

Munro, Jean, and R.W. Munro, eds. *Acts of the Lords of the Isles, 1336–1493*. Publications of the Scottish Historical Society, 4th series, 22. Edinburgh: Scottish Historical Society, 1986.

Napier, Sir Francis, 9th Baron, ed. *Evidence taken by Her Majesty's Commissioners of Inquiry into the condition of the crofters and cottars in the Highlands and Islands of Scotland*. 5 vols. Edinburgh: Neill, 1884.

Necker de Saussure, Louis A. *Voyage en Écosse et aux Îles Hébrides*. 3 vols. Geneva and Paris, 1821.

Newby, Andrew G. "Emigration and Clearance from the Island of Barra, c. 1770–1858." *Transactions of the Gaelic Society of Inverness* 61 (2003): 116–148.

Newte, Thomas. *Tour in England and Scotland, 1785. By an English Gentlemen*. London: Robinson, 1788, 1791.

Newton, Michael. *Bho Chluaidh gu Calasraid / From the Clyde to the Callander: Gaelic Tales, Songs and Traditions from the Lennox and Menteith*, rev. ed. Glasgow: Gimsay Press, 2010.

Newton, Michael. *A Handbook of the Gaelic World*. Dublin: Four Courts Press, 2000.

Newton, Michael. *Sgeulachdan an Dà Shaoghail*. Glasgow: Sandstone Press, 2007.

Newton, Michael. *Warriors of the Word: The World of the Scottish Highlanders*. Edinburgh: Birlinn, 2009.

Newton, Michael Steven. *The Everyday Life of the Clans of the Scottish Highlands*. [London?]: Michael Newton/Saora Media, 2020.

Nicholson, Ranald. "Domesticated Scots and Wild Scots: The Relationship Between Lowlanders and Highlanders in Medieval Scotland." *Proceedings of the First Colloquium on Scottish Studies*. Guelph: University of Guelph, 1968.

Ó Baoill, Colm. "Scotland in Early Gaelic Literature (600–1200 A.D.)." *Transactions of the Gaelic Society of Inverness* 48 (1972–1974): 382–394.

Ó Baoill, Colm. "The Scots-Gaelic Interface," in Charles Jones, ed., *The Edinburgh History of the Scots Language*. Edinburgh: Edinburgh University Press, 1997, 511–568.

Ò Baoill. Colm, ed. *Bàrdachd Shìlis na Ceapaich, c. 1660–c. 1729*. Edinburgh: Scottish Gaelic Texts Society, 1972 [woman of Keppoch, on 1689].

Ó Cuiv, Brian, ed. *The Impact of the Scandinavian Invasions on the Celtic Speaking Peoples c.800–1100 A.D.* Dublin: Dublin Institute for Advanced Studies, 1983.

Oftedal, Magne. "On the Frequency of Norse Loan-Words in Scottish Gaelic." *Scottish Gaelic Studies* 9 (1962): 116–127.

Oliver, Neil. *A History of Scotland*. London: Weidenfeld & Nicolson, 2009; London: Phoenix Books, 2010.

Oppenheimer, Stephen. *The Origins of the British*. London: Constable; New York: Carroll and Graf, 2006.

Oram, Richard, ed. *The Lordship of the Isles*. Leiden: Brill, 2014.

Òran na Comhachaig: A Critical Edition with English Translation and Annotations, ed. Pat Menzies. Glasgow: Scottish Gaelic Texts Society, New Series #4, 2012.

Orkneyinga Saga: The History of Orkney, ed. and trans. Hermann Pálsson and Paul Geoffrey Edwards. Harmondsworth: Penguin Classics, 1981.

Pennant, Thomas. *A Tour in Scotland and Voyage to the Hebrides*. Chester, 1772. Rpt. Edinburgh: Birlinn; Chester Springs: DuFour, 1998. See also Youngson, A.J. *Beyond the Highland Line*.

Pennant, Thomas. *A Tour in Scotland and Voyage to the Hebrides, MDCCLXXII, Part 1*. Chester: John Monk, 1774; London: Benjamin White, 1776.

Pennant, Thomas. *A Tour of Scotland, MDCCLXIX*. Chester: John Monk, 1771; rpt. Edinburgh: Birlinn, 2000.

Philip of Almerieclose, James. *The Gremeid, an heroic poem descriptive of the Campaign of Viscount Dundee in 1689* [epic poem in Latin, 1691], trans. and ed. Alexander D. Murdoch. Edinburgh: Scottish History Society, 1888.

Pictish Chronicle. See Skene, William Forbes, ed., *Chronicles of the Picts, Chronicles of the Scots and Other Early Memorials of Scottish History*.

Pinkerton, John. *Dissertation on the Origin and Progress of the Scythians or Goths*. London: George Nicol, 1787.

Pinkerton, John. *An Enquiry into the History of*

Scotland Preceding the Reign of Malcolm III or the year 1056 Including the Authentic History of that Period. 2 vols. Edinburgh: John Bell, 1789; London, 1794.

Pittock, Murray. *The Myth of the Jacobite Clans: The Jacobite Army in 1745*, 2nd ed. Edinburgh: Edinburgh University Press, 2009.

Pittock, Murray G.H. *Jacobitism*. Basingstoke: Macmillan; New York: St. Martin's, 1998.

Pocock, Isaac. *Rob Roy, or, Auld Lang Syne*. London: John Miller, 1818 [three-act operatic adaptation of Walter Scott].

Poppleton Manuscript. See Hudson, B.T., ed. and trans. *Scottish Historical Review*.

Powell, Michael, and Emeric Pressberger, dir. *Edge of the World*, sc. Powell and Pressberger [fictional portrayal of the evacuation of St. Kilda's]. Released 1937.

Powell, Michael, and Emeric Pressberger, dir. *I Know Where I'm Going!*, sc. Powell and Pressberger. Released, 1945.

Prebble, John. *Culloden*. Harmondsworth: Penguin, 1961.

Prebble, John. *The Highland Clearances*. Harmondsworth: Penguin, 1963.

Prendergast, Muríosa. "Scots Mercenary Forces in Sixteenth Century Ireland," in John France, ed., *Mercenaries and Paid Men: The Mercenary Identity in the Middle Ages*. Leiden: Brill, 2008, 363–382.

Rankin, Effie, ed. *As A Bhràighe/Beyond the Braes: The Gaelic Songs of Allan the Ridge MacDonald, 1794–1868*, 2nd ed. Sydney: Cape Breton University Press, 2005.

Rankin, Reginald, ed. *Mabou Pioneer II*. Mabou: Privately published, 1977. See also MacDonald, A.D.

Rankin, Robert A. "Òran na Camhachaig" Text and Tradition." *Transactions of the Gaelic Society of Glasgow* 5 (1957): 125–171.

Reich, David. *Who We Are and How We Got Here: Ancient DNA and the New Science of the Ancient Past*. New York: Pantheon, 2018.

Reid, Stuart. *The Campaigns of Montrose. The Military History of the Civil War in Scotland, 1639 to 1646*. Edinburgh: Mercat Press, 1990.

Reid, Stuart. *Like Hungry Wolves—Culloden Moor, 16 April 1746*. London: Windrow & Greene, 1994.

Reid, Stuart. *1745: A Military History of the Last Jacobite Rising*. Staplehurst: Spellmount; New York: Sarpedon, 1996.

Reid, Stuart, and Gerry Embleton. *Culloden Moor 1746: The Death of the Jacobite Cause*. Oxford: Osprey Press, 2002.

Reid, Stuart, and Gerry Embleton. *Cumberland's Culloden Army, 1745–45*. Oxford: Osprey Press, 2012.

Richards, Eric. *Debating the Highland Clearances*. Edinburgh: Edinburgh University Press, 2007.

Richards, Eric. *The Highland Clearances: People, Landlords and Rural Turmoil*. Edinburgh: Birlinn, 2000.

Richards, Eric. *A History of the Highland Clearances: Agrarian Transformation and the Evictions, 1746–1886*. 2 vols. London: Croom Helm, 1982–1985. 2nd ed., 2000.

Richards, Eric. "How Tame Were the Highlanders During the Clearances?" *Scottish Studies* 17, no. 1 (1973): 35–50.

Richards, Eric. *Patrick Sellar and the Highland Clearances; Homicide, Eviction and the Price of Progress*. Edinburgh: Polygon at Edinburgh, 1999.

Riding, Jacqueline. *Jacobites: A New History of the '45 Rebellion*. London: Bloomsbury, 2016.

Rob Donn [MacAoidh, MacKay]. *Songs and Poems in the Gaelic Language by Rob Donn, 1714–1778*, ed. Hew Morrison. Edinburgh: J. Grant, 1899; rpt. Charleston: Palala Press, 2015.

Roberts, John Lenox. *The Jacobite Wars: Scotland and the Military Campaigns of 1715 and 1745*. Edinburgh: Edinburgh University Press, 2002.

Roberts, John Leonard. *Feuds, Forays and Rebellions: History of the Highland Clans, 1475–1625*. Edinburgh: Edinburgh University Press, 1999.

Ross, Raymond J., and Joy Hendry, eds. *Sorley MacLean: Critical Essays*. Edinburgh: Scottish Academic Press, 1986.

Sadler, John. *Clan Donald's Greatest Defeat*. Stroud: Tempus, 2005.

Scarfe, Norman, ed. *To The Highlands in 1786: The Inquisitive Journey of a Young French Aristocrat*. [Selected translations from Alexandre de la Rochefoucauld and Maximilien de Lazowski.] Woodbridge: Boydell Press, 2001.

Schama, Simon. *Landscape and Memory*. New York: Vintage, 1996.

Scott, Sir Walter. *Manners, Customs and History of the Highlanders of Scotland/ Historical Account of the Clan MacGregor*. Glasgow: Morrison, 1893; rpt. New York: Barnes & Noble, 2004.

Scott, Sir Walter. *Tales of a Scottish Grandfather, Being Tales Taken from Scottish History*. London: Simpkins and Marshall, 1828. Portions edited by Dr. George Grant and issued under different titles, e.g., *From Montrose to Culloden: Bonnie Prince Charlie and Scotland's Romantic Age*. Nashville: Cumberland House, 2001.

Selkirk, 5th Earl of, Thomas Douglas. *Observations on the Present State of the Highlands of Scotland, with a View of the Causes and Probable Consequences of Emigration*. London: Longman, Hurst, Rees & Orme, 1805; 2nd ed., Edinburgh, 1806. Rpt. New York: S.R., 1969.

Sellar, Thomas. *The Sutherland Evictions of 1814*. London: Longmans, Green, 1883.

Sellar, W.D.H. "Divorce and Concubinage in Gaelic Scotland." *Transactions of the Gaelic Society of Inverness* 51 (1978): 464–493.

Sellar, W.D.H. "Gaelic Laws ad Institutions," in Michael Lynch, ed., *The Oxford Companion to Scottish History*. Oxford: Oxford University Press, 2001.

Sellar, W.D.H. "Hebridean Sea-Kings: The Successors of Somerled, 1164–1316,"in Edward J.Cowan and R. Andrew McDonald, eds, *Alba: Celtic*

Scotland and the Medieval Era. Edinburgh: John Donald, 2000, 2005.

Sellar, W.D.H. "The Origins and Ancestry of Somerled." *Scottish Historical Review* 45 (1966): 123–142.

Seton, Bruce Gordon, Sir, and Jean Gordon Arnot. *Prisoners of the '45*, edited from the State Papers 3. Edinburgh: Constable for the Scottish Historical Society, 1928–1929.

Sharpe, Richard. "The Thriving of Dalriada," in Simon Taylor, ed., *Kings, Clerics and Chronicles in Scotland, 500–1297*. Dublin: Four Courts, 2000.

Shaw, John. *Brìgh an Òran/ A Story in Every Song*. Montreal: McGill-Queen's University Press, 2000.

Shaw, John. "Language, Music and Local Aesthetics, Views from Gaeldom and Beyond." *Scottish Language* nos. 11–12 (1992–1993): 37–61.

Shields, Juliet. "From Family Roots to the Routes of Empire: National Tales and the Domestication of the Scottish Highlands." *ELH* 72, no. 4 (Winter 2005): 919–940.

Shields, Juliet. "Highland Emigration and the Transformations of Nostalgia in Romantic Poetry." *European Romantic Review* 23 (2012): 765–784.

Sims-Williams, Patrick. "An Alternative to 'Celtic from the East' and 'Celtic from the West.'" *Cambridge Archaeological Journal* 30, no. 3 (February 2020): 511–529.

Sims-Williams, Patrick. "Celtomania and Celto-scepticism." *Cambrian Celtic Medieval Studies* 36 (1998): 1–35.

Sims-Williams, Patrick. "Genetics, Linguistics and Pre-History: Thinking Big and Thinking Straight." *Antiquity* 72 (1998): 505–527.

Sinclair, A[lexander] Maclean. "The Gaelic Bards and the Collectors of Their Works." *Transactions of the Gaelic Society of Inverness* 24 (1899–1901): 259–276.

Sinclair, Sir John. *An Account of the Highland Society of London*, etc. London: Longman, 1813.

Sinclair, Sir John. *Statistical Account of Scotland*. 23 vols. Edinburgh, 1791–1799; rpt. ed. Donald J. Withrington and Ian R. Grant. East Ardsley: Wakefield, 1991.

Skene, William Forbes. *Celtic Scotland: History of Ancient Alban*. 3 vols. Edinburgh: Douglas, 1886.

Skene, William Forbes. *The Highlanders of Scotland*. Stirling: The Sentinel Press, 1902.

Skene, William Forbes, ed. *Chronicles of the Picts, Chronicles of the Scots and Other Early Memorials of Scottish History*. Edinburgh: HM General Register House, 1867.

Sledzinska, Paula. "Revisiting the Other: National Theatre of Scotland and the Mythologization of the Highlands and Islands." *Canadian Journal of Irish Studies* 39, no. 1 (2015), 118–141.

Smith, Iain Crichton. *Consider the Lilies*. London: Gollancz, 1968; rpt. London: Fontana Books, 1970.

Snorri Sturluson. *Heimskringla*. 3 vols. Trans. Alison Finlay and Anthony Faulkes. London: Viking Society, 2011–2015.

Steer, K.A,. and John Bannerman. *Late Medieval Monumental Sculpture in the West Highlands*. Edinburgh: Royal Commission of the Ancient and Historical Monuments of Scotland, 1977.

Stevenson, David. *Highland Warrior: Alasdair MacColla and the Civil Wars*. Edinburgh: The Saltire Society, 1994.

Stevenson, David. "The Irish Franciscan Mission to Scotland and the Irish Rebellion of 1641." *Innes Review* 45 (1980): 54–61.

Stewart, David of Garth. *Sketches of the Character, Manners and Present State of the Highlanders of Scotland*. 2 vols. Edinburgh, 1822, 1825. Rpt., *Sketches of the Character, Institutions, and Customs of the Scottish Highlanders of Scotland*. Inverness: Mackenzie; London: Simkin Marshall, 1885.

Stewart, Donald C. *The Setts of the Scottish Tartans*. Edinburgh: Oliver and Boyd, 1950; rpt. New York: Van Nostrand, 1974.

Stiùbhart, Dòmhnall Uilleam. "Murder in Barra, 1609? The Killing of the 'Peursan Mór.'" *Béascna* [Cork] 8 (2013): 144–178.

Stowe, Harriet Beecher. *Sunny Memories of Foreign Lands*. Boston: Phillips, Sampson; New York: Derby, 1854. See riposte by Macleod, Donald [also M'Leod]. *Gloomy Memories in the Highlands of Scotland: versus Mrs. Harriet Beecher Stowe's Sunny Memories in (England) A Foreign Land*. Toronto: Privately printed, 1857. Glasgow: A. Sinclair, 1892; rpt. Bettyhill: Strathnaver Museum, 1996.

Stroh, Silke. *Gaelic Scotland in the Colonial Imagination: Anglophone Writing from 1600 to 1900*. Evanston: Northwestern University Press, 2017.

Sykes, Brian. "Scotland," "The Picts," "The DNA of Scotland," *Saxons, Vikings and Celts: The Genetic Roots of Britain and Ireland*. New York: Norton, 2006; Toronto: Blood of the Isles, 177–218.

Szechi, Daniel. *The Jacobites, Britain & Europe, 1688–1788*. Manchester: Manchester University Press, 1994.

Szechi, Daniel. *1715: The Great Jacobite Rebellion*. New Haven: Yale University Press, 2006.

Taylor, Simon, ed. *Kings, Clerics and Chronicles in Scotland, 500–1297*. Dublin: Four Courts, 2000.

Thomson, Derick S. "Gaelic Learned Orders and Literati in Medieval Scotland." *Scottish Studies* 12 (1968): 57–78.

Thomson, Derick S. *The Gaelic Sources of Macpherson's Ossian*. Aberdeen: Aberdeen University Press, 1952.

Thomson, Derick S. "Scottish Gaelic Folk Poetry Ante 1650." *Scottish Gaelic Studies* 8, no. 1 (1955): 1–17.

Thomson, Derick S., ed. *The Companion Guide to Gaelic Scotland*. Oxford: Basil Blackwell, 1983.

Thomson, Oliver. *The Great Feud: The Campbells and the MacDonalds*. Stroud: Tempus, 2000.

Thoreau, Henry David. "Homer, Ossian, Chaucer." *The Dial: A Magazine for Literature, Philosophy and Religion* 4 (1844): 290–305.

Thornton, Thomas. *Sporting Tour Through the Northern Parts of England, and a Great Part of the Highlands of Scotland...* London: Vernor and Hood, 1804.

Thrasher, Harriette F. *The Clan Chisholm and Allied Clans.* New York: Privately printed, 1935.

Trevor-Roper, Hugh. "The Invented Tradition: The Highland Tradition of Scotland," in Eric Hobsbawm and Terence Ranger, eds., *The Invention of Tradition.* Cambridge: Cambridge University Press, 1983, 14–42. Cf. refutations of this thesis by Donald Meek (1991) and Howard Gaskill (1986).

Trevor-Roper, Hugh. *The Invention of Scotland: Myth and History.* New Haven: Yale University Press, 2008.

Wainright, F.T., ed. *The Problem of the Picts.* Edinburgh: Nelson, 1955.

Walker, John D., Rev. Dr. *Report on the Hebrides, 1764.* Rev. ed Margaret M. McKay. Edinburgh. John Donald, 1979.

Warner, Alan. *Morvern Callar.* New York: Vintage, 1995; filmed as *Morvern Callar,* dir. Lynne Ramsay, sc. Ramsay and Liana Rognin, 2001.

Warner, Alan. *The Sopranos.* London: Cape, 1998; adapted for the stage by Lee Hall as *Our Ladies of Perpetual Succour,* Edinburgh, 2015; London, 2017; stage text published in London by Faber, 2015; adapted for film under title *Our Ladies,* dir. Michael Caton-Jones, sc. Caton-Jones and Warner, 2019.

Watkins, Peter. *Culloden*; also known as *The Battle of Culloden* [film], sc. Peter Watkins, based on John Prebble's *Culloden* (1961), 1964.

Watson, Fiona. *Scotland: From Prehistory to the Present.* Cheltenham: Tempus, 2001.

Watson, Moray, and Michelle Macleod, eds. *The Edinburgh Companion to the Gaelic Language.* Edinburgh: Edinburgh University Press, 2010.

Watson, William J. *The History of Celtic Placenames of Scotland.* Edinburgh: Blackwood, 1926; rpt. *Celtic Placenames of Scotland.* Edinburgh: Berlinn, 1993.

Watson, W.J. "Early Irish Influences in Scotland." *Transactions of the Gaelic Society of Inverness* 35 (1929–1930): 178–202.

Way (of Plean), George, Romilly Squire. *Collins Scottish Clan & Family Encyclopedia.* Glasgow: HarperCollins, 1994.

Wenskus, Reinhard. *Stammesbildung und Verfassung: Das Werden der frühmittelalterlichen gentes.* Cologne: Böhlau, 1961.

Williams, Ronald. *The Heather and the Gale: Clan Donald and Clan Campbell and the Early Kingdom of the Scots.* Isle of Colonsay: House of Lochar, 1997.

Williams, Ronald. *The Lords of the Isles: The Clan Donald and the Early Kingdom of the Scots.* London: Chatto and Windus, 1984, 1999.

Wishart, George. *Memoirs of the Most Renowned James Graham, Marquis of Montrose 1639–1650* [original in Latin, 1647]. London: Longmans, 1893.

Withers, Charles W.J. *Gaelic in Scotland, 1698–1981: The Geographical History of a Language.* Edinburgh: John Donald; Atlantic Highlands: Humanities Press, 1984.

Withers, Charles W.J. *Gaelic Scotland: The Transformation of a Culture Region.* London: Routledge, 1988.

Withers, Charles W.J. "On the Geography and Social History of Gaelic," in William Gillies, ed., *Gaelic and Scotland/Alba agus á Ghàdhlig.* Edinburgh: Edinburgh University Press, 1989, 101–130.

Womack, Peter. *Improvement and Romance: Constructing the Myth of the Highlands.* Basingstoke: Macmillan,1989.

Woolf, Alex. "Dún Nechtain, Fortriu and the Geography of the Picts." *Scottish Historical Review* 85 (2006): 182–201.

Woolf, Alex. *From Pictland to Alba 789–1070.* Edinburgh: Edinburgh University Press, 2007.

Woolf, Alex. "On the Nature of the Picts." *Scottish Historical Review* 96 (2017): 214–217.

Woolf, Alex. "The Origins and Ancestry of Somerled: Gofraid [sic] mac Fergusa and the 'Annals of the Four Masters.'" *Mediaeval Scandinavia* 15 (2005): 119–213.

Woolf, Alex. "Pictish Matriliny Reconsidered:" *Innes Review* 49, no. 2 (Autumn 1998): 147–167.

Wordsworth, Dorothy. *Recollections of a Tour Made in Scotland, A.D. 1803.* Edinburgh: Edmonston and Douglas, 1874; rpt. New Haven: Yale, 1997.

Wordsworth, William. "To a Highland Girl," "The Solitary Reaper" [both written 1803, published 1807] *Poetical Works*, 2nd ed., ed. E. de Selincourt and Helen Darbishire [sic]. Vol 3. Oxford: Clarendon Press, 1959 73–75, 77. Also: "Glen Almain: or the NARROW Glen," "Sonnet in the Pass of Killycranky,""Rob Roy's Grave," "Effusion in the Pleasure-Ground on the Banks of the Bran Near Dunkeld" [composed 1814], *Memorials of a Tour in Scotland, 1803.* London, 1827; frequently reprinted and now available in e-text.

Wormald, Jenny. "Blood Feud, Kindred and Government in Early Modern Scotland." *Past and Present* 87 (1980): 54–97.

Wormald, Jenny. *Lords and Men in Scotland: Bonds of Manrent, 1442–1603.* Edinburgh: J. Donald, 1985.

Wormald, Jenny, ed. *Scottish Society in the Fifteenth Century.* New York: St. Martin's, 1977.

Worten, Jonathan. *The Battle of Glenshiel: The Jacobite Rising in 1719.* Warwick: Helion, 2018.

Youngson, A.J. *After the Forty-Five: The Economic Impact on the Scottish Highlands.* Edinburgh: Edinburgh University Press, 1973.

Youngson, A.J. *Beyond the Highland Line; Three*

Journals of Travel in Eighteenth Century Scotland: [Edward] *Burt,* [Thomas] *Pennant,* [Thomas] *Thornton.* London: Collins, 1974.

Youngson, A.J. *The Prince and the Pretender: A Study in the Writing of History.* London: Croom Helm, 1985; reissued as *The Prince and the Pretender: Two Views of the '45.* Edinburgh: Mercat Press, 1996.

Index

A dh'aindeoin có thiereadh 224
a' dol sìos 100
Abbotsford 170, 171
Abercorn, Lady 171
Aberdeen, city of 14, 27, 44, 63, 96, 98, 120, 134; post-1974 borders 14, 24; pre-1974 borders 15, 16, 32, 63, 103, 116, 165, 205; sack of 96, 101–102, 103; *see also* University of Aberdeen
Aberfeldy *see* "The Birks of Aberfeldy"
Aberystwyth 23
aborigines, generic *see* American native people; indigenous peoples; Maori
Aboyne, Viscount 98
Abrach dialec *see* Gàidhlig Abrach
Acallam na Senórach 158–159
Account of the Improvements on the Estate of the Earl of Sutherland 191–192
Achnacarry 123, 138, 145
Act for Settling Schools 112
Act of Proscription (1746) 119, 155, 162; *see also* Disarming Art and Dress Act
Act of Settlement 131
Act of Toleration 94, 115
Act of Union, Ireland 114
Act of Union, Treaty of 1707 93, 94, 105, 106, 107, 110, 114–115, 116, 131, 176, 207; anti-Union sentiment 128, 131
adaltrach 75
Adam, bishop of Caithness 59
Adam Smith's Legacy 140
Add river 24, 29
"Address to a Haggis" 224
"Address to the Unco Guid, or, The Rigidly Righteous" 125
Adirondacks 150
adultery 75, 87, 91; *see also* marriage
Advocates Library 156
Áedan mac Gabráin 26
affricated stop 50
Africa 21, 113, 168, 224; romanticizing 222
agricultural revolution 148
Aikman, Christian 122, 220

Aird, John 153–154
Airer Goídel 26
Aitkin, Thomas 226
Alasdair Buidhe (17th century) 106
Alaisdair MacDòmhnaill *see* Alexander of Islay
Alasdair mac Mhaighstir Alasdair 163, 164, 214
Alasdair Mòr 106
Alasdair of Inverlair 106
Alba 16, 24, 25, 30–31, 32, 36, 45, 50, 54–55, 69, 70; pronunciation 30
Albania, archaic name for Scotland 36
Albany *see* Robert, Duke of Albany
Albany Stewarts *see* Stuart dynasty
Albert, Prince 180–185
Albidosi 33
Aledaide, Australia 209
Alexander (ship) 149
Alexander I 58
Alexander II 58
Alexander III, king of Scotland 51, 59
Alexander Carrach 64, 65, 107
Alexander, the Earl of Buchan, "Wolf of Badenoch" 62, 63
Alexander of Islay, Earl of Ross 63, 64–65, 76
Alexander Stewart *see* Mar, Earl of
Alford, Battle of 103
Ali, name 67
Alien Act of 1705 114
allodial power 70
Almerieclose *see* Philip of Almerieclose, James
Alps 18, 102, 181
Amazon.com 221
American native people, Indians 34, 162; *see also* Métis, Mohawks
American Revolution, War of Independence 141, 147, 150
American West, romanticizing of 222
Amie mac Ruari 61
Amsterdam 33, 113, 121
Anatolia 20; *see also* Asia Minor

And No Quarter 105
And the Cock Crew 201
Anderson, James (19th century) 197
Andes Mountains 18
Andrew of Wyntoun 30
ANE, ancestral north Eurasians 20; *see also* Yamnaya
Angles, early people 2, 31
Anglicans 43, 52, 92, 99, 206
Anglicization 53, 55, 90, 96, 115, 125, 208, 210
Anglo-Irish 40–41, 210
Anglo-Irish War 43
Anglo-Normans 40–41, 42, 56, 75
Anglo-Saxon art 29
Anglo-Saxon Chronicle 45
Anglo-Saxons 142
Anglophone *see* English language
Angus, Angus-shire: post-1974 borders 14; pre-1974 borders 15, 16, 32, 67, 95, 99
Angus, Bishop of the Isles 63
Angus, son of Somerled 58, 69
Angus Mòr name 67
Angus Òg: 15th century, son of John Islay 66–67; mythic figure 25; name 67
Annandale, 4th Lord of 40
Annals of Tigernach 26
Annals of Ulster 24, 29, 30, 34, 45
Anne, Queen 115–116
Antichrist 93
Antigonish 149
Antipodes *see* Australia, New Zealand
Antiquité de la nation et de la Langue des Celtes 9
Antiquity journal 23, 27
Anton, A.E. 74
Antrim, County 27, 28, 37, 40, 41, 42, 44, 54, 83, 130; *see also* Ulster
Antrim, Earl of (17th century) 98, 100
Aonghas *see* Angus Òg, name
Apollo 25
Aporcrosan 38
Appalachian Mountains 43
Appin 186
Appin Regiment 132

251

Index

Applecross 38
"apprich" 4; *see also* Gàidhlig Abrach
Apurchrosan 38
aqua vitae 183
Arabs 33
Aran Islands 27
Arbroath, Declaration of 60
Archæologia Britannica 9
Archbishop of Canterbury 92
Arctic char 144
Ard-righ (Sc) *Ard Rí* (Ir) 57, 75; *see also rí*
Ardersier 146
Ardmore Bay 81
Ardnamurchan 56, 57, 80, 100, 205
Ardross 153
Ardtornish 57, 62, 66
Ardtornish-Westminster Treaty 66
Argentina 186
Argyll, Argyllshire 15, 16, 26, 27, 28, 35, 36, 38, 39, 43, 56, 57, 58, 69, 83, 84, 94, 100, 103, 121, 125, 132, 146, 159, 181, 182, 186, 198, 214, 223; etymology 26
Argyll, bishop of 24
Argyll, Duke of, creation of title 84
Argyll, 2nd Duke of 116
Argyll, 3rd Duke of 122
Argyll, 8th Duke of 7, 76, 84, 138
Argyll, 13th Duke of 84
Argyll, Earlship of 84, 90 *see also* Argyll, Duke of
Argyll, 2nd Earl of 66
Argyll, 3rd Earl of 39
Argyll, 9th Earl of 109
Argyll, 10th Earl of 84, 111
Argyll, Lords of 58
Argyll, Marquis of 98, 99, 102, 103
Argyll and Bute, post-1996, 14, 16, 17, 26
Argyll Street 84
Arisaig 137, 138, 149
Arkaig, Loch 3, 85, 137, 145
Arlen, Michael 2, 5
Armadale Castle 65, 145
Armenian people 2; language 6, 20
armigerous 82
Armstrong, Clan 82
Arnish 226
Arnold, Matthew 161
Aros 57
Arran, Isle of 15, 16, 47, 54, 56
Arthurian legends 159
artillery 133, 135, 136, 194
Aryan, Aryans 19
Ashmolean Museum 9
Asia 10, 21
Asia Minor 8; *see also* Anatolia
assassination 60
Assynt 194
Ath Fotla, Ath Fothla 35
Atholl 35, 70; rival etymologies 35; *see also* "Humble Petition ... Duke of Athole"

Atholl, Earl of 67
Atholl Brigade 132
Atlantic Celts: Ancient People or Modern Invention? 11–12
Atlantic provinces of Canada, also Maritime Provinces 140, 148
Atlantic Zone 9
Auchinbreck 84
Auel, Jean M. 69
Aughrim, Battle of 111
Augustinians 59
"Auld Alliance" 60
"Auld Kirk" *see* Kirk of Scotland
"Auld Land Syne" 139
Auldearn, Battle of 103
Austen, Jane 171
Australia, Antipodes 48, 190, 205, 209, 210, 214
Austria 8, 9, 11, 117; Austrian cause 128
Austrian Succession, War of 128
Avich, Loch 83
Awe, Loch 83, 84
Ayrshire 25, 84, 125, 164, 165, 223

baccalaureate, B.A. degree 219
Bacon, Sir Francis 89
Badenoch 4, 62, 86, 98, 155; *see also* Alexander, Earl of Buchan, "Wolf of"
Baghdad 45
bagpipes 4, 86, 162, 183, 184, 187, 215, 220; *see also* pibroch
Bahrain 22
baile, township 148
Baile Átha Cliath 46
Baillie, Henry 197
Baillie, James 198
Bakewell, Thomas 192
Balbridie 24–25
Balclutha (Macpherson ship) 159
Baldoon 190
Balerino, Lord 138
Ballachulish 95, 168
Ballad of the Tailor 178
ballads 63, 68, 157, 171, 178, 187; *see also* Border Ballads; folklore; oral tradition
ballet 85, 226
Balliol family 60
Ballycastle 44
Balmoral 165, 180–182, 183, 196, 205
Balmoralism 181–183, 209
Balnagown 151, 155
Baltic states 18, 33
Balto-Slavic languages 20
Banchory 24
Band of Union 86
bandits 94–96, 106, 108, 120; *see also* crime; rustling, cattle
Banff, Banffshire 15, 16
Bank of England 112
Bank of Scotland 112, 113, 183, 218
Bannockburn 40, 60, 70, 83, 114
Banquo, dramatic character 32
Barbour, John 41
Barcelona 18

The Bard (1757) 156
Bàrd na Ceapaich 105
bards, bardic poetry 38–39, 53, 63, 121, 156, 159, 163, 164, 166; Bard of Keppoch 105; "bard of the Clearances" 200
Bargarran, Battle of 58
Barra, Isle of 4, 49, 67, 77, 94, 128, 129, 198, 204; purchased by John Gordon of Cluny 205; *see also* Outer Hebrides
Barrach dialect *see* Gàidhlig Bharraidh
Barrington, Lord 146
barter 73, 111, 121, 122, 143
Basilikon Doron 89
basketball 10
Basque language 20, 33, 221
Bastille 166
"Battle of Alasdair," musical composition 104
"The Battle of Sherramuir" 165
Bavaria 31, 181
BBC, British Broadcasting 81
Beaton family 3, 220
Beaufort, Duke of (18th century) 128
Beauly 153
Beaune 184
Bede, Venerable 26, 27, 34, 37
Before Scotland: The Story of Scotland Before History 21
Behan, Brendan 223
beheading 97, 138
Beinn Dorain 200
Belfast 37
Belgium 17, 44, 203; *see also* Flanders
Ben Lee, hill 211
Ben Nevis 13, 17, 18; *see also* "Sonnet. Written Upon the Top of Ben Nevis"
Benbecula 137, 155
Bend of the Boyne 67
Benedictines 26
Beowulf 159
Bergen 44
berling *see* birlinn
Berlioz, Hector 173
Bernadotte, Jean-Baptiste 161
Bernera Riot 210
Bernicia 31
Berwick-upon-Tweed 133
Bettyhill 195
Beurla 51
Bible 53, 89; *see also* Gospel; New Testament; Old Testament; scripture
Biblical history 43, 136; *see also* Creation; creationism; Gospels
Biblical scholarship, Interpretive 207
"big music" 86
bilingual signage, bank notes 119, 218, 219
bilingualism 53
"The Birks of Aberfeldy" 165
birlinn, berling 41, 56, 59
Bishop of the Isles 52, 63

Index

bishops, offices of 91–92, 94, 99, 149
Bishops' Wars 92, 97, 99–100
Björnsson *see* Ketill Björnsson
Black, George 157
Black intellectuals 223
Black Isle 18, 197
Black John 95
Black Watch Regiment: earlier militia 119–120, 139, 146, 147, 153, 178; name explained 119; tartan 119, 178, 180
blackface 215
blackhouse, described 123, 210
black-faced sheep *see* Linton sheep
blackmail 95, 119; semantics of word 78
Blackwoods Magazine 199
Blair, Hugh 155
Blair Castle 100, 101, 110
Blake, William 161
Blàr Coire na Creiche 81
Blàr Millieadh a' Ghàraidh Milligearaih 81
Bliadhna an Losgaith 195, 196
Bliadhna nan Caorach 153–154
Bliadna na Thearlaic 130
"Blind Harry" 169
The Blood Is Strong 226
Blood of the Celts 21
Bloody Bay, Battle of 67
boar imagery 24, 35
"Bobbing John" 116; *see also* Erskine, John
Bochanan, Dùghall 163–164
"bodice-ripper fiction 222
"body snatcher" murders 143
Boece, Hector 32, 40
Bohemia 115–116
Bohuntin 163
Boil the Breakfast Early 104
Bolivia 17
"Bonie Dundee" 165
Bonn University 216
"The Bonnets o' Bonnie Dundee" 110
Bonnie Dundee *see* Dundee, Viscount
Bonnie Prince Charlie *see* Charles Edward Stuart, Prince
Bonnie Scotland 216
Book of Ballymote 28
Book of Common Prayer 92, 99
Book of Durrow 29
Book of Invasions/Conquests of Ireland 43
Book of Kells 11, 26, 45
Book of Lecan 28
Book of Leinster 158
Book of the Dean of Lismore 39
Book of the Dun Cow 157
Boone, Daniel 43
Bòrd na Gàidhlig 219
Border Ballads of the Scottish-English border 171
Borders region 78, 171, 186, 212
Boreraig 198
Borges, Jorge Luis 186

Borneo 4, 96
Borrodale 137
Boston 10
Boswell, James 36, 74, 80, 139, 143, 144, 164, 165, 166
Bothan Airigh am Bràigh Raithneach 52
Bothnagoune 32
Bouguereau, William-Adolphe 166
Boulton, Sir Harold Edwin 137
Bourbon dynasty 128
Bower, Walter 62
Boycott, Capt. Charles 210
Boyne, Battle of the 109, 111
Boyne Valley 37, 67
Bradwardine, Baron (Scott character) 172–173
Bradwardine, Rose (Scott character) 171–173
Brae Lochaber 3, 52, 63, 64, 107
Braemar 63, 116, 181, 184
Braes, Battle of the 211
"The Braes O' Killiecrankie" 165
Braes of Angus 95
Braes, on Skye 211, 212
Brahan Seer 86–88
Brahms, Johannes 161
brandy 184
Braveheart (film) 40, 169
Brazil 184
breacan 177, 178
Breadalbane *see* Campbell of Breadalbane
Brehon law 74–76
Bremen 49
Breton language 9, 20, 26
Bretons 220–221
Brian Boru 46–47
Brig of Dee 98
Brigadoon 74, 223
Bristol 198
Britain, Great Britain 8, 9, 10, 19, 45, 68, 90, 151, 152, 173; *see also* England; United Kingdom
Britanni 34
britheamh 61, 75
British Army 72, 123, 126, 148; Highland regiments 177, 184, 210, 215; recruitment of Highlanders for 146–147, 192, Secretary of War 146; *see also* Black Watch Regiment; Fraser's Highlanders; Montgomery's Highlanders; red coat
British Commonwealth 151, 217
British East India Company 96
British Empire 120, 147, 151, 210
British Empire Medal 226
British North America *see* Canada
British Parliament *see* Parliament, English later British
British television 140, 182
British Wool Society 152
British Zoology 143
Britons, pre-modern people 2, 31, 33–34, 83

Brittany 9, 11, 22, 25, 37, 60, 216, 221; woman's name 221
Brittonic 27, 33–34
Broad Scots *see* Scots language
broch, brochs 23–24, 36, 37
Brochel Castle 226
"broken men" 62, 77, 95, 121
Bronze Age 20, 23, 25, 85
Brora 197
Broster, D.K. 201
Brown, Dorothy 104
Brown, John (19th century) 181
Brown, Keith 79
Browning, Elizabeth Barrett 161
Brú na Bóinne 23, 67
the Bruce, Robert *see* Robert I, the Bruce
The Bruce see *The Brus*
Bruce, James 198
Bruce family 40–41, 51
Bruce invasion of Ireland 40–41, 50, 76
Brummell, Beau 176
Brunton, Mary 169
The Brus/The Bruce 41, 159
Bryggen 44
Brythonic 9
Buchan *see* Alexander, Earl of Buchan
Buchan, John 105
Buchanan, Dugald 163–164, 173
Buchanan, George 8, 30, 178
Buchanan, John Lane 143, 144, 148
Buidhe, cognomen 42
Burberry tartan 180
Burgundy 31, 184
Burke, Betty, imposture of 137
Burke, William 143
Burnet, Thomas 17
Burns, Robert 114, 121, 125, 161, 164–165, 166, 221; "To the immortal memory" 224
Burns Night dinner 224
"Burns of the North" 163
Burt, Edmund/Edward 17, 120–121, 123, 124, 125, 126, 141, 143
Burtisland 115
"The Butcher," slur on Cumberland, Duke of 136
The Butcher's Broom 201
Bute, Isle of 15, 16, 47, 56; *see also* Argyll and Bute
Byron, Lord 165, 169, 171, 181; quoted 165

cadet branch 72, 73, 83
Caesar, Julius 8
Cailean see Colin, name
Cairill 38
Cairngorm mountains 17
cairns, ancient monuments 23, 45
Cait 35
Caithness 15, 16, 17, 32, 35, 45, 46, 59, 152, 194, 203, 219
Caithness, Earl of 152
Caledonia 17, 23, 36, 215, 225; translated 17

Caledonian Canal 18, 87, 107, 145
Caledonian Forest 86
Caledonian Mercury 131
calendar, New Style vs. Old Style, Gregorian 129
California 184
Callanish, Callernish 23
Calum's Road (book) 226
"Calum's Road" (music) 226
Calum's Road (stage play) 226
Calvin, Jean 91
Calvinism 13, 44, 76, 89, 90, 91–93, 99, 107, 115, 126, 128, 132, 149, 150, 162, 173, 177, 206–209, 214, 215; moderate 90, 207–208; scholastic 93
Cambridgeshire 25
Cameron, Alexander 153
Cameron, Capt. Allan 153
Cameron, Archibald 138
Cameron, Donald 122
Cameron, Sir Ewen 117
Cameron, Clan 3, 52, 64, 80, 82, 108, 109, 117, 123, 145, 220
Cameron of Lochiel (17th century) 90, 94
Cameron of Lochiel (18th century) 117, 122, 131, 132, 138
Cameron of Lochiel (19th century) 208, 212
Campbell, Archibald (early 17th century) 98, 99, 102, 103
Campbell, Archibald (late 17th century) 109
Campbell, Archibald (18th century) 84, 122
Campbell, Lord Archibald (19th century) 187
Campbell, Colin (15th century) 66
Campbell, Colin (17th century) 39
Campbell, Ewan 27–28, 29
Campbell, George 7, 76
Campbell, John (18th century author) 142
Campbell, John (18th century soldier) 116
Campbell, John Francis, of Islay 187
Campbell, John Lorne 156–157
Campbell, Torquhil 84
Campbell, Clan 3, 4, 81, 82, 83–84, 85, 86, 90. 96, 98, 100, 101, 102, 103, 111–112, 117, 119, 130, 138, 173, 185, 220; Islay, gain possession of 81
Campbell name: etymology, Normanization, spelling 66, 83; folk etymology 83; prominence 84
Campbell of Argyll 84
Campbell of Breadalbane 84, 146; Earl of 146
Cambpell of Cawdor 84
Campbell of Glenlyon, Robert 111–112
Campbell of Loudon 84
Campbell of Possil 84

Canada, British North America 3, 4, 50, 90, 140, 146, 150, 180, 184, 185, 190, 192–193, 195, 198, 200, 202, 205, 208, 220; *see also* Atlantic provinces; Cape Breton Island; Gulf of St. Lawrence, Manitoba; Hudson's Bay Company, Ontario; Prince Edward Island, Quebec; Red River; St. Lawrence River; Saskatchewan; Upper Canada; Windsor
Canada Ard 150
"Canadian Boat Song," quoted 199, 202
Canan, Clan 70
Candide 128
Capercailie (musicians) 226
Canmore dynasty 32, 51
Canon Law 74, 76
Caorruill 38
Cape Breton Highlands National Park 199
Cape Breton Island 2, 4, 5, 6, 49, 124, 140, 197, 205, 209
Cape Fear 150
"capital of the Highlands" 217; *see* Inverness, city of
caput regionis 29
Carlisle 133, 137, 172, 175
Carolingian 25
Carrach *see* Alexander Carrach
Carrick 13
Carrickfergus 98
Carson, Kit 43
Carter-Campbell of Possil 84
Carver, Martin 35–36
cash economy 120, 121, 143, 189; *see also* free market economy
Cashel, Rock of 55
Caspian Sea 22
cat, linked to Chattan, Clan 85–86; Mackintosh coat of arms 86
Cat, Pictish region 35
cateran 62, 95, 121
Cath Gairbheach 63
"Cath-Loda: a Poem" 160
Cath Raon Ruairidh 100; *see also* Killicrankie, Battle of
Cathbat (Macpherson character) 160
Catholicism, Roman 5, 13, 32, 42, 43, 44, 74, 75, 90, 91, 93, 94, 98, 100, 105, 106, 107, 109, 110, 111, 114–115, 120, 128, 130, 135, 138, 148, 150, 163, 165, 173, 178, 192, 196, 205, 206, 208, 210, 223; anti–Catholicism, "Popery" 44, 79–80, 90, 91, 98, 105, 109, 111, 114, 120, 131, 132, 148, 149–150, 178, 196; Mass 44, 91, 93, 96; "yellow stick" 150; *see also* sectarian violence
Caton-Jones, Mihael 223
Catriona 186
cattle 144; droving 52, 73, 120, 144, 174, 175; kept in residences 123; mobile wealth 78–79; thievery 78–79, 94–95

"Cattle Raid of Cooley" 38, 78
Catullus 163
Cavaliers (17th century) 97, 101
cavalry 16, 102, 130, 132, 134, 135
Cavan, County 50
Cave of Francis 80–81
Cawdor Castle 32; *see also* Campell of Cawdor
CBE, Commander of the British Empire 188
ceann-cinnidh 193
ceatharnaich 62
ceilidh 5
Ceilidh Trail 5
Celestine (Gilleasbaig) 65
"Celt," "Celtic" caution in using words 8–12; "Celtics" used as a noun 10; etymology 8–9; favorable resonance 10, 75, 187; pronunciation 9, 216
Celtae 8
Celtiberia 9
Celtic Christianity 53
Celltic cross 35
Celtic languages 8–10; academic study 216
Celtic mythology 38, 157–158
"Celtic race" 10
Celtic Renaissance 187
The Celts: Origins, Myths and Inventions 12
Celts, viewed collectively 10, 12, 142–143, 177, 178
cenél, cenéla (pl) 29, 69 defined 29; *see also* clans
Cenél Comgaill 29
Cenél Conaill 69
Cenél Eógain 69
Cenél Loairn 29, 32, 69
Cenél nGabráin 29
Cenél nOengusa 29, 69
census 2, 39, 84, 197; pre-medieval 28
Central Board of Management for Highland Relief 204
ceòl mòr 86
Cesarotti, Melchiorre 161
cétmuinter 75, 76
Chad 17
Chadwick, W.H. 34
chainmail 80
Chair of Celtic 187
Chalcolithic period 20
chamber music 108
chambered tombs 23
Charlemagne 7, 25
Charles I 53, 92–93, 97–99, 101, 102–103, 105, 108, 109
Charles II 85, 94, 103, 104, 105, 107, 109
Charles XII of Sweden 117
Charles Edward Stuart, Prince (aka Bonnie Prince Charlie, the Young Pretender) 3, 63, 115, 118, 127, 128–138, 139, 146, 147, 163, 164–165, 172, 178, 183, 188, 220, 224; "Charlie's Song" 139; "The Chevalier's Lament" 164–165; described 128; "king

over water" toast 139; Prince Regent, named 129; *see also* "Pretender"; sobriquet
"Charlie Is My Darling" 139
"Charlie's Song" 139
Chartist movement 209
Chattan, Clan 82, 85–86, 107–108, 132
Chaucer, Geoffrey 156
Chelsea Magazine Company 225
Chelsea Pensioners 146
"The Chevalier's Lament" 164–165
Cheviot Hills 151
Cheviot sheep, True Mountain breed, Long Hill breed 140, 151–153, 162, 194
The Cheviot, the Stag and the Black, Black Oil 201
Chieftains, musicians 104
Childe, V. Gordon 24
Childe Harold's Pilgrimage 171
"Children of the Mist" 84–85
China 22, 177, 183
"Chinaman" 183
Chisholm, Annie Belle 4
Chisholm, Donald, "the Blacksmith" 192
Chisholm, Elizabeth MacDonell 192–193, 194
Chisholm, William 195
Chisholm family or Clan 3, 4, 132, 192–193, 194
Chisholm's Battalion 132
Christianity 25, 26, 27, 35, 36, 38, 53, 74, 75, 93, 118, 151, 209; *see also* Calvinism; Catholicism; Protestantism
Christmas 44, 79, 91
chromosomes, group numbers 36; *see also* haplogroup
Chronica gentis Scotorum 13–17
"Chronicle of the Kings of Alba" 30
Chronicles of England, Scotland and Ireland 32
Chronicles of Mann 55
Chronicles of Melrose 57
Church, Frederic Edwin 161
Church of England 91, 93 99, 109; *see also* Anglican, Episcopal
Church of Scotland *see* Kirk of Scotland
Church of Scotland Free *see* Free Church of Scotland
Churchill, Arabella 109
Churchill, Winston 215
Cille Choirill 5, 38, 98, 107
Cille Chuimein 119
Cináed mac Ailpín 30–31, 35, 45, 55, 56, 59
Cinderella 24
Cior Mhor overture 187
Ciotach, name explained 100
civil war 65, 92, 93, 97–105; *see also* English Civil Wars; Scottish Civil War
clachan, described 123

Clan Donald Centre and Museum of the Isles 65, 82, 145
Clan of the Cave Bear 69
"Clan Unity and Individual Freedom" 76
Clann Iain Dubh 95
Clann Iain Mòr 41, 100; *see also* MacDonald of Dunnyveg
Clanranald *see* MacDonald of Clanranald
Clanrickard 75
clans 28, 39, 41, 51, 54, 58, 68–86, 121, 225; chief, role of 76–77, 121, 125, 127, 138, 174, 204, 210; clan wars 61; confederation 85–86; criminals outside clans 174; definition 69–70; dwindling 146; economic liability 204; enumeration 82–86; etymology of word 69; "gathering of the clans" 176; Heritable Jurisdiction (Scotland) Act dismantles authority 138; loyalty betrayed 193; negative connotations 73, 77; pride and vanity 126; semantics 69, 73; tartans 176–180; *see also cenél; cenéla; tuath*
The Clans of the Scottish Highlands 177, 179
Clark, John (18th century) 159
Claverhouse, 7th Laird of *see* Dundee, Viscount
Clearance 87, 96, 140–143, 145, 151–154, 168, 175, 179, 185, 191, 195–199, 207, 210, 225, 226; distinguish from enclosure 148; in literature 200–202; semantic resonance 140, 147–148; two phases defined 148; *see also* eviction
clergy *see* ecclesiastics
Clonmacnoise 26
Clontarf 46–47
Cluny 198
Clyde, Robert 147, 167, 169, 214
Clyde Estuary 15, 59; *see also* Firth of Clyde
Clydesdale Bank 218
CnaG *see* [no preceding article] Comunn na Gàidhlig
Cnoc na nOs, Battle of 103, 104
An Cnota Bàn 133
coastline of the Gael 26
Cocktail Hour Under the Tree of Forgetfulness 224
Coe, River 83
Coffin, Sir Edward Pine 203–204, 206
Coilleag a' Phrionnsa 129
Coinneach mac Ailpein *see* Cináed mac Ailpín
Coinneach Odhar Fiosache 87; *see also* Brahan Seer
Coleridge, Samuel Taylor 161, 166, 168, 199
Colin, name 66; common among Campbells 83
Colkitto 2, 100; *see also* Mac Colla, Alasdair

Coll, Isle of 56
Collins Scottish Clan & Family Encyclopedia 82
Collis, John 12
Colloquy of the Elders 158–159
Colmóc 35–36
colonialism, colonization 89, 96, 113–114, 139, 142, 146, 147, 222, 224; *see also* post-colonialism
Colonsay, Isle of 56, 95, 100, 216
Colquhoun, Clan 81, 85
Colum Cille, St. Columba 11, 26, 37, 49, 91
Columba *see* Colum Cille
comedy 78, 127, 174, 176, 188, 213–216, 222, 223; farce 215, 224; *see also* Highlanders, comic and satirical
Comgall 29
Comhall (Macpherson character) 159
Commission on Pacifying the Highlands 96, 109
Commonwealth *see* British Commonwealth
Commonwealth (17th century) 93
Communicado Theatre Company 226
An Comunn Gàidhealach 217
Comunn na Gàidhlig, or CnaG 218
concubinage 74, 75, 76
Confederate States of America 59
Confederation Wars in Ireland 97, 99
The Confession of Faith of the Kirk of Scotland (more often known as *The Scots Confession*) 43, 79, 91, 149
Congested District Commission 213
Congregational, Congregationalists 91, 93
Conn Cétchathach 158
Conn of the Hundred Battles 158
Connacht 39, 49, 75
Connemara 50
Conradh na Gaeilge 217
conscription 77; *see also* "levies"; manrent
Conservative Party (UK) 213; *see also* Tory Party
Consider the Lilies 201
Constantín mac Cináeda 31
Continent, Europe 18, 21, 44, 56, 92, 110, 128, 134, 146, 173, 203
Continental Celtic languages 9
Cooper, James Fenimore 161
Cope, Sir John 130–131
Copenhagen 66
Copenhagen *see* University of Copenhagen
Copper Age *see* Chalcolithic period
Cornell University 186
Cornish language 9, 68
Cornwall 12, 25

Corpach 208
Corrie of the Spoil, Battle of 81
Corylus avellana 215
The Costume of the Clans 179
The Cotswolds 13
cottars 121; *see also* subtenant
Coubertin, de, Baron Pierre 184
Coul, location 153
country music 43
country of the Gael 26
Covenanter, Covenanters 92, 97–99, 101, 170, 206; origin 92; semantics of name 92; *see also* Solemn League and Covenant
Cowal Peninsula 28, 29
Cowoer, William 164
Craignish 84
Crannich 192–193
crannóg 27
Crathie 180
Crawford, Ross 78, 79–81, 85
creach 94, 126, semantics 78–79, 94, 126
Creag Bun-Ullidh 202
Creation, creationism 17
creideamh a' bhata-bhuidhe 150
Crichton Smith, Iain *see* Smith, Iain Crichton
crime 126; *see also* bandits
The Crofter and the Laird 80
Crofter Commission Delegation of Powers Act 213
crofters 121; defined 121; *see also* tenants
Crofters Commission 213
Crofters Common Grazing Regulation Act 213
Crofters Holdings (Scotland) Act 212
The Crofters' Party 212–213
Croick 198
cromach, walking stick, defined 214
Cromarty 203; *see also* Ross and Cromarty
Cromdale 110
Cromwell, Oliver 84, 93, 97, 104, 119, 210
Cromwell family 6, 84
Cromwellian Conquest of Ireland (war) 97, 104
Crown, English, royal family 28, 41, 67, 115–117, 137, 146, 165, 180, 182, 190, 205, 206
Crown, Scottish, seat of royal authority *see* Scotland, Kingdom of
Crown Jewels of Scotland 176
Cruthin, Cruithini, Cruthni 33, 34
Cuala Press 187
Cuchulain restaurant 38
Cúchulainn 38, 158
Cuillin Hills 81
cuisine 89, 125, 221; *see also* diet, daily; nutrition
Cùl Lodain, Cùil Lodair 134
Culloden (book) 131, 140
Culloden (film) 131, 136, 140

Culloden House 134
Culloden Moor 3, 78, 82, 101, 104, 116, 122, 125, 126, 127, 130, 139, 141, 142, 146, 147, 149, 174, 186, 192, 200, 211, 216, 223; Battle of 135–136, 164, 172; description and etymology of name 134; misreadings 127; Visitor Centre 222
Culrain 197
cultural appropriation 215
"culture province" 13, 36
Cumall (father of Fionn) 159
Cumberland, Duke of, William Augustus 131–132, 133, 134–137, 173
Cumberland, Richard 162, 214
Cumming, Alan 224
Cunliffe, Barry 9
Cunningham, Wlliam 154
cup-and-ring markings 23, 37
Currie, family or clan 2
An Cùrsa Comais 218–219
The Cycles of the Kings, Historical Cycle 38, 157–158
Cymro 31
Cyril 38
Czech language 161
Czech Republic 8

dà sheallach 87
Dafydd ap Gwilym 160
Dál Riada 24, 26–30, 32, 50, 51, 57, 69, 70, 157
Dál Riada nursery school 29
Dalits 126
Dalredini 26
Dalreudini 26
Dalrymple, John 111, 114
dance 44, 91, 94, 124, 184, 199, 206, 217, 224, 226, Highland and Irish compared 224
Danelaw 48
Danish language 68, 161; *see also* Denmark
"Danny Boy" 137
Dante 224
Danu 69
Danube Valley 9
daoine uaisle 122
Dar-thula (Macpherson character) 159
Darien Company 113
Darien Scheme 113–114, 120, 127
Daughters of the American Revolution 1
David, King, biblical 40
David I, king of Alba/Scotland 56, 57, 58, 60
David II, king of Scotland 60
David Copperfield 92
Davidson, Clan 86
Davies, Peter Maxwell 200
Davitt, Michael 210
"Day of Inverlochy" 102
deasil (ceremony) 175
Declaration of Achallader 111
Declaration of Independence 157
Dee, River 24, 98, 165, 180

deer 70, 103, 126, 158, 161, 175, 181, 182; *see also* stag
Defoe, Daniel 17, 120, 126
deforcement 211
Deirdre 38, 159
Dembling, Jonathan 6
Denis, Michael 161
Denmark 18; *see also* Danish language
deoch an doruis 15
depopulation 87, 99, 199, 216; *see also* Clearances; emigration
derbfhine, derbfine 29, 69; defined 69, 70; etymology 69
Derby 133
Derry, Siege of 110
Derwenterwater, 3rd Earl of 117
Description of the Western Isles of Scotland 74, 77, 178
Desmond Wars 39
Destiny, or the Chief's Daughter 169
Destitution Board 198
Devine, T.M. 17, 44, 120, 124, 140, 141, 145, 146, 149, 150, 189, 221
Devon, 12, 109, 203
Dhòmhnullach 61, 70; *see also* Donald, Clan
diacritical markings 50
The Dial 156
Diana, Princess 182
Diarmait and Gráinne story 186
Diarmid (opera) 186–187
diaspora, Highland 2, 3, 87–88, 146, 201, 204, 220, 223, 224, 225
Dick, Mr., fictional character 92
Dickens, Charles 92, 150, 203, 224
Diderot, Denis 156
"died for the law" 126
Dieffenbaker, John 195
diet, daily 125. 144; *see also* cuisine; nutrition
digraph 50
Dingwall Castle 63, 64
Dio Cassius 34
Diocese of Sodor and Man 47
Diorbhai Nic a'Bhiuthainn 104
"diphyletic" 28
Disarming Act 119, 139
Discipline (book) 169
A Dissertation on the Origin and Progress of the Scythians or Goths 142
distilleries 182, 184, 194, 218; *see also* whisky
Divided Gaels: Gaelic Cultural Identities in Scotland and Ireland 1200–1650 37, 38
divine right of kings 89, 109, 129
divorce, as subject 75; *see also* marriage
DNA (deoxyribonucleic acid) tests 3, 21, 22, 36, 48, 56; *see also* genome; haplogroup
Dochgarroch *see* MacLean of Dochgarroch
Doggerland 18
dolmen 25

Domesday Book 28–29
Dòmhnall Donn 163
Dòmhnall mac Ailpín 31
Dòmhnall Mac Dòmhnuill *see* Donald of Islay
Dòmhnall mac Fhionnlaigh na Dàn 98, 107
Dòmhnall Òg (17th century) 106
Dominiatus Insularum 15
Dominus Inchegal see Lord of the Isles
Dominus Insularum see Lord of the Isles
Don River (Russia) 20
Donaghadee 142
Donald Ballach ("the freckled") 64, 65, 66, 107
Donald, Clan 2, 4, 22, 41–42, 56, 57, 58, 65, 67, 69, 70, 76, 82–83, 84, 85, 98, 102, 106, 108, 109, 130, 150, 172; escutcheon 59; origin of name 61; *see also* MacDonald, clan
Donald of Islay, of Harlaw 62–63
"Donald the Blacksmith" 192
Donaldson, family name 4
Donegal, County 49, 69
Donnachaidh 70
Donnchad, historical figure, medieval 32
Donnchadh, first Campbell lord 83
Donnchadh Bàn Mac-an-t-Saoir 164
Donne, John 89
Donnelly, Peter 12
Don't Let's Go the Dogs Tonight 224
"door-knob" spear butts 37
Dorian, Nancy 216
Dornoch Firth 151
Douglas, Earl of 66
Douglas, Sir James 40
Douglas, Thomas 190
Douglas family and kindred 65–66
Doune Castle (Scott invention) 172
Doune Fair (Scott invention) 175
Dove of Aberdeen 145
Dreghorn 25
Dress Act 139, 162, 176, 178
droving *see* cattle droving
"druid circles" 23
druids 38, 107
Druimm Albin, Druim Albin. Drum Albyn, Drumalbin 27, 28, 35, 45
Drumalban *see* Druimm Albin
Drummond, James 113
Drummond, John 132
Drummond, Capt. Thomas 111–112, 113
Drumossie Moor, Muir 134, 174
Du Teillay, Dutillet (ship) 129, 188
Duart 67
Dublin 40, 45, 46–47, 187, 214
Dublin General Post Office 10

Duchomar (Macpherson character) 160
Duffy, Seán 36
Dugald, son of Somerled 58
Duich, Loch 117
Dumbarton 16, 98
Dumfries 112
Dùn Èideann 208
Dun Emer Press 187
Dún Scáthaige 38; *see also* Skye, Isle of
Dunadd 24, 26, 29, 35, 68; etymology 24
Dunbar 18
Dunbeath 48, 85
Duncan, John 187
Duncan, dramatic character
Duncan, historical figure 32
Duncan, name 70; *see also* Donnchadh
Duncanson, Major 111
Dundee 14, 16, 103, 109–110, 120, 172, 209
Dundee, Viscount, Bonnie Dundee 109–110, 114, 224; *see also* "Bonie Dundee"
Dunedin, New Zealand 208–209
Dunfermline 57, 60, 61
Dunkeld 119
Dunkeld, Battle of (17th century) 110
Dunkirk 115, 133
Dunluce Castle 42
Dunn, Clan 194
Dunnyvaig *see* Mac Domhnail South, MacDonald of Dunnyveg
Dunollie Castle 29
Dunrobin Castle 193, 194, 196
duns, ancient monument 23, 27, 37
Dunsinane 32
Dunyvaig 41, 83; *see also* MacDomhnaill South; MacDonald of Dunnyveg
Dürer, Albrecht 39
Durham 98, 169
Durie, Henry (Stevenson character) 186
Durie, Jamie (Stevenson character) 186
Durness 197
Dutch East India Company 113
Dutch language 161, 168; *see also* Netherlands
Dùthaich Mhic Aoidh 200
dùthchas, defined 72, 173, 210, 212
Dutillet see Du Teillay
Dwelly, Edward 72, 78, 214
Dyfed 31

earl, English term explained 57
"Earse" 36
East Lothian 113
Easter 44, 79, 91
Easter Rising 10
Easter Ross 35, 81, 153
Ecclesiastical History of the English People 26

ecclesiastics, clergy 38, 45, 86, 89; 91, 94, 127, 138, 149–150, 157, 158, 161, 164, 168, 188, 195, 198, 199, 201, 206, 207–208, 209; *see also* Augustinians; Franciscans; Jesuits; monasticism
Edinburgh 15, 16, 18, 29, 32, 37, 41, 42, 53, 60, 65, 66, 76, 79, 85, 89, 91, 92, 98, 103, 104, 115, 116, 125, 131, 132, 133, 139, 142, 143, 162, 164, 169, 170, 172, 176, 182, 185, 186, 207, 208–209, 213, 215, 218; becomes capital 60; City Guard 164; Jacobites capture 131 New Town 177; *see also* University of Edinburgh
Edinburgh Castle 51, 60, 131
Edinburgh Celtic Society 179
Edinburgh Festival 223
Edinburgh Highland Society 179
"Edinburgh of the South" 207–208
Edinburgh Weekly Chronicle 195–196
Education (Scotland) Act 216
Edward II, of England 40
Edward IV 66
Edward the Bruce 40–41
EEF (early European Farmers), ancient population 19
egalitarianism 89
Eigg, Isle of 38, 80–81, 138; slaughter 80–81, 87
Eilean Donan castle 38, 117
Eisteddfod, National 160, 217
El Cid 55, 159
Elcho, Lord (17th century) 101
Elcho, Lord David 136
"Eleemosynary Relief" 204, 208
"Elegy Written in a Country Church Yard" 156, 199
Elgin 32, 62, 63
Elizabeth 1 39, 42, 75, 89, 91, 108, 210
Elizabeth (ship) 129
Elizabeth, younger sister of Queen Anne
Elizabeth II 180, 182
Elizabeth Mure 62
Elizabethan drama 89
Elizabethan illustration 34
Elsick Mounth 24–25
emigration from Highlands 1, 2, 3, 4, 5, 139, 140–141, 145, 147, 148, 149, 150, 187, 190, 196, 199, 202, 204–206, 208
emigration from Scotland 9, 141,
Emmett, Robert 223
Emmons, Alma Randall 186, 221
enclosure, agricultural 148
Engaged 214
England 2, 23, 31, 36, 37, 39, 40, 43, 48, 60, 65–66, 90, 93, 96, 116, 117, 127, 131, 133, 140, 147, 159, 170, 184, 219, 224; *see also* Britain; Church of England; United Kingdom
English Channel 87, 115, 128
English Civil Wars (17th century)

93, 97, 99, 103; First 97; Second 97; Third 97
"English Kirk," pejorative term 94
English language 6, 49, 50, 51, 53, 68, 69, 112, 125, 128, 141; Anglophone 150; *see also* Anglicization
Enlightenment 76, 142, 174, 193
Eochu Riata 26
Eòin Mac Dòmhnuill *see* John of Islay
episcopacy 89; *see also* Bishop
Episcopal Church in Scotland 94, 128; *see also* Scottish Episcopal
Episcopalianism 13, 90, 93–94, 99, 107, 109, 110, 111, 114, 115, 118, 128, 138, 173, 206, non-juring 110, 118, 138, 163, 208; *see also* Anglican; Church of England; Scottish Episcopal Church
Eriboll, Loch 17
Eriskay 129, 187, 188, 223
Eriskay jersey 188
"An Eriskay Love Lilt" 188
Eriskay pony 188
Erra Ghaidheal 26
"Erse" 36, 155
Erskine, John 116
Essays on the Superstitions of the Highlanders of Scotland 168
essentialism 225
Estonians 33
ethnic cleansing 53, 90, 222
"ethnic fallacy," ancient 11
ethnic slurs 4, 40, 113, 176 183, 191, 198
ethnogenesis 25, 28
Etive, Loch 38
Eton 218
Ettrick Shepherd 145
Europe *see* continent, Europe
Eva of MacKintosh 85
evangelicals 93, 207–208
Evening in Balmoral 181
eviction 1, 3, 99, 140, 148, 150, 170, 181, 190, 193, 194, 195, 197, 198, 199, 200, 201, 202, 205, 207, 209, 210, 211, 212, 225; *see also* Clearance
Evidence Taken by Her Majesty's Commissioners ... (Napier Report) 212–213
Ewen Dhubh 95
Exchequer Rolls 183
Excise Act of 1823 184
execution, killing 59, 85, 91, 93, 105, 104, 126, 137–138, 149, 172, 175, 220
Exiles (sculpture) 202
Exploring the World of the Celts 12

factor, factors 149, 192, 193, 194, 195, 196, 198, 205, 210
fada, diacritical mark 50
The Fair Maid of Perth see Scott, Sir Walter
Falkirk 59, 162, 178
Falkirk Muir 134

Falkirk Tryst 162, 164
famine 11, 41, 81, 86, 124, 143, 147, 196, 198, 202, 203, 204, 208, 209; Irish potato 196, 198, 203, 204; Nova Scotia 198, 203; Scottish potato 147, 198, 202–206, 207, 209
"Farewell to the Highlands" 165
farming 3, 10, 19, 43, 52, 121, 148, 151, 152, 153, 184, 190, 193, 194, 195, 198, 202, 203, 208, 211, 224; *see also* EEF; runrig; subtenant; tenant
Farquharson, Clan 86
Farquharson-Macintosh, Lady Anne 132
Farr parish 194
The Fashionable Lover 162, 214
"father of English history" 26
Faughart, Battle of 41
Faulkner, William 78
Feannag 202; *see also* "lazy-bed"
fear thollaidh nan tighean 101
feminisn 75
Fenian Cycle 38, 157–158, 159, 163, 186, 187; *see also* Fianna; Fingal; Fionn mac Cumhaill
Fenyo, Krisztina 1
Ferdinand III 105
Fergus mac Eirc, Fergus Mór 26, 29
Ferriter, Susan 169
feudalism 56, 58, 61, 66, 69–70, 73, 95, 107, 131
Feuds, Forays and Rebellions: History of the Highland Clans 1475–1625 79
Fianna 156–158; *see also* Fenian Cycle; Fionn mac Cumhaill
Fib, Pictish region 34–35
fiction, historical *see* novels, historical, etc.
Fidach 35
fiddle music 5
Fife Adventurers 52, 90
Fife, Fifeshire 15, 34–35, 52
film noir 223
"Fine-Scale Genetic Structure of the British Population" 12, 21
Fingal (character) 25, 38, 155, 158, 159, 161, 162
Fingal (Irish place names) 158
Fingal, an Ancient Epic Poem ... 155, 157; *see also Poems of Ossian*
Fingal's Cave 25, 38, 161, 165, 186
Finlaggan 57, 62, 64, 70
Finland 160, 223
Finn MacCool *see* Fionn mac Cumhaill
Finnish language 20, 160
Finno-Ugric 33, 220
Fiona, Fíona, invention of name 158
Fionn gall 158
Fionn mac Cumhaill 25, 38, 158; antecedent of Fingal 158; etymology 158; variant forms of name 158

fir Alban 31
fir Éirenn 31
fir-tacsa 122
firearms 53
First War of Scottish Independence 59
Firth of Clyde 47, 54, 98; *see also* Clyde Estuary
Firth of Forth 15, 34, 60, 64, 94, 115; *see also* Forth-Clyde slash
Firth of Lorne 18
fish *see* Arctic char; salmon; shell fish; trout
Fisk, William Henry 182
Fitzpatrick family tartans 180
Flanders 119, 131, 133; *see also* Belgium
Fletcher, Andrew 113–114
Flatnose *see* Ketill Björnsson
Flight of the Earls 43, 90
Flodden Field 51, 68, 171, 183
The Flood, biblical 17
Flood in the Highlands 182
folklore 38, 156, 157, 159, 187, 188; coinage of word 159; *see also* ballad; oral tradition
Fontainebleau, Treaty of 129
Fontenoy, Battle of 129
"footprint of fealty" 24
Forays, Age of 68, 78
Forbes, Lord President Duncan 131
Forbes, family 220
Fordun. Johannis de, John 13–17, 51, 61, 125
Forres 32, 35, 62
Forsyth, Kathryn 34
Fort Apache 119
Fort Augustus 119, 137, 168; named for William Augustus 131; names, alternate 119
Fort Francis 119
Fort George 146, 194, 197
Fort William 3, 27, 49, 82, 85, 102, 107, 111, 112, 119, 130, 139, 181, 192, 208, 220; name, etymology and semantics 119, 183; rebuilt as garrison 119
Forth-Clyde line, lateral division, slash 13, 32, 33, 35, 36, 66, 103; *see also* Clyde Estuary; Firth of Forth
Fortiu 35
fosterage, definition of 73
Fotla 35
Fragments of Ancient Poetry ... 155, 159; *see also Poems of Ossian*
France 8, 9, 10, 22, 30, 60, 87, 109, 112, 117, 128, 129, 137, 146, 148, 155, 159, 172, 184, 189, 192, 220, 221
Franciscans, Irish 44, 90, 94
Franks, ancient 28
Fraser, Hugh 80
Fraser, James E. 28, 34
Fraser, Simon 132, 138; *see also* Lovat, 11th Lord
Fraser, Clan 80, 82, 119

Fraser-Mackintosh, Charles 85, 107
Fraser of Lovat 80
Fraser's Highlanders 146
fraudulent emigration scheme 142
Frears, Stephen 182
"The Freckled" *see* Ballach, Donald
Free Church of Scotland 90, 93, 203, 204, 207-209; colonizes New Zealand 208, founded with three competing names 207; Lay Association of 208
free market economy 140, 202, 203; *see also* cash economy
Free Protestant Church of Scotland *see* Free Church of Scotland
French army 129, 130, 132, 137, 138, 146; Irish Brigade of 129; *see also* Irish Picquets; *Royal-Ecossais*
French gold, legend of loss 137
French language 49, 60, 91, 128, 145, 161; *see also* Norman French
French Revolution 166, 167, 170
From Caledonia to Pictland: Scotland to 795 28, 34
From Rebel to Hero: The Image of the Highlander, 1745-1830 147, 214
Fruin, Glen 85
Fry, Michael 140, 201, 206, 208
A Full and Particular Description of the Highlands 142
Fuller, Alexandre 224
Fuller, Nicola 224, 225
Fyne, Loch 29, 83, 111, 181
Fyvie Castle 102

Gabaldon, Diana 88
Gabrán 29
Gabriel's Gully 208
"Gaelic Cowper" 164
Gaelic Development Agency 218
Gaelic-English Dictionary 72
Gaelic in Scotland 51
Gaelic Language Act 219
Gaelic Language Board 219
Gaelic language, Scottish 1-2, 4, 8, 9, 11, 13, 15, 16, 23, 25, 27, 28, 32, 34, 47, 48, 54-55, 68, 79, 82, 120, 155, 156-159, 166, 170, 171, 175, 187, 191, 196, 208; academic study 187, 216-217, 219; advocacy groups 217-219 anti-Gaelic slurs 4, 176, 191, 198, 200, 204, 212, 214, 226; compared with Irish language 49-53; dialogue quoted 156-157; divergence from Old Irish 36-37, 49; Norse influence 48; orthography 50; phonetics 48-50; pidgin Gaelic 215; vocabulary 50; *see also* Irish language; poetry in Gaelic; proverbs in Gaelic

Gaelic League 49
Gaelic Society 217
Gaelic League (Ireland) 217
Gaelic nationalism, Highland nationalism 51, 55, 68, 145, 183
Gaelic Revival 157
Gaelic Scotland in the Colonial Imagination 96
Gaelic Sources of Macpherson's Ossian 157
Gaelophobia 153; *see also* Lowland perceptions of Highlanders; scientific racism
Gaels 25-26, 29-30, 35, 69, 175, 177, 185, 187, 191, 203, 208, 210, 224; *see also* Goidel
Gaeltacht (Irish) 13, 223
Gaeta, siege of 128
Gàidhealtachd 3, 5, 6, 7, 13, 31, 32, 35, 53, 54, 61, 74, 75, 81, 83, 90, 91, 95, 100, 101, 117, 120, 123, 138, 140, 141, 144, 145, 159, 164, 168, 177, 187, 197, 199, 200, 202, 205, 208, 210, 212, 213, 216, 217, 219, 220, 223, 224
Gàidhlig Abrach 4, 49
Gàidhlig Bharraidh 4, 49
Gàighlig Strathglais 4
"Gainsay it who dares" 224
Gairloch 146
Gairm 200, 226
"gal," the phoneme 8
Galacia 8
Galahad 158
Galldacht 51, 53; *see also* Lowlands
Gallgáedil, Gall Gàidheall 46, 54, 56
Gallic Wars 8
Gallienus Redvivus, or Murther Will Out 112
Galloway 13, 46
gallowglass, galloglass 39, 41, 42; translation 39
Galway, County 50
games, Highland/Scottish 150, 181, 184-185, 220, 224
"Garden Province" 149
Garibaldi, Giuseppe 224
Garth *see* Stewart of Garth, David
Gascony 31
Gaskill, Howard 179
Gaul 9
Gavrinis 37
Gearsdan 119
Geddes, Jenny 88, 92
Geddes, Patrick (person) 187; *see also* Patrick Geddes, publisher
Geddes, Thomas 151-152
genealogy 1-2, 121, 126
General View of the Agriculture of the Counties of Ross and Cromarty 153
"Genetics, Linguistics and Pre-History: Thinking Big and Thinking Straight" 22-23
Geneva 91
genome 21, 22, 45; *see also* DNA;

haplogroup; Human Genome Project
The Gentleman's Magazine 155
George I, Georg Ludwig, George Louis 115-116
George II 131, 134
George III 147, 150, 176
George IV 139, 176-177, 178, 179, 180, 197, 213
George IV Bridge 177
George, Henry
George Square 170
George Street 207
Georgia, Colony of 150
Georgian language 20, 161
German language 49, 116
German scholarship, universities 9, 10, 13, 216
Germanic languages 8, 10, 20, 31
Germany 8, 93, 98, 115-116, 223
Gibbon, Lewis Grassic 189, 222
Gibson, Henry 150
Gibson, Mel 40, 169
Gigli, Beniamino 214
Gilbert, W.S. 214
Gildas 26
Gillanders, James 198
Gillanders, James Falconer 197
Gille Íosa family 145
GilleAdamnan 56
Gilleasbaig *see* Celestine
GilleBride 56
Gillespie, Thomas 150, 192
Gillis, Angus Bàn 5
Gillis, William 43
Gillis family 3, 5, 145
Givinchy 225
Gladstone, William Ewart 210, 211-212
Glamis 32
Glasgow 10, 16, 67, 114, 134, 148, 168, 170, 196, 206, 209, 211, 216, 225; *see also* University of Glasgow
Glasgow International Airport 58
An Gleann Mòr 18
Glen Albyn *see* Great Glen
"Glen-Almain; or, the Narrow Glen" 166
Glen Fruin, Battle of 81
Glen More *see* Great Glen
Glen Roy 38, 101, 108, 163
Glen Shiel 118, 130
Glenbucket *see* Gordon of Glenbucket, John
Glencalvie 197
Glencoe 80, 111-112, description 112
Glencoe (book) 140
Glencoe, Argyllshire (painting) 182
Glencoe, Massacre 83, 108, 111-112, 113, 114, 131
Glendale 211
Glenelg 198
Glenfinnal Viaduct 183
Glenfinnan 130, 131, 132, 133, 183, 188
Glengarry, Canada 150-151, 192

260　Index

Glengarry Glen Ross (stage play) 221
Glengarry, landform 83, 107, 192; *see also* MacDonell of Glengarry
Glenlivet 94, 184
Glenlochy 84
Glenloy 86G
Glenlyon *see* Campbell of Glenlyon, Robert
Glenn Albainn 18
Glenshiel 118
Glenstrae 84
Glenyla *see* Lochow and Glenyla
Gloomy Memories in the Highlands of Scotland 185, 196, 200, 201
"Glorious Revolution" 107, 108, 131, 149, 206
Glorious Twelfth 111
gneiss 17, 23
God, Biblical deity 70, 89, 92, 93, 125, 201
Godred 57, 58
Godred Crovan 47
Goethe, von, Johann Wolfgang 156, 161, 177
Goidelic, *Goídel* 9, 25, 27, 33; *see also* Gaels
"Gol na mBan san Ár" 104
gold 130, 137, 208; gold rush 208
Golspie 194, 196, 202
Goodare, Julian 53
Gordon, Catherine 165
Gordon, Duke and Duchess of 168, 184
Gordon, Elizabeth *see* Sutherland, 1st Duchess of
Gordon, George *see* Byron, Lord
Gordon of Cluny, John "Colonel" 198, 205–206
Gordon of Glenbucket, John 129
Gordonsburgh 119
Gorsedd 160
Gospel 45, 70, 91; authorship 207; *see also* Bible; New Testament; Scripture
Goths, ancient 28, 142
Gràdh Geal mo Chridhe 188
Graham, James *see* Montrose, Marquis of
Graham, John *see* Dundee, Viscount
Grameid 110
Grampian line 16, 27
Grampian Mountains 16, 25, 100, 165
Grand Ball, 1822 176
granite 17
Grant, Anne 168–169, 178, 185
Grant, Donald 108
Grant, I.F. 70
Grant, James 168
Grant, Clan 6, 80, 119
Grant, family name 85
Gray, Thomas 156, 199
Great Bernera 210
Great Britain *see* Britain

Great Disruption *see* Kirk of Scotland
"great drill square" 146
Great Feud: The Campbells and the MacDonalds 84
Great French Wine Blight 184
Great Glen 3, 18, 80, 83, 119, 168
Great Lakes 190
Great Moss 24
Greece 170, 185
Greek language 8, 9
"green winter" 196
Greenock 16, 149
Greenock-Dundee line 14
Gregor, alleged ancestor 84
Gregorian Calendar 129
Gregory, Donald 74
Grieve, Christopher Murray 189
Grimble, Ian 163, 196
Grimm, Jakob 159, 187
Grimm, Wilhelm 159, 187
Gruids 197
Gualda *see* Galda, Ronald
Gucci 225
A Guide to Early Irish Law 75
Gulf of St. Lawrence 148
Gunn, Neil 48, 201
Gunn, Clan 194
gunpowder 63
Gurkhas 147
Gwynedd 31

Haag, Carl 181
Haakon, King 58–59
Habsburg dynasty 128
Haggard, H. Rider 222
Hall, Betty Stuart 220
Hall, Lee 223
The Hall of Ossian 181
Hallaig 200, 226
Hallstatt 9, 11, 178
Hamburg 140
Hamilton, Ontario 206
"Hammer of the Norse" 48, 54–58
Handasyde, General 133
Handel, George Frideric 136
handfasting 74, 125
hanged, drawn and quartered 59, 104
hanging, execution 91, 59, 85, 104, 126, 137, 138
Hannibal 102
Hanover, House of, Dynasty 115–117, 128, 130, 131, 133, 138, 139, 172, 222; *see also* Cumberland, Duke of; George I; George II; George III; George IV
Hanoverians 77, 119, 122, 131, 132, 134–137, 146, 150, 164, 166, 172; term explained 134
haplogroup 21–22, 36, 70; *see also* chromosomes; DNA; genome
Harald Fairhair 46
Harbison, Janet 104
Harbour View 4
Hardy, Oliver 216
Hare, William 143
Harlaw, Battle of 2, 62–63, 79, 96

harp 91, 162
harper 67, 104
Harris, Isle of 46, 67, 142
Harrower, David 226
"Harry Lauder's walking stick" 214–215
Harry Potter films 183
Harvard University 21
haute couture 224–225
Havana 170
Hawthorne, Nova Scotia 4
Hay, Charles Allen 178
Hayne, Barrie 162
Heaney, Seamus 200, 224
heather 17, 51
Hebrew 10
Hebridean migrant workers 210–211
Hebrides, collectively 26, 39, 42, 45, 47, 56, 58, 82, 83, 150, 188, 199, 210, 223; *see also* Inner Hebrides; Outer Hebrides
Hebrides Overture 25, 161, 186
Hechter, Michael 96, 139
Hector (ship) 149
Hekla volcano 17, 19, 23
Helensburgh-Stonehaven line, 14, 16
Helmsdale 202
Hemingway, Ernest 221
henchman, semantics of 77–78
Henderson, Ewan 200
Henry II 41, 75
Henry VI 66
Henry VII 68, 91, 97
Henry VIII 61, 109
Heritable Jurisdictions (Scotland) Act 138
herring, herring industry 126, 195, 197
Hessian mercenaries 134
L'Heureux (ship) 137
Hibernia 25, 168; *see also* Ireland
Hiberno-Norman heroics 39
High King *see* Ard righ, Ard Rí
Highland and Island Emigration Society 204
Highland and Islands Development Board (HIDB) 213
"Highland Boundary Fault" 14, 16
"Highland charge" 100–101, 108, 110, 118, 136; origin 100; translation 100
The Highland Clans 82
The Highland Clearances (Prebble) 140, 196, 201
The Highland Clearances (Richards) 140, 197
Highland Council Area, post-1974 14, 16
Highland fling 224; *see also* dance
Highland Land Law Reform Association 211–213
Highland Land League 212–213
Highland line *see* Highlands, borders of

Index

"Highland Mary" 165
Highland Memories suite 187
Highland nationalism *see* Gaelic nationalism
"Highland Rape" 225
Highland River 48
highland romance 76, 77, 88, 168–169, 171, 181–182, 185, 201, 205, 221–222; erotic 222; *see also* novels, historical
"Highland Romance Fiction" 221–222; erotica 222
Highland Society of London 162, 165, 179
Highland Tours 145
Highland Warrior: Alasdair Mac Colla and the Civil Wars 100
"A Highland Widow" *see* Scott, Sir Walter
The Highlander (publication) 210–211
"The Highlander in Scottish Prose Fiction" 186
"Highlander," semantics of word 221
Highlanders, character: admirable 169; attributed 125–127; comic and satiric 47, 162, 213–216, 223; heroic 168–169; *see also* Lowland perceptions of Highlanders
Highlanders: A History of the Gaels 90
Highlands: borders 14–17, 132, 151; cultivation, agricultural 17–18; definition 1, 13–18; geology 17–18; landscapes 17; population 2, 17; rainfall 18
Highlands and Islands, electoral district 16–17
Highlands and Islands Enterprise (HIE) 213
Hill, Lt. John 111
Hiller, Wendy 223
hillforts 23, 37
hip-hop music 69
Historia Majoris Britanniae 16
Historic Scotland 24
Historical Cycle *see* The Cycles of the Kings
A History of Greater Britain as well England as Scotland 79
A History of Quadrupeds 143
History of the Destitution in Sutherlandshiire 196
A History of the feuds and conflicts among the clans ... from the year 1031 unto 1619 79, 128, 142, 162
History of the Highland Clearances 196
"The History of the Men of Scotland" 28–29
Hitler Diaries 179
Hobsbawm, Eric 179
Hogg, James 145
Holished, Raphael 32
Hollywood 119
Holy Roman Empire 105

Holyrood Castle, Palace 64, 92, 104, 172
Home Rule (Irish) 210, 211
Homer 156, 160, 162
homespun 52
homosexuality 75
Honours of Scotland 176
horse manure 124, 125, 145, 223
housing, described 123, 143
How the Scots Made America 140
Hudson Bay 191, 195, 202
Hudson River School 161
Hudson's Bay Company 190, 191
Hugh (Ùisdean), son of Alexander 65, 76
Human Genome Project 22, 45
"The Humble Petition of Bruar Water to the Noble Duke of Athole" 165
Hume, David 142, 155, 170, 176
humor 127
Hungary 8, 184; Hungarian language 20, 161
Huns 19
Hunter, James 142
hunter-gatherers *see* WHG
Hunterston Brooch 29
hunting 19, 70, 119, 126, 139, 181, 182, 209, 143
Hunting the Fairies 223
Huntly, Earl of 80, 91
Hussein, name 67
Hutchinson, Roger 226
Hyde, Douglas 217

I Know Where I'm Going! 223
Iain Dubh 95
Iain Lom 38, 65, 77, 95, 102, 104, 105–108, 110, 111, 112, 114, 127, 159, 162, 181, 224; commemorated 107; name explained 105; named Poet Laureate 107
Iain mac Dhòmhnaill mhic Iain mhic Dhòmhnaill mhic Iain Alainn *see* Iain Lom
Iain Mac Dòmhnuill *see* John of Islay
Iain Manntach 105
Iain Mòr, Clann *see* MacDomhnaill South
Iberia 8, 9, 22, 144; *see also* Celtiberia; Portugal; Spain
Ice Age 19
Iceland 17, 44, 45–46
IE *see* Indo-European family of languages
Iliad 10
illegitimate birth 6, 62, 63, 65, 66, 74, 76, 109, 125, 157, 176
Illinois 203
imperial *see* British Empire
impotence, sexual 75
"Improvement" 152, 168, 176, 191; semantics 191–192
Improvement and Romance: Constructing a Myth of the Highlands 124, 126, 214

indentured servitude 73, 142; *see also* manrent; thirlage
India 19, 20, 96, 147; Conquest of 96: Governor General of 212
Indies *see* West Indies
indigenous peoples 68, 62, 191, 220
Indo-European, IE, family of languages 8, 10, 19–20, 34
Indo-Europeans *see* PIE
Indonesia 184
Ingibiorg 32
Inglis 51
Ingre, Jean-August-Dominique 161
ingressive pulmonic speech, IPS 50
Inheritance (book) 169
An Illicit Still in the Highlands 182
Inner Hebrides 16, 25, 26 39, 46, 47, 48, 54, 83, 100, 198, 205; *see also* Coll, Isle of; Colonsay, Isle of; Eigg, Isle of; Iona, Isle of; Islay, Jura, Isle of; Isle of; Mull, Isle of; Raasay, Isle of; Rùm, Isle of; Skye, Isle of; Small Isles; Staffa; Tiree, Isle of
inoculation 141, 190
Insular Celtic languages 9
Insular Style 29
Internal Colonialism 96
International Phonetic Alphabet, IPA 50
Internet searches 33
interregnum 59
invasion of the British Isles by Celts, assumed 11
"Invented Tradition: The Highland Tradition of Scotland" 179
The Invention of Scotland: Myth and History 179
Invention of Tradition 179
Inverary 83, 84, 111
Inverary, Lord 84
Invergarry 106–107
Invergordon 203
Inverlair House 106, 107
Inverlochy 2, 65, 119, 182
Inverlochy, Battle of, first 64–65, 107
Inverlochy, Battle of, second 65, 96, 102, 104, 106, 121, 146
Inverlochy Castle Hotel 3, 220, 223
Inverness, city of, castle of 63, 64, 77, 86, 103, 116, 118, 119, 120, 134, 137, 146, 176, 192, 193, 217; "capital of the Highlands" 217; sheriff 77, 153, 211
Inverness-shire 4, 15, 16, 35, 36, 38, 43, 82, 85, 132, 136, 148, 150, 151, 153, 155, 168, 176, 197, 198, 211, 212, 218; *see also* Badenoch; Lochaber
Inversaid 167
Inversneyde 167
Inverurie 63

Iolo Morganwg *see* Williams, Edward
Iona, Isle of 11, 26, 27, 29, 30, 37, 45, 48, 49, 52–53, 56, 86, 91, 219; *see also* Statutes of Iona
IPA *see* International Phonetic Alphabet
IPS *see* ingressive pulmonic speech
Ireland 10, 11, 12, 13, 22, 23, 25, 27, 28, 31, 33, 34, 36, 45, 66, 70, 73, 75, 78, 84, 89, 97, 103, 106, 109, 114, 125, 141, 142, 144, 147, 156, 159, 164, 168, 170, 175, 183, 186, 198, 199, 202–206, 210, 216, 218; Irish whiskey 183, 184; Lordship of 97; relationships with Highlands 27–29, 36–44, 68; stage Irishman 214; tartans 180; *see also* famine, Irish
Ireland, Republic of 43, 49, 68
Irish Brigade, of the French army 129
Irish Christianity, Church 75
Irish Franciscans *see* Franciscans
Irish Free State 43, 49, 217, 218
Irish language 9, 11, 13, 20, 24, 27, 36, 39, 47, 156, 183; compared with Scottish Gaelic 49–53; phonetics 49, 50; Ulster dialect 44; vocabulary 50; *see also* Gaelic; ogham; Old Irish
Irish music 137
Irish Picquets 132; function defined 132
Irish pubs 223
The Irish Rebellion (17th century) 97, 99
The Irish-Scottish World in the Middle Ages 36
Irish Sea 26
Iron Age 20, 24, 33, 35, 178
Is Treasa Tuath na Tighearna 212
iska baha 183
Islay, Isle of 29, 37, 41, 56, 57, 60, 61, 64, 70, 81, 83, 84, 100, 143, 187, 219; awarded to Campbells 81; described 57; *see also* Alexander of Islay; Donald of Islay; John of Islay
Italian language 49, 128, 161
Italian restaurants 224
Italy 2, 8, 9, 79, 86, 117
itch, itching 124, 214
Ivanhoe see Scott, Sir Walter
Ivory, William 211

Jackson, Andrew 43
Jackson, Anthony 35
Jackson, Kenneth H. 34, 36, 49
Jacobean drama 89
Jacobins 167
Jacobite restoration of 1708, attempted 115
Jacobite Rising of 1715 77, 116–117, 127, 128, 130, 131, 133, 135, 146, 165, 173–174, 184

Jacobite Rising of 1719 117, 127, 129, 130, 131
Jacobite Rising of 1745–1746, 77, 79, 127–139, 146, 156, 162, 164, 171–173, 186, 220; Charles's Year 130; Jacobite Council 133; "Out," supportive clans enumerated 132; uniforms 132–133
Jacobite Cruises 200
The Jacobite Rising (opera) 200
Jacobite Steam Train 183
Jacobite Trilogy 201
Jacobites, Jacobite Rebellions 3, 33, 44, 53, 63, 82, 83, 90, 96, 104, 106, 110, 111, 112, 114–115–117, 122, 127–139, 142, 148, 149, 165, 167, 171, 181, 189, 192, 215, 220, 222, 224; Council 133; Manifesto 130; origin and naming of 110; "Out," definition and enumeration 131–132; Royal Standard unfurled 130
Jacobites: A New History of the '45 Rebellion 127
James, Henry 186
James, Simon 11–12
James I, of Scotland 60, 63, 64, 165; assassinated 60
James I (James VI of Scotland) 31, 43, 52–53, 67, 74, 79, 81, 85, 86, 89–90, 91, 107, 114, 129, 183, 204, 210, 213, 216
James II, of Scotland 65
James II, of England (James VII 0f Scotland) Duke of York 94, 96, 106, 107, 108–110, 115, 149; linked to New York 108
James III, of Scotland 65, 66, 67, 107
James III or England & James VII of Scotland (proposed titles) 115
James IV of Scotland 25, 51, 54, 59, 67–68, 183
James V of Scotland 171
James VI of Scotland *see* James I, of England
James VII of Scotland *see* James II, of England
James Francis Edward Stuart, the Old Pretender 96, 109, 110, 114–115, 116–117, 118, 128–129, 130; declared king of Scotland 131; *see also* "Pretender" sobriquet
Jamestown 89, 96
Jarvie, Bailie Nicol (Scott character) 174
Jeannie Deans 186
Jefferson, Thomas 156, 157, 161
Jeopardy! television show 2
Jesuit, Jesuits 91, 149
"Jesus and No Quarter" 92
jewelry 11, 24, 27, 29, 162
Jewish intellectuals 223
Jewish legends 40
Jews, in Scotland 149
Johannes Scotus Eriugena 25
John XXII, pope 40–41

John, younger brother of Donald of Islay 62
John Móideartach 76
John Muir Award 218
John Murray, publisher 141
John of Islay, Earl of Ross 65–67
John of Islay, the Good 60, 61–62, 96, 105; name explained 61
"John the Bungler" 65
John the Good *see* John of Islay
John the Irishman 25
Johnson, Dr. Samuel 3–4, 17, 36, 74, 80, 96, 122, 127, 139, 140, 143, 144, 156, 160, 164, 165, 166, 213
Johnstone, clan 82
Jolson, Al 215
A Journal of a Tour to the Hebrides 140
Journal of Genetic Genealogy 21
A Journey to the Western Islands of Scotland 140
Joyce, James 170, 224
Judas Maccabeus 136
judge, judges 61, 75–76; *see also* Brehon law
Jura, Isle of 56
justiciar 70

The Kalevala 160
Kalmar Union 65–66
Kansas 54
Keats, John 25, 145, 165, 181
Keith, George 117, 118
Keith, James 117, 118
Kells Monastery 45
Kelly, Cindy 226
Kelly, Fergus 75
Kelly, the Rev. George 130
Kelp, kelping industry 120, 144–145, 162, 189, 204, 205
Keltoí 8
Keneabin 197
Kennedy-Fraser, Marjory 187
Kenneth I, King 30; *see also* Cináed mac Ailpín
Kenneth Oaur, Kenneth Owir 87
Kennington Common 138
Keppoch, Chief of 106
Keppoch House 106, 107, 138; *see also* Bàrd na Ceappaich; Bard of Keppoch; Keppoch Murders; MacDonell of Keppoch
Keppoch Murders 77, 108
"kernel of tradition" 28
Kerouac, Jack 221
Kerrill 38
Ketill Björnsson, Ketil, Flatnose 46–47
Kettle, Charles 208
Kidnapped 133, 186
Kiev *see* Kyiv
Kilchrist 81, 85
Kildermorie 153
Kildonan, Strath of 194, 195, 202
Kiliwhimmin 119
Killechyrille 38
Killiecrankie, Battle of 108, 110, 112, 121, 178, 225; *see also* "The Braes O' Killiecrankie";

"Sonnet in the Pass of Killiecranky"
Killin *see* Stuart of the Rev. Killin, James
Killop, family name 4
Kilmarnock, Lord 138
Kilmartin Glen, Village 24, 29
Kilmuir 211
Kilravock *see* Rose of Kilravock
Kilsyth, Battle of 103
kilt 121, 124, 131, 133, 139, 147, 150, 176, 177, 189, 197, 214, 216, 222; first citation of word 121; Scott's promotion of 176–177
kiltie bands 4, 150
Kinadius 30; *see also* Cináed mac Ailpin
Kincardine, Kincardineshire, Mearns 15, 189
King James translation 89
"king of Argyll" 57
"King of the Isles" *see Rex Insularum*
The Kingdom of the Isles 56
Kingussie 156
Kinneil 34
Kintyre and Lorne, Marquess of 84
Kintyre Peninsula 16, 28, 29, 37, 41, 48, 56, 83, 84, 103, 110; name translated 29
Kirk of Scotland, also Established Church 44, 52, 90, 91–94, 97–98, 99, 110, 150, 170, 199, 203, 206–209; Disruption Assembly 207; General Assembly 92, 98, 207; Great Disruption 1843 198, 206, 207–208, 209; Moderates 90, 207, 208; Patronage Act of 1712 206–207; Veto Act 207
Klopstock, Freidrich Gottlieb 161
Knocknanuss, Battle of 103
Knox, Andrew 52
Knox, John 44, 90–91, 149
Knox, Robert 143
Knoydart 198
Koch, J.T. 9
Koh-i-noor 146
Kulturkries 13, 36
Kyiv, previously Kiev 45
Kyle Rhea 144
Kyned, son of Alpyne 30; *see also* Cináed mac Ailpín

Là Inbhir Lochaid 102, 105
"Lachin y Gair" 165
lacunae 33
The Lady of the Lake see Scott, Sir Walter
Laggan river 168
Laing, Gerald 202
laird, word, semantics of 73
Lairg parish 194
"The Lake Country" 13
Lallans *see* Scots language
"The Lament for Mulroy" 108
"Lament for the Women of the Massacre" 104
Lancashire 116

Lancastrians 65–66
Land Law (Ireland) Act 210, 212
Land League (Irish) 210
The Land of the Mountain and the Flood 186
land reform 209, 210–213
Land Rover 182
Landlord and Tenant (Ireland) Act 210, 212
landlords 76, 95, 121, 122, 140, 144, 147, 148,, 150, 151, 153, 155, 162, 185, 190, 193, 195, 198, 200, 203, 205, 207, 209, 210, 213; financial distress 140, 197, 203, 213
Landscape and Memory 18
Landseer, Sir Edwin 181–182, 188, 209
Laney, Battle of 100–101
lang nan daoine 142
Language Death: The Life Cycle of a Scottish Gaelic Dialect 216
Languedoc 184
Langwell 152
Laoidh an Tàilleir 178
Laoidhean Spioradall 164
Largs 59, 69
Larnach Castle 209
Larne 40
Laroch 95
La Rochefoucauld, de, Alexandre 145, 166
La Rochefoucauld, de, Francois 145, 166
La Tène 11
A Late Voyage to St. Kilda 120
Latin language 2, 25, 26, 28, 33, 36, 39, 104, 110, 149, 183; *see also* Roman commentators; Romans
Laud, William 92
Laudabiliter 40–41
Lauder, Sir Harry 214–216; quoted 215
Lauderdale, Duke of 95
Laurel, Stan 216
Laxdalers *see Saga of the Laxdalers*
The Lay of the Last Minstrel see Scott, Sir Walter
Lazowski, Maxmilian 145
"lazy-bed" 202
Leabhar na Féinne: Heroic Gaelic Ballads Collected in Scotland 187
Leatherstocking Tales 162
Lebor Gabála Érenn 43
Lebor na hUidre 157
A Legend of Montrose 105
Leicester sheep 151
Leiden 10
Leipzig, Battle of 171
Lent, season of 150
Lepontic 9
Lerner, Alan Jay 74
Lerwick 44
Leslie, Gen. Alexander 98
Leslie, Charles 112
Leslie, Stephen 12, 21, 37
Letters from a Gentleman ... (Burt) 17, 121–122

Letters from the Mountains 168
Levantine 5
Leven, Loch 83, 95
Leveson-Gower, George Granville *see* Sutherland, 1st Duke of
"levies" among Jacobites 131–132, 134
Lewis Chessmen 47
Lewis, Isle of 23, 46, 47, 48, 50, 52, 67, 87, 90, 117, 145, 205, 210; *see also* Outer Hebrides
Leyden, John 171
Lhuyd, Edward 9, 11
Lia Fáil 26
Liberal Party (UK) 209, 212, 213
Liffey River 46
"Light-headed Marjorie" 150
Ligurian 8
Limerick 46
Lindisfarne 45
"Lines Written in the Highlands After a Visit to Burns Country" 165
lingua Hiberniae 36
linker, diacritical marking 50
Linklater, Erik 136–137
Linn an Àigh 68
Linn nan Creach 68, 79–81, 86–88, 94
Linnhe, Loch 18, 168
Linton sheep, black-faced 151, 155, 197
the Lion *see* William I
Lion, HMS 129
The Lion's Tongue 217
Little Big Horn, Battle of 127
Livesay, Roger 223
Livingstone, Alastair 122, 220
Lloyd, Edward *see* Lhuyd, Edward
Loch, James 191–192, 193, 200, 201
Lochaber 3, 4, 32, 36, 64, 80, 81, 82, 83, 94, 95, 98, 102, 106, 107, 110, 153, 198, 208, 214; Lord of Lochaber 64; Thane of Lochaber 32; *see also* Brae Lochaber
Lochaber, Battle of 64
"Lochaber—The Last Bandit County, c. 1600–1750" 94
Lochalsh 38, 65, 117; *see also* MacDonald of Lochalsh
Lochcarron company 82
Lochgilphead 29
Lochiel *see* Cameron of Lochiel
Lochnagar 165, 181
Lochow and Glenyla, Viscount of 84
Lochy, Loch 80
Locke, John 76
Lockerbie 87
Lockhart, John 177
Lockhart-Ross, Sir John 151–152, 155
Loewe, Frederick 74
Logan, James 177, 178, 179, 180
Lomond, Loch 85, 166, 167, 173

Index

Lonach Games 184
London 48, 53, 76, 84, 89, 92, 94, 113, 114, 115, 121, 125, 133, 136, 137, 138, 146, 165, 169, 181, 214, 223, 225; *see also* Tower of London
Londonderry *see* Derry
"The Lone Shieling" 199
Long Hill breed *see* Cheviot sheep
longphort 46
Lönnrot, Eilias 160
Lord Lieutenant of Scotland 99, 103
Lord Lyon King of Arms 179–180
The Lord of the Isles (poem) *see* Scott, Sir Walter
Lord of the Isles, *Dominus Insularum, Rí Innse Gall, Dominus Inchegal, Triath nan Eilean* 41, 48, 57, 58–68, 70, 74, 78, 79, 81, 82, 94, 105, 126, 143; escutcheon 59; *see also* Donald of Islay; John of Islay
Lordship of the Isles 15, 37, 41, 51, 54, 55, 57, 58–68, 79, 83; initiated 60
Lorn, Lorne 29, 69; *see also* Kintyre and Lorne
Lost Tribe of Israel 8–9
Lothian counties 15
Loudon 84; *see also* Campbell of Loudon
Louis XIV 115
Louis XV 129
Louth, County 41
Louvain 44
Lovat *see* Fraser of Lovat
Lovat, 3rd Lord 80
Lovat, 11th Lord (18th century) 131, 132, 138; Regiment at Culloden 132
Low Countries 8; *see also* Belgium; Netherlands
Lowland perceptions of Highlanders, Gaelophobia 1, 13–17, 39, 73, 79, 85, 96, 101, 102, 123, 124, 12–126, 155, 171, 174, 189, 213–216, 223; "great malice of the Lowlander" 125, 214; intellectual elite 142–143; *see also* anti-Scottish sentiment; Scotland
Lowlands, later industrial Scotland 13, 18, 27, 31, 42, 43, 51–52, 61, 73, 78, 91, 94, 96, 99, 101, 102, 116, 120, 125, 132, 134, 137, 140, 141, 142, 148, 149, 151, 159, 164, 170, 174, 185, 189, 193, 197, 203, 208, 214; definition 1; population 12; *see also Galldacht*
Loyalists, American 147, 150
lumper potato 202–203
Lusitanian 8
Lynch, Michael 198
Lyon Court Books 180
Lyon King of Arms, Lord 82–83

Mabou, Nova Scotia 3, 4
Mabou Pioneers 3, 6
MacAlister, MacAllister, Clan 58, 83
MacAlpin, MacAlpine, Kenneth 30, 55; *see also* Cináed mac Ailpin
MacBean, Clan 86
Macbeth, drama 31–32, 35, 51, 89
Macbeth, historical figure 31–32, 33, 35, 51
Macbethad mac Findlaich 31–32, 35
MacCabe family 39
MacCallum brothers, Hugh and John 159
MacCodrum, John 156–157, 163
Mac Colla, Alasdair, Colkitto 6, 7, 95, 96–97, 100–105, 224; executed 103; heritage 104; name, ambiguities 6, 100, 104, 110, 131
Mac Colla Chiotaich MacDhòmhnaill 6
MacCola, Fionn 201
MacCulloch, Horatio 182
MacCunn, Hamish 186
MacDhomhnaill, Alasdair 100
MacDiarmid, Hugh 189, 201, 222
Mac Dòmhnaill, Iain (17th century) 95
Mac Domhnaill of Sleat, Sir Seumas 106
Mac Domhnaill South 41–42; aka MacDonald Dunnyveg, Clainn Iain Mòr
Macdonald (ship) 150
MacDonald, A.D. 3, 6
MacDonald, Aeneas 130
MacDonald, Alexander (17th cent.) 6, 100
MacDonald, Alexander, (18th century), 163; *see also* Alasdair mac Mhaighstir
MacDonald, Alexander (19th century), 2nd Baron MacDonald 179
MacDonald, Colin 226
MacDonald, Flora (18th century) 137, 147, 150
MacDonald, Flora (20th century) 137
MacDonald, Hugh 65
MacDonald, Hugh of Morar, Bishop 149
MacDonald, John (17th century) *see* Iain Lom
MacDonald, John of Glenaladale 148–149
MacDonald/MacDonnel, Sir John 130
MacDonald, Thomas Douglas *see* MacColla, Fionn
MacDonald family and Clan 4, 6, 52, 54, 56, 61, 63, 64, 65, 66, 67, 70, 76, 80–81, 82–83, 87, 96, 98, 100, 111–112, 185, 198, 220; origin of name 61; *see also* Donald, Clan

Macdonald, Lord in Outer Hebrides 198
MacDonald of Ardnamurchan 83
MacDonald of Boisdale, Lord Colin 150
MacDonald of Clanranald 76, 80–81, 82, 83, 91, 128, 148, 224; Regiment at Culloden 132
MacDonald of Dunnyveg 41, 83, 100
MacDonald of Glencoe 83, 95, 108, 111–112, 132; *see also* Glencoe
MacDonald of Glenaladale 148
MacDonald of Lochalsh 83; *see also* Lochalsh
MacDonald of Sleat 65, 77, 142, 145, 156, 163, 198, 211, 218; *see also* Sleat
MacDonell, Duncan 150
MacDonell, Marjorie 150, 192
Macdonell, Miles 191
MacDonell, Clan, 4, 42, 83, 86
MacDonnell family 39, 42; *see also* Sorley Boy
MacDonell of Glengarry 80, 81, 83, 106, 108, 111, 150, 198; forced removal of tenants 150; of Invergarry 106; Regiment at Culloden 132; *see also* Glengarry
MacDonell of Keppoch 4, 38, 77, 83, 86, 94–95, 105, 107–108, 110, 132, 138, 180; Regiment of at Culloden 132; *see also* Keppoch murders
MacDougall, Clan 29, 58, 83
MacEachráin family 39
Mac Fhearchair, Iain 156–157
MacGilp, family name 4
MacGill-eain, Somhairle *see* MacLean, Sorley
MacGillivray, Clan 86
MacGregor, Duncan 39
MacGregor, James 39
MacGregor, Clan 81, 82, 84–85, 9, 166; name translated 84; proscription 85; *see also* Rob Roy (historical figure)
Mac Ille Ruaidh, Donnchadh 217
MacInnes, 95, Clan 5
Macinnes, Allan I. 93–95
MacInnes, John 52
MacInnes, the Rev. John 76
MacInnes, Mary 188
MacIntyre, Clan 86
MacIntyre, Duncan Bàn 164, 200
Maciomhair 173
Mac-Ivor, Fergus (Scott character) 172
Mac-Ivor, Flora (Scott character) 170–172
MacIvor, MacIcer, Clan 173
Mac-Ivor, Clan (Scott characters) 172–173
MacKay, Alexander 154
MacKay, General 110, 119
Mackay, Margaret 195

Index

MacKay, Clan 163, 200
Mackellar, Mary 187
Mackenzie, Alexander 87, 140, 147, 196
Mackenzie, Sir Alexander 190
Mackenzie, Compton 51, 182, 188, 223
Mackenzie, the Rev. David 195
Mackenzie, Sir George, of Coul 153
MacKenzie, Hugh Breck 153–154
MacKenzie, Kenneth 87
MacKenzie, Clan 2, 81, 108, 117, 173
MacKid, Robert, sheriff-substitute 196
MacKenna, Maddie 222
Mackenzie River 190
MacKillop, family or Clan, 5; name 4; tartans of 180
MacKillop, Alexander 3
MacKillop, Colin 4
MacKillop, Finlay 4
MacKillop, Margaret Gillis 4
Mackinnon, Donald 187, 212, 216–217
Mackinnon, Iain 96
MacKinnon, Kenneth 217
MacKinnon, Clan 52; MacKinnon's Regiment 132
Mackintosh, John (18th century) 77
Mackintosh, Lady, Regiment at Culloden 132
Mackintosh, Brig. William 116
Mackintosh, MacKintosh Clan 64, 80, 85, 107–108, 132; coat of arms 86; name translated 64, 85
MacLachlainn, Iain 200
Maclachlan's Regiment 132
MacIain of Glencoe 111–112
MacIan, R.R. 177
Maclaymore of Lochaber (stage character) 214
Maclean, Lachlan 197
MacLean, Sorley 200, 201, 226
MacLean, Clan 62, 67, 82, 109; name translated 67
MacLean of Dochgarroch 86
MacLennan, Hugh 205
MacLeod, Alastair 5, 146
MacLeod, Calum 225–226
MacLeod, Charles 226
MacLeod, Colin (dramatic character) 162, 214
MacLeod, Dennis 202
Macleod, Donald (19th century) 185, 195–196, 200, 201
MacLeod, Donald, sheriff 153
MacLeod, Fiona 157
MacLeod, John Norman 176
Macleod, Kenneth 188
MacLeod, Màiri 81
MacLeod, Malcolm see MaLeod, Calum
MacLeod, Clan 6, 52, 54, 67, 80–81, 82
MacLeod of Dunvegan (18th century lord) 142

MacLeòid, Niall 200
MacLoughlin, family name 48
MacNeacail, Dòmhnall Bàn 178
MacNeil, Torquil (film character) 223
MacNeill, Eoin 10
MacNeill family or Clan 4, 67, 77, 128, 205
MacPhail, Clan 86
MacPhee 95
Macpherson, James 10, 25, 79, 141, 155–162, 163, 164, 165–166, 168, 170, 178, 179, 181, 187, 188, 189, 224; prose style reviled 160, 170; see also Poems of Ossian
MacPherson, Mary 200
MacPherson, Clan 82, 86
Macpherson's Ossian and the Ossianic Controversy 157
MacQuarrie, Clan 52
MacQueen, Clan 86, 224–225
MacQuillan family 42
MacRae-Gilstrap, John 117
MacRory, Clan 58
mac Ruaidri, Dubgall 39
MacSorley family 39, 55
MacSween, family name 4
MacSweeney family 39
MacTavish Mhor, Elspat (Scott character) 174–175
MacTavish Mhor, Hamish Bean (Scott character) 174–175
MacThomas, Clan 86
MacVicar family 168
Madagascar 21
Máel Ruba, Máelruba 38
Máel-Caluim 32; see also Malcolm
Máelruba see Máel Ruba
Maeshowe 45
magnates 61, 67, 75, 76
Magnus Barefoot, Barelegs, Olafsson, the III 47–48, 56
Magnus VI 59
Mair, John see Major, John
Maitland, James 95–96
Major, John (16th century) 16, 74, 79, 121
Malcolm II 85, 184
Malcolm III, historical figure 32, 48, 51, 60; also Malcolm Canmore (name translated 32)
Malcolm IV, "the Maiden" 57–58
Mallaig 183
Malmesbury see William of Malmesbury
malt tax of 1725 131
Malvina (Macpherson character) 159
Mamet, David 221
"Mammie" 215
Man, Isle of 40, 45, 47, 54, 56, 57; see also Chronicles of Mann
Man, Kingdom of 47, 56, 58
Manchester 133
Manchester Regiment 132
Manco, Jean 21
Mangar Castle 100
Manitoba 54, 151, 191, 195, 202

"Mannie" see Sutherland, 1st Duke of
manrent 73; see also conscription
Mantel, Hilary 186
Manx language 9, 20, 47, 68
Maol Ruadh, Maoile Ruaidh 107; see also Mulroy, Battle of
Maori 33
Mar, Earl of, Alexander Stewart 63, 64–65, 107
Mar, realm of 63, 116
Mar, 6th Earl of 116, 117, 118, 128, 135, 146, 165, 184
"the Marchioness" Prebble's term for Sutherland, Duchess of
Margaret, daughter of Robert II 61
Margaret, Maid of Norway 59
Margaret of Wessex, Saint 32, 51, 60; latterly of Scotland 51
Margaret Tudor 68
Maria Clementina Sobieska 118
Maria Theresa of Austria 128
Maritime Provinces of Canada, also Atlantic provinces 140, 148; see also Cape Breton Island; Nova Scotia; Prince Edward Island
Márkus, Gilbert 11
Marmion: A Tale of Flodden Field see Scott, Sir Walter
marriage 52–53, 74–76, 77, 85, 93, 125; see also divorce
Marriage (book) 169
"Marriage, Divorce and Concubinage in Gaelic Scotland" 74–76
Marsailidh Bhinneach 150
Martí, José 170
Martin, George R.R. 112
Martin, Martin 23, 74, 77, 120, 121, 125, 178
Marxism 191
Mary daughter of James II 109, 111; see also William and Mary
Mary of Modena 109
Mary Stuart, Queen of Scots 51, 52, 89, 91, 107, 108, 149
Maryland 17
Masonic Order, Lodge 165, 170
Mass see Catholicism
The Master of Ballantrae 186
Masterpiece Theatre 140
matchmaking 77
Matheson, Angus 104
Matheson, Sir James 205
Matheson, William 87
Maxwell, Clan 82
McConachy, Peter 138
McDonald, R. Andrew 56, 57–58
McDonald, Roderick 48
McGahern, John 39
McGrath, Douglas 224
McGrath, John 201
McHardy, Stuart 78
McLellan, John, Pipe Major 183
McLeod, Norman 209
McLeod, Wilson 36, 38–39
McNeill, Sir John 204–205

M'Combich, Robin Oig (Scott character) 175
McPhee, John 80
McQueen, Alexander 224–225
Mearns *see* Kincardine
the Mediterranean 223
Mediterranean appearance 5
Mediterranean culture 11
Meek, Donald 179
megaliths 23
Meikle, Maureen 79
Memoirs of a Highland Lady 178
Memoirs of the Most Renowned James Grahan, Marquis of Montrose 104–105
"men of Alba" 31
"men of Ireland" 31
Mendelssohn, Felix 25, 161, 186
menhir 25
Menzies, Patricia M. 78
mercantilism 128
Mercat Cross 85
mercenary soldiers 39; *see also* cateran; Hessian
Merino sheep 151
merk, coin 61
merkland 61
Mesolithic period 19, 21, 23
the Métis 191
Metropolitan Museum, New York 225
Middle East, southwest Asia 19, 21, 41
Middle Irish 26
Middle Stone Age *see* Mesolithic period
mightier than a lord (slogan) 209, 212–213
Milan 49
militia 119, 134, 197, 205
Milton, John 8
Minch 80
Mingary 57
minister, religious cited under ecclesiactics
Minstrelsy of the Scottish Border see Scott, Sir Walter
Mioran mòr nan Gall 125, 214
Mirren, Helen 182
Mitchell, James Leslie 189
Mitchell, Joni 221
Mòd *see* Royal National Mòd
Moderates *see* Calvinism, Kirk
Modern Irish *see* Irish language
Moffat, Alistair 21, 22, 36
Mohawk Valley 150
Mohawks, native Americans 168
Moidart 138, 149; *see also* Seven Men of Moidart
Móideatach, John 76
Mòine Mhòr 24
Moine Overthrust 17
The Monarch of the Glen, painting, novel, television series 182
monasticism, monastery 35–36, 38, 45, 67; *see also* ecclesiastics
Moncrieffe, Sir Iain 82

Monmouth, Duke of (17th century) 109
Monolith 23
Monro, Donald 154
Montgomerie of Ayrshire, Alexander 125, 223
Montgomery's Highlanders 146
Montrose, Marquis of (James Graham) 65, 96–97, 98, 99–105, 106, 109, 131, 224; executed 104, name, etymology of 99; switches affiliations 99
Montrose: A History 105
Montrose: The Captain General 105
Moore, Dafydd 160
Moore, John Robert 166
Moore, Thomas 199
Morar 138, 149
Moray, Morayshire: pre-1974 borders 15, 16, 32, 35, 46, 63, 94, 193; post-1974 borders 14
Morgan, Clan 70
Morganwg, Iola *see* Williams, Edward
Morier, David 132, 178
mormaer, great steward 32, 57, 70; explained 57
Morna (Macpherson character) 160
Morning in the Highlands—The Royal Family Ascending Lochnagar 181
mortar, weapon 118
Morven (Macpherson region) 159
Morvern 56, 57, 62, 159
Morvern Caller 223
Motte-and-bailey castles 58
Muir, John *see* John Muir Award
Muircetach Ua Briain 55
Mulgrew, Gerry 226
Mull, Isle of 11, 26, 48, 52, 56, 57, 62, 67, 155, 186
Mull of Kintyre 37, 82
Mulock, Thomas 198
Mulroy, Battle of 81, 107, 112, 163; causes 107–108
Munich 49
Munro, Donald 154
Munro, Hector 153
Munro, Hugh 197
Munro, Clan 117, 154
Munster 49
"Murderer's Monument" 196
Murdoch, John 210
Murlaggan 3
Murphy's Law 87–88
Murray, Lord George 130–131, 133, 134–135
Murray, John *see* John Murray, publisher
Murray, William 130, 132
Murray, family name 85
Murt Ghlinne Comhann 112
Murt na Ceapaich 77, 106
music 5, 10, 43, 44, 86, 91, 104, 108, 114, 124, 133, 136, 137, 160, 162, 150, 167, 173, 186–187, 188, 200, 203, 214, 219, 220, 226

Muslim discourse 67
Muslims in Scotland 149
mutton 151, 152, 197
"My Heart's in the Highlands" (Burns) 165, 221
"My Heart's in the Highlands" (Saroyan) 221
Mythological Cycle 157

Na Caimbeulaich 66; translated 83; *see also* Campbell, name
Na Caoraich Mòra 152
Nairn, Nairnshire 15, 16, 32, 63, 84, 103, 134, 135
Nairne, Lady 139
Naismyth, John 152
names, Highland Gaelic family: Norse names 48; uniqueness of 2
nan Uamh, Loch 137
Naoise 38
Napier, Francis, Lord 212–213
Napier Commission 210, 212–213, 217
Napoleon I, Napoleonic Wars 144, 145, 151, 161, 171, 173, 177, 197
Naseby, Battle of 103
Nashville 43
National Geographic 120
National Museum of Scotland 29
National Theatre of Scotland 226
Nature journal 12, 21, 37
Nelson's Column 181
Neolithic period 19, 21, 23, 24, 45; *see also* Stone Age, unspecified
Nepal 147
Ness, Loch 13, 18, 64, 80, 87, 131, 137, 192, 201
Ness, River 87
The Netherlands 2; Dutch Republic 103, 113, 117, 129; *see also* Dutch East India Company; Dutch language; Low Countries
Neuchâtel, Lake 11
New Amsterdam 108
New Caledonia (17th century) 113
The New Edinburgh History of Scotland 28, 34
New Jersey, colony of 113
New Model Army 102
New Perth 113
New Stone Age *see* Neolithic period
New Style Calendar 129
New Testament 93, 164 *see also* Bible
New Town *see* Edinburgh
New York (pre-Independence colony) 108, 150, 168
New York, state 2
New York City 5, 225
New Yorker magazine 2, 80
New Zealand, Antipodes 159, 190, 208–209, 210, 220
Newcastle 133
Newcastle-upon-Tyne *see* University of Newcastle-upon-Tyne

Newfoundland 18, 45
Newgrange 23, 25, 37, 67
Newton, Michael 127, 214
Niall Noígiallach 158
Niall of the Nine Hostages 22, 26, 38, 70, 158
Nicholas Nickleby (film) 224
Nicholson, R.G. 73
Nidaros 47
No Great Mischief 146
No Quarter Given 122, 220, 223
Nobel Laureate 186, 200
Noble, Iain 218-219
non-juring *see* Episcopal
Nordreys, Northryars 46-47
Norman barons 58, 63
Norman French 16, 31, 32, 39, 40, 45, 51, 56, 58, 60, 69, 99; *see also* Anglo-Normans; Hiberno-Normans; Scoto-Norman
Normandy 18, 45
Normanites 209
Norn language 68
Norsemen, aka Vikings 2, 16, 17, 18, 29, 30, 31, 35, 36, 44-48, 49, 50, 54, 56, 59, 69, 123, 189, 221; family names 48; mixed with Gaelic population 46, 54, 56, 82; *see also* Denmark; Norway; Old Norse language; Scandinavia
"north Britons" 170
North Carolina 43, 147, 150
North Channel, of the Irish Sea 26
North Island *see* New Zealand
North of the Tay 16
North Sea 18, 87
North Uist 94, 141, 155, 156, 163, 198; *see also* Uists
North West Company 191
the northerlies *see* Nordreys
Northern Ireland 42
Northryars see Nordreys
Northumberland Strait 149
Northumberlandshire 173, 194
Northumbria 30
Norway 19, 44, 47, 48, 54, 56, 57, 58-59, 65-66, 161
Nostradamus 86, 87
Nova Scotia 2, 3, 5, 124, 145, 148, 149, 151, 192, 197, 198, 199, 201, 209
Novar, 8th Laird (18th century) 153
Novar, Laird of (19th century) 197
novels, historical 48, 85, 88, 105, 112, 133, 169, 171-175, 185-186, 201, 221-223; criticized 172-173; prehistorical 69; *see also* Highland romance
nutrition 124, 125; *see also* potato

Oban 29, 112, 217, 223
Ó Baoill, Colm 49-50
O'Brien, Murtagh 55
Observations on the Present State of the Highlands of Scotland 190

Ó Cairbre, Diarmuid 67
O'Casey, Sean 224
Ó Conchobhair, Aedh 39
O'Connell, Daniel 223
O'Connor, Turlough 75
O'Conor, Charles the Elder 156
O'Donnell, Rory 90
O'Donnell family 39
Odyssey 10
OED *see Oxford English Dictionary*
Oftedal, Magne 48
Ogham, ogham pillar 24, 27; *see also* Irish language
Ogilvie, John 91
Oich, Loch 107
oighreachd, defined 72-73
Oilthigh na Gàidhealtachd agus nan Eilean 219
Oisín 158; antecedent for Ossian 158; etymology 158; pronunciation 158
Olaf I, King of Man 56, 57
Old English 33
Old Irish 25, 26, 27, 28, 30, 33, 36, 49, 68, 74, 78, 216; cycles of narrative 157-158, 159; *see also* Irish language
Old Mortality 110
Old Norse language 33, 44, 49, 68; *see also* Norsemen
"The Old Pretender" *see* James Francis Edward Stuart
Old Stone Age *see* Paleolithic period
Old Style Calendar 129
Old Testament 93; *see also* Bible
Oliphant, Cornelia 139
Olympic Games 184-185
O'Neill, Hugh 90
O'Neill, Shane 42
O'Neill family 42
Onondaga County, New York 2
Onondaga County Public Library 222
Ontario 119, 190, 192, 203, 206
Open University 219
Oppenheimer. Stephen 22
oral tradition 38, 57, 80, 81, 97, 100, 105, 142, 157, 158, 214; *see also* ballad; folklore
Òran an Aghaidh an Aonaidh 114
Òran na Comhachaig 86, 98, 107, 156, 162, 182
Orange, House of 109, *see also* William III, of Orange
Orange Lodge, Orangemen, Orangism 109, 110
Orangeman's Day 111
Orchy, Glen 84
Original Collection of Poems of Ossian, Orran, etc. 159
Original Succession Church 206
Origins of the British 22
Orkneys 15, 16, 17, 32, 36, 45, 46, 47, 48, 56, 59, 65, 104, 144, 212, 219
Ormonde, Duke of 117

Orygynale Cronykil of Scotland 30
Osbaldistone, Frank (Scott character) 173-174
Oscar (Macpherson character) 158-159, 161
Oscar (traditional) 158
Oscar I, King 161
Ossian 155, 158, 159, 161, 162, 181; invention of spelling 158; *see also Poems of Ossian*
"Ossian, Scott and Cooper's Indians" 162
Ossianic controversy, skepticism 156-157
"Ossianic," definitions of 158
Ossianic Society of Dublin 158
"Ossian's Address to the Sun" 165
Ostaig 218
O'Sullivan, John William 130, 131, 134
Otago Association 208
Otago Peninsula 209
Our Ladies (film) 223
Our Ladies of Perpetual Succour (stage play) 223
Outer Hebrides 4, 13, 15, 16, 17, 46, 47, 49, 52, 54, 57, 82, 87, 94, 117, 123, 129, 188, 198, 203, 205, 210; *see also* Barra, Isle of; Benbecula; Eriskay; Harris, Isle of; Lewis, Isle of; North Uist; South Uist; Uists; Western Isles
"Over the Sea to Skye" 137
"The Owl" 86
Oxford English Dictionary 77-78, 136, 150
Oxford University 9, 62, 140, 218
Oykel, Strath 197

P-Celtic 9, 20, 27, 28, 31, 33, 34, 36, 49, 83
Pacific Ocean 196
pagan 44, 45, 79, 91, 92, 175
painting, painters 181-182, 187
Paisley 67
Paleolithic period 19
paleontology 28
Palermo 49
Pan Am flight 103 87
Panama 113-114
papacy *see* the Pope
Papal States 117, 128
Paradise Lost 8
"parallel roads" 38
pariah class 126
Paris 87, 115, 129, 184, 130, 184
Paris Exposition of 1889 184
Paris Gazette (17th century) 112
Parliament *see* Scottish Parliament
Parliament, English, also Westminster government; after 1707 called British Parliament 98, 109, 114, 115, 116, 128, 131, 138, 157, 190, 206, 207, 212, 213; Secretary of War 146
Parliament of Scone 60
Parliamentarians (17th century) 93, 97, 98, 99, 101, 102, 107

passage grave 37
Passage to Ararat 2
Passenger Vessels Act 190, 192
Paterson, William 112–113
Pathans 147
patriarchy 71, 76
Patrick Geddes, publisher 157, 160
Patronage Act of 1712 *see* Kirk of Scotland
patronymic 5–6, 100; *see also* sloinneadh
Peanfahal 34
Peel 47
Peelites 209
Pennant, Thomas 87, 121, 143–144, 166, 188, 189
Pennsylvania 43
Persian language 20
Perth, Perthshire 15, 16, 32, 35, 52, 67, 100, 132, 146, 151, 173, 187
Perth, city of 59, 60, 61, 101, 113, 116, 130
Perth, 4th Earl of 113
Perth Amboy 113
Perth and Kinross 14
Peterhead 116
Pezron, Paul-Yves 9
Philadelphia 143
Philip V 129
Philip of Almerieclose, James 110
Philiphaugh, Battle of 103
Phillipson, family name 4
phylloxera bug 184
Phytophthora infestans 203
pibroch 86; *see also* bagpipe
Picasso, Pablo 221
picquet, picket, miliary unit defined 132
Pictavia 35
Pictish language 32–34, 49, 99
The Pictish Trail: A Traveller's Guide to the Old Pictish Kingdoms 35
Pictland 30; regions of 34–36
Pictou 145, 149, 192
Picts 2, 24, 25, 26, 27, 29, 30–31, 32–36, 45, 48, 59; genetic inheritance 36; King of the Picts 31; origins 33; presumed disappearance 36
PIE (Proto-Indo-European) 20, 21, 22, 36; *see also* Indo-European family of languages
pilgrimage 32, 130, 171
pingere 33
pink sea bindweed 129
Pinkerton, John 142
Pinkie Clough 79, 84
Piper Alpha oil rig 87
pit-, prefix 34
Pitcairn 34
Pitgaveny 32
Pitlochry 34
Pitmedden 34
Pitt the Elder, William 146
plaid (garment) 139, 177
plaid (solecism for tartan) 4, 71, 139, 177

Plains of Abraham 146
Plantagenet dynasty 41
Plantation of Ulster 28, 43, 52, 90, 99, 113; *see also* Ulster
Plymouth, colony 96
Poe, Edgar Allan 199
Poems of Ossian 10, 25, 141, 155–162, 168, 169, 170, 187, 189; contributing titles resolved 155–156; Gaelic "originals" 157, 168, 179; *see also Fingal, Temora*
Poems on Various Subjects 168
Poet Laureate 107, 167, 171
poetry in Gaelic 38, 39, 52, 53, 63, 104–106, 110, 121, 127, 142, 156, 158, 162–164, 179, 181, 200; *see also* Iain Lom; *Òran na Comhachaig*; Rob Donn
Poets' Corner 157
Poit Dhubh 218
polio 170
Polish language 161, 178
Polish nobility, royalty 118
Politician (ship) 188
poll tax 148
polygamy 75
poor laws, of Scotland and England compared 204–205
Pope, Alexander 163
Pope Innocent VI 61
Pope, papacy 40, 47, 60, 61, 75, 79, 91, 93; Popish Plot 128
Poppleton Manuscript 30–31
"popular antiquities" *see* folklore
Popular Tales of the West Highlands 187, 188
population, growth of 141, 198
Port Ellen 41
Port Hood, Nova Scotia 4
Port Mo Chalmaig 35–36
Porter, Jane 169, 221
Portmahomack 35–36
Portree 38, 203, 211, 225
Portugal 8
Possil *see* Campbell of Possil; Carter-Campbell of Possil
post-colonialism 96
potatoes 124–125, 126, 141–142, 189, 196, 202–206; fungus 203–205; lumper species 203; *see also* famine
Potter, Harry films 183
Powell, Michael 223
Powys 31
pre-aspiration 48, 50
Prebble, John 5, 131, 140–141, 148, 149, 151, 153, 175, 179, 189, 192, 193, 195, 196, 200, 201, 222
Pressberger, Emeric 223
Presbyterian Free Church 198
Presbyterians 43, 91, 93, 98, 99, 110, 117, 132
Preston 77, 116, 133
Prestonpans, Battle of 131, 134, 172, 173
"Pretender," sobriquet explained 115
primogeniture 69, 70

Prince Edward Island 148–149, 190
Prince Igor 159
The Prince in the Heather 137
Prince Regent (19th century) 176
Prince's Cockleshell Strand 129
Princes Street 170
Pritani 33–34
Privy Council of Scotland, Act of 53; *see also* Scotland, Kingdom of
Problem of the Picts 33
Progress and Poverty 211
Prosperity, Age of 68
Protestantism 42, 43, 52, 93, 98, 99, 100–101, 108, 109, 115, 117, 128, 131, 149, 150, 206, 207
proverbs in Gaelic, quoted 127
Provision for the Poor in Time of Dearth and Scarcity 120
Prussian army 118
pseudo-history 27, 43,
public school, schools 112
Public Television in U.S., PBS 140
Puritanism 92, 106, 127, 164; semantics 92
Putting Pants on Philip 216
"Puzzle of the Picts" 33
Pyrenees 221

Q-Celtic 9, 20, 27, 28, 31, 33, 34, 36, 49
Qritani 33
Quadruple Alliance, War of the 117
Quakers 91, 128
Quebec, city 146, 155
Quebec, province 150, 198, 206
The Queen (film) 182
quern 24
Quincey, de, Thomas 199
Quoich, Loch 150

Raasay, Isle of 35, 138, 200, 225–226
The Races of Men 143
racism 142; *see also* scientific racism
Radclyffe, James 117
Ragnhild, Ragnhildis, Ragnhilde 56
Raghnaill Òg (17th century) 106
Raghnall *see* Ranald Òg (16h century)
Ragnvald 58
rail, railway 87, 182, 183, 196, 203, 214, 218
Rainy, George 200
Ramsay, Lynne 223
Ranald, son of Somerled 58, 61
Ranald Òg 86 (16th century)
Ranger, Terence 179
Rankin family 3
Rannoch 98
rascal, Gaelic term 95
Rathlin Island 40, 54
Recollections of a Tour Made in Scotland, AD 1803
red coats 134, 146, 194, 197; term

explained 134; *see also* British Army; Hanoverians
"Red Harlaw" 63
Red River 191, 195, 202
Reform Act of 1832 170, 207
Reformation 79–80, 90, 91, 207
Reformed Presbyterian Church of Scotland 206
regulus of Argyll 57
Reich, David 7
Reid, Mr, Sutherland agent 194
Reid Harlaw 63
reiver, semantics of 78
The Reivers 78
Relief Church 206
Renfrewshire 16, 58
"rent-a-thug" 95
The Reprisal: or, The Tars of Old England 214
Rerum Scoticarum Historia 30
Restoration of Stuart dynasty 85, 92, 94, 95, 104, 107, 111
Reuda 26
revocable lease 107
rex, the Latin term explained 57
Rex Insularum 60
Rex Manniae et Insularum 47
Rex Pictorum 31
Rhodesia 224
rí, Gaelic and Irish term explained 57
Rí innse Gall see Lord of the Isles
Riasgan (Gunn creation) 201
Richard de Clare 41
Richards, Eric 140, 195, 196
Riding, Jacqueline 127, 132, 135–136
ringfort 27
Riot Act 194
Riverdance 224
road building 119, 226
Road Making & Maintenance: A Practical Treatise ... 226
"Road to the Isles" 183, 188
Roag, Loch 2
Roanoke Indians 34
Rob Donn 163, 224
Rob Roy (novel) *see* Scott, Sir Walter
Rob Roy, historical figure 85, 166, 167, 173–174, 175; *see also* MacGregor, Clan
"Rob Roy's Grave" 166, quoted
Robeson, Paul 137
Robert I, usually Robert the Bruce 31, 40, 54, 60, 69–70, 83, 84; distinguish from others with same name 40
Robert II 60, 61, 62, 180
Robert, Duke of Albany 62, 63
Robert of Poppleton 30
Roberts, John L. 79
Robertson, Clan 70
Robertson, William 198
Robin Hood 78, 166
Robson, farmer, quoted 152
Rock of Cashel 55
Rocky Mountains 18
Rodrigo Díaz de Vivar 55

Rokeby see Scott, Sir Walter
Ronald, Lord (fictional character) 55
Roman commentators 8, 33, 34; *see also* Latin language
Roman law 74–75
Romance languages 20
Romans, Roman Empire 17, 33–34, 36, 54, 159
romantic movement 17–18, 161, 165–177
Rome 32, 106, 117, 128, 170; *see also* Pope
Rona Light 226
Rose of Kilravock 94–95
Ross, Earldom of 62–63, 64–66
Ross, Ian 191
Ross, Malcolm 154
Ross and Cromarty, Ross-shire 15, 16, 35, 38, 46, 62–63, 64, 104, 121, 136, 146, 148, 151, 198, 203; Lord Lieutenant of 146; *see also* Easter Ross
"Ross-shire Sheep Riot" 153
Rothiemurchus 86, 178
Roundhead 92, 97
Roxburgh 120, 171
Roxburgh Castle 6
Royal burgh 60
Royal Commission on the Ancient and Historical Monuments 24
Royal-Ecossais 132
Royal family of the United Kingdom *see* Crown
"Royal Gift" 89
Royal Mile 91
Royal Navy 110, 117, 123, 135
Royal National Mòd 217
Royal Stewart Tartan 180
Royalists (17th century) 92, 95, 98, 99–101, 107; modest appearance of Highland fighters 101
Roybridge 3, 5, 83, 102, 181
The Ruins of Inverlochy Castle 182
Rùm, Rum, Isle of 150, 197
Runciman, Alexander 181
runic 45
runrig 73, 148; explained 123–124
Runrig, folk group 14, 226
Rupert's Land 191
Russia 20, 159, 160, 161
Russian literature 6, 211
rustling, cattle, "lifting" 78–79, 94–94, 96, 138
Ruthven 156
Ruthven Barracks 137

Saami *see* Sámi
Sabhal Mòr Ostaig 218–219; name translated with semantics 218
The Sacred Theory of the Earth 17
sadism 59, 62, 79, 96, 102, 112; depictions 225
Saga of the Laxdalers 46
saighdearan dearg 134
St. Andrew, Church of 207

St. Andrew, Cross of 114
St. Andrews 30, 47, 217; *see also* University of St. Andrews
St. Andrew's Society 224, 225
St. Augustine 75
St. Caorruill 38
St. Clair, Lake 190
St. Colmóc 35–36
St. Columba *see* Colum Cille
St. Donnán 38
St. George, Cross of 114
St. Germain-en-Laye, Palace of 115
St. John, island of 148
St. Kilda, island 120, 212
St. Margaret's Chapel 51
Saint-Nazaire 129
St. Patrick 158
St. Paul 8
Salen 57
salmon 125, 138, 197
Salmond, Alex 202
salt mining 11
saltire 114
Salzburg 11
Sámi, Saami 20, 220–221
Sanskrit 19
Sarah (ship) 190
Sardinia 22, 117
Saskatchewan 5
Sassenach, anti-English slur 40, 113
satire 126, 127, 178, 215; *see also* Highlander, comic and satiric
Saxon vs. Celt narratives 175
Saxony 31
Scandinavia 18, 19, 20, 31, 44–48, 54, 56, 57, 161, 187; *see also* Denmark; Iceland; Norse; Norway
Scandinavian appearance 4; *see also* Norse
Scandinavians and the Celtic West 48
Scáthach 38, 158
Schama, Simon 17–18
schiltron 63
The School of the Moon 78
Schubert, Franz 161, 188
Schumann, Robert 188
scientific racism 142–143
Scone 30, 32, 59–60; translation 59
Scotch *see* whisky
Scotch-Irish *see* Scots-Irish
Scotch Novel Reading: or, Modern Quackery, by a Cockney 185
"Scotchman," "Scotch" semantics of 89, 183, 205
Scotchman's Return 205
Scoti *see* Scotti
Scoti sylvestres 1, 16
Scotia, archaic name for Scotland 23, 30, 32; conflicting definitions 25
Scotichronicon 62–63
Scotland 2, 11, 12, 13, 30, 55, 69, 89, 90, 93, 116, 152; anti Scottish sentiment 89–90, 160, 179, 213, 219, 221; coinage of word 30

Scotland (magazine) 225
Scotland, Kingdom of, Scottish Crown 13, 15, 16, 32, 39, 41, 42, 45, 4, 51, 52, 54, 56, 57-58, 59, 61-63, 64-65, 66, 70, 76, 79, 80, 82, 83, 84, 89-97, 107, 108, 110, 111, 129; Department of Agriculture 226; Privy Council 53, 111, 130; Secretary of State 111, 116; unites with England 114; weakness 130
Scotland: A New History 198
Scotland as it was and as it is 76
"Scotland's greatest ever ambassador" 215
Scotland's Shame? 44, 149
"Scotland's vilest man" 62
Scoto-Normans 40, 51, 70, 83, 169
Scotorum Historiae 32
The Scots: A Genetic Journey 21, 22, 36
The Scots Confession aka *The Confession of Faith of the Kirk of Scotland* 43, 79
"Scots Dialect" 68
Scots-Irish, Scotch-Irish 43
Scots language, Broad Scots, Scottish language, Lallans 16, 31, 33, 39, 41, 51, 53, 63, 68, 78, 96, 122, 126, 141, 159, 163, 164, 174, 189, 214, 215, 224; *The Brus*, first epic 41; "language of the nation" 68
Scots Magazine 155
Scotsman 62, 70,
Scott, James 109
Scott, Sir Walter 40, 41, 55, 65, 69, 74, 79, 80, 85, 88, 105, 112, 136, 145, 156, 162, 166, 167, 169, 170-177, 178, 181, 184, 185, 186, 187, 188, 190, 196, 215; *The Bride of Lammermoor* 170; *The Fair Maid of Perth* 173; *Heart of Midlothian* 186; "A Highland Widow" 173, 174-175; *Ivanhoe* 173; *Lady of the Lake* 170, 171; *The Lay of the Last Minstrel* 171, 186; *A Legend of Montrose* 105, 173; *Lord of the Isles* 55, 171, 173; *Marmion: A Tale of Flodden Field* 171; *Minstrelsy of the Scottish Border* 171; *Old Mortality* 110, *Rob Roy* 85, 167, 173-174; *Rokeby* 171; *Tales of a Grandfather* 40, 173; "Two Drovers" 173, 175; *Waverley* 166, 169, 171-173, 178, 185, 196, 200
Scott Monument 170
Scotti, Scoti 25-26, 33; etymology 25
Scottish art 47
"Scottish baronial" style 180, 209
Scottish Benevolent Society 206
Scottish Chiefs 169, 185
Scottish Civil War 65, 77, 78, 79, 83, 85, 95, 97, 99-100, 131, 146
The Scottish Clearances 17, 140, 189

Scottish Crown *see* Scotland, Kingdom of
Scottish Episcopal Church 94, 170; *see also* Episcopal
Scottish Gaelic *see* Gaelic
Scottish Gaël, or Celtic Manners, as Preserved Among the Highlanders 177, 180
Scottish Land Restoration League 211, 213
Scottish National Gallery 182
Scottish National Party 215
Scottish Parliament 16-17, 52, 66, 67, 73, 98, 104, 112, 132; Kirk General Assembly takes role 207; post-1999 87, 114, 180, 202, 216, 219; votes self out of existence 114
The Scottish People, 1490-1625 79
Scottish Poor Law Boards, Board of Supervisors of 204-205
Scottish Register of Tartans Act, SRT 180
Scottish Tartans Authority, STA 180
Scottish Tartans Society, STS 180
Scottish Tartans World Register 180
scratching *see* itching
Scriptures 93; *see also* Gospel
Scythians 33, 142
Sea of Moyle 26, 27, 28
Seaforth, Earl of (17th century) 87
Seaforth, Earl of (18th century) 117
Séamus an chaca 109
Sean Dana le Oisian, Orran, Ulann 159
seanchaidh, defined 163
The Seasons 161
Second Interregnum 59
second sight 87, 175
sectarian violence 98, 149
Seduced by a Highland Thief 222
Self-Control (book) 169
Selkirk, 5th Earl of 190-191, 192, 195, 202
Selkirk, Canada 191
Selkirk, Scotland 103
Sellar, Patrick 191, 192, 193-196, 200, 201; trial of 196
Sellar, W.D.H. 74-76
Selma (Macpherson palace) 159
seminaries 94, 149
Semitic languages 10
Senchus fer nAlban 28-29
sept, defined and etymology of 4, 72, 73, 82
sett 82; defined 177
Seven Daughters of Eve 21-22
Seven Heads 107, 108
Seven Men of Moidart 130, 134
Seven Oaks, Battle of 191
Seven Years' War 146
Shakespeare, William 31-32, 35, 51, 89, 164, 170, 171
Shannon River 26
Sharp, William 157

Shaw, Clan 86
sheep 126, 140, 145, 150, 151-154, 176, 190, 191, 192, 194, 197, 210; Cheviot breed 151-153; early Highland sheep meager 151; Linton breed 151; resistance to introduction 151; "Ross-shire Sheep Riot" 153
sheep walk, run 150, 210
shell fish 19, 144
Shelley, Percy Bysshe 168
shepherd 151
Sheridan, Sir Thomas 130
sheriff, office of 70, 77
Sheriffmuir, Battle of 116; *see also* "The Battle of Sherramuir"
Shetland Islands 16, 17, 36, 44, 45, 46, 59, 212, 219
Shie, Loch 130
Shilric (Macpherson character) 159
Ships' Passenger Act *see* Passenger Vessels Act
Shirts, Battle of the 80, 96
Shrewsbury 102
Sibbald, Sir Robert 120
Sibelius, Jan 160, 223
Sicily 17, 117
Sigurd, Earl of Orkney 47, 48
Sikhs 147
Sims-William, Patrick 9, 22-23
Sinatra, Frank 224
Sinclair, Sir John 152-153
siol, term of patrimony defined 71
Siol Diarmait 71
Siol Dughaill 106
Six Counties of Northern Ireland 42, 43
Skene, W.F. 15, 37, 74
Sketches of the Character, Manners and Present State of the Highlanders 176
skuta 56
"The Skye Boat Song" 137
Skye, Isle of 13, 17, 35, 36, 38, 41, 45, 48, 57, 65, 67, 76, 81, 82, 83, 106, 120, 124, 132, 136, 142, 144, 147, 148, 150, 155, 158, 162, 183, 187, 198, 200, 203, 208, 211, 212, 214, 218-219, 223, 224, 225; "The Skye Boat Song"/"Over the Sea to Skye" 137; *see also* Dún Scáthaige
slavery, slave-trading 46, 142, 144, 185
Slavic languages 8
Sleat 65, 76, 106-107, 218, 219; *see also* MacDonald of Sleat
slender coronal stop 50
sloinneadh 5-7, 100; *see also* patronymic
Slovenia 8
Small Isles 80
Small Landholders (Scotland) Act 213
smallpox 115, 141, 190; inoculation for 141
Smith, Adam 125, 140, 142, 170, 191

Smith, Dr. (19th century) 107
Smith, George 184
Smith, Iain Crichton 201
Smith, Dr. John (18th century) 159
Smollet, Tobias 214
Sobieski, Jan 118
Sobieski dynasty, family 128, 129, 178
Sobieski Stuart family 178–180
soccer 10
Society in Scotland for Promoting Christian Knowledge *see* SSPCK
Sodor 47
sola scriptura, sola fide 93
Solemn League and Covenant 92, 94, 99, 207; *see also* Covenanters
"The Solitary Reaper" 167
Sollas 198
solstice, winter 37
Solway 32
"Somber Kenneth of the Prophesies" 87
Somerled 2, 18, 42, 55–58, 61, 67, 69, 70, 82, 96, 224; rival forms of his name 55
Somhairle *see* Somerled
Somhairle Buidhe *see* Sorley Boy
Somhairle, Clan 70
Somhairle Mòr MacGhillebhride 42, 48
"A Song Against the Union" 114
Song of Roland 159
Songs of the Hebrides 188
"Sonnet in the Pass of Killiecanky" 167
"Sonnet. Written Upon the Top of Ben Nevis" 165
Sophia, Electress of Hanover 115
The Sopranos (Warner) 223
Sorley *see* Somhairle, Clan
Sorley Boy 41–42
sorning 53
The Sorrows of a Young Werther 161
South Africa 214
South America 124, 202
South Carolina 43
South Island *see* New Zealand
South Uist 94, 129, 142, 149, 150, 155, 188, 198, 206; *see also* Uists
the southerlies *see* Sudreys
Southey, Robert 167–168, 171
Spain 9, 55, 105, 113, 117, 128, 144, 159, 221; *see also* Iberia
Spanish language 128, 161
Spanish Marines 117
Spean Bridge 16, 83, 102
Spey River, 16, 134
Speyside 6, 16, 182
"Spine of Britain" 27–28
Spiritual Hymns 164
"spiritual laager" 208
Spoiling or Spoiled Dike, Battle of the 81
sporran 147, 174 214 216
Squire, Romilly 82

SRT *see* Scottish Register of Tartans Act
Sruth na Maoile 26
SSPCK (Society in Scotland for Promoting Christian Knowledge) 53, 120, 148, 216
STA *see* Scottish Tartans Authority
Staffa 25, 38, 165
"Staffa" (poem) 165
Stafford, Lord and Lady *see* Sutherland, 1st Duke of, 1st Duchess of
stags, stag-hunting 181, 182, 201; *see also* deer
Stair, Lord, Master of 111, 112, 114
The Stamping Ground 226
standing stones, ancient 23
Statistical Account of North Uist 141
"Statutes of Icolmkill" 53
Statutes of Iona 36, 52–53, 74, 76, 79, 86, 90, 96, 125, 219
"A Steamy Scottish Historical Novel" 222
Steeleye Span 114
Stevenson, David 39, 100, 103
Stevenson, Robert Louis 133, 186, 187, 188
Stewart, David, of Garth 176
Stewart, Dugald 193
Stewart, Rod 137
Stewart dynasty *see* Stuart/Stewart dynasty
Stirling Bridge 59
Stirling Castle 133–134
Stirling, county, post 1974 borders 14
Stirling, town of 60, 63, 115, 133, 141–142, 171; *see also* University of Sterling
Stiùbhart *see* Stuart dynasty
Stockholm 44
Stolberg, Louise, Princess 178
Stone Age, unspecified 28; *see also* Neolithic period
Stone of Destiny 26
Stone of Scone 26
Stonehaven 14, 16
Stonehenge 23
Stornoway 52, 117, 190
Stowe, Harriet Beecher 185, 196
Strachnur 84
"strai-wash" *see* Gàighlig Strathghlais
"The Strange Case of Dr. Jekyll and Mr. Hyde" 186
Strathaird 198
Strathbogie 138
Strathclyde 32, 83; *see also* University of Strathclyde
Strathconan 197, 198
Strathdon 184
Strathglass 4, 132, 192–193, 194
Strathmore, in United States 221
Strathnaver 195
Strathrusdale 153
Strickland, Francis 130
Stroh, Silke 96, 139

Stromness 195
Strongbow 41
STS *see* Scottish Tartans Society
Stuart, Charles Edward 178–179
Stuart, John Sobieski Stolberg 178–179
Stuart of Killin, the Rev. James 164
Stuart/Stewart Dynasty 58, 60, 61, 63, 64–68, 83, 92, 105, 107, 108–110, 111, 127–129, 132, 138, 165, 173, 180, 181, 189, 222; Albany Stewarts 64; origins 60; spellings 60, 89; *see also* Anne, Queen; Atholl, Earl of; Charles I; Charles II; Charles Edward, Prince/Young Pretender; James I; James II of England, James II of Scotland; James III of Scotland; James IV; James Francis Edward/Old Pretender; Mary daughter of James II; Mary Queen of Scots; Restoration; Robert II; Robert, Duke of Albany; Royal Stewart Tartan
Stukeley, William 23
Suas Leis a' Ghàidhlig 216–219; choral work 217; as graffiti 217
subclade 22; *see also* haplogroup
subtenants, cottar 121, 124, 131, 142, 143, 144, 148, 150, 151, 155, 162, 163, 168, 173, 181, 190, 202, 204, 212; status described 121
"Such a Parcel of Rogues in a Nation" 114
Sudreys 47, 48, 54
Sueno's Stone 35
suicide 127
Suisnish 198
Sumatra 4
Sumbawa Volcano 196
Sumerledo *see* Somerled
Sunny Memories of Foreign Lands 185
Sussex 5
Sutherland, Clan 117
Sutherland, Countess of (early 19th century) 176
Sutherland, 1st Duchess of, Elizabeth, "the Marchioness" (mid-19th century) 185, 193, 194, 201
Sutherland, 2nd Duchess of 196
Sutherland, 1st Duke of, George 185, 192, 196, 197, 200, 201; statue ("Mannie") of abused 196, 202, 205
Sutherland, 2nd Duke of 196
Sutherland, Earl of (later Duke of) 192, 193
Sutherland, Sutherlandshire 15, 16, 17, 35, 46, 48, 193, 194–195, 197, 198, 200
Suthreyars *see* Sudreys
suzerainty 47, 57; defined 47
Swanson, family name 4
Sweden 44, 47, 117, 160
Swedish language 6, 68, 161

Sweeney, William 200
sweet William, flower 136
Sweyn Forkbeard 35
Switzerland 8, 9, 11, 221
sword pommels, bone 37
Sykes, Brian 21–22, 32
Symonds, James 140
Syracuse, New York 221
Syria 173

tack, Scots word 122
tacksmen 73, 121, 122, 124, 137, 144, 145, 150, 194; decline 148; duties 122; etymology of word 122
Táin, category of narrative 78
Táin Bó Cuailnge 38, 78, 158, 159
Tain peninsula 18
Tairrdelbach Mór ua Conchobhair 75
Talbot, Colonel (Scott character) 172
Tales of a Grandfather see Scott, Sir Walter
The Talisman see Scott, Sir Walter
tanistry, thanistry 31, 70
Tantallon Castle 64
Tara 159
Tarbat Peninsula 35
Tarbet 166
tartan 2, 4, 52, 69, 72, 82, 84, 113, 119, 131, 132, 139, 155, 177–182, 189, 197, 209, 220, 222; Advisory Committee on 180; banned 119; becomes national signifier 177–178; Black Watch 119, 178, 180; Burberry 180; commodifying 178–179; etymology 177; Lyon Court Books 180; origin 177–178; registration 179–180; Royal Stewart 180; *see also* Dress Act; plaid; sett
tartanism 168, 185, 205
tattoo 33
taxes 49, 61, 111, 144, 148, 183, 184, 204, 205, 212, 229
Tay, Loch 84
television 3, 11, 12, 182, 183; *see* British television; Public Television
Telford, Thomas 126–127, 168, 183
Temair 159
Temora 155, 157
Temora (Macpherson region) 159
tenants, crofter 1, 121, 123–124, 131, 140, 142, 143–144, 148, 150, 151, 152, 154, 155, 163, 168, 173, 181, 183, 190, 192, 193, 194, 195, 196, 197, 198, 199, 202, 204, 207, 209, 210, 211, 225; status described 121; *see also* Crofters' Party
Tennessee 43
teuchter defined and pronunciation of 4, 214, 222; *see also* anti-Gaelic slurs; Gaelic
"teuchters' umbrella" 197

Thames Estuary 129, 137
thanistry *see* tanistry
Thatcher, Margaret 140
theater 89, 127
thirlage 122
The 39 Steps 105
Thirty Years War 93, 98, 102
"thistle and the rose" 68
Thomas the Rhymer 87
Thoms, William John 159
Thomson, Derick S. 157, 163, 179
Thomson, James 160
Thomson, Oliver 84
Thoreau, Henry David 156, 161
Thorfinn the Mighty 47
Thornton, Thomas 121
Thornton, Col. Thomas 182
Thursteinn the Red 46
Tigh Litrichean 4
Tight Little Island 188
Tilbury Fort 137
Tioram, Castle 82
Tippermuir, Tippermore, Battle of 101
Tiree, Isle of 48, 54, 56
"To a Highland Girl" 167, quoted
Tobat-nan-Ceann 107
Tobermoray 67, 203
Tocharian 20
Toland, John 23
Tolbooth of Edinburgh 104
Tolmie, Frances 187–188
Tolstoy, Leo 211
Tom Aingeal 38, 107
Tomahourich, Janet of (Scott character) 175
Tor Castle 85
Torbay 109
Tordarroch *see* Shaw, Clan
Torman (Macpherson character) 160
Tory Party, Tories 114, 115, 116, 127, 128, 170, 171, 173, 181, 190, 209; *see also* Conservative Party
A Tour in Scotland, 1769 87, 143–144
Tour Thro' the Whole Island of Great Britain 17
tourism 17, 36, 38, 42, 49, 81, 91, 108, 112, 130, 144, 166, 182, 183, 199, 201, 213, 223, 225
Tower of London 60, 109, 130, 137
Towneley, Francis 132
Toyota Sports Utility Vehicle 221
Traditionskern 28
Trafalgar Square 181
trains *see* rail, railway
Transactions of the Gaelic Society of Inverness 217
transportation as punishment 153–154
Tranter, Nigel 105
"treachery of the people" 142
Treasure Island 186
Treaty of Perth 59
Treaty of 1707 *see* Act of Union
Trevelyan, Sir Charles 203, 204
Trevor-Roper, Hugh 142, 179

The Trial of Patrick Sellar 198
Triath nan Eilean see Lord of the Isles
tribute, to pay 108
Trinity, Christian dogma 93
Trinity College Dublin 28
Trinity College Medieval Symposium 36
Tristan und Isolde 187
Trondheim 47, 48, 58
Trossachs 168
trout 125
"true bloods" 165
True Mountain breed *see* Cheviot sheep
Trumpan Church 81
tuath 29, 69; definition 69
Tuatha Dé Danann 69
Tübingen University 216
Tudor dynasty 42; *see also* Elizabeth I; Henry VII; Henry VIII; Margaret Tudor
Tullibbardine, Marquis of 130
Turkey, Turks 20, 33, 118
Turnbull, clan 82
Turner, J.M.W. 181, 183
Twain, Mark 170
Tweed river 32, 65
23andMe, company 22, 36
"Two Drovers" Scott, Sir Walter
Tyne-Tees coal resources 115
Tyrone, County 43, 69

Un Uaimh Bhinn (*Un Uaimh Finn*) 25
Uaimh Fhraing 80–81
uamh 25
Uí Néill dynasty 26
Uilleam Uallas *see* Wallace, William
uisce beatha 183
uisge-beatha 183
Ùisdean *see* Hugh (Ùisdean)
Uist islands 48, 81, 82, 94; *see also* North Uist; South Uist
Ukraine 20, 33
Ulaid 31
Ulbster 152
Ulster 26, 27, 31, 33, 40, 42, 43, 49, 50, 76, 90, 98, 100, 113; *see also Annals of Ulster*; Antrim, County; Plantations of Ulster
Ulster Cycle 38, 157–158
Ulster Presbyterians 43
Uncle Tom's Cabin 185
Union Jack 114
"union of the thistle and the rose" 68
United Kingdom 43, 89, 93, 114, 128, 129, 155, 174, 199, 211, 213, 218; devolution 216, 218, 219; *see also* England
United States of America 3, 43, 90, 127, 128, 143, 156, 159, 161–162, 170, 184, 190, 218, 220; *see also* American West
University of Aberdeen 217
University of Copenhagen 21
University of Edinburgh 155, 187,

Index

188, 193, 212; Chair of Celtic 187, 212, 216
University of Glasgow 163, 217
University of Highlands and Islands 218–219
University of Newcastle-upon-Tyne 79
University of St. Andrews 217
University of Sterling 219
University of Strathclyde 219
Upanishads 19
Upper Canada 150–151, 192, 206
Urquhart castle 64, 80
usquebaugh 183

Valladolid 105
Van Dyke, Sir Anthony 92
Vandals 19
vassalage 70, 73
vellum codices 38
Venerable Bede *see* Bede, Venerable
Vernon, Diana (Scott character) 173–174
Verturiones 35
Vestiarium Scoticum 179
Victoria, Queen 25, 139, 180–185
Vienna 28, 118
Vikings, connotations of 44; *see also* Norsemen
Villon, François 163
Vinvela (Macpherson character) 159
violin, violinist 108; *see also* fiddle
Virginia 89, 203
volcano 17
Volga River 2
Voltaire 128, 156
Voyage to the Hebrides 143

Wade, Maj. Gen. George 119, 130, 133, 146
Wagner, Richard 186, 187
Waifs and Strays of Celtic Tradition 187, 188
Wainright, F.T. 33
Waipu 209
Wakefield, Harry (Scott character) 175
Wales, Prince of 67
"Wall of China/One Man" 226
The Wallace 169
Wallace, Alexander, "Big Wallace" 153
Wallace, Randall 169
Wallace, William 55, 59, 60, 114, 162, 169; actual names; Uilleam Uallas; William de Waleys
Wallaceburg 190
Walpole, Prime Minister Robert 128, 138
walrus 47
Walsh, Maurice 105
War of the Roses 65–66
"Warfare in the West Highlands and Isles of Scotland" 78, 79

Warner, Alan 223
Warriors of the Word: The World of the Scottish Highlanders 214
Wars of the Three Kingdoms 97–105
Washington, George 128
water transportation 44, 54, 58; *see also* birlinn
"water of life" 183
Waterford 46
Waterloo, Battle of 147
Waternish Peninsula 81
Watkins, Peter 131, 136, 140
Waverley see Scott, Sir Walter
Waverley, Edward (Scott character) 171–173
Waverley, Sir Everard (Scott character) 171–172
Waverley Novels 173, 186
Way (of Plean), George 82
Wealth of Nations 125
Weber, Max 206
Wedderburn, Jean 190
"A Wee Deoc-an-Dorris" 215
weem, human retreat 25
Well of the Heads 107
Welsh language 9, 20, 33, 156, 159–160
"Welsh Macpherson" 159; *see also* Williams, Edward
Welshmen 11, 12, 31, 34, 36, 68, 97, 127, 175, 191, 216, 217
Wemyss, Clan 82
Wenskus, Reinhard 28
"Were the Scots Irish?" 27–28
West Highland Museum 139
West Indies 52, 99, 113
West Virginia 43
Westbrook, Harriet 168
western hunter-gatherers *see* WHG
Western Isles, electoral district 17; *see also* Outer Hebrides
Westminster Abbey 157
The Westminster Confession of Faith 44, 93
Westminster Gazette 126
Westminster government 172; *see also* Parliament
Westminster, Treaty of 66
whales 47
"When I Roved a Young Highlander" 165
WHG, western hunter-gatherers 19, 20
Whig Party, Whigs 124, 126, 128, 165, 172, 209
whiskey, Irish 183, 184
whisky, Scotch 2, 16, 52, 182, 183–184; "black pot" in-joke 218; prestige 183–184; single malt 184, 218; spelling 183; tax 183–184, 215, 218; wee dram 139; *see also* distilleries
Whisky Galore 188, 223
White, John 34
White Boys 147
white cockade 133, 178

Who We Are and How We Got Here 7
Wick 203
Wightman, Joseph 118
Wikipedia 6, 55
wild Scots 1, 16, 74, 79, 141, 147
Wild Scots (book) 140–141
Wilde, Oscar 161
"Will Ye No' Come Back Again" 139
William I, of Scotland, the Lion 60
William II, of England 48
William III, of Orange 84, 85, 94, 108, 109–110, 111, 113, 115, 119
William, Windsor-Montbatten, Prince 67
William and Mary, reign of 94, 108, 109–110, 149, 206
William Augustus *see* Cumberland, Duke of
William le Waleys *see* Wallace, William
William of Malmesbury 48
Williamite 110, 112
Williams, Edward 159–
Williams, Elizabeth 138
Williams, Ronald 62
wine 52, 184
Winnipeg 202
Wishart, George 104–105
Wilson, James F. 21, 22, 36
Windsor, Ontario 5
wine 52
Witch Wood 105
witchcraft 87
Withers, Charles W.J. 51
"the Wolf of Badenoch" *see* Alexander, Earl of Buchan
Wolfe, Gen. James 146, 155
women, status of in Highlands 124, 125, 126, 143, 145, 194; *see also* marriage
wool 152, 189
Woolf, Alex 47
Womack, Peter 124, 126, 214
Wordsworth, Dorothy 166–168
Wordsworth, William 145, 165–168, 181; quoted 166, 167
The Works of Ossian (1765) *see* Poems of Ossian
Works of the Caledonian Bards 159
The World of Rob Donn 163
World War I 214
World War II 219
Wrath, Cape 46; name translated 46
Wu-Tang Clan 69
Wyeth, N.C. 169
Wyld, William 182

Yamnaya 20; *see also* ANE
"Year of the Burnings" 195, 196
"Year of the Sheep" 153–154
Yeats, William Butler 187
"yellow stick," yellow-stick belief 150

Yerevan, Armenia 5
Yiddish 214
York, Duke of (17th century) *see* James II, of England
York, England 30, 45, 137
Yorkists 65–66
Yorkshire 175, 182
Young, William 193–194
Young Folks magazine 186
The Young Montrose 105
Young Pretender *see* Charles Edward Stuart, Prince
YouTube 217

Zellweger, Renée 221